GOING DOWNHILL FAST

OTHER BOOKS BY JAY COWAN

Nonfiction:

The Best of the Alps

Hunter S. Thompson

In the Land of Living Dangerously

Scandal Aspen

Fiction:

The Time of the Heathen Rage

The Time of the Gold Snake

The Time of Chaos

GOING DOWNHILL FAST

AND OTHER STORIES FROM SKIING'S EXTREMES

JAY COWAN

BLUE TRAIN INK

Front Cover:
Valentina Greggio, women's speed skiing world record holder. Photo © Louis Billy.
Kite skier Jon Devore. Photo: Scott Serfas / Red Bull Content Pool.

Back Cover:
Japanese Nordic jumper Ryoyu Kobayashi. Photo: Limex Images / Red Bull Content Pool.
Kit Deslauriers skiing Everest. Photo © Bryce Brown.
Iceberg grotto, the British Antarctica Expedition 1911 – 1913. The National Library of New Zealand.

Cover design by Jay Cowan, executed by Elite Authors
Interior design and layout by Elite Authors.

Paperback ISBN: 9798861222570
Hardcover ISBN: 9798871759707

TABLE OF CONTENTS

ACKNOWLEDGMENTS

A book of such naïve scope and dimensions can't be entirely blamed on one person and I don't intend to let that happen. For starters, there were my amazing parents who got me hooked on the skiing life from the age of two and never quit encouraging a kid who may have ultimately taken it all a little too seriously.

The genesis of this project was provided by multiple stories I wrote for Skiing History magazine that appear here in extended forms and I thank them for the platform they've provided me the last 20 years. I am grateful for various editors and board members there including Dick Needham, the legendary John Fry, Kathleen James, Seth Masia and eternally patient Greg Ditrinco with whom I've worked on various magazines.

My writing for several Aspen-based magazines, and particularly my 5-year tenure as Editor-in-Chief at Aspen Sojourner, gave me the opportunity to pursue a number of stories and themes I'd always wanted to, some of which also led directly to this.

Editors at other magazines have helped sustain my bad habits and addictive behaviors (skiing and writing), especially Steve Cohen and Lauren Bernstein at SKI, where I started with a big assist from Martie Sterling. Les Anthony and Steve Casimiro at Powder gave me work that kept me in touch with the cutting edges, as it were, of skiing and boarding. No other magazine has been more faithfully supportive of the extremes of our sport and its lifestyle. And Dave Reddick in Powder's present iteration has been enormously helpful supplying images for this book.

Others who have kept the fires burning include Andy Bigford at Snow Country, Barb Sanders at SNOW, John Fayhee at Mountain Gazette, and a host of others at Couloir, Freeskier, Cross-Country Skier, Ski Press and on and on. The National Association of Snow-sports Journalists of America (NASJA) provided valuable contacts and backing for years. And I've also made some new media connections during this enterprise, including at The Avalanche Review (TAR), where they do valuable work that deserves our support, and went above and beyond the call to help me verify historic info.

I'm also deeply indebted to a number of heavy-hitting photographers who have let me use pics for this book I could not have afforded otherwise. When writing about the extremes of our sport, it's important to note that few athletes have gone to greater lengths to bring them to light than the photogs who risk life and limb to take the images that defined the modern era of riding. They include Scott Markewitz, Ace Kvale, Wade McKoy, Chris Noble, René Robert, Kim McHugh, Louis Billy, Bryce Brown and Cedric Bernardini. I hope my words are worthy of their work.

Another major underwriter of adventure sports that has been instrumental in their continuing existence, as well as in supplying me with photos, is Red Bull. Their financial support of athletes and events around the world has been second to none. And their Red Bull Content Pool for members of the media is both generous and smart.

One of the best things about an undertaking that sometimes seemed pointless and never-ending was the chance it gave me to make new contacts with people I've always admired in the sport, and to get help from others that I've known for years. My Aspen high school classmate Lou Dawson (the author of Wild Snow and host of the website of the same name) was of significant help. During my research I finally got to meet a longtime idol, Dick Dorworth who gave me the inspiration to keep at it. And Chris Davenport, a neighbor for years in Aspen, has never turned down a request for a quote or a photo or just a friendly chat.

Because of this strange sport and writing about it, I've gotten to meet and sometimes know a who's who list of its players that includes the Marolt family of Aspen, the Blitz from Kitz Anderl Molterer, Andrea Mead Lawrence, Toni Sailer, Christian Pravda, Nancy Greene (Raine), Ernst Hinterseer, Egon Zimmermann, Steve Podborski, Andy Mill, Klaus Obermeyer, Kiki Cutter, Dave Stapleton, Mark Tache, Christin Cooper, John McMurtry, Bob Beattie, and hundreds of others.

I also owe a big shout-out, as we all do, to the various tribes that support skiers and boarders in general: the vital National Ski Patrol that puts their lives on the line for us; professional ski instructors everywhere such as the PSIA which kept me gainfully employed at one time; and the National Ski Areas Association, which helps resorts function and follow some rules, and provides a deep well of information on the industry.

Finally, and most critically for me, are the friends, enablers and codependents who've kept me in the game over the decades. Several orthopedic surgeons make the list. So do a couple of ex-wives. Along with Anne Morningstar, Don Birnkrant and Jay Reader who're always there to ride with and talk about it, say yay or nay, and share the good, the bad and the weird. Along with Raoul, Star, Don, Ray, Eric, Jenkins, Wayne, Whit, Sal, Beaver, Watson, Casey, Kevin, Kirby, Lonnie and Mary, Matt and Heather, Kim, Liz and all the crews I've ridden with who've kept it fresh and fast.

INTRODUCTION

Going downhill fast on skis or a board is thrilling and fun. So are most of the other wild things you can do on them and I hope that comes across in this book. All of them can also have disastrous and tragic consequences. I've tried not to dwell on those but I haven't downplayed them either. After all, part of what makes some sports exciting is the potential for things to go badly wrong.

The ski industry overall has little appetite for talking about injuries and death, avalanches and lift disasters, and other unhappy occurrences on the slopes. While understandable from a marketing standpoint, these elements are facts of life and seem silly to ignore. Plenty of other sports are hazardous as well, such as surfing, cycling, football, hang-gliding, kayaking, pole-vaulting, bobsledding, hockey, car racing, and on and on. It's also true that driving to watch or do any of these including skiing and boarding is more dangerous than the sports themselves.

Ultimately, we buy the ticket and take the ride, to quote my old friend. And if we don't want to hear or think about what's the worst that can happen, that's our choice. But in the real world these things are all part of the package, as they are in this book.

I've also taken a fairly deep dive into worldwide snowfall patterns that may seem unnecessary, or at least over-wrought. However, as skiers we are as dependent on weather as farmers and sunbathers and a long list of other pursuits. Since accurate historical snowfall data can be very difficult to come by from region to region around the world, let alone aggregated in one place, I decided to make an attempt.

On a slightly more cosmic scale, it's vital to our planetary survival to acknowledge and respond to the crisis of climate change. And a huge part of that is understanding and anticipating its effect on weather, which requires an underlying knowledge of weather patterns I hadn't previously possessed. And may still not but I think it deserves attention.

Logistically speaking, in approaching a book like this it may help to know that while there are recurring themes and citations, it's easy to pick it up almost anywhere and start reading randomly without feeling like you need to have at least skimmed what comes before. I want it to be informative and usable as a reference work, while hoping its also readable. I haven't included an index because I think the TOC serves much the same purpose. And providing one would have not only driven me mad, but likely rendered the damned thing so long as to be un-publishable in any reasonable fashion, a status it's already flirting with.

So there you have it. Thanks for buying the ticket and I hope you enjoy the ride. Skol!

Jay Cowan
Montana
September 15, 2023

SECTION I
BIG AIR

Jesper Tjäder at Red Bull Playstreets event. Photo: Simon Rainer / Red Bull Content Pool.

CHAPTER 1
ALPINE JUMPING

Gelandes, Gap Jumps, Cliff Hucks, Freestyle Aerials and Terrain Parks

When Jesper Tjader explains to an event official what he wants to try on a practice run for the 2014 Suzuki Nine Knights terrain park comp in Watles, Italy, no one thinks its possible. But he casually skis onto the in-run anyway. He's planning a transfer from one big ramp to another one about 55 meters (180 feet) away on a completely different course. Coming up short means a face-full of vertical ice and serious injury at a minimum. Overshooting isn't even a consideration since nobody believes he'll clear the massive gap to begin with.

But the 20-year old Tjader is riding a wave of big air heroics along with a host of others who will define the first two decades of alpine ski jumping in the 2000s. The Swede sticks the landing three times that day on a jump no one else is even thinking about, and the last time he throws in a double back flip.

Skiing Big Air's debut at the 2022 Winter Olympics in China came on the back of some attention-grabbing feats over the last twenty years. Candide Thovex making the first successful jump on 120-foot Chad's Gap in 1999; Jamie Pierre dropping a 255-foot cliff huck in 2006, only to have Fred Syversen up the ante to a bonkers, and accidental, 351 feet two years later; Rolf Wilson laying down a 374-foot-long alpine jump in 2011; and David Wise popping 46.5 feet above a hip hit at Watles in 2016, upping that record by more than 10 feet.

The origins of intentionally taking flight on skis are murky. It may have been first done in order to cross a creek or dry area without removing the skis. Then they discovered it was fun and it went viral. Or it may have developed after various people fell off cliffs into snow and discovered that it was fun and survivable, and began to take it up deliberately. Whatever the case – and it gets explored further in the next chapter – it seems like something that could have developed spontaneously amongst skiing communities.

My parents had me on skis when I was two, and when I was 10 my dad figured I should be jumping. By the time I was 20 I'd been in more gelande comps than I can remember. The result was a lot of thrills, multiple knee surgeries, a lifetime of nervous dreams where I jump and never land, and a keen ongoing appreciation for what skiers are doing with bigger and bigger air.

Hannes Schneider likely introduced, or at least popularized, the gelandesprung (literally "terrain jump" in German) in the early 1900s in the Austrian Arlberg. Writing about it in *Skiing* magazine in 1964, G.S. Bush mentioned Schneider demonstrating a maneuver where he, "Used two ski poles instead of one, and, an accomplished jumper, he leaped even when there was no ramp. Rushing across a sharp break in a slope, he'd push himself up and forward on the poles, catapulting himself high over the hill's edge, and then, by twisting his body and skis, he'd change the direction his skis were facing in mid-flight. He called this spectacular trick, 'Gelandesprung'."

This explanation was as confusing as it was illuminating. The changing directions part sounded intrinsic to the maneuver, but nowhere represented in the term gelandesprung. It also seemed important for it to have been facilitated by a double pole plant. That narrow interpretation didn't last long, however, before the term gelandesprung, shortened to gelande, became a staple of the skiing lexicon when referring to nearly any jump made with alpine gear. Which means bindings with locked-down heels and ski poles in the hands, the major things that differentiate it from classic heads-and-tips-first nordic jumping.

 Gelandesprunging began to make regularly noted appearances in the U.S. in the 1930s where it was mentioned as an activity at areas from Glen Ellen, Vermont, to Badger Pass in Yosemite. Oddly, it also turned up on an American stamp issued in 1932, commemorating that year's third Winter Olympics, being held in Lake Placid.

As noted collector James Riddell remarked in an article, "The Scandinavian disciplines Langlauf and Springlauf only at Lake Placid! This stamp, strangely enough, depicted a Gelandesprung, which hardly suited either event." Mort Lund observed that the stamp displayed "a form of skiing for which there was no Olympic, world or local competitions…" It may have been the 1940s before the first known gelande events started occurring at places like Mount Ellen and Alta, Utah.

Ultimately, what has primarily propelled alpine jumping has been photography, which has proven both a blessing and a curse. Detractors claim that photo fame and peer pressure drive kids to do dangerously crazy things they wouldn't otherwise. I've always found this assessment to be nothing more than recognizing how a lot of kids do anything, which is often at least partly from peer pressure.

To suggest that GoPros or the clamoring of friends can inspire anyone to do wild things they might not do otherwise is both obvious and beside the point. As humans we will learn about and be driven by those kinds of things whether we see them carved on a cave wall, hear about them from someone or see them in magazines and films. The decision about what to do with that input is ours alone.

As the world rolled into the 1960s, photography was indeed a major driver for alpine ski jumping. Not because skiers were doing it expressly for the cameras, but because the audience craved it. Big air is dramatic and it has always sold. So if there was jumping going on, the photographers were usually there.

Jim McConkey was one of the early ones to figure that out and act on it. He first drew widespread attention for an image of him jumping 100 feet over a ski plane on a glacier in Canada in 1962. Next he dropped a 90-foot cliff in the Bugaboos, which was nearly unthinkable at the time. Ninety feet is still bragging material today. And it opened up the mountains to stuff so ridiculous that jumpers had to literally create wings to keep raising the bar. Tragically, one who did was McConkey's son Shane, who died in a skiing and base-jumping accident in the Italian Dolomites in 2009.

McConkey's plane-jumping image was followed by a 1963 Hans Truol photo of legendary Austrian downhill racer Egon Zimmerman jumping the Flexenpass highway above Lech, Austria, and clearing a new 356 Porsche in the process. Zimmerman personally gave visitors a postcard of the photo at his Hotel Kristberg in Lech right up until his death at 80 in 2019. He once told me that he'd done the jump mainly as a promo for Porsche, which he thought was ironic since he suffered a bad wreck in his own Porsche a few years later. The pic is still famous today and along with McConkey's plane jump helped create the modern concept of gap-jumping as an Evel Knievel form of showmanship.

 The value of film to big league ski jumping was cemented when skiing began appearing in James Bond movies being shot by Willy Bogner in some of the Alps most glamorous locales. It gave a big boost to the sport in general and to bat-shit crazy jumping in particular, the latter as a result of three deeply memorable sequences.

The first was in *On Her Majesty's Secret Service* in 1969, where star George Lazenby's stunt skiers were German racer Ludwig Leitner and Swiss downhill ace Bernhard Russi. Near the end of a long chase sequence at Murren, Switzerland, Bond jumps over a highway very reminiscent of Zimmerman's Porsche-clearing gelande. Only Bond did it over a huge snowplow with a snowblower that devours the pursuing bad guy who doesn't go big enough. Unfortunately, "Russi was injured when he crashed on the road," Bogner told me. But it definitely raised the stakes on gap-jumping and built on the Zimmerman/McConkey tricks.

Next came Rick Sylvester's mind-boggling jump off Mount Asgard on Baffin Island in 1977's *The Spy Who Loved Me* that ended 3,000 vertical feet later with a parachute landing. It was a game-changer that furthered the blending of skiing with base-jumping and fired up ski jumpers by exponentially extending the limits of what was possible. The movie scene took three tries for the camera crew to get the shots, but it awed a global audience and inspired people like Shane McConkey.

In 1981's *For Your Eyes Only*, extensive ski scenes in Cortina, Italy, are capped by former 6-time World Champion freestyle skier John Eaves standing in for Roger Moore and jumping off Cortina's famed 90-meter Olympic hill. On a pair of 205 Olin Mark VI slalom skis.

At that time almost everyone used at least 215 GS or downhill skis on gelande jumps a lot smaller than a 90-meter, and most of us used 220s. Plus he did it tandem, side-by-side with a regular, properly equipped nordic jumper.

"I had my own jump," Eaves told me. "It was set at 0 degrees. The Nordic take off was -11 degrees. They need that to get into the airfoil. Mine felt like a good kick when I hit it, allowing me to gain altitude over the nordic jumper immediately, then I would slowly lose altitude as he went ahead. I did 200 feet once," he said with pleasure, explaining it wasn't out of his wheel well. "I got second place at the Whistler gelande in 1974 on a pair of Dave Murray's lead weighted downhill skis."

That kind of competitive alpine ski jumping had been going on for some years. The first National Gelande Championships were staged at Alta in 1964 by the legendary skiing pioneer Alf Engen, and just for good measure he won it. The annual event lasted for ten years (plus occasional resurrections for anniversaries) before insurance companies and lawyers got involved, but by then there were gelande comps, and their direct descendants in the form of "ski splashes," going on everywhere.

At one point a North American gelande tour included 13 stops: Purgatory's famous Goliath Gelande; Steamboat Spring's Winter Carnival off the 70 and 90-meter jumps; wild Snowbowl, Montana; Mad River, Sugarbush, Jackson, Whistler, Alyeska, Aspen's Winterskol, and so on. but Alta's remained the granddaddy and the one everybody aimed for.

Interestingly, Porsche stayed allied with alpine ski jumping well beyond Zimmerman's promo jump, and they supplied a car as first prize for one of the early gelande events in Vail, won by Mark Jones in 1974 at the then-world-record distance of 213.5 feet. The prize got everyone's attention as much as the length, and helped jump-start (ahem) the tour.

According to an obit for Jones in 2005 in the Vail Daily Sentinel, he started doing gelande comps in high school and his world record distance stood for ten years. The obit added, "He drove away with a new Porsche, which lasted about nine years less than the world gelande record."

By this time the new discipline of freestyle skiing aerials had been going on for a few years in the US and around the world. Combining outrageously vertical air (20 feet above the kicker, up to 60 feet above the landing) with full-on gymnastics (three full back flips with five full twists for example), they've made for great TV.

Often done in conjunction with freestyle bump skiing events, they were formally recognized by the FIS in 1979 and first showcased at the Olympics in 1994. They also led directly to the jibbing movement and park and pipe riding that rewards tricks as much as amplitude or distance.

For the last 40 years, the sky has literally been the limit for gelandes, gap-jumps and cliff hucks, to the point where some of it has gone almost beyond the pale and stalled a bit as a result. There is no denying the inherent danger of all this. After Paul Ruff's fatal 150-foot jump in 1993 near Kirkwood, CA, in an attempt to set a world record, some industry insiders said it would slow the seemingly endless rush to push skiing's limits. The actual evidence is that it was barely a hiccup.

Beginning in 1997 the Winter X Games took the nascent park and pipe scene fully public, in the process combining most of the other forms of alpine jumping and adding some new wrinkles. Winter X was an instant success on ESPN, giving the events the kind of wide exposure and prize/sponsorship money that has both attracted and nurtured a lot of the jumping going forward.

Freestyle courses, super-pipes and big air kickers provide highly visible venues for people to go huge while not necessarily dying if something goes wrong. That's because the jumps are vaguely within reason, and are regular events instead of one-off stunts to set a record.

Which isn't to say they're danger-free by any means. Or that all record-setting attempts are, perforce, more dangerous. In 2010, the park crew at The Canyons Resort in Utah moved and shaped more than 45,000 yards of snow to create a huge special hip feature for freeskier and X Games medalist Grete Eliassen. Carefully designed and sculpted, separate from any other competition, it was able to accommodate a world-record effort with a maximum amount of safety.

The result was that Eliassen went up to 60 miles an hour on her inruns and eventually soared over 31 feet above the snow off the giant hit, with sponsor Red Bull announcing, "No woman has ever come close to reaching this height on skis."

The risk of regular competition super pipes can be some of the most serious because its possible to either case into the flat edges on the sides, or stray out into the middle of the pipe and land flat there. And when you're coming down from over 20 feet at good speed on the sides and twice that in the middle it can be ugly.

American snowboarder Kevin Pearce was 22 in 2009 when he struck his head just above the left eye, on the top of the sidewall during a training run on the Park City halfpipe at the US Ski Team facility. He was immediately airlifted to the University of Utah Medical Center in Salt Lake City where he was diagnosed with a traumatic brain injury (TBI). After extensive rehabilitation Pearce was able to board again, but not to compete.

The three-time medalist at the 2008 Winter X Games in Aspen had won numerous other big competitions, including the Swatch TTR World Snowboard Tour Champion title in 2007/'08. He's now a motivational speaker and founder of Love Your Brain Foundation, a nonprofit focused on improving the lives of people affected by TBI.

Superstar snowboarder Gretchen Bleiler was practicing a halfpipe maneuver on a training trampoline in Park City in 2012 when it went badly wrong. She smashed her eye socket with her own knee, breaking her nose and dislodging her eyeball. With a major concussion and ongoing double vision there were many questions about whether she would ever be able to snowboard again, let alone compete at the level that earned her five X Games golds and a silver medal in the 2006 Olympics.

"I've been hurt before, a blown ACL, a shoulder, but this was a whole different level," she told me. "I was first focused on getting back my vision and my quality of life. The biggest challenge was to be patient once I got my vision back. But I feel these challenges happen for a reason. To teach me more finesse, patience and humility." She made it back to the podium at 31, but didn't qualify for the 2014 Olympics in Sochi and announced her retirement soon after.

The movie featured Rick Sylvester's massive cliff huck.

The same year Bleiler was injured, Canadian super-skier Sarah Burke had an accident while training in January at the same big halfpipe in Park City where Kevin Pearce was so badly injured. One of the leading champions of including women's superpipe in the 2014 Sochi Olympics, Burke had often competed against the men early in her career. "She always asked, 'Why not?'" said the chief executive officer of the Canadian Freestyle Ski Association, Peter Judge. "It was: 'Why not ski with the men? Why not be in the Olympics?'"

The popular and charismatic four-time gold medalist at the Winter X Games was practicing a 540 flat spin when it appeared that she landed fine before awkwardly flipping over and striking her head in what onlookers described as an innocuous appearing crash. But she didn't get up, then went into cardiac arrest and stopped breathing. CPOR was administered at the scene without restoring her heartbeat and she was placed on life support at the University of Utah Medical Center in Salt Lake.

A ruptured vertebral artery had led to severe intracranial hemorrhaging. Even once surgeons operated to repair the rupture, Burke's brain had been deprived of oxygen for too long during the cardiac arrest and she died 9 days later in the hospital. It was a terrible blow to her family, husband, friends and fans, as well as the sport. In the end, though, the show went on, just as Burke would have wanted it to, with women competing on a par with men.

Maybe it was fitting that one of the biggest achievements in the superpipe also happened in that same tragic season. Standing at the start of the 2012 Winter X Games SuperPipe in Aspen for his final run of the comp, snowboarder Shaun White was the dominant and defending champion in the event and already a certified legend. Just to drive that point home he made a run that soared 15 to 20 feet above the shiny pipe walls, casually spinning and whirling like some enraptured snow dervish. When it was over he'd thrown the first-ever frontside double cork 1260 in a pipe (three full spins with a double horizontal twist), and scored the first perfect 100 in the event in X Games history.

In a rising tide of Scandinavians, Norwegian Torstein Horgmo scored a first-ever triple cork (three full backflips) in the Snowboard Big Air in Aspen to win gold in 2011. In 2013 Swedish skier Brian Harlaut threw an even more game changing Big Air in Aspen. His nose butter triple cork 1620 (three flips and five full spins) came in a tight comp on the last run for a perfect score of 50 to win, after fellow competitor Tanner Hall urged him to go for it.

"Tonight's big air competition will go down in skiing's history books as one of the most talked about events ever," declared one of the announcers in a booth where commentators and reporters were screaming and throwing clipboards in the air.

In 2020 skier Gus Kenworthy (5 medals and counting) threw the first ever switch triple rodeo 1440 (three backflips with four full rotations) in Slopestyle in Aspen as the barrage of high-flying aerials continued with no end in sight. It seemed like a fitting metaphor for the Winter X Games, still flying high, unleashing genius and breaking records, a quarter of a century after it all began.

With all of that, in the wide snowy world beyond the parks and pipes there were, and are, still athletes getting big air, of course. The market for it has remained strong, especially in ski-porn films that are more popular than ever with the proliferating platforms to show them.

The cameras were there when Candide Thovex made that first successful flight over Chad's Gap in Cottonwood Canyon, Utah in 1999 with a mute grab, and when he came back the next year and did it with a D-Spin. Yes, the same Chad's Gap where Tanner Hall, after sessioning it well all day in 2005, came up short trying a switch cork 900 and broke both ankles. On video. He returned for redemption in 2017.

Cameras were there in 2006 when Jamie Pierre stuck a 255-foot cliff drop in the Grand Targhee backcountry of the Tetons. Literally stuck it, going in almost headfirst and dart-like and having to be dug out. He'd worked his way up since 2003 from 165 feet off Wolverine Cirque near Alta, through a series of big leaps in Switzerland and Oregon.

"I just really wanted to hold the record, even if only for a day," said the 36-year-old who grew up skiing Buck's Hill in Minnesota and never wore a helmet. He had a young family and noted he could now "retire" to slightly less hazardous skiing. Sadly he died in 2011 in an avalanche in the Alta backcountry.

The heart-stopping heights of serious cliff hucks progressed to the point by the 1990s where no one was even trying to ski away from them. They plant their landings in deep snow, using the ski's tails when possible to absorb some impact, and just hope to survive. That was Fred Syversen's plan in 2008 when he made a filmed practice run to a cliff in Norway chosen to break Pierre's record by a few feet. But he turned too early in his fast moving descent, and realized it too late to avoid going off the wrong, and much higher, drop. "Braking or trying to stop was no longer an option, it simply went too fast," he posted on social media. "So that left one choice: go for it and do it right!"

He turned slightly to avoid rocks to his left, got out over snow and tilted so he didn't land on his ABS pack that could have damaged his spine, then cratered from 351 feet high like an unexploded mortar shell. His only slight injury came when someone hit him with a shovel digging him out. And they got all of it from start to finish on video.

Even though pure gelande still doesn't get much love, there are 9 seconds of wobbly bystander footage of Rolf Wilson setting the world record of 374 feet at Howelson Hill in Steamboat in 2011. You probably didn't see it even if you lived there, where most locals only read about it in the Steamboat Pilot newspaper the next day.

"It's such an odd sport," allows Wilson, who's from Missoula, Montana. "One of the sports that doesn't get a lot of recognition, because the guys that do it really just wanna jump, and see how far they go, and have fun. And we're a bunch of hooligans to be honest with you."

While Jesper Tjader's giant transfer in 2014, and David Wise's 2016 amplitude, have helped pace the park and pipe world's ongoing aerial assault, more traditional Big Air has seemed poised for the next big step. As some alpine jumping records near their survivable outer limits, no one has been lining up to try to beat Syverson's 351 or Wilson's 374. So what's on the horizon?

More XGames-style events; more ski movies; more genius films like Candide Thovex's with amazing stunts that aren't always potentially lethal; wing-suited jumpers landing on slopes from big drops without ever popping chutes (it will happen); and someone letting the true gelande crowd build the jump they yearn for with a lightning fast in-run, adjustable kicker, and endless run out.

Meanwhile, if you want to go really big the best bet is still Nordic ski flying on the 120-meter hills, where the current world record by Stefan Kraft of Austria at 831 feet is closing in on three football fields, no tricks involved. Check out the full story of the oldest and most traditional form of ski jumping in the next chapter.

Olympic gold medalist Egon Zimmermann jumping a Porsche.
Photo by Hans Truol.

CHAPTER 2
NORDIC JUMPING – PART ONE

Defying Gravity

One of the most infamous pieces of sports video in history ran for years at the start of every episode of ABC's Wide World of Sports television show from 1971 on. It accompanied broadcaster Jim McKay's voiceover about bringing viewers, "the thrill of victory and the agony of defeat." Over the years they rotated different clips through the "thrill of victory" section. But they ran the same one during the "agony of defeat" portion until the day the show ended in 1998.

During the World Ski Flying Championships in Oberstdorf, West Germany, on March 21, 1970, Yugoslavian jumper Vinko Bogataj authored, in the space of a few seconds, one of the most enduringly well-known moments in his sport's history. And he didn't even have to actually jump to do it.

Conditions were icy and windy at Oberstdorf that day and on his first jump Bogataj landed at 410 feet then fell partway down the outrun. On his second round he tried to tuck more on the in-run because of the wind and get lower on his skis. Going over 50 miles an hour he tipped over to his right before he ever reached the lip and crashed along the edge of the inrun until he bounced off the side of the jump itself and ended in a heap with a concussion and broken ankle. All while the cameras were rolling.

ABC executive Dennis Lewin decided in 1971 to put the clip of Bogataj falling in an intro reel, and it struck such a chord that while other elements of that reel continually changed, the Bogataj footage always remained. And as Jim McKay would later note, it meant that, over time, "he would appear more often on Wide World of Sports than anyone else."

Norwegian Reidar Andersen jumping at Holmenkollen, 1938.
Municipal Archives of Trondheim.

For a party in New York on the 20th anniversary of the show, ABC invited Bogataj to attend along with a host of famous athletes. It was when Muhammad Ali asked for his autograph that Bogataj understood for the first time the level of attention his accident continued to receive.

The whole episode can be seen as a parable of the way ski jumping is viewed by much of the world. Especially in the early years of the event, it was obviously dangerous and subject to largely uncontrollable vagaries such as the wind, the visibility and the condition of the hill.

So how did it get started as a deliberate sport that actually caught on? Tracing the roots of ski jumping back "through the foggy ruins of time" is as difficult as trying to do the same with skiing itself since they are so closely tied. Various peoples may well have been ski jumping independently for fun and games long before organized competitions began being recorded. But those currently appear to have begun in Norway, where skiing goes way back and of course so does jumping.

The first known ski jumping distance record was set by a Norwegian-Danish soldier named Olaf (Olav) Rye on November 22, 1808. Rye created a small hill of freshly piled snow at Lekum farm in Eidsberg, on the outskirts of Christiania (renamed Oslo in 1905), and was witnessed by an audience of his fellow soldiers going 9.4 meters (30 feet 10 inches) off of it.

It isn't hard to imagine bored soldiers making a competition out of something they were already doing when they were on maneuvers or trying to figure out how to overcome various problems on while soldiering on skis.

Any earlier or competing distance claims are difficult to pin down. Legendary pioneer skier Trysil Knut (or Knut from Trysil) lived concurrently with Rye and was once credited with jumping over 12 of the King's soldiers standing shoulder to shoulder. Tim Ashburner, in his interesting book *The History of Ski Jumping*, calculated that span as probably being a few meters further than what Rye cleared, but it has never been considered a formal record. It did give it some more color though and demonstrated an early flair for showmanship.

Ashburner also wrote that, "One of the very first competitions on record took place at Tromso, far beyond the Arctic Circle in 1843." Apparently the most noteworthy thing about it was that one of the competitors was Johannes Wilhelm Steen who would become Prime Minister from 1891 – 1893. This mattered in part because the PM's backing probably contributed to the acceptance of skiing and jumping as recognized sports in Norway.

It also seems like it might have indicated that the indigenous arctic peoples of the region could have been involved or even staged the event since it isn't clear why else it would have been held so far north. Upon close examination a number of aspects of the Norwegian trailblazing in the use of skis begins to seem like it may have resulted from close contact with people such as the Sammi, who were widely acknowledged as experienced skiers whose use of skis went back potentially thousands of years.

One of the biggest influences on early skiing as a sport undoubtedly came from the region of Norway that gave its name to skiing: Telemark. And much of that can be attributed to the "father of modern skiing" Sondre Norheim from Morgedal. In addition to having a profound impact on the mostly poverty-stricken children of the area by creating something to do in the winter that fully engaged them, he personally won several early skiing competitions and set records in the process, further inspiring the locals.

The first known ski event in Christiania took place in 1866, close to where Olaf Rye set his jumping record nearly 60 years earlier. It was a combination of a so-called "slalom" that was seen as a test of style, and a cross-country race with small jumps on the downhill sections. In 1868 invitations to the event were sent across the country and Norheim and two friends came from Telemark, on skis and across mountains, taking three days to get there. After that the event itself was relatively tame and Norheim won handily.

A month later, on March 8, 1868, a large competition was held on the Haugeli slopes of Kvitseide in the Telemark area. It consisted of three laps on a course that included 7 jumps and was considered a kind of skiing steeplechase. Norheim was credited with one jump of 50 *alen*, which translated to 34 meters.

But there was concern over exaggerations in the rest of the account, with newspapers in Christiania citing the correct number as 30 *alen*. According to Ashburner's book, "Most historians credit him with a longest jump of 27 meters [88 feet 7 inches] which was to remain a record until 1891." However, several official sources list it at only 19.5 meters (64 feet). Either was a record.

After this, spectator interest in the new sport lapsed and other similar events around the country were discontinued. However, a small group formed the Christiania Ski Club in Norway's capital, and in February of 1879 held a demonstration of ski jumping on Huseby Hill in the western part of the city, to which they invited a troupe of Telemark's renowned jumpers. As Ashburner wrote, "They were rewarded with a crowd of some 10,000 people, and from this point, ski jumping never looked back."

In addition to the demo it was also the inaugural King's Cup event that included a "leaping competition." Some game locals, determined not to be left out, provided unintentional comic relief. Not familiar with the concept of a jump, only moderately accomplished at skiing, and "checking their speed with frantic efforts, they slid downhill to the dreaded platform, or 'hopp' from which they were supposed to leap, but over which they but trickled, as it were," wrote English author Chrichton Somerville who was one of the throng of spectators.

He continued, "But then came the Telemark boys, erect at starting, pliant, confident, without anything but a fir branch in their hands, swooping downwards with ever increasing impetus until with a bound they were in the air, and 23 meters (76 feet) of space was cleared ere, with a resounding smack, their skis touched the slippery slope beneath, and they shot onwards to the plain… That was a sight worth seeing, and one never to be forgotten…"

In the modern era when humans have found multiple ways to fly, including without the aid of mechanical devices, "breaking the surly bonds of earth" and essentially defying gravity is a common occurrence. But in 1879 it had to be an exciting concept, however briefly they were airborne. And really, to anyone who has ever jumped on skis then or now, it can be a unique joy.

It seems in retrospect especially remarkable it was happening in the late 1800s considering the equipment involved. Professionally made skis were virtually non-existent for many years and very difficult to come by, especially for the poor country people who invariably made their own. Without much of a template to follow, materials that included everything from barrel staves to green trees to maple, ash and hickory were employed. And whatever was created was used for cross-country, going downhill and jumping, with specialization still decades away.

In a description carried in the Illustrated London News in 1894 about the jumping held at the Holmenkollen competition, the skis were described as "two wooden planks about 8 feet long, securely attached to the ski." That length was roughly consistent with what was used for most of the next century.

Getting them to slide successfully on whatever snow conditions prevailed became a kind of mad science early on. Untreated, relatively porous wood not only isn't slick on most snow, it often gathers it in large clumps on the base, an aggravating occurrence even with today's sophisticated cross-country gear. Developing ways to seal the wood was critical and pine tar was a constant in this process for many years.

Adding different coatings that would make them quicker in different conditions, turned into a secretive practice referred to as "doping" (not to be confused with today's steroids and human growth hormones) and practiced by virtual skiing shamans. Everything from animal lard to plant oils, machinery grease and bodily fluids were included in these obscure formulas that made the difference between the skis being usable or just clumsy impediments.

Another big consideration was how to attach the boots to the skis so they'd stay put and also allow the ski to be maneuvered. Methods included drilling holes through the width of the skis under where the foot would go and then looping straps through there and over the boots. Nails and screws were also used to affix the boot soles directly to the skis (if you were rich enough to have dedicated boots for the sport), or more usually to attach pieces of wood or metal to the top of the skis where straps around the boots could be anchored to them.

All of these devices were difficult to make work for regular skiing. Jumping enlarged the problems by making it more likely the skier would fall or land hard and damage important pieces of their gear and bodies.

And as Somerville observed, there was also the matter of the "fir branch in their hands." A single pole was a staple of most skiing for centuries because it was vital for balance and also propulsion on the flats. While it was logical that early jumpers would keep the pole, it didn't last long once it proved nothing but a hindrance.

As the sport continued and progressed, much of that growth hinged on the gear being able to keep up with the facilities. One of the most important aspects of making ski jumping a viable ongoing competitive event has been striking a balance between the hills, the gear, the techniques, and the abilities of the athletes. That process

Ragnar Omtvedt jumping at the Holmenkolrendet. National Library of Norway.

continues to this day with the FIS and other organizations trying to regulate the sport for safety and sanity while also satisfying the athletes and the audiences that make the whole show possible.

With ski jumping still very much in its infancy in 1879, the main interest was in popularizing it. Having finally galvanized the townsfolk with this "peasant sport" from the snowbound outback, the King's Cup enjoyed such success that it made stars of Jon Hauge, the first champion, and the Hemmestveit brothers of Morgedal who together won it four times.

The Hemmestveits started the first ski school in Christiania, but the country was poor and the economy struggling. Eventually, along with some of their students, they moved to America where they continued to win and spread the sport. Others in fallout range of the Norwegian skiing diaspora included Finland and Canada.

The first recognized world records in jumping took place in Norway between 1868 and 1886. In 1887, the first official ski jumping competition in America was held in Ishpeming, Michigan where freshly arrived Mikkel Hemmestveit won. No length was recorded. Then in 1891 at McSorley Hill in Red Wing, Minnesota, Mikkel set the first world record in the U.S. when he also became the only person to break the 100-foot barrier and land it. The official record books list it at 31.1 meters (102 feet). In 1893 Mikkel's brother Torjus upped it by a foot to 31.4 meters.

Jumping over a dozen soldiers was impressive nearly a century earlier. But 100 feet was a major milestone, something a little hard to fathom that truly began to resemble flight more than falling. Though many early devotees of the sport thought it should be judged on style alone, it was increasing in popularity at least in part due to the distances jumped and the world records being set. And in 1901 a scoring system for distance was finally introduced that has been a major component of jumping contests every since.

During the same period that many Norwegians were moving to North America, some were also being actively courted by rapidly developing ski centers in the Alps. Davos and Glarus, Switzerland, were two resorts that took to skiing very early on. In Glarus, native Christoph Iselin partnered with Norwegian immigrant Olaf Kjelsberg to further promote skiing and jumping in the region. Kjelsberg and another Norwegian named Krefting are credited by Ashburner "with the first ski jumps seen not just in Switzerland but also in Europe."

This happened on the heels of the Richardson brothers from England spreading their gospel of skiing in Davos. They'd been introduced to it in Norway in the winter of 1885/'86 on holiday with their parents. E.C. Richardson was especially taken with jumping and when the brothers appeared in Davos in 1901/'02 they built some small jumps, possibly the first ever seen there, and eventually enticed a few locals to join them.

That helped set the stage for Kjelsberg, Krefting, Iselin and others to hold ski jumping exhibitions in Glarus in 1903 where the big and appreciative crowds sparked such an enthusiasm for skiing that it "spread like a bush fire to every canton," according to Ashburner.

In Austria, skiing really arrived with Norwegian Frederick Wedel Jarlsberg's appointment as ambassador to Vienna in the winter of 1892/'93, where he immediately formed a ski club. Another Norwegian, W.B. Samson, was also in Vienna working on becoming a master baker. He built a jump on a manure heap (a novel act of repurposing) on the edge of the city and wowed the locals with leaps in the 8 to 10-meter range (25 to 30+ feet), the first of their kind to have been seen by crowds anywhere in Austria.

The first series of ski races in central Europe were held in the Steiermark of Austria in 1893 and lightly attended. But at the inaugural event, the biggest hit was W.B. Samson who won the race and then gave a jumping demonstration. As he described it later, "I had a jumping hill made and flew like a bird through the air. At any rate that is what the spectators said when they told others about it later. They swung their hats, shouted and cried out, and then beamed when I landed down on the outrun after the jump. I waved back again. It was a great day." Many of the spectators seemed to almost regard it as a magic act.

Germany joined the skiing trend a few years later when a Prussian named Wilhelm Paulcke attending the University in Freiberg made a series of pioneering ascents and traverses in the Feldberg region over a three-year period. Once races began to be staged, members of the Todtnau Ski Club started looking for an experienced Norwegian to provide their skiers with the best instruction. The perfect opportunity presented itself when Asbjorn 'Bjarne' Nilssen (24 and a winner of the Holmenkollen in 1897 as well as a world record holder in ski jumping in 1899 at 32.5 meters) applied for enrollment at Freiberg and was gleefully accepted.

"Nilssen pointed out that back in Norway all competitions included ski jumping, and after showing them how to build a small hill he proceeded to jump 15 meters," wrote Ashburner. Then at Neustadt they were able to build something bigger and he went 23 meters, considerably longer than what Krefting and Samson were doing elsewhere, and onlookers loved it. Ashburner notes, "It was decided at once that ski jumping should be included as an additional event in the second German Championships in 1901."

Back in North America, the US and Canada were building some of the biggest new hills in existence. In 1909 Oscar Gundersen set the world record at 42.1 meters (138 feet) at Chippewa Falls, Minnesota. And on February 16, 1913 at Curry Hill in Ironwood, Minnesota, Ragnar Omtvedt became the first in the world to break 150 feet by launching 51.5 meters (169 feet).

This was all happening while the concerns of some of the sport's originators in the old country had been transmitted to the new world and were causing a similar uproar. Central to all of it was what historian E. John B. Allen, in his remarkable book, The Culture and Sport of Skiing, described as the Norwegian notion of *Idraet*.

"One of *Idraet's* goals was the health of the individual. *Idraet* would also make one into a moral, or at least more moral, being." This in turn would presumably bestow greater physical and moral health on the nation as a whole. "Every country has these sort of self-delusions," noted Allen. And much of Norway's came about in a time when they were striving for independence from Sweden and trying to define themselves as a separate people and nation. So *Idraet* became their motto, their banner, their reason.

The effect of transferring this ideal onto skiing was far-reaching for a time, and a source of conflict. Skiing had begun as a necessity for travel, deliveries, hunting, farming and forestry in the impoverished countryside of Norway. When it was turned into a sport by skiing exhibitions in the cities, the wealthy became much more interested in it and began looking for ways to make it reflect the Norwegian *Idraet*.

As Allen noted, "the ideal of skiing as a bourgeois sport rather than skiing as a country mode of transport," seemed to fly in the face of Ski-*Idraet*, which celebrated skiing's immersion in nature, and the accomplishments of those who were proficient at all aspects of it. Suddenly ski jumping was being removed from an all-around context in competition and turned into its own specialized event, with material prizes being awarded rather than just the warm glow of a job well done.

With the 1890 publication of "The First Crossing of Greenland" by Fridtjof Nansen, Norwegians had an internationally best-selling author to serve as the very embodiment of Norway and its *Idraet*. It helped that he was from an affluent and royalty-connected Christiania family (his uncle was Baron Wedel Jarlsberg), rather than from the peasant outback of Telemark. And no one seemed to mind that he first became noticed for his excellence as a ski-jumper rather than an all-around competitor, or that he made a lot of money from his book that helped popularize skiing in the general public's imagination.

Meanwhile the principles of *Idraet* came to be seen as not only anti-specialization, but also anti-commerce. If one were to ski and jump for reasons of making money, or to teach others skiing and jumping for pay, it sullied the purity of the endeavor and of *Idraet* itself. This was very much an early aspect of the long-lasting and largely pointless conflict over amateurism versus professionalism in sports as a whole. It could also be placed into context as part of the class war brewing across Europe, where the wealthy elites viewed life in philosophical terms, while the working class was forced to deal with it in practical terms

Since most of the ski clubs and other promoters of the sport in America were founded by Norwegians who believed fiercely in *Idraet*, this caused complications across a broad front that included even staging competitions

H. Smith, Norwegian, 1907.

Holmenkolbakken in 1904. Photo by Anders Beer Wilse/Norwegian Museum of Cultural History.

to begin with that were only specialized jumping events; judging them on distance and records rather than style alone; letting jumpers who had made money as instructors participate; and finally handing out money as prizes.

It was only when these ideals butted hard up against towns and communities seeking to attract visitors and new residents – whether in America, Norway or the Alps – attitudes quickly changed. Skiers and jumpers themselves naturally favored anything that made the sport more popular and gave them a chance to earn a living at it. So they went to the events that paid the most money, and set records at them that thrilled everyone from the spectators to the merchants to the city councils. And *Idraet* became a quaint memory in the New World.

In the 1916/'17 season, more world records were set, this time at Howelson Hill in Steamboat Springs by Omtvedt and Henry Hall, who were the first to jump over 200 feet. It had taken nearly 100 years to reach 100 feet jumping, then about 20 to double that. And in 1919/'20, famed immigrant Anders Haugen established new records at his own Haugen Hill in Dillon, Colorado, by first soaring 64.6 meters (213 feet) and then a few months later, 65.2 meters (214 feet). Hall took the record back on February 9, 1921 on the Big Hill at Revelstoke, Canada, with 69.8 meters (229 feet).

More jumps were also being built at many of the traditional sites as well as new ones in Eastern Europe, the Alps and Scandinavia. For example, small ski jumps were first built by youngsters in the Engadine Valley of Switzerland in the early years of the 20th century, then a 40-meter was built in 1912, and in 1925 the Bernina-Val Roseg-Sprungschanze opened permitting jumps up to 80 meters. Using the hill in 1930 a local Swiss named Adolf Badrutt became the first in the world to go 75 meters (246 feet).

Starting in 1931 for a four-year period, Norwegians Birger and Sigmund Ruud and Reidar Andersen dominated the record books, setting 8 of the 11 new long distances, advancing them from 75 to 99 meters (324.8 feet). It started at Flubergbakken, Norway, then the new Bolgenschanze hill in Davos, then Tremplin de Bretaye at Villars three times, before Canadian Robert Lymburne at Revelstoke in 1933 returned the title to North America for a year.

In spite of the attention being attracted to the sport by the records quests, the FIS continued their crusade to throttle back the distance obsession. In the early 1930s they decided jump hills could only have a maximum 70-meter (230-foot) K point and that athletes would be banned from FIS competition if they jumped on hills with more than an 80-meter K-point. Ones with more than a 90-meter potential – a distance that's now considered a 'normal' hill' – were denounced as unsafe, somehow degrading to the sport, and strongly opposed. Still, the crowds called out for more, and bigger jumps were being built everywhere.

Vinko Bogataj falling in ABC Wide World of Sports clip. Screenshot from YouTube video.

CHAPTER 3
NORDIC JUMPING – PART TWO

There's a Reason It's Called Ski Flying

When the Bloudkova Velikanka ("Bloudek Giant") jump opened in 1934 in Planica, Yugoslavia, despite the FIS edicts against burgeoning jump size, its K-point of 90 meters was substantially bigger than anything else on the planet. Birger Ruud obligingly broke the world record there almost immediately. The next year's big event saw the record set four times in four days. And in 1936, 18-year-old Austrian Josef (Sepp) Bradl became the first to land a legal jump past the 100-meter mark at 101.5 m (333 feet).

As he later recalled, "The air pushed violently against my chest; I leaned right into it and let it carry me. I had only one wish: to fly as far as possible! I could hardly believe it when an additional '1' popped up on the scoreboard!"

Stanko Bloudek, the head engineer of the team that designed the jump, declared, "That was no longer ski jumping. That was ski flying!"

Up until this time the size of jumps usually depended on what your site was suited for and what you could afford to build. Uniform sizing didn't really exist. Since then a classification system has evolved with five categories. Small Hill: up to 45 meters. Medium Hill: up to 74 meters. Normal Hill: up to 99 meters. Large Hill: up to 169 meters. Ski Flying: anything over that.

These standards have obviously been adjusted from when the Bloudkova Velikanka at 90 meters was the largest in the world and the first designated as a ski flying venue. And it was soon enlarged to 106 meters.

The quick new world records at Planica cemented the future of ski flying hills and when two years later Bradl improved his mark to 107 meters (351 feet) there, it further fueled the public's interest in this 'extreme' form of ski jumping. In their 1938 meeting in Helsinki, the FIS finally compromised to allow for experimental hill design, and ski flying was formally sanctioned. But to this day the FIS refuses to keep or recognize distance records set on ski flying hills and it still isn't allowed in the Olympics.

By 1941 the K-point at Planica had been increased to 120 meters and the world record was broken 5 times after that. As America entered WWII, nordic ski jumpers were soaring *further than the average city block*. And after the war in 1948, Fritz Tschannen moved the mark to 120 meters (393 feet). From 1934 to 1948, 10 records were set at Bloudkova Velikanka, and then it didn't happen again for almost 20 years as other ski flying sites came on line.

To this day only 6 ski flying hills have been built in the world, and four are still in use. A 5th, at Certak, has been slated for rebuilding for several years. Others have been considered for construction, but they require lots of land, maintenance and money, and have traditionally had limited other uses. However, new materials and configurations are making them easier to care for, as well as more versatile and available for year-round purposes.

Beyond those 5 there are a lot of Normal and Large Hill jumps that the FIS World Cup tour and other events are conducted on around the world, including in Japan, China, Korea and Russia. The Four Hills Tournament and the Holmenkollen are two of the oldest and most prestigious competitions. The FIS also stages regular World Championships, and the Large Hill has been contested at every Olympic winter games since 1924, with the Normal Hill added starting in 1964.

Ski flying events are also part of the mix for determining season long World Cup champions. And there's always a little added interest in them because they can involve new world records. From 1808 through 2022, the bulk of those records have been set at the two Ski Flying jumps in Planica, Yugoslavia for a total of 38; Vikersund, Norway, where the 6 most recent were made, adds to a total of 25 records in Norway; and Oberstdorf, Germany, which has hosted 21.

The progression of ski flying, however, didn't get any easier in spite of its records and popularity. When in 1948 a new 120-meter hill started being built in Oberstdorf, West Germany, under the supervision of former jumper Heini Klopfer, the FIS refused to sanction it. They'd already denounced the last two events at Planica.

By the 1950 Obserstdorf opening, though, the organization softened and gave its approval for a weeklong event at the Heini-Klopfer-Skiflugschanze that attracted 100,000 spectators. They were well rewarded with the world record broken three times in two days, ending with Dan Netzell at 135 meters (443 feet). That was stretched by Tauno Luiro the next year to 139 meters (456 feet) and stayed there for a decade.

Yugoslavian Joze Slibar finally bumped it up to 141 meters (463 feet) in February of 1961, and that distance was tied twice, one of them on a new jump at Kulm in Tauplitz, Austria. The record passed back to Obserstdorf two years later before returning to Kulm in March of '65 at 145.5 meters (477 feet).

The top of the Bergisel jump, Innsbruck, Austria, opened in 2006. Designed by Zaha Hadid Architects. Photo by QEDquid.

In March of 1966, when Norwegian Bjorn Wirkola upped it to 146 meters (479 feet) it marked the first time in 31 years that the world record had returned to Norway. There was because there was now another major venue on the scene.

Jumping has been going on in Vikersund since at least 1894 when a local ski club was organized. They used 6 different hills until the 1930s when it was decided that "a proper jump" should be built and in 1936 they inaugurated a 50-meter hill. The longest jump on opening day was by Reidar Andersen at 86 meters. He had set three world records in two days at Planica the year before and was in the middle of becoming the only man to ever win the Holmenkollen three consecutive years. The Vikersundbakken was next enlarged to 100 meters in the 1950s, and on March 13, 1966, they opened a further expansion, where Wirkola set the new world record.

An event at Oberstdorf in February of 1967 saw the record advanced to Lars Gini's 150 meters (492 feet). Then in March that year Austrian Reinhold Bachler pushed the Vikersundbakken to 154 meters, becoming the first to pass 500 feet at 505. It turned out to be the last time Vikersund would host a record for 40 years.

Wirkola is still the only man to win the Four Hills Tournament three times in a row, doing it from '67 through '69. And he also set the world record again twice in 1969, at the new 153-meter Letalnica bratsov Gorisek jump in Planica, before Manfred Wolff of East Germany moved it to 165 meters (541 feet) on the last day of the opening event.

It doesn't take genius to discern a pattern of jumpers on hot streaks taking advantage of the grand openings at the biggest new jumps or after old ones have been enlarged. And the distances were progressively more astounding.

Planica, Yugoslavia is the largest jumping complex in the world with 8 hills total. Construction had begun on the Letalnica in 1967 and finished at the end of 1968. The initial K-point was at 153 meters, bumped up to 165 in 1972, then 185 in 1985. After the flurry of records in 1969, only one more was posted on the hill in the next 10 years and that was in 1974 when Austrian Walter Steiner tied a record set at Oberstdorf.

Then in March of 1976 at Oberstdorf, three different jumpers set records over four days, with the great Austrian Toni Innauer coming out on top at 176 meters (577 feet). And in 1979 East German Klaus Ostwald at Planica tied Innauer's Oberstdorf record, as did Armin Kogler from Austria the next year, this time at the newly expanded Certak ski flying hill in Harrachov, Czechoslovakia. Kogler then advanced it to 180 meters (591 feet) in 1981 at Oberstdorf.

When Czech jumper Pavel Ploc took the title back to Certak in 1983 by one meter, it was a great national victory for a controversial ski flying hill that has not seen another world record since.

Bjorn Wirkola at 1966 FIS World Championships.
Photo by Kjell Sjoberg/National Archives of Norway.

Jumps in Harrachov were first built on a site called Certova Hora, locally referred to as "The Devil's Mountain," in the 1920s. In 1979 they added a Large Hill and a Ski Flying hill, Certak, the latter seeming to justify the diabolical nickname. Both jumps opened in 1980 and Certak quickly became infamous for bad crashes that resulted primarily from the ridiculous amount of height jumpers were getting over the knoll of 13 to 18 meters (49-59 feet) that magnified the effects of wind and pilot error.

In the 1983 World Championships where Ploc set the world record, there were multiple "horrific accidents," as one account described them. Steinar Braten, who had won the Holmenkollen that year, fell headfirst but walked away. Horst Bulau did almost the same thing and got a bad concussion. And even Jens Weissflog, one of the most successful jumpers in history, fell badly. Ploc himself had bad wrecks there in 1980 and 1985, fortunately without serious injuries.

The FIS finally pulled the plug on the jump and it was rebuilt between 1989 and 1992, conforming to their requirements. Even so, Austrian Andreas Goldberger had a nasty crash on the hill when it reopened, where he broke an arm and collarbone and was choppered to the hospital. He fully recovered and went on to win the overall World Cup title three times, along with 7 Ski Jumping World Championships medals that included one gold, and three Ski Flying World Championships medals that included one of each.

At its maximum size of a 185-meter K-point, and Hill Size of 210 meters, Certak was never the biggest jump in the world, nor capable of sustaining world record assaults. Regular World Cup comps were held through 2014, but then the lights were turned out with, "an extensive renovation required," according to the FIS.

In 2019 representatives of the FIS conducted an inspection of the hill during which they received, per the FIS website, a briefing on "an ambitious project to completely renovate the Ski Flying facility on the Certak, presented by the Czech Ski Association." A proposal was scheduled to be submitted at the next FIS Congress in Thailand in 2020, but the Covid pandemic put everything on hold.

It was 1985 when the Gorisek jump at Planica claimed another record all it's own with Mike Holland from the US holding it briefly at 186 meters before the legendary Flying Finn Matti Nykanen took it another 5 meters to 191 (627 feet) that same day. These results were clearly attributable to the jump having its K-point expanded earlier that year. And from then until 2005, only one of the next 19 world records was even tied somewhere else, and that came in 1986 from Andreas Felder at Kulm.

Opening in 1950 the Kulm jump was one of the early purpose-built ski flying hills and it has frequently been enlarged. After the first time in 1962 Peter Lesser set a world record. The jump was completely torn down in 1984/'85 and replaced with a K-185 for the Ski Flying World Championships the next year.

Andreas Felder's world-record-tying mark that year was the third and last one at Kulm in what was an otherwise ruinous World Cup event. Treacherous crosswinds preyed on the hill's big weakness, which was an excessively high launch from the ramp that catapulted jumpers 9 to 10 meters (30+ feet) above the knoll.

Masahiro Akimoto was knocked over by the wind, fell on his back and sustained chest and shoulder injuries along with a fractured ankle. On his first jump Rolf Age Berg hit 70 mph on the inrun and lost control in the air but managed to land safely. On his second attempt he was knocked out of the sky, concussed by a ski, tore an ACL, and ended his career. Ulf Findeisen landed headfirst and cartwheeled down the landing, suffering a cardiac arrest but surviving. Former jumper and color commentator for ABC Jeff Hastings said on-air, "I'm feeling a little sick to my stomach…I've never seen ski flying like this… so many falls."

A direct result of this televised disaster was that the FIS decided distance points would no longer be awarded for jumps longer than 191 meters, which tapped the brakes on any more world records after Piotr Fijas at Planica in 1987 went 194 meters (636 feet). Once new regulations for jump characteristics were put in place, the edict was jettisoned in 1991.

With tweaks, Kulm continued to host events, and prior to the 2015 World Cup event and the 2016 World Championships, the jump was thoroughly renovated to a Hill Size of 235 meters and a K-point of 200 meters.

For 1984 the Heini-Klopfer-Skiflugschanze in Oberstdorf had received another of its periodic upgrades, and

Finland's superstar Matti Nykanen set or tied three world records in two days, ending up at 185 meters and becoming the first to break 600 feet by taking it to 607.

This Oberstdorf jump is an anomaly amongst the Ski Flying hills by virtue of being a tower-jump rather than one built into an existing mountainside. It bears more similarity to many of the Normal and Large Hills around the world, created where the terrain wasn't suited to the styles of the Letalnica, Vikersundbakken, Kulm and Certak sites.

Tower-based jumps are those where the inrun and ramp rise like wild sci-fi totems above their surrounding landscapes to heights up to 72 meters (236 feet). That's the equivalent of a 28-story building and they're expensive to construct. The 90 and 120-meter jumps at Lake Placid, for example, used a jacking system that lifted and poured concrete into the forms continuously, night and day for 15 days for the larger jump, and 9 days for the smaller one.

Freestanding jumps such as these in the early days were usually underpinned by the kind of sketchy scaffolding supporting old-time roller coasters. They were structural relics that were scarier than the jumps they produced. In the modern era the jump designs have become architectural statements that often serve as the pinup posters for Olympic games and entire winter sports regions around the world.

The normal and large hill inruns at the Beijing Olympics, in keeping with the overall futuristic tone of the 2022 games, looked like giant airline escape slides from the silver flying saucer that crowned them. Following the style at many current ski jumping centers, the jumps are positioned close enough to each other to offer adjoining (and enclosed) start areas in that flying saucer. And wind protection for the smaller hills is provided by the bigger jump structures.

At Oberstdorf they've incorporated those features and created a monumental edifice that appears to defy gravity while dispatching jumpers to do the same. Pitched at the same sharp angle as the inrun, the upper reaches of the cantilevered tower aren't visibly supported for the last 50 meters or so, instead jutting out over the surrounding countryside like a massive flying beam.

As with many of the bigger jumps today, the former shacks located at the top of the inruns have been replaced by much nicer enclosed staging areas with the capacity to hold many jumpers and coaches along with gear storage, restrooms and other facilities, including ones to support summer activities such as ziplines and chairlift rides.

GEAR

It wasn't just bigger jumps that were increasing distances by literal leaps and bounds throughout the 1900s and 2000s, but technique and equipment as well. One of the most important evolutions has occurred in the skis and their use. Clearly the most significant equipment in the sport, these have undergone multiple changes over time, just as in all skiing disciplines. Today they're made out of the most appropriate hi-tech materials available for lightness with flex, enough weight to keep them from being fluttery, and the tensile strength to not fall apart after a few hard landings.

Copper Peak jump in Ironwood, Michigan, the only ski flying hill in North America. Photo by CBradshaw at English Wikipedia.

The length and width of these missiles is also critical and regulated. The maximum ski length allowed is 145% of the total body height of the competitor based on a minimum Body Mass Index (BMI) of 21 for both ladies and men. BMI is determined by body weight divided by body height squared, in kilograms per meter squared. Okay.

The objective is to make it so skis can't be used to gain an advantage over other competitors by virtue of their length, compared to the weight of the jumper. A very light jumper isn't allowed to have enormously long skis that could be both a big edge as well as a potential hazard to the jumper. The rules state, "For athletes with less than minimum BMI a grading table of 0.125 BMI will be applied." This effectively limits the length of the skis for any lighter-than-average athletes.

During the post WWII era jumping skis were typically around 240 cm long, as opposed to alpine competition skis, where the longest are downhill models that rarely exceed 225. Today, the average good recreational skier's boards are in the 165 to 180 cm range. And the average length of jumping skis is 252 cm (8.2 feet), so that number has remained somewhat constant for over a century.

Regulations also state the skis must be no wider than 115 cm at the tips and tails, or 105 cm under foot, with a minimum under foot of 95 cm. That shape is roughly similar to some recreational fat/powder skis, only stretched over much more length. Any number of grooves are allowed on the base, as long as they don't constitute more than 50% of the running surface, and that no groove is wider than 10 mm. Jumping skis have typically had two or three grooves on the bottom, to make sure they track well on the inruns and outruns at speeds well over 60 mph. While the length, design and multiple grooves inhibit turning, skiers only need to turn once during each jump, and that's in the finish area.

The base must be flat polyethylene that may have a fine base structure but no other shapes beyond the grooves. There are also more detailed rules regarding side cut, edges, flex, amount of tip and tail rise, and what the ski can be made of (torsion box with no limitations regarding material and dimensions). They must also be of a minimum weight in relation to their length, which involves another formula. You are free to add weight for balancing the center of gravity since making the skis heavier confers no advantage. No additions such as fins, stabilizers, spoilers on tips or tails, and so on are permitted.

The principles behind the ski regulations extend to all of the gear, including such things as not having a boot sole that's wider than the ski, or clothes so loose fitting they perform like a flying squirrel's body. The latter has continued to be closely monitored to avoid having them become wing-suits that confer unfair and potentially dangerous advantages.

No heaters, chemical energy accumulators, electric batteries or mechanical aids are allowed. Neither is anything that could dispense materials onto the inrun that would change the condition of the pistes or snow to disadvantage fellow competitors. This is apparently meant to keep you or your skis from spraying motor oil, glue, anti-freeze or, say, Ice-9 onto the inrun or landing.

TECHNIQUE

From the very beginning, Nordic jumpers pressed their whole bodies forward at liftoff, jumping up and out and leaning against the wind. At first they also thrust their arms forward in a kind of superman pose and also out to the side for balance. In its infancy, ski jumping was much more about form than distance, so what jumpers did with their bodies and skis was much more about looking good and only loosely connected to going further.

As the sport developed and athletes began chasing records, the best position in the air was one that combined three elements: stability, slick aerodynamics to maintain speed, and a positioning of the skis and body to create an airfoil effect providing lift.

At this point the arms started getting tucked alongside the body on the inrun and in the air for less wind-resistance. And parallel skis were used to create more float by being held a little further apart, allowing the whole body-and-ski structure to perform as a wing. As the jumps started to get seriously big with increased amounts of hang-time, it didn't take long to realize that the arms could have a huge effect in the air. Moving them a little away from the body and slightly adjusting each hand could make significant differences in flight pattern, direction and balance.

The biggest and most noticeable technique change in the sport since WWII has been in the positioning of the skis while the jumper is in the air. The so-called Dascher technique, or parallel style, with the skis held close together and pointed straight ahead, became the norm in the 1950s. As jumpers began experimenting in search of more lift, Matti Nykanen started pointing his skis diagonally to the side in the 1980s to create more surface area and distance, but it was a difficult maneuver to control.

As jumps grew and the heights became more exaggerated due to the prevalence of very steep landing hills before they were re-contoured, sudden gusts of wind were causing havoc. American jumper Mike Holland noted that using the parallel style, "If you were hit by a gust of wind in the air, you would just flip over mid-flight." That caused a number of bad wrecks, and inspired jumpers to update their methods for the circumstances.

Swedish athlete Jan Boklov began using a V-shape in the late 1980s, flaring the tips apart in the air and pressing his body further forward between them. It was heretical to the tradition of the sport and especially irritating to older judges. It was also slower through the air by over 6 mph than the parallel style, and airspeed had always been considered vital for distance. But with the increased surface area and lift, Boklov was adding as much as 10 percent to his length, while also gaining stability through the air.

Judges took him to task for it on style points. But he was the Swedish National Champion on the Normal and Large hills for the second half of the 1980s, and between December 10, 1988, and January 28, 1989, in just 7 weeks with time off for the holidays, he scored 5 straight World Cup victories and ultimately won the Overall World Cup that season. Other jumpers immediately began following suit, of course, and once again the FIS gradually backed away from another of its institutional prejudices and quit deducting style points for the V.

By the mid-1990s the V was ubiquitous and already undergoing modifications, going from a narrower platform that retained some of the old parallel technique, to a much wider V, with the skis sometimes crossed at the tails, and bodies stretched so far forward and so flat between the skis that it looks yoga-like.

As has been seen in the last 30 years, it's possible for the V to go bad when the jumper loses air pressure under one ski and tumbles out of control. But the parallel style statistically tended to result in more catastrophic headfirst landings than the V where the jumpers crash primarily on backs and shoulders.

CHAPTER 4
NORDIC JUMPING – PART THREE

Crazy Dangerous

It was sometime in the 1920s when the genie really got out of the bottle in terms of the FIS trying to protect ski jumpers from themselves. And there's not much evidence it was a great idea to begin with. Once jumpers started flying 200 feet, they weren't going back. And there was only so much harder they could fall and deader they could die once the distances went beyond that.

Once humans could fly without mechanical assistance, like many thrills it became an addiction requiring ever-larger doses. We've gone from leaping off small mounds of garbage to flying off Everest, from simple-minded ski jumping to base jumping, wing-suits, and ski flying nearly the length of three football fields.

Certainly some of the viewer fascination with the sport is that it looks crazy dangerous to go over 60 miles an hour down a long narrow ramp and hurtle yourself off the end of it into a yawning void where you can soar 30 feet high for hundreds and hundreds of feet down to a steep landing area and, if you stay standing, reach speeds over 70 mph before you try to stop.

Men hadn't often publicly soared through the skies in any viable or intentional way when the English writer Crichton Somerville was rhapsodizing about watching it happen in 1879 in Christiania, Norway. Ski jumping was definitely a game-changer, forever altering man's concept of his limits.

But for a hundred years from 1808 to the early 1900s, it remained on the fringes of human endeavor. And even at its most extravagant early on it couldn't really be considered flying. Many ski jumps of modest size basically send a jumper into the air at speed and following the contour of the snow until they land. There is never any real weightlessness or the time to ponder it until they've gone radically high and been suspended for a moment, dangling at the apogee.

Chinese National Ski Jumping Center, designed by TeamMinus Architecture. Photo courtesy of TeamMinus and Beijing 2022.

When that finally happened, in truly mythical fashion it was at the point where ski jumpers became most god-like that they also became the most mortal.

My earliest jumping experiences with my dad were when I was about 10 on one of the small nordic jumps on Casper Mountain in Wyoming, and I was bolstered by his love and enthusiasm for it. But I was also hearing all the stories from other people about jumpers being hurt and even killed. They got blown off course while airborne on big hills and hit the judging platforms; over-jumped the hills and landed flat from high up; under-jumped and plowed into the level space between the kicker and the landing knoll; or just landed badly and egg-beatered all the way down the outrun. There was no shortage of the ways ski jumping could hurt you.

Many adjustments and changes over the decades have continually made the sport safer. More protection is now provided against wind effects: inruns have plastic tracks that make them much more consistent and easy to gauge for speed; hills have been reconfigured to reduce excessive heights; clothing and skis and techniques are monitored to make sure they don't provide too much lift; and even the weights of the jumpers are regulated so they don't get a dangerous advantage from being too light.

Today, nordic ski jumping is regularly referred to as being safer than alpine ski racing and roughly comparable to many other collegiate sports. A widely reported study supplied by the National Library of Medicine Case Reports in June of 1988 stated in their abstract, "Nordic ski-jumping fatalities are rare events. Six jumping fatalities have occurred in the United States during the past 50 years. The fatality rate for Nordic ski jumping, estimated to be roughly 12/100,000 participants annually, appears to be within the range of fatality rates for other 'risky' outdoor sports. Cervical fractures appear to be the most frequent fatal ski-jumping injury."

There are some significant modifiers in there, as is the situation with two other case reports written about by J.R. Wright, Junior – either alone or with coauthors – offering similarly benign conclusions about injury rates. One says, "Our study indicates that the dangers of Nordic ski jumping have been overestimated." Another makes this comparison: "The risk of injury per 100 participants was 9.4, a rate less than reported for most high school or college intramural sports."

Though these sound suspiciously boosterish, they may be accurate numbers within the constraints of the samples studied, and could possibly even be indicative of the sport as a whole. But they seem to downplay the fact that when athletes are injured ski jumping they tend to be worse than the calf tendon pulls of track sprinters, or the ankle sprains of basketball players. As stated above, cervical fractures are the leading cause of death. They can also come be badly disabling when non-lethal.

Furthermore, the impacts sustained by crashing ski jumpers rank at or above the collisions on a football field and can have similar long-term effects not apparently accounted for in these studies. And these aren't guys who are built like linebackers taking the hits. There are also valid questions about how many ski jumping accidents and injuries are actually reported among student athletes, for a variety of reasons.

In reality, its obvious even to a casual observer that the sport is more dangerous than many and only so much can be done to protect athletes who are willingly subjecting their bodies to extreme conditions. The key here once again is, "willingly." And you can see it across a spectrum of sports, from car and motorcycle racing to cycling and motocross, surfing and skydiving and on and on, where athletes subject their bodies to serious stresses and put their lives at risk on a regular basis. By choice.

In spite of all the precautions, the consequences when things go wrong can be severe. Vinko Bogataj is one example, where the injuries weren't life threatening, and where the video was life changing for the better. Other accidents have ended far worse.

On January 5, 1975, US National jumping team member Jeff Wright of Minneapolis was practicing in the morning for an event that afternoon on the recently redesigned 70-meter hill in Brattleboro, Vermont. The 22-year-old was an experienced jumper and the holder of the ski flying record for an American, set at 476 feet in Oberstdorf, Germany. But in mid-air on this January day he veered sideways and landed on his head.

It was a move, experts said, characteristic of letting too much air get under one ski, and something Wright had done the week before at Lake Placid but corrected for. Unconscious and bleeding this time, he was rushed to the local hospital, then to the Dartmouth College campus hospital, but died en route of a neck injury.

In 1983 at the World Ski Flying Championships at Harrachov in the Czech Republic, three jumpers were blown out of the air and injured. One of them was going over 71 mph on the inrun, which is blazing. In '86 at the World Championships in Kulm, Austria, something similar happened due to wind, resulting in what were described as "brutal crashes." One jumper suffered a broken ankle along with chest and shoulder injuries. Another had a cardiac arrest, and the third had a career-ending concussion and a torn ligament.

There have been a number of hard falls over the years that didn't stop the survivors. The great Austrian jumper Andreas Goldberger in 1992 went over 66 mph on the inrun at Harrachov and then plunged from 30 feet high in bad winds, breaking an arm and collarbone. He still got second in the event and had a very successful career ahead of him. Valery Kobalev of Russia lost pressure under one ski and crashed headfirst at Planica in 1999, sliding unconscious down the outrun. He was placed in an induced coma for several months but later resumed his career until 2006.

On the other hand there have been terrible wrecks with lasting effects. Austrian Lukas Mueller, a winner of the 2009 Junior World Championships on the normal hill, had just reached his competitive peak at 5th in the men's Continental Cup standings when he came into the 2016 Ski Flying World Championships in Tauplitz, Austria. It was there on the famed Kulm 120-meter hill where Mueller experienced every jumper's nightmare when a binding released in midair on a training run and he landed on his back at over 700 feet. He was hospitalized with serious spinal injuries that casued an incomplete paralysis of the legs and later required surgery and was career ending.

One of the more sensational crashes of all time occurred in 2021 when 2018 World Championship and Olympic gold-medal-winning jumper Daniel-Andre Tande fell disastrously at Planica on a training run. The 27-year-old Norwegian, who remembered nothing of what happened, watched endless replays of the video to determine that, "In the first phase of the jump, where I'm about to connect with the skis, the angle of my skis is too flat, and the pressure on the skis is too much. I try to push my skis a little away from my body, but I push my left ski too much."

This mid-flight adjustment caused him to completely lose control and begin flailing before bracing for impact. He was knocked unconscious and rag-dolled down the outrun. A doctor on the scene told his coach to prepare for the very worst. After 30 minutes of working on him at the hill he was airlifted to a hospital with four cerebral hemorrhages, a punctured lung and two broken collarbones, and was placed into an induced coma for four days. Then he went on to get 10 titanium screws put in the shattered collarbone and the following season won a World Cup event on the 120-meter jump in Oslo in 2022. The shoulder still bothers him.

Going long on a nordic hill is at the top of the list of things not to do if you want to extend your career. A friend of mine who was a nordic and gelande jumper, twice out jumped the 40-meter hill in Aspen – once in each discipline – breaking both ankles each time. I've broken a tibia plateau by out-jumping a gelande landing, so I'm sensitive to the issue.

But in the modern version of nordic jumping they make going too far difficult by raising and lowering the starting point on the inrun to adjust for conditions and how far jumpers are going. At the World Cup level I've only found 8 accidents caused by going too long, though the resources for digging into this are admittedly limited. None of the wrecks were catastrophic. Generally, jumpers are able to exert some influence at the last minute to come down sooner, and most long jumps end up past the redline but still in the transition where jumpers are skillfully able to lay it down and walk away.

In the end, of course, crashes are part of the consequences, and without the potential for them the great jumps would be less impressive. Knowing that the jumpers know, better than us, what they're facing if it goes badly, yet still getting up there and doing it, is a significant part of their accomplishment and the drama of watching them.

Austrian Stefan Kraft in 2017, the year he set the current world record. Photo by Christian Bier.

As for the possibility that some viewers are like those who watch car races just for the wrecks, consider this: Vinko Bogataj's best career finish was 57th on the normal hill at the Four Hills Tournament in Bischshofen, Austria, in 1969. In a country such as the U.S. where not one person in a hundred thousand could tell you the name of the current world-record holder in ski flying, a much higher percentage would still remember the crash Bogataj took on *Wide World of Sports* over half a century ago.

WOMEN'S JUMPING

Any time official discussions in skiing competitions about safety take place, it inevitably gets around to the longstanding excuses for excluding women from events that have been held for men for decades and longer.

As the venues, conditions, gear and technique all advanced, treatment of women ski jumpers remained stuck in the dark ages. Notwithstanding the fact that a 16-year-old girl named Ingrid Olsdatter Vestby became one of the first female jumpers in competition known to history, in Norway in 1863, they've only been allowed to compete at a high international level since the 2004/'05 Continental Cup season in Europe. The World Cup didn't have a women's jumping tour until 2011/'12, and the first Olympics to host them didn't happen until 2014 in Sochi.

The first "documented" female jumper in competition is said to have been in 1911, although other sources cite women's jumping records going back at least to 1897, when 10-year-old Norwegian Ragna Pettersen is reported to have gone 12 meters on Mesterbakken in Nydalen. In conservative Norway, though women jumped often for fun, they usually weren't allowed in competition and would sometimes dress as boys to get in to the events.

Some early references exist of the town of Asker near Oslo becoming known for hosting a few women's competitions at the end of the 19th century that may have been some of the first where they were allowed to compete publicly. Hilda Stang of Norway is credited with setting a mark of 14 ½ meters in 1902 and eventually stretching it to 22 meters by 1910.

An Austrian countess from Kitzbuhel, Paula Lamberg, is widely considered a leading pioneer of women's ski jumping in Central Europe, and is credited with also flying 22 meters, doing it in 1911 in a dress. That same year Lady hocking from England was said to have gone 7 meters during the British Ski Championships in Switzerland, and the trend seemed to be spreading. An event featuring 28 Norwegian lady jumpers was reported to have taken place in Trondheim, Norway on Grakalbakken in March of 2014.

Then, as Scandinavian immigrants were arriving in larger numbers in North America and bringing ski jumping with them, a 16-year-old girl born in Revelstoke, Canada, stepped up and sent the next world record jump for women to 25.6 meters (84 feet). It was 1922 and Isabell Coursier was the rare lady participating in any kind of sports in Canada, let alone ski jumping.

From 1916 to 1975, major jumping competitions were held at Revelstoke's Big Hill, eventually renamed the Nels Nelsen Historic Ski Jump. Coursier became one of its most legendary jumpers, and one of the first formal World Champions for women in the sport by virtue of her record.

When Norwegian Olga Balstaad-Eggen went 26 meters in 1926, Coursier responded by going 31.4 meters in 1928. Then Norwegian Johanna Kolstad went on a run, setting four records between 1931 and '38, jumping mainly in the US in those years and topping out with her last record of 72 meters in Berlin, New Hampshire.

After that, women's jumping stagnated for three decades due in part to a World War. Also the bizarre notions that lady's presence would "diminish the prestige" of some of the most famous jumping events, and that girls jumping after the age of 12 would later face the risk of becoming infertile. The reasoning was both insane and not uncommon across women's sports at the time.

Norway's Anne-Lisl Hexberg became famous in the 1950s as that country's best jumper. But it was up to Anita Wold from Trondheim, Norway to break the world record for the first time in 34 years with an 80-meter leap in Meldal, Norway in 1972. Over the next four years she cranked those numbers up to 97.5 meters. That wasn't passed until 1981 by Tiina Lehtola of Finland, who became the first woman to break the 100-meter barrier, doing it by a full 10 meters.

It was 1994 when Eva Ganster from Austria became a force in women's jumping by upping the record to 113.5 meters in Lillehammer, Norway, then doing it 6 more times in 1997, finally settling for 167 meters. In four years she added *more than 50 per cent* to the prior record – most of it in one season. It was a phenomenal show that caught the attention of the world, including the FIS, which approved Ladies Grand Prix competitions in the summer in 1999, followed by winter ones as the numbers of participants climbed.

In 2003, during practice for the Ski Flying World Championships in Bad Mittendorf, Daniela Iraschko (now Iraschko-Stolz) became the first female jumper to reach 200 meters with a practice jump on the Kulm ski flying hill of 656 feet. Her official world record was listed at 188 meters.

In addition she has three individual victories at the Holmenkollen Ski Festival, the overall women's Continental Cup in 2009/'10, gold at the 2011 Ski Jumping World Championships, a silver medal at the first ever women's ski jumping Olympics competition in Sochi in 2014, and 9 individual World Cup titles.

Other women's stars have included Lindsey Van of the US who became the first female world champion in 2009; German athlete Carina Vogt who won a gold medal on the normal hill in Sochi in 2014, and was World Champion twice in a row in 2015 and '17; and Maren Lunby of Norway who won the gold in 2018 in Pyeongchang and the World Championships the next year in Seefeld.

Throughout all of it has been Sara Takanashi of Japan, who, following the 2020/'21 season had achieved such unprecedented levels of wins that, to her surprise, they added up to three Guinness World Records, among many other honors. Takanashi has won more ski jumping World Cup individual titles in a career than anyone ever, man or woman, at 60. So of course she also has the most victories of any female jumper so far. And she has also achieved the most podiums in the Ski Jumping World Cup Tour with 109. Added to that are her four Overall World Cup titles, 7 World Championships medals and a Winter Olympic medal.

The trend amongst women jumpers has been visibly higher and further as they've been "allowed" to do it. Ema Klinec of Slovenia, for example, who first began jumping competitively in 2014, has been a fixture on the women's tour since 2016. She won a gold medal on the Normal Hill in the 2021 FIS Nordic World Championships. And on March 19, 2023 she won the first ever women's ski flying competition at Vikersund, and in the process set a world record of 226 meters (741 feet).

All of these women and thousands more have sent a resounding message to the sports world and the Federation International de Ski (FIS) that they have been too often guided by obvious gender bias. Jason Laurendeau and Carly Adams in their 2010 paper, 'Jumping like a girl': discursive silences, exclusionary practices and the controversy over women's ski jumping', succinctly stated that, "…the IOC dresses up the same paternalistic practices in new garb," when it denied women's ski jumping's inclusion in the 2010 Olympics. It's wonderful to see women prove that in every competition, but it should never have been necessary.

FREQUENT FLIER MILES

As far as men's world records go, none were set for 7 years starting in 1987 while war raged in the Balkans, temporarily suspending jumping events at Planica, and ultimately resulting in the breakup of the former Yugoslavia. When the Fijas record was finally surpassed by Austrian Martin Hollwarth in 1994 he nudged it up by two meters on what was clearly the only hill in the world where it could have been done: Planica's Velikanka bratov Gorisek – re-profiled for more length, reopened, and now in Slovenia.

The event didn't end there, either. Later that day legendary Toni Nieminen of Finland tacked on another 7 meters to raise the mark to 203 (666 beastly feet), becoming the first man to break the elusive 200-meter barrier. "I was very surprised and didn't expect such a great jump," Nieminen said later. "I didn't really aim for a world record at all. I just wanted to make a good jump. I had no expectations, didn't care at all, and that's probably

Women's world-record holder, Slovenian Ema Klinec in 2016. Photo by Ailura.

why I set a world record."

It lasted about 24 hours before Espen Bredesen of Norway shattered it by another 6 meters. In two days the newest world record had been jacked up by a remarkable 13 meters to 209 (686 feet). Finally back on the world's biggest ski flying hill, jumpers made the most of it by extending the record nearly 43 feet.

"Without any doubt this is my greatest career and life achievement," said Bredsen afterward. "Nothing can be compared with this world record. Not even my gold medal at the Olympics or the World Championships. Now I know how birds feel when they fly in the air."

Three years later in 1997, Bredesen and Lasse Ottesen exchanged records in the process of advancing the distance to 212 meters (696 feet). In 1999 Norwegian Tommy Ingebrigtsen added five meters to it for 219.5 (720 feet) and the next year Austrian Andreas Goldberger took it to 225 meters (738 feet).

And so it went until 2005. Between 1999 and then, Ingebrigtsen held the record twice and Matti Hautamaki of Finland had it four times, three of them on successive days in 2003 when he finished off at 231 meters (758 feet). In 2005, when the hill size at Planica was increased to 215 meters, Ingebrigtsen started March 20th by tying the record and Hautamaki took it back briefly before Bjorn Einar Romoren capped the event at 239 meters (784 feet).

Then a records drought set in and Planica made a number of upgrades and adjustments to the Letalnica jump to satisfy FIS conditions for hosting the 2010 Ski Flying World Championships. These included a chairlift for competitors, a tweaked profile, renovated judge tower, and a lowered ramp angle to take some of the notorious height out of the jumper's flight paths.

Swiss golden boy Simon Ammann is the only jumper to ever sweep the gold medals in both men's jumping events – the Normal and Large Hills – in two separate Olympics, in 2002 at Salt Lake and 2010 in Vancouver. His 2009/'10 season was a dominating performance where in addition to the Olympics he won all four events at the Nordic Tournament and 9 World Cup competitions throughout the season to capture the Overall World Cup title for the year. He ended by winning the World Ski Flying Championships at Planica where one of his jumps was the second longest ever at the time at 236.5 meters.

A new world record wouldn't come again until the next season in February of 2011. And not in Planica but at the revamped Vikersundbakken, where Johan Remen Evensen on February 11 raised it first to 243 meters and then 246.5, making him the first to clear 800 feet, pushing it to 809. Evensen pronounced the hill "perfect" in a post-jump interview.

That previous autumn the jump had been rebuilt for the 2012 Ski Flying World Championships to a Hill Size of 225 meters – the first in the world that big – with a K-point of 195 meters making it easier to stay standing at greater lengths. In charge of the overhaul were the Slovenian engineers Janez Gorisek (sometimes referred to as the father of modern ski flying) and his son Sebastian. Janez and his brother Lado were the creators of the Letalnica bratov Gorisek, and the Norwegians hiring Janez was a bow to his expertise as well as a shrewd way to insure building a jump that would be bigger than Letalnica.

The K-point was further expanded to 200 meters in time for a 2015 World Cup event where ski flying specialist Peter Prevc, fittingly enough a Slovenian, became the first ski flyer to reach the 250-meter mark. Norwegian Anders Fannemel upped it to 251.5 m (825 feet) the next day. In training Russian Dimitri Vassiliev went 254 meters but crashed hard.

The next season Prevc went into the 2016 Ski Flying World Championships on a roll. He and his younger brother had both made the podium in Engelberg in December, a first in World Cup ski jumping history. Then Peter won the prestigious Four Hills Tournament in Germany and Austria with three firsts and a third during the month leading up to the Worlds at Kulm in mid-January. He became World Champion with a jump of 244 meters (801 feet), that's still the hill record. And he went on to have one of history's great seasons, taking his first Overall World Cup jumping title with 15 wins, along with his third Overall World Cup ski flying title in a row. He would finish his career with 23 individual World Cup wins, four Olympic medals, and four World Cup season titles.

By 2016 Vikersund Hill had become a wonder of the jumping world and an imposing behemoth. Built into a well-suited hillside in 1936 it was rebuilt for ski flying in 1964 and has continued to be enlarged and heavily modified in its same location on a regular and expensive basis since then. For years the inrun was recessed into the timber and the natural contours of the hillside and thus less exposed than some jumps. Indeed where most hills boast of the heights from the base of the outrun to the top of the inrun, Vikersundbakken calls that measurement Not Applicable in its case.

As of 2017, after more than 7 million cubic feet of earth had been removed on the landing and outrun over the decades, it was as wide as a football field to allow for any in-air movement jumpers might be subjected to and still provide them with room to land on a snowy slope. And it follows such a well-calculated curvature that jumpers don't get more than a few meters high, thus putting them at less risk of wind interference while still flying further.

Above the jump ramp the inrun is literally carved into the rock and dirt, and mounded by gravel on either side to shield it from wind. It looks like an insane alpine slide, or some space-age water diversion project, with the inset white plastic groove the jumpers speed down gleaming like a liner in a high-tech water flume poured onto the hillside.

On top of the inrun squats a low, concrete, V-shaped building housing the same facilities as at the top of nearly all big new jumps. This architecturally rendered bunker completes a stylish Scandinavian minimalist interpretation of a modern ski flying venue.

It was the perfect stage for Austrian Stefan Kraft on March 18th to whistle down the inrun, press seemingly all the way out between his skis as he launched, then about a third of the way down to press still further and hold it well past the redline, telemark landing sweetly in the bottom of the compression, then squatting low before standing up and sweeping to a stop to the roar of the crowd, with a huge grin and his arms raised high.

Japanese Olympic gold medalist Ryoyu Kobayahsi in 2023. Photo by Limex Images / Red Bull Content Pool.

New Holmenkollen jump being built in 2012, 108 years after the photo in chapter two was taken.
Photo by Wilhelm Joys Andersen.

It took many minutes for judges to review the landing footage to insure he didn't touch any part of his body, like his butt, to the snow. When from the clearest angle it was obvious he avoided that by a couple of inches, it was ruled a new world record at 253.5 meters (832 feet).

Kraft, born in 1993 in Schwartzach im Pongau, Austria, has won the Ski Jumping World Cup and the Ski Flying World Cup season titles twice each, along with three gold medals at the World Championships. In March of 2022 he notched his 25th individual World Cup win at Oberstdorf.

A huge soccer fan, Kraft describes how he arrived where he is today in another sport entirely. "One day a friend took me to ski jump training and the rest is history. I was immediately fascinated by the flight feeling and the vastness you experience up there. Until this day, the fascination of flying is what keeps me going." On top of the kind of stellar career that represents consistency as well as excellence, the world record also means a lot. "It has always been a dream of mine to be the one that jumps the furthest. The fact that I actually achieved this is simply unbelievable and really hard to describe."

As of 2023 that record still stood, in part because many events were cancelled during the pandemic years, and no major improvements have been made to any of the ski flying hills.

Meanwhile the jumping sites continue to be a focus for communities that are discovering year-round uses for the unusual and expensive structures, including as restaurants with views, ziplining and alpine slide centers, and flamboyant architectural showcases. The Chinese National Jumping Center near Beijing debuted for the 2022 Winter Olympics with an ultra-futuristic Team Minus design that looks like a UFO parked on top of the jump hill, while also emphasizing safety and echoing an ancient Chinese symbol for good luck.

SECTION II
GOING HIGH AND LONG

Fred Harris, founder of the Dartmouth Outing Club and first to make a ski descent of Mount Washington in 1913.

CHAPTER 5
SKIING HIGH - PART ONE

Because It's There… And It Has Snow

Sir Arthur Conan Doyle, who tried to kill off his incredibly successful detective in the Swiss Alps, liked writing about the mountains. That was especially so after he and his ill wife moved to Davos in 1893 for her health, and he learned to ski. Always a sporting man, Doyle had become interested in skiing after seeing it in Norway. Once he moved to Davos he ordered some skis from Norway and set about learning to use them. He famously remarked that, "On any man suffering from too much dignity, a course of skis would have a fine moral effect."

He teamed up with a pair of local brothers named Branger who'd been skiing more or less in secret for about a year at that point, tired of being mocked by the locals to whom the idea was entirely novel and weird. Once Doyle was viably proficient the crew climbed the local 8,500-foot Jakobshorn and skied down it.

This was reportedly much to the delight of the locals who watched from town. Stories differ on his luck with the descent. Doyle reported that the descent was fine, it was the climb that nearly killed him. Others claim he also fell most of the way coming down, which would have been the norm for the time. The very rudimentary gear included skis that resisted turning, and novice skiers had little in the way of accepted technique to go by.

However it happened, upright or crawling, it was a very high descent for the day. So was the same group's trip over the Fuka Pass to Arosa, which was being promoted in the region as a new winter tour. The pass was nearly 8,000 feet high with rugged and dangerous terrain. Doyle wrote about it for The Strand magazine in 1894

noting that skis enhanced some of the climbing but were treacherous on the downhill sections, when he spent much of the time on his back trying to stop. "My tailor tells me that Harris Tweed cannot wear out. He will find samples of his wares on view from the Furka Pass to Arosa," he wrote.

There was also considerable good to be found on the journey, as he described in their descent to Arosa. "Now we had a pleasure which boots can never give. For a third of a mile we shot along over gently dipping curves, skimming down into the valley without a motion of our feet. In that great untrodden waste, with snow fields bounding our vision on every side and no marks of life save the tracks of chamois and of foxes, it was glorious to whiz along in this easy fashion."

It was this kind of enthusiasm expressed in widely-read print that helped stir interest in the fledgling sport and made his prophecy self-fulfilling when he wrote, "the time will come when hundreds of Englishmen will come to Switzerland for a skiing season."

Doyle's adventures were also emblematic of the burgeoning interest in making ever higher descents. Once skiers started going downhill and liking it, they sought longer runs on higher mountains. As Lou Dawson notes in his seminal book *Wild Snow*, the early history of first descents in America often went un-recorded. That was also more or less true in the rest of the world.

In Europe, those who first introduced skiing to their communities made many of the first descents and inspired others. But they didn't start keeping close track of them until much later. Going higher was done at first simply to get more skiing, until eventually the skiing was combined with serious climbing and became part of a culture that noted such things as the first people to make ski descents.

From then on there's been debate, from barstools to alpine clubs to letters to the editors, over what constitutes a true first descent. In its simplest terms it means to ski/snowboard from the summit to the base of a mountain

Armand Charlet, early Chamonix ski guide on Mont Blanc.

and be the first to document and record it. But there are many complicating factors. Some mountains rarely if ever have conditions where there's enough snow on their peaks for parts of the descent to be skiable. Sections may need to be down-climbed or abseiled. Couloirs and bottlenecks can be too skinny for traditional skis to negotiate.

Most authorities in recent years have agreed that a true first descent has to originate on the summit, or as close to it as best case conditions will historically permit. And it has to descend the mountain all the way on skis/snowboard until the snow runs out. The gear doesn't come off even if you're rappelling.

A lot of discussion has centered on whether certain mountains are ever totally skiable even under ideal conditions. And whether a descent is continuous only if it's all done on the same day. The latter is a sticky point for a number of important descents. Some of history's best alpinists haven't been able to meet all of these exacting standards. But that doesn't diminish the courage and passion of all those involved in taking the sport quite literally higher.

Scandinavians were well out in front of the Western world in using skis, though there is no written record to suggest they did much early ski mountaineering. Military cartographer Harald N.S. Wergeland made a first ascent of the then-highest point in Norway on the 2,481-meter (8,140-foot) Glitterind in 1841. His descent is said to have "probably" been on skis, which would make it one of the really pioneering ones on the continent that anyone knows about. The "probably" part is concerning. Norwegian Fritdjof Nansen likely set new standards for altitude in Scandinavia when he made his historic 310-mile crossing of Greenland on skis in 1888, and reported his highest point at 2,719 meters (8,921 feet).

In the Alps in the late 1800s the early ski pioneers steadily sought higher slopes. Franz Reisch in Kitzbuhel, Austria, for example, first began using skis sent there from Norway in 1890, soon climbing the nearly 2,000-meter (6,549-foot) Kitzuheler Horn on them and skiing down.

As was also the case with Doyle and the other early skiers in the Davos region, the skiing involved mostly trying to stay standing. What techniques as existed didn't discuss turning. The Scandinavian telemark wasn't designed for that in part because the skis weren't either. The long, rough-hewn, stiff, heavy and unmatched boards with leather straps for bindings were built for going straight, period. Just as with the early climbers in the Alps and Himalaya who were outfitted in loden and lightweight boots with hobnailed soles, what the first serious recreational skiers accomplished with the equipment they had was incredible as well as slightly mad.

And it was a widespread affliction. According to Amar Andalkar of skimountaineer.com, 5,642-meter (18,510-foot) Mount Elbrus in Russia was the site of a successful ski ascent and descent in 1914 by C. Egger. If true it could well have been the first recorded, genuinely high altitude ski in history. Elbrus, a stratovolcano with a stunning 3,505 meters (11,500 feet) of vertical, is considered the highest mountain in Europe, and one of the famed Seven Summits.

It was 14 years later before the first landmark ski descent was recorded in the Alps. Equipment and technique were progressing, making it possible to maneuver rather than just leaning on poles or falling to control speed. That mattered in the Alps where many of the biggest peaks are steep and challenging, unlike the relatively benign Elbrus routes.

On Mont Blanc, the Alps' highest mountain at 4,810 meters (15,781 feet), the first ski ascent was recorded in 1904 by Hugo Mylius from Germany. He was accompanied by guides from the Swiss Oberland named Tanner, Maurer and Zurfluh. There was no mention of them skiing on the descent.

According to recent research conducted by Carole Faessler of the Alpin Museum of Chamonix, a winter ascent was made by legendary Chamonix guide Armand Charlet and Jean Camille-Claret-Tournier with Norwegian ski coach Emil Petersen in 1928. An article of the time said the return "was conducted at great speed," indicating that it was on skis. Charlet and Marquette Bouvier (described by Kilian Jornet as "one of the pioneers in skiing") also made a recorded ski descent in 1929. But Faessler believes that the first actual unrecorded ski descents on the mountain probably preceded these two.

In the United States the first ski mountaineering on any real scale appears to have occurred in 1907 when Irving Langmuir (who would win the Nobel prize in chemistry in 1932) began to ski peaks in the Northeast that included Wittenberg Mountain, Slide Mountain and Mount Greylock. Alexander Addison McCoubrey of Winnipeg began introducing Canadians to ski alpinism around the same time.

The first big recorded ski descents in the northeastern US are mostly agreed to have started in 1913-14. Fred Harris, the legendary founder of the Dartmouth Outdoor Club, climbed and skied some or all of New Hampshire's 6,288-foot Mount Washington, the region's highest, in 1913 with two others. One of them was Carl Shumway who went on to publish his descriptions of the ascent and descent. Interestingly, Fred Harris never spoke nor wrote on the topic as far as anyone knows.

The New England Ski Museum, based primarily on the Shumway account, maintains that Harris made it all the way down on skis "in spite of many obstacles." Others believe that the next year Irving Langmuir and John Apperson may have been the first to make a full ski descent and describe it contemporaneously, though they made no claims of being first.

Graeme McGowan, a 17-year-old with two teenage friends, made the first descent of 14,115-foot Pikes Peak in Colorado in 1921, setting an altitude record for the U.S. Then another 22 years elapsed before John Ambler and a small group skied the highest of Colorado's peaks, 14,433-foot Mount Elbert.

In 1932, two expeditions went to Alaska to ski Denali (Mount McKinley), the highest mountain in North America at 20,308 feet. One ended in tragedy with two deaths. But the Erlin Strom group summited. They didn't ski from the top, but according to Wild Snow, Strom made some turns while high on the mountain "in order to say we'd skied above 17,000 feet." Strom later wrote, "We used our skis, which had been invaluable on the glacier, greatly increasing safety in negotiating crevasses and saving much time on the return from reconnaissance trips."

Strom was a big believer in the value of skis for climbing and anxious to prove it. He also wasn't above self-promotion that included seeking the record books and filming his Denali climb, a new trend in the sport.

Ski mountaineering flourished in the post-WWII years with the help of a generation of skiers armed with metal edges, and everything was up for grabs. Numerous first descents were accomplished in the Rockies and Pacific Northwest. And a complete ski of the biggest mountain in the lower 48 states, 14,494-foot Mount Whitney, was documented in 1956 for the first time. Larry Yout and 16-year-old Paul Arthur, hearing about ski pioneer Hans George's plans to make the trip, beat him to it.

Willi Schmidt, Helmut Tschaffert and Manfred Schroder, along with ski instructor Hans Metz, climbed Denali on skis in 1962 and descended on them 4,000 vertical feet. It isn't considered a full ski descent but was still a major accomplishment and the first time anyone skied from the top.

With ski-plane access to Denali's base camps, more climbers began arriving and in 1970, Tsuyoshi Ueki and Kazuo Hoshikawa from Japan made the first full ski descent. The historic event was filmed by Japanese TV crews and the skiers became heroes at home but remained largely unknown in North America.

THE GLASS SUMMIT
One Woman's Epic Journey Breaking Through

JAN REYNOLDS

Cover of famed ski mountaineer Jan Reynolds' book.

A year later, Arno Dennig, Gerwalt Pichler, Bruno Kraker and Hanns Schell made the first complete ski descent from the summit of 19,561-foot Mount Logan, Canada's highest peak and number two in North America. Ski mountaineers were rapidly raising their games, and with nowhere to go but up, the focus shifted to the planet's 7,000 and 8,000 meter peaks in South America and Asia.

According to the *United Kingdom Alpine Journal*, famed Swiss engineer and mountaineer Andre Roch joined an expedition to the Karakoram of northern Pakistan in 1934 where they recorded ski ascents up to 7,000 meters on Baltoro Kangri and the central summit of Sia Kangri at 7,350 meters. These were unquestionably the highest ski ascents in the world at the time. It's not clear whether they skied down any appreciable distance.

In 1963, young alpinist Barry Corbet took some five-foot Head skis on that year's American Everest Expedition and used them in the Western Cwm at about 22,000 feet. Mort Lund's book *The Skier's World* called it a record for skiing at altitude.

Irving Langmuir circa 1900. The pioneering ski mountaineer was also a chemist for General Electric and won the 1932 Nobel Prize.

Corbet had heard from previous climbers about good snow on "three miles of gently rolling terrain, like the world's finest bunny slope." What he found instead was skimpy coverage and vast ice relieved only by crevasses. He later told SKI magazine, "Add these problems to flat light, the difficulties of skiing with a heavy pack, and the lethargy attendant upon first arriving at 22,000 feet, and it will be understood why the world's greatest beginner slope remains untracked."

German/American super-climber Fritz Stammberger made the first-ever oxygen-free ascent of 8,462-meter (27,765-foot) Cho Oyu in Nepal in 1964, taking skis with him to the summit. Finding it undoable from the top he started his ski descent at 7,315 meters (24,000 feet), the highest ever at the time, and continued 8,000 vertical feet to base camp to get help for other members of the team who had collapsed and ultimately perished on the mountain.

Stammberger would later disappear in the mountains of northern Pakistan in 1975 while supposedly reconnoitering a solo climb of Tirich Mir. His longtime friend and climbing partner Bil Dunaway suspected Stammberger may have planned to actually climb the peak since permits for it were very hard to come by. And that he may have died in the attempt.

It was in a very sensitive/hostile border region where the Soviet Union, Afghanistan, China and Pakistan all came together. His wife, Price is Right television show model Janice Pennington, later wrote a book about him called *Husband, Lover, Spy* based on multiple interviews with American and Russian intelligence officers. She believed he could have been working for the mujahideen or the CIA or both, and either captured by the

Russians and thrown into a detention camp, or killed during fighting in Afghanistan. Search efforts produced no body, but it's a vast area where the searchers had little to go on.

As the 70s dawned, perhaps the most important ski descent in the world at the time was one that kicked off the decade by seriously upping the ante on the showmanship element that was part of a lucrative personal branding movement among alpinists.

Japanese ski star Yuichiro Muira spent the last half of the 1960s making notable descents around the world, including being the first to ski Mount Fuji in 1966. When he arrived in Nepal to take on Everest in 1970 with an unprecedented crew of 800 porters, climbers, researchers and photographers, it appeared both Quixotic and overwrought. The main result was a weirdly fascinating 1975 documentary film called *The Man Who Skied Down Everest.*

Reportedly not allowed to ski from the summit by the Nepalese government, Muira settled for starting at 26,516 feet on the South Col. He had decided to use a parachute to stop himself, which he described in the film by saying it would look like a lotus blossom on the slopes of Everest. Okay.

It mostly came off as a desperate fail-safe device. One he bizarrely decided to go all in on by starting down the 45-degree pitch in a tuck, planning to pop the chute only if necessary. Which it turned out to be almost immediately, but to no avail in the thin air, and he covered 6,600 vertical feet in less than two minutes, with no hindrance from the chute. Finally he hooked a rock and fell another 1,300 feet before clawing to a stop not far above a huge crevasse.

Even with him editing the movie, it looked like little more than a deranged stunt. Some suggested it be called *The Man Who Fell Down Everest*, and criticized his seeming recklessness. In fairness to Muira, he went on to complete skiing on all the Seven Summits and later climbed Everest multiple times, including last when he was 80.

Ultimately, Muira's 1970 expedition became a groundbreaking event with a strong cult following and influence. A book was produced, and the movie won an Academy award. It also spawned a brilliant poster that I first saw in the Nepal tourist office in Kathmandu in 1975, and it became famous around the world. It all helped dial up the exposure for ski mountaineering, which was only just starting to go big. Really big.

CHAPTER 6
SKIING HIGH – PART TWO

Into the Death Zone

When 30-year old Polish ski mountaineer Andrzej Bargiel skied from the summit of K2 in July of 2018, it was one of the last and greatest first full descents of the world's highest peaks. At 8,611 meters (28,251) feet in the Karakoram range of northern Pakistan, K2 is the second highest mountain on earth, and arguably the most challenging to climb or ski. To date, fewer than an estimated 450 people have summited it, compared to ten times that many on Everest. And only a handful were crazy enough to try skiing K2. When it finally happened it was instantly legendary, one of the big highlights of skiing's longtime obsession with going higher.

Ski mountaineering at this level has evolved into a highly specialized pursuit, demanding the best alpine gear and skills along with super-human physical endurance. All in order to survive at the very limits, in thin air, polar temperatures and brutal winds, on slopes that are mostly insane. This isn't some groomed black diamond at Deer Valley. The snow varies from concrete sastrugi whitecaps to steep sheets of sheer ice, on gnarly couloirs and exposed faces, in the shadows of tilting seracs and across snowfields stitched with crevasses.

On top of all that, Bargiel soloed the climb and descent without oxygen. That bears repeating but I won't. It is by any measure a remarkable achievement on those merits alone. But that he made the descent on skis, over conditions that were generally as skier-friendly as corrugated tin, is stunning. He made one 150-foot rappel with his skis on at the top of an aptly named feature called the Bottleneck, where other skiers have died. "I'm very happy that I managed to ski down… safely… To be honest it was my second attempt, so I'm glad that I won't be coming here again," he declared at the base.

Standing on the top of an 8,000-meter peak in the Himalaya or Karakoram is one of the great achievements in climbing. You are on hallowed ground that few on earth will ever touch. You've spent days or more in the

Davo Karnicar made a stunning 4.5-hour, first ski descent of Mount Everest in 2000.

"death zone" above 26,000 feet where your body is deteriorating just by being there. The sheer physical exertion of chiseling your way upward—foot by punishing foot, over rock and ice and cliffs in temperatures only fit for yetis and lichens—is fully extreme. And on top, having just expended this massive amount of energy and willpower, you still need to have something left in the tank. Because now you have to get down.

It may seem like a skiing descent would at least be easier and quicker than on foot, but that's not always the case. Quicker, yes, but dangerously so. And those who ski above 8,000 meters, who are all athletic beasts, say they are the hardest turns they've made in their lives, even on decent snow, which it rarely is.

Just keeping your concentration and staying aware and in the moment is difficult when you're fighting an oxygen-deprived brain and hemoglobin shortages in your blood. And it's especially sketchy on a 50-degree pitch slathered with wind-rippled boilerplate where one slip can be fatal and each turn requires maximum effort.

This kind of ski mountaineering is clearly not about simple transportation or pleasure. It's about constantly pushing the boundaries of yourself and the sport. And that was the realm ski mountaineering was entering as the 1970s progressed.

In North America, Bill Briggs' descent of Wyoming's 4,197-meter (13,770-foot) Grand Teton in 1971 wasn't as high as it was daring and unheralded. Just a year after hype had gone big league on Everest, Briggs authored one of the most visible and bold lines of the time with very little fanfare. Conventional wisdom said it was unskiable. Rather than make a big deal out of it beforehand, Briggs chartered a plane to fly over the mountain the next day so his tracks could be photographed as proof he'd been there. Please see chapter 10 for further details of this momentous descent that in retrospect marked the arrival of extreme skiing in America.

That same year Sylvain Saudan, a brash Swiss talent touted by the European press as the *"skier of l'impossible,"* came to America and made a first descent of 3,429-meter (11,239-foot) Mount Hood. In 1976 he skied 7,135-meter (23,409-foot) Nun Peak in the Indian Himalayas.

French super skiers Patrick Vellencant and Jean Marc Boivin in 1978 made the first descent of 22,205-foot Huascaran in Peru, the second highest peak in the southern hemisphere. The first descent of South America's highest peak, Argentina's 6,962-meter (22,841-foot) Aconcagua, took some time to accomplish for no taller than it is. But it's wind-lashed, boney and subject to severe weather, so not many people have ever skied it. "The only true ski descent route is the Polish Glacier," says Anton Sponar, who did it in 2009. Kit DesLauriers (a 2019 International Ski Hall of Fame inductee) was the first person to accomplish it in 2005.

Ultimately, the focus returned to Asia. In 1979, Yves Morin skied all of 8,091-meter (26,545-foot) Annapurna in Nepal, the 10th tallest mountain in the world, accomplishing it in several sections over the course of multiple days. The plan was to summit, then link all of the sections in one descent, but he fell during the attempt and perished at 6,600 meters (21,653 feet). He ratcheted up the highest altitude skied from by a bunch, but it isn't considered a full ski descent since it wasn't continuous and he died on the mountain.

The following year, Ned Gillette and Jan Reynolds were invited by John Fry and SKI magazine to China to help train their junior ski racers. From there Gillette and Reynolds met Galen Rowell and launched a National

Geographic-backed expedition to 7,546-meter (24,757-foot) Muztagata on the northern edge of the Tibetan plateau.

They made a successful first ski ascent and full ski descent and shared the record for what was the highest mountain skied from its summit in a single day. Reynolds held the record for the highest ski descent by a woman for the next 8 years. Almost equally impressive was the fact that they had a great ski, a nice perk in this line of work. "It was beautiful," recalls Reynolds. "It had just snowed and was pretty soft. There were crevasse fields and other things, but mostly it was really good."

All three of them used alpine touring gear, somewhat rare on big peaks at the time but well suited for this climb. Among other benefits they saved weight by not taking an extra pair of ski boots. Reynolds has typically preferred it even lighter. "I've used three pins [touring bindings and skis] and skating skis at high altitudes," she says, noting that she likes saving weight and being more adaptable.

Gear has always played a large role in the evolution of skiing and ski mountaineering, from generalized things such as camber, metal edges, and shape of the ski, to more specific advances like ski poles with ice axes built-in, dual-purpose climbing/skiing boots, and lighter weight materials all around.

When Fritz Stammberger skied from 24,000 feet on Cho Oyu in 1964, Mike Marolt estimates that, "He was carrying maybe 30 pounds more weight than we do today." Mike and his twin brother Steve (from Aspen's famous Marolt skiing family), along with friend Jim Gile, have been at the forefront of American ski alpinism for 20 years. And during that time, improvements in gear have made as much difference to their sport as modern climbing gear does to those who follow in the footsteps of the hobnail-boot-wearing likes of Mallory and Irvine from the 1930s.

Ever-improving equipment, monster training regimens and increased access to the highest mountains have kept pushing the records higher. In 1981, Josef Millinger and Peter Woergoetter of Austria skied from near the top (30 meters below) of 26,759-foot (8,163-meter) Manaslu in Nepal to Camp 5 where they over-nighted and then continued to Camp 1. Considering it wasn't from the summit or completed in a single day it isn't considered a full ski descent but did represent a new altitude record for skiing, starting at roughly 26,683 feet.

The next year, 46-year-old Sylvain Saudan put the exclamation mark on a remarkable career. He climbed 26,509-foot (8,089-meter) Gasherbrum I in Pakistan and skied from the summit to the base, in what is widely believed to be the first full descent of an 8,000-meter mountain. What's more, he did it on an uninterrupted 50-degree slope, using an estimated 3,000 jump turns on what is likely the longest such steep pitch ever skied. Saudan's controversial nature aside, it has to rank as one of the shining achievements in the sport.

In 1984 Patrice Bournat and Wim Pasqier skied from the summit of 26,362-foot (8,035-meter) Gasherbrum II, a feat duplicated the next year by Thierry Renard who went from the summit to a bivouac at 7,500 meters, then skied to Camp 1 the next day. Peter Woergoetter & Oswald Gassler made a full first descent of Shishapangma that same year. Then Flavio Spazzadeschi and Lino Zani did the same on 26,906-foot (8,188-meter) Cho Oyu in 1988.

Kit Deslauriers starting her ski descent of Mount Everest in 2006. Photo © Bryce Brown.

Also that year on Cho, the woman who broke Jan Reynolds' record, Veronique Perillat of France, did it by using a monoski and becoming the first woman to descend from the top of an 8,000-er and the first to ski from over 8,000 meters. And Pierre Tardivel in 1992 skied from the 28,772-foot (8,770-meter) South Summit of Mount Everest to Camp 2, a new altitude record.

The next big leap forward occurred in Nepal in 1995 when Slovenian high altitude pioneers Andrej and Davo Karnicar skied 26,545-foot (8,093-meter) Annapurna from summit to base in one day. The giant Nepalese massif is one of the Himalaya's marquee mountain groups and very deadly, claiming Yves Morin among many others. So a successful full ski descent, all in one long run on the same day, was a big deal.

As the number of unskied mountains narrowed and the summit races heated up, one of the most accomplished and well-known ski mountaineers of his time was Hans Kammerlander of Italy. He was Reinhold Messner's frequent partner, has climbed all but one of the 8,000-meter peaks, and was in the fray for first tracks on no fewer than five of them.

"Skiing has always been my great passion," he said in a 2000 interview. "Climbing came later and immediately became extremely important. Combining these two disciplines produces a really strong emotion." Unfortunately

Adrzej Bargiel, first to make a full ski descent of K2, skiing Pakistan's Yawash Sar II. Photo: Jakub Gzela / Bartlomiej Pawlikowski, Red Bull Content Pool.

he was unable to lay claim to any true first ski descents, due in part to a noble refusal to use supplemental oxygen.

Davo Karnicar felt differently, and using oxygen in 2000 made the first top-to-bottom descent of Everest without ever removing his skis, completing it in a stunning 4 hours and 40 minutes. The seemingly impossible had finally been done, after so many others had tried.

"Skiing down the Hillary Step proved to be a lot less difficult than the previous section, along the very thin and exposed crest. It's delicate and you really feel the altitude," said Karnicar. And in order to complete his descent on skis he had to maneuver around the infamous Khumbu Ice Fall near the base. The route he chose was, he said, "Exactly the kind of place you'd never want to be in: steep and exposed to the serac falls from above. What's more if you fell you'd certainly finish off right in the middle of the Ice Fall – they wouldn't even get you out in little pieces."

It seemed like the Holy Grail of ski mountaineering, but in the end it left room for improvement, and even Karnicar said, "In a few years someone will probably make the first complete descent without oxygen. Lets hope so." In fact, Andrzej Bargiel has tried and failed due to weather.

Karnicar's accomplishment somewhat overshadowed other significant ones that same year. Steve and Mike Marolt became the first North Americans to make a ski descent from above 8,000 meters on Shishapangma's central, but not highest, summit. And later in 2000 Laura Bakos became the first North American, man or woman, to ski from an 8,000-meter true summit when she descended from Cho Oyu to Camp 1 with an overnight at Camp 3. The latter meant it isn't considered a full first ski descent. Both the Marolts and Bakos carried all their own gear and went without oxygen.

In 2001 Italian snowboarder Marco Siffredi rode from the top of Everest to 6,400 meters on the north side, marking the first time a boarder had descended from the summit. He used oxygen that was carried to the top for him along with all of his gear by Sherpas, who also later assisted him during the descent. That said, it was the highest ride ever on a snowboard. Siffredi disappeared the next year trying to ride Everest's notorious Hornbein Couloir.

Kasha Rigby made the first telemark descent of Cho Oyu in 2005, with an overnight at advance base camp before continuing to Camp 2. The following year Kit DesLauriers became the first woman to ski off the summit of Everest (though she didn't make a full ski descent in a single day) and later all of the 7 Summits. There is some disagreement about how to credit her due to the two-day Everest descent, but no confusion over the magnitude of her achievements.

It just added to a series of big accomplishments in the high mountains for women in the new millennium when Telluride-based Hilaree Nelson and her "romantic and skiing partner" Jim Morrison (both in their 40s) made their remarkable first ski descent of Lhotse in 2018.

Lhotse was one of the last major unskied mountains, the fourth highest in the world and a close companion of Everest. Many have long admired what's called the "Dream Line" where Lhotse Couloir plunges off the summit at a sick 60 degrees for 1,500 vertical feet until it chokes down and spills out onto the Lhotse Face. Nelson and

Morrison skipped the traditional Camp 4 and carried all their own gear on a grueling 12-hour summit climb. After waiting to use oxygen until 1,400 feet below the top, both were nervous about having overspent themselves.

"We put our skis on right on the summit," said Nelson. "It's funny. Skis are so familiar to both of us that once you put them on it was this nervousness but excitement, like 'Oh my God, we're going to pull this off. We're going to do this, and we're going to really legit ski it. We're not side-slipping it; we're going to ski this thing.' It was pretty cool!"

The fire-pole-steep couloir featured "really variable snow conditions… really consequential breakable crust," said Nelson. Then, "We came through the choke and we were just looking at each other and we were afraid to say it. Holy shit, did that just happen? I was totally blown away. It was 100 percent a ski line. The conditions were pretty abysmal, but nothing worse than a really bad day at Telluride. Totally manageable."

That highly descriptive and inspired assessment was just one of the things that made Nelson such a beloved member of the world's high-altitude ski mountaineering club. And why it was such a blow when she perished in an avalanche on treacherous Manaslu in Nepal in September of 2022.

She and Morrison had just begun their ski descent from the 8,163-meter (26,781 feet) summit of the 8th highest mountain in the world when Nelson disappeared. Morrison said in post that he was skiing ahead of her when she "started a small avalanche" and "she was swept off her feet and carried down a narrow snow slope." He was unable to locate her and skied to base camp for help and there were some initial fears she'd been carried into a crevasse. Her body was recovered two days later and flown to Kathmandu.

Nelson left behind two children, Morrison, countless friends and admirers, and a record of dozens of first ski descents and more than 40 expeditions to 16 different countries. Her sponsors at North Face described her as "the most prolific ski mountaineer of her generation."

Hers and Morrison's descent of Lhotse only leaves three virgin 8,000-ers now: Kangchenjunga, Makalu and Dhaulagiri. The first two will need perfect conditions to be doable from the top. Meanwhile many top alpinists have already shifted gears to other efforts at altitude: new lines on the 8,000-ers; super-sized vertical like the Wickersham Wall on Denali and the north face of Mount Saint Elias; skiing all the 7 summits; and 7,000-meter "recreational" ski trips such as the Marolts enjoy now.

Internationally renowned mountaineer Hans Kammerlander has skied most of the 8,000-meter peaks, without oxygen. Photo by Thomas Mitterer.

Chris Davenport, one of the most widely accomplished skiers in the sport, expects to see more big, hard-to-reach lines done as gear and weather forecasting constantly improve. And big ski traverse projects such as Everest-Lhotse are on many ski mountaineers drawing boards, along with new speed records for ascents and descents.

In addition to winning the World Extremes and the grueling 24 Hours of Aspen competitions, Davenport has climbed and skied on Everest, the Matterhorn, all of the 7 Summits, and skied all 54 of Colorado's 14ers in 12 months. I asked him where he sees the future of ski mountaineering going, and will it become a crowded shit show of under qualified wannabes like we see sometimes on Everest?

"I really don't see that happening. The crowds and lines we see pictures of on Everest are partially a product of the press more than reality. They take one photo one day and make more of it than it is. My experience there was great, nothing like that, and most people's are. It's not always this crazy scene.

"And I don't see ski mountaineering going that way because it takes such specialized skills that only a handful have them. Almost anyone can pay their money and climb up Everest, but not everybody can ski down. I think it can be a concern that by writing about these things, as I did with my book on the 14ers, we might be encouraging people to flood these peaks. But I think we can report responsibly and hope that people use their heads and stay safe."

Amen to that.

Thin air acts like a drug on the brain and the body. Combined with wild snow it can produce amazing accomplishments in the mountains that no less an authority than Hans Kammerlander has said becomes an addiction. And that, as much as anything, insures that ski mountaineers will continue skiing high as long as there are mountains to do it on.

Skiing one of the world's longest vertical-foot runs in the Vallée Blanche in Chamonix. Photo © Jay Cowan.

CHAPTER 7
GOING LONG

Lift-Served High Speed Masochism, Chopper Assisted Records, The Penitents of Ski Mountaineering, The World's Longest Runs

MARATHON DOWNHILL RACING

Not many skiers have ever gone 90 to 100 miles an hour down Aspen Mountain. But of the few who have, most did it *80+ times in a day*, once a year. It happened in the 24 Hours of Aspen events where skiers on a course with virtually no gates regularly flirted with the 100-mile-an-hour mark. And they did it on every single run, all day and all night, non-stop and bumper-to-bumper with a teammate.

"Skiing so close together at high speed is amazingly dangerous," British Olympian Martin Bell told Sports Illustrated in 1996. "Which way will I go when he crashes? It's nerve-wracking. And when it gets dark and you can't see as well the danger is doubled."

Indeed. Imagine bombing down the roller-filled mountain at 4:00 a.m., on 240-centimeter downhill skis in a full tuck and speed suit, 18 hours into the gig and embracing the delirium. "The constant roar of wind starts to get to you," Ian McLendon said in a 2001 Aspen Times story. "And the whipping of your ski suit. It's like the wind is trying to pry it off your body."

Competitor Matt Ross described the night skiing to me as "really eerie" and "pretty trippy." And Chris Davenport, longtime local resident and 1998 winner with Tyler Williams, told me, "Words don't really do the mental state justice."

The stories of the physical and psychological traumas (frostbite, mega-blisters, severe cramps, permanent back issues, hallucinations, paranoia, vomiting, bad wrecks and so on) are legion. It starts to sound like a snowbound Death Race movie without the cars – the sort of thing convicts might have been forced into doing to earn their freedom. But it was actually very prestigious and the height of some skier's winters.

[DROP CAP] The first time I remember caring about the amount of vertical feet I skied in a day was when I went heli-skiing. Since they charge you by the foot, and a lot of bragging rights are also attached to those numbers, it quickly got my attention. Prior to heli-skiing, it's hard to trace exactly where and when racking up heavyweight amounts of vertical became an actual thing, and then a competition.

Even before watches and phone apps became available that made keeping track of such numbers easy, it was possible to get an idea of them simply from the number of runs you made. This presupposes that you had a reason to do it in the first place, other than just trying to keep track of the cash racing out of your bank account and into Mike Wiegle Heli Skiing's. You may want to see how you compare to others, how you rate in terms of your personal bests, or how your fitness regime is working. Or you may want to keep track of your world records.

There are inevitably issues about the legitimacy of some of the watch and phone app numbers, whether due to glitches or outright fraud. This can be frustrating as a user when you're not sure of the accuracy of your readings. But it becomes a bigger concern when users are establishing records based on their app readings with no one else monitoring or witnessing them.

Strava, a popular Internet service for cyclers and runners that utilizes GPS readings, has also become big with ski mountaineers. Many endurance athletes train solo and only have their altimeter watches and Strava to record their efforts. While many of the records are widely accepted when supplied by reputable athletes, they usually aren't officially recognized by Guinness, or the governing bodies of various sports.

Those commercial and competitive concerns aside, the fact is that a sizable segment of the snow-riding population has become enamored with tracking their vertical and the achievements of others. For those who hadn't given the whole idea much thought before, it also provides some context for the kinds of feats being racked up by the athletes in this section of the book.

Man being a generally competitive creature it's seems likely that comparing ones vertical, as it were, to another's, has been going on for a very long time and simply kept track of in the form of numbers and lengths of runs in whatever location.

That basic concept hasn't really changed in several millennia. As witness the 24 Hours of Aspen. Not your typical Aspen all-nighter, this was high-speed masochism for a cause. It ran from 1988 through 2002, as one of the first and craziest big time vertical-bagging competitions.

The race was a cross of team-speed-skiing with an Ironman endurance element, dreamt-up by snowcat operator and itinerant ski racer Ed McCaffrey. Thinking of his father's battle with multiple sclerosis, he conceived of the event as a unique challenge that might be entertaining enough to be an MS fundraiser.

Elite Wiegle Heli-Skiing pros set a world record for vertical feet in 1998. Unrelated photo courtesy of Mike Wiegle Heli-Skiing.

It took a couple of years to find a location and sponsor and the first race was in December of 1987 at Keystone, Colorado. Five two-man teams participated and McCaffrey and his partner won. They also raised $10,000 for the Jimmy Huega Center in Vail, which aids people with MS.

The race caused such a stir that the next year it attracted eight national teams and media attention from around the world. It also moved permanently to Aspen where the bottom-to-top gondola was the perfect facilitator, serving a 2.69-mile track that dropped 3,267 vertical feet.

Attempting to explain the torturous race's unexpected popularity with competitors – especially given there was no prize money – the 38-year-old McCaffrey said, "You push yourself so far out there that you reach this trance-like state of blissful exhaustion. It's truly amazing, it keeps people coming back every year."

If that sounds like the kind of thing you hear people in the Ironman Marathon in Hawaii saying, it's because the 24 Hours had that in common with many other ultra-marathon competitions: the toxic allure of the suffering. Competitions for endurance skiing records on any level are almost always pain-fests.

Special newspaper insert published by the Aspen Times for the 24 Hours of Aspen event.

With title sponsors Audi and the Aspen Skiing Company, the 24 Hours rapidly evolved into a high maintenance production unlike any other race in the world. Support was not only required across a broad front, but for *24 hours straight*. The 800 volunteers included physicians, ski patrol, ski techs, massage therapists, food handlers, lifties, lighting and course crews, and on and on. Fortunately, Aspenites have never needed much of an excuse to stay up all night.

On a course with a long flat start and little emphasis on turning, good ski-techs were vital and consisted of local savants like Bill Miller, Jeff Hamilton and Dave Stapleton, as well as pros from the World Cup and Speed Skiing tours.

The team of Hamilton and Miller had waxed the last two winners when Jeff told the Aspen Times, "The challenges facing us as techs are minimal compared with the challenges facing the athletes. But what we really need to be able to do is change and adapt… It's not a one lap race." Each racer had three to 10 pairs of skis they rotated through with techs providing an average 750 ski tunes/wax jobs per event.

A further distinction from other ski races was that the competitors spent most of their time (20 hours) on the lift. So the gondola became another major focal point. It was where they rested their legs and got massages – Dav reported at least 40 when he won. They also tried to warm up or cool down, using special comforters designed to help flush lactic acid from their muscles; changed clothes and boots; relieved themselves into Ziploc baggies and buckets of kitty litter; ate and drank – Asia Jenkins leaned on smoothies and sushi; and sank into fitful naps – Gella Sutro and Kate McBride once ate only Tums for hours and went semi-comatose.

In the end, despite all its crazed uniqueness, the comp couldn't survive. It was turned into a solo race with a cash award in 2002 in the hope of attracting bigger names. But when they couldn't find a sponsor the 2003 event had to be dropped and in 2004 it was scrapped for good. "I feel like I've lost a little bit of my heart. I absolutely adored that event," said local native McBride.

The record lap time was 2:10.98 in 1998 by Graham and Martin Bell from England. The women's record vertical for the event was 261,360 feet, 215.2 miles, 80 laps, by multiple winners Kate McBride and Anda Rojs of Aspen in 1997. The men's record was 271,161 vertical, 223.27 miles, 83 laps, by Chris Kent of Canada in 1991. And after 13 events over 16 seasons, with three weather cancellations, the event raised more than three million dollars for charity.

The concept sparked interest in other places as well. Using the Aspen competition as a template, the short-lived

16-hour Compaq 50K in Coronet, New Zealand, was run in July in 2000 and 2001. With three skiers each, 8 teams from 6 different countries and two from New Zealand skied from 7:00 p.m. through the night until 10:00 a.m. the following day. The goal was to achieve 50,000 vertical feet, but for the first event fog and white-out conditions caused timing problems and a two-hour delay during the night.

Six of the teams completed 101 laps, the Swedish women's trio did 98 and one of the New Zealand teams withdrew. Places were determined by the aggregate overall time on the snow. The Canadian team ran the fastest lap of the event early in the evening with 48.24 seconds, versus the six minutes the chairlift ride required. Average run times ranged between 50 and 53 seconds, with speeds clocked by radar up to 130 kilometers per hour (80.778 mph).

The German team won the inaugural event with 1:25.44, barely edging the Canadians at 1:26.01, and Australia finished third. In the subsequent two outings the Germans continued to win and speeds bumped up to the 140 kph (86.992 mph) mark. The number of competing teams rose to 10 with name-brand racers that included Austrian gold-medal-winning downhiller Patrick Ortleib, three-time 24 Hours of Aspen winner Chris Kent from Canada, and Martin Fiala from Germany.

Most importantly, in total during three years the event raised over $400,000 for the Cure Kids Charity while bringing some fast times to Coronet Peak. Ultimately, the event went the way of the original one in Aspen.

THE RECREATIONAL QUEST FOR MEGA-VERTICAL

On the purely recreational side there are some shocking numbers for what regular mortals can do over the course of a full ski season (or 8) during normal operating hours. This includes standing in lines, lift breakdowns and all the other travails that confront any civilian skier or boarder.

It also ups the ante on trust and taking the word of personal logs on whatever device or app is being used. For the folks at Guinness, that's rarely sufficient, which seems justifiable. But that doesn't necessarily diminish the things that some people claim to have done.

In 2018, 65-year-old Scott Howard of Stowe, Vermont, bagged almost *6.5 million vertical feet* in more than 170 days on the slopes in the Northeast. At Stowe he utilized, "a quad that gets you 2,100 vertical feet and it only takes a little over six minutes. You can do six laps an hour." Stowe also opens at 8:00 a.m. and 7:30 on weekends. Plus up to seven times a year, New Hampshire's Crotched Mountain stays open 18 hours. Howard was invited there for a vertical challenge where the record was 111 runs on an 850-foot hill. "I had 143 runs for 130,900 vertical."

Howard was chasing the official world record of Canadian Pierre Marc Jette established at Whistler in 2014/'15, from November 22nd to May 10th when he skied 6,025,751 feet. That was done in an effort to raise awareness for Alzheimer's in support of his relatives affected by the disease, and was fully monitored by officials at Whistler.

Howard clocked 6.4 million, but his only real witness is his Alpine Trace app and the word of some fellow skiers and a neglected girlfriend. Guinness has never recognized the mark, so for him the world record is only his on Alpine Trace.

Similarly, 62-year-old Brad Blacketor of Breckenridge reported skiing 188 days in 2020/'21, from November 6th to May 16th, and logging 12.4 million vertical feet. That was for an average of forty lift rides and 66,000 verts a day, according to EpicMix, and was two million more than he skied in 2018. His friends have dryly explained the highly unlikely accomplishment by saying "he skips lunch."

In a story for Snow Country magazine Sarah Corbett mentioned an "8 million foot man in Sun Valley." The story goes that Neal Holmes died at 72 in late 1996, but that season had skied every day from November 22nd to Aril 30th and accrued 8,614,600 vertical. It's cited as evidence that its not just rich people who chase vertical, though there's no mention of what Holmes did for a living in his life. Or any further substantiation of what would be a definite world record. Since it has never been acknowledged in Guinness or mentioned elsewhere its hard to know what to make of it.

On the other hand, a literally staggering long-range record has been officially recognized for Rainer Hertrich, a cat-skinner at Copper Mountain in Colorado. Starting on November 1st, 2003, *he skied at least one run every day – every damned day – for the next 2,992.* Eight years, two months and ten days, to be exact, and he only quit at his doctor's request because he was suffering cardiac arrhythmia.

He began this singular task after hearing about some skiers in Jackson, Wyoming, reaching six million vertical in a season. When he got to seven million in 2004 he just stayed after it. "You have to remain dedicated," Hertrich told Men's Journal writer Eugene Buchanan. "Some days were tough, and there were a lot of logistics to deal with. I also skied through some miserable conditions, as well as pain and illness. You just have to get up and deal. When I separated my shoulder, I still skied the next day. I just didn't plant my pole."

He was able to put in six months every day at Copper, then hit a series of late-closing areas on the way to Mount Hood where he drove cats all summer. To be able to pull it off meant South America in the fall which required lots of creativity including skinning, early morning runs before flying, and "anything as long as your skis are underfoot."

While the 2,992 days are an amazing record, what he's proudest of is the nearly 100 million vertical feet he amassed. His Guinness Book of Records entry is for accumulated vertical in consecutive days. Says Hertrich, "That's a million vertical feet per month, which is a lot."

But of course none of it came without a price. Not only couldn't he have had much of a life beyond his work and mission, but the physical toll has been significant and includes an amputated foot and full hip replacement, so far, with a myriad of other injuries and issues. It's all detailed in his book, The Longest Run: How a Colorado ski bum skied every day for more than eight years.

HELI-SKIING MADNESS

If you really want to set a power-assisted vertical record and can foot the tab, a chopper is the only way to go. In

February of 1997, oral surgeon Dr. Mark Bennett hired two of them in the Yukon to ski 294,380 feet in 14 hours. The effort was well enough monitored to earn him the world "daylight" vertical record, previously held by Martin Jones, a New Zealand speed skier who ran up over 212,000 feet on the top tram at Les Grands Montets in Chamonix in 12 hours. Bennett's feat also surpassed the prior 24-hour lift-assisted record set in the 24 Hours of Aspen of 271,161.

Bennett skied the same nearly 3,600-vertical-foot run 82 times and when it was over he couldn't walk or sleep. Snow Country magazine reported that he said, "Every time I closed my eyes I saw ski tracks rushing at me. I was nauseous. It was like falling into a nightmare."

But it didn't dampen his enthusiasm about getting a record that he felt all skiers craved. "Every recreational skier sits around after a day of skiing and talks about his runs," he told Snow Country. "What they're really talking about is the vertical feet they accumulated. It's at the heart of what every skier does... Everybody should be able to relate to my record."

A bit to unpack there, but in a word, no. Vertical isn't at the heart of what every skier does. And I say that after having spent one winter skiing 82 times and logging over a million feet on my Alpine Trace, just to see what I could do if I paid attention. But I haven't repeated the experiment because it just isn't at the heart of what I do. And I don't think it's at the heart of what most of the true skiers I know do.

However, for strong Type A people such as the doctor, it no doubt applies. As evidenced by what goes on at heli operations around the world, but especially in Canada. On any given week there are many individuals, groups and guides for whom it's all about the verts. They're the ones who covet the million-foot-club perks like the suits from CMH and the silver belt buckles from Wiegle. And if they're being honest, their bragging is as much about what it costs as it is about the accomplishment. For many others it's more about all the amazing powder skiing that they've been fortunate enough to be able to do.

Amongst the competitive crowd, however, Bennett's record wasn't taken lightly. Around places like the Wiegle operation in Blue River, British Columbia, there was talk about how some rich doctor shouldn't be able to just go out and buy the record. In Sarah Corbett's Snow Country story she cited criticisms of Bennett that ranged from the fact that he did his skiing alone instead of in a group of four as was the custom; to him using two choppers instead of one to save time on refueling; to having porters help him load and unload his skis; to the fact that he wasn't a ski pro and as such just a fluke to be in possession of such a record.

Fourteen months after Bennett's unpopular ego trip, former US Ski Team member, pro racer, and 24 Hours of Aspen competitor Rusty Squire set out to break it at his home mountain of Big Sky, Montana where he selected a run well known to locals. Big Horn is where my friends and I and many others have regularly used our Alpine Trace apps searching for high speeds.

The only difference between that and what Squire did on April 6,1998, is he went faster, for 10.5 hours, using a high-altitude Eurocopter 208sa "Lama," rather than the Thunder Wolf high-speed quad chairlift. He also, in keeping with the nature of such crusades, had a crew of 60 backing him up. Ultimately he made 220 laps on the backside of Andesite Mountain for 331,160 vertical feet, a new daylight world record by more than 35,000 feet.

I don't use the word "crusade" lightly, because the other thing Squire's effort had in common with many of those before and after is that it was done as a fundraiser. His was to support the pet project of one of his closest friends who was a big supporter of Montana's famous Eagle Mount program for kids with cancer. That friend died of cancer himself within days of Squire proposing the project, and that was at the heart of what prompted him to continue with it.

Meanwhile the heli operators continued to launch assaults on the mark, especially during Vertical Challenge week at Blue River. On April 28th of 1998 a team at Wiegle's consisting of Swiss extreme skier Dominique Perret, former Canadian ski team member and 24 Hours of Aspen winner Chris Kent, along with Ed Podivinsky and Luke Sauder of the Canadian Alpine Team, and Austrian guide Robert Reindl, tapped the 5,000-vertical-foot north face of Mount Albrada for 353,600 feet in 14.5 hours.

When all the snow settled that year, Rusty Squire had held the record for 22 days, and the Wiegle crew was the new daylight world record holder. Doctor Bennett got to enjoy his pricey glory for about 14 months.

Other more pedestrian records that have been noted for heli-skiing at Wiegle's include: 72,200 feet in a day for a regular group with a Bell 212 chopper rotating with two other groups; a daily vertical record for snowboarders using the private A Star, which doesn't rotate with any other groups, set in 1995 at 153,000 feet; the weekly record in an A Star at a hefty 375,000 set by Paul Sylvester, Sandro Gabrielli, Marc Arnold and Mike Wiegle in 95; and the weekly record for a regular group of 315,800 set in 96.

SKIMO PENITENTIALS

Soon it became increasingly obvious that further mechanized vertical-foot skiing records were going to continue to be as much about money and connections as about the skiing. Since then the big trend has been toward more egalitarian achievements that don't require a giant event, lifts that run for 24 hours, or helicopters. Instead they're based on the most self-powered vertical climbed and skied in whatever period of time is designated, and these have become some of the most pursued marks in the booming sport of ski mountaineering (SkiMo).

In 2009, Austrian Ekkehard Dorschlag set the 24-hour record at 60,350 feet. It was March of 2018 before someone bettered it when 34-year-old ski mountaineer Mike Foote skinned and skied Ed's Run on the front of Big Mountain in Whitefish, Montana. A sponsored North Face competitor in ultra running, Foote plotted his attempt carefully and had about 20 people helping, in a kind of one-man replication of Aspen's 24 hour event.

"I had a few people at the base drying out gear, putting on skins, and giving me food and drink," he told writer Jack Foersterling. "But after eight hours it's not really fun to eat. I had these sweet potato rice balls that were dope, though."

He also had pacers on the mountain to help keep him on track, and a groomer friend who laid down a line of corduroy several times during an otherwise icy night. "It was slick going up and teeth chattering frozen on the descents. The conditions were not ideal."

For gear he had flyweight carbon fiber skimo boots and a brace of Dynafit DNA race skis, each fitted with climbing skins so he could trade them out quickly. He set the official record seven minutes shy of the 24-hour mark when he logged 61,170 feet, or 77 miles, and then "just kind of fell asleep."

It was only a few months later that Norwegian Lars Erik cranked out a total of 68,697 feet, and countryperson Malene Blikken Haukoy put up 50,656 feet for a women's record. Then in February of 2019, superhuman trail runner and ski mountaineer Kilian Jornet threw down 51 laps on Tusten ski area in Molde, Norway, for what Nick Hell in Outside called "an absurd 78,274 feet." For reference, that would be like going up and down the Empire State Building more than 62 times. With skis. In 24 hours.

It was not a formally monitored effort, but verified on his Suunto watch and Strava as well as by observers and friends who assisted in the effort. And Jornet said he didn't consider his accomplishment a record, but rather just testing to "see how his body will perform."

"Still, informally, the endurance community tends to treat them as records, much like FKTs [Fastest Known Times] so long as they can be reasonably verified," wrote Hell. "Similar 24-hour endurance tests aren't uncommon in cycling and mountain running (in Italy, one such contest allows runners to take a lift down between laps), but the personal challenge may be what matters most."

FKTs are increasingly popular amongst runners and triathletes who use established tracks and courses and can time themselves on them via various apps, then post for comparison to others. While less formal than monitored official records, they can be very useful for training. Rapidly evolving technology is redefining how people train, monitor themselves and compare to others.

In the same story, Mike Foote summed up why he does SkiMo. "How many push-ups can I do in a minute? How long can I hold my breath? How far can I ski in a day? In the end it's all arbitrary and contrived, but it gets people to ask, What am I capable of?"

For some people, it turns out to be really a lot. Take Aaron Rice for example. He tracked his vertical climbed and skied in 2016 and it was 2.5 million feet skinning up and skiing down. It was motivated by a desire to inject some order and meaning into a ski bumming life that was starting to feel aimless, he said, and doing it by breaking a record set by Canadian Greg Hill in 2010. "I find that goal setting in itself can be a great motivator," he told writer Trevor Husted.

Ultra endurance super athlete Kilian Jornet competing in an ISMF World Cup event at Font Blanc in 2017. Photo by Jorge Millaruelo.

He followed the traditional snow route from Colorado to Oregon and California then South America, and finished on December 29th, 2016, in the Wasatch Range of Utah, when his Garmin watch displayed his vertical for the year at 2,500,000, and he celebrated with a beer and a run with friends.

Obviously these kinds of accomplishments demand an almost religious, not to say penitential, commitment. That brings up an important point about long-term endurance projects in any sports like cycling or running or skiing, which is that they require time commitments most people can't arrange in their lives. In this case it also suggests, perhaps unfairly, that Rice didn't find it necessary to work for a while. Especially since the task required 332 days of skinning and skiing, averaging 7,200 vertical for each of them. "I mostly skied, ate, slept, tried to fit in stretching and that was about it," he admitted.

THE WORLD'S LONGEST RUNS

For those who want to tackle the most vertical you can ski without losing your mind about it here's another of those lists that could have so many caveats it would be pointless. When talking about the longest ski runs on the planet, are we just including lift-served ones? Is it continuous vertical? Are we talking length in kilometers/miles, or vertical meters/feet? Are they maintained/groomed? Are they the longest steep runs, or the longest beginner runs, or the longest bump runs? Does size really matter? All of that aside, here we go for the longest lift-served runs with no other covenants.

The Vallee Blanche off the Aiguille du Midi in Chamonix is probably the most famous long run in skiing. Its lengthiest route is 22 kilometers (13.67 miles), all of it off-piste and littered with seracs, crevasses, glacial debris and avalanche danger. I got to ski it by variations on the classic and Montenvers routes on a spectacular powder day. The full 2,750 vertical meters (9,200 feet) is if the run is in all the way to the Chamonix Valley floor. It still boasts over 2,130 vertical meters (7,000+ feet) when you have to stop short and finish with an uphill hike.

As we were completing our run my guide looked up at Les Grand Montets (LGM) on the other side of the Vallee Blanche and said, "The Pas de Chevre is open. One of the few times all year. You want to go?"

Soon we were dropping into still fresh steep lines that took a very direct line 5 kilometers and 1,829-vertical-meters (6,000 feet) down to the Mer de Glace glacier. The views of everything from the Nant Blanc face of the Aiguille Verte that overhung us, to the vast expanse of the Vallee Blanche below, to Chamonix down the main valley toward Switzerland, to a namesake chamois posing on a high ridge, were jaw-dropping. And we skied all the way to the floor of the Vallee Blanche, which is rarely possible any more without a rappel. I only took two runs that day, but they were on legendary terrain covering nearly 4,000 vertical meters (13,000 feet).

Called the longest red run in the world, a 22-kilometer descent at Zermatt, Switzerland from the Klein Matterhorn to Valtournenche requires a lift ride in the middle of it. But it does deliver 2,359 vertical meters (7,739 feet), and you to another country (Italy) in the bargain.

Murren, Switzerland, where they host the Inferno (the world's longest amateur downhill ski race, cited in more detail in chapter 42), also lets regular skiers on the same route when there's no race. It stretches for 15 kilometers (9.258 miles) with a 2,170-vertical-meter (7,119 feet) drop when there's snow all the way down.

It takes the fastest racers, at an average of over 40 miles an hour including on traverses and an uphill section, over 13 minutes to ski in a tuck.

Engelberg, Switzerland's 2,023-vertical-meters (6,637 feet) includes a run from the glacier on top to the village at the base that encompasses it all in 12 kilometers (7.45 miles), making it what the resort calls, "One of the ten longest in the world." It also hosts the famous Laub, described by Powder magazine as "a 3,900-vertical-foot pyramid of perfect turns that stands as the longest continuous lift-served powder field in Europe."

The Guinness Book of World Records says that a run at Davos, Switzerland from the Weissflujoch to Parsenn is "the longest all-downhill ski run in the world" at 12.23 kilometers (7.6 miles). A number of others would disagree.

Les Cascades in Flaine, France is advertised as "one of the longest blue runs in Europe" at 14 kilometers (8.7 miles). It runs from 2,480 meters (8,136 feet) high down to the village of Sixt at 728 meters (2,388 feet) when snow allows.

Alpe d'Huez, France has installed lights for night skiing on their famous Sarenne run, a 16-kilometer (nearly 10-mile) black-rated descent where the entire 2,000 vertical meters (6,561 feet) is on-piste, albeit with highly variable conditions throughout.

The lift-served terrain at Alagna, Italy features a 2,063-meter vertical drop (6,769-foot) with the V3 run encompassing all of it. And local helicopter skiing can sometimes provide over 3000 vertical meters (nearly 10,000 feet).

For North America, Revelstoke, Canada claims the longest groomed trail at 13.35 kilometers (8.3 miles), over the most vertical on the continent at 1,713 meters (5,620 feet). The Peak to Creek trail at Whistler is 11 kilometers (6.8 miles) long on 1,529 vertical meters (5,016 feet).

Jackson Hole is often incorrectly credited with the most continuous vertical in the US at 1,261.5 meters (4,139 feet). In fact at Snowmass, Colorado you can go for 1,343 vertical meters (4,406 feet) continuously from the top of the Rocky Mountain High drag-lift to the base, all inbounds with no in-between lift rides required. Jackson's longest route down is around 7 miles while at Snowmass it's 5.3 miles.

SECTION III
GOING STEEP

2007 BUYER'S GUIDE

Powder

SEPTEMBER 2006

THE SKIER'S MAGAZINE

Remembering
a Legend

DOUG COOMBS

1957 ~ 2006

"DOUG WAS THE CHOSEN ONE. THE POINT OF THE SPEAR. IT WASN'T A NEW LEVEL; IT WAS A NEW WORLD." ~*Theo Meiners*

09

U.S. $4.99
CAN $5.99
DISPLAY UNTIL
SEPT. 19, 2006

0 79025 34948 7

+ KYE PETERSEN ON INJURIES, EDUCATION AND GROWING UP IN THE SPOTLIGHT

Powder magazine memorial cover for Doug Coombs.
Photo © Ace Kvale. Courtesy of Ace Kvale and Powder magazine / Dave Reddick.

CHAPTER 8
PART ONE – HOW STEEP IS STEEP

Metaphors, Expletives, Numbers and Systems

As my friend Raoul and I stood squinting into a thick gray fog that filled an unmarked chute near Zurs, Austria, the inevitable question arose. "How steep you think this is?" he asked with a nervous chuckle.

"I don't have a clue," I replied. It wasn't the answer he wanted but it was true. I'd never really checked out the run before when there was good visibility. Now we couldn't see past our tips and the trail map was useless on that part of the mountain. All we knew was that the run was discernibly steep and the snow was stable. So we dropped in and "felt" our way down one giddy, free-falling turn after another. And at the bottom the question still remained: How steep was it?

It's a question that confronts every skier from time to time, whether it's the first-day beginner who views the bunny hill as a thinly disguised cliff, or the extremist wannabe trying to convince his buds that he's skied more radical lines than they have. For those looking to test themselves, as well as those who want to make it a competition, steep skiing is perhaps the most complicated of all the ways that people can rate their riding.

As with most of skiing/boarding's varied disciplines, when it comes to setting records for skiing steep stuff, whether they're personal ones or Guinness ones, some kind of ground rules have to be established. And that's not easy.

I explored the most fundamental issue with steep skiing in a piece for SKI magazine in 2002 that was subtitled, How Steep Is Steep? I've updated it here.

For most recreational riders, the simplest way to judge the difficulty of what they're skiing is by the on-trail signs of the Green-Circle to Black-Diamond scale. Skiing at more than one resort should persuade almost anyone that those difficulty ratings are relative to the local mountain and not some international standard. And they are meant to include other factors than just the pitch.

What most of those who discuss these matters at any length use as their starting point is the degree of the slope. Ski pro Chris Stagg at famously steep Taos, New Mexico, where more than half the runs are black or double-blacks, told me, "I start introducing better skiers to the steeps on the middle of Al's Run, where it's just over 30 degrees." At the other end of the spectrum, most people who make a habit of this kind of thing don't even get interested until it goes over 45 degrees (think Transamerica Building).

The limit of what is skiable is still hotly debated, as is the term "skiable," and both are very dependent on conditions. Inevitably the talk turns to "angles of repose," and "mass wasting" on interminable threads on the Teton Gravity Research (TGR) site every time someone starts speculating about the steepest pitch that can be skied. Both of those terms are beholden not just to gravity, but the ability of snow to bond to a surface. That's important so there's something to ski on, and so you can be reasonably sure it won't slide when you do.

In America, coastal snowpacks will routinely provide steeper skiable lines than the drier snows of the Rocky Mountains. Under ideal conditions, many experts feel that slopes can be doable in the 70 to 80 degree range, and from there the discussion revolves around what can be considered skiing versus controlled falling or jumping.

You're definitely sniffing around the furthest edges of what's possible when you're dealing with details like how far it is between each time your skis actually contact the snow on your turns, and whether the hip drag is just an unavoidable function of the incline or, technically, a controlled fall.

The key word is "control." I've read opinions that for someone to be considered to have legitimately skied a pitch, they need to exhibit enough control that they could stop after each turn. Particularly in the current age of skiing I believe many would disagree with that. For one thing, if the slope is long at all, or has repercussions if you slide all the way down it, any sane rider will want to exert the most control they can throughout the descent. It will usually be necessary to a successful and survivable run.

For another thing, the trend now in descents is to do them with as much style, fluidity and speed as possible. Once many of the first descents have been done, the way to distinguish further ones on the same routes is to do them faster and a lot of riders consider faster to be more exciting and reflective of more skill.

Many of the earlier steep and extreme skiers tended to favor jump or hop turns, which allow the skis to be turned quickly so you don't gain too much speed. In the middle part of the turn where the skis would normally be pointed down the fall-line while still on the snow, they were just pivoting them in the air.

This turn, which isn't totally out of favor, was a staple of the likes of Sylvain Saudan who once estimated that he did 3,000 of them for his famed first descent of an 8,000-meter peak from summit to base. It was on Baruntse, and is still considered one of the most remarkable feats in the history of ski mountaineering.

In general, super steep skiing anywhere with consequences, has long been thought to be safest when it's done slowly and one turn at a time. Some of this has to do with being more alert to the ever-changing conditions. Some of it has to do with staying in balance and secure. And some to do with handling the fatigue of lots of turns on mixed snow in thin air.

In watching old videos of Saudan or Boivin or Vallencant and others who favored the jump turn, it looks very cautious and studied, and undoubtedly necessary in multiple different conditions. But it can also seem exaggerated and over-used. Some of that can be related to the fact that some of these athletes are not true skiers, they just use them as tools to accomplish their goals. They aren't concerning themselves with taking a beautiful line or the aesthetics of their technique, nor even the feel of it in terms of making smoothly transitioned carved turns. And I'm not either when I'm in survival mode.

But just as with climbing or surfing or wingsuit flying, the current trend is to do the traditionally most difficult lines and routes possible, and with a maximum of flow and grace. That can be attained even with jump turns, but there is a difference between doing them while skiing, or while executing a repeated form of exercise like jumping back and forth over a weight bench.

In the case of Saudan, I think his desire to showcase his endurance overcame common sense at times. It was also what he did best, when skiing wasn't necessarily his number one skill.

More to the point, however, is that the modern way of skiing big lines might not seem to be fully under control at all points, but I don't think that disqualifies it from being legitimate in terms of records and fair descents.

Jump turning continues to be a popular and smart way to deal with high degree angles, but raises questions about the line between jumping over steep terrain, versus maintaining contact with it.

How far should you be allowed to travel downhill in the air between turns to still be considered skiing? As long as you stay mostly upright and descending without excessive side-slipping, I'm not sure it matters. If someone can fire down the Wickersham Wall, launching out of turns and skipping over terrain features, keep it together and pull in to a stop at the end, I think that's not only completely legit but totally awesome.

Determining the relative difficulty of steep slopes also involves many variables other than pitch alone, of course. Forty-five degrees of blue ice is always going to ski harder than 45 degrees of foot-deep powder. A squeaky tight plunge through the timber on something like Telluride's Zulu Queen or Stowe's Goat will present different challenges from carving down a wide-open slope like Jackson's Rendezvous Bowl, or Liberty Bowl on Lone Peak at Big Sky.

Bumps are gnarlier than corduroy, and longer sustained steeps are tougher than shorter ones. Couloirs and runs right under the lift have a definite psych component. And 30 degrees with a cliff directly below it is a much scarier species than 45 degrees with a long gradual run-out. Immediate ugly consequences are what define all of the world's most dangerous steep lines.

Truthfully, everything else is subject to exceptions. Some skiers love to showboat under the lift, others don't think about it one way or the other. Ice can present a more predictable surface than mixed windslab and sun-cupping.

And while a long demanding bump run like Spiral Stairs at Telluride or Alta's High Rustler is a stiff workout, moguls also provide a way to control speed on a steep angle.

The Aspen Highlands Ski Patrol developed one of the most wide-ranging inbounds steep terrain areas in the country in Highland Bowl, along with a remarkably complete and award-winning map to accompany it. It lists the steepest pitch, average pitch, and aspect for each of more than 50 routes. Among the steepest are B-Cliffs in the Steeplechase area with an average of 46 degrees, and Go-Go Gully in the Bowl with an average of 42 degrees and one section that tilts in at 48.

Not everyone places high confidence in such empirical data, worrying about where the measurements are taken and when. Highlands takes theirs in summer because that's the only time they're consistent, barring rock slides or other natural events. But it doesn't take into account conditions in winter that can vary significantly according to snowfall, wind, previous slides, and so on.

I've been in the Bowl often with a pretty thin layer of form-fitting snow when the whole thing is big and steep and spooky looking. Other times after a big dump and some wind-loading it can create everything from formidable drops to something almost welcoming.

All of which simply means that there is no perfect way to calculate these things. Even slope readings done with watches or apps, at the time of the descent in multiple spots, can be tricky. Not to mention time-consuming and annoying when what you're really there to do is ski.

The most thorough approach, as always when its practicable, is to climb up whatever you're going to ski down, and check out all the conditions as well as take your slope angle readings on the way.

Beyond the realm of the numbers and science lies the other way of quantifying steep skiing, and that's with visceral adjectives. Common ones run the gamut from "staircase" to "elevator shaft" (which is the name of an infamous Aspen Mountain run). I've employed "firepole," and "windshield," and once called Aspen Mountain's S1 "steeper than drink prices in the town below." One of my favorite descriptions comes from a story about early trail-clearing on Aspen Highlands where one sawyer referred to a pitch as, "Steep as a cow's forehead, and her a-grazing."

A good metaphor can evoke an admiring response, yet still not give you much to go on. Resorts that specialize in steep terrain have developed colorful language to go with it, usually originating with ski patrol people and filtering through the copy writers. A Big Sky press kit one year read, "Most Testosterone-Charged Run Off the Tram: the Big Couloir at an average 42 degrees. Steepest Way Down, Castro's Shoulder at 50 degrees."

It's the same slick combination of numbers and hyperbole that Jackson Hole also employs. For America's most notorious steep run, Corbet's Couloir, they devised a fairly inclusive thumbnail: "A classic ski run, the couloir is world-renowned for it's nearly vertical entrance, steep pitch, and variable conditions." Following the cliff-like drop-in "the slope then 'flattens' to 50 degrees. The overall average steepness is 40 degrees."

I've skied it, and once past the jump-turn entry it's a surprisingly accommodating chute that flares out and can deliver some of the best powder on the mountain due to its north-facing exposure. I described it for SKI magazine as a place to "arrive by air and depart by body-bag," primarily because not everyone successfully lands that initial jump.

But with steep skiing progressing as it has in the last few decades, Corbett's is now seen as civilized enough to host the annual Kings and Queens of Corbett's event that features dozens of riders launching off the entry with multiple front and back flips and then roasting the run-out. In what seems almost like mocking this once terrifying landing, a recent trend has been to intentionally tap the imposing stone wall on skier's left while still airborne.

Some guides and resorts still prefer an old-school approach to describing runs that totally ignores the inclinometer in favor of a succinct synopsis of the runs. On the mountain map at La Grave, France, they've gotten so pithy they just use big yellow exclamation points to delineate their most dangerous runs.

Mad River Glen in Vermont, where 40% of the skiing is advanced, has an interactive trail map on its website where you can point and click at runs, and bring up photos and quick-hit assessments. "Gazelle – most difficult. Super steep and usually scratchy up top, nice bumps on the rest. Better ski it well since you'll have a big audience above on the Sunnyside lift." Another way to judge it would be to note that of all 20+ black runs at Mad, a number are called "most difficult," many are called "steep," but only Gazelle is labeled "super-steep."

My friend Chris Davenport, who knows steep skiing intimately (it's even the name of his website), says of rating pitches by degrees, "I don't really buy that stuff. There's a lot of inconsistencies." How, then, does he gauge the steepness of something? "Basically, if I have to think twice before dropping in, it's pretty steep for me. Usually things that are only moderately steep you can just ski right down. When every turn is very slow and deliberate, like on a 14er or in Alaska, that's steep."

Then he adds, "When it's the steepest, I'll use my uphill hand against the snow, to feel where it is and give me more stability. And that's when you know it's fairly vertical because otherwise you wouldn't be able to touch the snow without falling over."

In the end, Davenport uses the same phrase a lot of us do to refer to something really precipitous. The same one I used with Raoul in Zurs that day. "It's really fucking steep." And Chris thinks that may be the most basic criteria of all. "When you have to use an expletive to describe it, then it's steep."

Needless to say, there is a more complex system for grading both the steepness and exposure of runs than simple metaphors, curses or degrees of pitch. Called the Toponeige Cotation, famed alpinist Volodia Shashashani wrote it for alpine skiing descents along with climbing/mountaineering gradations. According to Wikipedia, the system has been improved by his collaboration with a number of local ski mountaineers and is in widespread use, including by the Topoguide books published by Volopress. In the United States ski mountaineers Andrew McClean and Lou Dawson have proposed a similar scheme.

The object of these systems is to quantify both exposure and skiing difficulty. While the challenge of any ski descent anywhere is always dependent on conditions, this rating scale assumes similar and good conditions equivalent to hard spring snow in all cases. As Kilian Jornet notes, "It does give us an idea of where we are getting into and the consequences of a fall."

Descents are rated from 1 to 5 with further specifications at each level. Level 1 includes slopes up to 30 degrees, while level 4 starts at 40 to 45 degrees sustained over at least 200 meters. Grade 5 descents are more than 45 degrees on big lines and over 50 degrees on shorter ones. "Extreme" ratings start at 5.4 in normal conditions, with Jornet citing the Mallory route on the Aiguile du Midi as an example.

The highest grades are 5.5 and 5.6 and, "require slopes of more than 50 or 55 degrees [long and short], with technical difficulties such as narrowing, rocky outcrops and navigation [issues], and major slopes such as Nant Blanc, the Austrians or the descent from Chantriaux in l'Artesonraju," explains Jornet.

That's half the formula. The 'difficulty' part is defined as a route's exposure, i.e. the consequences of a fall. It ranges from 1 where there are no considerations or obstacles other than the slope, to 4 which includes high walls that you can plunge off of or careen into and where a fall would be almost certain death.

This all results in some hieroglyphics and figures that sound simpler than they are to decode, and it doesn't sound simple. For starters, the first letters of the rating are for the difficulty of the climb, which we aren't that concerned with here, but is still good to know for determining how difficult it will be to access a given line of interest. The ratings go from W, for Walk, generally with no aids, through five ratings total, with D as the most difficult that may require ropes and climbing equipment, rappels, and so on.

According to Jornet, "in general terms one should consider that it is impossible to stop a fall on a 35° ice slope or from 45° on spring snow. From 50° a fall that is not immediately stopped, even in deep snow, is impossible to stop."

The danger levels in the toponeige cotation go from one through four, or "very little" to "death in the case of a fall is certain." A number of factors contribute to danger levels besides pitch and conditions, including altitude, length and width of the slope, timing, avalanche exposure, and of course weather.

Reduced to its most basic, the toponeige cotation confirms what any other rating system or just basic advice would: if you even have to ask what some of the specifications mean, you probably aren't ready for the most dangerous lines. As a recreational skier, it's always wise to consider, in essence, whether any given run is really worth your life.

CHAPTER 9

PART TWO – SOME OF THE WORLD'S STEEPEST LIFT-SERVED RUNS

A Fool's Errand

While there is widespread fascination with steep skiing and the steepest runs in the world, few can agree on what it takes to make the grade. It's not that there's a lack of opinions on the subject, as illustrated in the introduction, just a lack of agreement about how to accurately determine the steepness of a given run.

As you've already read, many authorities like using clinometers and arriving at empirical numbers. However, a substantial number of others don't think that should be the only or even dominant criteria. What's more, some resorts keep no stats, while others keep copious ones that are subject to interpretation and fluctuations. As has also been discussed, conditions play a huge role in how skiable and/or dangerous something is, and in what the pitch actually is on any given day.

Most of the steep lists in magazines and on the Internet include all the clichéd usual suspects that have been getting cited since the 1970s. That's because all are worthy and as with many such rankings, they're often most notable for what they leave out. That's always going to be the case given the large number of steep runs in the world and skier's differing tastes and opinions. That's why it would be worse than a fool's errand for me to try to assemble a comprehensive list of the world's steepest runs, and why I've copped out by just offering a tasting menu of some of the most legendary, while debunking a few internet myths along the way.

Reliable ski data is hard to come by anywhere, and often non-existent in much of the world when it comes to things other cultures have no interest in. Such as how steep a ski run is, which seems mostly a western obsession. That's due in part to the cost of running lifts into very steep terrain and then controlling them for avalanches.

When you include the expense of grooming really steep slopes, which some resorts do with winch cats, then it gets very spendy for the limited numbers of skiers and riders capable of using them.

So this chapter centers on the two continents (North America and Europe) where steep skiing is a significant part of the ski culture, plus Las Lenas as the representative of another continent where steep skiing has a real presence.

One troubling issue with writing about some of the world's steepest runs is the attention it draws to them from riders who have no business going anywhere near them. And this isn't just hazardous for those skiers and boarders, they're a danger to anyone else on the slopes, and a big problem for ski patrollers who all too often have to assist them off of life threatening slopes.

At Big Sky in Montana there was much debate amongst patrol and mountain personnel before the 2020/'21 season about whether to start designating some existing runs as triple black diamonds instead of double black. The hope was that it would discourage the gapers and yahoos who were continuously getting in trouble in places with potentially dire consequences. Unfortunately a side effect of going ahead with the plan was that it prompted still more poseurs to try them so they could brag that they'd done a triple black run, which was exactly what some had worried about from the beginning.

In fact, the runs are deserving of the extra diamond because of steady pitches in the 40s and low 50s, lots of unmarked obstacles, and serious exposure to rock ridges and cliffs. Frequently the only way for the patrol to evacuate those who are in way over their heads is to lower them by ropes, a time consuming and risky pain in the ass for everyone involved.

This terrain is abundantly visible from several different lifts and vantage points, so there is no excuse for not having scouted it at least a little, even involuntarily. The drops, mandatory airs, cliffs, close outs, rock buttresses and waterfall-steeps are impossible not to see. So it's beyond fathoming how anyone can look at it and not understand its dangers, or so misjudge their own skills.

But it's a fact that these drastic mistakes happen way too often all over the world and there is no certainty about how to deal with it. Screening those who want to access dangerous terrain is one way, with checkout systems where riders have to sign in, show their beacon, probe and shovel, and wait their turn to ski the terrain. It's an effective approach because having the proper rescue gear is one gauge of how serious riders are about what they want to do.

There are drawbacks though. It necessitates having patrollers manning screening stations, and works best where getting to the goods has to be done through a gate that allows it to be easily monitored. It's not foolproof of course, because fools can be crafty.

Beyond that, restricting access to their steepest and most challenging terrain keeps resorts from being able to include that acreage in its overall terrain figures, because they aren't technically considered open slopes. For some resorts that's a significant consideration in their advertising campaigns.

Lone Mountain at Big Sky, MT, with the Big Couloir run marked. Courtesy of Big Sky Resort.

Limiting publicity about super-steep slopes is another potential way of dialing down the lure to naïve riders. But it's a slippery slope, so to speak, because it can limit the amount of good information that gets out about the kinds of runs where having honest intel is very important. It also runs counter to the reason the resort has the terrain open to begin with, which is to be able to promote it to good riders. In the same way Pebble Beach likes being known as difficult golf, and Nazare, Portugal, likes its reputation as home to the world's biggest and baddest surfing, there is cachet in being able to say you have some very challenging slopes. In the case of the golf, all it costs you if you're not up to the challenge is a fistful of dollars and a piece of your pride. With the surfing it can cost your life, and that's also the case with super-steep/extreme skiing.

But in the end it's hard to protect people from themselves. So proceed at your own risk and do not interpret this chapter as a guide or a recommendation of any kind.

The steepest runs in North America are mostly well known, and I'll start with the granddaddy of the genre, Corbet's Couloir at Jackson Hole Mountain Resort in Wyoming. If its reputation is more fearsome than its reality its in large part because of the gnarly optics. That vertical entry I cited in the preceding chapter is almost always a mandatory air onto an icy 50-degree landing, unless you really send it. After that the widening 40-degree rollout to the bottom is benignly awesome. Truth be told, many Jackson locals consider Alta 1 Chute, Tower 3 Chute and the nearly mythical S&S Couloir to be steeper and more challenging than Corbet's.

The run was named for the ski mountaineer Barry Corbet, who predicted that someday someone would ski it. It was actually first skied by Lonnie Ball, a ski patrolman at the time and subsequent well-known ski photographer living in Montana who is modest about an historic achievement. But for anyone who suggests the run

Aiguille du Midi - 3842m

Entrance - 3575m

Exit (Glacier des Bossons) - 2800m

The deadly Cosmiques Couloir off the Aiguille du Midi at Chamonix, France. Courtesy of Chamonix Tourist Office.

should be named for Ball instead of Corbet it needs noting that Corbet had an illustrious career based out of Jackson and Exum Mountain Guides and discussed in later chapters of this book. He definitely had the chops to ski the couloir, he just never had the chance before a crippling helicopter crash while making a ski film.

Lone Peak at Big Sky, Montana, is a beast. The entire giant cone from The Wave and Castro's on the southern shoulder, to the Dictator Chutes staring due east, to the pure north-facing Big Couloir and Headwaters Bowl, to the west side wilds of the North Summit Snowfields, ranges from the low 40s to the low 50 degrees, with no-fall zones and mandatory airs. Most of it isn't where you want to be without serious skills and local knowledge.

That Highland Bowl trail map in Aspen, Colorado, I mentioned earlier lists the range of pitches across the sprawling caldera at 38 – 48 degrees as measured in the summer. The north-facing G-Zones are the most tilted in places like Full Curl and the pow stash of G-Spot. As the ski patrol's best selling t-shirt puts it, you can "Smoke the Whole Bowl," because it's all great. Most of it involves a hike at altitude to reach, and a speedy traverse at the bottom back to the lift.

Just next door on Aspen Mountain, S1 is the tightest and steepest of the mountain's glades and mine dumps. It's legend has surpassed even the likes of the Silver Queen run's Elevator Shaft, and the journeys to the east down Hyrup's and Christi's.

The Pallavacini Lift at Arapahoe Basin, Colorado delivers you to some of the highest, steepest chutes in Colorado resort skiing, with Gauthier, more familiarly known as 5th Alley, tipping in around 46 degrees.

Crazy Ivan 2 at Breckenridge, Colorado is unmarked on the map. Its 49-degree line requires a hike to the top of Peak 8 and preferably a guide to locate the cornice huck entry from there.

At a consistent 50-55 degrees Rambo at Crested Butte, Colorado is widely considered the steepest man-made resort run in North America and littered with enough gnarly small trees and spiky rocks to make it even more of a test.

A traverse from Chair 9 at Loveland ski area in Colorado and a short hike puts you on top of the Continental Divide at 3,870 meters (12,700 feet.) Wild Child dives off of it at 52 degrees, with either an airborne-from-a-cornice entry, or a ski-in side door.

A 15-minute hike to the nearly 3,657-meter (12,000-foot) summit of the Mirkwood area at Monarch Mountain, Colorado features Mexico, Staircase and East Trees in the mid to high 40-degree-range through tight timber.

All of Silverton Mountain in Colorado is fairly serious but amazing business. A prime example is a 30-minute boot pack up the west face of the big central ridge that delivers you to Tiger Claw, a dicey wind affected couloir at an honest and nerve-wracking 52 degrees.

Senior's in the Telluride, Colorado side-country is accessed from the top of the Prospect Peak lift and a two-hour-hike and obviously isn't an inbounds or controlled run. But wedged into a 52-degree rock gully off the top of 4,060-meter (13,320-foot) Palmyra Peak it's emblematic of the wild steeps all around Telluride. More accessible resort runs like Spiral Stairs and Kant-Make-M are two double-black mogul monsters that drop almost straight down into town and combine XL length with serious pitch to create some of the country's most daunting bump runs.

A good part of the Waterfall Area of the Wolf Creek Ski Area in Colorado is accessible with an easy skate from the Treasure Lift. Some of the Peak Chutes have been clocked at 46 degrees, and on past them is the Big Cornice at 49 degrees, and the headliner of 52 Degree Trees, which gives the whole plot away with its name.

In Alyeska, Alaska where many great lines are hike-to, the 305-vertical-meter (1,000-foot) double black Christmas Chute is fully inbounds, fully 50 degrees, and fully puckering.

Al's Run at Taos, New Mexico is one of the best known runs at a famously steep ski area. That's less for its relatively modest 35-degree tilt than because its 548 vertical meters (1,800 feet) of massive moguls are directly under Lift 1. That intimidation factor causes it to be included on lists of the best bump runs in America and the scariest runs in the world.

Great Scott at Snowbird, Utah is a steady 40-degree pitch that drops off the top of the Cirque underneath the tram for a 1,000 vertical feet of stone-studded slopes where you can get surprise-launched at any point.

KT-22 at Palisades Tahoe in California is one of the most infamous west coast drops, covering 357 vertical meters (1,500 feet) at a steady 35 degrees, and it totally slays on powder days.

"Nicknamed the 'Mothership', Steep and Deep Chair at Mammoth Mountain, California accesses the steepest terrain on the mountain," as per Teton Gravity Research. Wipeout, Dropout and the Noids, "range in pitch from slightly hair-raising to full-on breakneck."

Couloir Extreme (aka Saudan Couloir) at Blackcomb Mountain, British Columbia is a 762-vertical-meter (2,500-foot), 42-degree chute that Skiing Magazine ranked in its Top 10 Steepest Runs. Along with the shorter The Cirque and The Couloir at Whistler, they headline the two area's astounding 2,200 acres of black and double-black slopes.

Revelstoke, British Columbia's 's Kill the Banker run is called one of the longest sustained steep resort pitches in North America. Deserving of kudos just for its name, it plunges nearly 914 vertical meters (3,000 feet) with enough powder pillows and mushroom cap drops to keep it lively all the way.

Delirium Dive at Banff Sunshine in Alberta (known as "the Dive" by locals) is labeled as an "extreme off-piste ski zone" that CNN has called one of the most extreme ski runs in the world. Said to have pitches up to 60 degrees that figure is dependent on conditions and most of the skiing is in the 40s on a broad slope.

Smuggler's Notch, Vermont hosts a run called Black Hole with 53-degree section full of rocks, trees, bumps and spurs and described as "some of the eastern US's most intense glade skiing."

The Goat at Stowe, Vermont is considered one of the most difficult runs in the Northeast because it's 36 degrees is skinny, rocky and bumpy.

The deceptively mild 38-degree pitch of Paradise, an off-piste plunge at Mad River Glen, Vermont, is only attained after an 8 to 10-foot mandatory air and then you have to survive the lumps and stumps and a four-foot ice dam across the entire run.

When it comes to the steepest runs in the Alps and Andes, there are so many, on-piste and off, that all I can do is cite a selection of some of the best.

First, let's address a popular Internet story about a run called Harakiri in Mayrhofen, Austria. Cited as the steepest groomed/man-made run in the world by multiple sources, it serves as an object lesson in the inaccuracies of many similar online lists. The run's gradient is actually rated *at 78%,* but frequently gets misstated as *78 degrees*. As we know, 78 degrees would have a hard time holding snow, let alone a skier, but it would definitely qualify as the steepest groomed run on earth. On the other hand, 78% translates as 38 degrees, which isn't the steepest marked/groomed run in the world, or the Alps, or even Austria.

In 2020 the Kaunertal glacier area in the Tyrolean Oberland on the Italian border, opened the Black Ibex run with an average pitch of 41.3 degrees. And there is more steep skiing all over Austria at the likes of Sport Gastein, off the backside of the Kreuzkogel, on runs that aren't marked or maintained; at Ramsau am Dachstein where it also has very steep unmarked slopes off the Dachstein Massif; Ischgl, where their run 14a weighs in at 35 degrees; and Diabolo in Montafon at the Golm resort with a similar pitch.

Kitzbuhel's Streif run, where the world's most challenging downhill is held in the Hahnenkamm event (more on it in later chapters), has two very steep sections at the top. The Mausefalle (Moustrap) is the steepest at 40.5 degrees and racers cover most of it in the air. After a huge cranking turn comes the Steilhang (literally "steep slope") at nearly 36 degrees. Both are parts of the maintained Streif run and skied together will test any recreational rider due to their steepness and firm-to-icy conditions.

Then there's the massive Arlberg region where St. Anton is the acknowledged expert's mountain. Its most severe runs are centered around two lifts, significant side-country and massive off-piste. The Vallugagrat and the Schindlergrat lifts feature most of the steepest runs tucked into razor-rock pinnacles and cliffs that leave little room for error. I've been lucky to catch the Schindlergrat (aka "Schindler's Lift") in good powder on some very steep lines and didn't even destroy my skis.

The backside of the Vallugagrat begins a route that leads to Zurs (which you would otherwise reach by a half-hour drive over two big passes) and you aren't allowed to do it without a guide. Right off the top is a steep, exposed 40-degree pitch where several people have fallen over the years and died as a result of hitting a rock wall at the bottom.

It was one of only two places where my guide advised me not to fall the day we did it. The other was after a climb up out of Zurs on the way back to St. Anton, on a long funnel down a steep ridge with smooth, slick snow, a sustained pitch in the mid-40s, and bare rocks to either side and below. After which the mandatory air off a highway tunnel was easy.

Other well-known steep offerings in the region occur along the largely off-piste White Ring that starts in Zurs on the Flexenpass and passes through Lech on the way back to Zurs.

In Switzerland, many consider Verbier to be the country's steep capital, with a lot of wild, hike-to chutes and couloirs where extreme contests are held and that will get any good rider's attention. Inbounds, perhaps its most notorious maintained run is the Chassoure-Tortin itinerary on a wide, heavily moguled face with sections up to 40 degrees that can be icy. Whether you ski it, or traverse above it to reach steeper and less trafficked slopes beyond, a fall here probably won't kill you but can definitely beat you up.

Beyond Verbier, Switzerland is stuffed full of big, steep descents at resorts that include Murren, where some of the off-piste is all-world steep; Engelberg, with the legendary Laub wall, one of skiing's most famous powder playgrounds draped at 35 to 40 degrees for over 914 vertical meters (3,000 feet); Andermatt, which hosts excellent alpine ski touring with numerous notably steep options; and Saas Fee, where the Mittelallalin run is another long challenging outing with impressively steep elements like the rock-lined Langfluh and the skinny Altes Kanonenrohr ("Old Gun Barrel").

In another case of overly enthusiastic promotion, a run in the Portes du Soleil known as Chavanette or Le Mur Suisse ("The Swiss Wall"), is frequently described as "the steepest run in the world." Lately that's been finessed by noting, "locals claim it's the steepest in the world." With a 56% gradient (less than 30 degrees), it might not even be the steepest run in the Portes du Soleil let alone the world. But it's still a workout due to its ridiculous sea of bumps.

In the very vertical world of the Italian Dolomites there are some steep off-piste lines made especially dramatic by the mountains that enfold them. Most of the steepest maintained slopes in Italy are all in the 35 to 36 degree range. The 3 Zinnen Dolomites resorts feature what is widely called Italy's steepest piste on the Holzriese 2 run with a 36-degree average gradient for its 1,000 vertical feet. The steepest wall of the Thoeni–Chiesa Valmalenco is said to be almost 35 degrees, while the Spinale Direttissima at Madonna di Campiglio reportedly has gradients over that. And the Herrnegg-Kronplatz at Plan de Corones, part of the "black five" circuit of adjoining expert runs, is said to exceed 35 degrees in places.

In fact, Alagna in western Italy near the French border has steeper slopes than any of the above, though they're mostly unmaintained freeride slopes. The V3 run that leads from the 3,275-meter (10,745 feet) summit to the valley floor when conditions permit, includes pitches of up to 50 degrees on the upper part. And some other off-piste sections are rumored to weigh in at 60+ degrees. With a reputation as Italy's La Grave, like that area most of Alagna's best skiing is off-piste on runs with no signs or grooming and minimal avalanche control.

If you want to find the biggest variety of super-steep, ultra-challenging lift-served terrain in the Alps, the best way is to follow those who have been seeking it out for the last 50 years and head to France.

La Face (Face de Bellevarde) at Val-d'Isere is alleged to be 71 degrees in one place and demanding enough to host part of the World Cup Criterion Downhill course for nearly 1,000 meters (3,280 feet), and can be icy and crowded.

start

3200

3

1

0

2

Skierslodge/Guideservice

Route lines of the infamous Trifides Couloirs at La Grave, France. Courtesy of Skier's Lodge and Guide Service, La Grave.

In Courchevel, the Emile Allais Couloir is considered the narrowest and most difficult of the resort's trio of fearsome chutes, while the Grand Couloir is the least scary, and all are accessed by a usually icy ridge.

They've been digging tunnels through solid stone on the Alps for 150 years. So it's appropriate that the entry to The Tunnel at Alpe d'Huez runs through 200 meters of rough-hewn rock. It is sometimes also called the steepest resort run in the Alps, but since it's most tilted pitch is 35 degrees, it wouldn't even make a top twenty list.

The bulk of the steep skiing pioneers ended up in either Chamonix or La Grave, and the tradition continues with those chasing the extremes today. Both are the centers of vast mountains with more insane routes and lines than most mortals can even imagine.

Chamonix's include the E.N.S.A. Couloir on Brevent. At 47 degrees, 1,404 vertical meters (4,606 feet), and readily accessible from the Brevent cable car, this is a great intro to the real Chamonix. The spicy entry is testing at best and an abseil when necessary.

Cosmiques Couloir on the Aiguille du Midi requires some hiking/skinning to reach, followed by a short downclimb or rappel, and is considered one of the classic extreme lines in the Alps. At a sustained 900 meters (2,952 feet) of 50-degree pitch, with an overall descent of 1,646 vertical meters (5,400 feet), the route is exposed and demanding.

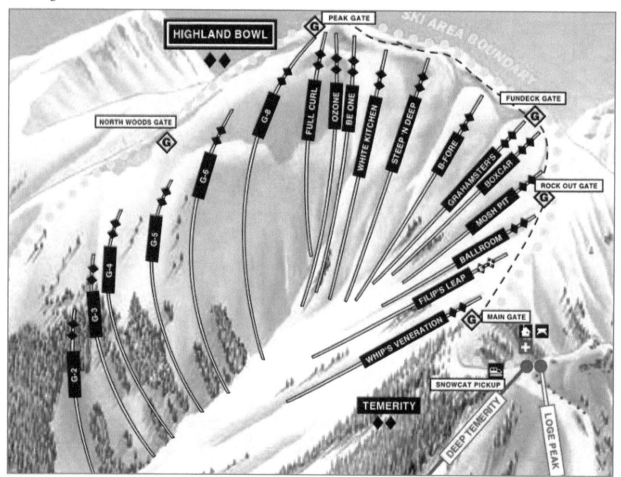

Highland Bowl Trail Map, courtesy of Aspen Skiing Company.

I got to ski the Vallee Blanche off the Aiguille du Midi cable car by variations on the classic and Montenvers routes on a spectacular powder day. The pitches were often on sustained 35+ degree slopes, with frequent seracs, crevasses and snow bridges, plus a ski-through blue ice cave and one section with an optional fixed rope for descent. And everywhere I looked, especially on Montenvers, were inspiringly steep walls and flanks. You can pick routes here that will be the equal of many of the steeps in the area, but still with lift access. And you should always have a guide, if for no other reason (and there are many) than to find the best lines on any given day.

Some of the less demanding lift-served, ski-in steep stuff around Chamonix is on Les Grand Montets (LGM). Both runs to either side of the top cable car are black rated. Of the latter, one online guide says, "The run is very steep but not suicidal." Chamois off the Bochard cable car is a black run that passes through a tunnel, a recurring theme in the Alps.

The crown jewel of LGM is the Pas de Chevre that drops straight down from the top lift station to the Mer de Glace glacier in the Vallee Blanche, 1,828 vertical meters (6,000 feet) below. It runs for about 4 miles with a maximum gradient of 51 degrees on a slightly tight couloir midway down, and the egress onto the glacier at the bottom has become so sketchy most of the time they advise everyone to rappel from a few fixed points. Either way you're delivered to the same place as the runs down the Vallee Blanche. And if you get as lucky as I did you can combine a morning jaunt down the VB with an afternoon drop into the Pas de Chevre and have a two-run day of consistently steep skiing on almost 4,000 total vertical meters (13,000 feet).

At La Grave, all of the lift-accessed runs on La Meije are unmaintained, generally steep and often exposed. As in Chamonix there are nearly endless backcountry lines in the surrounding mountains and on the peak of La Meije.

Just as with Chamonix, all I can do is note a few of the highlights.

Starting with the best known we have the Trifides Couloirs, a cluster of four narrowish, sometimes deadly drops near the top of the cablecar that are numbered 0, 1, 2, 3. Also known as Couloir de l'epaule (0), the lower part of the Grand Couloir (1), and Grand Couloir – Couloir Median (2). Three, on the far skier's right, is rarely ridden due to the 100-foot rappel or jump necessary to enter. They range from 40 to 45 degrees for roughly 716 vertical meters (2,350 feet). Between them they've racked up the lion's share of the 30 deaths in La Grave as of 2020.

At a steady 44 degrees the Grand Couloir has been the site of many of the fatal accidents. It is highly visible from the lift and slopes below, making it attractive to people who may want to ride it for the wrong reasons, and/or don't have the necessary skills. And it has an infamous wall on the left halfway down that a number of riders have hit after losing control and/or falling.

The popularity of the Grand is evidenced by the fact that it has moguls for much of the winter now, which was definitely not the case when I skied it the first time with friends including guide Gary Ashurst, who lived there. We caught it as it had just opened on a good powder day. There was a wind plume of snow trailing from the peak of La Meije just above us, about a foot and a half of snow with more in the lee-sides of the run, and it was stunning. Broader than Corbet's or the Big Couloir in the US and twice as long, it's immensely skiable and only mildly intimidating.

On the Chancel side of La Grave the north-facing Couloirs du Lac funnel down toward Lake Puy Vachier through a 500-foot-high cliff band. Choices include Patou, a straight pure line usually in the shadows so the snow stays soft on the 36 to 38 degree slope; the steeper, narrower and more exposed Le Banane that curves like, yes, a banana and can have a few icy spots; and the fast le Couloir du Lac with its melting hourglass shape dripping through the rocks in the mid-40 degrees.

Below those upper-mountain couloirs on the Chancel side are Les Couloirs de Freaux with 900 very vertical and tight meters (nearly 3,000 feet). The Couloir Polichinelle is a route variation of these couloirs that can involve skirting above a 500-foot cliff where famed American guide Doug Coombs went off and was killed while trying to help his friend Chad Vanderham who slipped on ice and went over the edge ahead of him and also died.

Perhaps the only other ski resort in the world that could be mentioned in the same breath as La Grave, Chamonix and the Arlberg for the scale and audacity of its seriously steep skiing is Las Lenas, Argentina.

At Las Lenas most of the wildest stuff is concentrated in one sprawling area served by the famed Marte lift. The eponymous under-the-lift run reaches 38 degrees in places and the choices beyond it are generally steeper, nearly endless and truly dazzling. Eduardo is a sweet chute with a 45 to 50-degree entrance that drops 1,200 meters (3,937 feet) all the way to the base and is named for instructor Eduardo Gutierrez who died there in 1986.

Cerro El Collar encloses, or "collars," a huge series of steep bowls. Cerro Martin is a 3,637-meter (11,900-foot) rock formation with a cornice and an eastern face that tilts in at 50 degrees and fills up with wind-loaded powder; and Mercurio starts with a tricky steep entrance and descends another 4,000 very vertical feet.

These runs are only a quick taste of the full Las Lenas buffet. And the same can be said for this whole list in general terms. In many cases, the best lines are the ones only you and a few of your friends know about, because anyone else you told you'd have to kill.

CHAPTER 10
PART THREE – GOING TO EXTREMES IN THE '60S & '70S

Long Hair and Steep Lines

Born in 1937 near Verbier, Switzerland, it was 30 years later in 1967 when Sylvain Saudan made his bones in Chamonix by executing the first ski descent of the Spencer Couloir, with slopes up to 55 degrees and until then considered impossible.

He and two companions climbed the couloir and on top Saudan put his skis on and roped up with his friends securing it. After some turns to test the snow, he was ready. "It was the most difficult moment, when I untied the knot and saw the rope go up to the top," he said later. At that point he was fully committed in the no-fall zone, and he says he asked himself why. "What would it get me? The answer was nothing. It was a completely free risk. But these ideas did not disturb me… I hunted them down and started skiing."

After that came a flurry of first descents in the Alps that included the Whymper Couloir on the Aiguille Verte, the Rothorn, the north face of the Piz Korvatsch, the north face of Bionnasay, the south face of the Grande Jorasses, the Marinelli corridor on the south face of the Monte Rosa, and the northwest face of the previously un-skied and wildly forbidding Eiger.

One of Saudan's most high profile early descents was on October 17, 1968, in the very exposed Gervasutti Couloir on the Mont Blanc du Tacul. With a 45-degree rating for most of the slope, and 55 degrees in the entrance below the seracs, the chute has proven deadly for dozens over the years. When he checked in at the Les Cosmiques hut Saudan was greeted by the guard with the comment that, "The Gervasutti has not made any dead this year, you will be the first."

As ultra-ski mountaineer and endurance athlete Kilian Jornet has written, "These descents are still considered great classics of extreme skiing, and only very experienced skiers dare to put their skis there. When I ski, my hands get sweaty imagining Saudan making turns with his varnished wooden skis and soft leather boots."

[DROP CAP] The vast majority of the most extreme and demanding lines being ridden since 1950 haven't been at resorts, but in the backcountry and on the big mountains where steep skiing became extreme skiing and created one of the most interesting and straight up crazy cultures on the planet.

Distinguishing steep skiing from extreme skiing is fairly straightforward: virtually all extreme skiing is also steep skiing, but not all steep skiing is extreme by any means. As many of those who have pursued the passion have defined it, extreme skiing is steep skiing with serious consequences. It is called no-fall because it can mean serious injury or death.

Jornet, who has lived in Chamonix for many years, began writing about steep skiing in 2020 for a Spanish magazine called Kiss the Snow. Out of a lifelong passion for skiing and a longtime involvement with extreme routes in Europe, he has a large trove of innate knowledge about the sport and has added to it with extensive research.

He cites, "first descents not yet extreme but visionary by the time of Marcel Kurtz, Louis Falisse and Robach or Sondre Norheim. Snowshoe Thompson. Or the first descents in terrain until then reserved for climbers with ice axes and crampons."

One such example was when Arnold Lunn, the famous English skiing pioneer, skied with guide Joseph Knubel from the summit of Dom des Mischabel at 4,545 meters (14,911 feet) in the Swiss Valais on July 18th of 1917. A pitch of 45 degrees just beneath the summit was negotiated by "his particular technique of descent, a wide-open wedge, the butt touching the ground and slowing down by nailing the poles." In other words, the basic five-year-old's wedge and its hard to imagine how it worked on something that steep.

Jornet goes on to cite Arthur Comey skiing Baxter Peak in Maine in 1926. Also three Swiss who in '28 descended the north face of the Fuscherkarkopf with a 50-degree slope. They did it "with their crampons tied to their backpacks with their tips out to – more out of faith than logic – stop them in case of a fall."

In 1938 legendary French ski racer Emille Allais skied the Glacier du Milieu in l'Aguille d'Argentiere, the same year Chamonix's famed guide Louis Lachenal was the first to ski les Droites.

Eminent glisse alpinist and historian Lou Dawson, in his book *Wild Snow*, suggests that when Bil Dunaway – the eventual longtime Aspenite and owner of the Aspen Times newspaper – and his famed guide Lionel Terray skied Mont Blanc in 1951, on wooden skis with metal edges, they "sired modern extreme skiing."

Jornet notes that, "Even if steep mountains have been skied since the beginning of the last [20th] century, the priority was to go up and down the mountain, not to look for a more difficult line." They were skiing from that particular summit which was accomplishment enough at the time with the equipment they were using.

Jornet agrees with other historians who believe that actively seeking out the most challenging lines on big mountains didn't really start until the 1960s. The first real provocateurs of the movement included Bill Briggs, Heini Holzer, Toni Valeruz, Yuichiro Miura, Serge Cachat, and a lithe and flamboyant Swiss named Sylvain Saudan.

SYLVAIN SAUDAN

After his numerous accomplishments starting in 1967, when Saudan first took his road show to the US in 1971 it was with major successes leavened by some controversy, which was not unusual throughout his career. On March 1, 1971, he attempted to be the first to ski from the summit of Mount Hood in Oregon at 3,425 meters (11,239 feet).

Anselme Baud, an early extremist who worked with Saudan on this descent, once worked as a ski instructor at Mount Hood Meadows. And the ski school director there, Rene Farwig, was responsible for inviting his friend Saudan to ski the big mountain.

In typical fashion Sylvain eschewed the fairly moderate south route down. "I wasn't looking for the easy one, I was looking for the difficult one," he said on a return visit to the area in 2009.

So he decided to try the, "Icy, cliffy, wind-scoured Newton Clark Headwall on the east side," wrote Asit Rathon for The Oregonian. Rathon was surprised in 2009 when he recreated Saudan's descent and discovered the route Saudan took was not the broad Wy'East Face that many accounts claim, but instead the "significantly steeper and more exposed" headwall.

Before Saudan could begin his ascent in 1971 he had to hunker down at the Timberline Lodge for two weeks of storms. Weather eventually forced him to decide to make his ascent via helicopter rather than climbing since he was running out of time and a Bell two-seater was available.

Choppers were being used by steep skiers fairly often during this period, an assist that is now widely rejected by serious alpinists. Modern extreme skiers are, and have been for awhile, often mountaineers who relish the climb as much as the descent.

Of course it's also far safer to climb whatever you're going to ski first, which Saudan acknowledged. But there he was anyway. They'd waited for the weather to clear so the heli could land on the summit, and it was late in the day as Saudan and Anselme Baud were dropped off in heavy winds, one at a time.

Baud glissaded the Wy'East Face. Then Saudan started down the east summit ridge in cold, brutal conditions, on a route he hadn't climbed, and he ended up taking the wrong chute into the Newton Clark headwall. It cliffed out and he had a "tense" 30-minute climb back up, sidestepping on ice, until he could traverse over to the proper entrance couloir.

From there he still had to deal with an icy crux out onto the glacier apron, along with crevasses on the headwall face and constant avalanche danger. "The run was much shorter than the ones I did in Europe, but it was just as dangerous," he said afterwards.

Poster advertising the Academy Award-winning movie of Yuichiro Muira skiing on Mount Everest.
A Crawley Films Production.

Regardless of how the ascent was conducted, the ski was epic and historic and within the accepted style of the time. It's still considered a gnarly line even with far more advanced gear.

Saudan's next big event in America was a descent of Denali in Alaska in 1972. Japanese skier Tsuyoshi Ueki had already skied from the summit in 1970, one of the major feats in a two-year period that took serious ski alpinism global.

According to several who were involved, the Saudan expedition had a heavy complement of support crews, toadies and publicity flaks. Some have also said the star himself was out of shape and heavily assisted on the ascent and that he never reached the summit, which he once claimed.

Whatever the case, everyone agrees that Saudan reached the summit plateau below the actual peak at 5,974 meters (19,600 feet). And that's where one of the most singular couloirs in all of mountaineering starts. It drops 1,828 vertical meters (6,000 feet) at a sustained pitch in the 40 to 50-degree range, and at that time it had never even been ascended, much less skied. Four years later, the GOAT Reinhold Messner would finally climb it and it's now known as the Messner Couloir. In 1972 Saudan windshield-wiper-turned his way down the entire thing, with its radically mixed conditions and lethal exposure.

Despite other questions, he had once again produced incredible extreme skiing that capped off a brilliant five-year run by him and several others who changed ski alpinism forever.

He would later crown his career with multiple high-altitude descents in the Himalaya, including the first ever, full ski-descent of an 8,000-meter peak. In 1982, at the age of 46, he skied Gasherbrum I, better known as Hidden Peak, from its 8,068-meter (26,470-foot) summit. Even more remarkable is that he did it on what is one of, if not *the*, longest sustained 50-degree pitches in the world. And he jump-turned nearly every foot of the way, estimating later that he made 3,000 of them in a bravura show of pure strength.

In the end he also did what many haven't in the "no country for old men" that is the world of extreme skiing. He survived, and had turned 85 as of this writing.

BILL BRIGGS AND AMERICA

Not many others in the world were even contemplating things like what the brash Saudan was accomplishing in the 1970s. Some who did were in North America. German-born mountaineer Fritz Stammberger (cited in chapter 6) moved to Aspen in the early '60s. On June 24, 1971, he cramponed up the north face of North Maroon Peak near Aspen and then skied back down it, falling over a 15-foot cliff at one point, and skiing a tight 50-degree plus section.

It was heralded locally and in some of the climbing press, but didn't garner much wider attention in spite of being a dazzling display that was done solo, with no ropes. It was definitely one of those defiant acts like Saudan's and Bill Briggs that was designed to get attention. And it added to the impact of these formative years in the sport.

The American who stood out the most in this period was that low-key ski instructor Bill Briggs (also cited in chapter 6) in Jackson Hole, Wyoming, who was quietly putting down lines on one of America's most famous and daunting mountain ranges, the Tetons.

He'd started at Dartmouth where Lou Dawson writes in his book Wild Snow that he would visit Tuckerman's Ravine and ski progressively steeper lines, saying it "scared the pants off me." But he began developing a "slow speed turn with an uphill stem and a jump of both tails to quickly get into a turn." Forms of jump turns are still popular on steeps today.

In 1967, after moving to Jackson full-time several years earlier, Briggs made first descents of the Middle and South Tetons, and the next year added the eternally tempting Skillet Glacier on Mount Moran. Then in June of 1971 he went from being a relative unknown to being hailed as the father of extreme skiing in America by solo climbing and skiing the Grand Teton, something many at the time doubted could be done.

"I've always had a thing about proving the experts wrong. Its kind of fun to do," said Briggs on the 50th anniversary of his ski down the Grand. "It's the idea of killing the sacred cow. I just had a bent to do that. It's about reasoning. You get fixed notions or fixed ideas about the way things are, but when you take a look at them, that's not always the way it is. Even if everybody says so. To say you can't ski the Grand Teton just didn't stand to reason."

Briggs was born without a left hip socket and had surgery to fix it at the age of two and then years later had it fused so he could still climb and ski. "The medical field said I'd be in a wheelchair by the time I was 40. But here I am, I'm 90 and still no wheelchair." He's been proving people wrong his whole life, and skiing the Grand was just one more opportunity.

His keen interest in skiing history from early on was given a big boost by meeting Sir Arnold Lunn while climbing in Wales in 1957. "What I really wanted to do was combine the sport of mountaineering and alpine skiing," he said, and talking with Lunn inspired him to continue pursuing the idea. While serving as the ski school director at Woodstock, New York, his assistant was a fellow Dartmouth alum named Barry Corbet, and they soon made the move to Jackson, Wyoming, to work with Exum Mountain Guides and live the dream.

"We were trying to figure out what the skills were that were needed to ski steep mountains," recalled Briggs. He began climbing the other Tetons as a calculated prelude to doing the Grand. "That one would make news," he said. "The rest of them don't really make the news. Skiing it would be worthy of recognition, and I was working my way up to being able to do it with confidence. I didn't want it to be a daredevil stunt. I don't want to risk my life."

His preparation was methodical. "I was mountain guiding at the time so I had guided that route like a hundred times. In the process of taking people up I could look at different portions of the route. So I knew pretty much what the snow route would entail, even though I'd never set foot on it."

His friend Corbet was there all the way for him. "You need inspiration coming from someone who is a little bit better than you. Not a lot better – that's overwhelming. But just a little bit better, so that you think to yourself, 'Yeah, I can do that.' And Barry was always just that little bit ahead. How lucky can you be to have someone like that, at the right time, come in and be a support?"

Corbet was also climbing and skiing in the Himalaya (as cited in chapter 6) and working as a partner in Summit Films. Increasingly occupied on those fronts he was going to film Brigg's descent but had a prior commitment when the time came.

There is a legend that no one even knew what Briggs had planned before he did it, but that wasn't the case. Corbet and a number of others knew. And the night before it happened, Briggs did a local radio interview and announced his plan. The interviewer introduced him by saying, "I've got this nut who thinks he's going to ski the Grand."

"So it was pretty much understood I was going to do this thing," said Briggs. "Except for the radio station, everyone was very supportive. It was a difficult challenge, let's put it that way. This wasn't about achieving some landmark in skiing, or doing – and achieving

Anselme Baud's book became a steep-skiing must-read.

– something scary. The highlight was running into challenge after challenge and then succeeding at each one. Every one of the problems you encounter that you solve is such a kick. That made the whole thing a fantastic adventure."

And there it was. On June 15th, 1971, after years of consideration and planning he climbed on mixed conditions with a broken crampon and up a tight, steep couloir near the summit. "I remember when I was at the top, all ready to ski down, and thinking, 'I've gotten through the hard parts, now all I have to do is ski. That's the easy part'." The top rock band was only spottily covered with snow and very tight. "There's just no room to turn. But then you get out of the rocky section and hit beautiful even snow. It's just plain fun to ski."

He stitched tracks down the very steep and exposed front of the mountain and made a 165-foot rappel with his skis on in the middle, all with no known audience, then went home and out to the bar. It was only after someone later that evening questioned whether he'd really done it that he called Virginia Huidekoper at the Jackson Hole News newspaper.

She owned a Cessna 182 plane and the next day flew over the Grand with Briggs and took some pictures of his very obvious tracks with a 35mm camera, while Briggs, who didn't fly, flew. News photographer Roger LaVake joined Hudekoper on a subsequent flight and took more images with his large format camera. Briggs' case was proven and posters with photos from these flights continue to be popular sellers to this day.

In the opinion of some, including Powder magazine, "Briggs' most technical descent may have come in '74 as he laid the first turns ever down one of the toughest in the Tetons, the steeple-like Mount Owens." In addition to this storied career on skis that includes over 50 years instructing and running the ski school at Snow King in Jackson, Briggs is an accomplished banjo picker and yodeler. He's played in the Stagecoach Band that he helped form at the Stagecoach Bar in Wilson, Wyoming, on Sunday nights since 1969. Bob Dylan even sat in with them once when they played at a private wedding near Jackson for some music industry VIPs.

His love of playing music has been as important in his life as his love of the mountains and skiing steep slopes. And they seem to have created a healthy balance that's helped him live for 91 happy years and counting.

When he retired from steep skiing after a scare on a descent, it undoubtedly helped his longevity. And of his reputation as the father of American extreme skiing, he has said, "I don't consider the skiing I did as extreme, it was alpinism. It was knowing how to be careful, it wasn't jumping over rocky bars."

YUICHIRO MUIRA

I've also written about Japanese alpinist Yuichiro Miura in the Skiing High section of this book. There will always be debate about his motives and the massive circus he created with an entourage and crew of 800 for his 1970 expedition when he skied, and mostly fell, down part of Everest. But that piece of theater and the Academy award winning film that resulted from it, were a big part of the five-year period from 1967 to 1972 that was the detonator cord for steep skiing extremism. It provided the justification for those who followed to tell themselves, 'If that crazy shit can be done, lots of other crazy shit can be, too.'

And in fairness, the Everest gig was by no means a one-off stunt. Muira put in time as a speed skier, including a very brief world record in the discipline in 1964 when he was 31. Following the Everest stunt he skied the rest of the 7 Summits, if not always from the summits. His first descents in Asia included Mount Fuji where he tried the idea of deploying a parachute to stop, after previously using one while speed skiing. But it was a spectacular failure in the thin air above 7,900 meters (26,000 feet) on Everest.

He was roundly mocked for the whole Everest expedition, especially for never summiting and only skiing from lower down on the South Col. Muira has always said that the government of Nepal wouldn't allow him to ski from the summit and assigned him to do it from the South Col instead. In any case, the movie was a big success. And over time he has gained well-deserved respect for his other accomplishments, including returning several times to summit Everest without skiing it. On his last climb in 2013 he became the oldest to ever reach the top at the age of 80.

SERGE CACHAT

While this Chamonix native didn't have the far-reaching impact of some others in the early years, his influence was definitely felt in Chamonix, which has always been the global center of glisse extremism. His exploits in the area inspired the likes of Kilian Jornet's father when they were living in the Pyrenees of Spain. Cachat's achievements included the first descent of the Couloir Couturier on the Aiguille Verte on August 1, 1972, paving the way for what Jornet describes as "this long corridor in the heart of Chamonix" to become the classic route it is today. The descent was an important component in the full flowering of ski mountaineering as an extreme sport that took place in those first two years of the '70s.

ANSELME BAUD

One of those everyone agrees was present at the creation of extreme skiing was Anselme Baud. Born in Morzine, France in 1948, he grew up skiing in the Chablais Massif where he participated in the beginnings of the Avoriaz Resort. After work in America where he assisted Saudan at Mount Hood, he partnered with Patrick Vallencant and other leading figures during the pioneering days of extreme skiing.

Baud has lived in Chamonix for most of his life and is still guiding, as of this writing, with the company he founded that his son Christopher, also a certified mountain guide, now runs. Anselme's book *Chamonix – Mont Blanc and the Aiguilles Rouges – a Guide for Skiers*, has been must reading for would-be alpinists for decades.

He and Vallencant also made the second descents of the Couloir Couturier, and of the Whymper corridor on the Aiguille Verte in '73. With many extreme descents throughout the world, from the Alps to the Andes, Antarctica and the Himalayas, his best known may be the filmed first ski of the arête de Peuterey and the Aiguille Blanche de Peuterey in the Mont Blanc massif in 1977 with Patrick Vallencant. Baud also made a first descent of the north face (the Mallory Line) of the Aiguille du Midi with Daniel Chauchefoin and Yves Detry that same year.

Several other first descents on telemark gear have also been recorded by Baud with clients in the Alps, Nepal and Himalaya. And he and Conrad Anker skied the Northwest Corridor of Mount Vinson in Antarctica in 1997. Baud has written four other outstanding books. In 2003 his son Edouard died in an accident in the Gervasutti Couoloir. And in 2008 Anselme was decorated with the French Legion of Honor for Extreme Descents.

TONI VALERUZ

His given name is actually Tone but he's been known by Toni since he was young. Born in Alba di Canazei in 1951, Valeruz was one of a trio of Italians who were very committed to extreme skiing during this period and who left their fingerprints on the early days of the sport.

Valeruz first took up off-piste skiing for the same reasons most do: he wanted some variety from the routine of lift-serviced slopes. His first ski of the Northwest Face of the Gran Vernel on March 23, 1973, was attention grabbing and he has called it among the most demanding north faces of the Italian Alps. Then he had a first on the North Face of the Lyskamm on June 1, 1974, a mountain he has revisited several times and descended faster each time, starting at 13 minutes and whittling it down to a very impressive 2 minutes and 58 seconds in 1993.

On May 14, 1975, he made a first descent from about 4,200 meters on the Hornli shoulder on the East Face of the Matterhorn on slopes of 60+ degrees, and repeated the descent on May 26 that year, and again on May 30, 1996.

He used a helicopter for an ascent of the Mont Blanc in 1978 when he skied the Gran Couloir della Brenva between the Via Major and the Sentinella Rossa in 35 minutes. And when he revisited the Gran vernel in 1980, he choppered to the top and descended in 30 minutes in front of a large crowd as it was being filmed.

As has been discussed, the use of helicopters was not uncommon during this era, but it was not always well received and soon fell out of favor as a legitimate part of first descents. Valeruz made no apologies for his methods. His view was shared by others who considered themselves to be primarily skiers, not climbers, and wanted to save their strength and energies for the descents, which was their real interest.

They were all criticized for being reckless because of not becoming familiar with the conditions of the slopes they were skiing by climbing them. Valeruz remains insistent that he always researched his descents very carefully and that his experience gave him an edge in knowing what to expect at all times.

And he didn't always use helicopters, as in the early years, or the cases of his landmark first descent in 1983 of the Northeast Face of the Eiger, and firsts on the Southeast and Northwest Walls of Ortles the same year. The same applies to the Southeast Face of Tofana di Mezzo in December 1993.

HEINI HOLZER

Born in 1945, this compact and powerful rock climber became known at a young age in his native Italian Tyrol for his numerous first ascents, "almost always alone," as Kilian Jornet notes. He met Reinhold Messner during their military service and "together they open some very difficult climbing routes at this time," wrote Jornet.

Holzer was an early believer in always climbing his routes before skiing them, even as helicopters were becoming the preferred option for others. He began making regular first descents in the Dolomites, including the north face of the Marmolada in June of 1970 on a 600-meter (1,968-foot) long wall pitched at 55 degrees. And soon followed it with the north corridor on Tosa Peak where he encountered frequent blue ice on a 50-degree slope that reached for 900 meters (2,952 feet). Imagine skiing a run as steep as an A-Frame roof, riddled with blue ice and nearly the length of all of Aspen Mountain, on heavy old wood and fiberglass skis in leather boots.

Grave site memorial to Heini Holzer. Photo by Friedhof Schenna.

When he made the first descent of the north face of the Piz Palu in the Bernina massif in 1972, famous Austrian mountaineer Toni Hiebeler declared him the most remarkable extreme skier in history. "That complex face of snow, seracs and rock is such a chaos," wrote Jornet, that in the 19th century guides would only consent to guide clients on it if they first signed their wills in the guide's favor.

On July 11, 1977, Holzer reached the summit of the Piz Rozerg in the Bernina in a 4-hour speed ascent before starting his ski down the northeast face. After one fall up high in a very steep section he managed to self-arrest. Then about a third of the way down, underneath a rock wall, he fell again and wasn't able to stop.

Holzer was always aware of the perils he faced. But he responded to questions about it by saying, "I wonder how many men don't see their family for weeks, just to earn money? Others immerse themselves in alcohol… but the risks are less calculable than those of my so-called madness?"

After what is reputed to be more than 88 first descents he perished the way he had lived, on the edge and straining for more.

STEFANO DE BENEDETTI

Another Italian would come along in Holzer's wake who chose a much different path. De Benedetti is said to have achieved more than 80 first descents beginning in 1976, including a legendary West Face Direct route on Mont Blanc. By 1986, after a challenging trip on Mont Blanc's Innominata Ridge, De Benedetti retired and donated a pair of his skis to Turin's National Museum of the Mountains. But in his short and spectacular career he helped Valeruz and Holzer put a permanent Italian stamp on the early days of extreme skiing.

Pierre TARDIVEL

mémaires de pleine pente

avec
Jack LESAGE

Préface de Sylvain SAUDAN

Book about Pierre Tardivel co-written by him.

CHAPTER 11
PART FOUR - GOING TO EXTREMES IN THE '80S

The French Revolution and an American Trailblazer

PATRICK VALLENCANT

In the October 1980 issue of SKI magazine, Peter Miller wrote, "The most passionate skier of the steeps is 34-year-old Frenchman Patrick Vallencant who has made 50 major descents on slopes over 50 degrees."

Vallencant was the first born (June 9, 1946) of the wave of French men who in the 70s and 80s continued the tradition begun by Sylvain Saudan. Several of Vallencant's descents were done with Saudan's sometimes partner Anselme Baud, including seconds of the Couturier and Whymper couloirs on the Aiguille Verte, and a filmed first on the ultra-difficult Arete de Peuterey in 1977.

His time really began in 1971 with a first descent of the North Face of the Grande Casse and Couloir des Italians; and the North Face of the Tour Ronde. In '72 and '73 he teamed with Marie Jo on the North Face of the Courtes and the Y Couloir on the Aiguille d'Argentiere. Then in the late '70s he went to South America and skied the Southwest side of Huascaran South in '78, and in '79 the Southeast side of Artesonraju, multiple first ascents and descents in the Cordillera Blanco, and an historic first on the West side of the 6,630-meter (21,750-foot) Yerupaja, with slopes of over 65 degrees.

To accomplish what he did he always climbed everything he skied, saying, "In my conception of *ski extreme*, the climb and descent are intimately tied one to the other." He felt that knowing every detail of the snow conditions was critical to success and studied them closely while climbing, which he did with his skis lashed on his pack, wearing crampons and using an ice ax in each hand.

He also created his own technique for descending, explaining to Miller, "It's quite evident that on a slope of 45 degrees or more the skier doesn't use a snowplow any more than he would *avalement*. Every skier who skis the steeps develops his own style. Mine is based on what I call the pedal-jump turn. I call it this because it is a jump turn to which a pedaling motion is added, or a lifting of the downhill ski. This turn does not require much physical effort and allows me to turn to a quick stop without sliding.

"I initiate a turn with my weight on the uphill ski, which breaks the rules of ordinary ski technique. I push off the uphill ski and because of the steep slope, drop into immediate weightlessness – what I call 'jumping into the void'. In the middle of this weightlessness I lift the downhill ski and rotate it, which initiates the turn and brings the uphill ski into the same position while both are in the air… In essence I load the uphill ski but carry my body weight on the downhill ski."

What this well analyzed technique led to for Vallencant was a form of Nirvana. "In the steeps, I feel the falling away of restraints. My head and heart are free… the light, the sky, all the world's beauty I feel through the quick rhythm that sings in my blood. It is during these moments that I am free, part of the mountain and the sky – of the world that is around me."

It was hard to tell if he was an aspiring ski instructor or poet. Apparently both. As he continued climbing and skiing into the '80s, Vallencant founded an extreme skiing camp called Stages Vallencant in Chamonix, and co-founded the Degre 7 apparel company with Iingrid Buchner in 1983, selling his interest in 1988. A year later in March of '89 he was killed in a climbing accident when a carabiner broke during a rappel from the top of La Beaume Rouge in France. In spite of the mythology at the time, it wasn't part of a skiing expedition.

JEAN-MARC BOIVIN

Born on April 6, 1951, in Dijon, Boivin began carving his own way in the world of extreme sports almost from the beginning, seeking originality and progression that would differentiate him from the growing ranks of extreme skiers.

When Killian Jornet writes about Boivin he cites a roll call of the great skiers who followed Saudan in the 70s and 80s. The list includes Vallencant and Marie Jo, Yves Derty and Daniel Chauchefoin, Tony Valeruz, Nino Viale and Diego Fiorito, Laurent Giacommini, Jacky Bessat, Velodia Shahshahani, and Pierre Tardivel. Then he concludes with, "But among them none leaves a trace as marked as Boivin."

Like Vallencant, Boivin was a climber first, a skier next and then for Boivin a variety of other disciplines. When he first started becoming known it was for solo ascents of some of the most challenging routes in the Alps, starting with the Albinoni-Gabarrou goulotte on Mont Blanch du Tacul in '72. He also teamed up with Gabarrou in '75 for first ascents of the direct north faces of Les Droites and the Aiguille Verte, and the Supercouloir on Mont Blanc du Tacul.

It was only in the latter part of the '70s that Boivin began making a name for his ski descents. A first on the Frendo Spur on the Aiguille du Midi on July 2, 1977, and the South Face of Huascaran and the north faces of Kitarahu and Pisco in '78. On June 6, 1980 he skied slopes of more than 60 degrees on the East Face of the

Matterhorn from the Shoulder, then soloed the Schmid route on the North Face in 4 hours and 10 minutes. He did the Y Gully on the Aiguille Verte in '85, and its Nant Blanc Face in '89.

The latter, on the North Face, is called the most difficult descent in the Mont Blanc massif. As Jornet describes it, "This wall of ice, snow and rock of more than 1,200 meters [3,937 feet] has sections… of more than 55 degrees, sections of ice, exposure to the seracs and a complicated itinerary." It was 10 years before the route was repeated when Marco Siffredi of Chamonix snowboarded it.

By the end of the '70s, Boivin had also started hang gliding and paragliding and setting altitude records with them, eventually making the first paraglider descent from the summit of Everest on September 26, 1988, after climbing the Southeast Ridge.

Learning to fly helped him pioneer what were dubbed *enchainement* routes that linked ascents and descents of multiple peaks using skis, parasails, hang gliders and BASE jumps.

On April 17, 1987, he enchained 5 descents: a first on the Southeast Face of the Aiguille du Moine; a first on the South Face of the Aiguille du Dru; the Whymper Couloir on the Aiguille Verte; the Northeast Face of Les Courtes; and ending with a ski down the Grandes Jorasses. It was a stunning achievement that combined climbing, skiing and paragliding.

Once again Boivin demonstrated what Jornet calls his "polyvalence, the word that defines him, without being the most gifted for a particular activity." Those activities also included, for example, being a member of a team of speleologists that set a world record on the Mer de Glace above Chamonix in 1986 for a sub-glacial scuba dive.

Interestingly, as Jornet suggests, he was able to set records at several of his disciplines without being the most accomplished at them. His climbing continued to be his strength, while other efforts were only just sufficient. Boivin's sometimes partner Laurent Giacommini is quoted as saying that with Boivin, "skiing was a luge! With the hang glider, he didn't know how to fly…"

In Wild Snow, Lou Dawson writes about someone who saw a movie of Boivin's descents at the Telluride Film Festival and said, "My hands broke a sweat as I watched. He'd make a turn, then slide for 40 feet with his skis shaking and uphill hand dragging on the snow, finally gaining enough control to make another 'turn'."

It was not, overall, the image of a highly skilled athlete so much as a multi-faceted and absolutely fearless one with enormous vision and a driving curiosity. Boivin was also, like so many of his contemporaries, anxious to push the boundaries not only to get his adrenalin going but also to make a living from his passion. Doing that traditionally requires attention-getting spectacles for your sponsors that center on being the first or setting world records.

Angel Falls in Venezuela has the longest drop of any known waterfall on the planet at roughly 1,000 meters (3,300 feet). On February 16, 1990, Boivin made the first-ever BASE Jump from the highest point of the falls while being filmed for a French television program. He liked it so much he decided to do it again the next day. Before he went a woman made the leap and was injured when she landed. "Boivin decided to make his jump immediately afterwards, carrying help for the injured woman," according to an entry in Wikipedia.

There are two slightly different versions of what happened next, but in both cases Boivin was seriously injured during his descent. Rescuers, however, believing he was alright, picked up the woman first. By the time they returned for him Boivin had died from internal injuries and blood loss. As with Vallencant, the initial stories said he died in a ski accident, though that wasn't the case.

BRUNO GOUVY

Perhaps the most controversial and flamboyant of the famous Frenchmen of these times, Bruno Gouvy was born in 1962 to parents who loved to sail. He took up windsailing and soon crossed the Mediterranean by board and that seemed to set the stage for future grand adventures. As he told SKI magazine in January of 1989, "After it's over, I want it again and again. But it's not just the risk and the thrill that are satisfying. It's the effort. I don't like things too easy."

It was a statement that echoes what many of the extreme pioneers have said. Setting a seemingly impossible goal and dealing with all of the challenges to accomplish it is one of the big payoffs.

Whereas relationships between the prior generation of French steep skiers and freeriders had been fairly collegial with frequent collaborations, by the 1980s things had changed. "Gouvy was a contemporary of Jean-Marc Boivin, Patrick Vallencant, and other ski mountaineering luminaries from the 1980s golden age of Chamonix steep skiing," Brook Sutton wrote in a 2016 magazine story. "The crew, linked through a love of the mountains more than friendship, had a healthy competition among its ranks."

In Gouvy's case, as an admirer of Boivin's he set himself some very large scale and complex tasks. Being a man who confessed that he "had problems with false modesty," as well as a telegenic one who had to make a living, he was filmed for many of his gigs.

He was also doing it all on a snowboard. That alone was a bold and pioneering move as he began racking up first snowboard descents all around Chamonix. Then he took it to the next level by accessing lines hitherto thought unreachable, presaging the wizardry of Shane McConkey and others to come.

Gouvy's most famous footage on YouTube epitomizes what was becoming an increasingly mechanized and bizarre series of sideshows by a number of different athletes trying to make names during this period. In this effort Gouvy assaults the Petite Aiguille du Dru in 1986 with every device he can summon.

Spoiler alert: the video is much more surprising and alarming if you don't know what's coming so you might want to watch it before reading this.

It begins with him circling the area he's planning to ride by helicopter, revealing the sharpened spire of the Dru, along with several different crews stationed on the mountain to assist in the elaborate production. Gouvy then parachutes from the chopper and spirals around with big stone walls on all sides until suddenly he seems to take aim at the one in the near foreground and roars into it like a half-blind James Bond.

Jean-Marc Boivin skiing the Nant Face of the Aiguille Verte, Chamonix, 1999. Photo © René Robert.

His arrival on the Aiguille du Dru is hard to overstate for what a reviewer describes as "his totally out of control landing." And "landing" is a charitable term. He crashes hard into a ledge below the summit and disappears from the camera view. There's an almost thirty second delay before a hand appears on one of the summit rocks and Gouvy follows it with a grin, apparently no worse for the wear.

Which is good because he still has a mission. Never mind that it seems in every phase like something Wile Coyote has dreamed up. Next, with assistance, he rappels two-thirds of the way down the mountain's face. Once he reaches a 50-degree hanging glacier he buckles into his board and with an ice axe in each hand proceeds to make a longish series of jump turns on very hard, loud snow, using his uphill hand and axe to stabilize himself. It's obvious that if he slips or falls he will die because the steep and slick snowfield ends in a sizable cliff. He stops above it, sheds the board and grabs a paraglider from the crew stationed there and flies on down to town.

There are many things about this whole escapade that are… disturbing. The size of the crew and the amount of money required to accomplish it are primary ones, along with the use of the chopper, and a "plan" that seemed to rely as much on luck as skill.

Some of that is a judgment call from the perspective of today, when so much of the emphasis in alpinism is on minimally assisted efforts. And Gouvy certainly did that in his early years when he was said to be a very good mountaineer. But like many others he needed to make his mark, distinguish himself and find sponsors. He admired Boivin's *enchainments* and wanted to add speed and grandeur to them. And helicopters were being widely employed at the time, along with the big crews it took to pull off many of the stunts.

Patrick Vallencant in the middle of one of his famous jump turns. Photo © Chris Noble.

Consider Gouvy's 1988 event when he climbed the Eiger and spent the night near the summit. He made the descent by snowboard the next morning, then met a helicopter at the base that took him to the top of the Matterhorn. After snowboarding it he was lifted to the top of the south face of the Les Grands Jorasses. He rode it down just before dark, logging a third major descent in one day and nearly having to amputate several fingers due to frostbite when it was over.

In that 1989 interview in SKI magazine Gouvy said, "I'm not strictly a climber, a snowboarder, a skydiver or a windsurfer. I'm happy to play whatever the conditions are right for." Like Boivin, he sampled from a wide range of disciplines. He held the world speed record for a monoski from 1986 to 1989, at 110 miles an hour, and also held a skydiving free-fall record at one point.

With all of that, and some grandstanding stunts, his greatest contribution to extreme riding was almost certainly as the point of the snowboarding spear. "Gouvy went as big on a snowboard as his contemporaries went on skis, which was unheard of at the time," wrote Sutton. He was with a group that made the first board descent of Mont Blanc and was the first to descend from above 8,000 meters when he started at 27,650 feet on Everest.

Gouvy died at 27 on June 15th, 1990, which meant that three of France's best-known extreme skiing stars had died within 15 months of each other. He was the last of that trio and the only one who did it riding.

He was dropped off on top of the Aiguille Verte near Chamonix by a helicopter carrying a film crew. And they watched in horror as he skidded on a slick patch near the summit and started a 914-vertical-meter (3,000-foot) fall that ended with him plunging into a crevasse without ever regaining control.

It was a story that spread instantly through the ski world, a nightmarish consequence that made the blood run cold of anyone who skied steep and dangerous terrain or followed those who did. The irony of Gouvy dying because of using a helicopter instead of climbing the route was lost on no one.

Indeed it probably marked the beginning of the end for involving choppers in respectable skiing/boarding first descents or *enchainments*, especially in the Alps. If it wasn't questionable ethically, it could obviously be an unsafe tactic. On the other hand, in very different conditions and circumstances, choppers are *de rigeur* for ski porn in Alaska and other remote parts of the globe.

PIERRE TARDIVEL

At the same time Boivin was taking his brand of mountaineering into more complicated combinations with other extreme disciplines, Pierre Tardivel was

toting up traditional first descents in the already well-skied Alps. Born in Annecy on November 26, 1963, Tardivel is said to have achieved anywhere from 55 to more than 100 such new routes on skis.

It started in 1980 when he and Daniel Chauchefoin began knocking them down in the Aravis Range, and the Vanoise, Beaufortain, Chablais and Bauges massifs. Their scores of first skis also included the attention-getting

East Slope of the Col du Diable in the Mont Blanc massif and the Corridor of the Cardinal on the Aiguille Verte in '81.

Tardivel also notably soloed the North Corridor of Trelod in the Bauges in '84. He did the same on the north side of the Grand Pilier d'Angle on the Italian side of Mont Blanc in '88. His descent from the South Summit of Everest at 8,770 meters was the altitude record at the time in '92. And he continued strongly throughout the '90s and on to 2007 when he opened the North Side of Aretes de Rochefort in the Mont Blanc massif, and 2010 with his first descent of the Caribou route on Mont Blanc. His multiple steep descents of all sides of Mont Blanc over the course of seven years were an epic achievement.

Tardivel's longevity is just one hallmark of a career that spanned more than three decades, illustrating his commitment, technique, long-term training regimen, and attention to safety. Ultimately, his old-fashioned approach to climbing what he skied and forsaking helicopters and the endless self-publicizing in favor of just getting it done in new and interesting ways, seemed to set the trend for the new millennium.

LOU DAWSON

In North America, after Bill Briggs semi-retired, steep skiers went several different ways. Some continued to climb and make first descents on their home continent. Others took to competing in World Extremes contests and starring in ski porn. A handful did everything.

On the mountaineering front Lou Dawson from Aspen, Colorado, set out in 1980 on a project to be the first person to climb and ski all 54 of Colorado's 14,000-foot peaks. He started on South Maroon Peak, near his hometown, with a solo descent. He got his last one 11 years later when he skied Kit Carson in the Sangre de Cristo Mountains with Glen Randall.

Dawson was scrupulous about skiing from the summits unless it was completely impossible. And though he wasn't generally looking for the gnarliest or steepest lines, sometimes the *only* lines were a little of both. For example, his descent of Little Bear Peak in 1991 was the first from the summit, "down the westerly climbing route couloir, with white and blue ice at 50 degrees."

He also descended notorious Capitol Peak near Aspen from its summit for the first time in 1988, doing it on northeast aspects that meant skiing the dangerous and corniced Knife Ridge. And, as he noted in his accounts, "Mount Democrat, in 1987, wasn't a first summit descent but it was the first of the Northwest Face via complex terrain."

Dawson's descent of North Maroon Peak in 1987 wasn't the first from the summit – that had been accomplished by Fritz Stammberger – but it was the first down complex terrain on the northeast to a narrow couloir on the North Face. "Pyramid Peak is of course the icon of all of this, what with Greg Landry's East Face descent and all. Davenport was the first one to repeat Landry's entire line, though Jeff Maus and I skied the upper part in 1989, and had to exit to another route because of avalanche danger. I did a cool almost-second descent of Pyramid via a very complex line I named Basket Weaver."

WILD SNOW

54 CLASSIC SKI AND SNOWBOARD DESCENTS OF NORTH AMERICA

Louis W. Dawson

Lou Dawson's groundbreaking book Wild Snow with his cover photo of Art Burrows. Courtesy of Lou Dawson.

The "ski the teeners" effort highlighted pure alpinism with little fanfare and almost no video. And in so doing it promoted traditional ski mountaineering techniques and ethics to a new generation at a time when stunt skiing was threatening to overwhelm the sport. In a decade where the Alps were seeing a revolution in goals and methods, there were still new lines and first descents to be had there, and in the mountains of North America.

Dawson's magazine articles and his seminal 1997 book *Wild Snow: A Historical Guide to North American Ski Mountaineering* played an important part in the upsurge of interest in backcountry steep skiing going into the new millennium. And it also helped justifiably land Dawson in the Colorado Ski Hall of Fame.

CHAPTER 12

PART FIVE – GOING TO EXTREMES IN THE '90S

The Real and the Unreal

MARCO SIFFREDI

As a snowboarder who may have benefitted most immediately and directly from Bruno Gouvy's groundbreaking work, Chamoniard super-boarder Marco Siffredi also acknowledged being inspired by Boivin and sometimes called himself "JMB Represent." Siffredi came from a climbing family: his father was an occasional mountain guide and his older brother died in an avalanche near Chamonix.

Kilian Jornet describes him as the "*enfant terrible*" of the 1990s who "surfed all the very difficult descents of the Mont Blanc massif." Born May 22, 1979, Siffredi was the first of the proto-punk riders, whose wild hair was multi-colored (though often bleached blonde) and his nickname was "the storm." Stylistically as well as soulfully he was the '90's logical successor to Gouvy's perfect cheekbones and '80s disco look.

At 17, only a year after taking up snowboarding, Siffredi rode the Mallory line on the North Face of the Aiguille du Midi, a 914-vertical-meter (3,000-foot) descent with pitches of 55 degrees. Following that he put down several impressive lines in the Andes of Peru and Bolivia

In 1999 when he was 20 he made only the second descent ever of the Nant Blanc on the Aiguille Verte, 10 years after JMB skied it, and Siffredi's was the first by board. That autumn he climbed and made the first snowboard descent of nearly 7,000-meter (22,965-foot) Dorje Lhakpa in Nepal.

Canadian ski mountaineering super-duo of Eric Pehota and Trevor Petersen. Photo © Scott Markewitz.

It's been said that he first saw Everest on this expedition and became very focused on making the first snowboard descent of it. Well-known New Zealand mountaineer Russell Brice, who owned a Kathmandu-based expedition company, agreed with him that he could do it. He also helped him "plan and successfully ride Cho Oyu, the world's sixth-highest peak at [8,188 meters] 26,864 feet" in the fall of 2000, according to a review of the Jeremy Evans book about Siffredi called *See You Tomorrow*.

Brice also put together a spring of 2001 expedition to Everest where Siffredi planned to snowboard the Hornbein Couloir, the steepest line on the mountain, but there wasn't enough snow to do it. After summiting he instead rode the more traditional Norton Couloir to the foot of the North Col where the Advanced Base Camp was. From there he began his descent of the Norton Couloir on the North Face, but broke a binding. After repairing it he descended over the next two hours to 6,400 meters (roughly 21,000 feet).

There were, however, several asterisks to the ascent and descent. He used oxygen on the climb and was assisted by sherpas who carried all of his equipment. And when the strap on his board broke, one of the sherpas helped him repair it. While none of those were disqualifying factors for the first snowboard descent, they were viewed askance by some, and noted in the accounts.

Another matter was that an Austrian climber Stefan Gatt had reached the summit the day before Siffredi, solo and without using supplemental oxygen. And then he had snowboarded down to the 8,600-meter (28,215-foot) level where he encountered such hard and difficult snow that he down-climbed for roughly 1,000 meters. The ultimate consensus among publications that track such things was that both men would be credited with the first snowboard descent of Everest, with their particular merits and demerits.

There are those who say that the reason Siffredi was hoping to ride the Hornbein was because he knew the Austrian was snowboarding from the summit before he got there, so he wanted to do a line that had never been done by anyone.

That fall he made an attempt at boarding 8,027-meter Shisha Pangma, but was rebuffed by heavy winds. And the next spring he returned to Everest late in the climbing season in the hopes there would be enough snow in the Hornbein to make it passable.

He was accompanied by three very experienced Sherpas: Pa Nuru, Da Tenzing and Phurba Tashi, the latter of whom had summited Everest 21 times. Two of them had been with Siffredi the previous year when they thought he was less distracted and climbed more like a Sherpa. A brutal 12-hour slog through waist-deep snows seemed to particularly sap him before they reached the top at 2:10 p.m. on September 8, 2002, where he complained of too much climbing and being too tired.

Though there was enough snow coverage for an attempt, based on changing weather conditions and Siffredi's fatigue, all of the Sherpas advised against him boarding the Hornbein. But just after 3:00 p.m. he went anyway, wearing a "full-body yellow snowboarding suit" and heading toward the couloir.

According to an account in Transworld Snowboarding, "His Sherpa companions lost sight of him periodically at times," as they descended on foot. "At the North Col, about 1,300 meters below Camp Three, Sherpas reported seeing the distant image of a man stand up, then slide silently down the mountain. As they reached the point of the sighting, Siffredi's snowboard tracks were not to be seen. His body has not been found."

He was 23 when he joined the ranks of several hundred who have disappeared on the flanks of Everest over the years, including, most famously, two of the first western climbers in the 1930s, Mallory and Irving, evidence of whose vanishing in the summit region was only found in the last two decades. And of course Siffredi's disappearance has also inspired speculation and myths.

Some feel his fatigue got the best of him and he sat down for a rest, fell asleep and never woke up. Others think he may have been swept to his death by an avalanche in the unstable spring conditions. Or he could have gotten caught in the crux of the couloir and his body could still be there.

His sister is said to have once believed he may have just gotten tired of the modern world and boarded on down into the valley and left to live a simpler and anonymous life in a local village somewhere.

He was extreme snowboarding's first tragic figure. Undeniably ambitious, "He seemed eccentric and crazy, and in some ways he was, but he was shy and reserved around most people," wrote Jeremy Evans in his book.

Mathew Renda, in reviewing the book, wrote that Siffredi was "wary of the trappings of fame and endorsements and the other accoutrements that accompanied superstar snowboarders at the time." He didn't spend time courting sponsors and worked for his family's business when he needed to finance his expeditions.

Having shunned celebrity and competitive freeriding in favor of doing what he wanted, it was perhaps fitting that he would just slide off into the wildest mountains on earth, forever an enigmatic mystery, leaving behind a family that lost two sons to their hearts.

In the end, the first two real snowboarding extreme stars, Gouvy and Siffredi, had gone down young and as the stuff of instant legends. And the body count was adding up. Whereas the earliest steep skiing stars have mostly lived to ripe old ages, their successors felt they needed to radically expand the realm of the possible in order to make their marks, and they were increasingly paying the price.

ERIC PEHOTA & TREVOR PETERSEN

As the 1980s rolled over into the '90s and touring gear started improving in quantum leaps, the backcountry of North America in all of its pristine glory began to get opened up by more ski mountaineers tired of the limitations of the lift-served resorts.

That meant new terrain coming on line in vast amounts throughout the western US , Canada and Alaska. Not surprisingly, some of the biggest talent of the time was coming from among those who cut their teeth on all that backcountry. Eric Pehota and Trevor Petersen were two British Columbia boys born and bred, and when they teamed up it changed the face of skiing in North America.

Born November 17, 1964, Pehota grew up in Mackenzie, a BC logging town where his father and brother

Steep skiing pro Kristen Ulmer's signature rock-jumping move. Photo © Adam Clark.

Marco Siffredi on the Nant Blanc, Aiguille Verte, 2003. Photo © René Robert.

worked. Eric went on to make a number of movies and more than 40 first descents, many of them with Petersen who he met shortly after high school. They met in Apex, moved back to Whistler in 1984, and started skiing the Coast Range and peaks like Decker, Tremor, Wedge, Mount Currie and Mount Waddington.

As per Powder magazine, "One of Pehota's greatest individual accomplishments was the 1990 first descent of Mount Waddington, but together the influence of Petersen and Pehota was often as a single unit, showcasing their skills together on mountains like Pontoon Peak in the Chugach or Canada's Mount Robson." The latter was featured in Peter Chrzanowski's 1987 film *Mount Robson the North Face*. Sponsored by Rossignol and Arcteryx, Pehota has remained BC to the core, living in Pemberton with his wife and family and staying active in the ski industry.

Trevor Petersen was born in New Westminster, BC, two years before Pehota, with a wild streak in him and a yearning for the outdoors and the mountains that took precedence over fame and commerce. He was an icon in Canada and at Whistler as his hard-charging skiing and his long blonde ponytail became trademarks of a series of RAP films in the 80s and 90s. He climbed in the summer and fall and boogie boarded Class V rapids, fully committed to an adrenaline-fueled lifestyle.

"He was a long-haired, crazy-intense fellow," said longtime partner Pehota. "It's the ultimate paradox. The closer you come to the edge, the more alive you feel. Trey lived for that. There's nothing like being the first to set foot where no one has gone before. Trevor wanted to be a pioneer and explorer. He always talked about Shackleton and all those hard-core dudes."

They both became "those hard-core dudes" but Petersen's run ended far too soon. It happened on February 26, 1996, on the Exit Couloir in the Cosmiques off-piste area above Chamonix. Skiing solo in an area he'd skied before, he was there late in the afternoon when the snow had started to loosen up. A slide was triggered in the steep, dog-legged chute and he was found by two Swedish skiers the next day, sitting upright and half-buried, at 34 another young casualty of the Mont Blanc massif.

When Yi-Wyn Yen wrote about it in Sports Illustrated she quoted pro-skier Johnny Chilton. "He called me that morning to vent. He felt like he hadn't done anything during the trip. They'd been shooting him all week. He called it posing for the mags. He hadn't skied anything big. He was psyched to be in Chamonix. He said he was going to ski something that would satisfy his itch."

RAP ski films principal James Angrove said, "He was a pioneer in the extreme skiing business and a featured skier in most of RAP's ski films. The cool thing about Trevor was that he didn't just talk about it or pose for the camera, he actually did it. Nothing was more difficult for Trevor than playing the image man. But that is what allowed him to pursue his dream of being a pioneer, a mountain man, being out in the wilderness skiing the steeps."

Petersen was survived by a wife and three kids. Son Kye, who skied the Exit Couloir at 15 to honor his father, has had his own stint as a young, high profile, Whistler-based skier on the park and pipe tour. The family's saga as a moving personal story as well as a metaphor for the steep skiing era, has been profiled in two movies and a book, *The Edge of Never* by Bill Kerig.

TROY JUNGEN & PTOR SPRICENIEKS

Another remarkable Canadian duo also loomed large in ski mountaineering in the 1990s, capturing widespread attention with the first descent of the North Face of Canada's Mount Robson in 1995. This 914-vertical-meter (3,000-foot), 55-degree line off the highest peak in the Canadian Rockies was the biggest prize left in the country. It had been attempted numerous times, including by Pehota and Petersen, and mountaineer/filmmaker Peter Chrzanowski, who made a film of one of his failed efforts in 1987.

A fundamental difficulty with the route is that it's too cold in the winter for the steep, glaciated, blue ice to hold snow. This isn't an uncommon issue on high and very steep terrain. While Spricenieks was in Pakistan trying to ski Nanga Parbat in the summer of '95, Jungen kept close tabs on Robson's conditions. Once Ptor had returned they set out on an ascent that saw them start climbing the 1,100-meter North Face to the summit at 3 a.m. on September 8th in a full moon. The face was a sustained 57-degree pitch before the last 20 meters up a 70-degree ice wall that they free-climbed.

Gripped Magazine has quoted Spricenieks as saying, "We dropped in right off the summit and it was really, really, really, really steep and really, really big and we were way scared… it was great."

In Wild Snow however, Lou Dawson reports that the two didn't go to the summit but just below it, cut over to the summit ridge and went straight to the face to take advantage of good conditions. "Without ropes they skied a terrifying 60-degree pitch, then enjoyed the relaxed 50-degree skiing below, with a final drop off a 15-foot bergschrund," wrote Dawson.

"We had to blow like 20 feet of air to get to safer exposures on the glacier because of all the crevasses," Spricenieks explained to Gripped. He went on to say, "It's a real gnarly place and if the weather came in it would be almost impossible to get off the mountain. The cosmic forces were definitely with us."

Ptor, who anchors a team that resembles Penn and Teller in that only one of them ever seems to talk, has said many times that their mission was to ski the North Face of Yuh-hai-has-kun, which is the original Shuswap indigenous people's name for Robson and means 'Mountain of the Spiritual Road.' That name not only more closely reflected his own spiritual leanings and the duos' general bohemian attitude, but, "As the King of the Rockies, it always seemed more fitting and respectful for it to be called by its traditional name than after some colonialist fur trapper who never climbed it," said Spricenieks. To which I would add, "Bravo!"

"For Troy Jungen and me, it was always the ultimate steep ski descent, a truly wild and mystical grail deemed impossible, a line that ventured into the unknown. Troy is the main instigator of this adventure, having monitored conditions all summer… Surely there is no one else who could have created the crucial combination of confidence and higher purpose for myself with such an undertaking," Spricenieks posted on his website.

While Jungen has preferred to stay out of the limelight, Spricenieks has traveled the world notching descents in Peru, Colombia, France, Italy, Alaska, India and so on. He also released a highly introspective movie in 2014 titled Dreamline, which Dawson announced on his website by saying, "Ski mountaineering's best loved mystic drops a compelling biopic. Ptor describes his feelings about dreams being a doorway to parallel universes… The film attempts to thread these metaphysical concepts along with foundational stuff like how ski touring gets us back to the primal purity we lose if we lead coddled citified lifestyles."

Dawson also noted that the movie contains a lot about Sprcienieks wife and children, "a welcome addition to a film that could have been way too self-involved." And finished by saying, "The real closing line of the flick is him [Ptor] wondering aloud, "why I'm such a crazy bastard to run around and piss in strange places."

Whatever it is he's still doing it with a successful guide business in La Grave, France called 40 Tribes, and the kind of deep curiosity and thoroughness that have been hallmarks of his life.

KRISTEN ULMER

Women such as Jan Reynolds, Hilaree Nelson and Kit Deslauriers were ripping the steeps fairly early on in their careers as part of their remarkable ski mountaineering exploits around the world. But Kristen Ulmer was one of the first and best female steep and extreme competition skiers who saw that as an end in itself.

Starting on the US Ski Team in 1991 in moguls she quickly moved on to became known as the best female big mountain extreme skier in the world for all of the 1990s and was voted the best overall female skier in the world in a 1997 Powder magazine survey. She also likes to climb and made the first ski descent of the Grand Teton by a woman in that same year. After being voted the most extreme woman athlete in North America in 2000 in a Women's Sports and Fitness magazine poll, Ulmer retired from professional athletics in 2003 and continued her writing career for outlets including SKI, Powder and Outside, while also authoring a book called The Art of Fear.

Joining the ranks of the handful of other women who were into freeskiing at the beginning included the likes of Wendy Fisher, Emily Gladstone, Wendy Brookbank and Kim Reichhelm. The latter began as on the US Ski Team, then became a pro ski racer and ultimately a two-time World Extreme Skiing Champion who was named one of the most influential skiers of all time by both Powder and Skiing magazines. She has gone on to guide adventure ski trips around the world and write a book To The Limits.

It might have been a little lonely at first, but those ladies broke trail for what has become a much broader movement that includes ski film and competition stars like Angel Collinson, Ingrid Backstrom, Michelle Parlor, Jaclyn Paaso, Tatum Monod, Elyse Saugstad and Kaya Turksi, who has won 8 Winter X Games slopestyle gold medals. Perhaps most importantly they let other women know that it could be done and they could charge hard too, whether competitively and as a career, or just for grins like most of the guys on the slopes. Only frequently better.

SCOTT SCHMIDT, GLEN PLAKE, DOUG COOMBS

Meanwhile, back in the States, the latest wave of extreme riders were competing in the new North American and World Extreme championships, and also finding renewed purpose for helicopters. This time, not to make first descents but rather as part of the resurgent ski porn industry. Choppers were being viewed the same way those who pay Wiegle to use them do: as tools to get to the goods.

In the case of the budding film stars listed above, they were getting paid to chopper in and ski for Greg Stump, Warren Miller, TGR, et al, in some of the best powder and most dramatic terrain on earth. They could make good money in Alaska and Canada, the Alps and Himalaya, using helicopters and not necessarily risking their lives on every run. While the terrain being skied can often be some of the steepest imaginable, it's not always fatal if you fall. Avalanches are a big concern, so are 1,000-vertical-meter (3,300-foot) beaters, looming bergschrunds and cliffs. But it was almost always powder instead of the absurdly mixed conditions of ski mountaineering.

And make no mistake. When Doug Coombs came out of nowhere (actually Bridger Bowl, Montana, and Jackson, Wyoming) to win the first World Extreme Skiing Championships at Valdez. Alaska in 1991, he was at heart a mountaineer. So were Glen Plake and Scott Schmidt when they started skiing for Greg Stump. The contests (Coombs won again in '93) and movies were means to ends and no one was too concerned about how the ski mountaineering community viewed it.

The Blizzard of Aaahs, Maltese Flamingo, License to Thrill, Fire and Ice and a flood of new ski movies helped rewrite the business model for making a living at steep skiing. Now you didn't have to be riding Everest, or sky-diving onto some hanging glacier in the Alps, or launching yourself off a cliff in Greenland, to make a splash. And once you'd done enough competitions and films you could buy a cat operation in Canada, or a heli operation in Alaska, or your own towable ski cabin in the Sierras, and go get paid to do what you *really* love.

Glen Plake's posters were on more apartment walls in ski resorts than Suzy Chapstick's in the 1980s and 90s. And if you didn't stop somewhere and just stare at the poster of Scott Schmidt and Doug Coombs skiing down

Ptor Spricenieks dropping in at his home base of La Grave in 2016. Photo © Cedric Bernardini.

a frozen waterfall, you weren't paying attention. They were the matinee idols of the ski world, the surf gods of winter, the representatives of what some purists in the mountaineering world sneered at as pure Hollywood.

But no one who thought the latter thought it for long once they saw any of them ski. Schmidt went from Squaw Valley ski tuner to being featured airing the Palisades in Warren Miller's *Ski Time* in 1983. But it was his "memorable performance in Greg Stump's classic *Blizzard of Ahhs* that cemented his reputation as the most revered skier of the 1980s," said Powder magazine. His Island Park Lodge became a cat-skiing legend and today he serves as an ambassador for the Yellowstone Club in Montana.

Powder also credited Plake's "ballsy star-turns in a handful of Greg Stump movies beginning with 1987's Maltese Flamingo" for elevating him to a mohawked poster boy for the era. Cartwheeling down the Aiguille du Midi may have also had something to do with it. But he has stayed devoted to his core beliefs of big bumps, long skis, family run mountains, community activism, and ski mountaineering, and earned the respect of many including Powder magazine "as one of skiing's most important icons and respected elder statesmen."

Boston native Coombs had become an internationally certified mountain guide (IFMGA/UIAGM) while working in Jackson for Exum Guides. And following his two World Extreme wins in Alaska he and his wife Emily became "infatuated with the Chugach terrain," as he put it, and started Valdez Heli-Ski Guides. In 1993 they branched out by starting the Steep Skiing Camps Worldwide in Jackson and then moving it to Europe in 1997. They sold the heli operation in 2001 and spent most of their winters in La Grave.

"When I first arrived at La Grave," Coombs wrote on his website, "and stared at the majestic glaciated peak of La Meije (13,065 feet), I imagined endless ski runs that would last a lifetime."

It turned out he was right, and would have been even if his lifetime hadn't been cut short. He immediately became known and liked as one of the top guides around. He and Rick Armstrong were making names for themselves in the La Grave climbing community when I first met them, and the sheer amount of ropes and gear they carried for a day of 'recreational' skiing was stunning.

Coombs had put comps and films mostly in the rear-view in favor of guiding for his income, and to satisfy his addiction to steep skiing and powder. While not stunt skiing for movies had reduced the risk factor for him, anyone who climbs and skis where he did nearly every day of the winter is still putting themselves in harm's way. It caught up with him on April 3, 2006 in the Couloir de Polichinelle above La Grave.

Chad Vanderham was a 31-year-old skier from Keystone, Colorado, who had been guiding and apprenticing with Coombs and become good friends with the 48-year-old. They were skiing one at a time with two other Americans that day in the steep, rock-encased chute, as related in an account submitted to the American Mountain Guides Association by one of those Americans, Matt Farmer.

VanderHam disappeared over a rib or precipice and, "Doug yelled up that 'Chad fell, come down with a rope'," wrote Farmer. "Christina and I heard Doug yelling Chad's name while side-stepping down and attempting to see over the cliff to his right. We saw his skis slip on the rock and he fell out of view over the rib."

Both men's bodies were found later by rescue teams at the base of that 137-meter (450-foot) cliff Coombs had been trying to see over. The slope above the drop was discovered to be almost solid ice. Friends in the area reported that when VanderHam disappeared Coombs was afraid he might be hanging above the cliff in urgent need of help and didn't wait for the rope to arrive before exposing himself to the same risk in an attempt to rescue his friend. It was a heroic act that left behind his wife and 3-year old son David.

The Valdez Heli-Ski Guides site released a statement saying, "Words can't describe the loss his friends feel right now. His impact on Alaska heli-skiing, alpine guiding and just plain fun-hogging is immeasurable."

CHAPTER 13
PART SIX — GOING TO EXTREMES IN THE NEW MILLENNIUM

Traditional Ski Mountaineering, Extreme Skiing and Big Mountain Freeriding

By the new millennium, steep skiing was settling into several different formats with lots of cross-pollination: traditional ski mountaineering, extreme skiing, and big mountain freeriding.

In the traditional ski mountaineering version the focus was still on climbing and skiing the world's un-skied mountains and lines. This meant the last of the big 8,000-meter peaks, as well as engaging lines on all of them. And it was increasingly coming to mean doing them cleanly, top to bottom without removing the skis or board. In the cases where that had already been accomplished, it might mean doing it faster than anyone before you. The latter has developed into one of the more recent mutations of extreme skiing on serious lines all over the world.

ANDREW MCLEAN

Born in Salt Lake City, Utah in 1961, Andrew McLean was described this way by Powder magazine in 2006: "From Denali to the Patagonian Icecap, from the Wasatch to Tibet, nobody has influenced backcountry skiers in the past decade more than he has."

McLean's family moved around when he was young, finally settling in Seattle. "I learned how to ski at a very small but steep area in the Pacific Northwest named Alpental," he told Andy Lewicky in an interview with Sierra Descents in 2007. "It had a lot of steep terrain in it, and for some unknown reason I just really enjoyed skiing steep terrain…"

With first descents on all 7 continents, and something like 19 in one trip alone to Baffin Island, McLean is perhaps best known for his 2003 first descent, with three friends, of Alaska's Mount Hunter, one of the last holy grails of North American descents. It came on the heels of him skiing the Orient Express and the Messner Couloir on Denali.

McLean is also the author of one of skiing's certified bibles, The Chuting Gallery – A Guide to Steep Skiing in the Wasatch Mountains, first published in 1998. And he designed equipment for Black Diamond where he developed several important pieces of technical ski mountaineering gear, including most notably the Whippet, "an ice axe/ski pole hybrid that's become a ski mountaineering standard," according to Backcountry magazine.

Working with Black Diamond brought him back to his birth city of Park City where he began really exploring the Wasatch with fellow employees such as Alex Lowe. He told Lewicky that Lowe, "turned me onto the idea of ski mountaineering – climbing up hard stuff, technical climbing, with technical steep skiing."

His lifelong love of the steeps led him to participate in a feature segment of the legendary 2007 film Steep, one of the few ski movie's he's been involved with. "Steep looked at the whole idea of big mountain skiing, and chose different episodes – they have the beginning history with Bill Briggs, the Blizzard of Ahs, and things like that, and I got involved because the type of skiing I do represents one of the specific niches."

In their interview Lewicky tells McLean that he likes the term 'big mountain skiing,' "because it encompasses the higher-risk aspects of the sport without the unwanted associations that the phrase 'Extreme Skiing' has picked up the years."

McLean's response makes an important point. "Yeah, extreme skiing is kind of a sport unto itself. Extreme skiing used to be purely the French term of it, and Steep has a really good segment on the original French extreme skiers, but then extreme skiing in North America morphed into going straight down big Alaska peaks, and that's really dynamic skiing but its not the true, original idea of extreme skiing. Shane McConkey was one of the first to come up with the idea of calling it free skiing, which is I think a much better description of that type of skiing."

It wasn't that extreme skiing had evolved into big mountain or freeskiing. Freeskiing grew out of lots of things, but it didn't supplant or replace any of them. Extreme skiing still exists today when you use the term in its intended sense of, 'you fall you die,' rather than as a pejorative for stunt skiing.

Some still pursue extreme skiing in and of itself. Others invariably become involved with it at times through ski mountaineering, or massive gap jumps, or free skiing porn when the consequences escalate from ugly high-speed powder-beaters to fatal cliffs, rock bands and avalanches.

SHANE MCCONKEY

None of those pushing the boundaries of what was possible on skis really worried about what to call it until after they started doing it. Going Mach on big lines in Alaska was following in the tracks of Dominique Perret, Steve McKinney and Jeremy Nobis and it wowed everyone on videos.

Ski-lord Shane McConkey, practice session for Red Bull Snow Thrill of Alaska, 2002. Photo: Ullrich Grill / Red Bull Content Pool.

And when Saucer Boy Shane McConkey went from alpine ski racing to bump skiing to freeskiing and hucker/BASE jumper, he was updating his father Jim jumping ski planes in Canada, and Rick Sylvester sending Mount Asgard on Baffin Island as Bond in 1976, and a legion of others on through Boivin, Gouvy and Vallencant.

Born December 30, 1969, in Vancouver, British Columbia, McConkey had an itinerant upbringing that always kept him skiing. As with most of the new freeriding generation (McConkey used that term as well as big mountain skiing), he built his reputation on extreme skiing comps and films starting in the 1990s. Eventually basing out of Squaw Valley, in 1994 he won the South American Freeskiing Championships, took second in the World Extreme Skiing championships and – shades of Glen Plake – finished 8th on the Pro Mogul Tour. That was also the year he was in TGR's The Realm.

He continued competing throughout the '90s, winning the US National and South American Freeskiing Championships the next year, the European Freeskiing Championships in '96, and finishing second in '98 IFSA World Tour of Freeskiing Championships, the European Freeskiing Championships, and the US Freeskiing Nationals. By the end of the decade he was also in the Winter X Games in Big Air and Skiercross.

As he phased out of comps in the early 2000s he appeared in more and more movies ripping huge, steep lines. McConkey eventually appeared in 27 films and counting (several have been made after his death). His filmography has included The Tribe in '95, Global Storming in '99, Warren Miller's Higher Ground in '05, '07s fateful Steep (also featuring Doug Coombs who died the year the movie was made, and McConkey died two

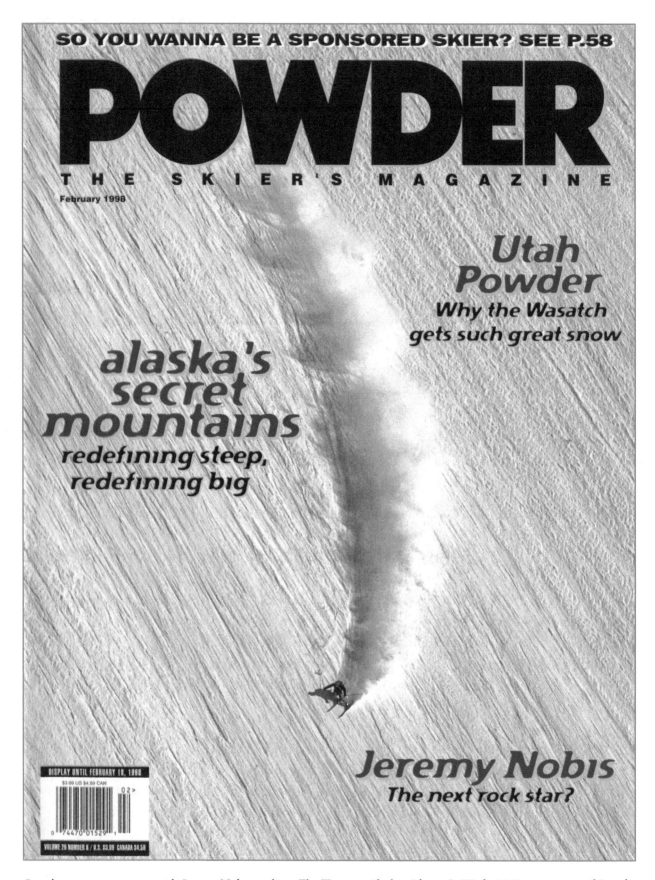

Powder magazine cover with Jeremy Nobis making The Turn in Alaska. Photo © Wade McKoy, courtesy of Powder magazine / Dave Reddick and McCoy.

years later), and Ultimate Rush in '12.

In 2001 ESPN gave him the Action Sport Award for Skier of the Year and he ranked first in Skiing Magazine's Top 25 Skiers in North America. From '02 through '05 he ranked 1st, 2nd, 2nd and 1st in Powder magazine's Reader's Poll, while also twice winning their Full Throttle Award.

The latter asked in a 2006 story, "What can you say about action man Shane McConkey that hasn't been said by a thousand wide-eyed wing-nuts in a hundred internet chatrooms? Just this: even when he seems fresh out of surprises, he finds a way to re-inspire a legion of fanatical followers."

For example, he started BASE-jumping in 2003, eventually making more than 700 of them, including a double front flip ski jump off the Eiger in 2004. In the tradition of Jean-Marc Boivin, the BASE jumps were often in pursuit of steep, wild routes not otherwise doable. These "close-out lines" were what he considered the last uncharted horizon that his ski-BASE jumping predecessors (mostly prematurely deceased) had only just begun exploring.

On March 25, 2009, McConkey posted to his account from Italy. "Today was quite cool! We finally nailed that line variation off the Val Scura couloir on Sassongher. This was extremely satisfying getting to ski such a unique line. Conditions in the couloir were still very hard and icy in places so the skiing was slow and careful… The snow on the slope above the cliff was firm and icy and not much fun but it was only about 3 or 4 four turns long before the jump… I must say that it seemed a bit more spicy than we were expecting."

McConkey did a straight BASE jump that day while JT Holmes flew his wingsuit. Shane's description of JT's flight was of one going properly. "No more than 30 seconds after I landed I see JT flying off the cliff with a lot of speed. He yanked his skis off right away and began to fly immediately. It was a perfectly executed wingsuit ski base. Skis off quick and stable and into forward flight with no potato chipping or instability. I was jealous. Today was a good day!"

The following day, close to where that jump took place, things didn't go nearly as well. In an email to Tim Mutrie on March 27th, McConkey's longtime ski/BASE partner and friend Holmes revealed what happened.

"Contacted by phone in Italy this afternoon, Holmes respectfully declined to field questions about the circumstances of McConkey's fatal ski-BASE-ing accident in Italy Thursday. Holmes, instead, emailed this statement:

"Yesterday, March 26, 2009, Shane died while skiing in Italy. There are some technical aspects that are left out from this statement, and it does not touch upon the beauty of the Dolomites and the skiing we shared before the accident or Shane's typical shining persona, full of adventure, humor and life experience.

"We chose to ski off of a cliff with our wingsuits and fly them away from the cliff wall before opening our parachutes for landing. We skied and hiked off of the Pordoi cable car to a spot Shane had base jumped once before, in the summer. We spent a bunch of time preparing for the jump, building a kicker, helping each other gear up, and finally we were pleased and prepared and went for it. Shane did a double back flip in perfect McConkey style. As planned, afterwards, he went to release his skis in order to fly away from the wall and safely deploy his parachute. This is where the jump went wrong.

"He was not able to release either of his skis. He remained focused on releasing them by reaching down towards his bindings. This put him into a spin/tumble/unstable falling style, that may have appeared out of his control, but in reality, Shane was not concerned about flying position or style; just concerned with reaching those skis so that he could get them off and fly or deploy his parachute. He succeeded in releasing both of skis and immediately transitioned into a perfect flying position; then he impacted the snow, and died at that moment.

"The whole thing took place in about 12 seconds. Once he released the skis, he was immediately in control of the flight and would have only seen the ground and imminent impact for a tiny fraction of a second before he hit. Shane's parachute did not malfunction; it was never deployed."

It was devastating to family, friends and fans, and a gut punch to the whole ski industry.

CHRIS DAVENPORT

Another of those who rose to prominence via competitions and film going into the new millennium was Chris Davenport, who's website, steepskiing.com, says it all.

Born in New Hampshire on January 4, 1971, Dav was a ski racer at Holderness School there, then CU in Boulder. He moved to Aspen in 1989 and won the first of his two World Extreme Championships in 1996. That vaulted him into the spotlight and he started assembling one of the most diverse and wide ranging portfolios in skiing. He also took second in the 24 Hours of Aspen that same year, and was the New Zealand Heli Challenge champion.

In '98 he won the 24 Hours of Aspen with partner Tyler Williams and got a bronze medal at the Winter XGames. In 2000 he racked up podiums at the Canadian Freeskiing Championships, NBC Gravity Games Big Mountain Contest, the North American Freeskiing Championships in Snowbird, and the Rip Curl Heli Challenge in New Zealand. And he won the IFSA World Freeskiing Championships again at the Red Bull Snowthrill of Alaska. In '01 he became the Red Bull Ultracross Champion and the following year won the first of 5 consecutive Powder Magazine Reader's Poll awards.

During this time he had become very interested in ski mountaineering and started skiing some of the Alps most classic steep routes. From January 22, 2006, to January 19, 2007, he skied all 54 of Colorado's 14,000-foot peaks. Only one person, Lou Dawson, had done it before, and he devoted 13 years to it. No one had even thought about trying it within a one-year span before, which Dav accomplished with two days to spare.

While some of those skis were fairly straightforward, many were complex and challenging with highly variable conditions, difficult route-finding, ever-present avalanche danger and numerous extreme pitches.

Capitol Peak, for example, in the Elk Range that separates Aspen from Crested Butte, is one of the most dramatic peaks in the state and the toughest to ski. Some of this is because of the infamous Knife Ridge that dominates the western approach to the summit. "A fall on either side of this ridge is the last one you'll ever take," wrote

Davenport in his book Ski the Fourteeners.

After summiting he concluded, "This was the hardest alpine climb I have done in the States (with skis on my back)."

He and his partner, Aspen native and professional mountain guide Neal Beidleman, planned to ski the South Face, which had never been done before. "I scouted the route from an airplane, looked at it from the ground and studied photos. With that said, when you are on the face itself, it is a maze of cliffs and traverses and Neal and I had some difficulty route finding. Anyway, we dropped in off the summit ridge and were immediately faced with several hundred feet of 60-degree turns. When you make a turn at this angle, you actually drop a few feet before your skis touch the snow again."

And that was just the beginning. Before long they were fully committed on a route that had never been climbed even in summer. "From our first turn off the top, to the last turn out the bottom, we had been exposed to massive cliffs below – basically a big no-fall zone. I am relieved and happy to put Capitol behind me," he wrote. "For those people who want to ski all of the fourteeners in the future, Capitol Peak will be by far the biggest hurdle."

In May of 2011 Davenport and Beidleman reached the top of Mount Everest, then skied 2,000 vertical feet of the Lhotse Face, one of the few such documented descents. It ranks as one of his proudest accomplishments he says, along with, "Lines like the Messner Couloir on Denali, the East Face of the Matterhorn, the West Face of the Eiger, and the SE Ridge of Baruntse."

Chris Davenport's website is called SteepSkiing.com. Enough said. Photo courtesy of Chris Davenport.

In addition to his ski mountaineering and competitions Dav has written his book on the fourteeners project, as well as 50 Classic Ski Descents of North America, and appeared in more than 20 feature ski films with the likes of Matchstick Productions and Warren Miller. During much of the first two decades of the 2000s he was also a reporter and color commentator for ESPN, ABC Sports and RSN TV. And all of this while guiding clients on adventure ski trips around the world.

He was inducted into the US Ski and Snowboard Hall of Fame in 2014 and the Colorado Snowsports Hall of Fame in 2017.

STEEP SPEED: DOMINIQUE PERRET, JEREMY NOBIS

As touched on earlier, a trend toward speed on both ascents and descents in general mountaineering has now taken firm hold of ski mountaineering and steep skiing as the sports grow and adapt. Of course, it hasn't come out of nowhere.

"The evolution in any sport has been since long ago a search for the most, the fastest, the most difficult, the highest, the farthest… and extreme skiing has not escaped from this either," wrote Kilian Jornet in Kiss the Snow magazine. "Alpine skiing is the conjuncture of 2 activities, skiing where from long ago speed has been sought, and alpinism that rewards difficulty."

Fast, fluid, technically crisp skiers have been charging steep lines from early on. World-record-setting speed skier Steve McKinney, brother to women's alpine racing legend Tamara McKinney, was straight-lining the steeps and backcountry of Squaw in the '70s. And Glen Plake rarely held back on that same terrain or anywhere else in the world, including the Aiguille du Midi.

Swiss superstar Dominique Perret, born November 20, 1962, was featured in 20 ski films around the world from 1990 to 2010. He started with alpine racing but wanted something less structured. In 1991 he set a speed-skiing record in Chile and after that made big fast arcs a hallmark of his steep descents, which included one from 8,500 meters on Everest in '96.

It seemed everyone who came in contact with Jeremy Nobis thought he was one of the best ever. Another technically sound former racer, he had trouble getting anyone to take him seriously about freeskiing for film, where he'd become convinced his future was. In 1997 when it finally happened it was almost by chance.

He was the guy in the chopper when the TGR crew wanted someone to take a crack at Alaska's 610-vertical-meter (2,000-foot) Pyramid Peak. From a cold start to a 30-second, minimal turn flashing of a steep hairy line, what he did stunned everyone present. The scene was featured in the movie Further, and Powder magazine cited his massive, screaming bottom turn near the end as "the turn that changed the world."

It wasn't some one-off. As Powder noted, "it has been his relentless, consistent straightlining at over 70 miles per hour on the biggest faces on the planet that has kept Nobis at the forefront of skiing's cutting edge. When it came to skiing a giant Alaskan slope in the late '90s, nobody charged harder than Nobis." It was a lifestyle he seemed made for, but in the end it took a big toll and he died down and out in a Utah jail cell in 2023.

JEREMIE HEITZ AND SAM ANTHAMATTEN

Born in 1989, Swiss big mountain ace Heitz spent the 2010s, "feverishly reimagining the lines laid down by his heroes nearly a half century ago," as Josefine As wrote in Ski Journal.

Coming up through the Freeride World Tour ranks (3rd overall in '14, 2nd overall in '15, 9th in '16) he became interested in reinterpreting some of the steepest big mountain lines in the world by doing "something incredible, joining extreme slopes with extreme speed," as Kilian Jornet wrote.

For a project and film titled La Liste, he skied "15 of the mythical steep descents of the Alps [all 4,000 meters with pitches of 50-degrees or more]… with his personal brand. Fluidity and great speed, putting his skis at more than 120kph on slopes that need two ice axes to climb," wrote Jornet.

They included the North Face of the Obergabelhorn in the Valais, the Gervasutti du Tacul, the Zinalhorn with pitches of 55 degrees, the Lyksam (650m 5.4/E3) and the Couloir Spencer where Sylvain Saudan began his career.

After spending two years making La Liste, at the premier Heitz said, "I would like to push my skiing to the limit, in a discipline that requires a lot of experience and know-how. That's why I attacked these summits, in an aggressive and fluid way no one had ever tried before."

Josefine As wrote about Heitz's descent of the Ober Gabelhorn, "There are no hop turns, just fast and fluid GS arcs – straight down. Where a traditional steep skier takes eight turns, Heitz makes one." Jornet wrote about him, "making an impeccable descent in a dozen turns at a high speed on this steep slope of almost 1,000 meters. The images of this descent will go down in the history of ski mountaineering."

One of Heitz's main partners who is featured in La Liste is 3 years older than him and a native of Zermatt, Switzerland. Sam Anthamatten was born into a mountain family in the shadow of the Matterhorn and got his UIAGM guide certification at 24. Together with two brothers who are also certified guides, they've done things like first ascents in the Himalaya, winning World Ice Climbing titles and summiting all of the Cerro Torre and Fitzroy chains in Patagonia. When he was young his idols were climbers like Walter Bonatti and extreme skiers Heini Holzer and Sylvain Saudan.

After getting a wildcard invite for the 2011 World Freeride Tour he made the most of it by winning at the stop in Sochi, Russia, and finishing the season in 2nd overall. "It completely changed my life," said Anthamatten. "I was an alpinist four months before and then all of a sudden I was a freerider."

Competitions led to stints in films such as Days of My Youth, Superheroes of Stoke, White Noise, Degrees North, This is Home and La Liste. Much of it is due to his unique and hard-charging style.

Whistler-based big mountain skier James Heim, who has skied with Anthamatten in South America and Alaska, told Tess Weaver Strokes for Freeskier: "The way he picks his lines is different from even the best skiers. Where the entrance might look sketchy or technical, he has no issue at all. He has a unique mountaineering approach of getting to a line that might seem off limits to most, then he'll ski it as well as anyone could."

Today Anthamatten is hoping to be "done with the crazy competition stuff" and to return to primarily guiding and combining alpinism with freeriding where "there is so much more that is doable." With the North Face of the Breithorn on Supersaxo, the South Face of the Weisshorn, and the East Face of the Matterhorn under his belt, he's looking more to South America and the Himalaya for future big mountain descents.

Wherever he goes it's likely to put a premium on challenging climbs to reach elegant lines that he can rip at autobahn speeds, with the occasional flip or 360 thrown in for good measure. Which makes him sound like the poster boy for when Kilian Jornet writes, "perhaps now it seems impossible for someone to descend the Nant Blanc or the Austrians in a few turns, jumping the rocky bars or doing a back flip where they made rappels… but surely sooner or later, someone will."

THE FUTURE

Using the speed, style and tricks of freeriding to take on some of the world's biggest mountains and lines is guaranteed to dial up the excitement for films of expeditions that have traditionally been more painstaking, methodical and buttoned-down. While the ski mountaineering accomplishments have been historic, they don't always make for gripping cinema. That started to change with Davo Karnicar on Everest, Andrzej Bargiel on K2, and Jornet himself in the Alps and elsewhere, as they simply picked up the pace for both the ascents and descents.

In fact, Bargiel's solo and oxygen-free ascent and descent of K2 in 2018 was not only completely beyond anything that had been thought possible just a few years earlier, it was done on pitches up to 55 degrees, in a multitude of conditions and constant you-fall-you-die circumstances, and was completed in 7 hours.

Certainly it wasn't Bargiel's intent to establish a record for the descent when he was already doing something completely unheard of by skiing it at all. But it was an indication of the kind of super athleticism that has swept through all of sports over the last few decades. With the level of conditioning and skills being exhibited in alpinism and ski mountaineering, it is possible to complete in hours what once took days.

There are getting to be more mutants and hyper-trainers all the time and their accomplishments are approaching and even surpassing the previously 'impossible' likes of Jornet and those who came before him. These blazing fast times can sometimes be risky, of course, but minimize exposure to the ever-changing elements and conditions.

Another direction that ski mountaineering has been taking for big lines is to first of all climb them cleanly, and second to ride them cleanly, including without ever removing your skis/board. Even rappelling with skis on has become viewed as less than pure. With the 8,000-meter peaks, "clean" has also increasingly come to mean without supplemental oxygen.

Backcountry guru Andrew McLean skiing Grizzly Gulch and Wolverine Cirque, Utah, 2013. Photo courtesy of Andrew McLean.

While most of this may not have seemed that new, certain aspects of it were, and in fairly remarkable ways. As Jornet wrote, "in downhill skiing some skiers began to ski the descents they knew without taking off their skis, avoiding the use of rappels or artificial means to descend."

As a bellwether example, in 2009 Pierre Tardivel and Stephane Brosse skied the Nant Blanc, which had only been done rarely in 30 years, the last time by Marco Siffredi on a snowboard. And previous successes had been accomplished with rappels over rock bars. This time the skiers, according to Jornet, "were able to find a couple of very exposed crossings to outline the goulottes and rocky bars that until then had required the use of ropes."

Similarly Jerome Ruby and Dede Rhem descended the Via Mallory on the Aiguille du Midi on their snowboards in the late '90s without rappelling. As did Ben Biggs, the noted Englishman living in Chamonix who did it on skis in 2013.

One of France's current top freeriding alpinists, Vivian Bruchez, was born in Chamonix in 1986 and he has been skiing since very early. According to his athlete bio for Mountain Hardwear, he was, "Inspired by the light-and-fast missions of his mentors, he wanted to find ways of exploring mountains that requires the highest level of skill and precision while showcasing his unique style and eye for exploration."

The result has been nearly 50 first descents in the Alps, in a time when it seemed almost impossible there were that many left. He has also accomplished some classically demanding descents such as the Nant Blanc, the West Face of Mont Blanc, the Northwest face of the Aiguille Verte, the Matterhorn East Face, and others, without rappelling.

"Kilian [Jornet] and Seb [Sebastien Montaz] have been great influences in my life: Kilian for his humility and strong performance, and Seb for his vision. I had the chance to share many ski lines in the Alps, Alaska and Himalaya with Kilian and learned lots of things from him," says Bruchez.

And Jornet has written about learning from him, including one of Bruchez's techniques for rappel-free skiing. Called "dry skiing," Jornet describes it as being basically de-climbing (or down climbing) with the skis on. Certainly its something many have done of necessity at times, but Bruchez has taken it to new levels.

Jornet described his descent with Bruchez on the Chardonnet in the fall of 2012, the first time they skied together. "In the middle of the descent there was a narrowing to overcome a rocky barrier, a wide chimney of a few meters. When I got there I saw Vivian approaching it until the spatulas and tails touched the stone, then he dropped his back until it was resting on one side of the chimney and he put his skis on the other side, and he started to descend, using his back, his hands and the skis as if he were de-climbing. 'This is dry ski,' he said to me as I tried to understand how he could get down there. "

As Jornet sees it, the method has both a logic and elegance. In some cases it can be considerably faster and easier than looking for places to put the protections, installing the rope and picking it up. The elegance comes "because the descent is more fluid, without the manipulations of removing and putting on the skis."

It does have drawbacks, including being more time consuming in complicated situations, and requiring more technical difficulty than "hanging with the security of a rope."

Ultimately there is much to admire in an approach that requires less aid, and thus less gear, and allows for a truer ski descent. Andrzej Bergiel recognized this on K2, where rather than choosing the route favored by previous attempts that required 610 meters (2,000 feet) of rappels, he skied all the way through on a complex route using multiple exposed traverses to link previously unexplored sections.

As we dive into the third decade of the 2000s, Jornet's roll call of those he sees as pursuing the purest and most original routes ("To imagine the line is half the way, and the other half is a display of technique and acceptance of a high commitment") includes Bruchez's sometimes partner Paul Bonhomme who has been making first descents "of great difficulty and commitment" in the Aravis; Herve Degonon in the Ecrins; Roberto and Luca Dallaville in the Dolomites; and Ben Briggs and New Zealander Tom Grant.

With lots left to explore in the mountains of the world and a variety of ways to do it, the art of steep and extreme riding should continue to evolve and expand minds for as long as the snow holds out.

SECTION IV
GOING DEEP

Skier Adam U snorkel-deep at Geto Kogen in Japan, one of the snowiest resorts in the world. Photo © Kevin McHugh.

CHAPTER 14

INTRO

Betting on the Weather

For 2021/'22 the snowfall totals in western North America got a lot of press attention, and the reporting was a perfect example of how hard it is to get accurate information about these kinds of numbers. In this case the same incomplete and badly reported data appeared in multiple different online outlets where the timelines are suggestive of one original source being picked up and reworded by the others.

The first I could find appeared in SKI magazine online on May 27, 2022. A bylined story titled Find Out Which North American Resorts Got the Most Snow This Season cites a list of those resorts by region. It can usually be considered as an authoritative enough source for the rest to rely on. SnowBrains.com followed suit on October 17, 2022, with the Top 9 Snowiest Resorts in North America Winter 2021/22. Onthesnow.com ran a signed column five days later with the tagline The Snowiest Ski Resorts in North America. And then came Outside Online on October 30th with a bylined story called These North American Ski Resorts Had the Most Snow Last Year.

A depressingly unoriginal similarity in the headlines is followed by virtually photo-copied data. The top three snowiest resorts are all the same, which might seem to confirm the data. But they all reported the leader as Alyeska, Alaska, which in fact by all normal standards was not the case. And all but one cited that season's total snowfall on Alyeska as 21.5 meters (848 inches/70 feet) without giving it an asterisk or explanation. Mount Baker, Washington was number two with 16.4 meters (647 inches/54 feet); and Timberline, Oregon came in third at 14.4 meters (568 inches/47.33 feet).

From there the lists went on to round out the top 9 or 10 with only slight variations. What all of the listed resorts had in common other than Alyeska was that their measurements were taken at mid-mountain. Alyeska's were taken at the top of their highest lift. On their website they provide measurements which they state are taken at the summit, mid-mountain and base, for their historic averages. And they have made it clear that the measurements they release to the press are taken from the summit. None of the online outlets bothered to include that info in their stories or to inquire where the other resorts measure and consider or make note of the difference and why it matters.

Obviously one of the most critical aspects about snow measurements is where they're conducted. Most agree that a summit isn't fair for obvious reasons, the primary being that it doesn't represent the altitude you ski at. The base has the same problem and in more than a few areas, especially in Europe, it's just a lowland staging area where you board a lift to take you to ski slopes up on the mountain.

So mid-mountain is the widely accepted standard in North America for where snowfall measurements are taken that resorts report to the public. Providing the depths at stations at the base, mid-mountain and summit is also done. In every case resorts have a responsibility to note those locations, and the media has the same responsibility to report them. That frequently doesn't happen mostly because the media outlets have very limited resources and tend to run press releases verbatim, or to incorporate their data without question into a story.

In my research, only a couple of resources make clear distinctions about where their number come from: weathertoski.uk, and snow-forecast.uk. The travel agency Onthesnow.com is also a prominent online snow stat provider, especially for European resorts. On their historical charts they list numbers for each season for the last 12 in the categories of Total Snowfall, Snowfall Days, Average Base Depth, Average Summit Depth, Maximum Base Depth, and Biggest Snowfall. Though they don't specifically say where the Total Snowfall stat comes from, it's obvious that they're taken at the base. Which explains why they can list Total Snowfall of 0 for some seasons while still having decent numbers for the Average Summit Depth.

It's a confusing approach. But they supply some of the most wide-ranging numbers on the Continent, and even venture into North America, though not altogether reliably. Their columnist in the October 22 story reported, "The snowiest ski area in North America is Alyeska, Alaska, where the annual snow dump on the slopes averages 669 inches. It has jumped as high as 848 inches but, during the 2021-2022 season, the total took a dip to a mere 394 inches."

The entirety of the paragraph was wrong. Alyeska's average at the summit is 656 inches over a 35-year period, so the column was at least close on that. But Alyeska *did* have 848 inches at its summit for the season being discussed, and around 500 inches at mid-mountain. Which means it obviously didn't dip to 349 inches in either place. Most likely that was a base reading. Onthesnow.com declines to divulge how they source their numbers, though they usually correspond pretty closely to the resort's. As with all the other outlets, the writer never mentions where on the mountain the measurements he's citing are taken, and they would seem to be a jumble of all three measuring stations.

Multiple other sources also identify Alyeska as the snowiest ski area in North America not just for that season but historically, even though those assessments are based on measurements taken at its summit. In fact Mount Baker Washington has significantly higher average snowfall totals (662 inches) at its mid-mountain station than Alyeska does (530 inches).

In a 2023 story titled Top 10 Snowiest Ski Resorts – North America, Weathertoski.uk noted, "There is a much stronger culture for measuring snowfall in North America than there is in Europe – nearly every resort publishes its snowfall figures. Measuring parameters are also more consistent…. Most (though not all) resorts record their snowfall somewhere around mid-mountain, where figures are more representative of the ski area as a whole, whereas most European figures relate to resort level [which is often the base]."

They go on to name Mount Baker number one, saying, "With an annual snowfall average of around 16.5 meters, Mount Baker is the snowiest ski resort in North America if not the world! Alyeska [which they place at number two] claims a similar average – but only at the very top of its ski area. Mount Baker's measuring point is mid-mountain, less exposed and generally considered as more reliable."

Figuring out where any given resort does its measuring and reports it from isn't always easy since not all snowfall reports are specific about the details. In addition to those issues, there are other important influences to be considered. Outright lying and outrageous spinning aside, some of the biggest problems with tracking snowfall are inherent in the process. For instance, where are the measuring stations located: in the shade, in the sun, under snow-sloughing trees, or exposed to wind drifting? Are measurements taken at dawn or noon or somewhere in between, before or after the snow has settled or melted? Are they hand-done with yardsticks by nearsighted lifties, or by remote measuring devices with NOAA-endorsed computerized recordings overseen by meteorologists?

In the end, even though the people collecting and collating the data may have the best of intentions, their results can be flawed by location and other procedural complications, and are always subject to being finessed by resort management when they're announced.

And no matter how it comes out the locals will scoff and moan: either their resort is shamelessly over-reporting or oddly under doing it. Most locals prefer the latter since it doesn't entice so many visitors, but business owners start fearing plots to undermine their profitability. So sometimes the easiest way to go is just tell the truth, which by and large most resorts try to do.

When you're talking about enough snow to completely bury most chairlifts, those are the kind of season-long total accumulations that can make many skiers drool. The truth is those amounts aren't always skiable or as unreservedly great as they sound, and certainly they aren't consistent from year to year. But when they're happening they make for amazing photos, press releases and wet dreams.

Skiers are like farmers in that our reliance on the weather is acute. For most, fresh snow in whatever format is an agreeable thing. Nearly all of us except for racers prefer natural snow to the processed substance. Some of us love it in large quantities and especially while it's falling.

For powder freaks and regular skiers who crave soft, pliable snow – and for any resident of any place that depends on skiing as a vital part of the economy – watching the weather is a part of their lives.

Storm-watching and tracking snowfall records turned into a necessary avocation centuries ago in some places for a variety of reasons unrelated to skiing. And while some ski areas have kept methodical records of their snowfall since the day they opened, many haven't and some still don't. The practice varies widely around the world, and can be as much a matter of marketing as factual reporting.

Whether it's at a small ski-club-run area in the western US, or the town t-bar hill in Greenland, or a yurt and a rope tow in Kazakhstan, some places just aren't positioned or inclined to keep track of snowfall. And indeed entire countries have come late to the realization that an accurate historical record of weather is fundamental to trying to understand the future and how to prepare for everything from flood and drought years, to avalanche closures of highways, to storms that devastate entire communities.

On the other hand, in many of the ski resorts across the planet, keeping accurate track of the weather and snowfall is just common sense for budgeting, staffing and snowmaking needs among other things. The PR massaging of the messaging has meant reinterpreting how we contextualize snow depths in the era of climate change for more than 20 years. As average annual snowfall amounts have declined across North America and Europe, new ways of representing those numbers have evolved. The way that occurs depends on the resort.

If it's a ski area that has traditionally gotten lots of snow, they will always favor the "historical average," taken from as far back as their records go. This methodology obviously weights recent, often less snowy, seasons far less that the other popular approach, which is to take the most recent ten or twenty-year period and average that. Resorts across the board also began reporting tallies for how much snow had fallen, in total as the seasons progressed, as well as what the accumulated depth was. The former is always more substantial than the latter, which condenses considerably and is what actually gets skied on.

Historic snowfall records can raise a number of concerns, especially when they are at substantial odds with nearby simultaneous measurements or a location's past records. These are sometimes attributed to operator/observer error, the always-popular human factor that gets the blame for so many things.

The US Weather Bureau keeps records that are mostly considered sacrosanct because they're very particular about such things. But it's rare that a national weather service station directly overlaps with ski area or resort operations. And it's not unheard of for disputes to arise about the Weather Bureau's official records and why they recognize some and not others.

When we talk about records, and someplace being the snowiest in the world or country or province, we are always only talking about such things within a larger subset of: those places for which there are reliable measurements. A huge chunk of the planet is still understandably lacking in those.

I have been careful to attribute all of my significant sources, but cannot totally vouch for any of them personally. Few are independent of financial motivations. Whether they're aggregators of unsupervised resort-supplied info trying to attract and keep advertisers, or travel agencies who want your business, or even subscriber-supported content providers, they can't be assumed to be free of prejudice.

With all of that in mind, what follows is as well documented as possible, while still being subject to updating, modification and reconsideration. It isn't meant to say unequivocally what resorts get the most snow. But rather to look at an array of ones that have gotten it historically, what happens when ski areas get huge amounts of it, what the weather patterns are that influence such things, and how resorts and riders deal with it.

Yuki-no-otani of Tateyama Kurobe Alpine Route, Japan's "Canyon of Snow." Photo by 663highland via Wikipedia.

My purpose in writing about big storms and big winters is first and foremost to tell stories about some of the really wild weather that makes our whole sport possible. That includes discussing the benefits as well as drawbacks of such things and is not meant to criticize resorts for weather that is beyond their control, or how they react to it. It's to point out that big amounts of snow are nearly always mixed blessings, and can be overwhelming, whether you're trying to shovel your sidewalk, get to work, or go skiing, let alone keep a ski resort open and avalanche-free. We tend to judge big storms not just by how deep they skied but how big a disaster they caused, and the collateral damage is a clear record of that.

To the extent that resorts can bear some of the blame if streets don't get plowed as fast as some would like, those are first-world problems that tend to get solved pretty quickly. Nevertheless, this is the main reason many resorts are afraid of looking incompetent in stories about big storms. But for the most part it's simply not practical or affordable for communities to be prepared for the worst snowstorms. It's very expensive and difficult to have the capacity to handle even the normal ones.

Denver, Colorado is one example of a city that has been notorious for more than 50 years for electing their Mayors based on how they respond to bad blizzards. Those may happen half a dozen times a year, or twice, or not at all, placing them way down the list of things that need managing on a regular basis. But residents expect their government to be able to respond quickly and competently so they can get to work, buy groceries and go skiing.

This ability requires large, well-supported emergency services departments, fully staffed and operational 24/7. Also a big fleet of monster, fuel-guzzling plows, industrial snowblowers and dump trucks for clearing highways and streets, with fully licensed drivers standing by and ready at a moment's notice. And those are just a few of the equipment and logistical nightmares that are costly, manpower intensive, and nearly impossible to adequately deal with.

Even in Denver, which sits on the flanks of the Rocky Mountains and the edge of the Great Plains where storms are not uncommon, these resources are only required on average a small handful of times a year. That's a really big ask when it comes to budgeting in any city, but that's the impossible task most communities in snow country face during heavy onslaughts.

It's also important to bear in mind that the damage inflicted on society at large by powerful snowstorms is far-reaching. By the time you tally up the car wrecks, the dead livestock, the collapsed roofs and destroyed crops and on and on, a few skier's missed powder day can end up being a humanitarian disaster for tens of thousands.

In the cases where lifts and runs are closed due to avalanche control work, that's something every skier and rider should applaud, because we know what can happen when proper safety precautions aren't taken. And there are persuasive forces in these situations that can run counter to public safety concerns or even common sense.

Not opening lifts on big weekends is a financial and public relations nightmare not totally dissimilar to what Roy Scheider encountered trying to close popular beaches in *Jaws*. It impacts everybody in the community and beyond, and has resulted in litigation in the Alps and America over everything from being charged for accommodations when you can't ski, to not being allowed to leave your resort, or sometimes even your hotel, for days at a time due to avalanche hazards.

Insurance policies and guest waivers have been developed to deal with those and other potential conflicts that arise from trying to keep resorts both safe and open. And of course there are always going to be those who insist that it's up to them personally what risks they're willing to take, not the resort. Which is absurd on multiple levels.

The industry has worked to get a handle on some of the obvious inherent risks of the sport, including those caused by major snowstorms, while also trying to put as much of the responsibility for those risks as possible on the ticket holders. That's understandable, and fair on certain levels, but there is still the matter of that ticket. If they are going to charge you money for their services, that implies some degree of trying to see to it that you get those services and aren't hurt or killed.

On the other side of the coin, observers, journalists, skiers, boarders and the general public need to not be quite so shocked and outraged that skiers can be injured or inconvenienced due to snow conditions. That's the equivalent of being angry that a surfer has drowned. It's only reasonable to expect that a weather-dependent sport like skiing will be subject to weather-related hazards and closures.

With climate change exacting a toll on winter, big snow years or lack thereof have become much more than a ski industry worry. And particularly as weather has become more unstable and extreme, being able to forecast it with greater reliability is vital to communities, hospitals, first responders, commerce, transportation, insurance companies, and many, many others.

The jet streams, atmospheric rivers and massive ocean currents of our planet, its polar vortices, sea oscillations, tides, lake-effect moisture, bomb cyclones, melting glaciers, and a thousand other influences affect everyone. Skiing is a bellwether of those trends.

The storm systems that break snowfall records in Colorado may also devastate crops across the Midwest, or bring shipping to a halt throughout Scandinavia, or bury half a dozen villages in Iran. The big storms can bring ruin and rescue in the same package: bad flooding in one place, vital moisture in another. All that skiers can do is try to understand the processes at work.

Given a scarcity of verifiable and usable snowfall data in the ski world beyond North America and Western Europe, I am only providing overviews of the weather and snow accumulations elsewhere. While less thorough than the western coverage, it still includes specific resorts along with epic skiing, scattered disasters, and a number of world records.

Alta interlodge sign, one of many posted in the resort when roads and the mountain are closed due to avalanche danger.

CHAPTER 15

PART ONE – SNOWFALL RECORDS IN NORTH AMERICA AND THE STORM OF THE CENTURY

Major storms and massive snow years are the stuff of dreams. And nightmares.

It was President's Day weekend of 2021 before Alta shook off a snow slump with an active weather pattern that dumped most of the weekend, eased slightly, then started another cycle. Highway officials closed highway 210 up Little Cottonwood Canyon to Snowbird and Alta at midnight on Sunday, February 14th for avalanche control work. And the Alta Marshall implemented a town-wide order requiring residents, employees and lodge guests to shelter in place until avalanche work had been completed.

Known as an "interlodge," it's a necessary pain to protect lives because 80% of the buildings in town are in avalanche paths. And it's a misdemeanor crime to ignore, punishable by up to a $1,000 fine and 6 months in jail. It's also one of the biggest daydreams of skier's the world over because it usually guarantees deep first tracks when the siege ends.

Ten more inches fell between midnight and 8:00 a.m., then a natural slide around 10 a.m. took out highway 210 and the Bypass Road between Alta and the Bird, and another interlodge order went out again at 11:00 a.m. Monday and everyone stayed locked down for another day and night. On Wednesday more avalanches buried 210 under 4.27 meters (14 feet) of snow and debris, and swept a UDOT truck and snowcat off the Seven Sisters area of the highway. It was a rare occurrence and luckily no one was hurt.

Sixty hours after it began, Alta's longest interlodge ever at the time (they've been doing it since at least 1975), ended early Thursday morning. Little Cottonwood Canyon was still closed but lifts opened at 11:00 a.m. The 1.65 meters (5+ feet) of fresh since the lockdown started was untouched. It contributed to 4.12 meters (162.5 inches) of snowfall that month, the most in a decade.

More importantly and immediately, no one from the outside world could get to the mountain until hours later on that big Thursday. It was what locals call a 'Country Club' day, for one of powder skiing's most exclusive clubs. But it had come with a price, making it the perfect example of all the good and bad that happens when ski resorts get buried.

[Drop Cap] Skiers love to talk and brag about the most snow they've ever skied and the biggest storms they've seen. And while you might think that such things would be fairly easy to track, and something everyone can agree on, that isn't always the case.

Many – though certainly not all – ski areas have kept snowfall records fairly consistently since their openings. But those numbers can be problematic in many ways and don't always tell the full story. For example, the largest all time single-storm total in the US as certified by NOAA, occurred in northern California in 1959 and dropped almost 5 meters (189 inches) on Mount Shasta's Ski Bowl in the Cascade Range over a 7-day period. It was said to not have disrupted local life that much, since residents were so used to big storms that waiting for plows to get the deluge moved wasn't out of the ordinary.

For the ski area, however, it *wasn't* normal because no one knew what normal was since it was their first year of operation. They had just that fall opened a double chairlift on the southern flank of 14,179-foot Mount Shasta, with a base lodge at 7,850 feet. On February 13th it started snowing and didn't quit until the 19th, delivering nearly 16 feet. Mount Shasta City, 4,000 feet lower, reported .83 meters (33 inches) during the first day of the storm.

There appear to be no accounts of the skiing that resulted, but with it coming down at an average of over two feet a day, the first days had to be insanely good – before things became impossible. Though it sounds like the kind of godsend that could mint a new ski area's reputation, Ski Bowl eventually had to be moved on the mountain, in part due to the severe snow conditions.

Just as one big storm can sometimes define a ski area's history, some seasons are emblematic of the full range of what seriously deep snow can mean.

1993 AND THE STORM OF THE CENTURY

Big storms and big snow years often concentrate on one region, but occasionally a winter comes along that crushes the whole country. It happened when 1993's "Storm of the Century" highlighted an already heavy season that broke records and blew minds.

Alyeska, Alaska, situated virtually at sea level just a few miles from the Turnagain Arm of the Gulf of Alaska, is understandably one of the snowiest ski areas in North America. For them 1993 wasn't anything special. But as per their website they average (based on a 35-year span) 16.66 meters (656 inches), at their summit, where

Mount Baker images of measurements for their world-record season of 1998/'99. Courtesy of Mount Baker Ski Area.

they received their high of nearly 25 meters (81½ feet) in 2011/'12. Many ski areas (Mount Baker included) take their measurements-of-record at mid-mountain. At Alyeska that average is 13.46 meters (530 inches/44+ feet). Which is still a ton of snow. Famous Alaskan backcountry and heli destination Thompson Pass gets an average of 14 meters (552 inches), and in 1963 reported an American-record-setting 1.98 meters (78 inches) in 24 hours: at more than three inches an hour that's literally pouring down.

Almost 3,000 miles south of Alaska, Hawaii also gets snow they ski on. But so far they've never had the kind of storm that disrupted basic island life the way the Storm of the Century did on the mainland. In 1978, 8 inches fell on 10,023-foot Haleakala volcano on Maui. It was the highest recorded amount in the islands until 2016 when 24 inches fell on the summit of Mauna Kea at 13,803 feet on the Big Island. That was also the first snowfall ever recorded on the island that extended below the 13,0000-foot level. Both Mauna Kea and Muana Loa on Hawaii can get snow in the winter and locals like to ski and surf on the same day, and pack some snow in the back of their pickups for keeping the après beer cold at the beach.

The Pacific Northwest (PNW) routinely ranks as one of America's snowiest regions. One reason is because they're visited by "extratropical cyclones" with the kind of high wind and snow amounts that knock out power and bring highways, airports and trains to a standstill. During one such 3-day La Nina-inspired pounding in January of 2012, parts of Oregon got 1.27 meters (50"). And in the fierce winter of 1993 Mount Bachelor, Oregon tallied its second snowiest year on record with over 15.24 meters (600 inches), compared to their healthy annual average of 11.7 meters (462 inches).

For '93, Mount Baker, Washington actually had one of their leaner seasons, belying their astounding *average* of 16.8 meters (622"/55+ feet), the most in the US when measured at mid-mountain. Then in 1998-99 they got a positively freakish, world-record 28.95 meters (1,140"/95 feet!) and were open for the entire year.

Already located on the western slope and crests of the Cascades, some of the wettest mountains in the continental US, Baker's specific orientation of northwest to southeast is a further bonus. Meteorologists describe what that causes as, "orographic/upslope enhanced precipitation at the perfect altitude range for maximum snow." While Baker obviously gets some huge storms it also snows almost constantly to achieve those numbers.

Whistler, BC, gets a 448-inch average from some of the same weather patterns that affect the southern reaches of the Cascade Range. '93 was about average, but they got walloped like Baker in '98/'99 with a record 11.38 meters (644 inches). Powder magazine editor Leslie Anthony commuted there multiple times that winter from his then home in Toronto.

"Records are nice and all, but what's it like to ski during a winter of endless snowfall? Pretty freakin' great. Glorious even," he recalls. "Like the hyenas gorging on a dead elephant that skiers resemble when it comes to powder, day after day after day of a foot or more of snow meant skiing bell to bell day after day after day until you simply couldn't do it anymore. And with the highway frequently closed locals had a lot of it to themselves. After 22 years living here now, I have yet to see people take days off to rest their legs the way they did that winter."

California has been racking up absurd amounts of snowfall since accounts have been kept, like the suffocating 9.9 meters (32½ feet) in a month in 1911 at Tamarack, near what's now the Bear Valley ski area. The Sierras are known for other prodigious dumps, such as in 1982 when Donner Summit – near Sugar Bowl, Boreal and Donner Ski Ranch areas – reported 2.22 meters (87½ inches) in a single 2-day storm.

Even by those standards, 1993 still rocked. At Mammoth, it snowed one meter (three feet) on the last night of September and the area opened on October 8th and closed for skiing in mid-August – an amazingly long season for a non-glacier-based resort. The downside included numerous gas line ruptures, explosions and fires because people couldn't keep their propane tanks and lines clear of the pressure of all the pow. And they're used to lots of snow, famously having to shovel out their lifts at times, and getting their biggest haul ever of nearly 17 meters (668.5 inches) in 2010/'11.

For '93, the Sierras picked up 2.74 meters (9 feet) between Christmas and New Year's Day, effectively barricading a huge chunk of Heavenly Valley's holiday business *out*. The same thing happened throughout the winter at Palisades at Tahoe (the former Squaw Valley) where locals savored every minute. And the resort stayed open all year for the first time ever, keeping the Bailey's Beach lift running through the summer until opening day in the fall.

"Everyone had a great old time skiing all the new runs in the trees when the passes and the upper mountain were closed," said then-local Seth Masia. "National Chute, on Palisades where Warren Miller films a lot, normally has an 8 to 10-foot drop at the entrance. Even on a good winter. Last year you just skied in." And it wasn't even their record snow season, which they posted in 2016/'17 with 18.49 meters (728 inches).

During the massive snowfall season of 2022/'23 from the Sierra Nevadas of California to the Wasatch Mountains of Utah, a number of online sources verged on hysteria about the records being set and their sometimes ruinous consequences. Once again it just proved what shouldn't need it: that it's always possible to have too much of a good thing.

When Palisades at Tahoe was closed for days on end while they tried to shovel out lifts buried under 50 feet of snow up to the tower tops, no skiers or boarders were happy. The resort wasn't generating any revenue and no real estate was being sold because it couldn't be shown since the streets were impassable and the properties were all completely buried.

On the bright side, most of the Sierra Nevada resorts extended their seasons from mid-April into at least the first week of May, giving them a chance to recoup some losses. "This is definitely a season to remember with incredible powder days – and there's still months for everyone to enjoy it," said the president and CEO of the Lake Tahoe Visitors Authority Carol Chapin in a statement at the time. "Overall businesses are experiencing a successful season with occupancy figures comparable to 2022 despite periods of inaccessibility due to weather."

At the UC Berkeley Central Sierra Snow Lab on Donner Pass near Lake Tahoe, where they've been tracking snowfall numbers since 1878, things went rapidly from the sublime to the ridiculous. On March 1 they were reporting 531 inches (44.25 feet), with 141.9 (nearly 12 feet) of it coming in a single week. By March 24 they had 692" (57.7 feet) and had gone from threatening their record for the past 50 years of 572.4 inches (47.7 feet) to totally eclipsing it. Depending on the rest of the season, their highest numbers ever of 811.8 inches (67.65 feet) in 1950/'51, once considered unassailable, could be in jeopardy.

As of March 24, 2023, Heavenly Mountain Resort's total snowfall for the year was 545 inches and only 19 short of its all-time record, set in 2016/'17, with more storms on the way. Kirkwood with 672 inches was closing fast on their record of 700 from 2010/'11. Sierra-at-Tahoe's 655 was their second highest total ever to that point. "This historic year is a sight to see," said a post on Facebook by S-at-T workers. "Lift shacks and ski patrol stations are completely buried. Chairs in West Bowl have been covered."

By the same date Palisades was at 678 inches, as compared to their historic average of 400 for the entire season, and it was wreaking some havoc. Fire officials announced that, "Unrelenting winter storms have damaged dozens of homes and businesses in the Greater South Lake Tahoe area since last week." Roof collapses and an "alarming" increase in gas leaks and carbon monoxide related emergencies (including at one high school that had to be evacuated) led the list of problems.

The blame for all of this abundance fell on "atmospheric rivers," of which the legendary Pineapple Express is a famous example. Defined as corridors of super-saturated air greater than 2,000 km long and less than 1,000 km wide with at least 2 centimeters (.78 inches) of vertically integrated precipitable water, they typically provide 50% of California's annual moisture.

Carrying water from the tropics to the poles, they're graded 1 to 5. The first three are mostly to moderately beneficial, with category 4 and 5 being mostly to primarily hazardous. In 1996/'97 a New Year's class 5 storm

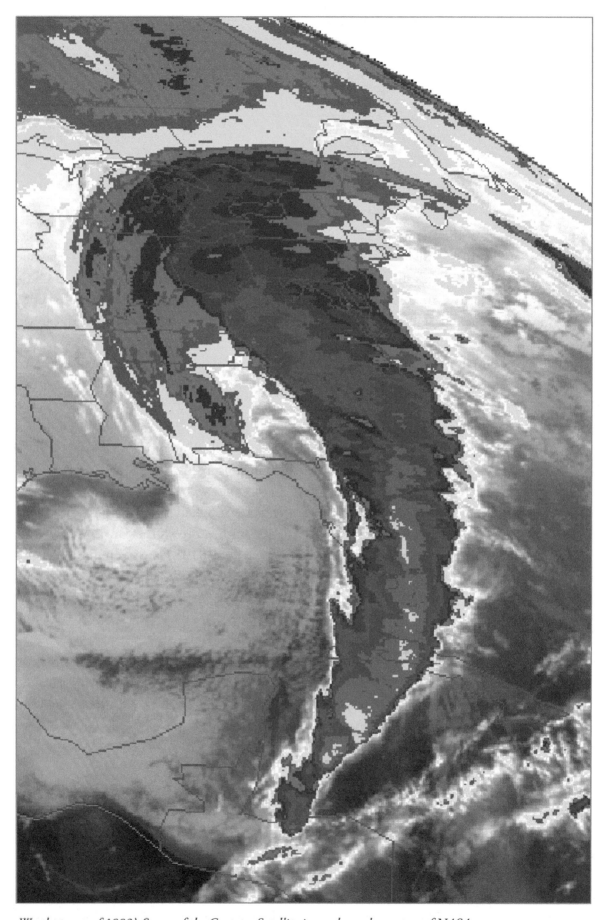

Weather map of 1993's Storm of the Century. Satellite image by and _courtesy of NASA.

over the Central California coast lasted over 100 hours and caused more than $100 billion in damage.

Much of the western US, which was in a prolonged drought, had mountain snowpacks running at anywhere from 150 to 300% of normal going into spring. At the UC Snow Lab in late March they noted online that, "We're still lagging behind a fair bit in terms of water content. We're nowhere near 2016/2017's SWE because of how cold/light the snow has been in the last couple of storms."

With more heavy wet storms in the forecast, the prospect of reservoirs and aquifers substantially refilling was still plausible. But it was offset by concerns about possibly disastrous runoff scenarios in the event of a warm spring.

Utah's Wasatch Range is legendary for being the first to get struck by big storms, including atmospheric rivers, moving in from the west coast with crazy amounts of moisture, then passing across a desert and adding heft over the Great Salt Lake before slamming into the mountains and releasing everything.

In Park City the booming real estate market took a hit in January of '93 because the weather was so consistently stormy no one wanted to go out and look at property. They had to dig out their high Jupiter Bowl lift in several places before closing on April 15 with more snow than they'd had all season. And they'd had plenty: just about 13 meters (42½ feet), which obliterated their previous record by over 7 feet.

One day in March of '93 Little Cottonwood Canyon had five avalanches and Alta ended the season with a heroic 16.5 meters (650.4 inches or 54+ feet) total compared to their remarkable average of 12.62 meters (497 inches) over an 82-year history.

With one of the most complete and carefully observed snowfall records in the country, Alta is meticulous about how and where they take measurements. The Alta Guard House study plot (at 2,656 meters/8,714 feet) has records dating back to 1944. In 1980 their new Collins study plot, located at 2,944 meters (9,662 feet) in Collins Gulch (near the literal mid-mountain elevation of 9,799), began making daily snowfall observations and continues in that role today.

At Alta, the "interlodge" experience can be great for non-claustrophobic guests when they finally get to be the first ones to the untracked bounty. But business-wise, the resort is out a day or two or three of lift ticket, mountain lunches and hot buttered rum sales, so it's a mixed blessing in the ledgers.

On March 24 of 2023, while the Sierra Nevada resorts of California were being buried to record levels, Alta also announced that they had just broken theirs of almost 19 meters (748 inches) set in 1981/'82. All that remained was to see by how much.

Though the Great Salt Lake, a big snow generator, had been drying up from drought, the resort and its neighbor at Snowbird benefitted enough from the atmospheric rivers to compensate for it. Then late in the season as La Nina faded and the jet-stream moisture dissipated, the lake effect took hold again and eventually by closing day Alta had received 22.93 meters (903 inches, or 75+ feet!).

In Canada, most of the Rocky Mountains of British Columbia missed out on the 1993 storm systems. Historically Fernie Resort has big years of over 10 meters (around 400 inches), but enough lower ones to drag its annual average down to 6.68 meters (263 inches) as per onthesnow.com. And Revelstoke, which only opened in 2007 and has no 1993 season to compare with, is said by the same source to average 5.8 meters (228 inches) and collected 11.35 meters (447 inches) in 2021/'22, a few inches more than Whistler on the year.

In 1993 Jackson, Wyoming's daunting Corbett's Couloir saw its traffic increase due to what locals described as "the lessened fear factor" from the much shorter mandatory drop to enter it. And Big Sky, Montana opened their steep and ragged Challenger Lift terrain earlier than ever before, on Thanksgiving.

Colorado also got blitzed in early November of '93 when Aspen had more than double its average snowfall for the month and opened weeks earlier than it ever had. Winter Park got a quick 2 meters (6½ feet) that month and was able to open their new Parsenn bowl November 18 instead of mid-January as planned.

With its formidable spine of the Rocky Mountains, Colorado has historically received lots of big storms. In 1921, Silver Lake (near skiing on St. Mary's Glacier) got nearly two meters (75.8 inches) in 24 hours out of a system that delivered another foot over the next few hours, making it one of the most intense of all time.

For the rest of '93, Keystone got 2.13 meters (7 feet) in February and promptly extended their closing date "indefinitely." Statewide snow totals didn't end up setting records, but most resorts reported an abundance of big powder days.

It wasn't all glad tidings of course. In Durango, Colorado – a town well accustomed to winter – they ran out of snow shovels. On January 14th. More were flown in from Denver but on the night of January 19 the roof of the empty Lewis State College auditorium collapsed under the weight of snow they couldn't remove in time.

"Bad news for the college, good news for skiers," said Mike Smedley, media relations director at nearby Purgatory, putting it bluntly. "As soon as that story hit the wire, our business shot up. People figured we must be buried and we were. There were days when we had 22 inches of new snow and less than a thousand skiers on the mountain."

In Taos, New Mexico Michael Blake, son of the ski area's founder, said he couldn't remember the last time he'd seen the snowbanks as high along their roads, and his plow crews ran out of places to put it.

Beginning March 11 and 12, an arctic high-pressure system formed over the Midwest at the same time an extratropical low-pressure front built over the Gulf of Mexico. The Storm of the Century was the cyclonic result of their collision over a big sweep of the East from the Deep South to New England. The most snow produced was at Mount Le Conte in Tennessee with 1.42 meters (56 inches). Birmingham, Alabama, got a shocking third of a meter (13) inches. Winds reached sustained speeds of 100 mph in some areas, temperatures plunged to record lows in 11 states, and a total of 318 fatalities were attributed to the storm.

Michigan's Boyne Mountain Resort was mostly out of the line of fire. This time. "We are within Michigan's Snowbelt and typically have a generous amount of lake effect snow," President and General Manager Ed Brice wrote to me. "Some of the most memorable winter storms would be in the late '70s to early '80s."

Alta's Katie Hitchcock in deep in January of their record season of 2022/'23. Photo by Chloe Jimenez, courtesy of Alta Ski Resort.

The great Blizzard of 1978 that clobbered the Ohio Valley and Great Lakes in late January was one of them. A National Weather Service meteorologist in Ann Arbor described it as, "The most extensive and very nearly the worst blizzard in Michigan history."

Brice remembers, "We had a period when we had so much snowfall and storming so hard that on a Friday local authorities closed the roads so guests could not get to the resort. During the following mid-week we dug out, roads were cleared and Mother Nature decided to give a repeat performance. Yep, on Friday the roads were closed again."

The Northeast gets hammered fairly regularly by serious storms, including in 1952 and '62 when big ones blanketed most of Maine and broke records in Bangor and Portland, the two main gateways to its skiing. The Eastern Canadian Blizzard of 1971 hit Quebec and Ontario with over two feet, creating memorable powder days at the likes of Mont-Sainte Anne and Mont Tremblant, which got about 20% of its average annual snow in that storm. Even more unusually, because of all the snow a Montreal Canadiens hockey home game had to be postponed for the first time since the pandemic of 1918.

The '92/'93 season started with a bang in New England when one of the most brutish nor'easters in history assaulted much of the Atlantic seaboard, handing Killington, VT, it's earliest opening (Oct. 1) in 31 years. The weather turned unseasonably mild in December then rebounded strongly starting in February when Vermont got anywhere from 1.8 to 3.5 meters (6 to 11½ feet) of snow and 98% of the state's skiing was open for the first time in years.

Then the Storm of the Century barreled in and dumped up to a meter (3½ feet) on March 12th and 13th. Okemo reported record base depths, and Killington went into April with the most skiing in their 35-year history.

"Sugarbush was incredible," reported frequent SKI magazine contributor Dana Gatlin. "Doug Lewis told me he was born there and had never seen it like that." They kept the steep and rugged Castle Rock area opened for two months on all natural snow, which hadn't happened since the '70s. "And traffic in town slowed to a crawl because no one could see over the snowbanks at intersections," reported Gatlin.

Writer David Goodman reported much the same thing from Stowe. "I've never seen conditions like it. The 'Storm of the Century' was a skier's blizzard because it was on a Saturday evening. Stowe got two feet and only one lift was running on Sunday. There was hardly anyone on the mountain because no one wanted to venture out. We hiked to runs like Lookout Trail, that hadn't been opened in a decade, and it was tremendous."

Stowe has been dealing with some of the most snow on average in the East (8 meters/314 inches) on lift-served slopes since 1933. Locals say mountain operations are rarely stymied by storms, '93 notwithstanding. However, as Town Manager Charles Safford notes, they have only one road in and, "We occasionally have a car that can't make it up Harlow Hill, blocking traffic." It doesn't happen often or for long, but when it does it can mean that those already on the mountain have it all to themselves for a few hours.

And that pretty much sums up the divine dilemma of large amounts of snow, whether it's at Whistler, Alta or Stowe, or anywhere in between. When the weather's really bad for most normal people, it can be great for skiers if we can just get to the goods.

CHAPTER 16

PART TWO - THE SAVAGE WINTER AND RECORDS IN THE ALPS

Germany, Italy and Austria

The last winter of the 20th century turned into one of the most severe in the recorded history of the Alps, shattering snowfall totals in many places and killing hundreds. It was the worst death toll in the mountains since the infamous Winter of Terror in 1951. And I spent six weeks right in the thick of it, driving to 12 different ski resorts for a book I was doing for the Best of the Alps organization.

Like the 1993 Storm of the Century in North America, the series of storms in January and February of 1999 across Europe represented all the good, the bad and the ugly that can happen any time ski resorts, cities and entire countries get completely overwhelmed by snow.

The Alps occupy a sizable chunk of the European continent, 1,200 kilometers (745 miles) long and up to four kilometers high, they comprise an amazingly dense and sculpted slab of terra-extra-firma. The Best of the Alps (BOTA) member resorts range across them from the lush Kitzbuhler Alps in the east to the brooding massif of Mont Blanc in the west, from the sudden limestone uprising of the Bavarian Alps in the north to the blushing pink spires of the Italian Dolomites in the south.

My wife and I managed to get to Munich in the midst of a cross-country blizzard in the US that had shut down most of the air traffic. And on the 5th of January we rolled out into Germany in the only vehicle Sixt car rentals could find to fit our needs. We needed it for long enough we should have probably bought it instead, and had multiple suitcases, three pairs of skis, an equal number of boots, several cameras, laptops, steamer trunks, hat boxes, packs, and coffins of dirt from our native land.

The author's rental van buried after two days of snowfall in Seefeld, Austria at the start of the record winter of 1999. Photo © Jay Cowan

Knowing we'd be on the road for 7 weeks and moving every four or five days, we'd come fully, and ridiculously, laden. Getting something big enough that was also outfitted for the mountains proved impossible so we were driving a bad-dream-looking purple Ford mini-van (aka "Moby Grape") with front wheel drive and slick street tires, into what would turn out to be the worst possible conditions for it. It came with some flashy looking disco tire chains because studded tires aren't allowed anywhere in Europe. At least the chains weren't necessary as we made the shortish drive to Garmisch-Partenkirchen.

GERMANY

The twin cities of G-P sit at a relatively low elevation at the confluence of two valleys on the edge of the German plains and the Bavarian Alps that levitate spectacularly up above the town. On the fringes of the storm patterns that affect much of the Austrian Alps, the resort is directly in the line of fire for big storm systems coming from the north and west.

The Hausberg/Alpspitze portion of the ski slopes come straight down into town and when we arrived the snow was thin there, befitting an area that averaged less than two meters from 2012 to 2022 and rarely gets storms of even half a meter (18") , according to Onthesnow.com using readings from the base.

The wide-ranging Zugspitze slopes just outside of G-P lap over into Austria and are well above tree-line for the most part. Their location on the Schneeferner, Germany's largest glacier on its highest peak the Zugspitze, is a huge boon for the resort's overall snowpack. Supplementing the glacier is a stout annual snowfall average of nearly 8 meters (26+ feet) from 2012 to 2022. That includes 10 meters (32 feet) in 2015/'16 and 2017/'18, followed by the next season topping a hefty 13.5 meters (44.3 feet).

Big days range from a half to almost a full meter. And they have some of the most snow-days in all of the Alps, averaging 58 per season, with totals of 70+ on 5 of those seasons. The amount of snowfall and number of snow-days are records for Germany by a wide margin.

From G-P we drove on dry roads over two high passes, through three countries and eight tunnels to reach Cortina, Italy at dusk. There was nothing but grass on the surrounding ski runs, but it started snowing as we pulled into our hotel.

ITALY

The next morning a full meter had blanketed everything, and it skied pretty well considering there was no base. Cortina is the kind of place where three-plus feet of snow overnight wasn't even a record, but even so, a fat meter in about 12 hours is a healthy wallop anywhere. Tucked at the base of the blushing pink Dolomites, Cortina is only 158 kilometers (98 miles) from Venice, and gets much of its weather from systems that form over the warm waters of the Adriatic and then merge with cold fronts over the mountains.

From 2012 through 2022, per onthesnow.com, they got an average annual total of 3 meters (just shy of 10 feet) in town, figures somewhat skewed by a couple of bad winters, which they are known to have. But they also include a serious 7.2-meter (23.6 feet) winter in 2013/'14. And that season didn't correspond to a really snowy winter anywhere else outside of Northern Italy, attesting to the sometimes unique sourcing of the region's moisture. They also had a record-setting single day that season with an astonishing 1.8 meters (almost 6 feet), in 24 hours.

In 2019 they got dumped on by a big storm system in the central Alps that left them 1.5 meters (nearly 5 feet) in one day. With an average of only 11 snow days per season, they tend to get a lot per storm, averaging a whopping .7 meters (over two feet). Nevertheless, by the reckoning of snow-online.com, Cortina is only Italy's 10th snowiest ski resort. Their ratings are based on how "snow-sure" resorts are and weighted heavily toward the ones with glacier access, thus guaranteeing skiing. They don't necessarily represent the resorts that get the most annual snowfall or the biggest storms.

For example, Ponte di Legno–Tonale–Temu (also known as Passo Tonale), a ski commune in the province of Breccia in the Rhaetian Alps, is number one on snow-online's list for Italy. It only averaged 5.5 meters (18 feet) of snowfall a year from 2012 through 2022, in a glacier-enhanced season that stretches from November into May, and none of the resort's snow stats are standouts.

Capracotta in the Apennine Mountains, on the other hand, has posted some mind-boggling numbers. On March 10/11 in 2015 they received a world-record-setting 2.58 meters (8.34 feet) in 18 hours, as certified by the Guinness Book of Records, obliterating the previous known amount for a single day anywhere. As recognized by the World Meteorological Organization that was 1.92 meters, or 6.3 feet and noted in the preceding chapter, at Silver Lake, Colorado in 1921.

Photos show a large front-loader trying to clear a street in Capracotta where the snow is higher than the very elevated cab on either side. There were no reports of how long it took to get the small ski area opened, but parts of the region were without power or water for hours. To add some confirmation to the numbers, the town of Prescocostanzo just down the road comes in at a close second in the record books with 2.4 meters during the same storm.

What produced this phenomenon was a deep low-pressure system over southern Italy that generated warm, heavily saturated winds off the Adriatic, which then hit the Apennines where the storm clouds rose rapidly and were forced to dump all the moisture as snow. Lots of it. Enough to eclipse a 94-year-old world record by more than two feet.

Cervinia, Italy, where I also skied on this trip, is routinely cited as one of the snowiest Italian resorts. It's situated on the opposite side of the Matterhorn from Zermatt, with which they share the Plateau Rosa glacier. At 2,050 meters (6,730 feet), Cervinia-Breuil is one of the highest resorts in the region, topping out at Piccolo Cervino at 3,880 meters (12,729 feet). They averaged just over 4 meters from 2012 through 2022, including seasons of 7.7, 5.35, 5.2, and 4.5, all of them decent numbers in Italy. That was generated by 20 snow days annually with storms that averaged a healthy .6 meters (two feet).

Courmayeur resembles Cervinia in that it's on the other side of another great mountain from another legendary resort (Mont Blanc/Chamonix), and also benefits from that mountain's weather influences. Their season-long totals weren't that striking from 2012 through 2022 (2.5 meters/8.2 feet), but their storm totals averaged half a meter (18+ inches), and that's top-three in Italy.

Arabba Marmolada, number 2 on the snow-online list, is one of their resorts that's snow-sure due to a glacier, and also gets large amounts of fresh snow regularly. With a lift nearly to the top of the Marmolada peak in the heart of the Dolomites, you can ski down the Marmolada glacier and then on pistes all the way to the village deep in the valley for 1820 vertical meters (nearly 6,000 feet). It's average snowfall of 4.25 meters (14 feet) was seriously buoyed by two seasons from 2012 through 2014 where it hit 10.97 meters (36 feet) and 11.36 (37.27 feet) – big by any reckoning. They haven't gotten near those numbers again since, but do average a strong .72 meters per storm which is the most of any major resort in Italy.

AUSTRIA

We drove from Cortina most of the way to St. Anton on dry roads. After that it was snowing so hard I had to chain up so we could cross the Arlberg and Flexen passes to reach Lech. For the next week there and in St. Anton, the snow came down in earnest and I got to ski some of the best the Arlberg has to offer. The powder off the back of St. Anton's Vallugagrat and all the way to Zurs was knee-deep. Zurs itself, on top of the Flexen Pass, has featured some of the deepest snow I've ever skied nearly every time I've been there, and the Weisse Ring around Lech was also prime.

After a meter of snow overnight in Cortina, Italy during the winter of 1999. Photo © Jay Cowan

With the amount and quality of the Arlberg's terrain, including lots of lift-served steeps and off-piste, it's some of the best powder skiing in the Alps. But in the snow-online ratings for Austria, Lech – very deceptively – only ranks 11th and St. Anton 13th. All but one of the resorts ahead of them have glaciers, but none get more average annual snow.

English ski journalist Fraser Wilkin, considered an authority on snow conditions in Europe, put Warth-Schrocken in the Voralberg at the top of his list of the five snowiest resorts *in the entire Alps* in a 2008 story for the British Daily Mail newspaper.

Relatively small, Warth is adjacent to the slopes of Lech at 1,44 meters (4,784 feet) and connected by a lift, but the road between them isn't open in the winter. Warth benefits from the same weather patterns as the Arlberg, and by Wilkins' calculations, over a 100-year period of recorded snowfall it has averaged a very hefty 10.7 meters (35+ feet) at their 1,269-meter base (4,163 feet). On the same basis, Lech/Zurs came in number two on Wilkin's list at 10.4 meters, due largely to the big volumes received at Zurs with the highest base elevation in the region at 1,717 meters (5,633 feet).

According to the Warth-Schrocken website they recorded an all-time high annual snowfall for the last 40 years in the brutal winter of 1998/'99 we were just embarking on. It ended up at a massive 16.5 meters (54 feet), yet barely edged out the winters of 1980/'81 and 1987/'88.

Damuls, boasting an annual average of 9.3 meters, is another ski resort in the Vorarlberg and claims to hold the European record as the village with the most snowfall, as well as an "honorary title" of "the snowiest village in the world." Both claims are steeped in questions, not the least of which is who has bestowed them with these titles. Furthermore Warth and Lech both have higher verifiable numbers. And it's also uncertain where Damul's measurements are taken since onthesnow's average for them from 2012 through 2022 was under three meters, during which time their biggest season was 4.3 meters.

But there is no doubt the region is one of the snowiest corners of the Alps when combined with the Arlberg. The Nordstau weather system gets the credit for the big and consistent storms that assail the area, the result of wet masses of air moving across the North Atlantic and plowing into their first obstacle in Europe – the Alps.

St. Anton, on the other side of the Arlberg and Flexen passes from Lech and Zurs, sits at 1,304 meters (4,278 feet). From 2012 through 2022 their average snowfall at the village level was 3.82 meters (12.5 feet), including one terrible season. Five were near the average and four ranged from about 5 to 7 meters (16 to 22.5+ feet). Their long-term average at the 2,000-meter level (6,561 feet), which is roughly their mid-mountain height, is a substantial 8 meters (26+ feet). So the onslaught of snow we experienced wasn't unusual, but a week later the bounty that I'd been charging gleefully around in would be turning into a disaster.

We took the A12 autobahn east across Austria to Kitzbuhel, about 200 kilometers and two and a half hours away, and in the process passed the turnoffs to a lot of snow-online's top 10 most snow-sure Austrian resorts.

Ischgl, 47 kilometers from St. Anton in the Paznaun Valley, weighs in at number 8 due largely to its glacier. Just up the road from it is the small resort of Galtur, a 600-year-old town that would be the scene of one of the worst tragedies of that savage winter. A days-long siege of heavy snow was capped on February 23rd when a massive avalanche swept across the valley floor and into the village killing 31 men, women and children. [More details in Chapter 24.]

The Pitztal at Imst is number 7 and located on the highest glacier in Austria with a top lift at 3,440 meters (11,286 feet). Considered a powder haven, their storms have averaged a half-meter each (about 20 inches) in recent years. The Kaunertal and the Serfaus-Fiss-Ladis complex also off the A12 on the way to Innsbruck, also make the list based on glacier access.

The Oetz Valley lies further to the east and also south of the A12 with the resort areas of Soelden, snow-online's number one, and Obergurgl-Hochgurgl at 5. Obergurgl, the highest parish in the country, is routinely cited as one of the biggest snow depositories in the Alps. Their average of less than 4.5 meters (14.5 feet) from 2012 to 2022, with a high of 7.1 meters (23+ feet), doesn't seem to support that. They do get single-storm totals fairly regularly between .75 and one meter (2.5 – 3.5 feet) while averaging a robust .64 meters (two feet).

The Brenner Pass lies immediately south of Innsbruck and a turnoff to the right near the bottom leads to the Stubai valley. The glacier at it's head can get single storms from .7 to 1.1 meters (27 inches to over 3.5 feet).

Further east along the A12/E45 is the turnoff to Mayerhofen and the Hintertux Glacier, ranked as the third most snow-sure resort in the country and a prime example of a rating due mostly to its glacier base.

Kitzbuhel, which was holding the world's most famous downhill race the weekend we were there, isn't one of Austria's snowiest resorts. The town sits at a relatively low altitude of 762 meters (2,500 feet) and isn't located in the path of the primary storm patterns in the region. They had to install snowmaking along the famous Strief downhill run and the lower part of the mountain after several bad snow years in the 1990s forced cancellation of the races.

However, other resorts that get upper-tier levels of snow are located in the surrounding region. Further east near Schladming is one of Fraser Wilkin's top 5 snowiest resorts in the Alps. The purpose-built Obertauern resort ranks fourth and sits at a base of 1,740 meters (5,708 feet) where it has received a strong long-term annual snowfall average of 8.8 meters (nearly 29 feet). From 2012 to 2022 that average was only slightly over 5 meters, though from 2017 through 2019 they got over 7.5 meters (25+ feet) both seasons. None of that came in huge dumps, but was dispersed across an average of 40 snow days, that ballooned up to 55 and 54 on those big winters. All of those numbers are substantial records versus the rest of the snow-online list of Top 10 resorts, with only Obergurgl getting close by racking up 54 snow days in 2017/'18 and a 36-day average over 10 years.

In January of 2019 Kitzbuhel, Saalbach and Zell am See all got hit with an unusually long and deep barrage, producing amounts not seen in Zell am See in decades. "It is certainly the most snow I can remember in these lower Austrian resorts and I have been following weather and snowfall patterns avidly for about 30 years," said Fraser Wilkins in an interview.

It started on January 5th and the village of Hohetauern in central Austria was snowed-in for 9 days with 270 people, including 60 children, cut-off by closed roads and avalanche danger. "The village is safe [from slides]

The Schindlergrat at St. Anton, Austria, in the region that gets the country's most snow. Photo © Jay Cowan.

and we are keeping the streets clear," reported a hotel owner on January 14th. "Nobody can go out and nobody get in. We are all good and the people in the town help each other. Everything is pretty cool here."

Kaprun, snow-online's 4th most snow-sure resort in Austria, accesses the Kitzsteinhorn Glacier. It's the highest ski area in a region served with a single pass that also includes Saalbach and Zell-am-See, and they all got buried. In early December of 2020 another blockbuster storm swept across the southern Alps striking eastern Austria and parts of the Italian Dolomites the hardest, with up to *three meters (9.8 feet)* in a multi-day deluge of historic proportions.

As Elena Protopopow of the Tirol Tourist Board reported, "Unusually large quantities of fresh snow have fallen in the Alps. In many places we are no longer talking about several centimeters, but several meters. Of course it is great to see the snowfall as we have been waiting for it in the last weeks and the snowfall has reached record levels. But…in many places in Tirol were avalanche warnings."

Marko Korosec of Severe Weather Europe reported, "After an intense snowstorm and ice storm just a few days and tons of rain yesterday, today produced several storms over the Adriatic Sea. Including a supercell storm in the evening with a tornado into the port of Trieste." Veneto and Trentino in northern Italy were put on avalanche alerts and railways were closed by heavy snow up higher and flooding down lower.

Snow-online's second most snow-sure Austrian resort is on the Molltaler Glacier at an unusually high base area for Austria of 2,108 meters (nearly 7,000 feet). From 2012 to 2022 it averaged almost four and a half meters (15 feet) of snowfall, going up to nearly 7 meters (23 feet). It isn't known for getting big individual storms, instead spreading the wealth over a laudable average of 30 snow days annually.

The common thread of most of these resorts is that they benefit from weather systems coming off the Adriatic as well as the fronts making their way from the north. They collide with a wall of towering Alps stretching close to the Italian/Austrian border from Piz Buin in the west (due south of St. Anton), to the Wildspitze (south of Innsbruck), and the Grossglockner, Austria's highest peak, straight south from Kitzbuhel. This formidable barrier not only generates great snow conditions on either side of it, but also monstrous hazards, as the year of 1999 was to prove.

The last occasion for such widespread disaster in the region was in the Winter of Terror of 1950/'51. It and the winter we were in shared similar weather patterns that are the most pronounced influences in the western and central Alps.

The catastrophe of '50/'51 was believed to have been caused be an unusually warm Atlantic front that met a polar cold mass right over some of the highest parts of the Alps. The trouble started with a huge two-day January snowstorm that dropped two-plus meters of snow on top of a base that was already double it's seasonal normal.

Accompanied by high winds it touched off a three-month-long siege that took place mostly along the Austrian/Swiss border, producing 649 avalanches "of note" that killed more than 265 people. Whole villages, hundreds of farm animals and thousands of acres of valuable forests were utterly destroyed. Austria suffered the worst loss of lives with 135 dead.

In Switzerland, Andermatt was hit by *6 avalanches in an hour* and 13 people died. In Munter a slide swept through town destroying 7 houses, the church and the schoolhouse, killing three. In Davos the railway station and part of the rail line were wiped out. The death toll reached 92 in the Valais Canton where there was this account of one avalanche: "Suddenly a dull rolling, then whistling, crashing, breaking and – darkness in the whole village – at that moment the houses and homes of entire families became their graves."

Fast forward to 1999 as we escaped Kitzbuhel to Seefeld, north of Innsbruck on a high bench. We didn't manage to escape the influenza that had been as common as schnapps in the streets during the Hahnenkamm. Harriet started feeling it midway through our stay there, while I was still trying to convince myself I was only getting a mild cold.

Small, largely car-free Seefeld is ultra-scenic and swank, possessed of more five-star hotels per-acre than any ski resort in Europe. We ensconced ourselves in one of them at the Klosterbrau just in time because by the next day I was truly and helplessly bedridden. We hunkered down and gobbled cold meds, hydrated and tried to get better so we could do our job.

At 1,200 meters (nearly 4,000 feet), Seefeld holds ample snow on its vast cross-country trails, small ski area, and nice nordic jumping hills. It got a respectable two meters of average snowfall from 2012 through 2022, and that included nearly 4 meters in 2017/'18, and almost 6 meters the following season. It doesn't generally include big single storms like the one that swept in on us 24 hours after our arrival.

Following a long walking tour on a beautiful day we returned to the hotel just as a storm started. In the morning there was a full meter of fresh on our van when I went to get my skis and it was still puking. Just like me.

I was miserable but I had to ski for the book, and conditions were exceptional. My guide and I proceeded to go hard in the heavy snow and the big workout turned my cold into the full-blown flu. By the next morning Moby Grape had all but vanished, becoming just a lump in the parking lot that took the better part of an hour for me to dig out. Seefeld had gotten a record two meters (nearly 7 feet) in 48 hours, an amount equal to their recent average season total.

We started driving on the worst day of the week in the Alps, a Saturday, when half of Europe takes to the highways. The shortest route to St. Moritz was closed by avalanches, so we took the Arlberg Tunnel as every ski resort in the region was flushing skiers, some of whom had been trapped for days by snowbound roads and avalanche danger.

While Seefeld was getting buried the Arlberg had gotten almost double that amount, 3.35 meters *(11 feet) in a little more than two days*. It was a shocking amount to see piled everywhere, and it had turned stylish resorts into high-end refugee camps where the slopes were closed completely due to avalanche danger and so were the roads and railways.

Irate visitors, many of them Germans only a few hours from home, were seething at being locked down and having to pay full fare for it besides. Lawsuits were threatened, guests were defying stay-put orders only to get stranded while trying to flee, and the tensions among the entitled had made their way onto CNN and into the European newspapers.

The barely plowed roads were crammed with cranky drivers and we crawled all the way through Lichtenstein into Switzerland under blue skies before the traffic volume eased. Then as we started up the Julier Pass toward St. Moritz, conditions deteriorated again and we had to chain up for the second time that day. As the storm jacked up its intensity levels we kept inching onwards when we moved at all, passing stuck cars, cars spinning out, cars turning around, cars chaining up, cars going sideways, while the plows were presumably laboring somewhere up ahead.

Conditions on the Arlberg and Flexen Passes when we were in Lech and St. Anton had been some of the gnarliest winter driving I'd done in years, even though I lived at 8,000 feet in the Colorado Rockies. This was uglier. And the last sprint over the summit was a free-for-all, power run with the few of us that were still moving betting everything on momentum as we drifted around switchback turns with trucks and cars off to every side, with us fish-tailing, crossing-up, but still climbing, blasting through the drifts that were growing by the minute as

Cross-country skiing by the Linderhof Palace near Garmisch-Partenkirchen, Germany's snowiest resort.
Photo © by Jay Cowan.

oncoming traffic materialized directly in front of us out of the stormy darkness like last-minute pop-ups in some seriously demented video game with real world consequences. And what should have been a three or four-hour drive, tops, had stretched to 9 by the time we crested the Julier Pass and drifted unsteadily down into St. Moritz.

Village of Andermatt, Switzerland is one of the snowiest in the country. Photo by W. Bulach.

CHAPTER 17

PART THREE – THE SAVAGE WINTER AND RECORDS IN THE ALPS

Switzerland and France

SWITZERLAND

It had been snowing and blowing in St. Moritz just like it was on top of the pass, and when both stopped the next day the temperature plummeted to -29 Celsius (20 below zero, Fahrenheit). The town was hosting its annual Polo on Snow Tournament along with their regular World Cup bobsled competition, and an internationally famous Gourmet Festival. In other words it was just another weekend in January in St. Moritz.

At almost 1,828 meters (6,000 feet), St. Moritz has four different ski areas in the immediate vicinity topping out at 3,303 meters (10,837 feet) at the summit of the Corvatsch cable car. So there is usually good snow somewhere. Thus St. Moritz/Corviglia is 5th in the snow-online snow-sure rankings for Switzerland. Their average annual snowfall from 2012 through 2022 was unexceptional at about 2.6 meters (9.5 feet), but they had numerous years in the three and four-meter (9.8 to 13.1 feet) range and had to cancel the women's World Cup races in early December of 2020 due to avalanche danger. That season their snowfall total was 1.3 meters above average.

Diavolezza/Lagalb on the Bernina Pass has snow coverage very similar to Corviglia, plus the Morteratsch Glacier right out Diavolezza's back door. The Corvatsch ski area, just across the narrow Engadine Valley floor from St. Moritz, also has similar snowfall with predominantly north facing slopes mostly sheltered in the shade giving it better snow retention than Corviglia. It wasn't snowing when we were there but much of the good stuff was closed from avalanche danger due to what had already fallen.

We ended up taking the long route from St. Moritz to Zermatt via Andermatt and then on the car-train through a tunnel from the Rhine to the Rhone Alps. The 7-hour drive across central Switzerland was another journey through a white universe and the results of the prodigious storms were amazing to see. The siege was starting to take a serious toll and the press had begun tracking the story. Getting to see it firsthand all across the Alps was a journalistic opportunity, the trick was to survive it as I continued gathering book material and filing stories with the Aspen Times newspaper back home.

We had to chain up again climbing to Andermatt in one of the snowier parts of Switzerland, at the center of the Saint-Gotthard Massif, and this winter it had drifts the size of buildings. The resort doesn't make the snow-online top 10, apparently for lack of a lift-accessed glacier. But the town's elevation is 1,437 meters (4,715 feet); its highest cable car reaches 2,955 meters (9,800 feet); and its average snowfall at the town of 4+ meters (13 feet) – with years of 5.03, 5.42, 6.55 and 6.83 meters in the mix – is some of the deepest in the country.

Historically, Andermatt has been in the middle of several of the Alps heaviest snow events. During the Winter of Terror, as noted in the previous chapter, it was struck by 6 avalanches where 13 people died. During a severe 2018 storm system they were cut off for days. And in March of 2021, following one of their biggest poundings in years, they reported a 5-meter (16.4 feet) base, with only Engelberg topping them in Switzerland at nearly 6 meters (18.5 feet).

Engelberg, not far from Lucerne and Zurich, averages well over 5 meters annually with 34 snow-days at more than half a meter each, ranking it number four on the snow-online Swiss list. With a summit at 3,028 meters (9,934 feet) it's famous for its powder, especially on the 1,190-vertical-meter (3,900-foot) Laub.

We made a grocery store stop then drove onto a train just above Andermatt and ate before we drove off at the other end of the tunnel into the high end of the Rhone Valley. The snow alongside the highway towered above us and was mounded so deep on buildings that they were virtually invisible.

In Zermatt the next day I found less snow up on the slopes than down in town, mainly due to the wind. Zermatt tops the snow-online list, thanks to several glaciers along with the Matterhorn and a cluster of other 4,000-meter (13,123 feet) peaks in the area creating heavy snowfall for a region that also includes Saas Fee one mountain range away and number two on the list behind Zermatt. The latter averaged 3.5 meters (11.5 feet) of annual snowfall from 2012 through 2022 with three seasons of well over 5 meters, and it has a top elevation of 3,899 meters (12,795 feet), one of the highest in Europe.

The seasonal average at Saas Fee beats Zermatt by over a meter, coming in at 4.66 (15.28 feet), with the 2017/'18 season registering a jaw-dropping (and record-setting) 11.36 meters (37.27 feet). That same winter a single storm dropped two full suffocating meters, helping boost their average storm total to .72 meters (2.33 feet), one of the highest in the Alps. In the big 2018 storm both Zermatt and Saas Fee were cut off for several days due to extreme avalanche danger.

The Loetschental is the largest valley that intersects the northern side of the Rhone Valley and is part of the Jungfrau-Aletsch Protected Area, the most glaciated in the Swiss Alps. Access to the Milibachgletscher endears it to snow-online which ranks it 8th on their list. Given its average annual snowfall of 6.36 meters (almost 21

Skiing deep in the Vallee Blanche in Chamonix in the Mont Blanc Massif. Photo © Jay Cowan.

feet), it should probably rank higher. That average has been achieved by breathtaking seasons of 12.65 (41.5 feet), 11.55 (37+ feet), and 10.52 meters (34.5 feet), with ones of 7.92 and 7.88 added for good measure, and 35 snow-days that average nearly .6 meters (almost two feet).

Arosa, not on snow-online's top 10, is nevertheless commonly considered one of Switzerland's snowiest resorts. Snow-online credits it with an average of 4.64 meters (15.22 feet) that included seasons of 8.12, 7.43 and 5.38 meters from 2012 through 2022, and never one less than 3 meters. Another source, Current Results, posts annual averages from a period of 1981 to 2010, and reports Arosa's as 7.22 meters (23.68 feet). WeatherToSki. co.uk, one of the most reliable sources on the continent, places it's historical average at 6.2 meters (20.34 feet) and ranks it as the snowiest major resort in the country.

Fraser Wilkin and WeatherToSki.co.uk (which he writes for) have listed Braunwald, an hour and half from Zurich, at number three or four of their snowiest resorts in the Alps in separate stories. Their historic record of 9 meters (29.5 feet) of average snowfall at midway includes three years starting in 2017 they averaged 9.68 meters, 7.77 meters and 7.86 meters *at the base*, as per OnTheSnow. Though Braunwald is easily the snowiest in Switzerland, it gets less attention than other resorts due to its relatively small size and vertical and lack of a glacier.

In mid-March of 2021 a major snowstorm battered Switzerland with up to 1.8 meters (6 feet) of snowfall over three days, inundating a number of resorts, Andermatt and Engelberg among them as mentioned earlier. Glacier 3000 and Les Diablerets near Gstaad also went deep, reporting a record-setting 1.57 meters (over 5 feet), accompanied by gale force winds.

Laax, number three on snow-online's list, got a meter out of that January 2021 storm that focused on the central Alps. Their 4.46-meter (14.63 feet) seasonal average is a result of getting successive seasons of 10.2, 8.47, 5.88, 7.16, and 5+ meters since 2017. Sadly they had five pretty dry years before that. They can get a lot of snow-days, averaging 32 but ranging up to 66, with .52 meters per storm. Add those numbers to a big glacier, and snow-online will love you every time.

After a leisurely lunch in a soft rain overlooking Lac Leman from the French side, we headed back into the mountains, thinking maybe the heavy weather was finished. We hadn't gone more than 10 or 15 miles, all uphill, before the drizzle became a thick snow and I chained up while cars and big trucks whizzed blithely past. We soon caught up to all of them, either pulled over, stuck on the side, or spinning to a halt in the middle of traffic.

FRANCE

Our grind on up to Chamonix was one of the tensest drives I've ever made anywhere due primarily to maniacal big truck drivers without chains who refused to give up when they were clearly going to spin out and seemed determined to take as many of the rest of us with them as possible. When we finally careened into town the snow was already nearing half a meter deep and the highway was shut down soon after that.

As it turned out, Zermatt had closed behind us, and Chamonix effectively shut down as soon as we got there. I was starting to feel unwanted as the legendary tourist office director Bernard Prud'homme explained all this to us the next morning.

The skiing was completely locked down in Chamonix due to avalanche hazard. It was still snowing and Prud'homme was Gallic in his apology. "It is the most snow we have in 20 years," he observed with a helpless shrug. Reservations were being cancelled by the thousands during one of their busiest weeks of the winter, so I was the least of their worries.

Word was coming in about a slide that had crushed a café and killed the owners in Wengen, very near where we were headed next. During what was being described as "the heaviest snow in decades" over the weekend, Reuters reported that 6,000 people were trapped in ski resorts in western Austria, primarily in the Arlberg of Lech and St. Anton, and the Paznaun Valley where Ischgl and Galtur are located.

Moreover, conditions all across non-mountainous Europe were horrendous. Planes, trains and automobiles were stopped altogether. Severe cold was gripping Scandinavia, heavy snow had closed the international airport in Sarajevo, and the army was called out in Belgium to clear motorways of hundreds of trucks that couldn't make it up icy hills.

Part of the magic of Mont Blanc, the highest mountain in Europe outside of Russia, is its favorable impact on snow conditions of the resorts located nearby. Courmayeur, as discussed earlier, is one of Italy's snowier resorts. And Chamonix's Aiguille du Midi and Le Grands Montets come in at 9 and 10 on the snow-online French list. Chamonix's snowfall history is derived from a weather station very near the base of the Aiguille du Midi cable car. Numbers for Les Grands Montets are from a slightly higher and snowier station.

The Chamonix average of 3.6 meters (almost 12 feet) at the Aiguille du Midi base from 2012 through 2022 may not be as much as some might expect, but not awful either. Big years of 5.08, 4.57 (twice), and 6.65 meters are bogged down by three weak seasons. The resort averages 31 snow-days at close to half a meter per storm. What makes all of this even better is the accessibility of the Mer de Glace and other glaciers. I've skied the Vallee Blanche and the Pas de Chevre on the same day in untracked, knee-deep snow, which doesn't happen every day but isn't totally unheard of either.

On February 9, 1993, while we were in Chamonix, a devastating avalanche tore down the mountains near the bottom of Les Grands Montets and 17 chalets in the villages of Montroc and Latour were buried. Eventually 12 people – tourists and locals alike – were confirmed dead, including four children. More than 20 were dug out of the rubble alive, two in critical condition. It was the worst such disaster in the region in 90 years. [For more details please see chapter 25].

The storm finally let up the next day (after depositing two more meters before, during and after the slide) so helicopters and rescue personnel were able to get to the scene. The day after that, they opened the bottom part of Les Grands Montets, within half a mile of where the Montroc avalanche was still being probed. I managed to get in some of the best powder lines of the trip, which felt good but pyrrhic at some level considering what this same snow had caused so nearby.

The rest of France's snowiest resorts include La Grave at number 6, where the terrain is unpatrolled and largely uncontrolled. One of the only times I've seen it shut down was when the top station of the telepherique was closed for a few hours because they had to dig it out. Its neighbors are Alpe d'Huez at 4 and Les Deux Alpes

Skiing La Grave/La Meije, France where they don't groom and deep powder lasts. Photo © Jay Cowan.

at 3. The Southern Alps where they're all located are one of the snowiest parts of France, with Alpe d'Huez raking in an average snowfall of 4 meters (13.1 feet) that can range well above 5, and storms consistently in the half-meter vicinity with big blasts up to a meter. The village is surrounded by glaciers and its altitude at 1,800 meters (6,102 feet) is also helpful.

Les Deux Alpes accesses one of Europe's biggest glaciers with a top elevation of 3,600 meters (12,200 feet). Their seasonal snowfall average is very similar to their close neighbor La Grave's at just under 3 meters (10 feet). They don't get a lot of snow-days or huge single storms, but benefit from the glacier.

Once again the numbers for these areas are deceptive because they're recorded at the bases. They all benefit from their high altitudes and storms boiling in from both the Atlantic and Mediterranean. La Grave especially is known as some of the best powder skiing in the Alps with it's ungroomed snow and big-time terrain.

It's probably no coincidence that positions one, two and 5 on the snow-online list are all concentrated in the Savoie Region in the Tarentaise Valley and include the most popular resorts in France.

L'Espace Killy in Val D'Isere/Tignes holds down the snow-online top spot with a nearly 5-meter snowfall average that can go well over the 6-meter level and is never less than 3, making it one of the most consistent resorts for fresh snow in the country. And that's before you factor in the glaciers. Its conditions are also assisted by an average of 40 snow-days annually, which is some of the most in France.

Fraser Wilkin writing for WeatherToSki.co.uk thinks one of the strengths of Val d'Isere/Tignes is that 60% of its slopes are above 2,500 meters (8,202 feet). And it also gets weather from the southeast out of Italy, which he notes is, "a privilege not extended to other nearby mega-resorts such as Courchevel or La Plagne."

However, WeatherToSki only ranks Val d'Isere/Tignes as third in France (and 9th in Europe) behind Avoriaz (at 6th in Europe), with an average of 32 snow days and a seasonal snowfall average of nearly 7.9 meters (26 feet) at the resort level, noting that "nowhere else even comes close" in France. And La Rosiere is second in the country with a 6.4-meter seasonal average.

Though Val d'Isere hasn't commonly gotten big storms like 1999 was generating, it did in February of 1970 with one that resulted in an horrific avalanche crashing into a hotel, killing 42 and injuring 60 in one of the worst such tragedies ever in the Alps. [Please see chapter 24 for more details]. Nearly 30 years later after major progress in predicting and preparing for avalanches across the Alps, it was still proving impossible to anticipate every freakish possibility.

Number two on the snow-online French list, the sprawling Les Trois Vallee with its 600 kilometers (372+ miles) of slopes, is spread across such an endless landscape that it's hard to pin down average snowfalls. The four settlements in Courchevel are scattered from 1,450 to 1,850 meters (4,757 – 6,069 feet). Meribel is 1,450. Val Thorens is the highest resort in Europe at 2,300 meters (7,545 feet). The lowest ski area included in the region is Brides-les-Bains at 600 meters (2,000 feet).

For Meribel/Courchevel/Val Thorens, the meters of average snowfall are 2.8/3.26/5.69. Snow days range from Meribel's 24 to Courchevel's 30, to VT's chart-topping 46 days, part of why it has a reputation as one of France's snowiest ski centers.

Paradiski at number 5 on the list includes Les Arcs, La Plagne and Peisey Vallendry, tucked into another part of the Tarentaise. Les Arcs gets around 3 meters annually, and La Plagne has a 4.77 meter average that includes seasons of 6.68, 5.24, 6.27 and 8.22 meters, spread across an average of 39 snow-days, which is top 10 in the country.

That still leaves out a few other French locales that get a lot of snow but not a lot of love from snow-online. Another of Wilkin's favorites is Flaine in the Haute Savoie, where it sits at 1,600 meters (nearly 5,250 feet) and tops out at 2,500 (8,202 feet). He cites its annual natural snowfall of close to 6 meters (19.6 feet) at the base and a colossal 15 (49.2 feet) at the top of Grandes Platieres, making it what Wilkin calls, "the snowiest skiable mountain in the Alps." It's location on "one of the highest points on the windward side of Mont Blanc," puts it directly in the path of the predominant storms from the northwest, in an area where the fronts are rising quickly against the mountain and purging moisture. Wilkin notes that the Haute Savoie area "generally has high snowfall averages relative to height."

SWITZERLAND, AGAIN

The morning after my day at Les Grands Montets we rolled out of Chamonix under bright blue skies bound for Switzerland with two more stops on our way back to Munich and a flight home. Behind us we left grief, confusion, and the strong chance for more of the same to follow. Other avalanches had already struck around Chamonix, closing the Mont Blanc tunnel and sweeping down near a small ski area that had continued running throughout the week. Until then.

And it wasn't necessarily any better where we were going. The death toll in avalanches in Switzerland so far had climbed to 12. According to the Swiss Federal Institute for Snow and Avalanche Research (SLF) in Davos, the country's Alps received 1.5 meters (5 feet) of new snow in three days at the start of the week. "This is one of the largest snowfalls we've had," the center's Martin Schneebeli told the press. "It's the worst since the winter of 1984/'85."

Earlier in the week heavy snows had forced airport closures in Zurich and Basel, as well as the Gotthard tunnel into Italy, and even the famously punctual Swiss postal system had succumbed to irregularities, having to deliver mail by boat to snowbound Interlaken.

We chained up just above Interlaken to start our short run up to Grindelwald where the road had finally opened after three days, just two hours before we got there. It had been closed due to fear of slides that could be set off by the traffic. Grindelwald's close neighbor Wengen had suffered a bad slide that took out a mountain restaurant and killed the two owners a few days earlier.

Veteran tourist office director Joe Lugen told us when we finally skittered into town that it was the most snow they'd had in 30 years. It was also the first time anyone could remember the road and train closing simultaneously for any length of time. The news of the couple being killed in their restaurant in Wengen, and a ski lift getting partially taken out by a slide at the Grindelwald First ski area, coupled with road closures and helicopter evacuations, had predictably dampened tourism at the resort.

Like others they were starting to feel they were getting unfair press and falling back on the inevitable strategy of blaming the messengers. Where Grindelwald felt most wronged was that they were closing roads and ski slopes to save lives, yet most of the focus was on the lives being lost and the inconveniences being suffered by paying guests because of the necessary safety measures.

It wasn't a situation anyone could remedy and it was unlikely that any news organization was going to ignore one of the most lethal winters ever in the Alps unless some other more sensational story came along.

In the meantime we went on about our business. The mind-boggling lineup of mountains over 13,000 feet which face Grindelwald, Wengen and Murren includes the Wetterhorn, the Shreckhorn, the Eiger, the Monch and the Jungfrau. As sheer and dazzling as any wall of mountains in the world, they are naturally the major influence on local weather.

Our first full day was bluebird but the only slopes open were the south-facing ones of First, rising above Grindelwald proper. Such a stellar Saturday would normally have generated big crowds but it was relatively deserted owing to bitterly cold temps and lingering fears about avalanches.

As I rode the lower chair with my guide we could see much of the off-piste scarred by gaping fracture lines, like the ruined marble palladiums of some lost civilization. There were also substantial sloughs and slides readily visible near the marked runs, and up higher we saw the remnants of the drag-lift that had been wiped out.

The snow that was stable was incredible, well over a meter deep in most places, and we managed to work in a little untracked off-piste as did a few others. Three-foot-deep slabs of the glistening fields would break off with us, well above ground level, and inch along on a lower layer of slick hard-pack, rarely gaining any momentum on the low angle pitches and huffing to a stop as soon as the slope flattened.

Grindelwald's snowfall history is for the combined region of Grindelwald-Wengen, with Grindelwald's base listed at 1,034 meters (3,392 feet), and car-free Wengen's elevation 240 meters (about 800 feet) higher. From 2012 through 2022 they averaged right at 3 meters (10 feet). That included four bad years in a row of 2 meters or less, along with one of nearly 7 meters (23 feet) in the big 2017/'18 season. Their average of 24 snow days doesn't historically include many large single snowfalls.

However, in January of 2021 the Jungfrau region of Grindelwald, Wengen and Murren received up to a meter of snow over a 48-hour period. Murren, perched at 1,638 meters (5,431 feet) on a shelf above the Lauterbrunnen Valley across from Wengen, has a snowfall history very similar to Grindelwald and Wengen's, albeit with fewer highs and lows.

Naturally, it had started snowing again on the morning we left. I never took the chains off while Moby Grape was parked and I left them on until we got most of the way to Davos. It was briefly sunny on the drive up to the resort, but quickly reverted to full deluge mode. I realized that the nervous tic in my eye when I parked the van in our already snowbound hotel parking lot was because I knew I'd be digging it out in a few days for the umpteenth time on the trip.

Davos-Klosters averages 4 meters (13.12 feet) of snow annually with a healthy 38 snow-days. And during the World Economic Forum earlier in the month powder poured down in the background of every reporter's shot as they filed stories. The result was the same as when the Denver Broncos play a home game in December and they have to plow a foot of snow off the field. Reservation lines in ski areas all over Colorado light up, and that's what had happened in Davos. It didn't matter what the economic news coming out of the Forum was, all the skiers of the world saw was snow piling up faster than it could be removed.

Alas, what looked like a godsend on the first of February had turned brutal by the middle of the month. There was a running daily tally in the Herald Trib for the avalanche and storm deaths throughout the Alps that frequently carried quotes from the avalanche center in Davos. So that even though no one in Davos had died so far from the weather, it was often the dateline for stories about death and destruction. And the tolls kept mounting in what was by then being called the biggest snow season in Europe in 50 years.

In addition to the human misery there was, of course, also a serious financial hit taking place. The "Hotel und Touismus Revue" in Switzerland announced that the storms had cost Swiss tourism in excess of $20 million for the first half of February alone. Estimates of the losses into the next winter season were too grim to even publicize at the time.

At that point Davos had plenty of customers since skiers had been making reservations while watching it snow on TV, and then they all showed up. And the four areas that surround the town had even managed to stay partially open. I got out with approximately one million others the next day on the Parsenn slopes directly above town.

Then it started to snow again and everything shut down for avalanche control as the hollow, long-range booms of avvy charges echoed over town. And it didn't change when the new day dawned with another two feet of fresh and no hope that anything worth skiing would open. Moods were turning ugly and tempers flared as hotel staff couldn't provide useful information about anything.

Unable to ski, it seemed like a visit to the Institute for Snow and Avalanche Research in Davos might be in order. Established in 1942 it had been tracking such info on the continent for over half a century. However, the institute's forecasters and scientists were overwhelmed with work and weren't accepting any visitors or doing interviews. Reporters were relying on the daily summaries being handed out by the center and it was clear the Institute had little interest in helping generate any more disaster-related press coverage than they could avoid. By the end of the winter they would announce a total of 36 avalanche deaths in Switzerland.

After I dug out our van in anticipation of leaving in the morning, it continued to snow and deposited yet another two feet overnight. You'd think I'd learn. And of course I got no help from the hotel in liberating my ride, leaving us with the uneasy feeling that if the lone open highway out of town wasn't already closed it would be soon. And we needed to get to Munich that day so we could catch our early morning flight home the next.

Le Serac hotel in La Grave, France, receiving a nice overnight storm. Photo © Jay Cowan.

Having to reschedule, given the *sturm und drang* of all travel anywhere at that time, was too much to contemplate. So I launched into an even more frenzied effort to free and load Moby Grape, incurring permanent tendonitis in my elbows and the wholesale wrath of the Sunstar management when I loudly bitched-out their total lack of service in a lobby full of other irate guests.

In spite of unplowed streets, highways full of stranded vehicles, a broken tire chain, murderous snowplow drivers on the autobahn and a general fuck-off-and-die attitude everywhere, we were one of only a handful of cars that made it out of town before the highway was closed for another three days. And we got home as scheduled.

But our absence in the Alps did nothing to change the weather. Two days later an avalanche in Evolene, Switzerland killed 12 [For more details please see chapter 25]. And the day after that, two massive avalanches came down in and near Galtur, Austria, destroying parts of two villages and killing 38 total. [For more details please see chapter 24.]

It took a while for the experts to unravel what had happened that winter, but when they did it clarified our experience. The North Atlantic Oscillation played an important role in a record-breaking and disastrous storm bombardment that was due primarily to a stable northwestern wind with heavy snow that produced a stunning number of avalanches. According to the Snow and Avalanche Research Center around 1,400 destructive avalanches occurred in the Swiss Alps that winter, compared with an annual average of 136.

As Timothy Oleson wrote in Earth Magazine, "Relatively light precipitation early that winter gave way in late January to the first of three major snowfalls that blanketed the Alps. From Jan. 27 to Jan. 31, about a meter of snow fell over large expanses of the mountain range, brought on by the combination of a high pressure system off Europe's Atlantic coast and a low-pressure front over Scandinavia."

Marie Rousselot and colleagues at the Snow Study Center at the National Center for Meteorological Research in France analyzed that winter for a piece in the Journal of Glaciology in 2010, writing that, "Fast altitude streams conveyed cold and wet air from the Arctic regions to the northern Alps." Those conditions also brought high winds from the northwest creating a system that is, "often associated with intense precipitation and major avalanche release in the northern Alps."

The pattern persisted with a second larger snowfall from February 5th to the 10th that produced about 1.3 meters of new snow around Galtur and almost 2 meters in Chamonix. And a third system from February 17th to the 25th "roared across the same areas that had been inundated by the earlier snowstorms,"wrote Oleson, with the result that "tens of thousands of people were stranded for days in remote mountain hamlets across the Alps as road and rail traffic ground to a halt." In sum, it created what Oleson described as "one of the most lethal [seasons] of the 20th century."

CHAPTER 18

PART FOUR – GLOBAL STORMING: NORTHERN AND SOUTHERN EUROPE

NORTHERN EUROPE

In a part of the world where substantial chunks of the countries lie north of the Arctic Circle – consisting more of ice caps, glaciers and tundra than soil and where much of their snow theoretically never melts – it stands to reason that they can also get large amounts of snowfall. Consider Norway, for example, where they get steady snow *every month of the year*, with the temperatures to sustain it for much of that time.

On April 8 of 2020, according to Watchers.news, "A number of snowfall records tumbled across Norway, particularly its northern region, over the weekend." State meteorologist Eirik Samuelsen observed that Northern Norway had been practically buried all season and with more heavy snow on the way it looked to be Tromso's snowiest ever. In Breivikeidet, 1.2 meters (4 feet) accumulated on April 5th to 6th. "I have never experienced so much snow in one day," said Samuelsen.

By mid-summer of 2020, headlines in the country announced, "Southern Norway Enters July With Record of 10 meters (32 feet) of Snow." A spokesperson for the company doing snow-clearing operations said they had never seen amounts like it before. Local media reported, "The region is currently so cold that the snow is hardly melting, but the situation could change with heavy rainfall, causing rapid melting. The goal of snow removal is to prevent melting into the almost full channels," which would then flood the lowlands. This was in mid-July, mind you, with snow still coming down.

Northern lights (aurora borealis) behind a lit ski area in Lapland, Finland. Photo © Hari Tarvainen, courtesy of VisitFinland.com.

A year later in September of 2021, early storms that were the remnants of Hurricane Larry hit parts of Norway, Sweden and Finland, combining heavy snowfall with record low temperatures for the season. It was just another example of the fact that no time of year is immune to epic storms in Scandinavia.

In mid-December of 2012, the southwest coast of Norway was battered by snow and winds that broke records set as far back as 1925. Over .7 meters (2.3 feet) piled up during the two-day storm in parts of Sandnes. One source noted, "Schools closed and hundreds of motorists were stranded in their cars on the E39 highway, prompting local Red Cross and other aid workers to use snowmobiles to offer some contact and reassurance until snowplows could make the road passable."

Bergen is said to be the snowiest city in Norway with an average of 2.2 meters (7.2 feet) a year. Kvitfjell and Hemsedal are two of it's snowiest ski resorts, with averages only slightly higher at around 2.5 meters that can inflate to double that on any given year. The snow falls during 30 to 60 snow days at each resort, spread out over a season that runs from late October to late April. Stryn Sommerski, the largest summer ski area in Northern Europe, is directly adjacent to a glacier though most of the skiing isn't on it. With an average of 6 meters (19.6 feet) snowfall a year, it doesn't have to be.

The most snow on record for a year in Norway's Nordland was in Dunderlandsdalen during the winter of 1919/'20, when 3.7 meters (12.13 feet) were recorded. That amount has been called into question, most notably by a study from Cryospheric Research at the University of Manchester in the UK in 2016.

Whether this number, which is similar to one in Sweden's far north in Kopparsen in 1927, is reliable or not, it's instructive that both are well below some of the record seasonal snowfalls in southern Sweden and Norway, not to mention single storm cycles in Lebanon and Iran. It's part of the evidence from all over the world showing that some of the biggest single snowfalls occur when it's warmer and in regions close to oceans and large lakes. Now it appears that its snowing more in areas above the Arctic Circle as they warm and their once permanent ice caps begin to melt and free up more surface water to generate precipitation.

Just as with Alaska, skiing in Northern Europe can have an extended season due to their far-north latitudes. July snowfalls are so common in Scandinavia there has been active debate about whether to consider them as part of the preceding winter's tally, or the upcoming one's (they go with the latter). Some years they're mostly inundated for 9 months. The only real drawback for skiers is that sunlight is low and brief during the shortest days of the year. But lighted slopes are common and fun.

With Sweden, as in most countries that receive appreciable amounts of snow, there has been an increased effort to understand and predict how snow-producing weather works. And they've discovered what other countries are finding: large cumulative snow totals over a season don't necessarily coincide or overlap with extreme snowfall events.

In their Bachelor of Science thesis from 2017, Matilda Cresso Nygren and Martina Frid concluded that, "The extreme snowfall give a much more scattered picture with no clear pattern, compared with the cumulative snowfall which suggest a relatively clear trend."

Historically the part of Sweden that has gotten the most snow is in the north in mountains along the Norwegian border because of the higher elevations and lower temperatures. However, the thesis confirmed that warmer temperatures (within reason) tend to create more snow in single storms than colder ones.

Northern Sweden does get some big snow events to bolster their season-long totals. In early February of 2015, a 50-year-old record was broken in the northern Swedish city of Lulea, more than 100 kilometers north of the Arctic Circle, when they received 1.13 meters of snow, passing the town's previous mark from 1966 by two centimeters. It was noted that a record for northern Sweden from 1926 still stood, when a snow depth of 3.27 meters (10 feet 9 inches) was measured in Kopparsen, north of the Arctic Circle. However, there has long been some question about those measurements.

On March 19, 2020, heavy snow fell over Sweden's northernmost town of Kiruna in Lapland, where four different ski areas, including cross-country and heli operations, benefitted from a season of 3.25 meters that broke the old record set in 1997-'98. The vice-chairman of the municipal council was quoted as saying, "We have already set a record and we know that it can be another meter before the season is over. It is positive when a winter town delivers." Indeed.

Some of Sweden's "snowiest ski resorts," as gauged by onthesnow.co.uk, are concentrated in the north, among them Hemavan, Bjorkliden, and Tarnaby (hometown to the likes of Ingemar Stenmark, Anja Paerson and Stig Strand).

True-color image showing much of Scandinavia covered by snow; acquired by Jacques Descloitres at NASA GSFC, courtesy of NASA.

Others (such as Are, Lofsdalen and Bydalsfjallen) are in central Sweden closer to Stockholm and the moisture-manufacturing waters of the Baltic Sea. On November 9/10 of 2016 in Stockholm they broke a 1985 record by getting .39 meters (15.35 inches) in a single day, with unconfirmed reports that most of it fell in 6 hours. They were hit by a *snokanoner* ("snow cannon") – lake-effect storms caused by a cold air mass moving across warm water (the gulf stream that runs through the Baltic) and producing rapid accumulation.

More predictable and reliable for skiing are the consistently snowy winter averages at the major ski areas of around a meter total, while sometimes burgeoning to two or three. That's accomplished a bit at a time, almost never more than .4 meters at a single storm during the 2012 through 2022 period.

In late February of 2020, most of Finnish Lapland was placed under a stage three avalanche advisory for the possibility of both natural and man-made avalanches in areas such as Kilpisjarvi, Ounas-Pallas, Yllas-Levi, Saariselka, Luosto-Pyha and Ruka . All of those also happen to be in the onthesnow top 10 for snowiest resorts in the country.

The Finnish Meteorological Institute (FMI) said that parts of Lapland had seen record amounts of snow for the winter to that point, though the all-time mark of 1.9 meters from April 19, 1997 in Kilpisjarvi wasn't broken. In data that has been kept in Finland since 1961, Kilpisjarvi holds the top three places, and 6 of the top 10.

Located in Lapland near the northernmost point in Finland, its subarctic climate almost qualifies as alpine tundra, with winters described as "very long, cold and snowy." Kilpisjarvi doesn't have any ski areas but most of the snowiest ones in Finland are in the province of Lapland, with Ruka, Yllas-Levi, Pallas and Luosto-Pyha rounding out the top 5.

The systems responsible for Finland's deepest storms are the product of "large, shore-parallel, quasi-stationary snow bands occasionally observed over the Gulf of Finland." They involve the Baltic Sea generating lake effect dynamics, along with a cold easterly large-scale flow along the gulf, and a cold local flow from the two near and opposite coastlines of Estonia and Finland that take the form of two land-breeze cells that collide offshore.

Parts of Iceland's northern coastline brush up against the Arctic Circle and only small parts of Norway, Sweden and Finland are further north. As an island, Iceland has two dominating weather influences. One is the notorious North Atlantic Oscillation that creates an enduring low-pressure system between Iceland and Greenland called the Icelandic Low. Were it not for the moderating effects of the North Atlantic Current that Iceland is directly in the path of, its winters would be decidedly icier.

"The Icelandic winter is relatively mild for its latitude, owing to maritime influences and proximity to the warm currents of the North Atlantic Gyre," says Wikipedia.

The country's subpolar oceanic climate along the coasts gives way to tundra in the interior and the weather can change abruptly, powered by fierce winds. Moisture rising off the surrounding seas cools rapidly in the subpolar air and then dumps where it encounters mountains that range up to 2,110 meters (6,922 feet) at Hyannadalshnjukur.

Being situated as far north as it is, it can snow right down to the ocean in Iceland from October through May. In early December of 2015, the nation's capital in Reykjavik, at sea level, received .42 meters (16.5 inches) of snow to make it the deepest for that month since records began. The previous record of .33 meters (13 inches) was on December 29, 2011. January of 1937's .55 meters is still their snowiest month of all time.

Iceland's biggest ski resort of Blafjoll, only a few minutes drive from the center of Reykjavik, gets very close to 4 meters (13 feet) of average snowfall at midway during their December through April season, as per snow-forecast.com. And if you throw in November, that's another .33 meters (13 inches).

The ski resort at Hlioarfjall is some 400 kilometers west of Reykjavik and many say it's the best skiing in the country. With a base (500 meters) that's higher than Blafjoll's summit, and a summit at 1,012 meters, according to snow-forecast.com, it also gets substantially more snow, 5+ meters (16.66 feet).

In both of the above resorts and most of the other 11 in the country, wind whipping across the North Atlantic and raking the country on a regular basis can have a profound effect on the snow. It can produce refills of powder on some slopes even when it doesn't snow much. But it can also create serious drifting and crust and make the perpetually dicey driving conditions even worse.

A larger and more northerly island nation than Iceland has been the focal point of skiing expeditions since the late 1800s. Greenland, though physically a part of North America, is geo-politically considered part of Northern Europe, at least in part because its still owned by Denmark (that despite the insane offer in 2018 by US President Trump to buy it).

The world's biggest snowy island, where Scandinavian explorers first started traipsing about on skis over 150 years ago, only has three small ski areas today. However it does have multiple guided glacier skiing opportunities via snowmobiles, or for boat and land-based touring and heli-skiing, as well as freeride ski camps and cross-country training experiences.

Greenland's base depths humble the biggest glaciers in the Alps, with an ice cap that's an average of 1,500 meters (4,900 feet) thick. But it doesn't get huge amounts of annual snowfall. For example, the snow season in relatively snowy Nuuk lasts from October to June, but its snowiest month is December with an average of only 9.7 inches. That can change abruptly, though it doesn't happen often.

Interest in the weather on Greenland has been keen for a while with some records going back to the 1870s. Most closely monitored is Greenland's "surface mass balance" that measures how much ice melt it loses every year versus what it gains. On balance that hasn't been going well for several decades as ablation (melting) has far outpaced accumulation and has become a leading bellwether of climate change, particularly given the impact on global ocean levels it has.

Since the new millennium several unusually big snow events have taken place, including in October of 2016 when a series of large storms struck the island dumping 264 millimeters of rain in the main town of Tasiilaq compared to an average for October of 83 mm. That spiked the accumulation numbers going into winter, but was the result of the warmest summer on record.

Near the end of September in 2021, Hurricane Larry, which would take a toll in Scandinavia, stopped in Greenland on the way. At that point it was a tropical storm accompanied by high winds and dropped heavy snowfall over the interior and southeast parts of the island. According to Lauren Andrews, a glaciologist with NASA's Global Modeling and Assimilation Office, "Such storms are quite rare. They generally dissipate well before reaching as far north as Greenland. Though there have been similar storms, including Noel in 2007 and Igor in 2010."

NASA called the snowfall "abundant" and parts of Greenland's east coast were estimated to have gotten two inches of liquid precipitation, the equivalent of two to three feet of snow. It was unusual to see such a big snowstorm so close to the end of the melting season, and helped offset what had been a summer with three notable melting events. There were no reports on how such early season powder skied.

THE BALTIC

In spite of their proximity to the moisture generator of the Baltic Sea, the Baltic States of Latvia, Lithuania and Estonia, don't get as much snow as their Scandinavian neighbors and as a result have little in the way of alpine skiing. Nevertheless, Tallinn, Estonia tops the Holidu "Top 10 Snowiest Cities in Europe" list with 20.5 snow-days per month in winter. Vilnius, Lithuania is second, Turku and Helsinki in Finland are 4th and 5th, Kaunas, Lithuania is 7th, and Riga, Latvia took 8th, giving the Baltic countries a near sweep of the top 10.

Heavy snowstorms "wreaked havoc" in Lithuania in late January of 2021, bringing over .32 meters (over a foot) of wet, weighty snow to Vilnius in two days, with tens of thousands losing power and roads not opening for days.

That these relatively modest snow amounts caused so much trouble is an indication of how little snow Lithuania is used to receiving.

The same is true for Latvia where Skiresort.info sums up the skiing by describing it as, "17 kilometers of slopes, served by 73 ski lifts." And Latvia.travel acknowledges, "Even though Latvia is not a land of mountains, skiing is a popular wintertime activity. Latvia's terrain is generally suitable for cross-country skiing." So is its snowfall, which is largely provided by machine.

Of course the region does get dumped on from time to time with wet lake-effect snowstorms off the Baltic Sea. In a study by the Royal Meteorological Society published in 2022, they examined the influence in the Baltic area of, "heavy snowfall events of possible sea-effect origin." As they noted, "The analyzed region is not very snowy, with an average of 40 days with snow cover in the winter season and a mean maximum snow depth of 8 – 12 centimeters."

In part they concluded that, "The bipolar pattern of sea level pressure with a high-pressure over Scandinavia and a low-pressure system southward of it was identified as favorable for sea-effect snowfall on the southern Baltic Sea coast." Just as with everywhere else on the planet, current climatic factors play a huge role, and the study observed, "global warming conditions seem to reduce the frequency of snow events over the Polish Baltic Sea coast."

RUSSIA

Russia stretches across a vast swath of the northern latitudes where it's easy to assume they must be loaded with snow, especially on the likes of the continent's tallest peak, Mount Elbrus, where there also happens to be a ski resort. And what about Siberia? The name alone is a synonym for cold, and if you've ever read *Tent Life in Siberia*, or even watched *Doctor Zhivago*, it seems like the region is mostly endless snowscapes with the occasional yurt, reindeer herd and gulag.

Befitting its immense scale, Russia gets snow in a variety of different ways, including moisture laden fronts off the Black Sea; seasonally rich lake-effect dumps powered by Lake Baikal before it freezes over; and almost daily snowfall in the far north of the Arctic Circle as well as the Great Caucasus Mountains in the towering heights of the Elbrus region's 5,000-meter peaks.

The latter reaches across 1,200 kilometers between the Black and Caspian seas, with over 2,000 glaciers and an annual snowfall of up to 55 feet. As per Geographic Expeditions, a climbing and skiing travel service specializing in the region, in the western part of the Caucasus winter lasts from October to April above 2,000 meters, with "abundant and frequent snowfall." In the eastern part, "Heavy snowfall is usual, sometimes with bad storms."

Formal snowfall measurements don't exist in most of Russia, but Mount Elbrus is considered the snowiest place in the country and is listed as getting up to 40 inches of precipitation some years, with no translation into what that amounts to in snow. One source reports that the Elbrus ski slopes get 8 to 13 inches of weekly snowfall on average throughout the winter, to go with what they call the "eternal" snow in its 134 square kilometers of glaciers and snowfields.

Of course a big reason Elbrus is thickly swaddled in ice and snow and also notoriously stormy is because it's the highest peak in Europe at 5,642 meters (18,510 feet). That combo makes it number one on the snow-online.com Russian list, offering both lift-served and heli-skiing.

The Cheget Ski Park, not far from Elbrus in the south of the Elbrus region, ranks number two on the list, also hosting glaciers and benefitting from the climate of the central Caucasus Mountains, which lie in the contact zone between Atlantic and Mediterranean humid air fronts, and dry continental air masses originating over inner Eurasia.

The Arkhyz Region in the middle of the Western Caucasus Mountains reportedly gets 50 feet of snow annually, and is surrounded by high mountains that protect it's lift-served and heli-skiing from wind and some of the more brutal temperatures associated with the rest of the range.

Then at the end of the Western Caucasus and less than 50 kilometers from the Black Sea, the Krasnaya Polyana Mountains are home to the Krasnaya Polyana complex of four ski mountains that fill out the rest of the top 6 of the snow-online.com list. The village of Achishko at 6,600 feet is said to have measured snow depths of as much as 315 inches. The Olympic venue of Sochi, the biggest ski resort in Russia, is also located in the region.

Snowy resort in Vostok, Primorsky Kray, Russia. Photo by Russian Dissident.

All are said to be "famous for dry and deep Alaskan quality powder," and draw frequent comparisons to Valdez and Niseki, Japan. That's because those cooler, drier arctic masses of the Central Caucasus collide with "moisture-laden breeze air from the Black Sea" creating "a unique environment for perfect powder," according to one of several heli-ski operators in the region. According to many sources, the Khamar-Daban region south of Lake Baikal is the best in the region from November through mid-January before the lake freezes over and the "massive snowfalls" and "huge quantity of low density powder snow" tapers off.

North of the Arctic Circle are resorts like Bolshoi Vudyavr where the copious snow lasts more than 250 days a year. And on the far frontiers of Russia in eastern Siberia are a number of lift-served ski areas, along with several heli operations and ski touring centers. In a story by Dmitri Vasin for the Moscow Times extolling the skiing, he opens with the stinging line, "Siberia is not generally known as a holiday resort."

Indeed, Vasin notes that in Tsarist and Soviet times criminals and political convicts were exiled there (and by most reports some still are). He also mentions that Sheregesh, one of the region's best ski resort towns, was founded in 1912 because of large iron ore deposits. Then he adds, "The mine they opened is still bringing out iron ore, and on a clear day you can see smoke from the mine's chimney rising up into the sky. Until the 1980s there was no real infrastructure for skiing here – just the mine and a maximum security prison, now closed."

Nothing in that quote is something you would find in any other country's promotional material for a resort. Nevertheless, Sheregesh's popularity has boomed, particularly with skiers from the Urals and Siberia and increasing numbers of Russians. And the reason is the snowpack of, "7 to 8 feet and sometimes more."

In a story by Andrew Lyle in March of 2022, his reasons to go to Siberia included its scale, its lack of crowds and the snow. A sampling of his plugs for the latter include: "The mountains are high enough for guaranteed snowpack… the snowfall is epic, with a heavy powder arriving as early as November and lasting well into spring…And snow it does! It is even possible for a meter of snow to fall within 24 hours… During the winter it can snow for more than 25 days in some areas."

The sheer scale of Siberia has led some commentators to call it the largest reach of unexplored skiing still remaining on earth. When bundled with the western Caucasus Mountains, Russia can legitimately lay claim to a large share of the planet's potentially last best ski places. Whether it's via lifts and snowcats, or touring and heli-skiing, more of it is being accessed every year, from the Baltic to Kamchatka, from the Arctic Ocean to the Black Sea. In a world assailed by climate change, the far northern outposts of Russia may hold hope for the survival of skiing into another century. Perhaps in the meantime they'll start really keeping track of their snowfall. On the other hand, they hardly have to bother.

SOUTHERN EUROPE

Especially as the climate changes, ski resorts located closer to the equator seem less likely to get and hold snow, and when they do it is generally at higher altitudes. This is true in the Pyrenees Mountains that separate Spain from France. With numerous summits over 3,000 meters, and big, sloppy wet fronts coming off the Atlantic and Mediterranean, they can get snowfall comparable in amounts to resorts in the Alps.

Baqueira/Beret, the ski resort for Val d'Aran and Valls de Aneu, Spain,had their best season ever in 2022, beginning with an early three-day storm that dumped two meters not long after opening. The international-caliber ski resort is perched on the "wetter" northern side of the Pyrenees and got 9 meters (29.5 feet) total by the end of March at its highest altitude of 2,655 meters (8,713 feet).

Measured at its base of 1,524 meters (5,000 feet), onthesnow.com has their average since 2012 at .91 meters (3 feet), though in the record season of 2021/'22 it was nearly three meters. In 2012/'13 they got 3.87 meters (12.7 feet) at the base, but struggled after that for 7 years with natural snowfall. They kept their ranking at number two on the list by having 70% coverage with snowmaking.

Number one in Spain is Valle Nevada, despite being the most southerly ski resort in Europe; having an annual average of only .2 meters with their biggest season since 2012 being .7 meters; and only 40% coverage by snowmaking. But their summit is at 10,826 feet, the highest in Spain, where they get considerably more snow and hold it well. Their base of nearly 7,000 feet also keeps the snow it gets longer than other Spanish resorts. All 5 of onthesnow's snowiest Spanish resorts have summit stations above 8,600 feet.

The Sierra Nevada range (which literally translates as "mountain range covered in snow" and is home to Valle Nevada), has a Mediterranean climate that above 2,500 meters (8,200 feet) becomes Mediterranean subalpine.

Mountain restaurant at Baqueira, Spain, with deep snow on roof. Photo by Faras.

And the Pyrenees Mountains in general, with their alpine and subarctic climate, have historically received heavy snowfall.

Portugal has only three ski areas and they're all in the Serra de Estrela, or Star Mountain range, that's roughly 100 kilometers (62 miles) long and gets most of its moisture from the Mediterranean. In 2018 the small Serra da Estrela ski resort had what may have been its snowiest season ever with a series of huge snowstorms that struck most of Portugal and left drifts up to 6 meters (19.6 feet) that took them two days to dig through on the highways and under the lifts. It's average annual snowfall figure since 2012 at the base from onthesnow is three centimeters, including 8 seasons with zero. However, by snow-forecast.com's midway measurements the seasonal average from 2007 through 2022 has been 1.5 meters (just under 5 feet).

Tiny Andorra, wedged into the Pyrenees between Spain and France, also has only three areas but they are higher, bigger and snowier than Portugal's, with an emphasis on natural snow. Grandvalira resort is the largest and most sophisticated in the Pyrenees and has averaged 1.13 meters annually since 2012, with higher numbers 5 different years, including 3.17 meters in 2017/'18.

Vallnord/Pal-Arinsal has averaged .91 meters (3 feet) since 2012 with 6 years deeper than that including 2.26 meters in that snowy 2017/'18 season. Snow-forecast since 2007 has them at roughly a 2.1-meter (7-foot) average.

Winter house in Jahorina, Bosnia and Herzogovinia after an avalanche. Photo by BrsJvnvc.

CHAPTER 19
PART FIVE – GLOBAL STORMING:
EASTERN EUROPE

Poland, Czech Republic, Slovakia, Romania, Ukraine, Greece, Serbia/Kosovo, Bosnia/Herzogovina, Greece, Bulgaria, Hungary, Croatia, Montenegro, North Macedonia, Belarus, Moldova

The skiing in Eastern Europe seems a little like Montana in the US. A lot of small, family-style hills with old chairlifts and platter-pulls and great atmosphere, plus a handful of heavy-hitting resorts that could compete anywhere in the world.

The first task at hand is to define "Eastern Europe" for the purposes of this chapter. The United Nation's official list encompasses 9 countries and part of another: Poland, Belarus, the Czech Republic, Ukraine, Hungary, Slovakia, Romania, Moldova, Bulgaria, and the eastern part of the Russian Federation. All of Russia was covered in the previous chapter. And for logistical reasons this section of the book also includes Croatia, Bosnia/Herzegovina, Greece, Serbia, Kosovo, Montenegro, Albania and North Macedonia.

With 269 ski resorts, Poland has more than any other EE country. Their nearly vowel-free resort of Szczyrk is the snowiest and also biggest in the country. Zakopane-Kasprowy Wierch (ZKW), at fourth, is the country's highest. As usual, the 'snowiest' stats are weighted toward glaciers and/or consistent coverage with snowmaking. Szczyrk has the latter wall-to-wall, or what onthesnow.co.uk calls 100%. Because ZKW is 2,400 feet higher at it's top station than Szczyrk, it gets a lot more natural snow, but has no snowmaking.

Szczyrk's annual snowfall is in the 1.1 to 1.4 meter range (onthesnow.co.uk measures from 2012 to 2022, snow-forecast.com from 2006). During that same period ZKW, with a large altitude advantage over most of the other resorts in the country, comes in at two to 4.6 meters.

Many older Poles say that cold and snowy winters used to be the norm, but now when they happen its news. Though several are cited, one comes up most often as Poland's 'Winter of the Century,' and that's the harsh 1978/'79 season.

An account from notesonpoland.com described it this way: "The extreme cold and snowdrifts paralyzed much of the country for weeks on end, starting around New Year's Day, when the coast bore the brunt of a storm coming in from Scandinavia and was buried under half a meter of snow, leading the Gdansk provincial governor to declare a state of natural disaster. Tanks were brought in to clear passages through the snow." That must have been disquieting given the country's not so distant history of being ruled by the military-backed communist party. Suwalki in northeastern Poland had .84 meters (2.75 feet) on the ground in mid-February and Warsaw had .7 meters cm (2.3 feet).

A December 2013 paper that analyzed heavy snow in the Polish and German lowlands found that "intense snowfalls" tended to result from deep low-pressure systems over central Europe, and that the snow stays on the ground a long time due to generally low winter temperatures. Though Poland isn't as mountainous as much of Eastern Europe, what they have in the southern part of the country can magnify those characteristics as moisture blows in from the North and Baltic seas and slams into Scandinavian and polar cold fronts. Storms of .2 to .3 meters (8 - 12 inches) aren't unusual at resorts like Zakopane and Szczyrk.

The Czech Republic is much smaller than Poland in square miles, but has nearly as many ski areas at 241. Mountain ranges are concentrated on the country's borders and include Snezka, the highest in the country at 1,603 meters. And in spite of being landlocked, they get a stout stream of wet weather pouring off the North Atlantic to the west and the Baltic Sea to the north that keeps their relative humidity high. The climate is temperate, between an oceanic and continental one with generally mild winters. When they get cold fronts over the mountains there is usually enough moisture to make it snow.

Two resorts in the Czech Republic (CR) rank in the top three for both 'snowiest resorts' and 'top ski resorts.' The smallish Sachty, with anemic natural snowfall – an average of .81 meters at the base since 2012. But it has full snowmaking coverage.

Number two on the snowiest list is the biggest resort in the country, 120 clicks northwest of Prague in Klinovec, spanning the border with Germany, which sends it a lot of visitors. With a top elevation of 4,081 feet and 1,578 feet of vertical, it's also credited with 90% manmade snow coverage and a presentable 1.5 meters of average annual snowfall (in a range of .47 to 2.48 meters since 2012).

Spindleruv Mlyn, number three on the list, gets the most natural snow of the top Czech resorts, with an average of 2 meters, ranging from .39 to 3.34 meters since 2012. It's located in the Krkonose Mountains with a top station at 1,235 meters (4,052 feet), and roughly 85% snowmaking coverage.

The highest ski resort is Praded in the Jeseniky Mountains in northern Moravia at 1,438 meters (4,717 feet), where the tourist office says, "there is usually around 2 – 3 meters of snow lying there. That is why the ski area is nicknamed 'The Moravian Iceberg' although, in fact, there has been no iceberg for a few thousand years there."

Though the CR has no ski resorts on glaciers, it does have a number of seasonally fluctuating snowfields, including one on Studnicni hora, the third highest peak in the country at 1,554 meters in the Giant Mountains. According to the tourist office, "The largest volume of snow fell there in the 1999/2000 winter season, when the depth of the snowfield reached a record 16 meters. Snow can usually be found there until July or August."

Slovakia is considerably higher than its former partner of the Czech Republic to the west, making it an even bigger beneficiary of the same high-precipitation fronts that roll across the CR. It's snowiest resort (per onthesnow) at Tatranska Lomnica in the High Tatras, tops out at 2,633 meters (8,641 feet). As might be expected, its annual snowfall comes in at double Spindleruv in the CR: nearly 4 meters (13 feet), in a range from .56 to 7.45 meters. From 2012 to 2022 it had three seasons over 7 meters (23 feet) and another over 5. Big league stuff. Throw in 90% manmade coverage and onthesnow will happily sing your glories.

The smaller resort of Strbske Pleso comes in at number two on the snowiest list. With a top elevation at 1,840 meters (6,574 feet) and a base of 1,376 meters (4,514 feet), it's the highest village in the High Tatras. Located in the Presov region, it has 100% snowmaking and its snowfall average has been 3.37 meters, in a range from 43 centimeters to 6.46 meters, including four seasons over 4.5 meters.

Number three is Jasna, probably the nation's most famous and largest resort, it hosts World Cup races, has a top station at 6,574 feet, and about 67% coverage with man-made snow. It, too, gets over three meters of snow annually, at 3.26, with no seasons under a meter in 2012 to 2022, and three in a row that averaged 5.5 meters.

Cable cars at Jasna, Slovakia, in the snowy Tatra Mountains. Photo © Pudelek (Marcin Szala).

Snow days at all three of these resorts number in the 40s, and storms are routinely in the .2 to .4 meter (8 – 16 inches) range with cold enough average temps to maintain them well into spring. Most of the rest of the country's 98 ski areas are lower and more in the elevation range of the Czech Republic.

Romania is typical of Eastern European countries with a strong skiing public served primarily by smaller more entry-level, family oriented areas. When you have 97 resorts with a total of 225 kilometers of slopes the average mountain doesn't have more than a couple of kilometers of runs.

Deep in Transylvania's Carpathian Mountains and only 23 kilometers from Dracula's Castle, Poiana Brasov ranks as Romania's "biggest and most luxurious mountain resort" according to the Romanian Tourist Office. At 1,783 meters (5,849 feet) on top and equipped with 100% snowmaking, it's also onthesnow's snowiest resort. Natural snowfall stats are iffy, but snow-forecast has them on average between 1.5 and 2 meters (5 and 6 feet).

Sinaia resort has a top station elevation of 2,090 meters (6,865 feet) and comes in second on the list. It appears to get around 2.5 natural meters (8.3 feet) annually, per snow-forecast, with 62% snowmaking coverage. In spite of its onthesnow rating, other reports say its conditions are unpredictable at best. "Romania, contrary to popular belief, has relatively dry winters," says the writer of a list called Emerging Europe's Top 10 Ski Resorts, who placed Sinaia 10th due to "unreliable snow" and frequent wind, which others have also written about. In fact, there is a suspicion that drifting may account for some of it's snow depth reports.

Screenshot of CNN story about a "snownado" in Greece.

Romania does get clobbered at times. As witness a mid-February storm in 2012 when "snow as deep as 15 feet isolated areas in Romania, Moldova and Albania." Starting in the end of January the region got some of "the heaviest snowfalls in recent memory" with tens of thousands snowed in and hundreds dead. In Romania they lost 79, many of them homeless. Four thousand Romanian coal miners volunteered to buy tins of foods from the money the company gives them for hot meals and donated it to some of the worst affected victims.

The Ukraine, with 58 ski areas, got pounded in some of that same 2013 weather as Romania with more than 120 people freezing to death on one weekend. It shares a border with Romania and that's where most of its mountains are, in the Carpathian chain that reaches for 1,700 kilometers from the Czech Republic through the Ukraine and a big swath of central Romania while also making appearances in Austria, Slovakia, Poland and Serbia.

The largest ski area is Bukovel, a contender for the title of "biggest ski resort in Eastern Europe," with 68 kilometers of runs and 19 lifts. Snowfall records are nearly impossible to come by and the Russian invasion hasn't helped. Bukovel, in the Ivano-Frankivsk province with a top station at 1,372 meters (5,250 feet), isn't renowned for its natural snow. It's said by unconfirmed sources that it gets less than a meter on average, but has 100% snowmaking coverage, to the point where they advertise a 6-month ski season from November through May.

The country is situated in a good flow of moisture originating off the Baltic to the north and the Black Sea to the south. But its relative lack of altitude and mountains are an impediment. And a savage and senseless war is far worse of one. At this point, climate change may be less of a business factor for ski resorts in Eastern Europe than local political instability and the regional wars that have gone on seemingly forever in the Balkans.

With 25 ski resorts, Greece is one of those countries that many people are surprised to hear has skiing at all. But it's actually quite mountainous, with 12 primary ranges and a number of lesser ones. And even though it's the southernmost of the Eastern European countries, it's about the same latitude as Denver, Colorado, which gets plenty of snow.

As the tip of the Balkan Peninsula, Greece has a lot of water around it generating moisture. And it has the elevation to turn it into snow. Even Athens, in the southeast of the country on the Attic plain, is surrounded by mountains on three sides and gets snow occasionally. Sometimes as much as Denver, such as in February of 1911, when a mind-boggling 1.5 meters (nearly 5 feet) covered the city following a multi-day storm. Not surprisingly that's still a record.

The stat got lots of circulation in 2021 when the country got clobbered again in February and .15 meters (6 inches) fell on the capital. That was one-tenth of what the storm of 1911 delivered, but probably caused as much havoc all told. They got hit again on December 11 that same year when satellite data showed 19% of the country under snow cover, breaking a 17-year-old record.

Late the following January of 2022, a 36-hour storm named Elpida assailed Greece and parts of Turkey, "causing chaos on the streets of major cities and forcing the evacuation of thousands of people," as CNN reported. Up until then, Athens had seen only 6 snow events since 2000, with an annual average of half an inch of snowfall. Elpida brought misery on a wholesale level with power outages, blocked highways, and closed schools, businesses and airports. It even spawned a rare and dramatic 'snownado' when a waterspout moved onshore over snow-covered land.

It was the biggest storm in Athens since 1968, with .4 to .5 meters of snow falling in the city. Weather services blamed the jet stream that had dipped down into the Balkans for several days, bringing polar cold with it. This caused an anticyclone to be blocked over part of southern Europe, forcing disturbed weather around it and into Scandinavia and the eastern Mediterranean.

What these mega-storms demonstrate is the extremes of a climate that, while it is rated as Mediterranean in its lower reaches, produces, "cold winters with strong snowfalls in the mountainous areas in the central and northern regions," as per Wikipedia. The biggest ski areas in Greece all have top stations near or above 2,000 meters (6,561 feet) and get enough natural snowfall that snowmaking is minimal.

The biggest resort in the country at Mount Parnassos tops out at 2,260 meters (7,415 feet) and ranks third on snow-online.com's snowiest ski resorts in Greece list. Snow-forecast.com lists their seasonal average as 2.865 meters (9.4 feet) at midway.

Number one is Voras Kaimaktsalan in central Greece, with its highest elevation at 2,480 meters (8,136 feet) on Kaimaktsalan Mountain. Its average annual snowfall December through April on snow-forecast.com is 3.4 meters (just over 11 feet) at midway.

Kalavryta-Helmos comes in number two while getting by far the most natural snow of the top three, at a commendable 4.66 meters (15.3 feet) on average at midway. With a top station at 2,325 meters (7,627 feet) in the Peloponnese Mountains of western Greece, it's one of the bigger and more remote of the nation's resorts, located 62 kilometers northwest of Tripoli.

In Serbia and Kosovo, where there are 25 ski areas total, there is no agreement between the two countries on whether Kosovo is part of Serbia or an independent state (as they declared themselves in 2008 after protracted hostilities). One of the results is that it further complicates getting to slopes that can be as much as four or five hours from any viable airport.

Kopaonik, "by far the largest and best" ski resort in the country according to Ski Serbia, is located in the Dinarske Mountains, four hours from Belgrade.

They also say it, "has a remarkable snow record considering its southerly latitude and...good sunshine record (200 days/year)." With a base elevation of 1,057 meters (3,467 feet) and the top at 2,017 meters (6,617 feet), it's also one of the highest resorts in the nation on one of its biggest mountain ranges. Those factors help produce average snowfall of 3.1 meters (12 feet 2 inches). Snow-forecast concludes, "Comprehensive artificial snow production and normally plentiful natural snowfall ensure a long season."

And then there is Brezovica. Yugoslavia used to be a dynamic European ski country, "from Kranjska Gora in the north to Papova Shanka in the south," as Tim Neville wrote in the New York Times in 2016. "Brezovica, about 250 miles southeast of Sarajevo, served as a backup" for the 1984 Sarajevo Olympics. "But Yugoslavia's most hard-bitten skiers already knew the place for offering the steepest slopes and deepest powder for the fewest dinars."

Starting from a base higher than most of the summits in Serbia at 1,718 meters (5,636), it rises to 2,522 meters (8,274 feet) in the Sharr Mountains, giving it a substantial advantage over any other resort in the region. And its deep powder has been the stuff of legends for decades. It's just been getting to it that's a problem.

Once one of the most popular resorts in the region, it flourished as an attraction for regional Serbs as well as Russian, German and UK tourists. But Brezovica became a ghost-resort during the Yugoslavian breakup and the Balkan wars, and ambitious plans to resurrect it have foundered.

Intrepid skiers who ventured there in most of the 2000s found it both "awful and awesome." Sometimes lifts run, sometimes you have to shop for rides up in snowcats, most of the time you sit and wait while the snow piles up, which by all accounts it does regularly. A foot a night isn't unusual. And the locals just shrug and hike it, which seems like the sensible approach since it is epic and mostly deserted when you finally get to it.

Bosnia/Herzegovina comes up next in the rotation with 22 ski areas, more or less, and again one of them is a relative colossus while most of the others have a couple of kilometers of runs each. In this case the big dog is Jahorina, which hosted some women's alpine events in the 1984 Olympics.

The central Dinaric Alps extend through BH and all the way down to Albania, ending only a short distance inland from the sea. In BH, which is mostly mountainous, the Dinaric reach heights of over 2,300 meters (nearly 8,000 feet), creating a formidable snowmaking landmass for the moisture coming off the water.

This includes the eastern part of the Dinaric's where the 1984 Olympics were held. Jahorina resort's namesake mountain gets 4.4 meters (14.5 feet) of annual snow. "Snowfalls are usually abundant and are complemented by artificial snow," according to skiresort.info.

The country as a whole seems to get hammered by crippling snowstorms fairly often thanks to its location and geography. In mid-December of 1995 according to AP reports, "Almost two feet of snow fell on Sarajevo in 24 hours, blocking public transportation and cutting water and power to much of the Bosnian capital." It was called the biggest snowfall the city had seen since before the 1984 Olympics.

WorldDataInfo.com reports that the most precipitation ever recorded in BH fell in December of 1999, at the rate of 15.1 millimeters per day. The Mostar weather station recorded it as the highest monthly average in 67 years. The 468.1 millimeters (18.42 inches) may have been roughly equal to about 5.6 meters (almost 18½ feet) of snow, in that single month. It is likely, however, that most of the precipitation actually fell as rain so ultimately those numbers are hard to believe since Mostar typically gets snow from December 13th through the end of February, and the average is one inch.

In early February of 2012 the AP headlined a story, "Evacuations underway after record snowfall in Bosnia." It went on to say, "Bosnia used helicopters on Sunday to evacuate the sick and deliver food to thousands of people left stranded by it's heaviest snowfall ever." More than 100 remote villages were left cut off by two meters

(6.5 feet) that fell in the mountains. The single meter that buried Sarajevo caused a state of emergency to be declared. Avalanches in eastern Bosnia stranded some in their cars on highways for 20 hours.

Bosnia, like much of Eastern Europe, had a refugee crisis in early December of 2020 when the first heavy snowfall of the year highlighted yet again the exposure of homeless immigrants sheltered in flimsy tents that were no match for the cold and snow. As the Euro-Med Monitor noted, "The snowfall since last Wednesday in Bosnia has dangerously worsened the conditions of almost 3,000 migrants and asylum-seekers."

Bulgaria has a great snow-producing combination of geography and location in the chubby part of the Balkan peninsula. With the Adriatic to the west, the Black Sea to the east and the Aegean to the south, Bulgaria is surrounded by water. And given that the word balkans is Turkish for "mountains," Bulgaria comes well-equipped with those too. In fact the namesake range of the Balkans exists almost exclusively in Bulgaria, running along the border between it and Serbia and then eastward across Bulgaria, dividing it into northern and southern halves. In the central and eastern sections of the country the range forms the divide for watersheds that feed either the Black Sea or the Mediterranean.

Of Bulgaria's 20 ski areas only three are reckoned to be on a par with western Europe, and those are Bansko, Borovets and Pamporovo, in the order they are listed for onthesnow.com's snowiest resorts, first through third. Once again the rankings are weighted according to their snowmaking capacities.

Jahorina Ski Resort is one of the snowiest in Bosnia and Herzogovinia. Photo courtesy of Wikimedia.

Bansko, in southwestern Bulgaria, gets a healthy average of 3.48 meters (11.4 feet) annually, as per snow-forecast. com's numbers at midway. It sits at 1,200 meters (3,937 feet) with a summit lift that reaches to 2,600 meters (8,500 feet). Second-place Borovets gets a strong 4.47 meters (14.66 feet) of the natural goods. Situated along the same highway as Bansko but an hour closer to the capital of Sofia, it's the oldest winter resort in the country. Pamporovo comes in third at 3.05 meters (10 feet) of actual snowfall. Considering their base elevation is 1,000 meters lower than Bansko and nearly 800 lower than Borovets, that's not bad.

In March of 2015, Bulgaria got hit with what was called their biggest snowstorm for 30 years that blocked roads and brought down power lines across the country. Ski resorts were reporting .6 to .9 meters (2 to 3 feet) in 48 hours, much of it in the 24-hour-period from Saturday to Sunday, when Borovets reported .6 meters (two feet). "Ski areas have attempted to continue operating despite the logistical problems the snow has caused," reported J2SkiNews. Pamporovo closed the whole ski area for a while, and Bansko closed their gondola for an hour on Saturday, and that same day three snowboarders were killed in an avalanche riding off-piste from Bansko.

Perhaps by virtue of its central location in the middle of Europe, Hungary is exposed to some of its harshest winter weather. Encircled by no fewer than six other countries it can sometimes serve as a clearinghouse for storms in the region. Their record number of snow days occurred in the winter of 1943/'44 with154, which is astounding. But it didn't account for the record snow depth of 1.51 meters that fell around Koszeg, which was measured in February of 1947. That was good news for skiers who had introduced the sport to the area in 1892.

On January 10, 1987 a fiercely cold blizzard struck creating drifts several meters high that blocked highways and buried cars. By January 12, .2 to .4 meters of snow covered the country.

In March of 2013, Al Jazeera reported, "Large parts of Hungary had to deal with crippling snow, causing major transport problems and leaving thousands without electricity." It was a rare assist to their 15 hills with ski lifts, most of which have snowmaking capacities but few slopes to apply them to.

Spread along more than a thousand miles of Adriatic coastline, Croatia had little in the way of skiing tradition following WWII. Today they host 11 ski areas along with a big reputation in World Cup racing based primarily on the brother and sister duo of Ivica and his sister Janica Kostelic, who was the best female racer of her time.

As in Hungary, all of the Croatian ski areas are quite small. The Kostelic's home hill is Sljeme, only 10K from the capital of Zagreb and the busiest resort in the country. Their 300 meters of vertical (nearly 1,000 feet), plus ample snowmaking, is enough for them to not only train Olympic and World Championships gold-medalists like the Kostelics, but to also host men's and women's World Cup slaloms.

The country is more than 50% lowlands, but the Dinaric Alps run through the other part of it and contain all of its highest summits, one of which is above 6,000 feet. Croatia has a moderately warm and rainy oceanic climate for the most part, with the bulk of its precipitation falling at the higher elevations in the Dinara Mountains and in Gorski Kotar, where, per Wikipedia, "some of the highest annual precipitation totals in Europe occur." It usually turns to snow above 1,200 meters (3,900 feet), which is higher than the top of most of its ski areas.

Nevertheless, Sljeme, with a summit at 1,030 meters, gets some natural snow, with an annual average of 1.34 meters (4.5 feet). Platak, the highest area in the country topping out at 1,363 meters (4,471 feet), gets almost double that, with 2.28 meters (7.5 feet), proving once again that height matters.

While their resort's snowfall records aren't exactly dazzling, the country is subject to occasionally heavy weather. When Zagreb got .68 meters (over two feet) in 24 hours in January of 2013, is shattered a record for the city that had stood since 1881. Of course, the ski area at Sljeme wasn't able to open to enjoy most of it.

And in February of 2018, according to Euronews, "record snowfall and sub-zero temperatures paralyzed parts of Croatia… causing havoc on highways and prompting authorities to evacuate several villages." Delnice in western Croatia, received 1.82 meters (almost 6 feet) in less than two days. Its nearby ski area of Petehovac was buried in what had to be an all-time record, but without the pitch to enjoy it even if they had been able to get dug out.

Close to two-thirds of Montenegro consists of mountains and river valleys, while their coastline on the Adriatic reaches for 294 kilometers (183 miles) and features the Bay (or Gulf) of Kotor that helps generate weather in the area. "Precipitation in Montenegro is plentiful," according to climatestotravel.com, "especially in the coastal strip and in hilly and mountainous regions overlooking the sea." In fact, areas such as Cetinje receive some of the highest amounts of rain on the entire European continent.

The predominantly Mediterranean climate of Montenegro becomes colder and is classified as continental as elevations rise. Cold air masses from Russia can turn all that precip into snow in a hurry in the mountains of the interior with downslope winds that help enforce temperatures more consistent with the Alps than the Adriatic. According to Wikipedia, "the high mountains of Montenegro include some of the most rugged terrain in Europe," and they average more than 2,000 meters (6,562 feet) in elevation.

The 11 ski areas in Montenegro include two notables. Kolasin 1450 & 1600 is located in the Sunjajovina Mountains of central Montenegro, with a top station at 2,072 meters (6.797 feet). Kolasin's "snowy period of the year" lasts from late October through April and January is generally the snowiest month with an average of .25 meters (10.2 inches), as per weatherspark.com. Nothing to write home about, but temperatures are consistently cold enough at elevation to create good snowmaking conditions.

Zabljak, northwest of Kolasin in the Durmitor Mountains, has more elevation and consistently colder temps, but snowfall stats of any kind seem to be virtually non-existent for it.

As with most of the Balkans, Montenegro is subject to fits of extreme weather. Their heaviest snowfall in 63 years took place in mid-February of 2012, "sealing off hundreds of villages, shutting down roads and railways and closing the main airport," as the Associate Press reported. The .52 meters (20 inches) that fell on the capital of Podgorica was the most since 1949. An avalanche closed the rail line into the resort of Kolasin and stopped a train with 50 passengers who had to be rescued by another engine. But such conditions appear to be strongly anomalous.

North Macedonia is one of the newest (2019) and smallest nations on earth. Made mostly of mountains, the former Yugoslavian Republic of Macedonia is north of Greece and its swath of ground carved out of the Balkans has been a crossroads in southeastern Europe for centuries. Most significantly for our purposes, it's also one of the snowiest parts of the whole region.

The country has no outlet to the sea, and is separated from the Adriatic and Aegean by high mountain ranges. Climatestotravel.com notes that their winters are cold and that the whole Balkan Peninsula is "exposed to cold waves from the north and east, and Macedonia is no exception." The northwest wind that blows down their dominant Vardar River Valley is called the *Vardec,* similar to the *Bora* that plagues the Adriatic, but less violent. What makes the cold winds so potent is a lack of offsetting warm fronts from the Mediterranean that have trouble making it through the mountains. Though Mediterranean moisture also has trouble reaching the country, it has three large lakes that provide precipitation to go with those aggressive cold fronts.

The February 12/13 snowstorm that swept over the Balkans in 2012 really punished North Macedonia and showed why it gets the kind of powder skiing they're (quietly) known for. It wasn't just the cold that made things brutal, and the snow depth of .5+ meters in Skopje and other cities before the wind got hold of it, but also the avalanches that came down in the mountains of western Macedonia, more than 30 in two days, stranding motorists and causing food and medicine shortages.

With 9 ski areas, Powderhounds.com says that, "Skiing and snowboarding in North Macedonia is not hinged on its couple of reasonable ski resorts, but mainly on backcountry powder and some of Europe's longest running and best cat skiing operations. [It's] attractive as a powder ski destination because of its abundance of snow and lack of local freeriders (lots of freshies for visitors!)."

Popova Sapka (aka the Priest's Hat) is considered the best resort in NM and has cat skiing as well as lift-served slopes. One of the oldest and best cat skiing operations in Europe is located 70 kilometers west of the capital of Skopje in the high Shar Mountains. Powderhounds reports that the Shar typically get annual snowfall between 5 and 10 meters, "but it can vary markedly from month to month and season to season."

From Popova's base at 1,700 meters (5,557 feet) you rise to the summit at 2,525 meters (8,284 feet) where the slopes are mostly above timberline and often get substantial snow with an annual average of 5.1 meters (16.7 feet), at midway from December through April, with an additional 10" in November, per snow-forecast.com.

One of the snowiest places in the country is Mount Karadzica in the Jakupica Mountains of north-central Macedonia. The highest peak in the range is 2,540 meters (8,333 feet) and Karadzica is next at 2,473. The ski area there is small but gets 5.2 meters (17 feet) of annual snowfall at midway, with another 22 inches in November.

On October 30, 2021, the director of the Macedonian Agency for Foreign Investments and Export promotion announced that three new luxury ski centers would be built on the site of several of their current areas. It was a project that will cost north of 800 million euros and was still seeking funding at the time. It's designed to promote the country as a top ski destination to attract not just Europeans but tourists from China and the Middle East. The sites were chosen due to their nearness to major airports, as well as famously good conditions, with the town of Krusevo at 1,350 meters cited as "a kingdom of snow."

It's obviously no coincidence that the Eastern European country with some of the fewest ski areas – Belarus with 6 – is also the one without much terrain. Tourism officials note that they have no mountains, "but there are high hills and steep ravines," though none are as high as the "skyscrapers in Shanghai."

It's hard to imagine they'd have skiing at all if it wasn't for the fact that they get a lot of snow. And they proudly point out that while they have no vertical feet at any of their ski areas over 100 meters (335 feet), they tout the advantages of quick lift rides on the small hills, and also a lack of avalanche danger. Seriously.

Though it's landlocked, Belarus is only separated from the Baltic Sea by smallish Lithuania, with no mountains to block the progress of sea-effect moisture toward them. The lack of elevation to help produce snow is offset by a steady flow of arctic cold fronts from Russia. The result is a country that can display almost total snow coverage during winter satellite observations, and get the occasional fierce storms that paralyze everything.

Weather-atlas.com states that, "Winter lasts on average about 100 – 120 days and sometimes can be accompanied by severe storms and high winds." In 2007 a record November snowfall of .17 meters struck the Homel region during "a cyclone from Scandinavia."

Cyclone Javier in March of 2013 crushed parts of the country for almost two days, delivering .2 meters of snow in 24 hours along with strong winds. Belarus Digest reported that, "Although the country is used to severe winters and well equipped to deal with large amounts of snow, public life has come to a halt this weekend." Some said the last time they'd seen anything similar was in the 1980s.

A January of 2017 storm was so severe it occasioned a reappraisal of the nation's Winter Emergency Plan. Snow piled up between .18 to .22 meters and was severely drifted by heavy winds across the entire country. Once again hundreds were hospitalized, thousands were stranded on highways and scores of villages went without power.

The upside, such as it is, to all of this is that they continue to get enough natural snow that there is no mention of snowmaking at any of their popular ski areas. These are set up like ski-park buffets, with tasting platters of everything from half-pipes to race-training runs to learning areas and jumping hills, all of it being eagerly consumed by thousands of locals. None of the areas are advertising powder skiing, but coverage on the largely smooth and grassy hills is good for everything else.

Moldova, sandwiched between Romania and Ukraine, has two ski areas with a high altitude of 375 meters (1,000 feet) and combined total of 3.7 kilometers of trails. It does snow there. Enough said.

CHAPTER 20
PART SIX – GLOBAL STORMING: THE MIDDLE EAST AND ASIA

Lebanon, Israel, Jordan, Turkey, Iran, Iraq, Kurdistan, Uzbekistan, Tajikistan, Pakistan, Afghanistan, India

Not surprisingly, there are quite a few ski areas scattered across the Middle East and Asia, including in places you might not expect, such as Lebanon, for example, which is mountainous enough to claim that, "some call it the Switzerland of the Middle East." It is home to the 10,000-foot peaks of the Mount Lebanon range, just off the Mediterranean, with a climate said to be similar to California's cool snowy winters that dump heavily in the mountains. They've been skiing in Lebanon at least since 1913, and today it hosts 6 ski resorts.

According to some dubious online sources, during one 5-day period in 2012, Lebanon got 40 feet of snow, for a fairly unbelievable 8 feet per day average. Other reports said that, "From February 17 to 19, a severe storm blasted the Lebanese coast with 100 kilometer-an hour winds and dropped as much as 2 meters (7 feet) of snow on parts of the country." That's a more realistic amount and still a bunch. It's not impossible that serious drifting could have occurred in places creating the alleged 40 feet.

What definitely did happen was that wet, heavy snow fell at altitudes down to 600 feet, and accompanied by those gale-force winds they decimated crops and shut down transportation. As reported by naharnet.com, "The heavy snow also forced the ski resorts of Farayya to close because of the inaccessibility of roads leading to these areas." A familiar refrain around the world.

The Global Times of China carried a Xinhua News Agency report that, "Civil Defense teams intervened in several areas of the country including Faqra and Kfardebian [where the Mzaar ski resort is] in Mount Lebanon to remove snow and allow smooth transportation of citizens in the area."

Oruu Sai Ski Resort, Kyrgyzstan. Photo by Thomas Depenbusch.

In a 2017 study by the Centre d'Etudes Spatiales de la Biosphere, snow observations were made on Mount Lebanon to contribute to understanding the weather systems at work in the region. As noted in more detail elsewhere in this section of the book, the Mediterranean has a far-reaching effect on precipitation throughout the Middle East and Asia. This study found that "the relationship between snow depth and snow density is specific to the Mediterranean climate."

Next door to Lebanon in Israel they are at the mercy of most of the same influences as Lebanon, though their mountains are fewer and smaller, reducing the amounts of snowfall in general. In terms of records, starting in January of 1950 it snowed for a two-week period that left depth totals still unequalled. It began in the northern mountains and swept to Jerusalem, where they got a meter total. It snowed in Samaria, the mountains surrounding the Sea of Galilee, in the Ngev Desert and even the Dead Sea, where .08 meters fell. It would be easy and obvious to call it Biblical. No accumulation of snow has occurred again since then in the Israeli Mediterranean coastal plain or the Dead Sea.

A two-day storm in December of 2013 dumped up to a meter in the Kefar Etzion area while the lower elevations got torrential, flood-producing rains that closed down Ben-Gurion airport. And in mid-February of 2021, "snow blanketed parts of Syria, Lebanon, Jordan and Israel…, covering areas it has not reached in years… in southern Lebanon… and in northeast Libya," the AP reported. The worst affected places, as usual in recent times, were the refugee camps for those displaced by local wars.

In a January of 2013 storm, three feet of snow was reported to have fallen on Mount Hermon in the Golan Heights, where Mount Hermon Ski Resort is the only one in Israel. The 2,814-meter (9,232-foot) Mount Hermon itself straddles the borders of Syria and Lebanon in territory annexed by the Israeli government decades ago, and is also the site of projected ski areas in Lebanon and Syria. Powder magazine once referred to Mount Hermon Ski Resort as, "The Israeli Ski Community on One of the World's Most Militarized Borders."

So snowfall might be down the list of things they worry about. But being just a two-hour drive from the desert, climate change has become an issue. With a top elevation of 2,050 meters (almost 6,700 feet), the resort has never felt compelled to make snow and have historically been open only when there's natural snowfall. That was typically January through March, but in the last three decades it has shrunk from two to three months to two to four weeks. In 1999 they didn't open at all.

Jordan would logically seem to get some sea-effect snow off the Mediterranean, they have plenty of mountains, and it's royal family were famous skiers for years. But it's impossible to find information on any ski areas and the highest mountains in the country are little more than 6,000 feet, which today may not be enough to sustain much skiing.

That January of 2013 storm that hit Mount Hermon was, "The fiercest winter storm to hit the Mideast in 30 years [and] brought a rare foot of snow to Jordan," reported the AP, noting that at least 8 people died across the region in weather related accidents. Once again war refugees were some of the hardest hit in Jordanian camps where tens of thousands were settled.

Turkey is partly in the same general fallout shadow for big winter storms off the Mediterranean, and has a reported 42 resorts to help take advantage of it. With the Black Sea bookending the country to the north they can get crossfire sea-effect storm systems. And those hit mountain ranges such as the Taurus and Pontic with numerous peaks over 3,650 meters (12,000 feet), and Mount Ararat at 5,137 meters (16,854 feet).

A 2018 report published in the International Journal of Environment and Geoinformation about the frequency of snowfall and its spatial distribution in Turkey used two data sets provided by the Turkish State Meteorological Service covering years from 1932 to 2006. The general conclusion was unsurprising in finding that the country-wide distribution of snowfall days depended heavily on factors of location, altitude, exposure and 'continentality' (the degree to which the climate of a region typifies that of the interior of a large landmass).

The results may seem obvious, but the study was necessary to establish a baseline for understanding where snow can be anticipated and how often, a process that hadn't previously taken place in Turkey. Prior to this report the trends were most graphically illustrated in the distribution of Turkey's ski areas and especially their snowiest ones. Where the country's high mountains are positioned near either the Black Sea or the Mediterranean, stunning amounts of snow can be produced, as witness the massive 1972 blizzard in Iran, immediately east of Turkey and described later in this chapter.

The city of Erzurum in northeastern Turkey sits at 1900 meters (6,233 feet) in one of the heaviest snowfall regions of the country, within hailing distance of the Pontus Mountains that front on the Black Sea. It averages 61 snow days every winter, nearly double that of most American and European ski resorts.

Mount Ararat rears up to the north of town. And Palandoken/Ejder 3200 ski resort, one of the country's largest, is just 7k away. Snow-online.com ranks them as the snowiest in Turkey. With a base elevation of 2,200 meters (7,200 feet), the top at 3,176 (10,420 feet), and so close to the Black Sea, it has averaged 3.5 meters (11.6 feet) at the base since 2006, per snow-forecast.com.

Erciyes Ski Resort, ranked second snowiest, is located near the city of Kayseri in central Turkey, in the Taurus Mountains as they join the high Central Anatolian Plateau. On the flanks of an eponymous 3,900-meter (12,795 feet) volcano, the ski area has a base at 2,088 meters and a summit of 3,346, making it the highest resort in the country. And its snowfall reflects that, with storms coming from both the Med and the Black Sea that tally up an average of 4.4 meters (14.43 feet).

Both of them very respectable, but they pale alongside Turkey Heliski-Ayder that comes in at a whopping 10.7 meters (35.33 feet) average, running from December through April. The operation is tucked into the northeastern corner of the country in the Kackar Massif, close to the Black Sea and home to some of the highest mountains in Turkey with summits at 3,900 meters in the Pontic Alps.

The country at large gets snow from stem to stern. In 2004, central and eastern Anatolia was crippled by a major three-day storm during the last week of November. At least 19 people were killed, more than 900 villages lost power and had phone lines go down, most domestic flights were cancelled, and 2,600 villages were classified as snowbound, all within 100 miles of the capital city of Ankara. In February of 2014 heavy snows paralyzed Instanbul for three straight days, breaking a 28-year-old record according to the Istanbul Metropolitan Municipality.

An extended period of heavy snowfall in late December of 2021 in the eastern Turkey province of Mus delivered up to four meters (well over 13 feet) of snow in a couple of days. A year later, at the end of January of 2022, "a strong storm hit much of Turkey, wreaking havoc," according to news reports. In Istanbul, authorities dispatched troops to clear highways and ordered military helicopters to shuttle the sick and injured to hospitals as most transportation in the city ground to a halt and 71 mosques were opened to provide shelter for those stranded. Their major new airport that opened in 2019 as one of the world's busiest, was closed down and the roof of one of the massive new cargo buildings collapsed.

On the other end of the country, "heavy snowfall and blizzards" disrupted life from Erzurum in the north to Hakkari in the south. Thousands of people were trapped on highways and schools were closed as avalanches, sub-zero temperatures and the steady accumulation of snow that completely buried single-story structures were problems throughout the province. The Gaziantep province in southern Turkey, "witnessed for the first time in 54 years snowfall with a depth of one meter."

These are the same kinds of conditions that can assail Turkey's neighbor Iran to the east. In fact, the Iran blizzard of 1972 is widely regarded as the *world's deadliest ever*, killing over 4,000 people during about a 10-day period of storms in early February that delivered anywhere from three to 8 meters (26 feet) of snow and brutally cold temperatures across northwestern, central and southern Iran. At the rate of over two and a half feet of snow falling every day, entire villages were completely buried with no survivors.

Thanks in large part to the Shah of Iran who was a devoted skier in the 1960s and '70s, there are some 34 ski areas in the country to take advantage of these storms. Most of the resorts are in the northern Alborz and Zagros mountains, roughly the same latitude as Denver, Colorado, and within two hours of the capitol of Tehran.

Skiing ropeway at Solang near Manali, India. Photo by Bleezebub.

The biggest in the country is Dizin with a top elevation of 3,600 meters (11,811 feet). They are said to average 7 meters (23 feet) of snow annually, on a par with some of Turkey and the Alp's best. And for a few years in the early 2000s Iran attracted attention as a hip new place for alpine touring in the mountains bordering Turkey and the Black Sea.

Iraq butts up against both Turkey and Iran. However, without as many mountains and being substantially further to the south, it doesn't catch as much precipitation and only has two ski areas, both of them iffy for snow.

The 'Stans' of Asia, on the other hand, are generally mountainous and can harbor huge amounts of powder, especially to the east of the Caspian Sea. But they have fewer ski areas and resorts than in Western Europe, and do far less rigorous tracking of snowfall except when something sensational happens. So instead of providing much in the way of stats they simply routinely describe their snow as both "plentiful and magical."

The Caspian, Black and Aral seas along with Lake Balkash, Lake Issyk-Kul and others have a huge influence throughout the Stans, creating some of the same kinds of weather patterns that make the areas around the Black Sea in Russia so deep.

In comparatively flat Turkmenistan, that doesn't help much and only a of hard-to-confirm ski areas are said to exist in the central highlands, while the country in general is reported to receive very little snow.

It's southern neighbor Uzbekistan, on the other hand, has a number of 4,000-meter peaks in several substantial mountain ranges. It's better known for its summer heat than winter snows, and even Tashkent in the north of the country rarely gets snow that lasts long. However, the plains of the far north reportedly get 100 snow-days a year, with 60 in the central region.

Conditions at the 9 ski areas and in the Chaktal Range for heli-skiing, are known for a deep snowpack that usually has good stability due to consistent winter temperatures. Even in their typically warmer winter weather the powder stays light for days because it's far enough from the sea that the snow is relatively low in moisture content.

Only one major, fully modern and professionally run resort has been built in the country. Called Amirsoy it's part of a billion-dollar project by a youngish oligarch in Uzbekistan, the first stage of which opened in 2019.

Amrisoy has wisely targeted the local market first, and are relying on their apparently copious and light snow to attract foreigners. One writer repeatedly referred to "waist-deep lines" at the resort and untracked snow that was days old and still blower.

View of snow-covered cabins from the Gulmarg Gondola in Gulmarg, Jammu and Kashmir, India.

Another, Sophie Ibbotson, noted in a 2020 story called The Cold Heart of the Silk Road, "The fact is that though the Russians and other hardcore skiers from the countries of the former Soviet Union knew that Uzbekistan has some of the best powder in the world, they kept the secret to themselves."

Hard to blame them, and it wasn't that difficult because the real stumbling block to skiing anywhere in the Stans has always been access. In an Al Jazeera story from 2018, for instance, Tajikistan was described as, "a country with an abundance of snow, but only one lone ski resort, 70 km north of Dushanbe, called Safed Dara."

That off-the-beaten-path aspect seems unlikely to last. The sprawling and mythical Tien Shan Mountains that cover a big swath of the Stans have gained a supernatural reputation in the ski-world that attracts more interest every year. The mountains stretch for 2,500 kilometers along the Chinese-Kyrgyzstan border and bisect Turkistan, with outlying ranges in Tajikistan and Kazakhstan. Very high altitudes throughout the Tien Shan help produce the generous quantities of snow they are said to receive, and include 7,439-meter (24,406-foot) Jengish Chokusu (aka Victory Peak), and 7,000-meter Khan Tengri Peak, the highest in Kazakhstan.

The saturated lake-effect fronts from the variety of big bodies of water in the region colliding with arctic cold masses over these giant mountains is said to produce snow of an exceptionally deep and light quality. Global skiing blogs have been raving about it for years.

Even more so than in countries prepared to deal with it, the abundance of snow in the Stans can be as catastrophic as it is welcome. In the notorious winter of 2008, "Heavy snowfalls and avalanches… disrupted public transport in many cities," and the lack of power for heating was a very serious additional problem that forced closures of schools and hospitals, and eventually "all plants, factories and other enterprises," until the end of January.

A harsh 2012 weather cycle plunged Pakistan, Afghanistan and Tajikistan into chaos and a single avalanche cycle resulted in over 100 fatalities. Then a record-breaking 3-day storm in February of 2014 was a nightmare for hundreds of thousands when airports, schools, highways and businesses closed. The capital city of Dushanbe was almost completely shut down and described as being "at the edge of a collapse."

The same thing can happen in Kazakhstan, which tends to get at least as much snow as Tajikistan and is a larger country with 6 ski resorts. In February of 2022 a bomb cyclone moved across most of Kazakhstan with precipitation that quickly turned to snow accompanied by strong winds. Several regions reported record amounts of snowfall by local standards, with major roads closed and avalanches an acute threat throughout the mountains.

As in so much of the world, skiing in the Stans in profoundly deep snow conditions is often as much a matter of reaching the slopes as it is the slopes being open and safe. The problems encountered are similar to many places around the world, from Denver to Davos to Dushanbe, and have as much to do with the financial and manpower resources of the cities and resorts as they do with the volumes of snow involved.

Of all the central Asian countries, Kyrgyzstan is said to have some of the best and most consistently good snow, along with a number of developed ski areas to enjoy it. According to one source, 94% of the country is "covered by mountains, and those mountains are slammed by snow systems fed by the world's second largest alpine lake."

If you're not totally up on such matters, that would be a reference to Lake Issyk-Kul, at over 1,600 meters high in the northern Tien Shan Mountains in the eastern part of the country. However, calling it the world's second largest alpine lake isn't totally accurate and conflicts with, among others, Lake Tahoe in the US that's given the same distinction.

Unlike Lake Tahoe, Issyk-Kul is endorheic, meaning it has no outflow. And it is almost certainly the second biggest endorheic alpine lake in the world. It's also the 7th deepest (over 2,000 feet) lake of any kind, and the 10th largest in volume, both of which are significant in terms of its ability to generate precipitation. Perhaps most importantly, it's the second biggest landlocked saline lake on the planet, after the Caspian Sea.

At roughly .6% salinity Issyk-Kul is half that of the Caspian; about a sixth the salinity of the world's oceans at 3.5%; and only a fraction of the Great Salt Lake, which is 27% in its main basin. But it's just salty enough that, when combined with its radical depth and a large number of hot springs that flow into it, Issyk-Kul doesn't freeze in the winter. Therefore, like the Great Salt Lake, it's a major weather influencer that keeps producing moisture throughout the ski season. As one source notes, "Because of the conveyor belt of winter storms pushing through the area, fresh tracks are all but guaranteed."

That helps explain the 23 ski areas in the country, including 10 within 45 kilometers the capital city of Bishkek. The town of Issyk-Kul on the shores of the eponymous lake is also a major ski center. And resorts at Karakol, Orlovka, Chunkurchak, and Kashka Suu have all garnered reputations for both their snow and post-Soviet-era facilities.

Backcountry touring is also gaining popularity in the vast and lightly developed Tien Shan Mountains. In Kyrgyzstan, Jyrgalan is a main touring center and acknowledged as one of the country's snowiest resorts. For heli-skiing the Suusamyr Valley and Too-Ashu resort also reportedly get trademark light and dry pow.

All of that said, none of the country is known for the kind of extreme depths found in North America and Japan. Once again reliable long-term numbers are nearly impossible to come by. But some estimates of average amounts over the last few decades place Bishket at around two meters annually, Karakol at 3 meters and the Jrygalan Valley at closer to four.

If Amirsoy in Uzbekistan and the increasingly upscale resorts of Krygzstan are hits, then similar projects in other of the Stans may find financing. If not, the skiing will still be there. Harder to reach perhaps, but still with all of that mystical pow and nobody to jump your line.

The remaining two Stans both have issues larger than snow to deal with at this point in time. Afghanistan has several things working for it as far as skiing goes. It's situated fairly far north, has a lot of big mountains, and gets a bunch of snow – in fact, sometimes way too much, especially in a country ill-equipped to deal with it.

In 2005, Kabul got hit by its "biggest snowstorms in the most severe winter weather in Afghanistan in over 15 years." More than a foot of snow during the first week of February overwhelmed municipal services along with refugee camps and was responsible for dozens of deaths in the capital, as well as the crash of a passenger plane that killed all 104 on board. Many residents said, "they have not seen a winter like this 50 years," wrote one reporter.

Five years later in 2010, more than 150 people were killed by avalanches in the high Salang Pass in the Hindu Kush Mountains. The winter was called the worst in 20 years, and there were fears that many deaths from exposure and collapsed shelters in hard hit provinces went unreported. After two months of heavy snows farmers ran out of pastures for their livestock and hundreds perished, causing food shortages that were exacerbated by closed roads to remote areas of the country so that not even basic supplies could get through.

In February of 2017, deadly avalanches in Pakistan and Afghanistan killed more than 100 in the mountain regions and put many more at high risk for heavy flooding in the spring. Obviously and terribly, these weren't the only problems in a country that has been at war for over 40 years.

The lone ski area of Sari Pul that was built around 1967, 10 miles south of Kabul at Chowk-e-Arghande, closed after the Soviet invasion in 1979. It wasn't until 40 years later that another area was opened, this time in the central highlands 100 miles west of Kabul at Bamyan.

It was generally considered an outgrowth of the Afghan Ski Challenge that was started by a Swiss Journalist in 2011, to help train and empower Afghani female athletes by holding a 1.8-mile ski touring race. Following the U.S. and allied withdrawal, the fate of this very successful program and the rope-tow area it spawned were shut down and their current status is unknown.

Afghanistan's neighbor Pakistan has some famous skiing right about where you might think it should be, in the heart of the Karakoram Range in the northern part of the country. That's where some of the planet's tallest mountains are, including the second highest in the world. When Andrzej Bargiel became the first person to ski K2 in 2018 (see earlier chapter) it marked one of the crowning achievements in more than a hundred years of organized ski mountaineering. It was also a highlight of skiing in Pakistan that has included ski descents of the rest of the 8,000-meter peaks in the country along with development of ski resorts such as Malam Jabba in the Hindu Kush range of the Himalayas, and Naltar at nearly 3,000 meters in the Karakoram near Gilgit.

The heaviest snowfall recorded in Pakistan from 1931 to 2020 as per the Pakistan Meteorological Department was 1.07 meters (3.5 feet) in 24 hours in Malam Jabba on February 4, 2013. The village is home to the ski resort that has a very checkered history. A partnership between the Pakistani and Austrian governments resulted in a chairlift and hotel that were completed in 1988, but not opened until 1999 after disputes about who should run it. After seven years of operation it was employing 20,000 people in the Swat Valley and then the Taliban occupied the area and turned it into a command center. During a military operation to liberate it in 2009, the chairlift and hotel were destroyed. It has since been reopened and still possesses one of the snowiest climates in the country.

Pakistan's snow derives mainly from the Western Disturbance (WD) that brings snowfall from November to February throughout the north and in the hill country of Baluchistan. Blizzards are frequent in the mountains, and in February of 2017 at least 14 people were killed and 9 injured by an avalanche in the Chitral district. The WD brings extratropical storms from the Mediterranean region – including moisture from the Med, the Caspian Sea and Black Sea – to the northern end of the Indian subcontinent as far as northern Bangladesh and southern Nepal, sweeping straight across the Karakoram and Hindu Kush mountains in the process.

Extratropical storms carry their precipitation in the upper atmosphere, moving strongly west to east in the subtropical jet stream. That moisture then consolidates in high pressure systems over Ukraine, introducing polar air to the mix that causes cyclogenesis and creates an extratropical depression that gathers momentum until it smacks into the mountains and disgorges its moisture, which can fall as snow any time of the year above 2,000 meters.

In the Northern Area and Abbotabad and Gallyat they "broke all records" by the third week of February in 2005 for amounts of snow received. That included 4.87 meters (16 feet) in the hill station of Murree, shattering a 29-year-old record. It followed 1.67 meters (5.5 feet) in 8 days, including two feet on the night of the 20th. Called the heaviest rains and snows in more than a decade, they killed at least 42 people across the country in everything from collapsed roofs to multiple avalanches.

Pakistan's northernmost province of Chitral, where various groups have explored skiing options, received over 1.5 meters (5 feet) of snow in the first 35 days of 2017, surpassing a 2006 record of 4.5 feet. One village got 40 inches in 24 hours.

In a very similar time period two years later the northwestern Khyber Pakhtunkhwa province not far from the Naltar and Malam Jabba ski resorts got almost literally buried. "During the last one month the country's northern hilly areas received heavy snowfall – up to six to seven feet [2.13 meters]," a senior office in the Khyber Pakhtunkhwa irrigation department reported, adding that it was the most in 48 years.

Early January turned ferocious in 2022 when the hilltop town of Murree got hit again and at least 21 people died "after heavy snow trapped them in their vehicles…. As many as 1,000 vehicles became stranded…" It was the result not just of the amount of snowfall, but a rush of tourists coming from as far away as Islamabad to see it. More than 155,000 cars arrived in the small town after photos of people "enjoying the snow" went viral online.

Authorities were quickly compelled to declare the region a disaster zone as the snow continued. Several feet fell in places and more than two-dozen trees were knocked down on highways where large numbers of unprepared drivers became trapped. From January 5th through the morning of the 8th, Murree got .8 meters (2.58 feet). An official of the Met Office told one newspaper it was normal snowfall, but no one was prepared for it to become a tourist-attracting spectacle. By the end of the month reports were saying that the entire country was witnessing "unprecedented snowfall during the ongoing winter season."

Kashmir in India gets much of the same extratropical storm flow as northern Pakistan. There are approximately 25 ski areas in India, including Gulmarg in Jammu-Kashmir, the best-known resort in Asia with the second-highest top station in the world at 3,979 meters (13,054 feet).

It makes Patrick Thorne's list of the Top 10 snowiest resorts in the world. He notes, "It's difficult to get any official stats from Gulmarg, but 14 meters (46 feet) [annual average snowfall] is the consensus, and the resort is certainly known for its spectacular snowfalls and deep powder."

Ladakh in Kashmir is another of the snowiest places in the country, with a season that begins in September, and "heavy snowfall during January and February leads to frequent road closures." The same early January 2022 storm that caused so much chaos in Murree, Pakistan also struck Ladakh with two successive Western Disturbances. Under their influence widespread snow hammered the Jammu, Kashmir and Ladakh regions.

The biggest snow year in Kashmir's long history of them was chronicled by English naturalist and writer Richard Lydekker, who reported on an "enormous quantity" in the winter and spring of 1877/'78. "So excessive indeed was the snowfall, that no tradition or record exists even among the oldest inhabitants of anything approaching to such a fall. "

The storms started early in October and continued with little letup until May. Inhabitants told him that it frequently snowed without intermission for upwards of 10 days at a time. With little in the way of written

Iranian newspaper's front page during the world's deadliest blizzard there, 1972. Headline: "King and Queen in St. Moritz."

records, estimates were that at Dras at 10,000 feet, the depth was from 12 to 24 meters (40 - 80 feet) on the flats. It crushed cabins and log houses throughout the region, including at Gulmarg where "most of the huts of the European visitors have been utterly broken down by the snow."

Avalanches decimated vegetation and soil in the high country and choked valleys with debris. The road over 11,800-foot-high Zogi-pas still had snow near the top that was *at least 150 feet thick in late August, when it was normally snow-free by the first of June*. Wildlife devastation was highlighted by hundreds of corpses of Ibex being discovered embedded in the snow, and an almost total absence of live ones that summer in the mountains. The red bear and marmots suffered similar fates.

Not surprisingly, some of the biggest storms in northern Pakistan have also generated record snows in recent years in neighboring northern India. Late January and early February in 2014 saw 30 and 40-year-old precipitation records in Kashmir broken by heavy snows, with little further snow until mid-March. Then with a WD lying over northern Pakistan along with Kashmir and Jammu in India, many areas got an unseasonably large three to four feet of snow.

In January of 2017, as Chitral, Pakistan was being pounded, a meteorological official in Srinagar announced, "We witnessed major snowfall in 1992 and 2006 but the present snowfall has broken the record of the last 25 years." Gulmarg had recorded more than 2.13 meters (7 feet) to that point (January), and Gurez, which had at least three avalanches in 72 hours, was up to 3.5 meters (11 feet) following three straight days of heavy dumping.

The Srinagar-Jammu national highway, the only road linking Kashmir with the rest of the valley, was closed for four days as a combination of avalanches and landslides piled snow up to 12 feet deep on them. One slide killed 24 people including 20 Indian Army personnel. A subsequent study revealed that the area's accumulated snowfall was the highest of recent decades, in a region already considered among the world's most sensitive for landslides, avalanches and lake-outburst floods.

According to that study of the exposure of the Jammu-Srinagar National Highway, in 2019/'20 "heavy snow again fell across much of Kashmir, which broke all previous records." That included a hundred-year-old mark for the most to fall in a single day at Kokernag, which received 1.22 meters (just shy of 4 feet). Multiple avalanches on December 4, 2019 occurred in the same place as the 2017 tragedy, killing four more Indian Army soldiers. Then more slides on January 14, 2020, killed another 10 people. By early February, snowfall in the Himalaya was 20% above normal.

"Our mid-winter assessment released this month reveals that the snowfall received from November 2019 through January 2020 has been the highest in the past 30 years," said Naresh Kumar, Director, Snow and Avalanche Studies Establishment (SASE).

India's ski areas are scattered across the five mostly northern provinces of Jammu-Kashmir, Himachal Pradesh, Uttarakhand, Sikkim, and Arunchal Pradesh. While J-K is considered the most reliably snowy in the country, Manali and Kufri in Himachal Pradesh are also notable for large amounts of powder from November through April.

Gulmarg in Kashmir is considered "the winter sports capital" of India and at an altitude of 2,650 meters (just under 8.700 feet) has the consistent fresh snow to justify its title. Popular Kashmir tourist destination Pahalgam is slightly higher at 2,740 meters (almost 9,000 feet).

Manali, at 2,050 meters (6,725 feet) is one of India's most famous mountain towns and has some of the best skiing in the Himachal Pradesh district in the Solang Valley near town. In February of 2015 Manali got .6 meters of snow in 12 hours, breaking a 17-year-old record.

Munsiyari, Uttarkhand is also gaining skiing popularity in the HP district. With an elevation of 2,200 meters (7,218 feet) and a name that means "a place with snow," it seems like a natural. And the "quaint little resort hill station" of Kufri, with its own ski area, is considered by some to "witness the most snowfall in India." Its neighbor Shimla also gets a lot, with records for single days in January going over half a meter.

Sikkim in northeastern India hosts some of the highest ski areas in the world. Phuni Valley at 3,352 meters (right at 11,000 feet) is known for its powder. And the Yamthang (or Yumthang) Valley's base at 3,564 meters (11,693 feet) insures that it gets and holds copious snow through its winter season.

Sun Mountain ski resort, Yabuli, China, one of the country's snowiest. Photo via Wikimedia Commons.

CHAPTER 21
PART SEVEN – GLOBAL STORMING: NORTHERN ASIA

China, Japan, Korea

CHINA

With more than 700 resorts and 12 million skiers, China has emerged as a full-blown ski nation since it landed the 2022 Winter Olympics. The burgeoning middle class was looking for ways to spend newfound time and money in the young millennium, and since they have plenty of mountains with a history of skiing that goes back 10,000 years, it was obviously a good fit.

Some of the ski areas located close to urban centers have been developed more as "a novelty than a serious athletic pursuit," as one story on the boom puts it. Intended so that thousands don't have to travel long distances to utilize, many of these, like the primary alpine ski venues at the 2022 Olympics, exist on lower, re-contoured hills with a heavy dependence on man-made snow. The Yanging National Alpine Ski Centre in Beijing is one example.

As was widely reported, it was rare for the region, where the average annual snowfall is less than 6 inches, to receive any snow at all. So naturally it happened twice during 10 days of the Olympics and caused far more problems than if it hadn't snowed. But as everyone knows, the surest way to make it snow at any ski resort is to schedule a major ski race, and it will happen on the day of the event, often in epic proportions.

Moving away from the Beijing area, in Yunnan Province just across the border from Myanmar in the Golden Triangle, is the famous Yulong Xueshan resort, aka Jade Dragon Snow Mountain. It's number one on the snow-online.com snowiest list, with the southernmost glacier of the Northern Hemisphere. It also has the world's highest cablecar top station at 4,516 meters (14,816 feet) helping it get fresh annual snow. All well and good except that much of the glacier is hard to access and there is no skiing permitted on the mountain.

While the ski scene is just developing around Beijing and north-central China, resorts in the Changbai Mountains on the North Korean border are well established in one of the snowiest parts of the country. Yabuli Sun Mountain is one of the biggest and best-known areas, with 3,100 vertical feet and lots of natural snow. Its relatively low top station at 1,345 meters (4,413 feet) is offset by its northerly location, and snow-online.com puts it at number 7 in China.

The Alshan Alpine Resort, used for race training and recreational skiing, is in the same general region as Yabuli and also benefits from its latitude that places it almost on the border with Outer Mongolia.

In Xinjiang Province the Tianshan International Ski Resort borders Kazakhstan, in the same endless mountain range that serves much of central Asia. Indeed, Stone Age cave paintings in the Tien Shan show hunters on skis stalking game, and may date back further than anywhere else in the world.

China has been facing some resistance to their push for more and bigger ski resorts in these homelands of ethnic Kazakhs, Mongolians and Tibetans. The projects are justifiably seen as preludes to the destruction of traditional cultures, as they have been elsewhere in China and the world. Emei Shan in Sichuan Province is one of the prime examples, built as it is on one of the Four Sacred Buddhist Mountains of China. With its many temples, deep religious significance and nearness to the local capital of Chengdu, there is concern that ski crowds will overwhelm an important spiritual site.

A proposed project near Lhasa, Tibet, has raised even more alarm. As with Emei Shan, planners believe that even in a warmer future, such elevations will assure the resorts of snow. It would be the highest ski resort in the world, built in the heartland of Tibetan Buddhism in a formerly independent nation that China controversially "annexed" in 1951. Many worry about the impact on a major cultural landmark. What's more the ski area would have a top elevation of 5,486 meters (18,000 feet), raising serious doubts about the environmental consequences of building in such sensitive climatic zones. Not to mention serious potential health issues for normal skiers at such high altitude.

Several online sites that list record-setting snowstorms around the world include one in 2008 that hit normally arid Lhunze County, Tibet, with up to 1.83 meters (6 feet) of snow over a 36-hour period. Officials in the China Daily Mail reported an average of 1.5 meters (nearly 5 feet) of snowfall as buildings collapsed, roads closed for days, and 144,000 head of livestock perished.

Such an unusual snow event was regarded as an anomaly in China's high and dry Tibetan plateau. However, with the world's highest mountains and influences from the Western Disturbances, as well as the Bay of Bengal to the southeast and the South China Sea to the northeast, China gets its fair share of winter weather.

That 2008 storm cycle affected the entire central and southern parts of the country where it doesn't usually snow much. From January 10th to the 6th of February most of the region was hit with heavy snows, ice and cold, that became China's worst winter weather in 50 years and claimed at least 129 lives.

It was all set up by a large dome of cold air that blanketed much of China starting on January 10th, causing heavy snow in 6 major provinces and Shanghai. The snow persisted for several days and the cold for even longer, with an eventual very high cost in crops and livestock; 80 billion Yuan (12 billion dollars) worth of overall losses to the economy; and 111 billion Yuan (16.8 billion dollars) in physical damages, making it arguably the most expensive blizzard in history.

On Nov. 11, 2021, a Reuters story reported, "Snowstorms have wreaked havoc in northeast China this week, with record snowfall in some parts snarling traffic, disrupting train services and raising concerns about power supplies…" Meteorological departments in Jilin province issued red alerts – their most severe – for snowstorms.

The chief forecaster at the Liaoning Provincial Meteorological Observatory said that snowfall in western Liaoning was the heaviest since records began there in 1951, with depths up to .53 meters (21 inches). The state outlet of Xinhua said it was the highest recorded snowfall there since 1905. In Inner Mongolia deaths were reported along with 5,600 people being displaced. Researchers in the Mongolian city of Tongliao called the snowstorm "a random and sudden extreme weather event."

In China, snowfall statistics can be as confusing as anywhere else in the world. For example, available data for Yabuli Sun Mountain indicates that a mountain billed as having "lots of natural snow" actually averages a pretty marginal 1.32 meters (4+ feet) annually. Changbai also has a reputation as one of China's snowiest counties, yet their deepest month (November) apparently only averages 2.7 inches.

Alpensia Ski Resort Korea. The country's popular night skiing preserves their snow. Photo by Albert Lee1.

Inaccuracies could arise in what figures can be found due to possible misinterpretations of what periods of time they cover, or erroneous translations, or questions about where the measurements are taken. And there is little consistent history – stats in some places only go back to 1996, others to 1951, and others as far as 1905.

On top of that there's a sense that no one regards natural snowfall as that important since as long as they can make enough snow, their facilities will work.

In 2015 during their Olympic bid Chinese officials noted that, "Whereas downtown Beijing sees little snow in winter, Yanqing is fairly humid." That primary Olympic venue, less than 75 kilometers from downtown, gets around .20 meters (8 inches). Annually. They also said that the more distant site of Zhanjiakou gets up to .72 meters on an average year. None of these numbers would have been remotely reassuring if it wasn't for the wall-to-wall snowmaking at the resorts and a history of low temperatures to make it viable.

With that approach, many of China's ski areas will have reliably adequate snow to ski on every winter, barring severe warming trends or serious water shortages. But where does it reliably snow enough, often enough, to provide consistently great powder?

Setting aside that Jade Mountain Snow Resort is primarily a sightseeing attraction with a cablecar, rather than a fully-fledged ski area, it's categorized by nearly everyone as the country's snowiest. It seems a likely candidate given its glacier location, altitude, and the fact that it gets massive amounts of precipitation all summer long, some of which is almost always snow above a certain altitude (3,000 meters). The numbers show that in the period from 2009 through 2022, the resort only had three winters where snowfall totaled above .15 meters.

Powder face shots are the signature of Geto Kogen Resort, Japan. Photo © Kevin McHugh.

But those measurements were taken at the base of the ski area.

Changbaishan International Ski Resort is described as sitting directly in the line of fire for Siberian snow fronts, and "getting cans of wind-whipped, dry snow from December through March." But no amounts are provided.

Alshan Alpine Ski Resort in the Tien Shan mountains, "is honoured with unending snowfall; the slants [slopes] are generally weighed down with new powder, so it's a skier's heaven." The actual stats describe a "snowy period" of 4.3 weeks from mid-January thru mid-February, where the latter is the snowiest month and averages 1.2 inches for the month. Once again the assumption is the numbers come from the base, but it isn't specified.

Chengdu Xiling Snow Mountain Ski Field is on the side of a 5,364-meter (17,600 feet) peak that's draped with permanent snowfields. They don't ski from the summit and its annual fresh snowfall at the base is in the .6 to .8 meter range (23 – 31 inches).

Numerous studies of China's avalanches reveal more information about snow conditions in its mountains. In order to determine how best to protect against them it has been vital to determine what causes slides in various localities. Sometimes they're the result of big storms with attendant wind-loading. Some are triggered by climate changes, i.e. the long-term thawing of the ice that binds many mountains together. Others are unleashed by earthquakes.

In the Tien Shan, a 1992 study published in the Annals of Glaciology confirmed that snow cover there is low density, low liquid-water content, and low temperature. "It is known as typical dry snow," they wrote, noting that it also has substantial temperature layering. But the conclusion was, "full-depth depth-hoar avalanches seldom occur. Avalanches in the Tien Shan Mountains are mostly loose-snow avalanches. Although not large in size, they are the most dangerous type."

A paper titled, "An outline of avalanches in the southeastern Tibet Plateau, China," was published online by Cambridge University Press in January of 2017. Based on that 1992 research article in the Annals of Glaciology, it described the area as "a special region geographically," noting, "Precipitation is plentiful in the region due to the southwestern monsoon from the Indian Ocean. The maximum depth of snow cover is always over 2 meters," and concluding, "These are advantageous conditions for avalanches."

The results of a 7-year study by the Xinjiang Institute of Ecology and Geography on the "characteristics of snow avalanche drivers in the western Tienshan Mountains," were published in the Journal of Mountain Science in 2009. In considering factors that included weather conditions, slope steepness and orientation, terrain, vegetation, etc, "Results showed that snowfall is the largely contributory factor that trigger natural avalanches." While that conclusion wasn't unusual, the low amounts of snow involved were. "There is a high probability of avalanche release with snowfall exceeding 20.4 millimeters during a snowfall period," reported the team leader. A rise in temperatures was also cited as causal.

Snowfall in the Tien Shan was determined to occur about 10 times a season, with less than 10 millimeters of water equivalent per system. To no one's surprise, avalanche activity increased following each cycle and was more prevalent in the snowier areas than the less snowy ones.

In another study published in Cold Regions Science and Technology in 1986, the authors wrote that maritime region seasonal avalanches are characterized by lots of solid precipitation, while the continental region is distinguished by severe cold and sparse solid precipitation. The latter is more typical of the western Tibetan plateau and the parts of the country centered around the Tien Shan mountains. The maritime regions occur mostly in southern and eastern China where the primary weather influences are from the South China Sea and Indian Ocean.

Improved detection of avalanches via satellites and high tech ground-based weather stations are also leading to new conclusions about the frequency of "glacier detachments" as sources for major snow and landslides. While many of them occur deep in the mountains and are largely unseen, a May 2019 "avalanche" at Jade Dragon Snow Mountain turned out to have actually been a landslide triggered by a rock collapse from a "free-thaw effect."

A 2022 television story about a January avalanche in the same Yunnan province showed close-up video of skiers being engulfed in what appeared to be a powder-avalanche of equal parts snow and wind. No deaths or injuries were reported.

For the most part ski resorts aren't locating in the areas of heaviest "solid precipitation," because they tend to be remote and inaccessible – and thus hard to reliably reach with public transportation – as well as clearly dangerous.

KOREA

North Korea has ski areas, mostly in the mountains bordering China, and we've seen photos of Kim Jung Il skiing at them, but it's no easier to get information about their snow conditions and significant snow events than it is about the country's nuclear program.

South Korea has quite a bit of skiing and hosted the 2018 Winter Olympics, although it's telling that their racers are said to frequently train in China because the snow conditions are more reliable. Geographically, South Korea is much like China and that means they get the same weather patterns as eastern maritime China does, producing good natural snow in their mountains. But they also have to depend on manmade.

One of the few sources for long-term snow depth records in Asia reports that the "average snowfall depth in South Korea" from 1973 through 2020 was .363 meters (1.2 feet). How the figures are arrived at isn't explained, and it's obviously a very broad statement and ipso facto almost meaningless, other than to indicate they do get snow. But not a lot.

In early January of 2010 NBC News reported that Seoul was battling "the heaviest snowfall in modern Korean history after a winter storm dumped more than 10 inches." While not huge it was paralyzing for the big city and the worst since the country began conducting meteorological surveys in 1937. Roads were blocked, flights were cancelled, and a regional bottleneck was created by large parts of China being hit with the same storm. Downtown Beijing got three inches with up to 8 inches in the suburbs.

A year later in mid-February "the heaviest snowfall in more than a century on South Korea's east coast" caused "widespread chaos." One city on the eastern coast recorded .8 meters (2.6 feet) in a single day, the most since they started keeping track in 1911. Hundreds of houses collapsed under the weight of what was called a "snow bomb" and 12,000 troops were deployed to rescue stranded residents.

In mid-December of 2021 and a month later in January of 2022, heavy snows hit Seoul and two other provinces with anywhere from .195 to .35 meters (.63 to 1.14 feet). South Korea's snowiest province of Gangwon was one of them and was the home of the 2018 Winter Olympics and the resort of Yongpyong that hosted the alpine skiing events.

Because of its nearness to the ocean combined with being high in the Taebaek Mountains, Yongpyong is said to have "one of the best snowfall records in the country" by a source that also admits, "that still isn't saying much though!" Snow-forecast.com says from 2007 through 2020 they averaged a little over .5 meters (1.64 feet) from December through April.

As another tour company puts it: "By the standards of Korean ski resorts, Yongpyong is as good as it gets and doesn't have any particular negatives other than the lack of powder days and off-piste skiing – issues which apply to all resorts in Korea." As with China, they rely on man-made snow, and the big natural snow events the country gets are very few and far between.

JAPAN

In all of Asia, and really most of the world, Japan is the snowiest country there is, thanks to the northern island of Honshu. The town of Tsukayama got 1.73 meters (over 5.5 feet) in a single 24-hour-period on December 30/31, 1960.

Niseko Resort, with an annual snow accumulation average of 15.1 meters (49.5 feet), ranks number 5 on Patrick Thorne's list of "what are (probably) the world's ten snowiest ski resorts." And Nozawa Onsen comes in 7th with 14.44 meters (47 feet 4 inches).

On February 14, 1927, Mt. Ibuki in the Japanese Alps of Honshu recorded a snow depth of 465.4 inches (38.78 feet) at the 5,000-foot level. That edges out Tamarack in California for the world record. In the 24-hour period just before this measurement, 2.3 meters (7.54 feet) fell at the station, eclipsing the North American record of 2.01 meters (6.6 feet) at Silver Lake, Colorado, in 1921.

The Yuki-no-Otani Snow Canyon road in these mountains is a big tourist attraction because it is kept plowed and open all winter, with banks on either side that get over 65 feet deep.

What generates these insane numbers, and on such a regular basis? Harshly cold Siberian winds from the northwest whip across the relatively warm Sea of Japan, picking up moisture and getting funneled upwards as the fronts hit the Japanese Alps and then start dumping.

Low-pressure areas in the winter move northeast off the east coast of Japan and combine with high pressure coming off the southeastern portions of the Asian mainland. This starts the whole storm process as winds spin clockwise around the high-pressure system over the land, and counter-clockwise over the ocean's low-pressure, with Japan's snow belt in the middle. "Strong winds over the Sea of Japan help skim moisture off the water and deliver it to the archipelago in the form of copious snow," is how a story on @EarthUncutTV put it.

These systems can turn into the same kind of "bomb cyclones" that affect the US and other parts of the planet when a storm drops at least 24 millibars in central pressure in 24 hours. During the winter of 2022, one system plunged a shocking 38 millibars, "whipping up fierce winds that combined with the snow to cause blizzard conditions."

Record snow in Japan became a common story starting in November of 2021 as "round after round of intense wintry weather caused big disruptions in regions that know big snow," wrote Ian Livingston.

One monster struck just before Christmas and two towns on the northern island of Honshu set records for 24-hour accumulations. Hikone got .68 meters (2.23 feet) and Asago received .71 meters (2.32 feet). Aomori City, where they average 8 meters (26 feet) every winter and are frequently cited as the world's snowiest city, recorded two meters (over 6.5 feet) in five days. In a country well prepared for heavy winters, road, rail and airline closures were commonplace for days and avalanche watches were put into effect for much of Honshu's

2008 snowstorm broke records dating to 1905 in northeastern China. Photo Benlisquare, English Wikipedia.

western slopes. The issue in Japan's mountainous north isn't just the large amount of snow that falls but how fast it does it.

By late February snow depths were surpassing 4.57 meters (15 feet) in places, "enough for modern records to be tested and bested," wrote Livingston. The bomb cyclone storm alone delivered as much as 3.65 meters (12 feet) over the course of several days.

Storm chaser James Reynolds @EarthUncutTV arrived in Yuzawa "after the snow started and left before it stopped," and posted that he "measured an astounding 165 centimeters or 5 feet 5 inches," in 48 hours.

Tsunan, another town unofficially known as one of the world's snowiest, broke a record for the deepest snow ever by the end of February with 4.16 meters (13.64 feet). A skier interviewed by ABC News said, "It's the first time I've ever seen such heavy and incessant snow. It's really shocking."

Anyone who watches ski porn at all has seen clips of over-the-shoulder blower powder in the skeletal looking forests of northern Japan. Myoko Kogen in the Niigata Prefecture is accorded as "one of the regions with the heaviest snowfall in Japan," by snowexplorers.com in their guide to Japan's snowiest resorts. It's proximity to the coast accounts for an average annual snowfall of 14 to 15 meters (46 to 49 feet). Because of the nearness to the ocean the snow is plentiful and also heavier than higher up. They had 16.11 meters (almost 53 feet) by the end of February during the big 2021/'22 season.

Appi Kogen in northernmost Honshu is much colder than Myoko, with lighter snow if a bit less of it at 12 meters annually. They also tend to get snow when others aren't, as in the grim season of 2019/2020. And their famous tree zones are less crowded than some.

Very popular with locals and international powder chasers, Niseko, just off the western coast, is Japan's most famous ski resort. It's also generally tagged as it's snowiest with 14 to 15 meters (46 to 49.2 feet) annual average, coming straight off the Sea of Japan and fully dehydrated by Hokkaido's frigid temps.

Japan's so-called "King of Snow" at Geto Kogen credits its location in a mountain divide for its annual 15 meters, enough to require good avalanche awareness from those who ride there. Geto is also sought out by knowledgeable powder sniffers for it's trees and steeps in a country that isn't long on the latter.

In the epochal season of 2021/'22, when virtually all of Japan's top resorts except Niseko set records, Geto was reporting 24 meters (nearly 79 feet!) at the summit by the end of February. Photos of the ski patrol digging out pathways for the lifts went viral. Base measurements for the overall season came in at 18.42 meters or 60.4 feet.

Australian snowfields rejoice after 'Blizzard of Oz' turns slopes into winter wonderland

By Riley Stuart and Stephanie Anderson

Posted Mon 7 Aug 2017 at 1:17am, updated Mon 7 Aug 2017 at 3:11am

More than 1.15 metres of snow has been dumped at Thredbo. *(Instagram: @_carlyt)*

Australia's 2017 "Blizzard of Oz" brought record snows. Screenshot of coverage by <u>ABC.net.au</u>.

CHAPTER 22
PART EIGHT – GLOBAL STORMING: SOUTHERN LATITUDES

New Zealand, Australia, Africa, South America

NEW ZEALAND AND AUSTRALIA

Three of the top 5 positions in pedalchile.com's list of "snowiest cities in the southern hemisphere" are in New Zealand and Australia. Wanaka and Queenstown, NZ, are third and fourth, sharing adjoining locations and weather on the South Island. "For years these have been some of the snowiest places in the Southern Hemisphere," says the story, which also notes that storms can go on here for days, "leading to major road shutdowns."

The 5 big ski resorts on the South Island consist of The Remarkables, Cardrona, Coronet Peak, Snow Farm and Treble Cone. According to one tour agency, "As part of the South Island's snowy climate, these areas receive precarious snowfalls that can go up to 53 centimeters [1.7 feet], creating extremely thick and dense veils of snow everywhere."

Coronet Peak ranks as onthesnow.com's snowiest in New Zealand, thanks in part to the requisite glacier at their door coupled with widespread snowmaking. It's fresh snowfall average of 3 feet annually is measured at the base, where they've received up to 5 feet in the last ten years. Their biggest storms deliver an average of one foot, with some as big as two.

Mount Hutt, at number 4 on the list and owned by NZSki like Coronet and The Remarkables, touts their "monster snowfalls" on their website. Their annual average at their base from 2012 through 2022 is 1.5 meters.

In a story from September 11, 2015, Coronet Peak announced that they had just broken their total annual snowfall record with a depth of 3 meters (9.8 feet). Since onthesnow's total number for that season was 20 inches it seems likely that the resort's number was being reported at least from mid-mountain.

There is no doubt the country gets serious amounts of snow. On August 19, 2008, Turoa on Mount Ruapehu "claimed the biggest snow base ever recorded for a New Zealand skifield with over 4.5 meters (14.7 feet) of snow on the ground," according to their marketing manager who reported that, "The record-breaking snow base at Turoa and the great levels at Whakapapa will be paradise for skiers and boarders, and the good news is that with such large bases we expect to be able to extend the season and potentially keep going into November."

A storm in May of 2009 brought over half a meter to Mount Hutt and the Remarkables ski areas. And a series of Antarctic cold fronts that generated major snow in 2011 were described by MetService as a once-in-a-lifetime experience that affected the entire country. They began on July 24/25 on the North Island and spread to the south, subsiding in later July then returning in August.

A Wikipedia entry on the storm system says, "It was the worst winter storm to hit New Zealand in seventy years." That's confusing since other reports talk about an entire storm system that lasted for weeks, not a single event. The original source for several stories appears to be the reputable weatherwatch.co.nz. And what it reported was that a two-day storm on July 25/26 was, "the most widespread snowfall in New Zealand in 16 years." Altogether Christchurch got .45 meters (almost a foot and a half) over the two days, which was a lot, and again described as the most in 16 years. Later in the story it reported that one site, Greytown in Wairarapa, received its first snow in 70 years.

When the weather returned for four days in mid-August, what was predicted to be the "perfect snowstorm" dumped consistently down to the sea in Wellington for the first time since 1976, and fell briefly in Aukland for the first time in 80 years. The South Island got hit the hardest this time with some regions receiving .2 to .3 meters. "As much as a metre of snow fell at Banks Peninsula, and 50 cm on Port Hill," according to one report, which added that, "Many ski resorts were completely closed due to being covered in dangerous amounts of snow and damage to infrastructure."

The Tasman Glacier, the largest in New Zealand and famed for its heli-skiing since the early 1970s, has been losing mass steadily like nearly every other glacier in the world over the last century. It still covers 39 square miles, with a high point of 3,000 meters (9,800 feet). According to Wikipedia, "Snowfall during the winter and spring seasons may accumulate up to 50 meters (160 feet). After the summer melt, 7 meters (23 feet) may remain in the high altitude glacier head."

That info is questionable however. It has to be given latitude for qualifying it with the "up to 50 meters" part. But the source they cite for it reads as follows: "The neve receives 20 – 30 metres of snow annually, of which 6 – 7 metres survives the summer melting." Twenty to 30 meters (65.6 to 98.4 feet) is what's known in the scientific community as a shit ton of snow, anywhere.

Aerial view of upper Tasman Glacier with some of New Zealand's best snow. Image via Wikipedia.

Fifty meters is a world-beating amount, and may have occurred somewhere, and may even do so regularly. It may even have happened on the Tasman Glacier. But its not possible to find reliable confirmation of it. The 20 to 30 substantiated meters is enough to qualify the Tasman as one of the world's snowiest ski areas.

What causes it? New Zealand's climate is dominated by the eastward movement of depressions and anticyclones across the Pacific, Antarctic and Indian oceans that surround it. According to an Aoraki/Mount Cook National Park educational resource document from 2010 compiled by the New Zealand Department of Conservation, seasonal variations mean that anticyclones can be found further south in winter, "which causes more cold southerly flows."

What results is dependent on the mountains, which in Aoraki/Mount Cook rise up to a Main Divide that averages about 3,000 meters (9,542 feet) and is "a major obstacle to the prevailing westerly flow… Moisture-laden westerlies roll in off the Tasman Sea and are forced to rise over the Main Divide," with most of the precipitation falling to the west of it around the 1,200-meter (3,937-foot) level. Snow falls at Aoraki/Mount Cook Village for about 21 days per year – the largest fall was 1200 mm (November 1967).

The fast-retreating Lewis Glacier is Mount Kenya's largest with skiing since the 1930s. Photo by Josski, Dutch Wikipedia.

In Australia, the Snowy Mountains in southern New South Wales is part of the continent's Great Dividing Range, the tallest on the mainland, with 5 of Australia's highest peaks, all near or above 2,134 meters (7,000 feet). According to Wikipedia, "The Snowy Mountains experiences large natural snowfalls every winter, normally during June, July, August and early September, with the snow cover melting by late spring. It is considered to be one of the centers of the Australian ski industry... with all four snow resorts in New South Wales being located in the region." It's also, not incidentally, where skiing in Australia originated in 1861 after the discovery of gold in Kiandra in 1859 sparked a brief rush of people to the region's high mountains above the snowline.

Snow-online.com's Australia list gives its top two places to Snowy Range resorts in New South Wales (NSW). Thredbo and Perisher are also the country's two most famous ski areas. In the onthesnow.com snowfall histories, Thredbo averaged 2.05 meters (6.75 feet) annually from 2012 through 2022. They're generally closer to 2.5 meters (8.3 feet), with a high of 3.04 meters (nearly 10 feet), but a low of .25 meters (.83 feet), and are subject to single storm systems dumping .6 meters (two feet) or more. Perisher came in at nearly two meters (6.3 feet), with a high of nearly double that at 3.6 meters (12 feet), but low years of almost nothing.

As an indication of the general snowiness of NSW, Oberon, a town in its central tablelands, is cited by pedal-chile.com as number 5 on their list of snowiest cities in the entire southern hemisphere. Owing to its elevation at 1,113 meters (3,652 feet) and windward location in the Great Dividing Range, moderate to heavy snowfall is normal, and can occur at nearly any time of the year.

The next four places on snow-online's rankings of snowiest Australian resorts are in Victoria, with Mount Buller at third averaging 1.1 meters (3.75 feet) at its base in the onthesnow records and lots of man-made. Charlotte Pass averaged 1.7 meters (5.7 feet), Hotham Alpine Resort 1.4 meters (4.75 feet), and Falls Creek 1.3 meters.

Australia and its ski resorts can get clobbered from time to time. From July 3rd through the 7th in 1900, what is known as The Extraordinary Snowstorm delivered in excess of a suspected four feet in the Snowies, but no one was keeping track at that point. The town of Rydal at 914 meters (3,000 feet) in NSW got that much. Blayney, not far from Bathurst, got .68 meters (2.23 feet) in 12 hours. According to one report, "Exceptional snowfalls were reported over the central districts of NSW. Record falls in the central tablelands resulted in blocked railways and extensive damage to buildings." Another account from the time reported that, "In places snow 8 feet [2.4 meters] deep on the rails."

The biggest 7-day snowfall on record at the time was from June 12 to 19 in 1956 with 1.32 meters (4.33 feet). It was responsible for a slab avalanche that crushed a hut in Kosciusko National Park, killing a 20-year-old woman. According to an Australian source named Barclay on Unofficial Networks, in early July of 1964, "it is said that around 3 meters of snow fell in less than two weeks." Data from Spencer's Creek showed a gain of 1.52 meters from July 6 to 20 during what many called "one of the best snow years this country has seen."

A storm for the first four days of August in 2010 dumped 1.2 meters (almost 4 feet) at Thredbo, while overall contributing to the snowiest month in 18 years with over 2 meters (6.5 feet) in 31 days. And in the biggest June snowfall since 1991, the 2014 Snowmageddon storm from June 24 through 26 brought 1.2 meters to the tops of Thredbo and Perisher.

Arguably the biggest and most famous snow cycle ever in Australia took place during the legendary Blizzards of Oz from August into September of 2017. A week in early August saw over a meter fall across Victoria and NSW ski resorts, with Threbo picking up 1.3 meters (4.25 feet) in 7 days. Then up to another half meter came on August 18/19. And the final piece of the trifecta started on September 6, which some called one of the best days ever. The final tally after 72 hours was as much as 1.2 meters at the resorts with conditions at Perisher described as, "the best in 17 years."

The Australian state of Tasmania is a mountainous isle located off of eastern Oz's south coast, and host to the country's southernmost ski slopes. It isn't to be confused with the Tasman Glacier in New Zealand. Or the Tasmanian Devil cartoon character from Warner Brothers.

Multiple cross-country areas and three lift-served resorts serve the island's skiers, with Ben Lomond Ski Fields ranked 8th on the snow-online list. All of the ski areas get and keep decent snow due to cold temperatures and higher elevations. Those influences can have profound impact on mainland Australia's weather, as in the record dumps of August 2010.

Australia has the same problems the rest of the world does when they get too much snow too quickly in the wrong places. Their airports and railways close, along with the two main alpine highways that access the ski areas. Avalanches, particularly in the Victorian Alps, are also a threat. Plus they have one more feature that not everywhere else in the word does: thundersnow. It's not that unusual for lightning and thunder to occur during snowstorms, which immediately causes lift closures and can shutter mountains until it's done. Fortunately it doesn't usually last long and it makes for good stories. And songs: "Can't you hear, can't you hear the thunder? Better run, better take cover."

AFRICA

While snow skiing in Africa is limited, it not only exists but there are some impressive snowfalls in the northern part of the continent in the Atlas Mountains stretching for 2,500 kilometers across Morocco, Tunisia and Algeria. And of course there are the snow-capped likes of Kilimanjaro and Mount Kenya, located just barely into the southern hemisphere.

The only substantive skiing in North Africa is in Morocco which hosts four or five lift-equipped ski resorts and multiple well-known backcountry guide services. Tours can include excellent desert-cured powder on the west slope of the Atlas, as well as ascents and descents of the highest mountain in North Africa, Jbel Toubkal, at 13,671 feet for some massive vertical. But the summit is often too windy to climb.

Heliski Marrakech, started by the French company

Evolution 2, is reportedly only heliski operator in Africa.

Founder Herve Favre told CNN, "We have just a few days of very bad weather in the Atlas Mountains, but when it's snowing it snows a lot – we can have a meter of fresh snow a day." He also noted that the snow in Africa can change quickly due to the high temperatures, and go from mid-winter conditions to spring overnight.

The country's primary ski resort at Okaimeden, 55 kilometers from Marrakech, is smallish but with a high enough base altitude at 8,530 feet to get and keep snow fairly reliably, averaging 2.76 meters (just over 9 feet) annually.

Morocco has been known to get treacherously big snowstorms. In January of 2018, 5,000 kilometers (3,100 miles) of roads and highways were closed due to what was described as "exceptional" snowfall that culminated by bringing heavy amounts to the country's southern region for the first time in 50 years. And in February of 2023 the southeast of Morocco was besieged by an "unprecedented" multi-day snowstorm that dumped up to 2.2 meters (7.2 feet), isolating 87 villages and leaving "24,000 families in need of assistance," as reported on Atalyar.com.

As several different studies have established, the Atlas Mountains account for a huge percentage of Morocco's fresh water, where annual precipitation (a "significant portion" of it in the form of snowfall) can "exceed 800 mm in the highest regions." While big snowfall winters are incidentally good for the skiing, they are vital to the country's well being, and "characterized by very strong inter- and intra-annual variability." And the North Atlantic Oscillation plays a dynamic role due to its influence on temperatures. Forecasts are, not surprisingly, for continued instability in water supplies due to the unpredictability of precipitation in the mountains.

Further south in Africa, the snows of Kilimanjaro were famous long before Hemingway wrote about them. At 5,894 meters (19,340 feet) and the highest summit in Africa, it has been crowned by snow since time immemorial. It was especially noticed by the first European explorers who tried to explain the distant vision of a white peak in equatorial Africa in any number of ways other than snow, from optical illusions to a summit of solid white quartz. One of the leading scientists of the time flatly declared that it was impossible for there to be a snowcapped mountain that close to the equator.

It was many years before any expeditions were able to make it to the summit to see that there were actual glaciers there. In fact the mountain gets snow down to 3,048 meters (10,000) feet and lower in the winter and can receive up to 3 meters (10 feet) a year. That would have to be the most of any place in sub-Saharan Africa. However, it's extremely rare that any of it lasts through the long spring, summer and fall. And over the last century the glaciers have been retreating at an alarming rate.

Kilimanjaro, however, isn't open for skiing or snowboarding. It's a National Park and the staff there is not adequately trained to perform mountain rescues in winter conditions, and not in a position to add those skills to their job descriptions. Which is not to say Kili has never been ridden, albeit illegally, and I will add editorially, disrespectfully.

Nevertheless, the summit region of Kilimanjaro, which lies at 3 degrees south latitude, undoubtedly gets the most snow of anywhere in the southern hemisphere of Africa. Snow-forecast.com says that the snowiest week on the mountain is the second one in December, which averages .41 meters (1.25 feet). A comprehensive small weather station has been located on Kili's Northern Icefield since 2000, monitored by a group from the University of Massachusetts.

Beyond that, Mount Meru at almost 4,572 meters (15,000 feet) and not far from Kili, also gets snow, though not much, and any skiing done there is brief. Next door in Kenya the second highest mountain in Africa is Mount Kenya at 5,199 meters (17,057 feet) and is said to straddle the equator in places, but to hew to northern hemisphere weather patterns. It gets decent snow every winter though its glaciers are still retreating, too, and 7 of it's former 18 ones identified in the 19th century have vanished.

According to SkiMountaineer.com, "the terminus of the Lewis Glacier now reaches only to 4,600 meters (15,000 feet). [But unlike on Kilimanjaro] the glaciers of Mount Kenya have been skied and snowboarded numerous times, including an extreme descent from the Gate of the Mists down the Diamond Glacier, which is normally considered the finest ice climb on the mountain."

The difference between it and Kilimanjaro is that Mount Kenya has had a well-trained Mountain Rescue group for many years. And people have been skiing there since Bill Delap pioneered it on the Lewis Glacier in 1933. The first African Ski Championship was held there in 1936. You can watch YouTube videos of people still skiing the mountain in the last 10 years, though its getting more difficult as the glaciers retreat. October through December is its snowiest time, providing about one-third of the mountain's total annual precipitation.

Some 2,750 kilometers (1,700 miles) south of Kilimanjaro, Southern Africa gets snowstorms deep enough to help a couple of small ski resorts and to cause headaches in the metropolitan areas in the world, just like everywhere else in the world.

Located in the Drakensberg section of the Great Escarpment in the country of South Africa, Tiffendell's ski area base sits at nearly 2,743 meters (9,000 feet), so if anywhere gets snow, they're usually included and have been since opening in 1993. An average season's natural snowfall during the last 14 years as reported on snow-fore-cast.com is around .38 meters (1.25 feet)

Afriski, just over the border from South Africa in Lesotho, is the only other ski area in southern Africa. With a base at 2,917 meters (9,570 feet), it too gets some natural snow, an average of a little over .45 meters (1.5) feet a year during the last 14. It's quite small and also has full coverage capability from snow-making equipment.

The UPI reported "the heaviest snowstorm of the century today" in Johannesburg and much of South Africa in June of 1964, with resultant heavy crop and livestock losses. There were no ski areas in the region at the time. There were by July of 1996, when some parts of southern Africa got up to a meter (over three feet) of snowfall and the Drakensberg mountains had 1.82-meter (6-foot) drifts.

According to the Associated Press Archive, it was the largest snowfall in southern Africa in 32 years. Over a hundred hikers were stranded for days and had to be rescued by helicopter. Power went down for thousands in sub-freezing temperatures. Airports and highways were closed and of course so were the ski areas.

When the next big snowstorm struck the region 20 years later, Lesotho took the brunt of it. "This particular snowfall was an extreme event, but it's only extreme in the context that we haven't had something like this in a long time," noted a professor at the University of Witwatersrand, SA. "In the first half of the 20th century, or certainly in the 19th century, these were very common."

SOUTH AMERICA

There are ostensibly 44 ski resorts in South America according to skiresort.info, though some are "temporarily closed" or "planned" or have .4 kilometers of trails. The best skiing in South America has been hamstrung by severe drought on the continent that persisted through much of the period from 2010 to 2022. According to onthesnow.com, during that time Portillo, Chile, averaged 34 inches at the base for the entire season. In Las Lenas it was 17. Even their relatively good seasons brought less than 7 feet, total.

Historically, the Andes of South America (SA) have tended to have their best snow and precipitation years during La Nina events, though that's not an infallible predictor. It depends on numerous factors including the strength of the La Nina itself. But since the La Nina–Southern Oscillation (ENSO) occurs directly off the Pacific coast of SA, it's a formidable player in much of the continent's weather, with greater direct impact there than in North America.

The warm pool of its currents feeds thunderstorms and increases rainfall across portions of the South American coast. Given the aridity of that region, the rains are a blessing. And the snow in the Andes helps transfuse that lifeblood of water throughout the mountains and plains, while vastly improving the skiing and thus the tourism economy.

It doesn't come without a price, however, since strong La Ninas inevitably cause widespread flooding, and create havoc for the fishing industry by reducing the normal cold-water upwelling in the ocean that feeds much of the fish population.

And when it's a strong La Nina and the precipitation comes down as snow in feet at a time in the mountains it causes avalanches and road and rail closures, along with livestock and crop losses, roof collapses, power outages and other mayhem. What weather and precipitation records there are seem to indicate that La Ninas are occurring less frequently and dramatically. But it's only recently that concerted efforts have been made to research the history of weather patterns in these areas, so historical trends aren't fully understood.

Certainly the ski areas of the Andes haven't always been drought stricken. Portillo was awarded the 1966 FIS World Championships at least partly based on its record of getting copious snow. And as if to prove it, when a major international ski race was scheduled there for August of 1965 to see how prepared they would be, it had to be cancelled because of a series of disaster-level storms that left up to 1.5 meters (5 feet) a day for three days and caused multiple avalanches. One destroyed a new lift built for the event, and another killed 5 ski patrolmen as they slept in a building at the base of the mountain.

Up until the new millennium, according to some sources Portillo reliably averaged 7.4 meters (roughly 25 feet) a winter. Since 2010, onthesnow.com says they've averaged .86 meters (2.83 feet) at their base. But even in this dry new century they've gotten some action.

A July storm in 2007 was described as the heaviest winter in Argentina in almost 40 years. It occurred when low-pressure systems across central Argentina encountered a "massive polar cold snap" that produced a three-day barrage of blizzards and severe snowfalls. Along with .6 meters (two feet) in Concorvado and Chubut, and half that (which was still overwhelming) in Rio Cuarto and Cordoba, it snowed in some places it never had before. Ultimately the storm was blamed for at least 55 deaths in three countries.

In 2013 a powerful Antarctic air mass hit Peru, Bolivia and Paraguay, producing very cold temps and snowfall in even one of the driest places on earth – the Atacama dessert of northern Chile. Thousands of cattle, llamas and alpacas were killed in the three countries, and weather reports said it was the most snowfall in the area in three decades.

Another decent season compared to most in the 2000s happened in 2015. *Snowbrains* announced that, "5 South American Ski Resorts Saw Over 200% of Their Last 6 Years Snowfall Average in 2015." Portillo supposed got a three-day dump of 2.69 meters (8.83 feet) in mid-July, and some ski areas had to close repeatedly due to avalanche danger from the large volumes of powder they were getting.

According to *Snowbrains*, Cerro Castor in Argentina got 3.83 meters (12.75 feet) that season, up 253% over the average for the prior 6 seasons. Portillo got 2.79 meters (9.16 feet) up 182%; La Parva, Chile, got 3.75

meters (12.33 feet) up 155%; Corralco, Chile, got 17.65 meters (57.9 feet) which was up 147% from its 7.13 meter average; and Cerro Catedral in Argentina was up 79% to 8.9 meters.

Several things in those numbers stand out. Portillo, which was listed in onthesnow.com as getting 76 inches total that year, is credited by Snowbrains with 110 inches, including 106 inches in three days in July. So apparently they only got another 4 inches in the next two months.

Also of interest is that Corralco's average for the "dry" 6 years was 7.13 meters (23.4 feet), which wasn't awful. And in 2015 it allegedly got 17.65 meters (almost 58 feet), which is Top 5 on the planet and strongly disputed by other knowledgeable sources on the region.

Several online sources agree that Chillan/Corralco "get the most snow among lift-served skiing in South America," according to Tony Crocker, a longtime observer of skiing in SA. He also believes it's long-term average could be 7.62 meters (25 feet) or more. But as with most South American resorts, there is little in the way of accurate long-term records. And in a reply to *Snowbrains* Crocker insisted that 17.65 meters in 2015 is simply not believable or supported.

In 2017 Santiago, Chile, got a couple of inches of snow, with up to .4 meters (1.3 feet) falling in the region. The nearby ski resort of Valle Nevado got nearly a foot from the storm. According to the Associate Press, "Chile's Meteorological Office said it was the biggest snowfall in the capital in 46 years."

And by the middle of July in 2020, 3.9 meters (13 feet) of fresh snow had fallen in the Andes in places such as Corralco, where it was crazy-deep for so early. Mendoza City in Argentina recorded 1.5 meters (5 feet) from one storm system, the highest ever that soon in the season according to the Argentine National Weather Service. And experts said they'd never seen so much snow so early in Las Lenas, either. Unfortunately nearly all of the South American resorts were closed for the season due to Covid.

As with numerous other areas of the world, it was noted in a statement from the Department of Climatology of the Argentine National Weather Service that the weather wasn't 'extreme' by historical standards, but the abnormal thing was that it hadn't been snowing the way it used to, so when it finally did, "that is why now it seems strange to us."

Snow-online.com's list of the 10 snowiest ski resorts in South America puts Valle Nevado at number one. Some websites report its annual average snowfall at 8.23 meters (27 feet), though that is clearly a long-term average, and uncertain even at that. Onthesnow reports Valle Nevado's average from 2012 through 2021 as 32 inches at the base. The altitude at the top of the resort of 3,670 meters (12,040 feet) contributes to its snowiness. La Parva in Chile comes in at two, and Las Lenas is 3rd.

Corralco, Chile, which many say gets more snow than any resort on the continent, only squeaked in at number 10 on snow-online's list, due yet again to their heavy favoring of snowmaking (which remains scarce in South America and especially Corralco) to insure skiable snow conditions, rather than snowfall records.

Some of the respect accorded Las Lenas is due to the presence of several dozen snow-cannons. And some is residual from when it was the home to awesome seasons. As Tony Crocker pointed out, snow measurements at Las Lenas are only taken at the base of the mountain due to wind/avalanche exposure up higher that precludes doing it safely or reliably. "There is no doubt it snows more, and sometimes a lot more up high," he wrote in response to the Snowbrains story. Then he noted that in 2005 Las Lenas got 8.53 meters (28 feet), and that their long-term average is 6.27 meters (20.58). Both of those are solid, especially in relation to many other resorts in S.A.

Bariloche, Argentina, places second on pedalchile.com's 2020 list of the snowiest cities in the southern hemisphere, based on their historic snowfall records, behind Villa Las Estrelas in *Antarctica*. In Bariloche, pedalchile wrote, "It's temperatures can go as low as 2 degrees F (-16 degrees C), and heavy snow has been recorded countless times, with the most recent (in 2019) depth of 4 feet recorded in Cerro Catedral Ski Resort in Bariloche," adding that, "the winters are as long as they are cold, precisely why there's a skiing culture predominant in the town."

Brazil is known to get the rare storms that deliver over a meter, but they have no real skiing e6tt78=20cept=806 on mats. The only other legitimate skiing in South America is at the southern end of the continent in Patagonia. The Andes extend deep into the region which is encompassed by both Chile and Argentina. The combination of high altitudes, cold latitudes, and steady ocean-born storm systems augmented by fronts from Antarctica, adds up to consistent precipitation. So much so that the region is famously clouded over much of the time.

Sigi Grabner in Las Lenas, Argentina. Photo: Gustavo Cherro / Red Bull Content Pool.

However, that doesn't always guarantee snow, and it makes it difficult to monitor snow coverage from satellites. That's why when images came in from a June 26, 2020, overflight by NASA's Aqua satellite that showed the one- million-square-kilometer entirety of Patagonia virtually cloud-free, it was a big deal, and a considerable help in studying the snowfall.

The "blocking high" system that diverted the normally westerly winds, stayed in place for nearly a week. During that time temperatures plummeted because the land surface heat could more easily escape, and sub-zero cold blanketed parts of the continent all the way to Bolivia. The diverted westerlies brought cold from Antarctica and spread it across Patagonia, guaranteeing that the snow from a major storm on June 23rd and 24th didn't melt off quickly. Coverage was visible in the photos from the western slope of the Andes in Chile to the coastal lowlands in Argentina.

A study *Assessing Snow Accumulation Patterns and Changes on the Patagonian Icefields* was conducted in 2019 by the University of Leeds in England, in cooperation with universities in Chile. The lead line in the summary reads, "Recent evidence shows that most Patagonian glaciers are receding rapidly." Meaning that they're part of the global trend. There was also some evidence to suggest that on certain Patagonian glaciers with "positive and stable elevation and frontal changes," snow accumulation had increased during the period 2000 – 2015. The summary concluded with, "This suggests that increases in snow accumulation are attenuating the response of some Patagonian glaciers to warming in a regional context of overall glacier retreat."

All of which is a long-winded version of skiers fervent hopes that the snow isn't melting everywhere faster than it's being replaced. Certainly for the ski areas in Patagonia it would be good news if it turns out some of the region is still getting more than its losing. Cerro Catedral Alta Patagonia near Bariloche, Argentina, has the largest lift-accessed ski terrain in South America (and some say the Southern Hemisphere) at 3,000 acres, with 120 kilometers of lifts and 3,770 vertical feet

Widely described as getting in the range of 6 meters (nearly 20 feet) of snow annually, that figure is taken from the top of the resort at 2,100 meters (7,151 feet), which is said to be fairly snowy, while the base of the mountain at 3,378 feet is routinely called "patchy." Powderhounds.com notes that, "Snow is probably not Catedral's forte." And onthesnow.com puts their average snowfall since 2012 at 1.47 meters (4.83 feet) at the base. However, 2021 went over 2.54 meters (8.33 feet) and at this writing, 2022 is looking awesome, with 3.1 meters (10 feet) so far and it's only the middle of their winter.

To give some context, Cerro Catedral is number two on snow-online.com's list for Patagonia, behind only Caviahue. Inasmuch as Cerro Catedral tops out at 7,152 feet, while Caviahue goes to 9,700, that makes sense. Onthesnow.com puts their average since 2012 at .6 meters (just under two feet) at the base, including 3.1 meters in 2021. Clearly between there and the nearly 3,048-meter (10,000-foot-high) summit, the snow is much more abundant.

Certainly, though its glaciers are mostly withdrawing, and the prevailing drought conditions in the rest of the Andes are bleeding into Patagonia, it does appear to be continuing to get regular snowfall at higher elevations. And the first two years of the 2020s were closer to long-term average snowfall.

SECTION V

GOING IN SNOWY TORRENTS

CHAPTER 23
AVALANCHES - INTRODUCTION

The Great White Sharks of the Mountains

My parents saw movement through the trees above us, and mom said it sounded like elk bugling. Instead it was an avalanche. I was 5 years old and we were on Togwotee Pass in Wyoming at a rope-tow ski area in 1957. The bugling sound was actually lift pulleys squealing under the tidal weight and force of the slide.

We stood in an alcove in the trees alongside a run where dozens of people had been skiing just an hour earlier. It was the end of the day and everyone was gone but us. The big March slide released from a ridge 1,000 vertical feet above, charged onto the ski-packed slopes, then slabbed-up and stopped on a bench just above us. My teeth didn't stop chattering for hours, and I didn't even understand what an avalanche was or what one could do. But I could tell it was a big deal.

One of the infamous avalanche stories my parents talked about on the drive home was of a man filming a big slide above him and not realizing that it might reach him, and that a powerful blast of wind would precede it. The film was recovered from the camera, buried some distance from his corpse, and it showed the concussive force slam him well before the slide as the camera went tumbling.

That story, I learned much later, was especially relevant because it had just happened that year on Berthoud Pass, Colorado to John Hermann. And it became, as Lou Dawson would write many years later in Wild Snow, "the most famous avalanche footage ever filmed."

Walt Disney films had contracted Hermann and his assistant Roland Wyatt to make a documentary about avalanches. Hermann wanted to capture one in action and consulted people who lived around the Continental Divide west of Denver about where ones usually occurred. Many of them mentioned what was called the "Dam Slide," an avalanche path above Berthoud Pass on US Highway 40, which leads from I-70 to Winter Park.

In a 2019 lecture on avalanches sponsored by the Colorado Department of Transportation at the Frisco Historic Park and Museum, longtime CDOT avalanche mitigation and snow removal expert Ray Mumford showed a video of Hermann's film. It was part of a review of the previous winter's record-breaking avalanche conditions along I-70, placing the events in historical context.

The Colorado Highway Department had agreed to trigger a slide in 1957 for Hermann, who set up on US 40 along with highway department supervisor Wayne Whitlock. Hermann's partner Wyatt positioned himself off to one side of the path. Locals and the highway department thought there was no way a Dam Slide avalanche could ever reach the road.

"So both men set up the camera on the highway and filmed, and continued filming the avalanche until it reached the highway. This is that avalanche," Mumford is quoted as telling the audience, in a story for the Summit Daily newspaper by Antonio Olivero. When he played the footage it elicited gasps and he said, "Imagine standing there watching that coming and not getting out of there."

The grainy footage is stunning to behold. The triggered slide released a much larger second one almost instantly and it was a true monster, with a powder cloud several hundred feet high and an air blast that snapped mature trees and "hurled them 200 feet in the air," according to a 9News.com story. Both Hermann and Whitlock were buried under hundreds of feet of snow and killed instantly. Wyatt, who missed the brunt of the beast, was able to dig himself out.

1984 Chevrolet Suburban parked on backcountry road near Aspen, compressed to 2/3s its width by slide. Photo © Jay Cowan

Taken in total, avalanches account for fewer skier deaths than any number of other things, from heart attacks to head traumas. It's much the same as a surfer who is more likely to drown or get pummeled on a reef than they are to be attacked by a shark.

But there's something wild and nightmarish about shark attacks and avalanches that creates a fascination. For most sane people, the basic interest is in how to avoid both. For those whose pursuits make contact with either inevitable, it's important to be as knowledgeable about them as possible.

Even non-skiers can have a prurient interest in avalanches due to their incredible destructive power, and their obvious lack of discrimination. An avalanche will devour anything in its way: young, old, male, female, fit or obese. It does not care. And it can change the shape of mountainsides, deposit thousands of tons of debris in the middle of highways and rivers, and wipe out entire communities.

It's possible to die in avalanches while climbing, driving, cross-country skiing, sleeping in your lodge, riding in a train, eating in a restaurant, and in any number of other reasonably innocent circumstances. But the odds are much greater of it happening to us if we intentionally

put ourselves in harm's way and keep doing it, accidentally or otherwise, for many decades.

Why? Powder snow is a big temptation, the canvas where sport and art meet most visibly in skiing and boarding. And ultimately, it's just pure, transcendent, free-falling fun. Plus some of us need an occasional rush in our lives to satisfy our ancient survival instincts.

Uncontrolled powder slopes can be very risky, and as anyone will tell you, no powder run is ever worth your life. Still we do it. Many friends and acquaintances of mine have been caught in – and some killed by – avalanches, and I've had multiple encounters myself.

The fact is that avalanches occur every day somewhere in the world, due to earthquakes, glacier activity, heavy snowfall, major wind events, sonic booms and a variety of other influences both geologic and human, including trying to ski on unsafe snow. When they've killed the most skiers at once, it hasn't been ones who are skiing but those in hotels, restaurants and their homes. So you don't even have to be doing anything riskier than eating raclette in the wrong place at the wrong time to die.

The good news is that, of the world's 100 deadliest known avalanches in Wikipedia, only a handful were connected to skiing and ski resorts. When skiers die in slides, they're often alone or in small groups where not necessarily everyone in a group is killed. And only a fraction of those deaths have been on controlled pistes. So it is still statistically very rare that a skier inbounds at a resort will die in a slide.

Avalanches have been with us throughout recorded history and the most powerful and destructive of them have been triggered seismically or by glaciers. Huascaran Mountain in Peru has been the site of some particularly large-scale destruction. In 1962, 4,000 people perished in an avalanche from its slopes caused by a calving glacier. And in 1970, another 22,000 died in an avalanche/landslide set off by the Ancash earthquake.

The Himalaya, Karakoram and Hindu Kush ranges of Asia have witnessed some of the worst death-toll avalanches, in countries in geologically active mountains with villages and/or whole troops of soldiers involved.

The second deadliest cluster of avalanches in recorded history took place during World War I in Italy. In what became known as White Friday on December 13, 1916, hundreds of Austrian soldiers died at once when a big slide took out their barracks near the top of Mount Marmolada, in the Dolomites near Cortina. And during the next week a series of avalanches roared down Marmolada, which was heavily occupied by both Italian and Austrian soldiers, and an estimated 9,000 to 10,000 died.

There have always been largely unproven stories that some of the slides were triggered as weapons of war. And one Austrian officer was famously quoted as saying, "The mountains in winter are more dangerous than the Italians."

The worst known avalanche in U.S. history is in 16th on the admittedly incomplete Wikipedia list. It took place in the state of Washington in 1910 when one train, trapped by one avalanche, was wiped out by another slide that killed 96 passengers. It was the result of a massive storm system that pounded the northwest in late February and early March and also caused a lethal avalanche on Rogers Pass in Canada, not far from Revelstoke, that killed 58 men who were digging out a rail line.

A museum exhibit opened in Revelstoke in 2015 called "Thundering Snow" and dedicated to documenting the history of avalanches in North America. "Avalanches and snow define our area," said curator Cathy English. Many of the earliest big avalanche accidents on the continent involved miners and railroad workers, and construction in unsafe locations.

One of the earliest accounts is from 1782 in a small aboriginal village on the East Coast of Canada where, against the advice of the locals, settlers built a church at the foot of a slope that later slid and killed 22 people inside.

It's not a unique story by any means. There's a church near Davos, Switzerland that a guide pointed out to us in the summer of 1998, only months before avalanches ravaged the region during the trip I described in the last section. This church had been built years earlier, directly in an avalanche path that locals had warned them about. Soon enough a big slide completely destroyed it, though no one was hurt or killed. So they rebuilt in the same spot, only now the church resembles a big bunker with a reinforced concrete prow facing uphill into the slide path, designed to divert any avalanche around it.

That's one solution, perhaps, though arguably not the best. Relocating would seem smarter but maybe they couldn't afford property anywhere else. And they may have gotten a deal on the location they had due to that one serious drawback.

A similar tactic to what they did in rebuilding the church was deployed in Galtur, Austria in the summer following the tragic avalanche there. Rather than moving the entire 600-year-old village, they elected to build two large walls of heavily reinforced concrete, angled and shaped to deflect any future slides into unoccupied sections of the valley floor to run out. The concrete has been covered with local stone to blend into the hillside.

The tiny village of Stuben in the Arlberg near St. Anton is just a valley away from Galtur and suffered through terrible avalanches in 1737 and 1807 that led them to also build a wall in 1849 that has helped protect the town ever since.

Avalanche deaths weren't uncommon amongst miners in late the 1800s in America, including around Aspen, Colorado. Most of those deaths occurred to men caught in their cabins or mines. One winter alone suffered six such known fatalities.

Probing an avalanche in Vals, Switzerland, in the Winter of Terror, 1951. Photo courtesy of WSL Swiss Federal Institute for Snow and Avalanche Research SLF.

One of the early misapprehensions about avalanches before much study had been devoted to them was that slide paths and avalanche-prone slopes were similar to hundred-year flood plains. The attitude was that, yes they might have avalanches, but they also might not. And when they did, it was incredibly rare, which of course begged the question of how you define rare.

Today we know there are a number of obvious indications that some topography is simply slide-prone on a regular basis, but it took time to acquire such knowledge and instincts. And just as that was finally happening, humans further complicated their own situations by adding widespread recreational activities in the mountains in winter to their ever-evolving ways of placing themselves in mortal peril.

Skiing, for example. Cathy English in Revelstoke points out that it wasn't until the '60s and '70s that the leading cause of the "white death" switched from mining to recreation. And tracking the results of that interaction, much like gauging the impact of building in the urban/wildlands interfaces around the world, is a complicated and developing science. And only in the last few decades have studies been conducted to determine how avalanches have historically affected life on our planet.

We are still in the process of understanding the impact they have today on everything from sports to transportation, power supplies, infrastructure integrity and the natural environment, including their wholesale rearranging of topography.

Clearing debris from 2006 avalanche on rail line from Saint Gervais to Vallorcine, France. Photo by Poudou.

A 1998 paper out of Norway examined prehistoric avalanche-related data to help reveal things such as, "signals related to extreme weather events." Using material gathered from "post glacial colluvium" in case studies from western Norway showed, "a detailed pattern of winter climatic conditions (snowfall rates and the frequency of winter storms.)" One consequence will be a better understanding of past weather in order to predict future weather, especially during periods of drastic climate change.

In multiple studies of avalanche fatalities off-piste and in the backcountry, they are shown to be increasing more or less steadily in the U.S. while perhaps leveling off or even decreasing in Europe. However, there are so many variables left unexamined that it makes the results difficult to interpret.

For instance, on the surface it would seem to make sense that as the volume of those skiing off-piste and in the backcountry increases, so would avalanche-related accidents. But that doesn't necessarily take into account factors such as increased avalanche awareness and understanding, increased traffic in specific areas leading to safer conditions due to man-made snow compaction, and overall snow conditions.

Of these and many more possible influences, snow conditions will always be a major determinant that's felt across the board. Whether backcountry and off-piste usage is static, declining or increasing is partly a function of population size, and also very much a function of snow conditions – not always in a totally predictable manner.

Good snow years will almost inevitably generate more skiers at lift-served areas, and in the backcountry as well. But not always. If the economy is bad and people are broke, for example, the conditions are less of a factor in their decision-making. And a good snow year can sometimes actually lead to less off-piste and backcountry activity because the conditions on lift-served terrain are so good it's not necessary to go elsewhere. Conversely, a good snow year can produce so many skiers at resorts that more people go into the backcountry to avoid the crowds.

Another issue in big snow years, as discussed in the Going Deep chapters, is that getting to the slopes can be difficult, and sometimes the lifts can't open. If major storms happen over holiday periods and shut down transportation and lifts, it can have a profound impact on all skier numbers in a region, for the entire season.

Some statistical anomalies can be smoothed over via complicated formulas, but not without leaving conclusions subject to disagreement. And snow amounts aren't the only yardsticks. Massive snow will always be a danger, but even more so if it's accompanied by wind. And when there is wind involved, smaller amounts of snow can still be treacherous.

Increased avalanche awareness can certainly be a factor in skier's behavior if for no other reason than fear alone. When fatal slides occur where people realize, "that could have been me," then it may lead to them thinking more before they make bad decisions. All of that is very subjective and hard to quantify or measure. And it is offset by the influence of the increasing numbers of people choosing to ride in uncontrolled terrain who lack any avalanche knowledge, or even a sense of reality, at all.

Several aspects of the modern ski industry may contribute to increased backcountry usage. Videos and photos are always going to get blamed, especially in an age of proliferating social media, cell phones and body cams. When the hold-my-beer impulse meets the you're-streaming-live response, anything can happen, not all of it good.

The changes in equipment that have fueled the rise in backcountry riding are easier to gauge. When fatter, softer skis began making powder much easier to ride, it opened up new markets for the commodity. That was not only unfortunate for the skiers who previously had most of the goods to themselves, it was dangerous because it allowed people with relatively little experience at the sport to push beyond the limits of their knowledge and safety levels. And that put a lot of others around them at risk as collateral damage.

I heard this complaint repeatedly during the 1990s everywhere from Chamonix to Jackson, from Alaska to La Grave. And it was completely valid. On the other hand, one unanticipated consequence of this was that increased usage was actually making conditions safer in some previously sketchy areas, because it was stabilizing what had been largely uncontrolled slopes.

The concern has been that this user compaction was lulling inexperienced riders into false senses of security in places where that's never a good idea, and the consequences of uninformed decisions can be lethal not just to the riders involved but also innocent bystanders.

It's worth noting that it wasn't until 2018 that avalanche risk management was recognized by UNESCO as a cultural heritage. It made the Representative List of the Intangible Cultural Heritage of Humanity on the basis of a dossier supporting the application from Switzerland's Institute for Snow and Avalanche Research. That it took so long to understand the importance of such work is an indication both of the lack of overall comprehension of the issue, and the increasing impact avalanches were having on country's economies.

On a personal level, when you're swimming with sharks you don't have to swim faster than the shark, you just have to swim faster than who you're with. In heavily used backcountry terrain, you don't have to set the first tracks, you can always wait until someone else takes that chance.

That isn't to say you should let your friends be crash test dummies. The point is that if there are other tracks in a questionable area, they give you a lot more to go on. And if it's an area you're unfamiliar with, there might be a reason for it being untracked, such as it slides a lot or is very boney. But in the end, unless you're with a fully certified mountain guide, you have to rely on your own knowledge and no one else's. And if you have a lot of experience and something feels wrong or off, it's prudent to honor that.

I've honestly lost count of the potentially compromising avalanche situations I've found myself in. That's not smart, of course, and I'm just lucky to have made good decisions most of the time. But no one's luck lasts forever, and all it takes is one bad call to find out really quickly how hard it can be to survive a single simple mistake.

I grew up always hearing that you should first try to get out of your skis if a slide is coming, which is no longer common advice. But trying to more or less swim when it overtakes you and stay on top, is. Failing that, as the slide comes to a halt you're supposed to keep a space cleared around your mouth to hold oxygen long enough for someone to dig you out. While that's all more or less good advice, it begs the issue of how easy any of it is to accomplish when you need to.

Large, 3,000-meter-long avalanche in Nepal. Photo © Jay Cowan

The truth of any large slide is that you have little to no control over what it does to you. The concussive force preceding it can blow you off your feet. The billowing powder surrounding the slide can suffocate you by itself. A serious avalanche can Maytag you worse than any ocean or river, pounding your body into ruin and straining you through all the trees in its path. It can fill your mouth with snow packed so hard you can't dig it out. And when it stops it can settle around you as hard as the concrete around Jimmy Hoffa's body.

After all is said and done, after all the classes, beacons, dogs and best laid plans, it comes down to choices. Whether calculated, stupid, greedy, unlucky, thrill-seeking or divinely observed, we make the call and keep moving because then we're harder to hit.

The purpose of this section of the book is to focus on the risks and consequences of avalanches for skiers and the resort industry at large as illustrated by some of the most devastating resort avalanches in history.

CHAPTER 24
THE WORST SKI RESORT AVALANCHE DISASTERS — PART ONE

The Winter of Terror 1950/'51; Val d'Isere France, 1970; Galtur, Austria, 1999

THE WINTER OF TERROR IN AUSTRIA AND SWITZERLAND

Number 5 on the Wikipedia list of the 100 deadliest avalanches in history is what was called The Winter of Terror in 1950/'51, when a three-month series of 649 recorded avalanches decimated parts of Austria and Switzerland along their mutual border. It's one of the first and still the deadliest winter of avalanches in and around ski resorts in the Alps since the sport began flourishing.

In Austria 135 people died, and big swaths of economically vital forests in both countries were leveled. On January 20/21 three villages in the Tirol – Tux, Hippach and Soelden – were struck, killing 26. In addition Heiligenblut, Malinitz and Bad Gastein also suffered catastrophic avalanches taking 31 lives, including 14 who perished in their farmhouses near Bad Gastein.

It was just the start of a bad four-year period in Austria that still stands as the worst for avalanche deaths in their history. February and March of 1952 saw 27 die, and in December, 29 more were killed in the Tirol and Vorarlberg, including 24 in a bus swept off the road near Langen. Then 1954 saw a stunning 143 lost. A heavy snowfall from a northwesterly frontal zone started on January 9th dumping onto almost no base. On the single day of January 11 in the Vorarlberg, 116 perished, including in the town of Blons where two huge slides in 9 hours killed 57, with another 22 presumed dead. And on January 12 another 10 died in Dalaas.

Back in The Winter of Teror in the Valais Canton of Switzerland, 92 people were killed along with 500 head of cattle, and 900 buildings were destroyed. Andermatt, Switzerland, (as mentioned in a previous chapter), was

Clearing road from Zernez to Brail, Switzerland after avalanche, Winter of Terror, 1951. Photo from the ETH-Bibliothek.

blitzed by 6 avalanches in 60 minutes that killed 13. The village of Munter was virtually obliterated, with the church, schoolhouse, 7 homes and 8 stables destroyed and three lives lost.

An atypical and very saturated warm front off the Atlantic had collided with a polar cold front over the region creating a three-day January blizzard that dumped from two to 4.5 meters (6.5 to 15 feet) of snow on top of a base already twice the seasonal average. Heavy winds caused major drifting, buildings collapsed, avalanches thundered down almost constantly, and according to one report, "more than 40,000 people were buried under snow." Obviously the vast majority survived, but the human and financial tolls were unprecedented and prompted the first modern wave of serious avalanche-mitigation barrier construction throughout the Alps.

VAL D'ISERE, FRANCE

The next really serious slide at a ski resort happened in 1970 at Val d'Isere, France. At about 8:05 a.m. on February 10th a massive avalanche tore down the ski slopes, killing three trail workers before slamming into a student hostel at the base owned by a youth club called the Union of Fresh Air Centers.

Breaking loose from a 2,133-meter (7,000-foot) high ridge called le Dome, a slide of more than 100,000 cubic yards (roughly a football-stadium's worth, full to the rafters) reached the valley floor, barreled 640 meters (2,100 feet) across the Isere River and a section of National Route 202 before plowing into the three-story chalet with its 200 occupants. Thirty-nine died and twice that many were injured. Most were French, some Belgians, primarily in their early 20s. To this day it remains the worst avalanche disaster in French history.

French President Georges Pompidou declared it a national tragedy and evacuations of other resorts in the region were ordered. That paid off when more avalanches came down over the next few days, and the abandoned hostel in Val d'Isere got hit again two days later.

"Freakishly warm weather and high winds were held responsible for the avalanche," the New York Times reported. Heavy snows had fallen in the region in the previous days. Then temps rose above freezing and the mayor of Val d'Isere reported winds in excess of 100 miles per hour caused serious drifting and helped further destabilize the snowpack.

Survivors reported being at breakfast on the ground floor of the hostel when they heard "a terrible noise" that some compared to an explosion or thunder, followed quickly by a mountain of snow crashing through the eight-year-old concrete building. Few had time to even move.

One reported from the hospital that the slide came through a window and carried him down a corridor and out a back window. A young woman was dragged unconscious but alive from an air hole under stairs in the dining room where many took refuge. And a father wandering the halls of a local hospital trying to find out anything about his son told reporters, "They really don't know anything."

A student named Jacques Sifferlen who was trapped in the slide told the New York Times, "I tried to get people out. But a lot of them were stuck like in concrete. You couldn't pull them out and had to cut people out with steel blades."

To make matters worse, the blizzard continued to rage throughout the day and into the night, badly hampering rescue efforts. The Swiss Federal Institute for Snow and Avalanche Research (SLF) in Davos, Switzerland, reported that it was the worst loss of life in a single avalanche in Europe since 1900.

The Times pointedly noted that, "Responsibility for measures against avalanches and for evacuations when one threatens, normally lies with local authorities in France." In a statement to the press, Melchior Schild of the SLF called the procedure in Val d'Isere haphazard and amateurish.

GALTUR, AUSTRIA

The tragedy in Galtur, Austria during the "winter of avalanches" throughout the Alps in 1999 was an awful example of how the worst can happen to skiers and their families when they aren't even on the slopes. Just as in Val d'Isere, scores of people died when something happened that never had before in the town. In the case of Galtur, in more than 600 years of recorded history, no avalanche had ever come off the Grieskogel mountain directly to the northwest and reached across the valley floor to the village.

I first visited the Paznaun Valley on a press trip in 1996 when they took us to Galtur for the skiing on the Ballunspitze Mountain, just up the road from the village, and we also went off-piste for a circumnavigation of the Piz Buin mountain on the border with Switzerland.

In a trip the next winter on assignment to Ischgl, a few kilometers down the road from Galtur, we stopped in to visit with the friends we'd made there. And the following summer, researching my Best of the Alps book, which didn't include Galtur, we nevertheless visited the area for a day because we'd grown so fond of it.

So this avalanche in 1999, as much as the one near Chamonix while we were there, felt personal. Over the course of multiple phone calls to the resort, and a trip back there the next winter, I came to understand more about one of the worst avalanches ever in a ski resort in the Alps. And I wrote the following (with some more recent updates) for the Aspen Times newspaper while I was in the resort in 2000.

In the Paznaun Valley of Austria, in the high Silvretta Alps once frequented by Ernest Hemingway, they are used to avalanches. Called *lawine* in Austrian, they've been rumbling down these steep-walled mountains since time immemorial. As I drive up the valley on the last day of January 2000, in the 12 kilometers between the resorts of Ischgl and Galtur we count at least 30 big slab slides serious enough to tear down trees and move the earth beneath them. But these aren't unusual features anywhere in the Alps, and they wouldn't be especially noteworthy now if not for what happened here last year.

The *Pfarrkirche* (parish church) Mariae Geburt has stood in its location near the high end of the Paznaun for 7 centuries. And the village of Galtur that nestles around it has over 600 years of recorded history. In all that time the towering Gorfenspitze to the southwest and the Grieskogel to the northwest have sloughed off countless thousands of avalanches that could seriously ruin anyone's day, but they had never once actually encroached on the village.

Now, however, there are three fresh wooden crosses in the northeast corner of the church yard commemorating the 31 lives that were lost last February 23rd, when the slide heard 'round the world slammed into the quiet snowbound town. "Since then," says our hotelier Franz Lorenz, "things are not the same."

Alongside the wood crosses are six small metal ones draped in white and black lace with wilted blue rose buds stuck in the snow by each. They represent the 6 local people who died that day, all women and children. Two of them were members of the Lorenz family, at whose Alpentirol Hotel we're staying.

When last winter's savage storms battered the Alps they produced death and destruction from one end of the mountains to the other for the 6 weeks we were there. And when we returned home in the middle of February, feeling lucky to have made it out alive, the stormy rampage in the Alps still wasn't over. When we saw on the news that two killer slides had come down in and near Galtur claiming 38 lives altogether, we wondered immediately if we knew any of them.

Galtur calls itself a "headstrong" village because they're one of the only ones in the Paznaun Valley not to opt for developing skiing on the glaciers above town to that stretch all along the Swiss border. In a distance of a little more than 100 kilometers from the upper end of the Paznaun to Innsbruck there are four major glacier-skiing resorts that do in excess of a million skier-visits a year each.

Galtur, with 3,700 guest beds, gets about half a million overnights a year and sells less than 200,000 lift tickets [at that time] in a season. It's skiing is just a few klicks away in tiny Wirl, at the base of the almost cartoonishly pointed Ballunspitze mountain.

Graveyard at parish church, Galtur, Austria. Three large crosses for 31 lives lost, 6 small metal ones for the local women and children. Photo © Jay Cowan.

Galtur has intentionally and repeatedly chosen to remain small, friendly and quaint. Everyone greets you with a real smile. They all speak at least some English and attempt it with ingratiating warmth. On a sunny afternoon you can always smell some cattle manure in the streets where they roam pretty freely during summers. And it doesn't get a lot more rural than that in Austria.

Their skiing is by no means limited to the 2,500-vertical feet of lift-served slopes, and it may be most famous for its off-piste and alpine touring. It's one of the reasons families like the Lorenz's have been here so long. Franz Lorenz's grandfather built a small stone hut at 2,165 meters (7,100 feet) up the Jamtal in 1882. At first it was just for summer hikers and climbers, in a valley that intersects the Paznaun right at Galtur. When Franz took charge over 40 years ago [at the time], the hut kept expanding and so did the season which now includes late winter and early spring skiers and is exceedingly popular, especially with Germans.

I'd had a chance to experience bits of all their on-slope offerings in the area, including the only legitimate barrel-stave skiing I've ever done, at a weekly race in Galtur. It's pure mayhem wrapped in liberal doses of *gluhwein* and *enzian* schnaaps. But with all of its potential for personal disaster, the race had undoubtedly saved lives in the winter of '99.

The month of February that year had started in Galtur as it did everywhere in the Alps, with one major storm system after another pummeling the area. Usually February in the Tirol isn't a big snow month, but heavy moisture off the Atlantic kept meeting Arctic cold fronts right over the mountains and dumping unprecedented amounts of snow. The month would end up as the snowiest ever in Galtur's *123 years* of keeping records. Combined with this gross excess of snow were three weeks of strong 80 to 90 kilometer per hour winds. They came out of the northwest and wind-loaded the southeast-facing slopes of the Grieskogel, the heights of which remained invisible for most of the month, obscured by storm clouds. By mid-February there had been 16 Level 5 avalanche warnings – the highest possible – issued in the Tirol, something that had only happened three times ever before.

Avalanche experts would later determine that over 20 different types of snow fell in this period, producing continual unstable layering. Manfred Lorenz, one of Franz's three sons, is a state certified mountain and ski guide, as well as a trained avalanche specialist and mountaineer of some repute. He has made ski descents of 8,000-meter Broad Peak in the Karakoram, and Shisha Pangma in Tibet [at the time he was one of the first to do so].

I'd skied with him with a press group two years earlier and didn't know any of this. This time he's touring me around again and he starts off by explaining what happened a year ago. "For 10 days straight we had snow and rain, warm and cold, with lots of wind," he says as he points toward the avalanche-ridden slopes of the Grieskogel from the other side of the valley where the Jam River comes in. "Then two days before the catastrophe we had many smaller slides, like we see now. And we thought, good, because that brings the snow down, but it doesn't reach the village, and that makes things safer. But we couldn't see that it was still piling more and more snow on the same places that had already slid."

Construction of huge avalanche-deflecting wall, Galtur, Austria, after tragic slides of 1999. Photo © Jay Cowan.

Hilary Slater and her family had arrived on holiday from their home in Germany on the 13th of February, after the road up the Paznaun had already been closed once and re-opened. In an account she wrote and sent to Manfred in March of 1999, she tells of continuing snows and high winds that finally shut all the skiing down by February 17, and closed the roads out of to their planned departure on the 19th. As she wrote, "The roads were closed in the evening, both down the valley and also to Wirl. We have experienced one day blizzards in the past, followed by glorious sunshine the next day, so there was no cause for concern."

On the 21st the temps rose and snow started thawing. Helicopters were shuttling in fresh food, water and medicine and taking out those who wanted to leave and could foot the costs of the chopper shuttle to Landeck. But there were priority passengers and 20 flights that day were all booked. The Slaters agreed with the call not to open the roads due to avalanche danger, and they never ran out of food, water or electricity.

On the 22nd the weather again turned too bad for any flights as another meter of new snow fell on the mountains. At the Lorenz's Jamtalhutte a slide crashed into the building destroying one wing and rattling the six occupants. They included Gottfried Lorenz, the brother of Manfred and twin of Peter, who ran the Alpenhotel Tirol with his older sister Maria Luise.

It was the 23rd before Gottfried could call down to Galtur to let them know what happened. "The building was all scrambled," 74-year-old Franz tells us. "But they were okay. And so my wife, Hildegard, and my daughter and I decided to go visit Gottfried's wife in the village to keep her company." But Peter needed help at the hotel so Franz stayed while the women went.

Meanwhile on that brooding day, Manfred was in a parking lot at the mouth of the Jamtal, waiting for possible helicopter landings bringing more medicine and food. The Tourist office had been trying to keep stir-crazy visitors entertained and were staging some of their famous barrel stave races down the snow-closed street that sloped past the church, with a course that ended in front of the city hall.

As the race finished around four o'clock people were gathered in the *Dorfplatz* to await the awards. A couple from Germany, Christa and Helmut Kapellner, recorded the moment on their video camera. That tape was later broadcast on a BBC special that we watched on video at the Alpenhotel. Manfred had seen the program but the rest of the family still had not. The tragedy was still that fresh and raw.

On the Kapellner's tape it was snowing furiously and they joked about Helmut looking like an abominable snowman. Hilary Slater would later write of that day, "We awoke to another whiteout." Fresh snow was blown in everywhere." They went to watch the barrel-stave races and on their way back to their apartment, "We heard a strange noise which we assumed came from the Dorfplatz, followed by a cloud moving from left to right quite quickly…. Everything went completely white, we couldn't see anything, we were enveloped by a snowstorm coming hard from all sides. We tried to turn away but it was impossible… We hung on to each other and waited. It was somewhat frightening," she added.

It lasted for several minutes, though it seemed longer, and they later heard it was what was called a *staublawine*, or a powder avalanche. They went straight to their apartment and were told not to leave, and at 6:30 were told that a big avalanche had come down between the church and the Hotel Ballunspitze. Slater wrote, "Fifty-five people we unaccounted for. TV reports claimed 25 missing, 10 badly injured and 7 dead… we didn't sleep well."

In the helicopter landing lot outside of the town center, Manfred heard and saw nothing, but instantly felt the blast of wind and powder generated by the slide. Christa and Helmut Zellner had just switched off their video camera. Later she would worry that if they hadn't stopped to film, they might both have lived. Helmut only had time to yell "Christa!" as they were struck, and it was the last time she saw or heard him.

Manfred Lorenz has participated in many avalanche rescues, and was on the scene in Nepal in 1986 a day after a big slide killed 25 Japanese trekkers. "But I have never seen anything like this," he tells us. The BBC broadcast would say later that experts estimated more than a million tons of snow had come down the mountainside in a tsunami-like wave *reaching 100 meters (well over 300 feet) high and travelling at nearly 200 miles per hour.* It lasted about two minutes from fracture point to finish. Eye-witnesses and victims later described it variously as a "steamroller," "a tidal wave," and "like being inside a washing machine."

About 300 vertical meters above town the slide split in two. One side ran down the Grosses Valley, the other sheared off into the Wasserleiter, narrowly missing a 400-year-old farmhouse. It continued to plow unimpeded across the road that leads to Wirl. The Grosses Tal Lawine was 400 meters (1,300 feet) wide and set up over 9 meters (30 feet) deep. It smashed into 17 buildings, completely destroying 7, all homes and lodges. If it hadn't first collided with the small but stout firehouse just across the street, it would certainly have hit the ancient church.

At Gottlieb Lorenz's home, his sister had decided to try to run some errands in the village and was safe, while her mother and sister-in-law drank coffee in the kitchen. That was where they eventually found them, dead under snow that had set up like concrete, like great white slabs of marble.

For 40 years Franz Lorenz had been up at the Jamtalhutte every winter, taking care of guests, while down in the valley his wife raised their four children and greeted guests on the way to the hut. In the summers the whole family was together at the cabin.

"For four generations we have always been very careful in the mountains because we know the risks," Franz tells us, his eyes watery. "Not like some new people who don't understand and are reckless. And then for this to happen, here in the village, where we thought we were safe." He sighs and shakes his head. "So now they must end in the snow," he says of his 78-year-old wife, Hildegard, and their 34-year-old daughter-in-law Edith.

First the slides seemed to seek out his son Gottlieb, but narrowly missed him. Then they cane for Gottlieb's wife and mother. And the cruel ironies of the disaster weren't through. "We have a very old friend, Herr Zangerl, who for years was proprietor of the highest hut in these mountains," says Franz. "But then he and his wife became old and had moved back into the valley, into a new house they built. And there his 84-year-old wife, their 56-year-old daughter and 16-year-old granddaughter all perished too, sparing only the father who was away."

For the first 24 hours after the avalanche Galtur was completely shut off, isolated from the outside world. What was always a tight-knit village became even closer, bonded in the aftermath, digging through the night in rubble that looked like the result of some massive bomb blast.

There was one trained avalanche dog in the town, a 6-year-old German Shepherd/Labrador mix named Heiko that became a hero. He was the one that found Christa Kapellner after she had been buried beneath two cars for nearly three hours. The body of her husband Helmut, who had been only feet away from her when the slide struck, was eventually found nearly 150 meters (500 feet) away.

"This wasn't like an avalanche that traps skiers," Manfred explains. "There they usually have Pieps [avalanche beacons], so you locate them quickly and then dig. Here, we didn't even know where to start." The next day as helicopters began arriving with 200 rescuers to help, they tried using infrared devices from the air, but it was no good. "There was too much debris, too much electricity running in the snow. It didn't help at all," says Manfred.

The avalanche hit on Tuesday and the last body was dug out on Saturday. Of the 31 dead, 12 were children. All were either locals or visiting Germans and Dutch. Two entire families of tourists were wiped out: four Schulz's, four Albingers. Hilary Slater's family was eventually evacuated on an American Blackhawk chopper with Bosnian military markings. They left with a Dutch man who had lost his wife. And the nightmare wasn't over.

Within hours another major avalanche tore through the tiny hamlet of Valzur, a part of the Ischgl township just down the road, killing 7 more. With 38 dead in less than 24 hours, it was the worst avalanche disaster in Austria in 50 years. And now the valley was left with the approbation, the trauma and the confusion over how such a thing could happen and where to go from there.

Put bluntly, the tragedy was an existential event. It was precipitated by conditions no one could have foreseen, resulting in an avalanche of such freakish proportions that, at first, not even computer-simulated models of worst case scenarios could recreate it. Think of that.

After a variety of avalanche experts in Austria and Switzerland worked together for 6 months, they finally determined that one of the weakest of the snow layers in the long-running series of storms, held for far longer than it probably should have. And once the slide started it had gathered snow as it went, doubling in mass. Then the big dense slabs at the bottom had churned up to the top, mixing with a "salt-snow" layer in the middle and powder on top. It all accelerated and advanced much further out across the more than two football-field-lengths (200 meters) between the bottom of the mountain and the village than any slide ever had before.

The sheer, unimaginable force simply leveled some buildings. Ice, rock trees and other slide debris strafed many structures like heavy war-time shelling, and the powder cloud invaded others through windows and doors, filling and exploding them like houses of cards. Most of the fatalities, it was concluded, had resulted from asphyxiation.

Beyond the obvious and devastating gravity of the disaster itself were a host of other problems. Many evacuees had left their cars and most of their belongings in order to be ferried out by helicopter, and would spend the spring returning for them. Some tourists had been incensed at not being allowed to leave to begin with, at being, in their minds, trapped in the path of the destruction. City officials had been forced to make decisions with the good of everyone in mind, and were working from historic knowledge that avalanches were poised to happen, especially if long caravans of cars began rumbling down the valley.

Some visitors had a different perspective, especially when they were being charged (albeit at a reduced rate) for their room and board after not being allowed to leave. "It was very difficult because the lodges had to work and provide the rooms and food, and they couldn't do it for free," Tourist Office director Gerhard Walter explains to us. "But this angered many people."

As in other Tirolean resorts that were also closed to arrivals and departures, such anger sometimes almost came to blows. Stories out of the Arlberg while we were making our way from Austria to Switzerland during that winter were of chaos and near rioting as visitors had been barred from leaving for days. And they hadn't even ended up getting avalanched on.

In Galtur, tourists were furious that they weren't being allowed to make a run for it, and that more chopper flights weren't being laid on to evacuate them sooner. The consequences of both of those gripes were that they had essentially been held captive in harm's way. It was all the stuff of big lawsuits and terrible press. And indeed some local politicians were brought to trial for negligence in not doing more to protect the village and its visitors. However, unlike similar cases in Switzerland and France, they weren't convicted.

Eighty percent of Galtur's business comes from Germany, and the publicity there was scathing. It was awful enough what the village had faced from the physical impact of the avalanche, and next came the question not of individual deaths, but possibly that of the whole community.

Left to quite literally pick up the pieces and start over, the first decision Galtur faced was whether to continue at all. "At first we discussed if we had other choices for making a living," says Gerhard Walter. "But we really didn't. For the 200 families who live here, tourism was the base for our survival. The farming of the old days was no longer an option and there was nothing else." The question then was, would the tourists return? "So we had to do everything we could to make it safe again."

Fortifying against a catastrophe of such unpredictable proportions might seem nearly impossible, but in fact avalanche protection has become a high science in the Alps. The real test was in executing the engineering and construction needed.

It all started with widespread support, both moral and financial from throughout Austria and Europe. The main costs of rebuilding that weren't covered by insurance were assisted by the national, Tirolean and local governments. Once the absurd amounts of snow finally melted, expedited construction permits were issued and construction began in mid-July. They accomplished in 7 to 8 months what would normally have taken at least two years.

Villagers were all given the choice of new land and new locations on which to start again, but all chose to stay where they had been. It was an important sign, and for that to work, it meant building differently, with stronger structures that had no door or window openings on the sides facing the slide paths. By winter most of the buildings that were damaged or destroyed had been rebuilt except for two.

Most importantly of course, were the external protections for the whole village. Up on the top ridges of the Grieskogel, new snow fences of the types that ribbon most mountains in the Alps, were added where they had

EN IMAGES

En 1970, 111 morts dans deux avalanches à Val d'Isère et au Plateau d'Assy

Le Dauphiné Libéré - 19 janv. 2017 à 11:16 | mis à jour le 13 avr. 2019 à 08:57

Le 10 février 1970, une énorme avalanche défonçait l'immeuble de l'UCPA à Val d'Isère (Savoie). 250 personnes déjeunaient à 8 heures du matin quand la neige a envahi le bâtiment. Des voitures ont été projetées à plus de 100 mètres. Le bilan est très lourd : 39 morts et 37 blessés. Photo Archives Le DL

Screenshot story of 1970 avalanche, Val d'Isere, France, killing 39. Archives of ledauphine.co.

never before been thought necessary, helping allay wind-drifting and cornice buildups. The project continued for 5 years with steel fences 5 meters (16½ feet) high, anchored a minimum of 2.5 meters (7 feet) into solid rock. If they don't at first strike rock, they keep drilling until they do. "Some of the holes are twelve and a half meters deep," says Manfred Lorenz, who helped in all phases of their planning and construction.

On the southeastern perimeter of the village, two long, beefy, concrete and steel dams were erected to deflect the initial impact of any future killer slides from the Grieskogel. One is 150 meters (492 feet) long, the other 350 meters (1,150 feet), and they range from 9 to 14 meters (30-50 feet) high. These mega-retaining walls are fronted with a gray and black stone from the area that helps them blend in.

Both are also anchored on the village sides by big buildings. One is a concrete and block private house, the other is an all-new concrete building housing a parking garage, fire/rescue station, and an alpine academy devoted to studying mountains and working with similar universities throughout Europe. Included in their studies are avalanches. The community wanted this to be another way of learning and somehow benefitting from the tragedy.

Along with Ischgl they also became the first resorts in Austria to initiate an insurance program for the community. In the event that guests should ever again be forced to stay past their scheduled departure dates, the town will pay for their food and lodgings and collect on their premiums for it. It has become a major tool for many resorts in the Alps to reassure their visitors.

With most of the rebuilding completed in record time, Galtur held a big winter opening with special package rates and a big open-air concert at the base of the Ballunspitze that was a great success.

Then on December 28th, 9 German tourists on an alpine touring trek near the Jamtalhutte were killed in another avalanche. It was 15 kilometers (9 miles) away from Galtur, nowhere near the lift-served slopes, but right away the news hit the wires and Internet with Galtur as the dateline.

Even a month later when we arrived the accident still wasn't well understood. The group was accompanied in front and back by German and Austrian guides, and the relatively small slide missed all of them. The skiers who were caught all had transceivers and were dug out quickly, but none survived. Soon, the question once again was, would Galtur survive, after taking another hit so soon?

The answer, looking back as this book is written, was a resounding yes. Even that next winter with the unfortunate start, business was down less than other Tirolean resorts on average. Galtur has added many new diversions and facilities. The Lorenz family's Jamtalhutte was beautifully rebuilt and preparing to re-open just after we left in that winter of 2000.

On our departure day we watched 74-year-old Franz Lorenz heading up the Jamtal to the hut in the snowcat with his son Gottlieb driving. Two men who had lost wives to the *lawine*, but been somehow spared themselves, returning to the high mountains. Hemingway himself might have paused to ponder it.

CHAPTER 25

THE WORST SKI RESORT AVALANCHE DISASTERS – PART TWO

Montroc and Le Tour, France 1999; Evolene, Switzerland 1999; Rigopiano, Italy 2017.

MONTROC AND LE TOUR, FRANCE, 1999

Chamonix was one of our last stops in the wild winter of 1999 and when we arrived the snow was still coming down with a fury. As one of the world's great mountain towns and the unquestioned center for ski alpinism, Chamonix is familiar with avalanches and the deaths and devastation they bring. Mont Blanc alone – at 15,815 feet the highest in the Alps – sloughs off major slides on a regular basis. Those include increasing numbers of calving glaciers and landslides, one of which I mentioned in a preceding chapter as being responsible for the death of skiers at Courmayeur.

In the very sheer mountain environment all around Chamonix, with so much stone at steep pitches, bonding between snow and the rest of the planet is never a certain thing. In the "avalanche winter" of 1999, it was the perfect breeding ground for a catastrophic slide.

An overview of that winter in Switzerland was presented by researchers at the Swiss Federal Institute for Snow and Avalanche Research (SLF) to International Snow Science Workshop Proceedings under the auspices of the Montana State University Library, and also issued as a press release by the SLF on February 21, 2019. Among several aspects examined, it outlined the root cause for the disastrous winter. "Three intensive snowfall periods accompanied by stormy northwesterly winds brought over 5 meters of new snow within one month to the northern side of the Alps."

The dates of the three heavy snow events were roughly January 26 – 31, February 5 – 10 and 17 – 24. The storms were induced by a high-pressure system off the Atlantic coast of Europe and a low-pressure Scandinavian front colliding over the mountains.

An analysis by the Snow Study Center at the National Center for Meteorological Research in France, published in the Journal of Glaciology in 2010, concluded, "As a result, fast altitude streams conveyed cold and wet air from the Arctic regions to the northern Alps," and also produced high winds from the northwest, conditions that are "often associated with

Memorial for 12 killed in a 1999 avalanche that devastated Le Tour and Montroc, near Chamonix, France. Photo by 503PM Pierre Martin.

intense precipitation and major avalanche release in the northern Alps." The relentlessly cold weather had several high temperature spikes that were slide triggers, particularly during the second storm system.

On our first day in Chamonix it was still snowing hard and all of the ski areas were closed. The tourist office, concerned that I might not get to ski at all in my time there, arranged for a guide (Gilles Claret, a former ski tuner for my friend Christin Cooper on the World Cup tour) to take me through the Mont Blanc tunnel to Courmayeur, where it wasn't snowing and hadn't gotten hit quite as hard.

We ate lunch at a mid-mountain restaurant there and my guide showed me some framed photos on the wall of a massive landslide/avalanche that had happened a few years earlier. A glacier had calved and cut loose a huge volume of snow, ice and rock from thousands of feet up on a flank of Mont Blanc across a very steep, narrow valley from where we were. It blasted down into that valley and then up the side we were on, burying some skiers on the slope below us and blowing completely up and over the restaurant we were in, 3,000 vertical feet up the mountain. The people in the restaurant who took the photos survived by pure luck.

That avalanche wasn't caused by large amounts of fresh snow so much as by climate change that was continuing to wreak havoc in all of the Alps. Around Mont Blanc the warmer temperatures are thawing the ice that has held together the high stone towers of *dents, drus and aiguilles* for eons, and entire sides of them are peeling off. It happened a couple of summers after this trip when the Aiguille Vert shed a large slab from near the summit and the resulting landslide covered the whole valley with several inches of dust for miles around.

On the day after my visit to Courmayeur, February 9, there was still nothing good open in Chamonix and it was still dumping. Our departure was pushed back a day and more avalanches had come down all over the Swiss canton of Valais around Zermatt, right after we left there for Chamonix, destroying buildings but fortunately taking no lives. And St. Anton had gotten another two meters of snow in as many days, stranding thousands of visitors because of closed roads and rail lines. It was being called the biggest winter in 20 years all over Europe.

We visited Chamonix's renowned Alpine Museum that afternoon and were being guided around when a siren went off causing obvious consternation amongst some in the museum. We completed our visit without giving it much more thought, and it wasn't until the next morning that we saw the local papers and heard on CNN there had been a massive avalanche just up the valley that had wiped out numerous chalets and killed people.

It had finally stopped snowing and the sun was shining on the mounds of new powder. But all the skiing was still locked down due to the extreme avalanche danger, and there was a noticeable pall on the normally bustling town. When I spoke to Xavier Chappaz, the head of the Companie de Guides de Chamonix, he told me, "Here, everyone knows someone who was killed. We feel for the visitors, and we feel for our own."

The usually gregarious staff at our hotel was subdued. One of the women at the front desk told us that there was widespread fear about where the next slide would hit. Then she gave a nervous glance over her shoulder and up toward the mountain that loomed almost directly above us. The Hotel du Mont Blanc has been in its location in one form or another since 1849 without major incident. And the tourist office is located in one of end of it, which presumably means they have faith in its security. But at that point, no one felt safe anywhere.

Apparently with good reason, as the shocking details of the deadly slide became clearer. In all, 17 chalets in the villages of Montroc and Le Tour had been, as the French daily newspaper Le Figaro put it, "souffled." Eventually 12 people, locals and tourists alike, were confirmed dead, including four children. More than 20 were dug out of the rubble alive, two in critical condition.

The scale of the avalanche was hard to imagine. It had come like the wrath of god down a mountain above where it ended, crossing the Arve River and a road and consuming all the buildings in its path. In the end it was from 120 to 185 meters (400 - 600 feet) wide, over 30 meters (100 feet) deep where it damned up the river, and 6 to 9 meters (20 - 30 feet) deep where it stopped.

One of the first big issues beyond the rescue operation was to excavate the massive snow dam as quickly as possible or they risked having a lake form that would flood the surrounding area.

Gilles Claret, my guide to Courmayeur, and 200 other guides and rescuers with dogs, sensors and heavy machinery delivered by helicopters, worked for days on end driven by a fear that there were still some people unaccounted for. It was the worst such catastrophe in the area in more than 90 years, and all around the valley, other homes in possible jeopardy were evacuated. Then the question inevitably arose, why hadn't evacuations come sooner?

The big storm at the end of January had delivered a meter of snow to the Chamonix region. Then a second period of intense snowfall started on February 5th and brought at least two meters over the next 5 days with serious wind-loading. Avalanche danger rose to Extreme.

While all of this was going on, concerns grew over the situation because construction of new houses in the Chamonix valley was booming and some were built too close to known slide paths. Evacuations were discussed but no decisions were made, "with disastrous consequences," as one report concluded. A local politician was soon held responsible, tried and sent to prison for negligence.

I was able to ski the following day on the bottom of Les Grands Montet, just next door to where the avalanche rescue work was ongoing. Choppers shuttled in and out of the ski area parking lot, and it had started to snow again. In spite of the singular warning that such close proximity to the disaster constituted, in spite of the fact that all off-piste was still closed and off limits, in spite of stellar skiing on-piste and the presence of ski patrol everywhere, people raged all over the out-of-bounds like nothing had ever happened or could.

In all, more than two-dozen major avalanches were reported in the vicinity of Mont Blanc during the February 5 through 10 storm cycle. Ultimately 19 people would die within a week in the Haute Savoie region of the French Alps, including three in Les Arcs, two in Val d'Isere, and one in Courchevel, all skiing in closed off-piste areas. It was hard to comprehend. And indeed a few days later in Chamonix two American snowboarders landed in court for riding out-of-bounds and setting off a slide that swept across open and marked ski trails.

EVOLENE, SWITZERLAND, 1999

Barely 12 days after the slide in Montroc and Le Tour, when we'd already returned home and two days before the Galtur tragedy, another Swiss ski resort was struck on February 21st. The municipality of Evolene is in the Valais canton, just one valley west of Zermatt. The snow that had been stacking up all February was reaching such absurd proportions that the community would have been on a higher avalanche alert than 3 as they entered the third week of the month. But cold temperatures had remained constant for most of the month, and the new snow was adhering well to the old and not layering up.

Then on the 18th weather reports indicated a warming trend and during that night the temperature climbed by 5 degrees Celsius. This rapid rise caused snow layers to mix, but the situation still wasn't viewed as critical enough to instigate emergency measures.

On The 20th of February the surrounding mountain got another .2 to .3 meters (8 - 12 inches) of snow and the avalanche alert was raised to level 4. The temperature stayed constant until midday on the 21st when it started rising quickly due to prolonged sun exposure. At 8:27 that evening, a fracture line nearly 4 kilometers long ran across a mountainside between the summits of Sasseneire and Ponte du Tsate, above the Vill section of Evolene.

A combination of new snow and the old roared 1,000 meters (3,300 vertical feet) down two adjacent gullies of the three avalanche paths of Le Brequet, Torrent des Maures and Mayens de Cotter, taking out trees and chalets and joining together near the valley floor to pile debris up almost 50 feet high.

Twelve people were killed, including 7 French, three Swiss and two Germans. Eight houses, four chalets, 5 barns and several alpine huts were completely destroyed along with 25 hectares of forest and 9 cars, while 10 other houses and chalets were damaged. Telephone and power lines were torn out and two main roads in and out of town were buried.

A 21-year-old Swiss man who had been skiing outside marked runs when the avalanche occurred was found alive 17 hours after the avalanche due to a small pocket of air in the snow that entombed him. What he was doing skiing at night through the forest wasn't explained, and the fact that he only had mild hypothermia as a result was considered a miracle. He wasn't carrying a transceiver and was found after an aerial helicopter search was initiated when reports came in that he was missing.

In a subsequent study by the Agroscope Reckenholz-Tanikon Research Station, they used dendrochronological methods to date one of the cottages that was obliterated by the slides. Portions of the wood in it were found to go back to 1693. The study noted, "The age of the dated construction wood suggests that the flow path of the 1999 avalanche was unusual and that it affected a sector that has, most probably, not suffered from similar events for at least 300 years."

The Swiss daily newspaper Le Matin on February 23 carried an entire front page dedicated to covering Evolene and the collective avalanche disaster of the winter so far. The banner headline was simple: La Mort Blanche (The White Death), in all caps.

After the end of the worst avalanche winter in Switzerland in 50 years, the SLF announced that some 3,000 slides occurred in the Swiss Alps alone during the siege, more than 1,000 of which did damage to structures, power lines and agricultural land and caused "havoc to the country's lucrative tourist industry."

Screenshot of front page of Swiss daily Le Matin, 1999, La Mort Blanche (The White Death) in/re Evolene, Switzerland tragedy.

In the SLF report they discussed Evolene and pointed out that, "the avalanche gave rise to protracted criminal proceedings." In 2006 the Federal Supreme Court upheld findings of negligent homicide, injury and disrupting public transport against the former head of the village council and the safety chief, handing them three- and two-month suspended jail sentences and fines of $17,000 and $25,500, respectively.

On the morning of the day of he avalanches the town's safety chief, with 25 years experience as a mountain guide, told the mayor he had performed an analysis of the snow at the village of La Sage at 1,727 meters, and that he deemed to avalanche hazard to be "very large." This required the evacuation of un-reinforced building in certain areas and the closure of certain roads. This was done though it was argued that it wasn't done thoroughly enough.

Ultimately the outcome hinged on whether the buildup to the slides was so exceptional that neither man could have predicted that they would reach the village. The court concluded that given the situation the defendants could have done more, though the punishment was light enough to suggest that they agreed the circumstances were extenuating. And such was the case in other convictions from that winter in Switzerland and France.

Hotel Rigopiano, Rigopiano, 65010 Farindola, Itali

Catastrophic 2017 avalanche at Rigopiano, Italy, destroyed hotel and killed 29 people. Image via Creative Commons/ YouTube.

RIGOPIANO, ITALY 2017

As has been demonstrated time and again, the worst ski resort avalanches in terms of fatalities are those that strike lodges, homes and on-mountain facilities. Whether in Val d'Isere, Galtur, Montroc and Le Tour and numerous other places, it's much the same story. Occurring without warning, often when the ski slopes are closed due to the hour or conditions, they catch groups of people unawares in difficult conditions.

In one of the most devastating accidents to strike a village or resort in the Alps in several decades, the Rigopiano avalanche on January 18, 2017 destroyed a four-star hotel and killed 29 people in and around it. It was the greatest loss of life in an Italian avalanche since 1916, and the deadliest in Europe since Galtur, Austria in 1999.

Several aspects made it unusual and controversial. As is typical in such cases, record snowfall preceded the disaster. But a complication in determining its cause was created by a series of earthquakes that hit the region earlier the day of the avalanche. A research paper published in 2020 in scientific reports at nature.com entitled "Seismic signature of the deadly snow avalanche of January 18, 2017, at Rigopiano (Italy)", offered some conclusions and insights about the unobserved slide.

Chief amongst them was this: "Given the large epicentral distance [of the quakes from the slide] and a minimum 2h time offset between the latest M5 event and the snow mass detachment, we consider it as very unlikely that the avalanche was released by ground oscillations from those events, while temperature increase in the course of the day may, however, play an important role for triggering the avalanche."

Crucial to the unfolding of the tragedy was an extreme weather event in the Appenines, which is the snowiest region of Italy. Another scientific paper on the avalanche (A Reverse Dynamical Investigation of the Catastrophic Wood-Snow Avalanche of 18 January 2017 at Rigopiano Gran Sasso National Park, Italy) noted the significance of the storm.

"A snow emergency occurred in Central and South Italy in mid-January 2017. Due to a low-pressure area trapped in the Western Mediterranean, Italy was affected by cold eastern currents that led to hard winter conditions with heavy snowfalls accompanied by strong winds, even at low elevations… Thus, the avalanche danger degree was stable at level "4-HIGH" for several days in the Central and Abruzzo Apennines."

Because no automatic or manual weather stations were available in the area, reference data for the storm was extrapolated from the "synoptic meteorological models" and "these data proved consistent" with other stations located in the Central Appenines. The upshot was that due to fluctuating temperatures, differing densities of snow layers accumulated rapidly on the mountains above the resort, with .7 to .8 meters (2.5 feet) falling daily and a total amounting to more than 3.5 meters (11.5 feet). These already unstable layers were also seriously wind-affected.

When the massive wood-and-snow avalanche struck the hotel around 5:00 p.m. on January 18, 28 guests and 12 employees were on premises. The three earlier earthquakes had been felt at the resort and created panic amongst visitors who wanted to leave the area. The hotel owner made a request to local authorities for guests to be evacuated and many were reportedly waiting on the ground floor for that to happen. But it wasn't possible at the time due to the closure of the 8-kilometer-long road to the resort by two meters of accumulated snowfall and the ongoing blizzard that grounded all helicopter rescue services.

The slide's estimated 100 kilometers per hour (62 mph) impact crushed part of the hotel roof and moved it 10 meters (33 feet) down the mountain. Estimates were that it weighed between 40,000 and 60,000 tons, and settled down at double that amount as it stopped. It left the hotel under four-plus meters (13 feet) of snow and debris that included a large amount of trees it carried with it, which inhibited rescue work.

Also challenging in the aftermath was a breakdown of communications with local authorities who reportedly considered initial first-hand calls about the accident to be untrue. Whatever the case, bad weather and the large snow accumulation deefinitely slowed the rescue response time. The first survivors inside the hotel weren't located for 30 hours and the last were pulled out 58 hours after the slide struck.

Subsequent autopsies stated that most of the victims died quickly from the initial impact, rather than of hypothermia during the protracted response. This information didn't completely eliminate concern over the response. Controversy also stemmed from the location of the hotel in an historic slide path, and it was even claimed that it was built on slide debris.

As happens so often following such tragedies, lawsuits ensued. So did years of investigations and delays after charges were filed against 30 people for a variety of alleged malfeasances including manslaughter, possible negligence leading to injury and death, and illegal construction. Finally in February of 2023, 25 of the 30 defendants were acquitted, while five were convicted on lesser charges such as failure to clear the road for prompt rescue. Frequently such legal decisions hinge on factors such as who has the ultimate responsibility for regulating building sites and managing emergency responses, as much as they do the facts of the case.

CHAPTER 26
THE WORST SKI RESORT AVALANCHE DISASTERS – PART THREE

Alpine Meadows, California 1982; St. Anton, Austria 1988; Davos, Switzerland 1968; Valfrejus, France and Geier, Austria 2016

ALPINE MEADOWS, CALIFORNIA, 1982

The 1982 Alpine Meadows avalanche near Lake Tahoe in California was such a nightmarish game-changer that its still talked about today. In fact, a new award-winning documentary about it was released in 2021, nearly 40 years later. That the slide killed more people than any other in-bounds avalanche at an American ski resort ever is one reason for its enduring importance. But in the end it may have been the story of one survivor that really gripped people.

The snow base at Alpine Meadows stood at 2.2 meters (7.25 feet) when a big storm rumbled in on March 27th that eventually left mountain operations and ski patrol scrambling to control their 2,000 acres of slopes and stay open. On March 30th mountain manager Bernie Kingery, 52, faced with an ongoing blizzard with 100 mile per hour winds, shut down the upper part of the mountain. It was impossible to run the higher lifts, but ski patrol continued using snowmobiles and snowcats to reach the avalanche routes they could and continued their control work in spite of whiteout conditions.

Alpine Meadows mild-sounding name belies a very avalanche prone ski area, with lots of steep terrain and 300 inbounds slide paths they work to control during storm cycles. According to Tahoetopia.com, "It annually records the largest numbers of avalanches of any ski area in the United States."

By the morning of March 31ˢᵗ a fresh 2.8 meters (7.5 feet) of snow had accumulated on top of the already deep base. Some avalanche control routes were still being managed with handheld charges, the results of which appeared to be normal.

Local snow scientist Norm Wilson wrote about the disaster for the inaugural issue of The Avalanche Review magazine on October 1, 1982. He related that, by Tuesday, "the slidepaths that threaten the base area were engaged with artillery: a 75mm recoilless rifle fired from a fixed position on Gunner's Knob, some 60m above the lodge, and a road-fired 75mm pack howitzer."

A sun crust below the new snow sat atop a water saturated layer and ,"slides were expected to go as deep as the suncrust. On both Monday and Tuesday the artillery was fired 'blind' on critical targets – each morning and evening – with extra shots high and low in the target zones, during each firing missions."

With winds still raging at 100 to 120 miles per hour, on Wednesday the ski area was closed to the public. Only the avalanche control crew, maintenance crews, a few management personnel and some stranded visitors remained in the area.

"The artillery was fired again on all the critical targets Wednesday morning," wrote Wilson. "Firing was completed at 10:30 a.m. After firing the howitzer the crew observed the run-outs of Pond and Buttress slides as well as they could through the intense snowfall. They saw what they thought was avalanche debris just above the road and parking lot. They assumed from this observation that the slidepaths had responded to the artillery."

In mid-afternoon 5 patrollers went to Palisades at Tahoe (called Squaw Valley then) hoping to ride their KT-22 Chairlift in order to ski off its backside and bomb chutes threatening the road from Highway 89 to Alpine Meadows. This was standard procedure at the time and for many years after.

Mountain operations assistant Jake Smith had driven a snowmobile down to make sure the road was closed. He was coming back through the Alpine Meadows base parking lot when he radioed the Summit Chair's Base 4 Room with one garbled word: "Avalanche!"

It was around 3:45 p.m. when several huge avalanches combined, releasing on a 975-meter (3,200-foot) long fracture line across the steep Poma Rocks, Buttress and Don's Nose terrain above the northeastern slopes of Alpine. It roared down 244 vertical meters (800 feet) in a matter of seconds, crashing through the lower Summit Chair terminal building like it wasn't even there. Then it pummeled two other lifts and the main lodge and tore through multiple snowcats and snowmobiles on its way through the parking lot where it finally stopped, depositing 15 feet of snow and debris as it did.

"To this day, unless you witnessed the results of that avalanche, its hard to describe just how monstrous it was," said Larry Heywood, the assistant patrol leader at the time. "This was no ordinary slide, but a once-in-a-century catastrophe."

Randy Buck was in the main lodge at the time and heard the radio call from Smith. "About five seconds later the avalanche hit us," he told reporters later. "You could hear a rumble and then the building started to shake

Movie poster for the 2021 film "Buried" about the 1982 avalanche at Alpine Meadows, California.

violently. Then there was a powerful air blast. When the snow stopped moving, I was about one and a half feet under." He had broken ribs and a fractured vertebra, but was able to free his arms and dig himself out as was Tad DeFelice. Along with arriving rescuers they also uncovered fellow employee and survivor Jeff Skover.

Mountain manager Kingery and employee Frank Yeatman weren't as lucky. Yeatman's corpse was found in the terminal building, Kingery's was 100 feet away and not discovered until April 5th. No one survived who was caught in the parking lot where rescuers eventually recovered the bodies of Jake Smith and three tourists – Doctor Leroy Nelson, his daughter Laura, and family friend David Hahn – who had been snowbound for several days and finally decided to brave the storm to try to find a restaurant.

Search efforts continued for days after the slide and a missing avalanche rescue dog was remarkably found buried alive. Then efforts were suspended after another meter (3.3 feet) of snow fell, threatening the site with further slides. When the search resumed on April 5th, a U.S. Forest Service worker's avalanche dog Bridget became animated in the building site. And at 1:10 p.m. two other rescuers spotted Anna Conrad's hand and found her conscious, talking and alert.

Conrad, a 22-year-old lift operator, had been with her boyfriend Frank Yeatman in the locker room on the second floor of the building preparing to leave when the slide hit. "I had no idea what had happened, it was so instantaneous," she recalled, and had thought it was an explosion of some kind. She was saved by a wall of the locker room crashing over onto a bench and the snow completely pinning her underneath in an air pocket. She ate nothing but snow and didn't know where she had ended up or that she'd been there for 5 days. "I just kept telling myself I could do it, I could do it. They'd find me."

As Larry Heywood later recounted, "Finding Anna and the commotion of pulling her out alive was an intense experience. There were probably 100 searchers in the vicinity at the time. Each person stopped and watched her get loaded into a helicopter. You could feel this incredible release and exhilaration from everyone. It was a very powerful moment."

Conrad lost her right leg below the knee and all the toes on her left foot from frostbite. And she was back skiing the next December. After teaching high school science in the Bay area she moved to Mammoth Lakes and worked as a director of their Mountain Host program.

"I don't dwell on what happened, but it's not something ever far from my mind. Not so long ago I was coming home with the kids from skiing. It was incredibly beautiful and impressive. I smiled all the way home. I felt like the luckiest person in the world."

The legal ramifications took years to sort out, and Alpine Meadows was absolved of any negligence in 1985. The case drew attention from the ski industry around the world. Attorney John Fagan, who defended the resort along with Gary Bunshoft, said, "There were over 100 witnesses called. The leading snow experts argued for both sides, but the jury correctly ruled that Alpine Meadows was not negligent. Basically, they found that despite the best efforts of highly trained professionals, an event like this could occur. We argued that it was a precedent storm that yielded an unprecedented avalanche."

Says former assistant patrol chief Heywood, "There was certainly some sentiment throughout the industry at first, that somehow we had messed up. People later learned just how unusual this event was."

It's worth noting that even though this was an inbounds avalanche, which is rare in the industry, it didn't strike anyone who was actually skiing because the lifts and slopes were closed. And that was done by ski area management the day before. That action undoubtedly helped mitigate in their favor in court.

Such was not the case when a skier was killed at Alpine Meadows by an avalanche while skiing on an open, inbounds run in 2020. It took place at 10:16 on the morning of January 17th in an area near Scott Chair. The resort had reported almost .4 meters (1.25 feet) fresh overnight and just over .6 meters (two feet) in the last 24 hours. There was a Winter Storm Warning out from the National Weather Service and the Lake Tahoe area had been under an avalanche watch starting at 7:00 a.m. the previous day. In April of 2022 it was announced that the resort had settled two lawsuits that resulted from the accident.

ST. ANTON, AUSTRIA, 1988

When a resort such as St. Anton, Austria is famous for its steep terrain, dazzling off-piste, and getting lots of snow, serious avalanche danger is sure to be part of its DNA. One of its famous ski racers, the 1969 0verall World Cup women's champion Gertrud Gabl, was killed in an avalanche on the Rendl side of the area on January 28 in 1976. Skiing off-piste with two friends, they were caught and buried in a slide. The friends were dug out alive.

As with Chamonix and Verbier and other free-ride centers, most of the slides that involve skiers and boarders occur off-piste and not on the regular, controlled, inbounds runs. Part of the reason for this is that the resorts attract riders who go off the controlled pistes into terrain that they don't know at all, or well enough, trying to get first tracks and avoid the crowds on the regular slopes. The result is that for decades, any substantial new snow can produce multiple avalanches triggered by riders being at the wrong place at the wrong time.

As just a brief example, in January of 2015 alone, St. Anton saw a slab slide on the back of the Valluga Grat that killed two guided skiers on January 19th. It was the same place a similar fatal avalanche took place in 2008. And that same month four Australian boarders were caught in a huge off-piste slide on the Rendl side that killed one.

Such fairly commonplace accidents are bad enough for the riders involved. But they can extend to others who are either also off-piste in the same area, or on-piste where a slide comes inbounds. All ski areas work diligently to insure that even avalanches triggered from outside their boundaries that can reach the public runs are controlled and prevented. But this isn't always successful any more than controlling inbounds avalanche areas is 100% foolproof.

Even when a slide started somewhere else doesn't reach lift-served slopes – which is about 99% of the time – more lives are put at risk on the rescue crews who can be in harm's way as they work to get the survivors and victims off the mountain.

Possibly the most infamous and disastrous slide in St. Anton occurred on Sunday, March 13, 1988, when 7 were killed in their hotels and chalets. Blizzards had dumped over .76 meters (2.5 feet) of snow in western Austria on Saturday and Sunday, trapping more than 40,000 in the local Arlberg resorts. On Saturday three avalanches came down within a 65-kilometer (40-mile) radius of St. Anton, killing 2 and injuring two others.

Then at 6:50 a.m. on Sunday morning, two slides originating on the Rendl side of the resort tore their way down a part of the mountain without ski slopes and across the main rail line in the valley before smashing into a group of guesthouses and hotels. Local mountain rescue leader Walter Strolz's 75-year-old mother was killed. "My parent's home was just ripped apart," he said.

Another 57-year-old local woman, Theresia Zangerl also died. The remaining fatalities were all Swedish visitors staying at the Haus Tscholl, which took the main hit from the slide. It had 31 guests and 5 staff and was buried under 12.2 meters (40 feet) of snow. "Some of the dead were still sleeping at the time. They were killed before they knew what hit them," a police official said. One Swedish survivor was recovered mostly unharmed while 20 to 30 others, some buried alive before being dug out, were injured and choppered to hospitals nearby.

Longtime St. Anton residents said the avalanche was the worst to hit the area in more than 80 years. Experts estimated it must have been 1200 feet wide and nearly 10 meters (30 feet) high, travelling at speeds up to 100 miles per hour down Mount Swoelerkopf. Hundreds of trees were uprooted on the mountainside, and on the valley floor, four buildings were destroyed along with half a dozen houses and a gas station, and the main east-west rail line in Austria was blocked. One witness said, "We heard a great roar. We saw the roof of one guest house blown off completely. It landed on top of another building across the road."

The Pension Nassereiner-hof was ripped in two leaving half of it under a mountain of snow. The 40-year-old owner Zdenka Crodin described the harrowing ordeal. "All of a sudden there was this great pressure of air and my husband yelled at me an avalanche was coming. It was a sound like I have never heard, it must have been like great bombs falling." She couldn't see anything but seconds later the snow burst through the doors and windows and they were buried up to their armpits.

Soon she realized that a greater disaster had probably been avoided. Had it happened 30 minutes later, her destroyed breakfast room would have been filled with 60 tourists. "My god," she said, "it would have been a catastrophe."

For St. Anton, it's nothing new to have their lone road and rail line cut-off from time to time. With their only means of access and egress seriously exposed to slide danger the trick is to keep them open as long as possible, then close them before avalanches happen and kill people. That's why the community has Ferdinand Alber.

Trained as a civil engineer he started work with the town's lift company Arlberger Bergbahnen AG in 1996. In an undated Arcteryx blog he's described as having become the Head of the Avalanche Commission in town and the Chief of Operations for the Osterreichischer Bergrettungsdienst St. Anton in 1999. It's his duty to lead the efforts to keep the ski runs and the town safe. No small responsibility in one of Austria's major ski resorts in a very challenging location.

The avalanche control teams on the mountain behave proactively and go out heavy, using Gazex tube-fired propane/gas mixtures and Wyssen detonation towers, plus a warlord-level 4½ tons annually of handheld charges.

Keeping the roads, railways and town safe used to be more of a passive, "watchful eye" approach that Alber spent a decade trying to convince the community to change. They finally agreed and have embarked on a program more similar to the on-mountain ones, with strategically situated remote detonation systems that can be triggered safely from afar.

"We can protect these areas by avalanche control," Alber told Mike Berard, writing for Arcteryx. "These systems keep the roads open," rather than waiting until they get slid on, then clearing them. "If that happens – if the road and railway is open and gets hit by an avalanche – well, I don't want to think about it."

Once again, it seems that for every step backwards, another two forward come with the experience. The Mount Swoelerkopf slide will have had a benefit if it helped persuade St. Anton to take a new direction in protecting themselves.

DAVOS, SWITZERLAND 1968

The Davos, Switzerland home of the world's premier avalanche analysis group, the WSL Institute for Snow and Avalanche Research SLF, has not itself been immune from such disasters. The SLF and the town held an event in Davos in 2018 commemorating the 50th anniversary of one of the worst.

On January 26/27 of 1968, some 41 avalanches thundered down in the surrounding areas, killing 13, destroying 51 residences, 14 barns and 11 hectares of forests. Similar to other avalanche swarms in the likes of Andermatt, it was a stunning siege. Forty-one bad slides in 48 hours constituted such a hellish barrage as to seem like some kind of Old Testament retribution.

"Even seen from today's perspective, such a localized concentration of highly destructive avalanches following unfamiliar or very seldom affected paths within a very short time is highly unusual," the SLF noted in its 2018 press release about the lethal onslaught.

The largest and most destructive was the Dorfbach avalanche that occurred at 10:40 p.m. on the 26th on the eastern side of the Schiahorn. It wiped out the Parsennbahn railway bridge over the Dorfbach, and blasted through the villages of Auf der Egga and Auf den Boden, killing four as it went.

The "In den Arelen" slide in the Wolfgang district of Davos on the 27th was another "annihilating incident," as the SLF described it, as were the Bildjibach and Bramabuel slides. Over all, the Rhatische Bahn rail line was blocked in 9 places; electrical pylons were toppled cutting power; and the community's primary road was hit by 11 avalanches. The situation resembled nothing so much as a wartime invasion, seemingly plotted to completely cripple the region.

"For three days Davos was for all practical purposes cut off from the outside world," noted the SLF release.

41 avalanches in 48 hours in Davos in1968 killed 13 people and this one that buried a road and rail line. Photo by E. Wengi, courtesy of the SLF.

"Only a few helicopter flights were available for the people and goods that needed to be moved most urgently."

Since that widespread devastation that threatened the future of all of Davos, the community has invested serious money to try to prevent a recurrence. The results include an avalanche dam in the Parsenn resort below the Schiahorn; a 390-meter-long avalanche "gallery" tunnel alongside Lake Davos; and extensive danger zoning, avalanche warning systems and slide mitigation procedures.

When we were there in 1999 it sounded like a war zone once again, but that was due to the ongoing avalanche control work being conducted with hand charges and howitzers while skiers hunkered down in the hotels and hoped for the roads to re-open so they could flee. As the longtime host of The World Economic Forum, Davos had managed to hold that annual event earlier in the winter and benefit from the publicity of the snow piling up during television coverage of the conference.

By the time we got there the consequences of those continuous storms was markedly less beneficial. But even though they were seeing business plummet as customers deserted in droves, they weren't seeing the kind of desolation and loss of life that the SLF was reporting elsewhere in the country and the Alps. And there was reason to believe that all of the work on protecting the area was paying off.

VALFREJUS, FRANCE AND GEIER, AUSTRIA, 2016.
AND THE BEAT GOES ON.

While the big slides that plow into towns and buildings tend to rack up large numbers of single-incident deaths, it's the ones that strike small groups and individuals off-piste that mount up.

All over the mountains of the world where it snows there are paths that slide regularly. It's because these back-country and side-country areas aren't as busy, and sometimes aren't controlled, that some skiers and riders seek them out. And it's for the same reason they die. Such deaths, while tragic, occur so constantly now that it's virtually impossible to keep track of them all. And in the end they are simply proof of the dangers of skiing uncontrolled terrain with little or no knowledge of what you're doing.

On January 18, 2016, a division of 51 French Legionnaires was part of an off-piste ski exercise to receive their Skier Certificate, called a BSM. It was taking place 60 kilometers south of the former Winter Olympic town of Albertville near the Valfrejus ski resort.

Strong winds had accompanied a heavy winter storm in the region. Avalanche warnings were at three and a bulletin was issued saying that single skiers could trigger slides up to two meters deep. The company was at 2,600 meters (8,500 feet) at 1:50 p.m. when a 100-meter-wide slab of ice broke off a ridge, initiating a fracture about 457 meters (1,500 feet) wide.

View from the lower ski slopes above St. Anton, looking across the valley at path of 1988 Wolfgrubben avalanche (the upper right). Photo © Jay Cowan.

The resulting slide swallowed 13 skiers on a steep slope and buried or roughed up 18 altogether, while the rest of the company remained at the foot of the pitch. All 13 were found under three feet of snow with the help of dogs and avalanche victim detection kits (DVAs). The six who did not survive had suffered cardiac arrest and were "a mix of veterans and new recruits," as well as a striking example of the Legionnaires diversity, hailing from Madagascar, Italy, Nepal, Moldova, Albania and Hungary.

The area around Valfrejus, near the Italian border, is known to be avalanche-prone. And a year later on February 5, one Russian skier was killed in a slide in the off-piste Seuil Couloir near Valfrejus. And a month after that, on March 7, 2017, three Dutch tourists reported by cell phone that they were lost in the same area, and they all died in an avalanche in the same couloir. One body wasn't found for 12 days.

A two-kilometer-wide avalanche in the Wattental Valley of Austria on February 6, 2016, came in the midst of a flurry of 19 slides reported on that date in the Tyrol after recent snowfall and thawing temperatures. It followed the Legionnaires avalanche in France by about three weeks and also struck groups of skiers, this time from a freeride camp in an area designated as an "absolute risk zone."

The group of experienced Czech skiers, accompanied by two guides, had been warned repeatedly by locals about the avalanche danger in that specific area of the Geier mountain range. The risk level was rated at a three (or "considerable") that day when 17 skiers in two parties were caught in the slide that occurred during midday near the Lizumer Hutte. Some were able to free themselves while others were reached by rescue workers using dogs and helicopters. Ultimately 5 people died and several more were injured.

Four days earlier two teenage French students and a Ukrainian tourist were killed when a teacher took them onto a closed piste at the Deux-Alpes resort in France. The badly injured teacher was later charged with involuntary manslaughter.

All of these incidents and more came during periods of increased avalanche activity spurred by dangerous conditions in areas known to be slide-prone. And they demonstrate how difficult the situation has become with ever-increasing numbers of poorly prepared skiers and boarders crowding into the mountains every winter.

CHAPTER 27
THE WORST SKI RESORT AVALANCHE DISASTERS – PART FOUR

High Impact Colorado Slides: Aspen, Highland Bowl, 1984; Breckenridge Peak 7, 1987; Loveland Pass, 2013/2020

ASPEN, HIGHLAND BOWL, 1984

The Rocky Mountains of North America are as active with avalanche danger as nearly any mountain range on earth for multiple reasons. The mountains are young and steep and high, which means they get a lot of snow, a lot of wind, and slides release easily and often on very sheer slopes. Like the Alps, due to rapidly rising populations throughout the mountain chain, dangers to skiers and boarders have increased exponentially as more recreationalists take to the mountains, and more frequently than ever before to the backcountry, side-country and off-piste slopes surrounding lift-served ski resorts.

Aspen, Colorado, where I skied for 50 years, is one of those places that has a lot of people who ride uncontrolled snow, and as a result a relatively high incidence of avalanche deaths occur in the surrounding Elk Mountains every season. It has been that way since the mining days, as cited earlier. Once lift-served slopes started being built, the rates of off-piste slide fatalities ticked up, especially in regions like McFarlane Bowl and Hurricane Gulch accessed from Aspen Mountain; or Highland Bowl, Maroon Bowl and the Five Towers Chutes at Aspen Highlands; or the Hanging Valley, Cirque and backside routes at Snowmass.

Much of that terrain is now included in the controlled terrain of each resort. At Aspen Highlands, their legendary out of bounds terrain for years included almost everything on either side of the lift-served area that's arranged along a large spine between Castle and Maroon Creeks. Highland Bowl was always on everyone's must-poach list, in spite of (and perhaps sometimes because of) the fact that it's a very large basin covering 270 degrees of utterly uncontrolled exposures that tended to slide spontaneously.

Local guy, backcountry-legend-to-be and longtime friend of mine Lou Dawson was one of several who got slid on in there over the years while it was still OB. The acclaimed author of the book Wild Snow wrote the following recollection for a story I did for Aspen Sojourner magazine.

"The large slide I triggered in Highland Bowl in 1982 (when the bowl was still backcountry) worked me like a tsunami. My left femur broke with a quaking explosion. My other leg was broken as well, up near the hip. I remember rag-dolling like someone had stuffed me into a clothes dryer – so violent and fast I had no body control. When it was over, I was partially buried. My partner John soon found me and did what first-aid he could with our minimal supplies… After making me as comfortable as possible John hiked out of the bowl in record time to fetch help."

Dawson would go on to become the first person to ski all 54 of Colorado's 14ers (peaks over 14,000 feet) and is cited multiple times in this book. Unfortunately his accident was just a harbinger of worse to come in the Bowl.

The avalanche with the most lasting reverberations in the Roaring Fork Valley took place a little after 2:40 p.m. on March 31, 1984. During control work in Highland Bowl, years before it opened, a massive slide was triggered and three patrolmen perished.

Starting at a small, exposed knob a few hundred feet below Highland Peak, a fracture in response to a bomb toss propagated below the patrolmen. Then another quickly spread above them and all the way across the bowl. When it ripped out it was full climax, with an estimated 7 to 8-foot crown all the way to the ground. Chris Kessler, Craig Soddy and Tom Snyder never stood a chance. It was the worst avalanche control accident ever in the U.S.

Snyder had been one of those to help rescue Dawson a few years earlier. And Chris Kessler had been in a slide at Highlands recorded in the annual Snowy Torrents compilation in 1981 where he was buried upside down, dug out hypothermic and hypoxic but was back at work the next day.

In the 1984 tragedy, "They were supposed to have long fuses and go back to the trees," said Highlands patrol director Mac Smith. "They didn't, and must have decided between them that it looked safe."

Smith and others soon concluded that conditions weren't the same in the Elk Mountains of Colorado as those where the rules for avalanche control were then made, in completely different climates that were dominated by marine snowpacks.

As a result of the accident, a whole new set of parameters were developed for the region and no more patrol people have died in Aspen from avalanches since. Runs in Steeplechase at Highlands (the formerly out of bounds 5-Towers Chutes) were named for the dead. Another of their legacies was that Chris Kessler was training Chopper, the forerunner of many avalanche rescue dogs working around Aspen since.

Unfortunately, civilians continued to die in slides around Aspen, 7 of them in the 1990s alone. In 2001 two separate accidents killed three men, all widely described as experienced backcountry skiers. But they were just as dead. Two more skiers perished in 2002. And in 2005, a locally guided group had a student die in a slide

A patrol-triggered avalanche in Highland Bowl at Aspen Highlands, CO, replicated 1984 slide that killed three patrolmen. Photo © Matt Power.

triggered by the student in the backcountry Five Fingers area above Maroon Creek. John Jensen from New Mexico veered away from the prescribed ridgeline route set by the guide and fell hard on exposed terrain. According to the report, "He appeared to attempt to 'swim' with the moving snow, but then the fracture propagated up the gully dramatically and John disappeared over a convexity with the slide."

Longtime Aspenite and certified mountain guide Dick Jackson, like many of us, has had friends die in slides. "Why do we continue to put ourselves in harm's way?" he asks, thoughtfully. "Well, first, I'm not sure skiing the backcountry is any more dangerous than driving on Highway 82 [that serves Aspen]. But people have a passion for soft snow and there's lots of it out there. Most of the time, it isn't whether to ski, but where to ski. You just have to know the limits of your judgment and training. It's not to be taken lightly and requires experience and formal education."

PEAK 7, BRECKENRIDGE, 1987

Since the 1950s Colorado has regularly lead the nation in avalanche fatalities. The winter of 1986/'87 brought a "shallow and weak" snowpack to the Ten Mile Range where the Breckenridge ski area is located. Naturally caused slides are constant winter features there and rigorously patrolled for and controlled within the ski area boundaries by the Breckenridge Ski Patrol. At the time, the very visible and appealing Peak 7 Bowl on top of the mountain was not within the ski area boundaries. But it got skied almost like it was, with patrol counting hundreds and even thousands going there on powder days.

In their avalanche report, patrollers Nick and Mary Logan wrote that, "it attracted a number of skiers. Many of them had no knowledge of avalanches, or of the hazards and risks when skiing backcountry terrain. The typical out-of-bounds skiers in Breckenridge claimed knowledge of snow and stability, but most disregarded basic avalanche safety. Many skied without transceiver or shovel and only a select few carried them religiously."

For these reasons and more Peak 7 was an ongoing topic of deep concern for the Breckenridge ski resort, patrol and local residents. The patrol had no legal duty to respond to any accident that might occur there, yet they were "the closest trained rescue organization and felt a moral duty to help if necessary," wrote the Logans. But there were a lot of questions about conflicts with their duties at the ski area, timing, and logistics. The decision about who would respond was left up to the patrol personnel when and if it happened, and was strictly voluntary.

Due to decisions by the U.S. Forest Service that many lauded, Colorado ski areas were told they could not prevent access to public lands that were adjacent to their ski area boundaries. All they could do was locate gates for the egress in the safest places they could find. Aware that providing those gates might make it seem like the area was saying it was safe, Breckenridge posted large (4 by 6 feet), blunt warnings, "Extremely Dangerous Avalanche Paths" at the gates that winter, with details about avalanches that had already occurred in the area.

In spite of the signs and numerous other efforts by the resort, the Colorado Avalanche Information Center (CAIC), the ski patrol, the local paper and radio station and others to encourage and help skiers to become more aware and educated, the results weren't encouraging. Riders continued to swarm onto uncontrolled terrain with little or no apparent concern. By mid-February, that "when and if" speculation about an avalanche in the Peak 7 Bowl had become a firm "when."

The Bowl got skied for the first time that season on January 1, 1987, and the first slide in it – skier triggered – happened the next day, revealing "weak stratigraphy in a shallow snow cover, 60% of which was comprised of 2-5 millimeter depth hoar grains trying to support a thick, collapsible slab. Not a good combination," noted the Logans.

Toward the middle of February the Ten Mile Range received nearly .6 meters (two feet) of snow over a period of several days, along with 15 to 30 mph winds. The CAIC's local hotline posted a "moderate to high" hazard warning, and four avalanche fatalities had already occurred elsewhere in the state.

On February 18th, .15 to .25 meters of new snow had fallen above treeline and people were headed into the Bowl in droves. Ski patroller Nick Logan, also working for the CAIC, "sat on the rim of Peak 7 Bowl, handing out CAIC hotline cards and asking people if they were carrying shovels and transceivers (only one was)."

Logan left around 2:00 p.m., about the same time patrol director Kevin Ahern, avalanche supervisor Paul Miller, and Mary Logan, were riding a T-bar servicing Horseshoe Bowl. From the top it provides easy access to Peak 7 Bowl. As they neared the top the patrollers noticed two skiers at the top of Peak 7. One made a couple of turns then cut south toward more gentle terrain. The second skier dropped in and as they reached a transition area, the pocket of snow collapsed. A fracture line appeared 150 feet above him, then "zippered its way down the ridge to the north for 1,600 feet! He was able to ski out of the slower moving snow along the south flank and onto the same gentle terrain his partner had sought earlier," wrote the Logans.

The avalanche was classified as HS-AS-4-G: Hard Slab, Artificially Triggered by a Skier, size 4 to the Ground. None of the patrollers had ever observed an avalanche of that magnitude. The average crown height was three to 5 feet with a maximum of 8 feet in two locations. It plunged for 341 meters (1,120 feet) down a slope ranging from 32 degrees at the start to 44 degrees breaking into the bowl, leaving a 244-meter (800-foot) wide deposition almost 400 meters (1,300 feet) long. The slide swept up 8 people altogether, and rescuers were left with "an enormous area to search" of nearly 24 acres.

Over the course of that evening and the next day, as many as 400 volunteers probing relentlessly eventually uncovered four victims at depths ranging from four to 6 feet under dense debris as hard as cement.

George Cates, 35, and his 17-year-old-stepbrother, both from New York, were taking their first lap ever in Peak 7 Bowl when George saw the avalanche and yelled at Alex to ski to the side. George was buried up to his knees, dug himself out and dug up someone buried near him. It turned out to be 16-year-old Marc Radicci, also from New York, who lived. But Alex Cates wasn't found for two days, the last of the four who died.

Below them in the bowl, a 22-year-old New Zealander named Nicholas Casey who was living and working in Breck for the season had been digging for a ski that he'd lost in the bowl when he was buried. Tim Kirkland, a 25-year-old Aussie who was one of three friends who'd been waiting on Casey for about 20 minutes, heard someone yell avalanche and skied to safety. Martin Donnellan, 19, another of the friends, was the first victim found that evening under four feet of debris. Paul Wray, 23, and Casey were found around noon the next day 6 feet deep.

The two skiers who triggered the slide helped in the rescue efforts until they got word that the sheriff planned to arrest them. They then made themselves scarce until rescue crews persuaded the sheriff to rescind his threat because the two were able to give them valuable information about where the skiers who were caught were located when it happened. The return of those two to the site helped in finding the last victim.

The slide turned into a full-blown media circus by the next morning with Denver news outlets competing for space with national news teams amid parking lots full of mobile uplink trucks. More than 130 reporters showed up for the next morning briefing, and to the locals it felt like they were all looking for someone to blame. If the ski patrol had been consistently warning about the dangers posed by Peak 7 for as long as it appeared, why had something like this been allowed to happen?

That season turned out to be one of the worst on record for Colorado skiers in avalanches with 11 deaths altogether. Along with the high-profile nature of the Peak 7 accident, these were big factors in sparking a re-evaluation of how Breckenridge and other Colorado resorts handled avalanche management going forward. A story in the Colorado Sun newspaper in 2022 included a dek that read: "How a Breckenridge avalanche 35 years ago changed the trajectory of Colorado skiing."

The story went on to say that, "The Peak 7 slide triggered sweeping changes in avalanche awareness, education and messaging. It created a region-wide, communal response to avalanches. It solidified a Forest Service policy to never close access between resorts and public lands. It set in motion a statewide expansion of ski terrain, with resorts opening steeper-and-deeper slopes that appealed to a new generation of powder-chasing skiers."

Some of that is hyperbolic and makes it sound, unfairly and no doubt unintentionally, as though there were no really effective avalanche policies in effect prior to this deadly season. But adjustments needed to be made for the times. And the changes were already in the wind by the mid-1980s as the skier demographics began noticeably shifting.

"It was just a whole different user group," said Dale Atkins, one of the four forecasters for the CAIC in 1987. "That accident of Peak 7 triggered a big switch for us. It showed us – the avalanche professionals, the forecasters, the patrollers – that we had a serious recreational problem. We kind of already knew it, but it showed us we had a new customer who was going to be involved in more avalanches moving forward."

Some lobbied hard for the USFS to allow ski areas to close their boundaries to public lands, and many in Breckenridge were incensed when they didn't agree to do that with Peak 7 access following the accident. Ken Kownyia was the snow manager at the time for the Whiter River National Forest (the most skied forest in America) in the Dillon Ranger District. He convened meetings for a year before the accident, and many more after it, to get input from everyone on one issue in particular, and that was whether ski resorts, often operating on USFS leases, were allowed to close off access to public lands adjoining their property.

The sometimes fiery meetings included the public, which as a whole were, and continue to be, recreating on public lands in ever-larger numbers. A vast majority of them who got involved weren't enthused about big, expensive ski resorts being able to control access to lands belonging to them, the public.

Kownyia had visited with patrollers at Breckenridge a week before the avalanche and saw dozens of skiers venturing into the dangerous terrain. As he said later, "Yeah, we had a lot of second guessing after such a horrible situation. But you have to understand the Forest Service cannot be in the position of opening and closing the national forest. You just always have to assume it's dangerous all the time."

One response by the White River National Forest Service was to develop a boundary management policy that was incorporated into local ski area permits and ultimately national policy.

At the same time some resorts decided to use what the Colorado Sun described as "an unusual rule that allowed them to close about 10 feet of space between a boundary rope and open Forest Service Land. They called it a strip closure."

Boots Ferguson, an attorney who worked for decades for the Aspen Skiing Company (which owned Breck from 1970 through 1987), noted that the approach was largely unenforceable. Some resorts claimed the strip closure right on behalf of protecting their customers from themselves. Ferguson called it "protectionist and a slippery slope." The ASC favored education over regulation and opted to inform skiers about the risks with large, aggressive signage and a much stronger push for education aimed at more than just ski professionals.

Ferguson said, "We got into some real philosophical discussions. It went something like this: Freedom is critical and part of the price of freedom is taking risk. So the question was – and really remains today – if we are going to be proponents of freedom, how can we best apprise people of the risks so they could make the best decisions?"

This approach eventually caught on at most American ski resorts, and in the process touched off another round of terrain expansions. The thinking was that if people wanted to ride these dangerous places so badly, then the smartest way to deal with it might be to include it in the resort's permit boundaries and directly control the avalanche hazards and the access to the terrain threatened by them.

In 1994 Breckenridge annexed Peak 7 into an expanded special use permit, which the USFS began to view much more favorably than it did brand new ski areas being built. The ASC did the same with Highland Bowl, and other ski areas around Colorado joined the movement. Taken altogether it was a boon to skiers and boarders as long as they didn't mind buying lift tickets, which many had been doing for years when skiing side-country and other terrain that the Colorado Ski Safety Act specifically included in a 2004 update.

The added education and safety measures include better funded operations by the CAIC to get their forecasts and daily information more widely and rapidly distributed; many more opportunities for civilian skiers to take avalanche awareness and search and rescue classes; more stringent transceiver and shovel policies on some inbounds terrain; and rapid, well-equipped response units for faster search and rescue missions.

The 70-member Colorado Rapid Avalanche Deployment program can get a chopper and dogs and crew to any slope in Summit, Eagle, Clear Creek and Grand counties within 15 minutes, and it was a direct result of the Peak 7 slide.

A big component of all of this should also be the recognition of our own responsibilities when exercising what Boots Ferguson called the "risks of freedom." If we don't take responsibility for our actions and the harm they may put us – and those around us – in the way of, we can't expect resorts or anyone else to do it for us.

And there is still a lot left to do. One of the situations that needs addressing is snowmobile-accessed skiing, which has been growing rapidly, especially in the western US. And avalanche fatalities for snowmobilers are surpassing skiers in many locations. Due to the more remote nature of the skiing and snowmobiling, well away from lift-served slopes, there is little chance to regulate or enforce these activities, nor inclination for many participants to pay attention if it's tried.

Yet the fact that much of it is being done on public lands does give the USFS some jurisdiction, and an obligation to protect all members of the public from the actions of a particular group. Especially when those actions can injure or kill others in the vicinity, as well as have grievous impact on the environment and wildlife. It's a multi-faceted and thorny issue that reflects some of society's most vexing current problems revolving around the limitations of personal freedoms in an increasingly crowded world.

LOVELAND PASS, 2013/2020

Another situation with far-reaching consequences has been going on for years at one of Colorado's most famous backcountry skiing sites on Loveland Pass. Due to the easy access of the pass from a highway going over it, as well as the Loveland Pass ski area directly adjacent to it, the potential for skier-triggered avalanches to endanger others is sizable. Those at risk include other off-piste riders, as well as highway traffic and cars and people in roadside parking areas, in a heavily trafficked area that looms directly above the portals to Interstate 70's always busy Eisenhower Tunnel cutting through the Continental Divide.

Snow avalanches regularly on both sides of the Divide, often unprovoked. The terrain is steep with few trees, and gullies, runnels and slide paths everywhere. Such obvious red flags don't deter everyone, especially since the easy accessibility makes the Pass one of the most popular backcountry sites in the state.

More than a few have died there, with fatalities occurring every season. An avalanche on Saturday, April 20, 2013, that buried 6 and killed 5 of them is especially infamous because it was the most people killed by a slide in Colorado since 1962. And that one hit a town, not backcountry riders. The other most publicized aspect of the massive 2013 Loveland Pass avalanche was that all of the victims were experienced backcountry riders.

Yes, that's the kind of refrain that does little to inspire confidence any more since it's too often associated with avalanche obituaries. There are clear issues with who is really 'experienced' or 'an expert,' and what those terms even cover. But this was definitely a test case of all of the above, almost as if it had been specifically devised to prove yet again that being an 'experienced expert' is no get-out-of-death-free card.

One of the worst things about that 2013 accident is that the people caught in the slide were the definition of ski industry insiders who on that particular day were on a mission to educate the public about the dangers of avalanches. They felt that was part of their responsibility to their consumers who were buying their backcountry skiing and boarding gear in rapidly escalating numbers each season.

In a truly terrible irony, "Joe Timlin – the sales manager for Jones Snowboards, Yes Snowboards and Now Bindings – [had] organized the weekend's Rocky Mountain High Backcountry Gathering as a backcountry safety and splitboard gear demo," according to a story from Outsideonline.com.

A fundraiser for the CAIC the previous day had been very successful and included presentations from Rick Gaukel, 33, a certified avalanche safety instructor from Estes Park who also gave a briefing on the dangerous snow conditions Saturday morning.

Gaukel was in the group on Loveland Pass, along with Joe Timlin, 32, from Gypsum; Timlin's best friend Chris Peters, 32, from Lakewood, who came to support the backcountry safety demo; Ian Lanphere, 36, from Crested Butte and co-founder of Gecko Climbing Skins; and Ryan Novack, 33, a photographer from Boulder who was a friend of Jerome Boulay, the group's other member.

David Carrier Porcheron, the owner of Yes Snowboards and Timlin's brother-in-law, stressed in interviews that, "These weren't just some yahoos throwing an event. Joe was definitely aware of the dangers of backcountry snowboarding – he'd made it his life – and everyone in that crew was fully aware of the specific dangers that day. After assessing the risk, they opted to take a shorter hike they thought would be safer."

All of which made it even scarier. Not because they got taken by surprise, but because they all should have known better. The avalanche forecast from CAIC delivered that morning by Gaukel was "considerable" (3 on a 1–5 scale), citing an ongoing weak layer in the snowpack that everyone had been aware of for days. A slide near Vail Pass just a few days earlier in similar conditions had killed a skier that several of the people at this gathering knew.

In the CAIC's report on the Loveland slide, written by its deputy director Brian Lazar, it was noted that spring storms had deposited over a meter (3.4 feet) of wet, heavy snow on the slopes the week before. As the group began their attempt to ski the Sheep's Creek drainage, Timlin, Gaukel and Bouray skinned one at a time across a danger zone to a stand of trees they used as a safety zone while waiting for the other three skiers to come across. But a slide broke above them, "as their collective weight pulled down on a layer of heavy snow," according to the report.

Much bigger than anything the riders had envisioned possible, the huge slide instantly overwhelmed both groups in spite of their perceived safety zones. The average crown of the fracture was 1.5 meters (5 feet), but over 3.6 meters (12 feet) in places. It was 243 meters (800 feet) wide and ran for 182 vertical meters (600 vertical feet).

Bouray was buried with one hand semi-free so he could clear an airway to the surface, but was otherwise pinned and unable to move any further for four hours. He was the only one who survived. Gaukel and Tomlin were found buried near him but much deeper. The other three were eventually found further down-slope under more than 3.6 meters (12 feet) of debris.

Kurt Olesek, co-founder of the Colorado Snowboard Archive Collection at the Colorado Ski & Snowboard Museum in Vail, was on Loveland Pass that day for the gathering but opted to ski somewhere different, due to the daily CAIC forecast.

In the Outside story he's quoted as saying, "They were all experienced people, and they let their guard down. I think there was just too much enthusiasm. They were gonna do a quick lap, thinking, 'It's not far, it's not steep.' They shouldn't have crossed that slope to begin with… It's easy to get excited: 'I'm gonna do a great run – I'm safe here with my bros.' Then you don't follow protocol. That's when shit goes down."

Ethan Greene, the CAIC director, noted that the group hadn't adequately adapted their behavior to their understanding of the conditions. "With the known risk of a deep hard-slab avalanche like this one, you really have to give yourself a huge margin for error. Although this accident was really tragic, it was avoidable."

In the same way that the Highland Bowl slide forced avalanche control people to re-examine the differences between Colorado's Rocky Mountain snowpack versus that of the coastal ranges, and that Peak 7 occasioned a much closer look at the burgeoning backcountry movement, the Sheep's Creek avalanche forced a lot of backcountry enthusiasts to gaze inward. Wild Snow author Lou Dawson and host of one of the most popular online backcountry sites by the same name, wrote about it online. So did friends of those who perished. The big takeaway was that even when you think you're doing the right thing, sometimes the *only* smart call is to just not go.

For those who skipped class that day, the point was made clear on Loveland Pass again 7 years later, in a much different way.

When Evan Hannibal and Tyler DeWitt triggered an avalanche above the Eisenhower/Johnson Memorial Tunnels on Loveland Pass in March of 2020, they videoed the whole experience, reported it, and waited around to answer questions from law enforcement. They also voluntarily reported it to the CAIC. No one was injured or killed but the slide did damage a remote-controlled avalanche mitigation device and buried the Loop Road running above the tunnels in up to 20 feet of debris. That road is closed to the public and only used for service and emergency vehicles. Tens of thousands of dollars worth of property damage resulted.

So did an unprecedented chain of legal consequences when they were charged with misdemeanor reckless endangerment by the Summit County Sheriff's Office. That was based on the report and video they had given to the CAIC, which had in turn been handed over to the sheriff's office. This is the same sheriff's office, but different sheriff, who threatened to prosecute the pair of skiers who triggered the Peak 7 avalanche.

Though it created a firestorm of controversy that still hasn't been entirely addressed, and though such charges had never been leveled before in the state of Colorado following any skier-triggered slides, it was still a case with merits. Especially in an ongoing atmosphere of rising backcountry avalanche deaths set amidst an epidemic of ignorant and reckless behavior that didn't seem to be abating.

The report and video, which can be seen on YouTube, are self-indicting. The video shows the two accidentally setting off a small slide that quickly balloons, running further than they imagined to hit the road, and capturing them saying, "Fuck, dude." "I know dude, that's what I was worried about." And, "I sure hope no one was on that road."

Pretty damning stuff, especially when coupled with the report they filed. And therein lies the rub. Was such incriminating material, delivered in good faith to an agency that strongly urges the reporting of any and all damaging snow slides, a violation of the right against self-incrimination, and the right to privacy regarding the report and video they voluntarily provided?

A defense attorney unsuccessfully argued the latter point, saying that use of the evidence provided to law enforcement by the CAIC represented an unreasonable search and seizure because his clients didn't know the information they shared could be used against them in court. In essence, he argued that they hadn't been advised of their rights. The court didn't agree.

It was a complicated case, in part because the defendants were not especially laudable themselves, beyond having properly reported the slide. Both claimed to be seasoned veterans of such backcountry boarding who's experience prepared them to be in dangerous situations, and that nothing they did was wrong or something to regret.

Apparently the comment, "I hope no one was on that road," was either a bad joke or part of the evidence that they didn't want shared. In either case, there seemed to be no regret expressed for having made a wrong decision that could have killed someone else. And one that did, in any case, result in considerable property damage. In the end it seemed that the most intractable aspect of backcountry safety continues to be riders unwilling to take any personal responsibility for their actions, as they affect themselves or most importantly, others.

The worst fallout came from them going on to defend themselves on the basis that such charges had never happened before, no one died in their accident, and they had self-reported everything. Therefore, the use of that information was unfair by law enforcement, and furthermore would have a chilling effect on others reporting avalanches.

The latter was most concerning to the CAIC and many others in the backcountry skiing community. The CAIC properly defended its actions saying their obligation was to the skiing public, not the privacy of a given individual. But they also understood it could have negative ramifications for the future of avalanche reporting. On that basis, Colorado Attorney General Phil Weiser filed a motion to quash subpoenas by prosecutors for CAIC employees to testify in the case. That motion was dismissed.

Ultimately the case was basically punted when prosecutors and defendants reached a plea agreement where Hannibal and DeWitt would plead guilty to reduced charges, get 20 hours of community service, and fines for their violation of the law. But they would owe no restitution for the damaged equipment, in the form of a $168,000 fine that was previously going to be levied against them.

Tyler DeWitt further endeared himself to those concerned about the important legal issues that were far greater than either him or his cohort, by later telling the Summit Daily newspaper, "It's very disappointing to take a guilty plea because at no point did we feel guilty. At no point did we act recklessly out there, but this was just an opportunity we couldn't pass up… and this isn't going to change the way I recreate at all." It was a statement that, in one selfish blast, succinctly summed up the problems with self-centered riders operating solely on the impulse that something was "too good to pass up."

Ethan Greene at the CAIC acknowledged that, "I do think information sharing has always been a delicate topic, and I don't see that changing in the future. I don't know what the impacts of this particular case are on that. I do think everyone benefits from information sharing, whether it's through us or other platforms."

In that vein, Evan Hannibal said he had talked with other backcountry users who were already saying they weren't going to report avalanches to state agencies in the future. But he didn't necessarily agree with that, saying that you could report things anonymously and still get the information out there without waiving your rights.

That's helpful. The discouraging part is that neither of them seem to recognize that they effectively waived their rights when they made an unnecessary and calculated mistake that resulted in harm to others, and now needs to be atoned for. Absent that, everyone who rides in the backcountry or anywhere near it – in fact, anyone who even drives, walks, eats or sleeps anywhere near it – is at the mercy of similar selfishness.

CHAPTER 28
AVALANCHES — PART FIVE

The Avalanche Hunters

[Note: Legendary first-generation avalanche authority Montgomery Atwater published a famous book of his reminiscences in 1968 entitled The Avalanche Hunters. We are indebted to him for the term, though it no longer seems in vogue in the trade. But I liked it well enough to pirate it for the title of this chapter. Snow White (aka Sue Ferguson), writing in the maiden issue of The Avalanche Review, defined Avalanche Hunter this way: "That part of humanity allowed free expression due to current prison overcrowding. As part of their discipline, avalanche hunters constantly search the steep and deep for socially accepted instabilities which result in the 'avalanche'." Okay.]

Parkin Costain is a sponsored skier out of Big Sky, Montana who won the Kings and Queens of Corbet's competition at Jackson Hole in 2020 when he was 20. Then in midwinter of 2021 he was featured in one of the most watched ski clips in years. The video showed him dropping into a steep backcountry pitch for his movie MIXTAPES and charging down the slope in a handful of turns with a big floaty 360 off a mound in the middle of it. Then he took dead aim at a rock promontory and just as he launched it the snow across the entire face above him settled loudly, tore loose and started flushing down the mountain.

There was speculation when the video was posted that the avalanche had been deliberately triggered for added drama. That has certainly been done often over the last several decades. As of this writing in 2023 Snowbrains was still 'reporting' that it wasn't clear if it had been intentional or not, in spite of the fact that Costain gave an interview to the Low Pressure podcast later the same year it happened where he made it clear it wasn't planned.

They were shooting in some backcountry in the Tetons "over toward Jackson," as Costain put it, and followed some locals into territory where they'd never been before. "Probably a big red flag," as Costain admitted in the interview. And he also wrote, "Looking back, mistakes were made and lessons were definitely learned."

Avalanche blasting in French resort Tignes at 3,600 meters. Photo by Alexander Joss.

In the podcast interview he gave details. "We skied this whole face and there was this little bit more southerly aspect that was kinda getting heated up by the sun all day and skied right on the edge of it most of the way down and I was like all right nothings slid yet lets head out for this backflip towards the bottom."

He got two-thirds of the way down, still ripping along when, "There was a propagation like I hadn't ever seen before where I was all the way at the bottom of the slope and it just like cracked all the way back to the top of the mountain. And I didn't see any of it until I was like taking off… I was so focused on this like next takeoff I was about to do that I had no idea until mid-flip… before I saw snow was moving right under me and I realized it was sliding."

During his long, layout backflip the slide hit full speed and barreled straight into his landing zone. And when he stuck a perfect landing only a yard or two in front of the 100-foot-wide slide moving at probably 60 miles an hour, someone in the film crew is yelling, "Avalanche, avalanche!" Someone else responds, "I got eyes on Parkin, he's on his feet."

As Costain explained to a clueless interviewer who hadn't seen the clip, he had to be concerned about the landing. Not just where it was in relation to the slide, but to how he hit. He knew some of the snow he was jumping into was "punchy," and he was thinking, "Oh my god I can't punch-front on this." Which meant he couldn't punch through the crust and front roll out of the landing without risking getting caught by the avalanche. He adjusted to sit back on his tails so he could straight-line coming out of it.

Then as he raced against multiple tentacles of the fast moving slide he realized, "I had a once in a lifetime opportunity," and showboated a little on the rest of the way down. And as he importantly noted, "We always have safe zones, that's the nice part about filming with a crew, and we got eyes on us from like six different angles."

That's one of the key reasons why the talent working with the bigger film crews can take some extra risks, because they know they have lots of backup keeping track of where they are who are ready to start probing and digging if necessary.

This is what has allowed some filmmakers to actually hunt for avalanche possibilities that will add some excitement to the footage without unduly endangering cast and crew. And it's certainly not a recent trend for skiers and riders to play around with skiing in slides on their own, even absent any kind of cameras or ready help. I've done it.

It really started for film when riders dropping cliff bands began intentionally triggering powder sloughs above the cliffs to pour over them as they were jumping. It makes a nice, action-packed sequence that usually ends with no one being worse for the wear because the powder slide can be skied through without being knocked down and run over as can easily happen in a slab slide.

We used to trigger short slides on cut banks and ride them down, and that's how I had the difference between slab slides and powder ones really brought home to me. On short pitches you can go with either kind and survive as long as you go straight. If you want to actually ski in one and make turns or try to exit to one side, you can do it in a middling powder slide. But any sizeable slabs will knock you on your ass instantly.

So there are several important things to remember about avalanche hunting. Number one, don't do it. Secondly, film crews are prepared for eventualities that you and a couple of friends probably aren't. Third, any slide you intentionally trigger can turn into something more than you're planning on. Fourth and very importantly, slab slides and powder sloughs are two entirely different animals. As with house cats and mountain lions, it's a really good idea not to confuse them.

A far more intelligent and important form of avalanche hunting is going on all the time somewhere on the planet. Avalanche forecasters are collecting data, ski patrol personnel are cutting lines and setting off charges to protect resort slopes, quick rescue units in helicopters are responding to people caught in slides in the backcountry, and when resort slides do happen the ski patrol serve as combination medics/firemen who have to be medical first responders as well as rescuers. And all of these professionals often have had to do their jobs while the possibility still exists of more avalanches coming down on top of them.

Any number of people put themselves in harms way on a regular basis to deal with the possibilities and consequences of lethal snow. These avalanche hunters are as much on the frontlines as firemen rushing into burning buildings, and their stories are both heroic and encouraging about the state of the science/voodoo of predicting and coping with the white death.

How real is the threat they work under? Way too. One story can't speak for the many who have perished doing their jobs, but maybe it can serve as an example. In an article for GQ.com, Joshua Hammer related a story about one of the guides for the Air-Glaciers rescue operation in Switzerland. His name is Pascal Gaspoz, an ex-cop who joined the team in 1995, and has flown hundreds of missions with them.

In 2002, an avalanche caught 6 climbers above Zinal in the Val d'Annivers. One woman was swept away and Air-Glaciers dispatched a dog-team and 23 rescuers to the scene. Then a second slide broke loose and buried six of the rescuers. Four were "pulled out alive," but one of the two who wasn't was Pascal's older brother Nicolas, 36. They found his body the next day in what was "one of the most tragic [events] in Air-Glaciers long history."

Throughout this avalanche section the organization that I've referred to most often is known as the Swiss Federal Institute for Snow and Avalanche Research, or more commonly the SLF. Their mission began in Davos in 1931, making them one of the first and most continuously reliable sources for information on avalanches throughout Switzerland, the Alps, Europe and much of the world.

The need for more thorough monitoring and eventually forecasting of avalanches in Europe wasn't really emphasized until the gradual development of the tourist industry put more at risk than the mountain farmers and their livestock. As the SLF website explains, "Promoters of ski tourism, railway companies and hydropower plant operators were making louder pleas for scientific methods to be adopted for avalanche research from the 1920s, and they supported the establishment of the Commission for Snow and avalanche Research in 1931. It became the first central agency in Switzerland dedicated to researching avalanches systematically."

It didn't take them long to figure out that they needed to make first-hand observations of avalanches and they built a post for that purpose on top of the 2,693-meter (8,835-foot) Weissfluhjoch above Davos in 1935. It was appropriately made of snow, like a square igloo. In 1936 they got their first facility that wouldn't melt and never looked back. In 1942 the commission was replaced by the SLF and an official "home office" on the Weissfluhjoch in 1943.

Following WWII more countries reached out to the SLF, "to assist with local avalanche protection programs. The SLF was soon recognized as the center of snow and avalanche research and is still acknowledged as such today." In a post from the SLF in the early 2020s they noted, "Avalanches are a fascinating, but above all else, a supremely dangerous phenomenon. We are therefore researching how they form and travel and how we can optimally protect ourselves. By issuing avalanche warnings for the Swiss Alps, we perform an important national service." It provides a "twice-daily national avalanche bulletin using data gathered by 200 people trained to do the job and 170 automatic measuring stations dotted across the Swiss Alps."

In order to more accurately forecast and prevent disastrous slides scientists need to understand the "complex physical processes at work" inside of them. "Our Vallee de la Sionne avalanche test site at Arbaz in the canton of Valais has been operating since 1997. The only facility of its kind in the world, it has technical equipment that allows us to gain just this kind of insight. The data collected helps us, among other things, to develop and improve avalanche simulation programs, which are used by engineers worldwide to assess hazards and design protection measures."

Digging snowpits is one of the most fundamental ways of making avalanche evaluations. Photo by <u>Clayoquot</u> via Creative Commons.

In November of 2018 Switzerland and Austria's knowledge, experiences and strategies of managing avalanche risks were officially recognized as a global cultural treasure by the United Nations.

In the United States, Ed and Dolores LaChapelle became living testimony to the fact that there were, indeed, some old avalanche experts in the world, in spite of the famous ski patrol aphorism to the contrary. And they achieved longevity in the field of avalanche research and forecasting when it was still in its infancy and at its most dangerous.

Easy to characterize as the poet and the scientist, Dolores and Ed also shared many of the same traits, including a love of the mountains and skiing. And they were at the forefront of studying snowpack and avalanches, starting with stints in Davos at the SLF in 1950-'52.

Ed went straight from there to Alta where he worked as a snow ranger for the Forest Service for 20 years, while also going on expeditions like one in 1953 to the Greenland ice sheet. His focus on research also included teaching geophysics and atmospheric sciences at the University of Washington; studying avalanches in Silverton with the University of Colorado's Institute for Arctic and Alpine Research; and developing the first avalanche transceiver (the Skadi) with John Lawton. He also turned his groundbreaking 1961 US Forest Service avalanche

Mountain rescue services in the Alps fly searchers, dogs and doctors to avalanche sites and evacuate victims.
Photo by Matthias Zepper.

handbook into what he described as "a handy pocket reference for people going out on a tour," titled the ABCs of Avalanche Safety, still a must-have today.

Dolores was a mountaineer and skier in her soul who famously wrote, "Powder snow skiing is not fun. It's life, fully lived, life lived in a blaze of reality." She climbed all of Colorado's 14ers by the time she turned 21, taught skiing in Aspen for several seasons, made the first known ski descent of Baldy Chute in Alta in 1956, and moved to Telluride where she was the director of the Way of Mountain Learning. She was also a deep ecologist before anyone else even knew there were ecologists, let alone radical ones.

Her numerous books included Deep Powder Snow that lyrically pointed the way toward how to chase the powder dragon for your whole life and survive. She understood in her blood about avalanches what her husband verified in his research and they combined to deliver that information and a path toward better understanding of the phenomenon to the skiers of the world. Though no longer married both died separately within a few weeks of each other of natural causes in 2007.

The SLF and dedicated individuals like the LaChapelles brought avalanche awareness out of the stone age and into the second half of the 20th century to the point where today, well into the 21st century, tens of thousands are actively involved in the science, engineering and white-magic of avalanche hunting and mitigation.

One of the pioneers arrived in the Tetons of Wyoming at just about the time the LaChapelles were getting settled in Alta. Rod Newcomb's first summer in Jackson was 1953 and after compulsory military duty and dropping out of college in Los Angeles, he moved to Wyoming to stay.

"My background in snow and avalanches began on Snow King [in Jackson], where I learned to ski. Right away, I caught on to the fact that if you were gonna ski off the packed run, you had to be aware of slab avalanches," he said in an interview for Mountain Time online. In the summers he worked for the famous Exum Guides in the Tetons, in winter he got a job on the ski patrol in Alta one year, and was "sort of the avalanche expert" at Vail when it opened in 1963, then in '64 moved back to Jackson for the opening of the new ski mountain there.

By the early '70s Americans were discovering skiing in the backcountry in droves due to gear advances that made it much easier. "Right away, we began encountering avalanches," noted Newcomb. "And I said to myself, 'There is a market here to run a private avalanche school.' So in 1974 I founded what became the American Avalanche Institute (AAI). I think of myself foremost as an innovator of avalanche education, more than I do as a mountaineer or climber or ski mountaineer."

Sarah and Don Carpenter and Don Sharaf bought AAI in 2009 from Newcomb, and in 2018 Sarah talked to Backcountry magazine about her mentor and colleague. "Rod is a pioneer in our industry. He started the oldest avalanche education school in the country, so he paved the way for all of us. The inspiring thing about Rod – I have worked quite a few courses with him now – is that he has been studying snow for a long time and teaching avalanche courses since the '70s, and he's remained curious. He's always reading about the next thing and is always willing to say, "Well, I don't know the answer to that. Let's call Karl Birkeland or Kelly Elder or whomever else."

When the residents of Innsbruck, Austria are awakened by explosions in the Nordkette Mountains south of the city, it isn't because the Italians are invading. It's because heavy snow has fallen overnight and the community's avalanche safety commission is hard at work setting off charges to trigger slides on overloaded slopes that may pose avalanche risks to the town and its surrounding ski resorts.

These kinds of bomb squads work on most major ski areas in the world, as well as for highway departments, railways and towns with exposure to the same problems. Every day of the year around the world enough explosives are deployed for avalanche control to invade and conquer New Zealand.

In Innsbruck in 2019, Werner Haberfellner and a "master of explosions" were part of a crew that used cablecars, Gazex canons and fused 2.5-kilo Emulex AV bombs to control the slide activity. "If the wind is blowing in the right direction, the windows rattle in certain parts of the city when we blast," he tells interviewers.

Haberfellner's considerable responsibility also includes issuing daily avalanche reports to local authorities, and it all requires him to be on the front lines. "You have to be out there yourself on skis and observe the snowpack up close," he explained to Tyrol.com. It's a duty that has earned him the nickname "the guardian angel of the city," by the local media.

It also means he's always the first one up the mountain. "When there is half a meter of powder and we are up on the ridge as the sun appears on the horizon and lights up the peaks, that is an amazing feeling. There are plenty of people who would pay a lot of money to join us at those moments as we ski down through the fresh powder to check the conditions before the day begins."

A 2003 avalanche on famed Rogers Pass in British Columbia, Canada, eventually resulted in alpine guide Abby Watkins creating the Mountain Conditions Report. Starting in 2006 skiers and climbers could go to their site (acmg.ca/mcr) and find weather and snowpack reports from members of the Association of Canadian Mountain Guides, including Watkins. "As guides, we know what's going on because we exchange info on conditions all the time that should be made available to the public," she told SKI magazine.

She realized the necessity for such a service after she and her husband Rich Marshall came upon a slide that had buried 14 high school students and their three chaperones on the Balu Pass Trail. They dug out 5 skiers in the next 40 minutes and began a rescue effort that saved 5 more. "Witnessing something like that leaves you with a physical understanding of the consequences of an avalanche," said Watkins. "It's more real than anything you can learn in a textbook."

Her Mountain Conditions Report has contributed immeasurably to helping backcountry users obtain vital information, potentially saving many more lives than she did that day on Rogers Pass. And so might her pointed advice. "Are you present? Do you know every layer that's between you and the ground? Situational awareness – that's what we call it in the avalanche and guiding industry."

National Geographic has written that, "Avalanches kill more than 150 people worldwide each year, most of whom are snowmobilers, skiers and snowboarders." And they've also noted that experts from the American Geophysical Union are "available to comment on the science of avalanches and the hazards they pose."

As of this writing that list included Chris Borstad, an associate professor of Snow and Ice Physics at the University Centre in Svalbad, Norway, where he studies cracks and failures involved in avalanches, iceberg calving, and ice shelf collapse. Natalie Vriend is a fellow at Cambridge who studies the dynamics of snow avalanches and sand dune migration. And physicist Dieter Issler at the Norwegian Geotechnical Institute in Oslo has been researching the modeling of snow avalanches and conducting experimental work on their dynamics.

Such scientists are contributing steadily to the information flow necessary to understanding and reacting to the conditions surrounding dangerous slides, whether by forecasters, researchers, resort managers or backcountry skiers. Another important link in that process is the National Avalanche Center (NAC). In view of the fact that "avalanches kill more people on National Forest lands than any other natural hazard," their "goal is to improve backcountry and ski area safety by reducing avalanche risk on and around National Forests." They accomplish this by providing support and guidance to Forest Service avalanche centers, along with field support and transfer of information and technology.

Meanwhile the science has also benefitted from the likes of Doug Fesler and Jill Fredston who work in the Chugach Range of Alaska and have been developing new ways of studying conditions firsthand. Since they established the Alaska Mountain Safety Center in Anchorage in 1986, they have, "identified how we make decisions and mistakes in the backcountry," Dale Atkins, a forecaster at the Colorado Avalanche Information Center, told Rebecca Stokes for SKI magazine in 2006. "They came up with better ways to evaluate conditions. Their work was cutting edge in the '80s, and it still is today."

No matter how good forecasters and those working on avalanche control get, there are still going to be accidents and victims. And that's where the ski patrol come in yet again along with other first responders such as the local police and gendarmerie, specialized army mountain troops when available, local fire departments along with doctors, nurses, mountaineers and any other trained and untrained volunteers available.

Key to all of this is how fast and effectively a response can be organized. Victims buried up to 18 minutes have a 91% survival rate. By 35 minutes that's dropped to 34%. After that the rate declines to around 20% and stays there for up to an hour and a half before living becomes a very long shot.

This is why emergency services helicopter response units have become more common throughout the alpine resort regions of the world, as exemplified by the Colorado Rapid Avalanche Deployment program cited in chapter 27 that can get a chopper and dogs and crew to any slope within a four-county radius inside of 15 minutes.

And that brings us back to Air-Glaciers in Switzerland, mentioned at the beginning of this chapter. Started in 1965 in the Valais canton they are now spread across 6 alpine bases with a squadron of 16 high-altitude

Radar station for avalanche monitoring in Zermatt. Photo by Avalaw.

helicopters flying an average of 2,500 missions annually – or nearly 7 every single day. They help raise operational finances by selling Rescue Cards that give their subscribers (some 80,000+) financial coverage for all costs not picked up by their private insurers.

France has had something similar for many years called Carte Neige, which is available at resorts throughout the country for 60 to 80 euros a year and can also be purchased daily. It covers you while on the mountains throughout France, including helicopter evacs.

Depending on circumstances each Air-Glaciers mission involves an initial helicopter pilot and crew of two plus a doctor, along with standard equipment such as probe poles, transceivers, shovels, a stretcher and an antenna attached to the chopper's underbelly for detecting avalanche beacon signals. Then depending on necessity and accessibility, as soon as possible at least one more chopper is dispatched with a handler and dogs.

As Joshua Hammer described it for GQ, the whole concept originated when Swiss military pilots rescued the crew and passengers of an American plane that crashed in the Bernese Oberland in 1946. They attached skis to a plane and landed it on site on a glacier to make the extraction. Then in 1963 guide and helicopter pilot Hermann Geiger responded to an emergency call where he couldn't reach the victim in his small Bell 47 helicopter due to high winds. So he and two partners Bruno Bagnoud and Fernand Martignoni then borrowed money and bought a jet-powered Aerospatiale Alouette III chopper that could reach high altitudes, and then 'launched' Air-Glaciers, one of the world's first full-time professional mountain rescue air services. It has since become one of the most successful and well-known businesses of its kind.

 "They've extracted the injured from deep crevasses and carried them down from towering ledges on high mountain walls," wrote Hammer. In 2018 they flew into the Pennine Alps after 14 cross-country skiers got lost in the fog at 12,000 feet and searched for them for 18 hours, saving all but 5 who froze to death overnight.

And there are always the odds-defying miracles. In 2005 a huge avalanche at the Verbier resort carried off a mountain lodge caretaker. More than 120 searchers with dogs probed fruitlessly for hours until it got dark. The accompanying doctor reluctantly returned to the ski cabin fearing the worst. Then the cabin phone rang and a woman who answered handed it to the physician and said, "It's the avalanche." When the doctor took the phone he heard a muffled voice saying, "When are you going to pick me up? I'm freezing!"

A 2019 search for a missing skier in a massive avalanche in the Valais had been called off after darkness set in and there was fear of a second slide. The next morning a chopper circled above the zone until something caught the pilot's attention. "I suddenly saw a face sticking out from the snow," he recalled. The skier, encased but alive with his head exposed for the long freezing night, was dug out largely uninjured and taken to the hospital.

As we've established, not all avalanche hunters are humans. The widely mythologized Saint Bernard was first used in the 1700s when the monks of the St. Bernard monastery, high on a pass between Italy and Switzerland, began using dogs to search for lost travelers in the winter. They proved so effective that one dog alone was credited with saving 40 people in 12 years.

The big slobbery beasts with kegs on their collars aren't the poster dogs for the modern avalanche dog but they've served well as the longtime symbol for mountain rescue canines. Many ski resorts around the world host ski patrol dogs of all varieties, although labs and golden retrievers are some of the most popular choices due to their temperaments and trainability.

In a world that's gone increasingly high tech with avalanche beacons, ultrasonic body locators and aerial spectrographic capabilities, usage of dogs has actually increased. They can smell people through 15 to 20 feet of snow, do it more quickly than some other methods, and help with the digging. Unfortunately, as with all location methods, they end up too often being for corpses rather than survivors. And that has primarily to do with how fast rescue services can get them to the scenes.

In 2014 a rescue dog located and helped save a mountain employee at the resort of Karellis in France who was trapped under a meter of snow for 40 minutes. "I was completely covered – I couldn't hear anything or see anything. It was completely dark. The snow was right up against my face. After a while I passed out, all I could breathe was the carbon dioxide trapped in the small pocket in front of my mouth – that was my last memory. The next thing I knew I was waking up in the hospital in Grenoble."

In the end, the best way to survive an avalanche is by never getting in one, of course. But if it happens its vital to have companions on the scene with avalanche beacons and transceivers on every member of the party. They also need to be equipped with probe poles and shovels and to be adequately trained in how to use them. If you ride often, or really at all, in slide prone circumstances, you absolutely should have taken an avalanche course and the occasional refresher on how to use the transceivers, how and where to probe, and how to dig most effectively. And in an ideal world everyone should have avvy vests that can be inflated if you're caught in a slide and have been proven to save lives. The biggest issue with them is that for many riders, as of 2023, they're just too expensive.

Once you've been caught in an avalanche, the old maxim of trying to swim with it still applies, with the primary objective being to stay on top of it. If you remain conscious and feel it slowing down you need to make the best effort you can to get to the surface, if you still know where that is. As you come to a stop and if you're still buried, it's critical to use your hands as much as possible to clear a space in front of your face so you can breath. In a serious avalanche your mouth may become packed with snow so hard you can't spit it out and will need to be able to dig it out with your fingers. And you need to try to do all of this urgently but without panicking and consuming what little oxygen you may have. If a hand or foot feels like it may be exposed and you can move it or wave it to attract attention, so much the better. And if your head is exposed, or you can dig yourself out, then clearly your survival odds have just improved tremendously.

Good luck and safe travels.

SECTION VI

GOING CRAZY

CHAPTER 29
THE WORST LIFT ACCIDENTS - INTRODUCTION

Fear of Flying

On March 9, 1976 in Cavalese, Italy in the Dolomites a cable car descending from Mount Cermis in strong winds began swaying, causing an overlap between the carrier cable and a support cable at the first lift tower. The carrier cable sheared the support cable and the cabin fell 60 meters (200 feet) down the mountain, then was dragged by the carrier cable another 100 to 200 meters (328 – 656 feet) along the snowy ground before coming to a halt. In the fall the 3-ton overhead carriage assembly came down on top of the cabin, and the resulting crushing and dragging were horrific.

The car had a capacity of 40 people or 7,000 pounds. When the crash happened there were 44 on board including the lift attendant. The operator justified this overage by noting that many of the passengers were young and smaller. That may sound like a good excuse but for the fact that most died: forty-three altogether, many from suffocation rather than trauma from the crash. Fifteen were children between the ages of 7 and 15, along with the 18-year-old lift worker. The only survivor was a 14-year-old girl from Milano, Alessandra Piovesana.

"I was going down with two of my friends… We stood at the front of the cabin facing Cavalese. The ride seemed to be normal until we reached the middle pylon [tower] when the car had suddenly stopped. We stood still for maybe a minute. Then it had started again, had winced, someone in the cabin had started laughing… when the rocking got stronger they all laughed as if it were a game. Then there was a loud noise. I knew immediately something dangerous was happening. I clung to Francesca. Then the cabin jerked backwards and I felt lifted, then pulled in the gin by the legs, I couldn't breathe. The fall… did not last more than three or four seconds… Four seconds are a moment, but they are also an eternity. I thought I was going to die. After hitting the ground everyone seemed to stop screaming and I heard only my voice. Then I passed out, but then woke up before help arrived. I tried to talk to Francesca, but she wasn't communicating… A child was screaming 'mom' and a man was saying 'I will be back in Milan very soon' before he silenced forever. Then I tried to open the door

The 1976 Cavalese, Italy cablecar disaster was caused by a low-flying jet cutting cables. Photo by Jag via Skistar.

in the roof of the cabin. Help arrived shortly and I wanted to call my mother to tell her I was OK. Next I was being taken to a hospital."

According to Wikipedia, an investigation concluded that a contributing factor to the cables getting crossed was likely that the cabin was going faster than normal, or than it should have been, when it went over the pulleys on the tower. This was because it was being run at a higher speed than usual in order to get all the people standing in long lines down the mountain a little faster. It was found that "many regulations given by the cable car manufacturer were broken, including manual alterations to a programme that regulates the speed of cabins near the pylons [towers]."

Witness accounts varied with some saying that in the days before the accident, speeds on the cable car hadn't been slowing as they were supposed to when passing the towers. Whether that was the case on this day was unclear. Once the cables crossed, an important safety mechanism activated that brought the cabin to an abrupt, swinging halt, as described by Piovesana.

At that point, having experienced personnel handling the situation might have made all the difference. Instead, the report stated that the cable car companies had replaced licensed workers with cheaper unlicensed ones in order to cut costs. One of them, a seasonal worker not licensed to operate this kind of lift, was the onboard operator that day.

He didn't know what to do when the cabin stopped and he called a colleague at the base terminal who told him to disable the automatic stop system. According to the report, "This maneuver was apparently done repeatedly on this particular cable car as cables often briefly touched each other on a long stretch between the station and the pylon, possibly as a result of the excessive speed of the cabins."

This time, however, the cables had completely crossed and by disabling the safety device it caused the engine to keep pulling the cabin. "Intense sparks" and noise from the cables were noticed by the operator and lone occupant of the ascending cable car that was parallel with the descending car at this point. He tried to report it but the cabin's phone didn't work. Within roughly a minute and half from the time the auto stop was disabled, the supporting cable gave way. The full cable car crashed to the ground and then was dragged because initially no one shut off the engine, another probable consequence of inexperienced operators.

It was a god-awful debacle, the worst aerial lift accident in history, and it rocked the resort and all of Italy. After a protracted series of trials and legal rulings, four lift officials were found guilty and jailed for their parts in the disaster. The world was left with a nightmarish image of a worst-case scenario on a cablecar, where the exposure is often significant.

[DROP CAP] Multiple aspects of skiing are dangerous. The physical risk of careening over snow on half-inch-thick planks as fast as you might drive to work when you're late is one of them. So is the prospect of being in an avalanche [see previous chapters]. And riding the carnival-like lifts ranks right up there for being daunting. There's no doubt that you're safer riding most ski lifts than you are driving to get to the resort, but no ski lift is perfect. Just like the weather that affects them or the people who run and ride them, machines can go crazy at any time.

These conveyances generally rely on hoisting you into the air in or on everything from open-air metal benches to beer-can-shaped multi-passenger buckets, to large cabins usually crammed full of other people and suspended at heights where military jets can, and do, slice through their cables.

It's not hard to see why when I taught skiing for years a couple out of every class of first-timers were more worried about the lift than anything else. And those were probably just the ones being honest.

Any ski resort as well as the National Ski Areas Association (NSAA) will tell you that the most frequent injuries involving lifts are caused by the skiers and boarders trying to use them. It's both true and a bit of PR-speak to emphasize how safe ski lifts are in general, and how reliable the machinery is compared to the humans using it. That should also include a disclaimer for the humans running it. And yes, most ski lifts are generally reliable, inspected frequently and subject to strict safety regulations. Today.

Tracking and trying to ensure the safe operations of ski lifts around the world is still a developing process, in part because new technology is constantly being introduced that has to be assimilated, tested and tried. What's more, regulations and inspections are not uniform, varying from country to country and even province to province and state to state.

In spite of these caveats, statistics show that the industry isn't plagued by defective and dangerous lifts. In fact, just the opposite. According to the NSAA, which started keeping stats in 1973, only 13 people died in ski lift accidents between 1975 and 2019 in the US, and two accidents accounted for most of those. According to the NSAA, during that period the industry provided more than 17.1 billion lift rides, so that's a very low number.

You're five times more likely to die in an elevator. And the lift accidents occur on machinery operating in winter in harsh conditions where the rates include people falling out of them on their own accord and not knowing how to load or unload safely.

Of course it's necessary to consider that the overall accident statistics (including more than just fatalities) may be a little higher due to the minor incidents that don't attract attention and go unreported. We also need to factor in under-reporting of serious incidents in countries still developing their ski resort industries and regulations. And looking at long term lift accident statistics its necessary to note that no one really kept track of them anywhere in the early years up through the 1960s. But even with all of that, and in consideration of the fairly specialized nature of ski lifts, they are still relatively very safe.

I tend to treat them the way I do airplanes. In spite of the fact that they seem to maximize the chance for carnage when something goes wrong, I like them and I trust them because I believe in the science and the self-serving stats, and because I have to trust them since they take me somewhere I very much want to go. And let's face it, unless you have serious agoraphobia or other issues, they're also usually fun.

Usually. The next couple of chapters are about those times when they aren't.

I spent 10 years of my youth riding rope-tows, t-bars and platter-lifts, and am lucky to have survived. And none of those ever left the ground, at least not intentionally.

Rope-tows, which debuted in Shawbridge, Quebec in 1931, could wear through gloves and other parts of your clothing like chainsaws when you tried to grab hold of them as they were moving, and that was how they worked. They could also pin you under them and drag you kicking and yelling up the hillside until you reached the big metal bullwheel at the top. In the early days those were infrequently protected by any kind of trip switch that you might hit before you were pulled into them. Getting knocked down and then hauled full length up the hill by the rope was scary and painful – it happened to me once when I was seven or eight – but bullwheel accidents were much worse, sometimes fatal.

J-bars and T-bars were invented by Swiss engineer Ernst Constam in Switzerland in 1934/'35 and caught on quickly. They were considered a huge luxury at the Hogadon Basin ski area in Casper, Wyoming, where I skied after doing an apprenticeship on a rope tow on Togwotee Pass out of Dubois.

For adults the T-bars were good although cumbersome and not entirely safe. For kids they were fun but dangerous. The big springs were calibrated for two adults so a single kid could, and did, get picked completely off the snow in certain places. That was challenging but also entertaining, until they spun you around so that when you did land again it was backwards. And this was long before twin tips.

The other active threat on the Constam T-bars at Hogadon was the bar itself. It was a thick, polished and shaped piece of wood that formed the T you stood against. It was bolted to the base of the thick metal upright post that was attached to the cable with that mega-spring. The whole device was a weapon against the unwary.

When you unloaded, the spring would cause the whole apparatus to recoil abruptly back up toward the cable.

High tram car in St. Anton illustrates why when something goes wrong it can be disastrous. Photo © Jay Cowan.

If you botched the dismount you could get whacked hard on the head with that wood bar and the big bolt that held it to the post. All of this was decades before regular helmet usage and for small adults it was infuriating. For kids it was borderline lethal. If the same lifts were around today they'd require a concussion protocol.

Fortunately T-bars do still exist because they serve a great purpose at places where chairlifts aren't always appropriate due to wind concerns. And the modern versions are far less heavy and dangerous. Other drag-lifts include platters, which we used to call Poma lifts because that company seemed to make all of them. Of course they only take one person at a time but like all drag-lifts are invaluable in areas above timberline where the wind exposure mitigates against chairlifts. They're also useful as connectors between other lifts or as ways to get across long flat areas and other special circumstances.

Platter-lifts are also about as safe as such things can ever be because they can't brain you or damage you too many other ways unless you're unusually creative. And the great advantage to all of the surface lifts has always been that if the power goes out or the lift quits working for some reason, you just get off and ski down. No elaborate evacuation procedures required.

Chairlifts, essentially adapted from equipment used to transport cargo onboard ships, joined cablecars as the first airborne ski lifts nearly a century ago, and all of them seriously upped the ante for potential injuries. One of the first cablecars in the Alps was opened in Kitzbuhel, Austria in 1928, and the Galzigbahn in St. Anton

80 riders evacuated from Aspen's Tiehack chairlift

Local FOLLOW LOCAL | Dec 24, 2015

Scott Condon
The Aspen Times

A skier gets belayed off the chairlift onto the ground below.
Jeremy Wallace/The Aspen Times |

Chairlift evacuation at Buttermilk, CO. Photo by Jeremy Wallace for the Aspen Times.

opened in 1937. Sun Valley, Idaho opened in December of 1936 with the first two known chairlifts in the world, both single chairs.

Reports of accidents with any of those lifts didn't start appearing until the 1950s. Cablecars, also called trams, have been used around the world for sightseeing as well as skiing. Given the nascent state of the engineering and manufacturing of trams and chairlifts in the pre-Word War II era, it's hard to believe there weren't some problems. But as with many things, stats just weren't kept until it became necessary due to increased regulatory and insurance issues.

Lift accidents have a variety of causes, from low-flying jets to weather to equipment failures caused or compounded by human errors. Cables snap, fray or unravel. Lift towers topple, mid-air collisions occur between gondolas when one comes loose and plows into others, and runaway lifts of every stripe can smash into base terminals when braking systems don't function. Almost any terrifying thing you can imagine with gondolas, telepheriques, trams and the like have either happened in real life or been staged for thriller movies. Desperate tourists or spies hanging by filaments from cablecars have become cinematic clichés on a par with collapsing wooden suspension bridges over deep river gorges.

Current lift options include some that never leave the ground, such as funicular trains on ratchet rail systems, as well as drag-lifts and moving carpets. But given the death-defying nature of most ski lifts – with chairs that suspend their passengers far higher above the slopes than they can safely fall, and cable cars that travel up to 700 feet above the ground and look insane just on the face of it – they're enough to cause pause for anyone even when they're working properly. And it's not uncommon to wonder what happens on some of them if things go wrong.

That's where the lift evacuation business comes in, when something happens and a lift stops running and can't be re-started. There are lifts everywhere that most people are grateful not to have to evacuate from: chairlifts over cliffs, cable cars so high they should be equipped with parachutes, gorge-spanning gondolas.

One of the most obvious options for an emergency exit from a lift that's relatively low is jumping. And of course, jumping from any lift is strictly and justifiably verboten. The danger to the jumper is obvious, plus it can cause a cable derailment that puts the rest of the lift at risk. The only legitimate, no-other-choice situations for jumping are in the event of a severe rollback; if you've somehow gotten yourself on a lift that's then closed for the night; or you're in a James Bond or action ski flick.

If it's a rollback it will depend on how much choice you have. In general terms you need to bail sooner rather than later. Waiting until near the bottom generally increases your chance of a lower jump. But it also exponentially increases the odds that you'll be going really fast at that point, and land on other people, or get landed on by them. In all but extraordinary situations, jumping is dangerously unviable, not to mention illegal.

One of those circumstances would be if you're well and truly stranded on a stopped lift with no immediate prospect of rescue. But if you're too high or confronted with other risks to jumping, your options get limited. Shedding your skis and trying to go hand-over-hand along the cable to the closest tower, or a lower place to drop, is a very long shot.

Unless you're close to a tower. In which case if you feel like you can make a move from the chair to it – no easy task – you'll need to bear in mind that you have on big, clumsy, slick boots (unless you're a boarder) and you'll be going down metal rungs on the tower that are often nothing more than skinny, slippery rebar. Move cautiously.

Failing the tower-assisted evac being tenable, there may be some possibility of lowering yourself part way by hanging from your ski poles, pack, and/or skis/board. If there are two of you, opportunities for assisted lowering utilizing your basic ski gear vastly increase.

Once again, all of these situations pre-suppose very extenuating conditions. In 99% of lift evac cases, you will be assisted by trained professionals who are prepared to handle most of the conditions thrown at them, including snowstorms, high winds and working in the dark. It may seem cavalier to suggest, but one way to think of any well-run aerial lift evac is that you're having a complimentary experience you'd pay a fat fee for in an adventure park.

The only time I've ever been evacuated was on Aspen Mountain at the end of the day after the lifts had closed to the public. I was part of a ski instructor's clinic and our group was asked if we'd stay late to participate in an evac drill on the Number Three chair going to the top. This would have been in the mid to late 1980s. I think there were four of us on the chair and a patrolman we all knew was working our section of cable.

We were in a steepish spot maybe 30 feet high over Dipsy Doodle Bowl, and we watched the patrolman climb up the lift tower above us, attach his rescue trolley (also called cable gliders) to the cable and careen down toward us. About 20 feet away he calmly announced, "Coming in hot," and hit us pretty stoutly as we braced to catch him. His hand brake was only partially working, but it was all good.

He dropped a rope from his pack that was looped through a pulley system on the cable, then handed us a loop of the rope to go over our heads and around our torsos. After that came a small J-shaped chair attached to the rope to sit on, and we did that and scooted off the chair on it. There was no abrupt drop then or as they lowered us. No tippiness or imbalance, we just reached overhead and steadied ourselves holding on to the rope and were on the snow seconds later, with our skis still on.

There are several variations on this approach, including using full harness slings for the evacuation and dropping the skis before you get lowered. And how the rescuer reaches the chair will depend on the situation. If they elect not to climb the tower and descend the cable (it may be too steep, too windy, or a variety of other influences could be in play), then they can shoot a rope launcher up from the ground below the chair to loop a rope over the cable. Then a rescuer, belayed from below just as they are when they descend the cable from a tower, is hoisted up to each chair from directly below them.

Bags for babies and harnesses for dogs are included in evac equipment for cablecars and gondolas. The process for gondolas is very similar to chairlifts. The patrol person, tethered to the cable, hangs in front of the gondola door – guarding against anyone falling out – and helps passengers get into harnesses and clip into the lowering rope.

All of this obviously begs several questions. What happens when you're too high for a standard rope evacuation to work because the weight of the rope becomes unsustainable and/or the wind is too strong or other factors are at work? And what do they do when you're over water or cliffs or canyons? Or say its dark out or a raging blizzard?

Starting with the last situations first: all ski patrol and lift evac personnel are extensively trained for bad weather situations (we're talking about ski resorts, after all), especially since lift breakdowns can be weather related. Most normal belaying operations from chairlifts and gondolas, etc, can be conducted in the wind up to a certain threshold depending on the location, and at night as long as lights can be brought to the position. It's not unheard of for some stranded passengers to have to spend the night on a lift when there is no other choice.

In September of 2016, 33 passengers had to spend the night in gondola cars traveling between the Aiguille du

Midi near Chamonix to Pointe Helbronner in Italy, across the Glacier du Geant and ice fields at over 3,000 meters on the flanks of Mont Blanc.

Operation of the lift was halted when towing cables and supporting cables became crossed in several places and they weren't able to get them all uncrossed. Some passengers were rescued by standard means from the glacier on the Italian side where the cars were fairly low.

Mathew Dechavanne, the chief executive of the lift company, said that when they decided to start evacuations at 5:00 p.m., "We had to do it by helicopter vertically [on the French side] and not like we can do it in other places, because the ground underneath is of a glacial type so there is a risk of crevasses and it could lead to accidents."

Passengers were provided with food and blankets but, "We had to stop the rescuing operations when the night came because the helicopters can't do the rescuing operation when it is dark," a spokesperson for the prefecture said. Rescue workers spent the night in all but two of the cars with the remaining stranded passengers. The next day the last passengers were safely removed and everyone caught in the ordeal was refunded the price of their lift tickets.

In some cases where lifts pass over water, such as on Lake Como in Italy, passengers can be evacuated directly down to boats on the lake. In other circumstances where they may pass over chasms or cliffs, rappelling evacs to the ground can be conducted at an angle to avoid the problems.

T-Bar in Sweden, example of an early surface lift that is still in use around the world. Photo via Wikipedia.

In all the rest of the cases, especially where the cars are just too high to rappel from, or the rescue needs to be conducted quickly before it gets dark, rescue workers are ferried in by chopper to help with the efforts from each car. Depending on the helicopters used, passengers may be plucked off the cars one at a time or in groups of up to four, all in slings and then roped together. Then you've joined a pretty exclusive fraternity of thrill-seekers (Navy Seals, Army Special Teams, US Coast Guard, etc.), more or less for free. And it beats the alternative, which you won't be offered anyway, of staying put until they get the lift fixed.

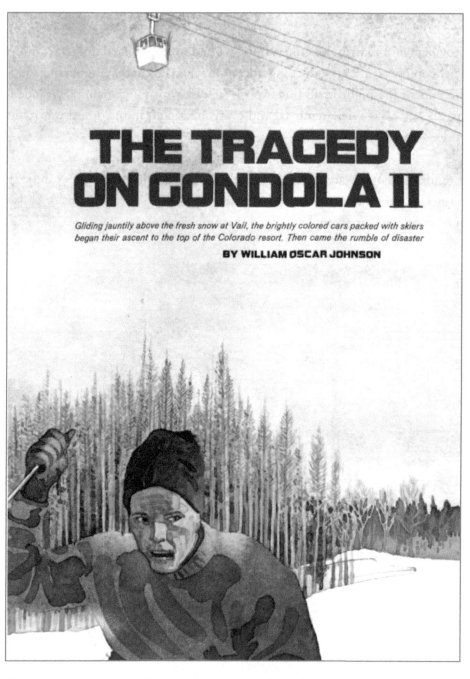

The first page of the Sports Illustrated story on the Vail gondola tragedy.

CHAPTER 30
THE WORST LIFT ACCIDENTS – PART ONE

Bad Luck, Bad Maintenance, and the Hand of God

Some of the earliest ski lift accidents on record in the U.S. and Europe involved summer operations for maintenance and/or sightseeing. In July of 1956 at Rowe Mountain, New Hampshire, a chairlift cable snapped while it was carrying 30 people. One died and 7 were injured. In August of 1957 a cable car in Cogne, Val d'Aosta, Italy, crashed carrying workers, killing one and injuring 11. On many years there are more fatal accidents on aerial lifts in the summer – involving lift maintenance workers, tourists and the occasional skiers going to summer slopes on glaciers – than there are during the winters.

One of the most terrifying of all accident possibilities first presented itself in August of 1962. A support cable for gondola-style cable cars on the Aiguille du Midi above Chamonix was clipped by a French pilot in his F-84F fighter jet. Three cabins with two summer sightseers each plunged to the ground killing all 6, and it took all night to rescue the remaining 81 people in the other cars. The pilot was never prosecuted.

Three years later the first really bad ski season accident that made the news occurred on Christmas Day in 1965 at Puy de Sancy in France. In a horrifying disaster, 100 meters from the top station a cable car suddenly lost power, pitching some of its 50 passengers forward where the cabin gave way, ejecting 17 of them out onto the snow and rocks 20 meters (65 feet) below. Ten survived.

VAIL GONDOLA NIGHTMARE

In 1976, 17 days after the tragedy in Cavalese that was discussed in the preceding chapter, the worst ski lift accident in U.S. history up to that time took place in Vail, Colorado on March 26. It made the front page of the New York Times and created enough of a shock that Sports Illustrated devoted nearly 10,000 words to it in their next issue. Some of this account is taken from that staff-written story.

Shortly before 9:30 a.m. on a school holiday with fresh powder on the slopes, two gondola cabins with six passengers each got knocked off the cables and crashed 125 feet to the ground. Four people died and several were severely injured. One other gondola car was left literally dangling from a fraying steel cable, and 176 more skiers were stranded for up to six hours while rescue operations proceeded. Evacuating the gondolas closest to the accident and/or involved with it was the most challenging.

It was around 9:15 when reports started coming in of problems on Vail's Gondola II to the Eagle's Nest terminal. A chairlift serving the Lionshead slopes ran adjacent to Gondola II, around fifty feet away on the other side of a run called Bwana. Passengers on it could clearly see and hear the gondola cars in operation and began telling the lift attendant at the top of the chair that the gondola cable was making weird rumbling noises. That liftie, Greg Bemis, called a patrolman who contacted a maintenance foreman.

Gondola operators at the Eagle's Nest were simultaneously hearing similar complaints from gondola passengers, one of whom reported seeing a strand of wire hanging from one of the gondola cables at Tower Four. But he wasn't sure if maybe it was a length of rope or strand of grease since such sightings had happened before.

Passengers still coming up the mountain, however, were becoming convinced something was very wrong. Two reports of cars bouncing violently at Tower Four came in accompanied by one passenger saying that they could see a piece of fraying cable hanging down 30 to 40 feet. Following that report the lift was shut down, according to protocol.

One of the patrolmen who took the report, Dennis Mikottis, recalled, "I got on the radio and started calling for a maintenance man to contact me by telephone. I didn't want to say anything about unraveling cables on the radio because the system goes all over the mountain. I didn't want to start any false alarms. We logged this report at 9:23 a.m. We were told to stand by and 10 seconds later we had another call from dispatcher Hesseltine who said, "We have a report that two cars are on the ground near Tower 5. We immediately went down to rescue."

A woman skiing nearby the run was one of the first to notice cars on the ground and was hysterical when she called it in on a ski patrol phone box nearby. Another skier who was a witness said later, "Through the trees I heard, then saw, a gondola car bang hard against the tower, veer away, then slam against it again…. I watched as it shuddered and then… the car simply separated and fell slowly. Then a second car approached and slammed into the arm on the tower. There were people inside. They beat their fists against the glass. Then it, too, fell."

Ira Potashner was in the first car to fall. "We reached one tower and the noise was much greater than usual and there was a lot more buffeting. Then we hit the next tower and it seemed as if we got stuck. There was a great deal of shaking… There was a lot of screaming inside… and we were dropping!"

Another passenger in the same car, Greg Dietrich, recalled banging against Tower 5 repeatedly as all the windows in the car shattered. And behind them another car was, "just jumping up and down, vibrating and making one hellish commotion," said Gene Reese who was on it. "I turned around… and just as I did I saw it. And my sister saw it at the same time. The first car fell. It went tumbling down. Everybody in our car got panicky…"

Le Mont-Dore cablecar similar to one in 1965 accident near place where it killed 7. Photo by Arie M. dem Toom

The car in between them and the one that had dropped jammed up at Tower 5, then started sliding backward down the cable. "Oh God, did we ever hit!" said Reese of the ensuing collision. "I saw the fiberglass kind of shattering and then we just tipped off. We just kind of pitched over."

The eventual accident report revealed that several cars had passed over the fraying cable at Tower 4 before it untracked the front set of wheels on the car Potashner was in. But the haul cable continued dragging the car upwards between towers four and 5. At Tower 5 it jammed while the haul cable kept tugging at it as the clamp that attached the car to the haul cable gradually loosened. When it gave way the heavy haul cable was freed and sawed against the wheel carriage, slicing through the steel casing that kept the car hanging on the line until it gave way and the car plummeted.

This same process was more or less repeated with the next car but the sawing action inexplicably stopped with one eighth of an inch of cable left intact. However, with its clamp broken the cart skidded back down the cable and slammed into the next car coming up. Somehow the car hanging by a thread stayed on the line but the one it hit came off the cable with its heavy wheel carriage still attached to its rooftop. That was weight enough to tip

The front page of the New York Times ran a photo of the 1976 Vail gondola tragedy.

the cabin upside down as it fell and when it struck the snow the carriage was forced through the roof, "lethally battering the passengers on their heads just as they hit the ground," according to a later accident summary.

At that point the lift finally shut down and the message was relayed to the patrol that there was a report of gondola cars on the ground. From this point on, the response from the Vail ski patrol and medically trained skiers in the area was nothing short of outstanding. Patrol with first aid kits and toboggans arrived on the scene within two to three minutes. Other entities from the Vail police to search and rescue units, the ski school, the snowcat operators, ambulance drivers, fire department and medical clinic were all alerted and flight-for-life helicopters were queued up in Denver.

The site of the accident was hellacious, with skull fractures, spinal injuries, broken bones, internal organ damage, lacerations, dislocations, concussions, and a nearly severed arm. Massive head injuries resulted in the first three deaths. One volunteer described the inside of the worst gondola car as "a gory mess."

Two doctors from the Vail clinic were dispatched to the scene while others prepped for incoming casualties. When the two arrived on site, four of the most critically injured victims had already been sent down by toboggans, and 8 patrolmen were at work on the rest along with two doctors who happened to ski by. Eventually there were 30 to 35 volunteer doctors on hand at the Vail Valley Medical Center, with specialists available for some of the worst injuries. Sports Illustrated noted that, "Each patient ultimately had at least one doctor and one nurse in attendance." It was a strong community-wide response that may have saved some lives.

One of the skiers at the scene who volunteered to help was Dick Pasterkamp, who that morning had gone to buy lift tickets for his two daughters and a friend of theirs while they waited in the lift line. When he returned the line was so long he was asked not to join the girls so he rode up a chairlift to meet them at the Eagle's Nest on top. While waiting for them he heard there was trouble but didn't think it involved his girls.

"I decided maybe I could help. I had some first-aid training years ago," he explained later. "I helped carry some people and load them on toboggans. I was there quite a while… I never thought for a moment that my kids were involved in this." Janice Pasterkamp, 14, died at the scene. His other daughter Carol, 18, was one of the most seriously injured and among the first evacuated to Denver where she was in a coma. Her friend Karen Togtman also perished. Dick Pasterkamp didn't learn any of this until later that evening. Carol, though severely traumatized, would survive.

Mrs. Darlene Reese was the other casualty at the scene. Steve Meoli, who had been significantly injured but stabilized at the scene, was transferred to St. Anthony's in Denver where he appeared to be recovering before suffering a setback and then dying suddenly of a ruptured blood vessel leading from the heart.

U.S. Forest Service investigators spent weeks piecing together what led to the tragedy. Per S.I. "They interviewed dozens of witnesses, workers and victims and compiled a detailed report." According to it, a section of track cable came loose at Tower Four and got longer. The track cable, made of layers of tightly wrapped steel, is stationary and the wheel carriage on top of each car runs along it. The weight of the gondola car and passengers, around 1,900 pounds, caused one strand to unravel and broke several more. Almost 1,500 feet of cable had unraveled before the lift was shut down. The strands caused the gondola cars to shake violently as they passed over it.

So why did the cable unravel? The morning after the accident the Vail police chief checked on the possibility of some kind of sabotage and found nothing. Vail Associates, Inc. – a publicly traded company – temporarily suspended trading in its stock the next day and hired consulting firms to examine the cable. The State of Colorado Passenger Tramway Safety Board, with jurisdiction over all ski lifts in Colorado, had an engineer do the same.

Three months later they issued reports that arrived at the same conclusion. The sheathing strands on the cable were likely weakened by stresses that were the result of a design flaw in the original placement of the towers for Gondola II. Vail Associates eventually spent two million dollars to correct it, then when Gondola I was found to have the same problem they sold it and replaced it with two chairlifts.

Eleven lawsuits were ultimately filed against Vail Associates, Bell Machinenfabrik A.G. of Switzerland the makers of the gondolas, and St. Egydyer, Stahl and Drathwerke, the Austrian manufacturer and seller of the cable. Eight were filed in the U.S. Court for the District of Colorado as a class action said to be for $20.2 million. Separately, Ira Potashner sued Vail and Bell jointly for $30 million. Vail Associates, Inc. reportedly settled "certain of the claims" and sought contributions from the European companies that supplied the lift.

BRAKING BAD

Another wrinkle in the way ski lifts can kill you was known amongst those familiar with the mechanics of them for years before it went public. Then suddenly everyone knew about the chaos that ensues when the braking system fails and a lift cable begins running backwards, unimpeded. The first time I heard that it was even a possibility I was about 10 and was actively alarmed. Of course I wasn't riding many chairlifts at that time, and if a T-bar cable went backwards you just jumped off.

But chairlifts are a different matter. They're often much higher than most people would care to jump from, and can be over everything from rivers and creeks to parking lots and canyons and rocky ridges. It isn't always just nice pillowy powder below you. So the thought of them suddenly starting to roar the wrong way was unsettling and I probably spent more time than I should have plotting how I'd bail if the time ever came.

First of all, it's not that simple to just jump off a chair with your skis on. Secondly, it will result in the cable bouncing and possibly coming off the pulleys. More than one chairlift accident over the years (including a 1981 cable-drop at Heavenly Valley, California) has been blamed on riders intentionally bouncing their chairs and causing the cables to ripple and jump the pulleys. Third, as mentioned, you can't just jump off any old place. And when you do you'll be landing backwards going downhill if you don't spin yourself around in the air. And when/if you do find a good place to jump you may be doing it on top of others also bailing. And others may land on you once you're down. And so on.

But riding it out on the lift out isn't really advisable either. You can get ejected at any given tower, and you will definitely plow back into the base terminal area eventually, which may involve hitting buildings, towers and other wrecked passengers. Nothing good will come from any of it.

Rumors of such things had been around for years when the Vail accident. What happened there was that the clamps on several cars came loose from the cable and the gondolas careened backwards, striking other cars. But that's quite different from the haul cable itself going backwards. When that happens, all of the trams/gondolas/chairs go with it.

I first heard stories about it happening well before a January 10, 1977 accident at Jiminy Peak, Massachusetts, that's one of the earliest I've found records of involving a rollback. Eleven skiers were hospitalized and scores had to be evacuated after a brake system failure that resulted in a high-speed rumble in reverse.

These incidents were more common than was well publicized in the two decades following WWII, as were a variety of other glitches and engineering fiascos that occurred before anyone was keeping track and appropriate regulatory agencies were virtually nonexistent.

SQUAW VALLEY CABLE CAR DISASTER

A little over two years after the tragedy at Vail, Palisades at Tahoe (formerly Squaw Valley), California, equaled Vail's sad record for the highest death toll of a lift accident in America. In 1969 Squaw began an expensive ($5.5 million) three-year project to build one of America's first aerial trams. The two-car system, with one going up as the other came down, could deliver 120 people to the top at a time. It helped catapult the area, which had hosted the 1960 Winter Olympics, into the top echelon of ski resorts in America and Europe by 1978 and the resort was hosting as many as 14,000 people on busy weekends.

Photo of destroyed tram car from 1978 cablecar accident at Squaw Valley.

None of this success had come easily. Avalanches destroyed lift towers several times, the original lodge capped a series of misfortunes by burning down in 1956, and there had also been a few lift accidents in the years following the Olympics.

None of it compared to what happened on April 15, 1978, when a gale-force wind known locally as the 'Shirley Zephyr' cranked up, creating a full-on blizzard. By 3:45 in the afternoon, many people were riding down instead of skiing due to the howling whiteout.

A partially full cabin with 44 people was descending at 11 miles per hour and had gone about 200 feet when it started skewing sideways, presumably due to the wind. After that, for reasons never understood, the car derailed from the outside cable of its two-cable system. The single remaining cable holding it was then double-loaded and the car abruptly dropped 23 meters (75 feet) before the cable tightened and the car bounced back in a bungee-jump-style rebound.

At this moment one of the 17-ton cables, with no weight on it as the car snapped upwards, came off the carriage and struck the 9-ton cabin, slicing through a wall, the roof and a door like a cosmic can-opener. When the devastated cabin came to a stop it was suspended 80 feet above the ground. One passenger had tumbled out, but survived almost unscathed. Three others were killed instantly and another dozen were pinned to the floor of the car by the weight of the massive cable. The rest had been knocked around the cabin and badly beaten.

The story then became even more monstrously melodramatic. A winter storm raged around the site on one of the most inaccessible parts of the entire mountain, where no snowmobiles or snowcats could be used, and it would be dark soon. Badly injured people were stranded and swaying in space. And 64 people in an up-bound car were also trapped when the lift stopped, 800 feet above the base terminal, stuck over the Tower One cliffs that would make their evacuation doubly challenging.

Once again a tight knit mountain community rallied. Volunteers from 8 fire departments arrived. A triage center and emergency hospitals were set up in the base Olympic House and in two day-lodges on the mountain. Ski patrol and sheriff's deputies broke a trail into the rugged site and lit it with flares. A fixed rope line that a chain of volunteers clipped into was established between the site and the High Camp terminal.

The on-board winch system for lowering passengers in case of an emergency was destroyed in the wreck, but the cable for it was intact. Twenty-five-year-old cable car operator Dan Gutowsky lowered it to veteran ski patroller Chris Phillips who was the first on the scene. Soon he and patrol director Jim Mott were hoisted up by hand by men on the car and they began organizing for its evacuation and stabilizing the injured as possible.

Local residents and famed climbers Jim Bridwell, Rick Sylvester and Malcolm Jolly all arrived on scene and helped set up a system of ropes and belays to get Doctor Charles Kellermyer up to the car to provide further medical care until the injured could be safely removed.

Maintenance worker Jon Krauss who had the expertise to figure out how to lift the 17-ton cable off the victims, climbed Tower Two and used a shimmy sling to work his way down the cable and then descended 75 feet to the car and entered through the slashed roof. He and the two patrolmen, the cable car operator and the doctor all worked as quickly as possible knowing that the badly damaged car could fall at anytime.

As per Robert Frohlich's 2008 story on the tragedy, "Over 300 volunteers took part in the rescue that lasted more than ten hours in blizzard conditions (at 9:30 p.m. winds were clocked at 60mph). The last body was removed from the smashed cable car at 1:15 a.m. The final person out of the car was lead rescuer Jim Mott, descending a climbing rope so frayed at that point he didn't know if it would hold. Meanwhile Hugh Bryce was the last person self-rescued out of the green [upbound] cable car. By the time he rappelled 800 feet to the ground it was 2:30 a.m."

Dean Wisniewski was one of the three men killed instantly by the cable. His wife Gina was also critically injured and it took 5 hours to free her from under the cable without killing her in the process. But then she died in a volunteer's arms as they were desperately rushing her to a field hospital.

Larry Hinkle was another of those killed immediately. His wife was with him on the tram and later wrote a comment to a 2015 story by Matthew Renda in the TahoeQuarterly.com about the accident. "I was one of the rescued – my husband Larry Hinkle died under the cable and I sat on his body with our best friend's (they were in the up car and helped get the people out of that one) little boy in my arms and listened to Mrs. W scream as well as Diane Fielding, a young girl who a man called Chris held until we could get her out of a mass of skis and poles at the front of the car – his son who was only 18 gave me his New Mexico hat and helped keep the pieces of roof off the Doctor and his wife who were just behind me – he was so brave and calm. Jim Mott and all the rescue folks – what can I say except thank you for you saved not just me but all of us, in the middle of a blizzard, in the dark, in the wind and cold – all of you define courage to me to this day, 40 years later."

Unable to find one thing, such as wind, or even a combination of them that would plausibly account for the accident, investigators for the Placer County District Attorney's office and Cal-OSHA officially declared it "an act of God." Resort owner Alex Cushing hired an authority on tram design, Karl Bittner, to look into it and he, too, was unable to pinpoint an exact cause. He did provide suggestions to make it safer going forward and a new cable car was installed 8 months later. In 1998 the entire system was upgraded.

A woman named Amy was also on the wrecked cable car and replied to the Tahoe Quarterly story online and expressed a not uncommon reaction to the investigations. "We live in a world in something that honestly could've been prevented ends up being deemed an act of God!" And she noted further on, "To be perfectly honest there are days I look up and think where was God. Because after all the time God was going to be blamed for the catastrophe."

CHAPTER 31

THE WORST LIFT ACCIDENTS – PART TWO

Shoddy Construction Practices, Low Flying Military Jets, a Raging Inferno, and Bad Brakes

Bad accidents with ski lifts are similar in some ways to when amusement park rides fail or run amok. Or when someone gets injured ziplining. It isn't unusual for some people's reactions to be, "Well, what were you thinking when you did it to begin with?"

As mentioned earlier, these are after all fairly complex pieces of machinery designed for purposes fraught with unhappy potential and operated in extreme weather conditions. When things go seriously wrong, we shouldn't necessarily be surprised. That said, it's still alarming and concerning when they do.

Witnesses to a February 13, 1983 accident in Champoluc, Italy reported that it occurred about 100 feet from the departure station when one gondola came loose from its braked position and hurtled back down the cable, crashing into two others before they all fell 160 feet to the snow. A total of 11 people eventually died as a result.

Investigators determined that, "It cannot be excluded that some negligence may have been responsible," according to Elveno Pastorelli, the chief of civil protection for Italy, who had coordinated helicopter rescue efforts at the site. The cablecar was 20 years old but was reportedly inspected and overhauled the previous fall, and had been found to be in good order according to lift company officials. Officials were never able to determine exactly what caused a braking mechanism failure.

CHAIRLIFT FAILS

A critical chairlift malfunction in Keystone on December 14, 1985, highlighted the shoddy practices of the soon-to-be infamous Yan Lift Engineering company that eventually became the target of criminal complaints following multiple accidents involving their lifts. In this case, when a faulty weld broke on the main pulley of the Teller chairlift, 50 people were thrown from their chairs, killing two and inuring 48.

Two years later, March 1, 1987, the anchor tower of a three-week-old chairlift in Luz-Ardiden, in the Pyrenees of France, failed. It threw 50 chairs as far as 150 feet onto the rocks and snow below, killing 6 and injuring 80, 41 of them seriously. The director of the resort, Daniel Toulou, was quoted as saying the concrete base that anchored the top tower of the lift and served as a counterweight, broke, but he didn't know why.

The Associated Press reported that Bernard Drevet, head of the Montaz-Mautino Company that built the lift, said a local subcontractor had not followed design specifications. During an inspection following the accident Drevet said he saw only 8 pieces of steel in the reinforced concrete platform for the tower, instead of the 24 the plans required. "It's the only anomaly we noted but it's sufficient. The concrete gave way, causing the pulley to fall, the pulley caused the derailing of the cable, and the cable went."

French Transport Minister Jacques Douffiagues visited the scene and told a news conference, "I saw an uprooted pylon, it's concrete base broken, another pylon ejected from its base and thrown 20 meters downward. We are accountable for the security of the skiers who frequent the ski slopes," he emphasized. "We are trying to inform ourselves and understand what happened in such a way as to avoid such accidents happening again."

Long delays in the arrival of emergency responders didn't help the situation. Some blamed it on the resort failing to report the accident expeditiously, complicated by heavy holiday traffic in the region. The director of the regional medical emergency teams, Louis Lareng, told a French radio station that the emergency team at nearby Tarbes wasn't notified until more than an hour after the accident, and that the regional center at Toulouse didn't learn of it for an hour and half.

"We immediately sent helicopters from the hospitals, police and military with men and equipment. When we arrived, there were volunteers working there who were enthusiastic but in anarchy and disorder," said Lareng.

United Press International reported that there had been 6 cable car accidents in France since 1981, with 28 deaths and 92 injuries. The figures supported resort manager Poulou's contention, "These machines are dependable. Accidents are rare, statistics prove that. This is a tough break for us." Also, one might think, a tough break for their customers.

Lift building has always been a complicated process involving a variety of components, from the planning, layout and engineering, to the manufacturing, installation, testing and maintenance. Issues anywhere along the line can create big problems, and they can combine for disastrous results.

During a final test run of a brand new cable car at Alpe d'Huez, France on January 13, 1989 – a week before the lift's scheduled opening – a cabin detached from the cable and plunged over 600 feet to the snow. Eight technicians were killed on what was going to be the biggest and fastest cable car in the world.

The victims worked for the lift's builder, Pomagalski, hired by the SATA lift company in Alpe d'Huez. A later report said that the cable car was built hastily and that corners were cut in an effort to be ready for the ski season. One expert witness claimed that the Vaujany cable car was a poor copy of an existing, and dangerously flawed, Swiss cable car system.

The report also revealed that at the time of the construction Pomagalski, "did not have sufficient expertise in building such lifts." In fact, they had agreed to have it finished in 10 months when other prospective builders had said it would take two years. Transport Ministry inspectors were also found to have failed to do their jobs. Ultimately three executives of Pomagalski were found guilty of manslaughter and given suspended sentences and fined.

On January 29, 1992, four people were killed and 10 injured at Nassfeld, Austria, when a cable jumped off the guide wheels, causing passengers from several of the four-person chairs to be ejected onto the ground and stranding nearly 100 others left hanging in the air for several hours until they were rescued by helicopter. All four of the fatalities were Slovenians. And 10 other people were seriously injured. Further details of the accident are very difficult to locate.

In the third well-publicized accident for lift-maker YAN Engineering, on December 23, 1995, four chairs at Whistler in Canada detached, killing two and injuring 10. The Quicksilver Express high-speed shuttle lift was downloading skiers due to thin snow on the lower mountain. It was nothing unusual on a mountain where skiing can be great on top and non-existent 5,000 vertical feet lower at the base. And the Quicksilver Express was said by Whistler officials to be "designed and certified for 100 percent download capacity."

Around 3:00 p.m. one of the detachable chairs on a steeper section of the lift came loose from its cable grip and slid down the cable, colliding with the chair in front of it. The detached chair with its passengers came off the cable and crashed more than 30 feet onto rocks. The chair it struck was knocked loose from its grip on the cable and slid forward striking another chair, which slid and struck another. The chain reaction left three chairs dangling until the cable took them over the next tower pulleys and they all came off and plunged to the ground. All were carrying passengers and in addition to an immediate fatality, 9 were injured, some seriously.

Detachable high-speed chairs revolutionized chairlift design starting in the 1980s, allowing much faster uphill speeds for the cables while letting the chairs detach on command and slow down at the bottom and top stations for easier and safer loading and unloading. The chairs are never supposed to detach on their own anywhere in between. But these did.

Some reports say that the cause of the accident turned out to be poorly designed cable grips on the chairs that failed following a sudden emergency stop. And it was reported by a Nevada newspaper to be YAN's 5th accident in 10 years. It turned out to be the one that put the company out of business.

MILITARY JET CUTS TRAM CABLE

On February 3, 1998, 20 skiers were killed when a military jet cut a support cable for a cablecar. Similar to the summer 1962 accident near Chamonix, this one struck Cavalese, Italy with another awful tragedy. As reported in The Aviationist, a U.S. Marine EA-6B Prowler jet on low altitude training missions in the region, was traveling 870 kilometers per hour (540 mph) at 80 to 100 meters (260 to 330 feet) above the ground when it severed a support cable for an aerial tram from Cavalese. A cabin plummeted 80 meters, leaving no survivors in what

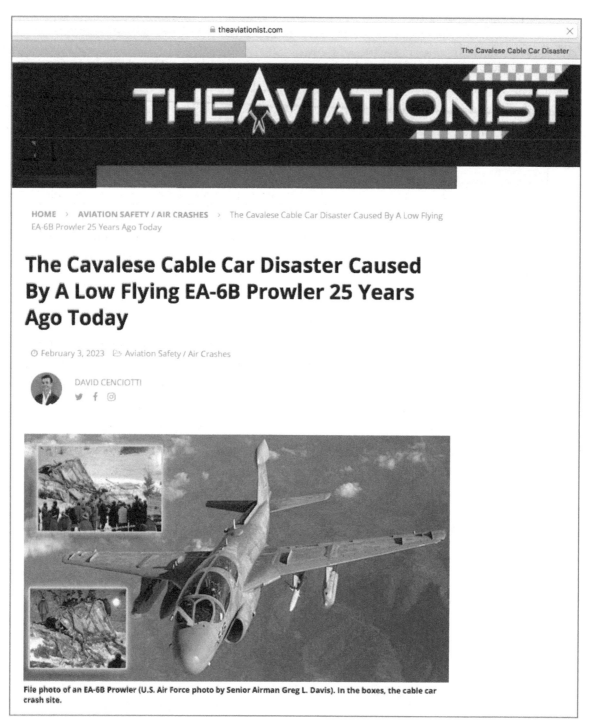

1998 Cavalese, Italy cablecar disaster. Screenshot of story in theaviationist.com. Photo by Senior Airman Greg Davis, © by the US Air Force.

became known as the 'Cermis Massacre.' The pilot and navigator were described as flying too low and against regulations in order to "have fun" and "take videos of the scenery."

Captains Richard J. Ashby, the pilot, and navigator Joseph Schweitzer, were put on trial in the U.S. Minimum altitude for the missions was supposed to be 610 meters (2,000 feet), and the cable was cut at 100 meters (360 feet). From underneath. So the plane had been *between the cable and the ground,* and sustained tail and wing damage, but was able to return to its base.

When the pilot claimed at his trial that the plane's altimeter was malfunctioning and that he was unaware of the speed restrictions he was also violating, he was found not guilty of involuntary manslaughter and negligent homicide, allegedly due to a lack of hard evidence that he knew he was violating regulations. Charges against Schweitzer were then dropped.

The entire country of Italy was outraged and American President Bill Clinton offered a pubic apology. Monetary compensations of nearly two million dollars each to the families were eventually delivered via the Italian government. Then information surfaced about an onboard videotape that was destroyed after the flight. And after the other two officers on board the flight agreed to cooperate with prosecutors, navigator Schweitzer made a plea deal for no prison time and eventually confessed he had burned the incriminating video when they returned to Aviano Air Base. He and the pilot Ashby were subsequently found guilty of obstruction of justice and conduct unbecoming and dismissed from the Marines. Ashby received a 6-month prison sentence and served 4½ of them. For killing 20 people.

On the 11th of November of 2000 an unimaginable tragedy happened in Kaprun, Austria that completely overshadowed all others that came before it. The worst accident of any kind in ski resort history, it was truly shocking and appalling.

Kaprun is 12 kilometers (7.5 miles) from Zell-am-See in Austria and together they combine to form a joint tourism area that attracts 2.5 million visits a year. Many of them come to ski on the 3,201-meter (10,505-foot) Kitzsteinhorn, served by 15 cable cars and funiculars.

A funicular railway is one that can climb fairly steep grades (the steepest grade in the world climbed by a conventional train is 10.5 degrees) employing a kind of ratcheting system and using one up-bound car and one down-bound, like many trams, but this system is on the ground, on a single track, except where they pass.

I've ridden in them in several places and they're interesting, if somewhat plodding. But they have always seemed comparatively safe because they were on the ground. The one at Kaprun opened in 1974 and was modernized in 1993 with a Jetsons-looking re-styling that made it the pride and joy of the Kaprun marketing department. And they gave each train a name: 'Gletscherdrache' (Glacier Dragon) and 'Kitzsteingams,' (for the Kitzsteinhorn and its gams, which are goats.)

Considered one of the most advanced lifts in the Alps, the Gletscherbahn Kaprun 2 was fully electric with no on board engine or fuel. Both trains used the same cable, which was underneath instead of above them as on a tram, and they acted as counterweights to each other while one ascended and one descended. A motor at the Alpincenter where the line terminated on top provided the power to the pulley that operated the cable's winch.

The 95-foot length of each train was split into two sections with a total carrying capacity of 180 people each way. It also included a control cab that had little real function except to reassure passengers that a human was running the largely automatic system. Each train had it's own hydraulic braking system that held 42 gallons of oil for brakes and doors. They also carried low voltage electronics fed by a 16-kilovolt-cable running right next to the track.

Travelling between 16 and 23 miles per hour, the Gletscherbahn Kaprun 2 lift climbed a distance of 3,900 meters (12,800 feet) up an average 26.6-degree slope in about 8½ minutes. After a nearly 610-meter-long (2,000-foot) uphill bridge right out of the bottom terminal, the rest of the track was inside a tunnel that ended in the basement of the Alpincenter. The unlit tunnel also held a small maintenance/emergency catwalk, pipes bringing water to the center, and that electric cable providing power to the train and the Alpincenter.

KAPRUN CATASTROPHE

On the morning of November 11th 161 passengers and the attendant were on board the Kitzsteingams as it departed the lower terminal at 9:02 a.m. for its first run of the day. By the time it crossed the bridge and reached the tunnel, unbeknownst to anyone on board, a fire had started at the back of the rear unattended car. Why and how that happened was the focal point of multiple investigations and reports that are still debated more than two decades later.

The original source of the fire was an electric fan heater that was later blamed in official court proceedings for having a fatal design flaw. In fact, it was not the fan heater provided with the original train or an acceptable and safe replacement as mandated by the train's manufacturer.

A key issue that was never resolved was whether the fan heater first caught fire and then burned through the adjacent hydraulic fluid lines. Or if leaking hydraulic fluid in the small compartment started the fire after coming in contact with the dangerously hot heater. Several different pieces of evidence seem to point to the latter, but the initial Austrian court ruling decided it was the former in part of a much criticized decision.

Either way, the train was 533 meters (1,750 feet) inside the tunnel when the fire became noticeable to passengers and the attendant radioed it in. Right after that the train was automatically halted as per the protocol for its response to a dramatic drop in hydraulic fluid pressure. Almost simultaneously, the now heavy smoke and fire, fueled by highly flammable hydraulic fluid and toxic high tech plastic in the cabins, burned through the electrical cable running alongside the train. This caused a blackout on the train, in the Alpincenter and other parts of the resort.

When the attendant tried to open the automated doors so passengers could exit the flaming funicular, the doors didn't respond. And whether it was because of the power loss or the low hydraulic fluid pressure didn't matter. The 161 occupants were trapped.

At this point panic erupted and people started trying to get out by pounding on the acrylic windows, which had been installed specifically because they were difficult to break. A dozen people near the back of the train finally succeeded in smashing one with their skis, and led by a former firefighter who knew the fire would burn upwards, they tumbled out of the train and ran downhill, toward flames now burning in the tunnel, but past them and finally outside in the open air at the lower tunnel entrance. They were coughing, terrified and half blinded by the smoke, but alive.

Back on the train, all communications were severed between the attendant and the top and bottom terminals and the attendant finally managed to open the doors manually. By this time hyper-toxic fumes and smoke

The Dallas Morning News

PHOTOS

Today in photo history - 2000: Skiers die in Austrian cable car fire

By Chris Wilkins
8:30 AM on Nov 11, 2012 CST

Screenshot from dallasmorningnews.com story about the Kaprun funicular tragedy.

were overcoming some passengers as those still standing scrambled out into the tunnel and uphill, thinking it was away from the fire. But the heat and lethal smoke actually raged up the tunnel like a huge chimney and none of them survived, likely overcome by the fumes before they were incinerated. The attendant and a lone passenger on the down-bound train were also stranded in the tunnel and killed.

In the Alpincenter on top when the lift operators started to see smoke coming from the tunnel they warned employees and customers to evacuate, then the lifties escaped through an emergency exit and left the doors open. This exaggerated the natural draft of the tunnel, feeding the fury of the flames and filling the center with smoke. Three more people died there from asphyxiation.

In a literally hellish inferno that was publicized around the world, from the Dallas Morning News to The Guardian, Die Welt and outlets in China, Japan and Australia, 155 skiers and employees perished from a lift fire at a ski resort. News photos showed a completely incinerated and mostly melted train that looked like it had been caught in a blast furnace. It was difficult for anyone to wrap their heads around – just too awful to fully comprehend.

In some ways it was reminiscent of the Mont Blanc tunnel fire less than a year earlier. Roughly a month after they had suffered an horrific avalanche while we were there, and then soon after that a bad fire in the historic downtown, on March 24, 1999, a Belgian transport truck carrying flour and margarine entered the tunnel from the French side and inexplicably caught fire about halfway through the tunnel. When the driver stopped and tried to extinguish it, the truck exploded and he fled.

The margarine turned out to burn like the equivalent of an oil tanker carrying 5,100 gallons. It took 53 hours to go out and 39 people died. Similarly to Kaprun 7½ months later, major components of the disaster were the chimney effect of the tunnel with winds coming in from the Italian side, and toxic fumes (mostly cyanide) that overcame people before they could flee. Twenty-nine died in their vehicles while 9 perished trying to run away.

Kaprun had also been through its own series of disasters, including an avalanche that killed 12 in March of 2000, just 7 months before their funicular catastrophe. Now a community already reeling was plunged into the aftermath of one of the most lethal accidents in Austrian history. And it wasn't like cable car disasters or avalanches where there are rescue efforts and the town comes together with everyone helping. This was a done deal within half an hour of when it started. There were no heroes to speak of, no survivors beyond the 12, and no full and satisfactory explanations for what happened.

In the coverage of the accident at the time, everyone interviewed was dumbstruck by how quickly the train was consumed in a firestorm, with some of the materials in the cars burning like incendiaries.

The grim statistics soon came out. The nationalities of the deceased were comprehensive, with 92 Austrians, 37 Germans, 10 Japanese, 8 Americans, four Slovenians, two from the Netherlands and one each from the U.K. and the Czech Republic. Thirty-two of them were under 18. Most of the bodies were so badly immolated that it required DNA testing to identify them.

The only thing that could have made it worse was if the Austrian justice system basically whitewashed the whole horror show. There was a justifiable fear amongst some that Austrian courts had historically exhibited a reluctance to find against ski resorts or the ski industry, which are substantial drivers of the Austrian economy.

Sixteen people were charged with causing a conflagration through negligence, and negligent public risk. They included three of the upper management and employees of several Austrian and German companies, including Gletscherbahn Kaprun AG, the company that owned and ran the lifts and oversaw their construction and operation. Others included the companies who bought and installed the wrong fan heaters; the company that installed the lines for the flammable hydraulic oil directly adjacent to the fan heaters; the workers who installed the fire exits in the Alpincenter; and various Transportation Ministry officials and inspectors that were charged with licensing the lift operations in spite of known failures to comply with safety regulations.

It sounded pretty daunting on paper, but on February 19, 2004 Judge Manfred Seiss in Salzburg acquitted all 16. Some of that ruling was based on the legal standards of the time as they related to funicular railways. Some was based on a lack of absolute evidence of intentional wrongdoing or negligence. And many felt some of the ruling hinged on questionable conduct by a judge who repeatedly disallowed key evidence and arrived at conclusions unsupported by the facts.

The entrance to the Kaprun, Austria funicular tunnel where the 2000 disaster happened can be seen in the background. Photo by Adrain Pingstone via Wikimedia.

A key one of those was his assertion that, "The fire trigger was a design, production and material defect in the fan heater housing and no dirt residues or oil leaks." The reference to dirt residues and oil leaks was a pointed reply to repeated claims that evidence of hydraulic oil leaks had been previously reported and even photographed but not allowed as evidence.

The court ruling caused the Kaprun lift company to sue the makers of the fan heaters that were incorrectly acquired and installed. When prosecutors in Salzburg turned for assistance to the public prosecutor's office in Heilbronn, Germany in the province where the fan company was located, that triggered an investigation by the Heilbronn office.

It's subsequent report, based on a much fuller look at the evidence than the Austrian court, stated that they found no criminal conduct on the part of the company that made the fan heaters that the Swoboda company improperly purchased and installed on the trains.

Instead they learned that when Swoboda replaced old fan heaters on both trains during what should have been a routine process, they found that the recommended fans weren't available. So they bought alternatives that were converted and then installed even though they were in no way designed for that purpose, and were in fact packaged with warnings and prohibitions to that effect. Then during the conversion process that violated the fans prescribed use to begin with, a further lethal mistake was made when the heater's built-in safety systems to prevent overheating were bypassed.

The final report from Heilbronn concluded: "It can be stated that the accident on November 11, 2000 could have been avoided if the Swoboda company had installed fan heaters suitable for vehicles that were available on the market." In relation to the new evidence that emerged from their investigations, the last sentence stated: "Thus, a different outcome of the trial would have been expected."

Some of this information was never heard in the Austrian court that attributed the critical mistakes to uninformed purchasing personnel and installers, and a breakdown in communications with their supervisors who never bothered to make sure the correct fans were being used. None of this had satisfied the court's standard for criminal negligence.

Chairlift rollback accident in Gudauri, the Republic of Georgia. Screenshot of YouTube video.

was acquitted, while most of those taken to court in France for the Mont Blanc tunnel fire were convicted, fined and some sentenced to short jail terms.

In what was taken by many as a political rubber-stamping process, a ministerial commission established right after the accident to investigate it issued a very similar final report to the Austrian court's ruling. They also offered numerous suggestions for changes to the safety procedures of funicular railroads and those proposals soon became law.

Following the accident the Gletscherbahn Kaprun 2 funicular line was closed and sealed off with two new, re-situated gondolas replacing its services.

EJECTIONS

For the first 22 years of the new millennium, lift accidents after the Kaprun tragedy were relatively minor, with one significant exception. In early September of 2005, a gondola car was transporting summer skiers up to the glaciers above Solden, Austria, when all 9 of them were thrown from cars and killed. Seven others were injured.

A helicopter ferrying construction supplies to a mountain site accidentally dropped a 750 kilogram concrete block onto one of the gondola cars, knocking it to the ground and killing three of its 5 passengers. That initial impact set off vibrations in the cable that caused passengers of nearby cars to be ejected. Six of 8 passengers were flung out of one car and died, and one was thrown from another and injured. Six of the fatalities were under 15.

An investigation reportedly found that there was a metal burr on the mechanism that controlled the helicopter cable that gripped and released the payloads. And it was what caused the mechanism to release the concrete block at an incredibly unfortunate random moment.

However, in March of 2006 the prosecutor's office in Innsbruck charged the pilot with negligence and contravening air transport regulations by flying with loads over the area used by the cable cars. The Judge who rendered a guilty decision said the pilot had performed a wrong maneuver that caused the mechanism to release. According to the BBC, the pilot said he was "very, very sorry about what happened," but denied it was his fault. He was handed a 15 month suspended prison sentence by the Austrian court.

A 2009 chairlift wreck at Devil's Head in Wisconsin was another rollback incident that injured 14 and stranded many for hours. The cause was ruled to be a gearbox failure that rendered the main braking system inoperable, and two backup braking systems also failed.

Then in 2018, probably the most famous rollback accident in history happened in the country of Georgia at the ski resort of Gudauri. It caught the world's attention when multiple videos appeared online showing skiers being hurled off a chairlift at the base as it raced backwards around the bullwheel. Many of them were fully airborne in what seemed almost like a staged parody. It was slapstick enough to just about be funny except that 11 skiers were injured and no one was laughing. Others could be seen jumping from the fully loaded lift up higher to save themselves from the pileup at the base.

The accident occurred on the lift to the Sadzele, at 3,279 meters (10,758 feet), the highest point at the resort. The four-seater chair built by Dopplemayr Garaventa Group (DDG) was installed in 2007. According to an account in the Georgian Journal online, "the lift is rarely open due to the avalanche hazard." That same story, posted the day after the accident, went on to say, "Despite the horrifying incident, Gudauri continues receiving the tourists," apparently letting the general public know they were still open.

The resort's initial response was a combination of damage control by letting the public know that there would be investigations into what happened, and shifting the conversation to asking the lift's manufacturer to explain it.

Meanwhile the international press coverage was not good. The BBC showed video with the title, "Skiers jump from speeding lift in Georgia." The Daily Mail called it "the ski lift from Hell." And the Washington Post warned its online readers, "Do not watch this video of a malfunctioning chair lift if you ever plan to ski again."

CNN interviewed a skier from Belarus who was on the lift with two friends when it happened and managed to jump. "The lift stopped and started going in reverse. We had to jump from it because at the bottom it was total trash and no chance to stay safe. We jumped, moved to a safe area, and made a short video."

Al Jazeera reported, "Videos of a horrifying ski-lift accident at a tourist resort in Georgia have hurt the country's hard-fought image as an attractive winter sports destination."

To combat it, Giorgi Chogovadze, the head of Georgia's tourism administration, said that in addition to paying for all the victim's expenses, the government invited them and their families to return to Georgia. "It made us very happy that all of them are interested and expressed their wish to visit us again. In the next winter season those injured and their companions will be invited and all of their expenses will be covered by the Georgian Mountain Resorts Development Company."

It seemed, in an era of multi-million-dollar lawsuits, to be the very least the resort and the country could do. Especially for what was quickly ruled the result of human error. As per Agenda.de, Georgia's Economy Minister Dimitry Kumishvilli released a statement on March 23rd about the findings of expert investigators from the international Bureau Veritas. He said, "Based on the records from a memory device installed on the equipment, it was determined that on March 16, there was a voltage drop, which stopped the ski lift. However, after the ski lift stopped, the operator should have turned on a nearby diesel generator to bring skiers to a point from where they would have been able to get off and vacate the lift."

In a meeting with Dopplemayr Garaventa Group in Gudauri at the end of March it was agreed that all people employed at the ski lifts would go through additional training in Georgia, assisted by a special simulator provided by the DGG. The Gudauri lift company would also be advised by experts from world-recognized companies about what type of inspections are required for their lifts.

Three years later, on April 23, 2021, the Prosecutor's Office of Georgia filed charges against two of the lift operators following an ongoing investigation by the Ministry of Internal Affairs. The two operators, who hadn't been tried as of this writing, faced from two to 5 years if convicted.

CHAPTER 32
SKIJORING

Dragged By Wild Horses

A pastime that's been around for at least a thousand years, skijoring has come back into vogue in recent years in a fairly genteel fashion via the increasingly popular dog-powered variation, whether you're being pulled around a cross-country track by your own fleet of giddy Corgis, or using huskies supplied by an outfitter. This soft version somewhat belies its long and radical history. As you might imagine, anything that originated with being dragged around on skis by elk and reindeer a thousand years ago, and progressed to getting towed by snowmobiles, sports cars and planes, has a fairly crazed back-story.

As with skiing itself, it's hard to precisely pinpoint when skijoring started, or for that matter, which of the two came first. Certainly animals pulling things such as plows, chariots and sledges/sleighs has been going on for a very long time – roughly since the mid 4th millennium BC according to many historians. I'm of the opinion that it was only a matter of days, if not hours, between when someone first figured out they could tow a sled full of stuff behind a beast of burden, until they realized it could pull them, too.

The term skijoring comes from the Norwegian *snorekjoring* and means "ski driving." Ancient rock art in Scandinavia shows humans skiing as early as the 5th century AD. Some also depicts skiers being pulled by elk – likely while being captured – and possibly domesticated reindeer. The first written record of what we might call skijoring seems to come from the Altai Mountains of central Asia, via a Persian historian, Raschid ed-Din. He wrote in the 1200s AD, citing earlier use of skijoring from historical records of the Tang Dynasty (618 - 907 AD).

In *The Culture and Sport of Skiing: Antiquity to WWII*, Historian E. John B. Allen notes that there are numerous references in literature over the years, starting in 1878, to the Persian account. Allen also studied translations of a 1993 book, *A History of Chinese Skiing*, edited by Zhang Caizhen, which reports that during the Yuan and

Skijoring with motorcycles, Augustusburg, Germany, 1963. Photo courtesy of the Bundesarchiv Bild.

Ming dynasties, starting in 1279 AD, "…tens of dogs pull a person on a pair of wooden boards… galloping on the same snow and ice faster than a horse."

Skijoring with whatever animals were available likely arose spontaneously in various parts of the world as people adopted skiing in general. The canine version mentioned in China has also long been popular in Sweden, where skijoring has traditionally been closely connected to *pulka*, which involves sleds being pulled by dogs. The tradition makes sense in countries where snow is a major condition of life. So it was logical that it got introduced in northern Canada and Alaska for the same reasons, culminating in events such as the Iditarod.

In Lapland and Siberia, reindeer have long been the designated pullers of sleighs and skiers. And *A History of Chinese Skiing* also refers to horses being used in the Altai during the Yuan/Ming era.

Skijoring likely started as a mode of transportation, then, after about half an hour, the inevitable racing introduced a competitive side to it and made it a sport. Informal competitions probably went on when opportunities arose. The first time one was recorded at a major venue in Europe may have been in the Stockholm Nordic Games of 1901, where it was the reindeer-powered version. Similar events are still held today in Norway, Finland and Russia.

By 1912 in the Alps and Poland's Tatra Mountains, equine skijoring was all the rage. In 1926 the Chamonix International Sports Week included it. St. Moritz began hosting horse-powered skijoring races in 1906, introduced to the region by a couple of Norwegian brothers, and made it a demonstration sport at the 1928 Winter Olympics.

The St. Moritz style features multiple teams going at the same time around an oval track, like regular horse racing, and the skier travels directly behind the riderless horse, tethered by reins that steer the animal. It's an insane but exciting event, with chaotic conditions and impressive skills required to handle the skiing, the steering, and the stampeding traffic.

Alternative forms of the sport have also involved horse-drawn cutter-sleighs towing skiers. While this is no simple stunt it seems slightly more civilized than the Viking-ish approach that excludes the sleigh and driver.

The horse-drawn skijoring that surfaced in America came from Scandinavia in another form still. A rider was installed on the horse, the ropes pulling the skiers got longer, and most of the tracks were straight and contained gates for the skiers, along with jumps and other bells and whistles as local events dictated. This new North American winter pastime seemed to appear almost simultaneously in 1915/'16 in Lake Placid, New York; the Dartmouth Winter Carnival in Hanover, New Hampshire; and the annual Steamboat Springs Winter Carnival in Colorado, where it has been featured continuously every since.

Heather Adeney skijoring with dogs at IFSS World Championship race, Dawson City, Yukon. Photo by Heathera skidog.

Skijoring team at 2009 Leadville, CO, event. Photo by Kaila Angello.

Just in case regular skijoring behind hard-charging horses going 40 mph wasn't sporty enough, it began going fully motorized in the early 1900s. In John Allen's book he has a drawing of Norwegians behind motorcycles in 1906, photos of the French doing the same in 1914, the Swiss in 1929 and the Russians in 1931. Swiss and Canadians started using airplanes in the 1920s. Given the low level flight required it's one of the few forms of skijoring that might be as dangerous to the driver as the skier.

Cars and trucks were naturally employed anywhere there were skiers, mostly as entertainment when roads were snowy enough, but sometimes also in search of pure speed records. Famous 1955 footage from Bavaria of motorcycles and sports cars towing skiers running simultaneously on a track at speeds said to be upwards of 100 mph., can be seen on YouTube in a video titled "The World's Most Dangerous Sport." [www.britishpathe.com]

The military applications of skijoring came into full play in WWII, whether it was in the Appenines of Italy with the 10th Mountain Division, or in Norway where their resistance soldiers trained and frequently used reindeer to pull skiers and supply sleds. The US Army has released photos of current day mountain troops skijoring behind large, military-grade snowcats.

The rebirth of skijoring is pretty much across the board. More than a dozen different countries and numerous states are now hosting races. In 2019, eight events were scheduled in Colorado, Wyoming, Idaho and all over Montana under the auspices of Skijoring America, with numerous other independent events on tap across the country.

What attracts competitors isn't just the thrill, but increasingly hefty purses at the bigger comps, currently topping $20,000. At the 2019 Best in the West Showdown in Big Sky, Montana, top teams in multiple disciplines walked away with as much as $2,000.00 and rodeo-style belt buckles. And what appeals to spectators and competitors alike isn't just the novelty and action but the frequent side betting. With Calcuttas — an auction in which contestants and others bid on contestants— there's often enough money involved to make for a profitable weekend all around, including charities which are sometimes given a portion of the proceeds.

So, as it turns out, wild horses *can* drag you away, if you let them. Yaks, too. While it seems like these prehistoric-style cows might have been harnessed for this purpose long ago, it's only been in more recent times that yak skijoring has surfaced as an actual thing. Not surprisingly it happens in India in the Himalayas where yaks are indigenous fixtures. In the hill resort of Manali, Himachal Pradesh, a local Tibetan yak herder will take groups of 5 up to the hills above town where they make an overnight camp.

In the morning he gives one end of a rope to a skier, takes the animal up a steep hill, attaches a pulley to a tree and loops the other end of the rope through and ties it to the Yak. The Yak herder has left a bucket of pony nuts (oats or some other yak-attracting grain) and instructed the skier to shake it when everything is ready. His main piece of advice is, "Never shake the bucket of oats before you're tied to the yak rope." Otherwise, according to a story in Time magazine, "You'll be flattened by two tons of hairy behemoth."

Skijoring races in St. Moritz, 1928, with horses controlled by the skier rather than a rider. Courtesy of Wikimedia.

When ready, the skier shakes the nuts, then quickly puts them down, and the yak sprints downhill to get them, hauling the skier up at what are described as "terrifying speeds."

While much of the evolution of skijoring seems to make some kind logical sense, this one completely defies that model. But it does make a good ski lift that's unlikely to have many of the hazards of the mechanical version discussed in a previous chapter. With the yak-lift you get a thrill ride going up and if you survive (which isn't that kind of a metaphor for the whole sport of skiing?) then you have the chance to get some good turns coming down.

A more representative type of modern skijoring is highlighted by the Arctic Man event in Alaska that started as a bar bet in 1985. It combines regular ski racing with snowmobile ski- and board-joring over a 5.5-mile course with a record speed of 91.6 mph. With 13,000 spectators, the Arctic Man has been a kind of far north X Games. Speaking of which, it's probably only a matter of time before snowmobile skijoring debuts at an X Games somewhere, and one of skiing's oldest competitions will merge with one of its newest.

TECHNIQUES, GEAR AND THE LAW

I first got involved with skijoring in Aspen in the early 1970s via "skitching," the common (and highly illegal) ski-town practice of grabbing onto car bumpers to get towed along the snowy streets. The biggest obstacles, aside from the cops, have always been uncooperative drivers, other traffic, and manhole covers that melt off before the rest of the street.

What seemed like a good way to barhop, as well as have fun after barhopping, quickly turned into a pursuit of its own. Soon we had waterskiing ropes attached to our own vehicles and gravitated toward late nights on deserted, unplowed and unpatrolled roads, replacing Sorels with ski boots and whatever rock-skis we had handy. Today, most skijoring pros use shorter skis with lots of sidecut and soft tails.

Our best pull came from a powerful pickup with a boom winch in the back. With ropes tied high to the boom, you could keep the towlines clear of collateral problems like parked cars and pesky pedestrians. Slaloming through town was really fun if we waited until late enough, but side roads near town were the best. We liked cruising along McClain Flats, or up Castle Creek, in and out of the bar ditches for freshies while keeping a sharp eye out for career-ending culverts.

We started horse-powered skijoring in the early 70s and several fundamentals quickly became obvious. You need a quarter horse or something similarly fast over short distances. They need to be able to ignore crowds, the idiot they're pulling, and the safety hay bales that often line the tracks, which they need to understand aren't feeding stations.

Any horse good enough to win will accelerate faster than a skier can keep up with, as they cross back and forth behind the horse to take gates and jumps. So the rider has to rate the horse to match the skier's ability. Also, the rope will go slack at times. Failing to reel it in can result in having your arms yanked from their sockets, and getting dragged until you remember to let go.

Doggie-style skijoring (get your mind out of the gutter) with cross-country gear can be highly entertaining, especially if you forget your heels aren't clamped down, and it's a good workout for both parties. Getting pulled by snowmobiles is always fun, and a polite driver occasionally checks to see that you're still with them. There are several reasons you may not be, including that you fell because you're drunk, or that you hit the top strand of a not fully buried but almost impossible to see fence line. The latter can be especially disastrous.

Random acts of skijoring and skitching on public roads used to be treated by the police on a "no harm, no foul" basis. But in the modern litigious climate, and after some bad accidents, tickets for "reckless endangerment" tend to be quickly issued.

Shaun White in the Aspen Super Pipe for Winter X Games. Photo © Matt Power.

CHAPTER 33
THE WINTER X GAMES

The X Factor

Standing at the start of the 2012 Winter X Games SuperPipe in Aspen for his final run of the event, snowboarder Shaun White was the dominant and defending champion in the event and already a certified legend. Just to drive that point home, he made a run that soared 15 to 20 feet above the shiny pipe walls, casually spinning and whirling like some enraptured snow dervish. When it was over, he'd thrown the first-ever frontside double cork 1260 (three full spins with a double horizontal twist) in a pipe in competition, and scored the first and only perfect 100 in the event in X Games history.

"I've waited for that one hundred for a long time!" said the jubilant 25-year old, with no trace of irony. He also picked up another gold to add to an overall medal stash of 18 as of this writing. It's all part of a stellar career that will undoubtedly see him headed into the US Ski and Snowboard Hall of Fame one day.

In January of 2020, Mark McMorris tied White's medal record with a silver at Snowboard Big Air in Aspen, then topped it at the Norway X Games with a gold. Whether this major achievement will help propel him into the Hall of Fame remains to be seen. But that it could, illustrates the status the Winter X Games have attained.

Coverage of the Games run live on ESPN and ABC throughout the multi-day event, and rerun almost incessantly across ESPN's many platforms for the rest of the year. That's because the overall X Games generate some of the network's biggest ratings outside of professional and college football, basketball and baseball. And Winter X gives skiing and snowboarding their biggest global audience other than the Olympics, reaching up to 215 countries and territories and 400 million households.

This transformative and deeply lucrative franchise arose from brainstorming at ESPN in 1993 aimed at creating a world-championship-level gathering of action – or alternative or extreme (take your pick) – sports. The concept was unveiled at a press conference at the New York Planet Hollywood in 1994, just to emphasize the showbiz nature of the undertaking. In 1995, 27 events in 9 different categories were held at the first X Games during the last week of July in Rhode Island.

With an enthusiastic response from everyone – the athletes, the hosts,198,000 spectators and, critically, the high-profile sponsors – ESPN realized they were on to something. Plans began evolving and expanding, an ongoing process today. The network scheduled events annually instead of every two years as originally conceived, and cloned the product. That resulted in the first Winter X Games, at Snow Summit in Big Bear Lake, California, in 1997. The following two years the Games were held at Crested Butte in Colorado, then they moved to Mount Snow, Vermont, and since 2002 have been held in Aspen.

The 1997 inaugural lineup consisted of five categories of competitions held over four days: Snowboarding (BoarderCross, Big Air and Slopestyle), Ice Climbing, Snow Mountain Bike Racing, Super Modified Shovel Racing, and a crossover multi-sport event.

For the first time ever, ESPN's sister channel ABC broadcast an X Games event, and coverage reached nearly 200 countries. Shaun Palmer won both the BoarderCross and the Snow Mountain Bike race for what would be the first two of his six total Winter X medals, all of them gold. Sweden's Jennie Waara won gold, silver and bronze in three separate snowboard events, still a Winter X record.

Striking in retrospect is that skiing itself wasn't even included. The glaringly insane – and not widely followed – shovel race was axed after one year. The treacherous mountain bike downhill racing on snow didn't survive much longer. But the snowboard events flourished. And new skiing comps along similar lines were introduced in 1998 with Freeskiing and Skiboarding (a terrain-park oddity on tiny skis jettisoned in 2001) at the new venue of Crested Butte.

This second Winter X also added snowmobiles. Skiing and snowboarding today form the bulk of the Winter X Games and drive their broadcast popularity. But snowmobiles (and for awhile motocross bikes) have played a prominent role, too, and routinely attracted some of the biggest live crowds in Aspen, who come for the noise, danger and NASCAR-style action. After some bad accidents pro motocross riders declined to do any more on-snow aerial events going into the second decade of the 2000s. And in 2023 snowmobiles were also dropped completely from the Winter X menu.

Skiing and snowboarding's dangerous head-to-head events have been popular but controversial. BoarderCross (or Boarder X), featuring multiple riders on a wild course, was in the games from the start for both men and women. SkierCross was soon added, and both are now in the Olympic Games. A kind of roller-derby on snow they can easily involve physical contact between competitors. Part of the thrill for viewers is the imminent possibility of disaster. Sure enough when the events debuted at Winter X, carnage ensued. After 20 years they were dropped in 2013 for what ESPN described as business reasons. Boarder Cross was briefly reintroduced in 2014, but currently neither is part of the event lineup.

Much of the Buttermilk Winter X Games venue under the lights at night. Courtesy of Aspen/Snowmass.

The first five years saw the introduction of women's Freeskiing, and Shaun Palmer was the first to win gold three years in a row, doing it in BoarderCross ('97-'99). The SuperPipe replaced the original Halfpipe competition in 2000 when organizers raised the walls from 11.5 feet to 15, and they grew again to 22 feet in 2009. Todd Richards, Barrett Christy, Ross Powers and Tara Dakides were tough to beat in the early years when frontside and backside 720s (two full spins) won gold in Snowboard Halfpipe and Slopestyle.

In 2002 Aspen Skiing Company officials finally reversed a longtime ban on snowboards on Aspen Mountain and needed a way to publicize their change of attitude. X Games honchos were attracted by Aspen's fame, and by the opportunity to present all the winter events at one venue: Buttermilk ski area.

Killeen Brettman, head of communications for ASC at the time, said, "When we sensed there was a chance to get the X Games, we decided this would be a bigger bang than anything else we were considering. The fact that a resort of Aspen's stature was interested in hosting their event was appealing to ESPN in that they felt being accepted here gave their event tremendous credibility."

Not everyone in Aspen was thrilled, of course. Some feared X Games crowds were just rowdy hip-hoppers with bad attitudes and no money. Even after the games succeeded, familiar questions around town were, "What do people see in all of this? And why do they like it better than the World Cup races?" Even early on, Winter X outdrew Aspen's World Cup races, live and on TV. Sponsors noticed.

Super-pipe skier with crossed skis in an appropriate X at the Aspen Winter X Games. Photo © Jay Cowan.

With three full rings of the Winter X circus going off simultaneously, either you got it or you didn't. Skiers arcing high above the walls of the SuperPipe, padded gladiators battling down a full-contact BoarderCross course, airborne snowmobiles in the tear-ass SnoCross races, music pounding and Jumbotrons flashing images of it all to every corner of the premises, was and is action-packed snow theater tailor-made for our short-attention-span times. Not incidentally that stage has also featured great athletes doing incredible things from day one.

As an index of the event's importance, the entire U.S. Olympic freestyle snowboarding team showed up in Aspen to compete in the 2002 SuperPipe, just a few weeks before the Winter Olympics in Salt Lake City.

Aspen's own three-time Winter X gold medalist Gretchen Bleiler boiled it down when she said, "For me the Olympics will always be huge, but the X Games are becoming the modern Olympics because the kids are really into them."

On the business side, ESPN ramped up world domination plans by launching the X Games Global Championship in May 2003. A team event with both winter and summer sports, it was held simultaneously in Austin, Texas and Whistler Blackcomb, British Columbia. More than 69,000 spectators attended live, Team USA won, and women's ski SuperPipe was introduced with rising star Sarah Burke taking gold. That said, there wasn't a second edition, though becoming an international brand proceeded.

During the rest of the new millennium's first decade, live annual attendance blew past 80,000. The games were carried across all ABC and ESPN media platforms, including clips on iPod, nightly X Center highlights, and daily mobile content.

In 2004, the first time ESPN and ABC broadcast the games live, they added massive lighting for night events during primetime viewing. It helped juice up television viewership over 30 percent from the previous year. And by 2006 viewers hit a record of more than 747,000 households, raising the 2005 numbers by 45 percent. The audience in every form was expanding exponentially.

The juggernaut helped create big stars such as Bleiler, White, Kelly Clark, Travis Rice, Lindsey Jacobellis, Tanner Hall and Sarah Burke. Winter X raised the bar every year on what could be done, expanding the limits of the sports and providing unprecedented opportunities for riders who had few other options at the time.

The Games also became labs for advancements in park and pipe gear, as well as ski features like twin tips that made their way to the general public. The entire new hard and soft goods industry that had sprung up for boarding got a huge boost as dedicated park and pipe ski lines such as Armada and 4FRNT joined pioneers like Burton and Jones, and crossovers from the surfing and skateboarding worlds like Oakley and Quiksilver, all flourishing in the bright lights of the X Games.

"Winter X has brought sports like skiing and snowboarding into people's living rooms that probably would never have seen them before," said Chris Davenport in 2004, when he became an announcer for them. Davenport got a bronze in Skier X at Crested Butte in 1998. "It's one of my prize possessions, seeing how big the X Games have become," he said, adding that they've "helped mainstream our sports and the athletes that participate, leading to more money from sponsors. Today we see more kids getting into skiing and snowboarding because they have been exposed to them through Winter X."

Meanwhile, ESPN's longshot bet on crazy youth looked brilliant. "In 10 years the X Games have become, pound for pound, one of the most valuable enterprises in television sports – and a favorite venue for Sony, Gillette and other marketers eager to reach an elusive audience: 12-19-year olds," wrote Monte Burke in *Forbes* in February of 2004. It was no secret ESPN targeted generations X and Y, and succeeded. Burke also noted that in four years TV ratings for the winter games increased 88 percent, and that in 2003, 37 million people watched some slice of them.

He further pointed out that the astronomical cost of buying major league sports rights was predicted by Morgan Stanley to cause "billions of dollars in losses for the four major broadcast networks in the next four years." On the other hand, the X Games, winter and summer, were expected to bring in up to $70 million for 2003 and net $15 million, "though ESPN executives insist the franchise's overall profit is only $1 million."

However much they're cashing in, it's in large part because they own the games outright, coughing up zero for TV rights, with no risk of losing them to a rival network in a bidding war. Disney, ESPN's owner, doesn't break out ESPN's financial performance, so it's hard to know how much that network makes, let alone its X Games brand. But the fact that reruns air constantly suggests healthy ad sales.

One important question Burke raised in *Forbes* was whether athletes are fairly compensated given the amount of money the games generate. Some athletes said no, and made attempts to unionize and launch competing events. But many of the top competitors seemed to agree with Barrett Christy, who made $100,000 annually in endorsements, when she said, "They're not paying us enough, but I'm where I am because of ESPN."

For ESPN's part, President George Bodenheimer said, "No one is holding a gun to anyone's head to participate." Then they began adjusting their awards scale.

"When the X Games first started, the total prize money was $186,000," said ESPN PR director Katie Moses Swope. She then explained that as the games and athletes were progressing, so were the financial rewards. For 2007, gold medal wins were reportedly worth $20,000, and by 2008 were up to $30,000 out of a total purse of a million dollars.

Meanwhile athletes understood that winning Winter X metal, and the constant drumbeat of media coverage on ESPN, helped them earn name recognition with kids everywhere. The program guide became a Who's Who of extreme sports.

In 2007 ESPN introduced disabled sports at Winter X with a combined men's and women's MonoSkier X event, with Tyler Walker taking home the first gold, and Sarah Will, the top female finisher, coming in fourth overall.

In 2010, Winter X went global with an event in Tignes, France. Games followed around the world, but 10 years later only Norway plays host outside North America. Now ESPN has licensed Winter X Games in China and Asia in 2021 and beyond, and is optimistic about further franchising.

In a surprise move in 2013 ESPN discontinued the snowmobile and MotoX best tricks events, largely for safety reasons. Other snowmobile events continued, including the very popular SnoCross which was part of the games from the beginning.

In April of 2020 Luis Sanchez followed up on Monte Burke's story 16 years earlier by doing "some detective work" for a financial website on Disney's media properties. Sanchez concluded that "ESPN likely generated at least $11.4 billion of revenue last year." Assuming total expenses of around $9 billion, "it implies that ESPN generates over $2 billion of annual operating income… and probably a good deal more."

Given that profits are hard to come by in the major sports league coverage, it isn't unreasonable to think that the X Games could be earning hundreds of millions or more of that total. Perhaps reflecting these impressive figures, an X Games gold medal in 2020 came with a $50,000 check.

A new generation of stars is rising to the occasion. Former teen sensation Chloe Kim already has eight medals, including six gold, for Snowboard SuperPipe starting in 2015 when she was 14. Added to her two Olympic golds in Korea and China, the haul cements her reputation as one of snowboarding's biggest legends ever for a career that can take her anywhere.

Reigning Snowboard Big Air queen Jamie Anderson takes lots of risks and gets lots of injuries. Also, lots of medals: 16 so far, more than any other female snowboarder in Winter X, ever. And in 2020 skier Gus Kenworthy (five medals and counting) threw the first ever switch triple rodeo 1440 (three backflips with four full rotations) in Slopestyle, as the barrage of high-flying aerials continued. It's a fitting metaphor for the Winter X Games, still going big, unleashing genius and breaking records, over a quarter of a century later.

For 2021 all snowmobile and the recently added snobike competitions were eliminated as ESPN continued to tinker with the lineup for business and scheduling reasons. They were also reflecting an increasing interest in reducing the environmental footprint of the games and their noise pollution. It was a jolt to the snowmobilers whose participation had already been scaled back, and it had a noticeable effect on local live attendance. Others were glad to see Winter X become ski and snowboard centric and to bid motorized comps adieu.

Another major change took place in December of 2022 when ESPN sold the majority interest in the X Games franchise to a private equity firm called MSP Sports Capital which also has interests in Formula One car racing and soccer teams around the world. Sports Content

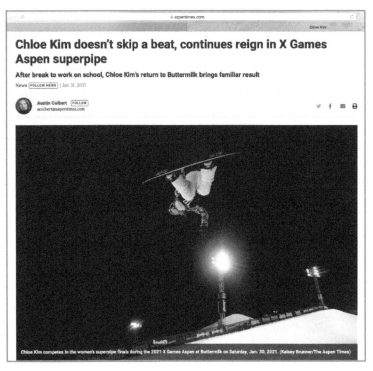

Screenshot of Aspen Times story about Chloe Kim's return to the Games following a break to finish college. Photo by Kelsey Brunner.

Creation LLC, an affiliate of the parent company, presented the 2023 games with largely the same staff as the event has used for years.

The new owners stated desire of "bringing X Games back to what it used to be," was an indication that in spite of constantly changing and adjusting, the Winter X Aspen version has suffered some diminished interest, with several factors figuring into that. A watering-down of the Aspen event's uniqueness by expanding the brand around the world was one. And eliminating fan favorite events like motocross, snowmobiling, and the skier- and boarder-crosses were also impacting viewership.

Reining in crowd sizes to a maximum of 15,000 at any given time has also been necessary. In the beginning, a cumulative crowd of 100,000 spectators overwhelmed the county's ability to handle it. "I must say, in the first few years it was a shit show," said Pitkin County Sheriff Joe DiSalvo in 2022. "We've come a long way since then."

CHAPTER 34
RIDING WATER

Skiing and Surfing: Separated at Birth

Life magazine was probably the first national media to acknowledge surfing's impact on skiing, and it wasn't favorable. In a March 12, 1965 issue they ran a feature headlined, "Aspen's Awful Surfer Problem." The story described Aspen as "one of the toniest ski resorts in the country – until the surfers arrive. Then the town fills with youngsters... there's wild skiing and wilder parties rock the nights. These surfers-turned-skiers are a new breed on the slopes."

While the story insisted, "the new invasion makes Aspen very unhappy," it gave skiing the same glamorous and sexy national spotlight that was already making surfing explode. Skiing not only grew in popularity amongst surfers, it received serious amounts of publicity in the world at large that attracted people who had never even considered surfing or skiing before, but wanted to try something wild and fun. Including the partying.

Snow riding and wave riding have many of the same followers who pursue both passions with one love. Both are action-based outdoor recreations that employ water in some form as their medium for artistic expressions of freedom in beautiful and exciting places. And the lifestyles surrounding them can be alluringly hedonistic.

Of course, not all the surfer/skiers were "bums" and "vagabonds," as the Life story labeled them. Joey Cabell from Hawaii was one of the most famous surfers of the 60s. He started skiing at 19 in Alta and moved to Aspen in 1960 to take up ski racing. "In the early 60s, Europeans still dominated the Aspen ski scene," he told me. "And we weren't what they were used to. But as long as crossovers with surfing exist, surfers will be also be there."

Cabell teamed up with local Herbie Balderson, and surf-god Buzzy Bent from California (who had gone to Colorado University and taken up skiing), to open the first Chart House restaurant ever, in Aspen in 1962. It turned into a very successful chain in California and Hawaii, becoming what one aficionado described as "a

Photo-shopped image of Bruce Irons, designed by Aspen Sojourner magazine. Background by David Hiser. Irons photo by Brian Bielmann, courtesy of Bruce Irons.

kind of surfing institution." Restaurants were good for surfers and skiers in general because it gave them jobs at night and freed up their days for riding.

Cabell lives in Oahu but still returns to Aspen every winter. "It's a very natural combination," he said of skiing and surfing. "The similarities are such that it put a lot of people from Hawaii and California in Aspen and other ski areas, and vice versa."

That fueled the fusion between the sports on a broader scale, and it was furthered following the introduction of mono-skis, snowboards and shaped skis. One of snowboarding's pioneers, Vermont's Jake Burton, had as a co-founder of Burton Snowboards in 1977 an east coast surfer named Dimitrije Milovich, who started Winterstick.

In 1981, in a striking reflection of the inner-sport synergies at the time, Surfer Publications, which began publishing Surfer magazine in 1959, bought 9-year-old Powder magazine. "One imagines that they saw the writing on the wall… and figured that the experiential, photo-driven, lifestyle-oriented material they were doing in surfing would translate easily into this new milieu," says longtime Powder editor Les Anthony. And Powder begat Snowboarder in 1987.

The magazines undoubtedly helped spur the merging of terminologies between the sports that had been happening from early on. Life mentioned it in 1965. "Groms" has been a nickname for both fledgling surfers and snowboarders since forever; "avalanche" is used to describe particular surf breaks; a line of Salomon skis were once called "guns" (surf slang for big boards); "bottom turns" show up almost as frequently on big mountains as big waves; and the list goes on and on.

In the late 1980s, a former Bulgarian World Cup ski racer named Ivan Petkov got into windsurfing on the Black Sea while recouping from injuries. That sport eventually took him to Hawaii where he ran a Naish Surfing shop. His experience shaping surfboards led him to try it with skis and resulted in the famous S Skis, one of the first super-sidecut designs, introduced in 1993. Shaped skis were a seismic event in the history of ski design.

"I was looking for a way to make carving moves on skis like in surfing and windsurfing," Petkov told me. It transformed skiing for everyone and the new skis and boards attracted even more surfers.

Cliff Ahumada's Pure Carve boards brought the likes of surfing legends Nat Young, JR Richards, Micki Munoz, Mike Doyle, Dickie Moon, Herbie Fletcher and Cabell into the boarding ranks, and to Pure Carve Expression Sessions at Park City, Buttermilk and Mount Hood in the early 2000s.

"Where powder on snowboards is like longboarding in surfing, alpine-style carving on snowboards is more like power-surfing," says Ahumada, who learned to surf in La Jolla when he was 16. "Carving is very intense and powerful, with a g-force through the turn like powerful bottom turns off a wave."

Pure carving became a distinct subculture in snowboarding. "Our average age customer was about 50," said Ahumada. "It was all about that crossover feeling from surfing. We had unbelievable support from the surfing communities. At a Legends event in Park City, I'd see Jay "Sparky" Longley at 5:00 a.m. just so stoked to go carve. It was so classic for a 60-year-old." For his part, Sparky, who is the hard-surfing founder and owner of California-based Rainbow Sandals, has had a home in Sun Valley where he's been riding for years.

As the links between the sports proliferated, so did the influences. The new fat skis that followed the sidecut revolution were largely made possible by being able to incorporate enough shape that you could actually turn them, allowing some to get nearly as fat as surfboards. Shane McConkey and other ski designers even started tapering them toward the front and back like surfboards.

When big-league surfing star Gerry Lopez moved from Hawaii to Bend, Oregon, in the early 1990s and started Gerry Lopez Snowboards, it was a dramatic indication of the widespread cross-pollination between the sports. The relocation surprised more than a few surfing fans. But as Lopez told the White Lines website in 2016, "The wind blows the snow into these shapes that are waves; they look every bit as great as a wave in the ocean… so Mt. Bachelor is a hell of a surf spot."

Today Lopez is still in Bend, shaping surfboards, working as an ambassador for Patagonia, and directing the Big Wave Challenge, a winter event he created that looks like a cross between a halfpipe and a slopestyle course and brings big-names in surfing and snowsports to Mount Bachelor every year.

The presence of surfing companies that have expanded into skiing/snowboarding markets, and the other way around, has been a strong trend throughout the industry for decades. It includes brands such as Patagonia, O'Neil, Lib Tech, Volcom, Nils, Quiksilver, Da Kine, Burton/Channel Islands and Oakley, along with almost every other sunglasses company in the world.

In 2011, skiers started paying surfing back by skiing waves. At Hawaii's massive Jaws break, professional skier and surfer Chuck Patterson took on 40-foot walls with ski poles, alpine boots and "modified" skis. And French superstar skier Candide Thovex featured some of his stylish wide-track turns on smaller waves and his regular skis in a 2018 video.

With all the crossovers it's no surprise that techniques among the sports have been comingling. Surfers apply their carving abilities to skiing and boarding. And when all-world surfers Andy and Bruce Irons talked to me for a story, both commented on how surfing was looking to snowboarding events for new tricks on the waves they were riding in competition. Soon everyone on the surfing tour was throwing major new moves that take them completely off the water, along with spins, rolls and big-air exits, as well as the kind of super-sharp cutbacks you see kids using to rip snowboard terrain parks everywhere.

The Irons brothers from Hawaii are the perfect personifications of the union between snow and surf. Their mother, Danielle Tache, grew up in one of Aspen's best-known skiing families. Her Quebec-born father Yvan was a top ski racer in his day, as was her Californian mother Marie (who dated a surfer before meeting Yvan), and her brother Mark. On summer break from college Danielle went to Kauai and fell in love with full-time surfer Phil Irons, whose nephew became the publisher of Surfer magazine.

Their sons were the beneficiaries of some super-genes. "I know for a fact it's helped. Good DNA," Andy told me, and they became two of the world's best surfers in the 2000s. Andy won three World Championship Tours in a row before an untimely death in 2010. Bruce has continued riding big waves all over the planet and is famed for his radical aerial maneuvers.

Both of them were just getting into snowboarding back in 2004 and had taken a trip to Park City for some carving that had them stoked. "It was a lot of fun," said Bruce. "I hope to do it every year. I think for a surfer to be boarding down a big mountain is like a big, never-ending wave, but sped up a hundred times. It's great!"

Andy was equally enthused, and also noted the challenges. "It's fairly different, being on frozen water. And the boards are thicker, heavier, with bindings. But they still do these amazing aerials that're starting to come into surfing now. Surfing's aren't as crazy or as high, but really inspired out of snowboarding."

In September of 2018, the first-ever World Surfing League Championship Tour stop at an artificial wave was held at the inland California Surf Ranch created by11-time world champion surfer Kelly Slater. WSL chief executive Sophie Goldschmidt told CNN that she sees surfing comps on such man-made wave systems as being "like halfpipes in skiing and snowboarding" and "pushing performance much more significantly."

Teton Gravity Research noted in a 2016 online post, "Surfing and snowsports will forever be compared. With similarities in their demographics, industry icons and adrenaline-seeking mindsets, it's no wonder why there is a hefty amount of crossover between these two action sports."

Life Magazine's 1965 fretting notwithstanding, that's been a good thing for everyone. And one of the latest examples of the popularity of this symbiosis was when world-renowned big wave surfer Kai Lenny took a spring trip in 2023 to Alaska with snowboarding legend Travis Rice. When Lenny released a teaser about it for his Life of Kai video series courtesy of Red Bull, it went seriously viral.

Historically, when snowboarding came along, a strong skateboarding connection to snow sports became obvious, dating back to 1963. A press release for 2018 U.S. Ski Hall of Fame inductee, the late Tom Sims of California, read, "In 1963 Tom built a 'skiboard,' combining the sports of skiing, skateboarding and surfing. He founded Sims Snowboards and Skateboards in 1976 and was World Champion in both sports."

That opened the door for Shaun White to win three Olympic gold medals in snowboarding, and more X Games medals than anyone can really keep track of, including golds in both skateboarding (where he turned pro at 17) and snowboarding (where he got his first sponsorship at 7).

The question of whether skateboarding or surfing had more of an influence on snowboarding may depend a little on which sport the people who do them all, did first. Virginia Beach, Virginia, pro skateboarder Othello Clark started with that, then took up snowboarding and moved to Aspen in 1994, becoming a pro at it too and eventually adding surfing to his repertoire just for fun.

"At the end of the day, all board-sports are similar," he says, and included kiteboarding and windsurfing in the mix. "Snowboarding for me was second nature, with the same dynamics, stance, balance and technique as skateboarding. Surfing and snowboarding both give you the same sense of being one with nature. And water is softer and more changeable than concrete and pavement, so it's like powder snowboarding."

Unlike either surfing or skateboarding, snowboards are attached to your feet, which Othello notes makes a big difference in what kinds of air you can do on them. Overall, "Snowboarding is a little of both skateboarding and surfing. But there are definitely more similarities between snowboarding and skateboarding, and I think skateboarding has been even more influential on snowboarding than surfing."

Today, Clark still pursues all the board sports. But his first love will always be skateboarding because, "It has stayed true to the game. You can do it anywhere. It's not expensive or complicated. All you need is a board and for it not to rain."

Alana Nichols competing in Alpine sit-ski. Photo courtesy of International Paralympic Committee.

CHAPTER 35
RIDING THE FRINGE

Car-top Skiing, The Bash for Cash, High Speed Synchro-Skiing, Barrel Stave Races, Pond Skimming, Ski Biking and Sit-Skiing

SKI BIKING AND SIT SKIING

This group of disciplines doesn't encompass mountain biking on snow. That's also a thing, and there have been competitions that included carnage-inducing mass starts and disastrous straight-lining speed trials. In 2017 Teton Gravity Research invited two world-class mountain bikers to drop into Corbett's Couloir at Jackson Hole, on snow. They survived but it didn't look like something that bore repeating. Ultimately, foir the purposes of this book, using regular mountain bikes on snow recreationally has no real connection to skiing or boarding.

However, ski biking (also known as snow biking and skibobbing) does, and has been around in this country since at least 1892 when the first patent was issued for a skibob in the US. The original ski bobs, which always had devotees in Europe, took awhile longer to enjoy any popularity in the US. But in the early 1960s they experienced a mini-boom in the States. Look magazine wrote about them in 1958 and so did Time magazine a couple of years later. After a false start or two introducing the sport in the US by European enthusiasts, a California man named William Cartwright succeeded in 1963. In 1965 he formed the only official skibob organization in the states, the Skibob Club of Santa Rosa.

The first versions of the US bobs were made of wood and included a front ski attached to a steerable handlebar, bicycle-style. Another ski was positioned under the seat, in a straight line behind the front ski. The skibobber was outfitted with mini-skis on each foot, equipped with metal claws on the undersides of the tails for braking.

They were bulky, heavy and fast, with only the illusion of control once you really got moving. My parents stocked some at their ski shop in Wyoming, and when we moved to Aspen we still had two. A friends and I beat ourselves up on them at Aspen Highlands until they eventually broke.

While skibobs have always roamed pretty freely in Europe, that hasn't always been the case in America. Taking them up most lifts requires adaptations, and there was initially a justifiable concern about their safety, both for the riders and others on the mountain.

Years later I got to try out the latest versions at Vail in one of their parks dedicated to them. The modern skibob is made of lightweight aluminum and steel alloys and equipped with shocks on the steering column, along with declawed goony skis for the rider.

My first thought was the same as years ago, that it looked like a great way to crush my nuts. In truth, I had a really good time, even in the bumps, and remained a viable sperm donor. It was much more maneuverable and controllable than the ski bobs I remembered and I had to talk myself out of buying one.

The next season I met a man named Darin Schultz who had developed a conversion kit so a regular mountain bike could double as a snowbike that would transport you from your car to the hill, and then uphill, if you wished, as well as down.

Since I'm not much of a mountain biker I was skeptical about how I'd do at but agreed to demo one at Buttermilk. There's a ski under each wheel and none for your feet since they're on the pedals. My initial goal was to avoid going too fast in spite of my natural inclinations, and that lasted about 30 seconds.

The bike was way easier to use than I imagined, and, a little scarily, almost impossible not to want to go fast on. Darin got special permission in 2008 to take his into the extreme terrain of Highland Bowl at Aspen Highlands, where he straight-lined a double-black section, stayed upright and reached estimated speeds of 50 miles per hour.

This would probably not be the typical usage for his kits. He has videos of himself on single-track dirt bike routes in the middle of winter, and it looks really fun. They also work nicely in powder if its not too crusty. For speed trials and gate-racing, the traditional snowbike design is definitely superior. It's lighter, more maneuverable, and faster. Much faster.

As skibobbing slowly developed in the US it was adopted as one of three National Wintersports by the American Athletic Union (AAU). Bill Cartwright moved to Missoula, Montana, where he continued to actively promote skibobbing at Missoula Snowbowl ski area by staging demonstrations and races. The Swiss national team performed there and in Park City, Utah, and at the Broadmoor in Colorado.

In 1967 another organization was formed called the American Skibob Association (ASBA) in Colorado and included the likes of famed ski coach Willy Scheffler. He predicted skibobbing would grow to be two to three times as popular as skiing, an odd endorsement that was never bourn out.

The ASBA sponsored an event at Arapaho Basin in 1968 and brought Austrian skibob star and manufacturer

Erich Brenter in for a clinic. He had posted a world record speed of 102 mph that year (today the speed record is over 120 mph). The first non-demo competition staged by the ASBA was held at Aspen Highlands a week later on the same slopes we where we skibobbed.

In Europe skibobbing was going full bore, and still is, as an accredited sport under the Federation Internationale de Ski (FIS) umbrella as FISB. In America two skibob organizations, the ASSBA and Cartwright's United States Skibob Association (USSBA) merged in 1970 to form the United States Skibob Federation (USSBF). The latter worked to stage the Third FSIB World Championships in 1971 at Mount Rose, Nevada. It was a big deal for the US to host and was considered a sign of the country coming of age as a skibobbing nation.

The USSBF issued a press release afterwards under the headline, "Skibobbing Achieves Major Sport Competitive Status." It went on to say, "Commencement exercises were held for the fastest growing winter sport March 22 – 28, 1971 at Mt. Rose, Reno, Nevada. The Third World Skibob Championships with 11 nations represented showed skibobbing had truly graduated into a major competitive activity worthy of Olympic sanction."

Getting included in the Olympics as at least a demonstration sport had been the aim of the sport's promoters for several years. Giant Slalom and Downhill events also produced a Combined result, and the DH course was considered the "greatest challenge ever in the world skibob competition," according to a USSBF press release. It had a 500-vertical-foot headwall so steep that it was melodramatically claimed, "skiers would not venture down it. The Swiss Team coach predicted 10 racers would be killed and refused to let his racers run. At the bottom of the pitch, ski bobbers were said to be going over 70 mph.

The combined championships were dominated by Austrians, although German Josef Estner won the Men's Elite Division, with Austrians in second and third. The Junior Men's group was swept by Austria with Franz Schwab winning. A German woman, Annemarie Hascher won the Junior Women's Division, followed by two Austrians. And an Austrian man won the Men's Senior Division with American Gene Zenger a surprise second.

Unfortunately, what had been hyped as a turning point when America would be won over by skibobbing, was its first, and last, major international event as interest in the sport soon stalled. Despite endorsements from the likes of Jean Claude Killy, Colorado Governor John Love, and Vail co-founder Earl Eaton, by the mid-70s ski-bobbing in America was a sport in decline and the USSBF was officially dissolved. It continues to be enjoyed in Europe where updated snowbikes are continuously being developed and occasionally make their way to America.

Where skibobs continue to exert significant and important influence in the US is in the adaptive skiing field. Sit skis are a game-changing piece of gear for many physically challenged snow sports participants, and they share similarities with ski bikes while being endlessly modified for adaptive skiers. They are also, confusingly, referred to as monoskis, a term that originally described skinny snowboards developed in the 1970s and ridden with both feet side-by-side facing forward.

Some of the descents being accomplished by adaptive skiers in sit-skis/mono-skis are exceptional and heroic.

Considering that many have already suffered traumatizing and disabling injuries, its incredibly gutsy they even want to expose themselves to such risks again. But having that opportunity is, paradoxically, incredibly life-affirming.

In 2015, Bozeman, Montana snowboarder Rob Enigl was in a car accident that left him no use of his legs. Just months later he learned how to sit-ski and three years later, in 2018, took on some of the steepest slopes at Big Sky. Gullies 1 and 2 had never been sit-skied before, and the legendary Big Couloir only once.

"Learning to sit-ski was kind of like learning how to snowboard," he told Powder.com. "That first day you're on your butt most of the day, but then after a couple of days doing it you start to figure it out. Sooner or later you'll catch an edge and eat it, but that's just how it goes. Monoskiing is great for people in wheelchairs. Especially on powder days, you can just point the thing down the mountain over and over again and you don't have to worry about your knees getting tired. I like doing steeper and scarier stuff just because I feel like a lot of people on monoskis kind of stay on the safe area, and I want to show that you can do more than what you think or what's been done before."

Alana Nichols was born in Farmington, New Mexico and was in high school when she injured herself in 2000 at 17 in the backcountry of the San Juan Mountains in Colorado. She was attempting a backflip on her snow-board when she landed on a rock and was paralyzed from the waist down. By the time she was 32 she was a four-time Paralympic athlete in wheelchair basketball and alpine skiing who had become the first American woman to win gold medals in both the summer and winter games.

On January 5, 2016, she added to that amazing resume by becoming the first adaptive skier to ride Silverton Mountain on a monoski. The famously steep, ungroomed and wild mountain is a serious challenge for the best skiers and boarders. She threw down four largely unassisted runs in two days and said, "I feel at home every time I come back here." A resident of San Diego now, she added, "The San Juan Mountains have been a blessing for me through and through. I learned how to snowboard at Purgatory and then broke my back and re-learned how to sit-ski at Purgatory. This area has taken part of me and given it back."

THE BASH FOR CASH: CORDITE AND MAYHEM AT ASPEN HIGHLANDS

From its inception in a market dominated by Aspen Mountain and eventually two other Aspen Skiing Company areas, Aspen Highlands always needed to stand out. So owner/founder Whipple Van Ness Jones, a maverick by nature, centered his ski area on being fun and entertaining.

Ski school director Stein Eriksen did flips at the bottom of the mountain every day after they opened in 1958/59. Soon enough ski patrolmen were jumping over a restaurant deck high on the mountain pulling toboggans. And Eriksen's replacement Fred Iselin performed Reuel Christies down the mountain while reading his own book. So it was probably inevitable that something as ballsy, doomed and fundamentally American as the Bash for Cash would be created there.

Jones blamed the race, where skiers charged en masse down a steep run for a pot of money at the finish, on the original head of the ski patrol. "There's no question that Charlie Bolte was the biggest character I ever knew at Highlands," Jones told me. "On the job he had a fondness for explosives. And after work he was quite

The Bash for Cash at Aspen Highlands race produced carnage and a popular poster. Photo by Tony Gauba. Poster image courtesy of Vintage Ski World.

a prominent member of the customers at the bar. He also came up with the idea, maybe at the bar, for our famous race the Bash for Cash."

Early versions of this obvious insanity with a mass start, no gates and few rules, were run down Lower Stein's near the area's base. Then it was moved higher up the mountain, with the start above the original Cloud 9 restaurant. It plunged down the Olympic run face and cut across to The Wall, a vertical and punishing mogul field with a run-out finish to the $100 cash prize. The winner was the first one there without falling.

"We started it each week by blowing up a case of dynamite. That was a hell of a charge," recalled Jones. Indeed. And almost as crazed as the fact that they ran the race *every week,* conditions permitting.

Not surprisingly, it occasionally produced chaos like that in a well-known poster, part of a sequence of three images taken by the late Tony Gauba on the Olympic face right after the start. Longtime Highlands instructor and patrolman Paul Dudley is one of those in the photo, and one of the few who didn't get hurt.

"I'm the one still standing in the poster," he laughs. "Then the shit hit the fan and people started colliding." He remembers, "twenty or less of us lined up side by side at the start and right away the run narrowed to about five feet wide with powder on either side." He and his friend Doug Rowley had practiced for the event and decided Dudley would try to shoot that gap, and Rowley would follow a little behind everyone and pick his way through in case Dudley didn't make it.

"When the chaos started I skied off to my left into the powder and stopped and then the screaming started. Everyone was hurt. Broken bones, concussions, cuts. Some of them skied down, they hauled others off, and they found one guy later halfway down the mountain just walking in a daze."

The photo on the poster has been dated by some as being from 1965, and Dudley isn't sure whether it was '64 or '65. But a story and an accompanying editorial in the Aspen Times about that particular race are dated February 28, 1964.

The editorial led with, "In the worst accident of the Aspen skiing season, two men were hospitalized following a collision during the Aspen Highlands first Bash for Cash race of the winter last Sunday, Feb. 23."

Highlands president Whip Jones, who witnessed the carnage, said no one was sure what happened. "Two of them fell or collided," the story quoted him, adding their own summary: "The other contestants either fell trying to avoid the first two or ran into them."

Attending physicians at the Aspen Valley Hospital were doctors Robert Oden and Robert Barnard. Myron Leafblad of Wisconsin had, "the worst spiral fracture I've ever seen," according to Oden. And Highlands instructor Mike Riddell "had his upper jaw broken in two places and his upper front teeth torn away," said the Times.

An angry letter from the doctors to the Aspen Times about the race was followed by the appalled editorial that read in part, "Racers and race organizers are lucky that more were not hurt, or that no one died." Alarm from the Forest Service, which owns most of the Highlands property, and panic from the Highlands insurance company, are said to have caused the event's demise. But a faint whiff of mayhem and cordite still lingers over the mountain.

INTERSKI AND HIGH SPEED SYNCHRO-SKIING

It may seem to the uninitiated that teaching skiing is far from extreme unless you try doing it with bickering couples, disagreeable children, or unpopular politicians, billionaires and celebrities who may be the objects of harassment and even assassination plots. However, ski instructor demo teams composed of some of the best in the business put on synchronized skiing and riding displays for a variety of events and clinics that will grab anyone's attention because, especially when performed at speed, there are obvious consequences if they go badly.

Collisions on the ski slopes are unfortunately not unheard of and can seriously injure or even kill people. But they are very rare in skiing and boarding competitions. The exceptions are dual slalom and giant slalom events as held on various pro tours and even at the Olympics, or skier and boarder-cross events at X Games as discussed elsewhere in this book. But even in those, collisions between competitors are scarce.

The same holds true for instructor demo team presentations. But unlike in the other events where collisions aren't a directly implied risk, they're obviously in play when instructors put on synchronized skiing shows.

These theatrics first became a staple of the instructing world in Zurs, Austria in 1951, when a relatively obscure quadrennial gathering of ski teachers from around the globe known as the Interski Congress was first held. Rather than spending all of their time sitting around discussing and comparing various techniques, they also take them to the slopes with demonstrations. These include public exhibitions featuring national teams, often in synchronized fashion, in what are tightly choreographed team-skiing drills.

Some of these are basic progressions as taught by various ski schools, and not particularly scintillating even to those performing them. But competitively judged advanced skiing techniques demonstrated by a dozen or more instructors in unison while showcasing high-speed crossover patterns, are impressive and exciting.

While accidents are almost non-existent at this level, they certainly occur in practice, though even when things go wrong good skiers can generally minimize the severity of the collisions. But it is the possibility of them that helps make synchronized skiing more exciting than, say, synchronized swimming. In both cases viewers may be dazzled by the formations, but in the latter no one fears for the safety of the swimmers.

BARREL STAVE RACING

The idea of skiing on barrel staves has been around for a long time, but it has mostly seemed like a cartoonish notion dreamt up by someone who never actually skied. In fact, it was done in earlier days of the sport by people who were looking for anything they could slide downhill on. In one possibly apocryphal story, a doctor in Norway needed to get to a woman outside of town on an emergency one snowy day and rather than try to posthole all the way there, he dismantled a barrel and used the staves and some leather straps to ski to his house call.

In the 1960s in Aspen there were several people working actively on the very first versions of reverse camber skis, which barrel staves are certainly the prototypes for. One of the things they discovered was that because of the rocking-chair-runner configuration they were fairly easy to turn, but highly unstable.

When actual rockered skis hit the market 40 years later they dealt with some of those problems by combining them with big side cuts and experimenting with lengths to see what would allow them to still keep a substantial portion of the ski in contact with the snow.

I got a chance to try skiing on actual barrel staves one evening on a press trip in Galtur, Austria. After a fine meal and numerous rounds of schnapps, our tourist office host shepherded us out to a halogen-lit slope near the village. We had agreed that barrel stave racing sounded like something fun to watch, and several of us were talking about actually trying it, until we got there.

The slope had no lift, was steeper than I'd expected and smooth as a bowling ball. There were 7 or 8 gates total in a simple back-and-forth pattern that on regular skis would have been easy even for a drunk. Nevertheless, some of our group concluded that watching was the sensible course of action. Others were undecided.

I was fed a large tankard of gluhwein, and then handed another one in a go cup. Next someone gave me a pair of three-foot-long, honest-to-god barrel staves fitted with straps for bindings, and a stout branch for my single ski pole. And then I was walking up the hill with only one other member of our party.

As I strapped on the seriously concave boards (I use the word 'board' literally), I realized the well-manicured slope was windshield hard and slick. But I didn't have a lot of time to mull that over – or the fact that I could barely stand up on the snow *without* the staves let alone using them – when someone gave me a little shove and I was on my way.

I hunkered down, old-school style, cranking furiously around the first gate, sighting in on the next flag and skidding past it, then rolled onto the steepest part of the slope, careening around two more gates. I could hear people cheering in the shocked way they do when someone hasn't wrecked so far. And I thought, 'Damn! I've got this!'

I hadn't seen anyone make it that far yet and in a moment of pure cockiness tried to lay one stave over on a non-existent edge and lost everything – balance, branch, sangfroid – and slammed down on my ass and cracked the back of my head onto that boilerplate snow.

Even then I had a crazed moment of thinking that if I could get upright I might still finish in the money. I spun around, lurching to my feet, weaving and flailing like I was wearing dress loafers on an icy sidewalk, and falling again. When I finally drifted across the finish line with only a mild concussion I felt much prouder than I should have.

Fortunately there was more schnapps at the finish. And soon the ringer local kids started coming down just to show that it could be done, if not gracefully at least a hell of a lot more professionally than the rest of us. And for the first time I had to accept that maybe people really had once skied on these things and lived to tell the tale.

Mammoth Mountain, CA's annual pond skim always showcases plenty of bikinis. Photo courtesy of Mammoth Mountain.

THE WAY OF WATER: POND SKIMS, SKI SPLASHES AND SLUSH CUPS

Over the years the French have gleefully taken various aspects of skiing and made them 'extreme'. They turned steep skiing into a dance with death on the world's most impossible lines. They flipped traditional technique on its head with *avalement* and created a generation of racers starting with Killy who won by skiing on the very edge. And they have even taken the simple pagan spring ritual of pond skimming and turned it into a Gallic flirt with drowning.

In the annual Defi Foly contest at La Clusaz they don't zip across a man-made slush hole, they take on an actual lake where the ice is only partially breaking up by the second half of April when the event is staged. Helmets and life jackets are mandatory for participants who start on a steep hill above the lake, tuck all the way onto the water and try to glide across some 525+ feet of it. Typically for this fatalistic mountain culture, by 2022 there had yet to be any winners. The half dozen rescue boats stay busy all day. The best anyone has done was in 2010 when Philippe Troubat made it 509 feet.

On this level, the sport itself sounds like the invention of some bored existentialists in a Chamonix bar. But all indications are it began with bored hillbillies in a Banff bar. And they didn't come up with it as a way to prove their indifference to death, but as an end-of-winter party to celebrate the coming of spring and new life. And another good excuse to drink heavily.

This was in 1928 and the concept eventually went global to the point where it may be the single most copied ski event in the world today, featured at resorts from the family rope tow hill of Leavenworth, Washington to Wild Mountain, Minnesota to Verbier, Switzerland, to Dorset in the UK and Mount Hutt in New Zealand.

And unlike at La Clusaz, the object isn't usually just to survive. It's to get wild, costume-up or strip down, and take your skis, snowboard, monoski, ski-bike, cardboard airplane, toboggan, sled or styrofoam Eiffel Tower and see how far you can make it across a small, purpose-built body of water surrounded by live music, paramedics, sponsor tents and a few thousand hard-partying sadists.

There have doubtless been many random, one-off pond skimming happenings around the world over the years. Anywhere that skiers had beer and tailgates and a half-flooded parking lot was a possibility, as were the inevitable spring slush ponds at the bottom of many ski resorts, and the glacial lakes that melt out at ski training camps throughout the summer.

The oldest official, continuing event in the US is claimed by Sugarbush, Vermont, where they say they also have the longest pond in the US at 120 feet. The most influential of the long-running events in America may be the Mount Baker Slush Cup, started in 1953 and held in July. Warren Miller said that a film segment he did about it in 1954 caused slush cups, pond skims and ski splashes to start appearing everywhere.

The unique and notorious Ski Splash at Snowmass, Colorado, began in the early 1970s and persisted for nearly two decades before the plug was pulled over liability concerns. The event had a kicker on the ski slope above the Silvertree Hotel's outdoor swimming pool and instead of skimming across it the often scantily clad and well-oiled participants did their aerials and landed *in* the pool. Hopefully. But not always. Hence the cancellation.

Factors from snow conditions to Covid have caused more attrition amongst events recently while some others have flourished. After a pandemic hiatus the "Cushing Crossing" at Palisades Tahoe re-surfaced, so to speak, and presented its 32nd edition in the spring of 2023 on Cushing Lake at the base of the resort. Sometimes erroneously referred to as the "original" pond-skimming event, it draws huge and raucous crowds.

Big Sky, Montana, annually held one of the most innovative pond skims in the country prior to Covid, but hasn't yet announced its return. Every year the spectacular man-made ponds changed, sometimes featuring two side by side or end to end, with kickers, rails, live music, a couple thousand crazed fans and nowhere to park anywhere near the resort.

Today there's hardly a ski area that doesn't hold some kind of skim or splash, usually on the last weekend of the season, with bulletproof competitor waivers and sponsors like Red Bull, Jagermeister and local breweries.

Parc de Snow at Val d'Irene, Quebec, claims the longest pond in North America at 215 feet; Vail claims, spoofingly, the World Championships of Pond Skim; Whitefish, Montana, gives over a $1,000 cash prize to its winner; and Les Arcs in France has a water slide open from March onwards for those who want to try it.

CAR-TOP SKIING: THE POOR MAN'S WIND TUNNEL

If riding your skis while they're in the rack on your car-top as it races down the highway seems like just one more dumb way to die, you're right. And you may be surprised to learn that it's an actual sport. Kind of.

It was initially first done to test a skier's tuck and other aerodynamics for downhill racing. Legendary Olympic bronze-medal-winning Canadian downhiller and wild-man Jungle Jim Hunter is credited with starting the trend in the early 1970s. He built a rack on the roof of his dad's old pickup, strapped his skis to it and climbed on board, riding on all kinds of roads and reaching a top speed of just under 200 kilometers per hour (62 mph).

Cartop world-record holder Sean Cridland says, "What Jim was doing was different from what we did later. He liked bouncy dirt roads for downhill training. We were going for speed records."

When Steve McKinney and Tom Simons went to their first Flying Kilometer speed skiing trials in Cervinia, Italy in 1974, they knew it could be useful to have some wind tunnel time under their belts. But wind tunnels were scarce and spendy. So they found a straight stretch of the Italian autostrada and, along with famous Finn Kalevi Hakkinen, took turns getting in their skis in the rack and taking a ride, "just to feel what it was like going 100 mph." It may have helped because McKinney set a new world record on snow that year.

Hakkinen, considered the father of speed skiing, continued to train on car tops for several years, and set a record for it in 1978 of 190 kilometers per hour (118 mph). He did it on top of a rally-equipped Saab as a promotion for the company which was one of his skiing sponsors. Swedish downhiller Benny Lindberg also did an ad on top of a Saab 900 Turbo driven by his teammate Ingemar Stenmark. A few years later Lasse Nyhlen officially upped Hakkinen's mark to 196.34 (122 mph) on top of an Alfa Romeo sedan.

In 1985, British speed skiing brothers Graham and Stuart Wilkie convinced an English car racing team to take them on top of a Jaguar to do some gear testing, and they reached 201.168 kilometers per hour (125 mph). Two years later Graham set the world speed skiing record on snow at 209.858 (130.4 mph).

But it was when they established the car-top record that American speed skier Sean Cridland, who was competing against them on snow, decided it was time to try the dry-land version. And to take it up a notch. The fastest people were doing it on production cars at racetracks and airports, all of which limited their top ends. So Cridland went to the Bonneville Salt Flats in Utah, where all the motorcycle, car and truck speed records were being set.

Legendary veteran Bonneville racer Rick Vesco agreed to work with him and developed a special chassis for his famous 300+mph "444" car in order to carry Cridland. Kirsten Culver, who held the women's speed skiing record in 1983 through '84 and had been training on an airport runway near Reno, joined him.

"We really don't get to train between races because there aren't any real speed training facilities," she explained to me at the time. "You end up just sort of training during the race."

Sean Cridland setting cartop skiing world record of 162 mph on Utah's Bonneville Salt Flats, 1985. Photo by Wade McKoy, courtesy of McKoy and Sean Cridland.

Their first day on the salt flats in the fall of 1985 proved enlightening, "These cars are geared so high they have to get pushed for about half a mile before they're going fast enough to drop into gear," said Cridland. Then to make it official they have to be timed for a full mile and coast a long ways to a stop afterwards, with the skier still in a tuck for most of it.

Cridland torched his legs on a practice run, so for his official one, "My legs started cramping and I was screaming into my helmet." He clocked a 238.18 kilometers per hour (148 mph), and Culver went 244.62 (152). The next morning, September 29th, Cridland went back out and turned in a 260.714 (162 mph) run. The Wilkie brothers were some of the first people he told. Cridland's men's record, and Culver's for women (or any other man but Cridland), still stand.

Scotsman Norman Clark set the cartop record for Europe in 1987 on top of a BMW 745i driven by his brother Alan who was a director at Aitken Motorsport, one of Norman's speed skiing sponsors. While the 227.72 kilometers per hour (141.5 mph) wasn't fast enough to unseat Cridland's world record it opened a sizable gap on the former Euro-record. That had been established when the Wilkie brothers had gone on to better their own European mark by pushing it to 215.65 kilometers per hour (134 mph) in a Sierra Cosworth.

The Clark brothers took their efforts to the Royal Air Force's Machrihanish Base near Campbeltown where the main runway is 10,000 feet. Both the ski rack and the car were raked to improve airflow and make the car as nose-heavy as possible. And it was recorded with light beams in a speed trap accurate to within a thousandth of a second.

Clark donated money raised by the effort to the charity Back Up. And because he couldn't afford to train on snow for speed skiing and he could only reach 120 mph at his local training hill in Scotland, he used car-tops and airplanes to test his tuck position. When he was 26 he regularly donned his full speed-skiing regalia and fastened his skis to the top of a stunt bi-plane for a ride, looking like a Marvel movies version of a wing-walker.

"It's all about aerodynamics," he explained to a local newspaper. "It helps me learn to hold my position at high speed. And it's the only way I can compete with my rivals. I hit on the idea of using a plane because it allows me to practice at speeds in excess of [225 kilometers per hour] 140 mph."

The use of car-tops for speed skiing testing and training has continued sporadically. American speed skiers Greg Abramowitz and Jim Trino spent the first half of the 1990s getting deeper into the gig than anyone else so far. "What we did was different," says Abramowitz. "Everyone else did the cartopping as a stunt. We developed it as an off-mountain training and testing method."

To be fair, that's really how the whole thing started with Jim Hunter and Simons and McKinney. But after that it did become an object in itself, to set records and get attention. So in 1990 Abramowitz and Trino took it back to its original intent with Greg's 1986 Toyota Supra Turbo and Jim's close connections to the man who ran the Civilian Test Flight Center at the Mohave Airport.

They had the benefit of a two-mile-long airstrip and virtually unlimited free usage as long as they yielded to the occasional actual airplanes they were sharing it with. They used it long enough every day they were there that it was a serious workout as they refined their tuck shapes and stances at speeds around 120 mph. They also occasionally used and filmed at El Mirage Dry Lake up to 145 mph, but it was too dusty for prolonged testing.

From all of their efforts over 5 years, "We got real indisputable data," related Abramowitz. "We discovered that different body shapes were more aerodynamic in different positions. The racers with more muscular upper bodies were more aerodynamic when we had our hands jammed up against our chins and biceps directly in front of our shins. While the racers with less muscular upper bodies were faster when they kept their hands stretched out front."

Something else Abramowitz liked to do "was to close my eyes while cartopping and FEEL what was happening with the pressures on my body," he wrote to me. The Cartop testing also gave them the chance to experiment with equipment improvements including their much safer and faster, "Invader helmet design using oil drop testing."

In 2000, Brazilian Christian Blanco was photographed cartopping at Sao Paulo's Interlagos Race Track while training for the 24 Hours of Megeve race. And in 2018, speed skier Jan Farrell posted video with the caption, "I raced on top of a BMW M2 in the Jarama circuit in Madrid." He reached 111.85 mph (180 kph) while doing "aerodynamic training," that he also admitted, "was really fun!"

Kite skiing on the Col du Lauteret Pass, France. Photo © Jay Cowan.

CHAPTER 36
PARAGLIDING, KITE SKIING, SPEED RIDING

It's Not Just Red Bull That Gives You Wings

I became mesmerized by hang-gliding the first time I saw someone do it off of Aspen Mountain and land in Wagner Park in the middle of town in the early 1970s. Within a few years a couple of friends and I bought Chandel hang-gliders with three to one glide ratios and soon flew them off Aspen Mountain one summer. I eventually crashed my glider in Montana and decided not to replace it. When I went on a press trip to Austria with my wife and a small group twenty years later we were offered a chance to take tandem paraglider rides at a ski resort in Alpbach.

Our hotel had a good view of the church across the street and the ski slopes rising behind it. Way above them, three or four thousand vertical feet higher, we could see multiple paragliders floating peacefully around. The broader view revealed a cross on the church steeple, and below it the tidy little graveyard that accompanies most churches in the Alps. It was a disquieting juxtaposition.

I'd been non-committal up until that point about the paragliding, but this seemed like a clear and disturbing omen to me. However several of the group expressed an interest in doing it, including my wife. We were told that it would be weather dependent and the next morning, which was our only available chance, was looking sketchy.

I went to sleep thinking the matter would be taken out of our hands. I also figured that this was the way the Austrian tourist office guides probably handled these situations. Everyone might seem gung-ho until it came right down to it, then they looked for ways out. So the guides were offering us one the night before.

But the next morning everything was a go, and my wife was still up for it. Given that, two other members of the group said they were in, and I had no choice but to agree. Or duck out the back door, take a flight home and start a new life somewhere else under a different name.

Up on the mountain, after consulting with our pilots, they decided that since I'd flown before and Harriet was very enthused, we should fly off the morning side of the mountain, where the wind was coming upslope at that hour and we could get some legitimate altitude. Then if the other two still wanted to go they could do it off the other side where the wind came uphill in the afternoons. Those flights would be much lower and quicker, since both of them were novices and understandably nervous about the whole thing.

Harriet weighed 110 pounds soaking wet and her pilot wasn't a big guy either. They went first, took off and immediately started climbing in a series of slow spirals. I was still processing the fact that we wouldn't be taking off and flying with our skis on, but it isn't really feasible in a tandem situation.

I'd done all my flying solo and in the summer up until then, so always had to run to take off and run to land. I had looked forward to being able to easily reach take-off velocity by just pointing my skis downhill, and having a nice smooth ski landing at the end. Instead we were suddenly loping down a moguled ski run and failing to gain any real air, with my pilot shouting at me, "Run. Run!"

I *was* running, but he was a big guy and I'm 6'5" and around 200 pounds with my gear on. Furthermore, running through the bumps wasn't easy and since I was in front of him I was getting lifted before he was and almost immediately my feet weren't touching the ground any more. So running was useless. And I had enough experience at this to realize we might not actually take off.

Then we gained just enough air that my pilot was finally lifted too, so he couldn't run any more either, but we weren't high enough to clear the chairlift we were veering toward. At that stage, you go where the wind takes you. But there were skiers on the slope and the lift yelling at us and gesturing, as if maybe we didn't see the lift and cable. My pilot was silent and I pretended to trust him.

At the literal last second we caught a little pop of air and glided up nicely over the lift and headed out over the deep valley beyond. Harriet and her pilot had already climbed 500 feet above us. We couldn't make it that high due to our combined weight and the stall indicator started beeping after we climbed just a couple of hundred feet before we leveled off.

I adjusted myself to get my camera in position and started taking pictures with my pilot suggesting I get my feet in the shots to emphasize where I was and what was going on. I'd been thinking my big yellow Nordicas would look like a thumb in the photos and was trying to keep them out of the frame. But it was actually a great idea to have them there. Next he asked if I wanted to drive.

"Umm…" I hesitated. I'd only flown a regallo wing glider with a fixed nylon wing. This was a huge, rectangular parachute that I wasn't sure behaved the same way at all. "I've never flown one of these," I pointed out.

"No worries," he replied. "You just pull on the lines on the right to go that way and on the left to go that way."

Okay. Still… I had visions of me yanking too hard on the lines and having one break, or me inadvertently putting us in a death spiral. "You know, I think I'm good with you in charge. I'll just take pictures."

As the landscape below us dropped down toward the main valley floor we maintained our altitude and were soon 3,500 feet above the nearest terra firma. It was breathtaking in every sense of the word. And even though I incline toward being a control freak I was actually enjoying letting someone else drive, leaving me time to enjoy the view.

My prior experiences had been so largely untutored and crazed that I spent most of my flights completely absorbed with trying to find a place to land and to breath normally to slow down my raging heartbeat. I'd discovered that all my best-laid plans immediately went out the window as soon as I got in the air. I went where the wind took me and just tried not to fuck it up. But I never spent enough time just enjoying the ride the way I was able to this time.

We followed the side valley we were over to the main valley it intersected and were eventually dangling ridiculously high over that same church and steeple that had freaked me out the day before. Then he asked if I'd like to try a spiral. "Well… sure," I replied, not that convincingly.

"Have you ever done one before?" he asked.

"No."

I couldn't see his face but I just knew he was grinning. "Okay. Well you should. Hang on, we get going pretty fast," he said and then tugged on the left lines and we dove that direction. It was a nice tight spiral that ate up about 2,000 vertical feet in half a dozen quick 360s and generated what felt like a couple of Gs of centrifugal force. I was about to say that I'd had enough when he turned out and took aim at a big grassy field with a slight skein of snow.

Later, after we'd all exchanged high fives and big smiles, my pilot asked me for their helmet back. It took awhile for me to convince him he'd never given me one. The other pilot agreed with me and they found the helmet in question in my pilot's pack.

This oversight, combined with our sketchy take off, left me wondering about the overall operation. Harriet's guy seemed fully pro, my guy not so much. It's the take offs and landings that are crucial in the sport, just as with flying a plane. Actually flying, while it definitely has its challenges, isn't usually the part that gets you hurt or killed. That happens when you botch the take offs and landings.

Andy Farrington kite skis off a cliff into a spiraling barrel roll during filming of The Unrideables. Photo: Scott Serfas / Red Bull Content Pool.

Three speed gliders – Jon Devore, Filippo Fabbi and Andy Farington – fly through a glacial canyon. Photo: Scott Serfas / Red Bull Content Pool.

By and large, the commercial paragliding operations around the world have very good safety records. Like hot air balloons, however, they aren't entirely predictable and are very weather-affected.

Though I've still never done it with skis on, it's extremely common now as fliers swoop down mountainsides, taking off from the top, then coming down on slopes along the way to ski for a ways before taking to the air again. This practice, as also described in a Steep Skiing chapter, is one of the hairiest and most amazing things you can do on skis. Whether as part of an enchainment to link several ascents and descents, or as a way to access difficult to reach snowfields on the sides of mountains, or just to take a hairball ride down the mountain, I think it's brilliant. And so dangerous I've never even considered getting good enough to try it.

Kite skiing seemed like the love child of kite surfing and paragliding when I first saw it on Lac St. Moritz where a guy was stitching his way back and forth across the frozen water, tacking into the wind and hauling ass when he was running with it. The lake wasn't completely smooth so there was rippled ice and drifted snow that made it sporty, and the man looked like maybe he was just getting the hang of it. But it seemed to me, at first glance, to be something that was confined to a flat surface with the intent being to see how fast you could get the wind to propel you.

The next time I saw it a few years later was on the Col du Lauteret in France, and it looked a lot more interesting. Some of the kite skiers and boarders liked to pick a ridgeline or small bowl and work back and forth across them like they were windsurfing: arcing big turns, catching indefinite air, looping casually across a fall line, defying gravity and making it look normal.

Others had also started using them to ascend routes that took a couple of hours to climb or skin up, and they were sailing (literally) up them in 15 minutes. Then they'd either take a breather on top, or just turn right around and kite-ski all the way down, including some flights off cliffs and knolls on the way.

This was a major progression from the armpit batwings that skiers had been using for Willy Bogner and Warren Miller movies since the 1960s to bomb down a regular ski area and amplify whatever jumps and air they could find on the way. The batwings were pretty limited, whereas kite skiing provided multiple options for how to descend a mountain.

Combining and melding kite skiing, paragliding and BASE jumping was a natural evolution, and pioneers like Shane McConkey began using them to link up big descents. Sometimes it was done to set new, previously unskiable lines. And sometimes it was done just to reach what looked like good skiing or super steep pitches that couldn't be accessed any other way.

The degrees of risk on the incredible routes that pioneers of these sports around the globe were laying down were illustrated by the annual death tolls. There weren't really that many people with enough skills to even be attempting this kind of next-level madness and some of them were dying every year.

As with other aspects of skiing such as cliff drops, gelandes and super pipes, survivable limits for how far or high you can go seem to eventually establish themselves. Then the focus changes to some other new insanity for a while, or to variants on the existing disciplines with more emphasis on style than size.

The base-jumping/paragliding/kite skiing realm may have reached that point. Or not. McConkey's process was to break descents into sections using several methods – including rappelling and base-jumping – to get into and out of skiable terrain. This allowed for timeouts in between the skiing to regroup and repack gear and consider the next phase. In terms of safety, in a very unsafe endeavor, it was considered and thoughtful. And then he died doing a signature kind of line in Italy in 2009 as recounted in the Steep Skiing Section.

His success before he got killed caused others to consider doing the same thing, and then they upped the ante by doing it without taking the breaks. They devised lines where they could just ski the kite all the way, touching down here and there for some turns then taking off again until they'd completed whole routes non-stop. This was raising the bar enough to exponentially increase what was already a high degree of risk.

These new variants developed as mutations of kite skiing, falling somewhere between it and wingsuit flying on the spectrum. And wingsuits are really just an elaboration on the armpit batwings concept, with new designs, more advanced technology in the materials, and ice water in the veins of the flyers. The variants are known as speed flying and speed riding. Both employ speed wings that are smaller, more maneuverable (also more twitchy) sails that are less lofted and notably less safe than traditional kite skiing wings.

They're meant for more low-level flights than para-gliders, allowing for big pops off of peaks and cliffs, but also letting the pilot swoop really low over, around and between terrain features that would be much less doable in gliders or standard kite wings. Their responsiveness also enables aerobatics like barrel rolls, loops and speed dives. And it's absolutely riveting to watch.

It's also difficult to accurately assess death tolls and injury rates in sports that are largely unmonitored. This isn't to say there's no regulation of them, particularly in terms of where they're allowed to fly and land in busy recreation areas. Ski resorts generally have specified take off spots and landing zones as well as kite skiing zones, and require that flyers maintain certain heights above the lift cables and don't present a danger to regular skiers and boarders. In Chamonix for example, speed riders must fly 100 meters over cables and 50 meters away from groomed slopes.

The deaths that do occur fall into a couple of broad categories. One of the major causes of problems is, of course, the wind. Turbulence and gusts and unpredictable wind direction shifts can be especially dangerous on take offs and anywhere near cliffs or the ground. Equipment malfunctions, line tangling, and faulty preparations

Kite skier Jon Devore. Photo: Scott Serfas / Red Bull Content Pool.

also figure prominently in recorded fatalities. Impacting rocks, cliffs, trees and the ground is a leading cause of death due primarily to the fact that they fly and maneuver so close to the terrain.

Thirty-six-year-old speed rider Manuel Muerner may have suffered from two of these issues when he died at Les Diablerets ski resort in France in March of 2009. It happened when he was reportedly flying too close to rocks for the conditions on the Les Diablerets Glacier with gusting winds blowing around 30 kph. Based on video from his helmet camera it appeared he attempted a 90-degree hook turn, got dropped from the air, touched down on the snow too hard and his kite collapsed. Investigators think he then slid down a steep slope and over a cliff.

A popular speed-riding site from the ski resort of Murren into the Lauterbrunnen Valley in Switzerland was the scene of a fatal 2006 crash. The flyer, Patrick Notl, on his last flight of the day may have forgotten to close the 8-centimeter trimmers on the back risers of his speed wing. Because the trimmers on speed wings are smaller, they can require more space in which to take off. Patrick and his friends were launching from the Acro-Takeoff called "Tennisplatz," a steep but short field with trees that have to be flown over within two seconds. For paragliders it's not a problem, but for a speed wing everything needs to go just right. They did for 7 prior flights that day but not for the 8th. It was determined that he probably partially struck a tree then tumbled over a hundred-foot cliff below it.

In Montafon, Austria in 2012, a 25-year-old speed rider hit a massive avalanche control structure shortly after takeoff, sustaining bad neck and head injuries and dying at the scene. Florian Haller, a 33-year-old who was speed riding at Punta Cervinia, Italy in 2014 crashed down a steep couloir after takeoff when a line from the wing got stuck in one of his ski boot buckles. How unsettling is that? His friends probably started duct-taping over their buckles.

An accident near Breckenridge, Colorado in 2022 claimed the life of a 26-year-old military Special Forces veteran named Zacharia Bolster. He and a friend took off from Peak 6 intending to land on the Copper Mountain side of the Tenmile Range, in the vicinity of a popular backcountry skiing destination and speed riding venue called the Sky Chutes. Bolster was using a speed wing while his friend was flying a paraglider. When Bolster didn't show up at the scheduled landing point his friend tried to contact him then called for help. He was subsequently spotted on a flyover and found dead at the scene with a broken-off treetop tangled in his speed wing.

The point of this depressing roll call is that while kite skiing is dangerous enough, especially when it includes cliff-hucking and other significant terrain features, speed riding, wingsuits and BASE jumping are next level crazy. And it doesn't matter how good you are.

One of the best known figures in speed riding and BASE jumping, Antoine Montant, was a ski and paragliding instructor in the Portes du Soleil ski area, and widely known as a Red Bull sponsored pilot whose incredible feats in films earned him a big following and attracted many to the sports he was passionate about. Those movies included *Claim*, from Matchsticks Productions and the 2010 one I cited earlier, *Can't Stop*, that stunned me with some of the most incredible footage I've ever seen.

And the current crop of videos in 2023 are even more mind-boggling, regularly featuring fliers in narrow couloirs and slots at making loops at high speeds within the very narrow terrain confines, then touching down briefly on one side or another and repeating the process for thousands of vertical feet with frequent other flourishes and aerobatics. It's like a real life video game with the best CGI of all time.

Redbull.com has quoted Montant as saying, "I started out on skis but I made my name in acro paragliding, because there's more room in that than in skiing, and yet I spend 80 percent of my winter skiing. I'd like to do more to get the word out on this way of mixing freeriding, steep slope and speed riding."

Montant won three consecutive titles at the Speed Flying Pro, an invite-only event for the world's best speed fliers at Les Arcs resort in France. International free-flying magazine Cross Country wrote, "He was a key exponent of the sport of speed-riding, and regularly attracted huge attention and acclaim for his videos and films… [and] regularly pushed boundaries, including a spectacular cable-car slide in Chamonix."

The same year he did that, in 2011, he perished in a wing-suit BASE jump in the Collet d'Anterne area north of Chamonix. He was jumping alone at the time and some reports have indicated his parachute failed to open at the end of his flight. He was 30 years old.

SECTION VII
GOING WILD

Skiing couples near Golden Gate of Yellowstone Park, early 1900s. Courtesy National Park Service.

CHAPTER 37
SKIING YELLOWSTONE PARK

The Torrid and the Frigid

Geyser plumes and steam rise through the brittle air like smoke from hundreds of scattered campfires. Impossibly stoic ice-rimed bison browse while eagles and ravens glide just above rivers warmed by hoit springs and floated by trumpeter swans. Elk and moose plow through chest-high drifts, coyotes pattern the snow-covered fields with their wandering paw prints in search of voles and rabbits, and shaggy white mountain goats roost on sunburned cliffs. Waterfalls are frozen into stunning ice stalactites, domes and walls. And from the summits and passes the visibility stretches across half a dozen mountain ranges, three states and eons of geologic time.

In March of 1893, Army Scout Burgess was probably aware of all of these unique and amazing features of Yellowstone Park in winter. But it wasn't his focus as he skied across a reach of the northwestern corner of the snowbound wilderness. He was in search of the biggest single wildlife poacher still working in the park, ten years after hunting had finally been outlawed there.

Edgar Howell was notorious in the region and may have been responsible for the slaughter of more American bison than any other individual in the country. And now, as the fate of the times would have it, he was in the position of being on the verge of making them extinct by invading their last refuge: Yellowstone National Park.

In Paul Schullery's excellent book *Yellowstone's Ski Pioneers*, he writes that trappers and Native Americans were almost certainly skiing there before it became the world's first national park in March of 1872. The earliest written reference he found of skiing in the region is from a journal by A. Barr Henderson, a miner who started prospecting in the Yellowstone Valley in 1866.

Around Christmas of 1871 Henderson left his camp near present-day Emigrant, Montana, and "went to Bozeman on a pair of 15 foot snow shoes." At that time his route would likely have taken him very near or through the northern reaches of what would become the park a few months later.

As a method of winter transportation, skiing was growing in popularity in these mountains. Winter visitors to the Mammoth Hot Springs were also taking up the activity for sightseeing and fun. After the park opened, the first winter expeditions into it were conducted largely on skis. And so was the winter business of the army scouts stationed there to monitor and protect the park and its wildlife.

Unfortunately the other primary skiers of the time were the wildlife poachers, who were at their busiest in winter. The region was known for its deep snows and harsh conditions that forced bison, elk and deer into valleys where they could become trapped. Hunters on skis had been overwhelming them in large numbers for years.

"The 1870s was a time of incredible waste and destruction among western wildlife populations, and Yellowstone Park was no exception," writes Schullery.

General W.E. Strong, who explored Yellowstone on an expedition in 1872, wrote, "In 1870, when Lieutenant Doane first entered the Yellowstone Basin, it was without a doubt unsurpassed on this continent for big game… During the past five years the large game has been slaughtered here by professional hunters by the thousands, and for their hides alone." The meat was left to rot.

The army in Yellowstone had been trying to catch Edgar Howell in the act of poaching in the park for years when they got word of where he might be camped in 1893. In a daring and difficult maneuver, army scout Burgess managed to arrest the well-armed poacher on March 12th in the Pelican Valley with hides and other evidence all around him. Getting him back over the course of two days to Fort Yellowstone at Mammoth Hot Springs was like Jack London material that involved the mostly single-handed transportation of a dangerous criminal through harsh conditions, with one of Burgess's feet ending up so badly frozen that parts of it had to be amputated.

Burgess was unassuming and understated. About what he'd done. But the fact is the bison was making its last stand on the North American continent at that time. Their wholesale slaughter was running unchecked virtually everywhere else. Yellowstone was one of the last places where there was still enough room that a big, roaming species like it might survive if the ski patrol could put an end to its killing. It was years later before it was fully understood what accomplishing that meant on a broad historic scale for the survival of a species that was a national symbol as much as the bald eagle.

Between the poachers, ski patrols, expeditions, the mail delivery system, a growing string of small lodges and ranger stations that were inhabited year-round, and increasing numbers of skiing tourists at Mammoth Hot Springs, it wouldn't be a huge stretch to say that early Yellowstone was one of the most active ski sites in the country in the late 1800s.

As Schullery notes, it would be hard to say when skiing in Yellowstone became less about poaching and patrolling, and more of a recreation. "Indeed it probably always was," he writes. "Skiing was certainly a popular local activity by the time Fort Yellowstone was built in 1891." Accounts in 1894 mentioned children at the

Fort skiing regularly and told of skis of varying sizes outside the doors of many of the houses. "Just as in the park today," observes Schullery.

Henry Maguire, author of 1878's *The Coming Empire: A Complete and Reliable Treatise on the Black Hills, Yellowstone and Big Horn Regions*, wrote about an attempt to get to Yellowstone Falls and the geyser (most likely on skis) in December of 1873, when he was turned back by deep snows and avalanche conditions. Having returned to Mammoth Hot Springs, he wrote, "I felt amply repaid, however, for making the trip that far. It seemed as though the torrid and frigid zones had met at the spot, and flung together the phenomena peculiar to each. Bright-green ferns, and other water-plants, grew in rank profusion, along the rims of the myriads of perpetually boiling springs, in the hot breath of which descending snowflakes were converted into water before they reached the earth; while hard by were colossal icicles and trees thickly encased in frost, the surrounding landscape being deeply buried in snow."

When a much ballyhooed 1886/'87 winter expedition by explorers from outside the region was launched by Lieutenant Frederick Schwatka and soon-to-be-legendary photographer F. J. Haynes to catalog the 'mysteries' of that season, locals scoffed that it was no new thing to ski around the park in the winter.

"As well talk of 'exploring' Central Park, New York, as the National Park. The National Park is a well known country, everything worth seeing is mapped out," declared seasoned Yellowstone skier Thomas Elwood ("Uncle Billy") Hofer in a series of stories for *Forest and Stream* magazine titled, *Winter in Wonderland, through the*

Modern day cross-country skier stopped near bison in the road. Photo by Jacob W. Frank courtesy National Park Service.

Modern skiers at eruption of Old Faithful geyser. Photo by Neal Herbert courtesy National Park Service.

Yellowstone Park on snowshoes. Probably a little overstated, but a typical local's response even today to visitors making big claims.

In April of 1902 even President Theodore Roosevelt, who had been instrumental in the park's creation and was a skier, went skiing out of Mammoth with nature writer John Burroughs.

Certainly no one, including Uncle Billy, was minimizing the risks of a deep dive into winter in country where nighttime temperatures can plunge to 50 below zero and the days aren't always much warmer. Where blizzards can strike any time, it's easy to become disoriented and lost, and at that time you had to carry enough food and warm weather gear to survive if that happened. Breaking through the ice on any of the many stream and river crossings was potentially fatal. Some seriously hardcore *Revenant*-style hardships were regularly endured in a place where any untimely mishaps could quickly become life threatening. And still can today.

The normal Wyoming/Montana winter experience is rugged. Concealed but unfrozen thermals, mud pots and 200-degree-geysers in the park present a whole additional class of difficulties. As does the altitude that ranges from 6,000 to 11,000 feet, exaggerating the cold and exposing anyone outside to heavy winds and whiteouts. Natural phenomena like avalanches and ice dams on the rivers are ongoing hazards. And wildlife can also be an issue.

While bears are usually well hibernated until early March, elk and moose feeling hemmed in by deep snow and protective of their offspring can be complicating factors if you get too close to them. And even though wolves have never been conclusively proven to attack humans under any but extraordinary circumstances, it can still be disconcerting to be skiing back down a trail you've broken, come around a corner and confront a wolf using

US Army patrol with captured poacher Ed Howell, 1893. Photo by Frank Jay Haynes courtesy National Park Service.

it to move about. They're known to do the same thing with plowed roads and highways, which is smart and bold of them while also being potentially unnerving.

But the stark and surreal beauty, along with only a fraction of its summer visitors, makes it a one-of-a-kind ski adventure in a big slice of the classic Wild West that's literally frozen in time about six months out of every year.

By 1941, according to Stan Cohen's comprehensive book *Downhill in Montana*, a Yellowstone Winter Sports Association was founded "for the purpose of purchasing a ski lift for the use of Yellowstone Park residents and for the promotion of other winter sports activities." That winter a rope-tow was installed on the north side of Mount Washburn. The next season a thousand-foot-long tow with a 250 vertical-foot rise was operating east of Mammoth Hot Springs near Undine Falls.

For 50 years it was a regular recreation for park employees and Gardiner and Mammoth residents, with an emphasis on kids instruction that became part of the curriculum at local schools. Then in 1994 several public controversies over safety issues and possible ski area expansion resulted in the National Park Service pulling the plug on the area and restoring the area it once occupied. In the meantime lift-serviced skiing had sprung up all around the Park, in Cody, Jackson, Grand Targhee and Big Sky.

Today cross-country skiing within Yellowstone and Grand Teton is flourishing to the point where concerns have dramatically increased about the impact of all the skiers, snowmobilers, snowshoers and snow-coach riders on the delicate winter ecosystem.

Yellowstone under snow is a harsh enough challenge for the flora and fauna without adding increasingly high levels of human interaction to the mix. The average frost-free period is barely more than a month. Annuals, and even perennials, have a tough time some years, and that directly affects wildlife populations that are already stressed.

Winter can be deadly for many of the park's species, especially bison, which get scalded by geysers and hot springs, mired in thermal bogs, and fall through iced over rivers. One winter 39 broke through and drowned in one episode on the Yellowstone River.

Over-winter survival rates among the newborn of most large animals are often less than 50%. Moose calves spend their first two years with their mother, who is vital to their survival that first winter because she provides protection from predators and helps the calves reach foraging areas. Deer, elk, moose and bison sometimes team up to take turns breaking trail.

The frequent thermal areas are some of the few havens, offering oases of green and blooming plants in midwinter so temperate they're actually accompanied by insect populations. Mosquitoes in January may be annoying, but they're a small price to pay for making it through another bitter winter.

With all of its challenges, Yellowstone in winter remains a place of exceptional beauty and wonder that can verge on the spiritual. As all 139 square miles of Yellowstone Lake freezes over it produces "music," variously described as sounding like a great pipe organ, or the ringing of telegraph wires. "Sometimes the music plays throughout the night – melodious, vast and harmonious. It stops within a few days when snow begins to accumulate on the ice," writes Steve Fuller in *Snow Country: Autumn, Winter & Spring in Yellowstone.* Add to that a full-moon night with a chorus of wolves and coyotes joining in, and the experience can be nothing short of transcendent.

Australian polar explorer extraordinaire Jade Hameister's book.

CHAPTER 38
HISTORIC POLAR AND ICEFIELD TREKS

Monochrome Poetry and Harsh Art in the Lands of Endless Winters

Completing a 373-mile trek across Antarctica on skis while pulling a 220-pound sled is a remarkable feat. To do it as the last part of a polar-explorer's hat-trick that also includes traversing the North Pole and Greenland's largest icecap, is a much rarer accomplishment. When Jade Hameister from Australia did it in 2018, only a few women before her had ever skied in similar tracks. And there was one more distinguishing feature to Jade's achievement: she was only 16.

She became the youngest person to ski from the Amundsen Coast to the South Pole without support, and the first woman to set a new route from the Amundsen Coast to the South Pole through the unexplored Kansas Glacier. She was also a part of the first all-Australian team to set a new route through Antarctica. In the process she spent Christmas in a tent with a temperature of 58 below zero. "It was a really hard day with extreme weather conditions and I realized why only 20 women have made this journey before," she said later.

This is the same kind of trip that 106 years earlier had killed Robert F. Scott and a crew of four that became the second team to ever reach the South Pole then perished on the return. One of the many differences in the two expeditions was that Scott's group wasn't skiing.

Recorded polar explorations probably began in 1827 with British naval officer William Edward Parry's unsuccessful attempt at reaching the North Pole. It was Fridtjof Nansen's first successful traverse of Greenland [cited in the Skiing High section] in 1888 that really alerted the world's adventurers to the advantages of using skis as opposed to hiking.

Robert Scott's first expedition to Antarctica from 1901 to 1904 took skis with them, but because only one of the crew was an accomplished skier, the team as a whole found them very difficult to use. Scott brought skis again on his 1911 expedition, but again hardly used them.

Norwegian Roald Amundsen, on the other hand, was a disciple of Nansen's and both had benefitted from their ongoing contact with the Sami people of Scandinavia and other aboriginals of Siberia, who were experienced skiers and dog-sled handlers. Two Sami accompanied Nansen's Greenland expedition. And Amundsen's success at leading the first team to make it to the South Pole on a 1,600-mile-roundtrip, was widely attributed to their skill with skis.

They got there on December 14, 1911, over a month before Scott arrived on January 17, 1912. They were safely back in their camp on the coast when they heard that Scott and his crew had reached the pole but then died later in a blizzard just 11 miles from a fuel and food depot on the way back to the coast.

American Robert Peary was, along with Robert F. Scott, America's most famous early polar explorer. He made his first foray into the frozen netherworlds in 1886 in Greenland, intending to cross its icecap by dog sled. Alone. A young Danish official convinced him that was suicide and the two made it nearly 100 miles due east of Godhavn before turning back because they were running out of food. It was the second farthest anyone had gotten across the icecap.

Though Peary is widely credited with being the pioneer of using skis for polar exploration, there is little to demonstrate that he was particularly successful at it. Part of that may have been due to a significant difference between him and Nansen. The latter went light with small groups making sustained pushes. Peary established the so-called "Peary system" of using support teams to establish supply caches. It relied on a siege approach for establishing supply lines and moving forward in waves of men who would then retreat to base camp and let the next wave break trail and extend the supply line.

Peary was verifiably the first American to employ the clothing and camping style of the northern Inuit peoples, wearing furs and mukluks and building igloos for shelter rather than hauling heavy tents and sleeping bags with them. He also used Inuit as hunters and dog-drivers on his expeditions, much like Nansen.

However, both his and Nansen's seemingly shoddy treatment of their indispensible indigenous crews came under scrutiny from early on. During an expedition in Greenland in 1894 or thereabouts, Peary became the first westerner to reach the Cape York meteorite site. Its fragments were taken back to America despite the fact that Inuits had depended on it for tool-making. Peary lied to the Inuit on his expedition and convinced them to come to America with promises that they would return home within a year with gifts of tools and weapons. It never happened and four of the six men died within months.

It wasn't the first or last such misconduct by the man, who made a number of significant discoveries, including proving that Greenland was an island. But he also either exaggerated or completely fabricated a number of other important claims, likely including having been the first to reach the North Pole on April 6, 1909. Never mind that Frederick Cook declared that he'd done it in 1908, though with virtually no proof. Many knowledgeable polar explorers have cast serious doubts on both Peary's and Cook's claims.

Plumb-bobbing on Roald Amundsen's 1911 South Pole expedition. From The Photographic Archive of Roald Amundsen's Icy Expedition, Lomography.com.

There were numerous inconsistencies about Peary's trip and record keeping, including him expressly excluding from the final stage of the trip the only member of the expedition qualified to take the navigational readings that would have verified their real locations. Furthermore, according to Wikipedia, "Many modern explorers, including Olympic skiers using modern equipment, contend that Peary could not have reached the pole on foot in the time that he claimed."

The Wikipedia account also mentions that, "A reassessment of Peary's notebook in 1988 by polar explorer Walter Herbert found it 'lacking in essential data,' thus renewing doubts about Peary's discovery." And it goes on to note that later, "By his lobbying, Peary headed off a move among some U.S. Congressmen to have his claim to the pole evaluated by other explorers." This ensured that Congress wound up formally honoring him for the dubious achievement.

Importantly, Peary and Nansen did establish that skis were a vital part of any polar expedition, and that there was a lot to be learned from the indigenous peoples of the Arctic, though treating them properly apparently wasn't one of the lessons.

Jeff Blumenfeld wrote for Skiing History magazine in 2017 about the importance of skis to polar expeditions and gave an account of Will Steger's 1986 expedition to the North Pole. He noted it as being, "the first confirmed, non-mechanized and unsupported dogsled and ski journey" there. And he provided vivid descriptions of the conditions that Steger and other polar explorers faced, including, "temperatures as low as minus 68 degrees F, raging storms and surging 60 to 100-foot pressure ridges of ice."

Of Nansen's 78-day marathon across the Greenland icecap in 1888, Blumenfeld observed that it succeeded, "Despite challenges such as treacherous surfaces with many hidden crevasses, violent storms and rain, ascents up to 8,900 feet and temperatures dropping to minus 49 degrees."

The conditions of the Greenland trek were somewhat different from the Arctic and Antarctica in several respects, primarily that Greenland generally had more terrain to contend with. When a 27-year-old Norwegian named Bjorn Staib recreated Nansen's crossing in 1962, he wrote in a SKI magazine story that, "There were steep slopes in the west, but we never knew where the crevasses would be. So we zipped across as fast as possible… and hoped that we were safe and wouldn't break through."

When Staib tried, and failed, to reach the North Pole two years later he defined the difference between it and Greenland or Norway. "Skiing in the Arctic is not like skiing at home. There's no real variety, there isn't even any waxing. There is no wax for snow so cold and, anyway, there is no need for it. There are no hills to climb or descend."

The Arctic is largely a flat, featureless plain of ice and snow. Antarctica has some spectacular mountains, but the routes to the South Pole have usually been plotted through the flatter icefields and glacial valleys. Either

British naval officer Robert F. Scott and men at South Pole. Photo by Lawrence Oates.

arctic is bitterly, lung-freezingly cold, very exposed to the wind and barely frozen sections of sea, and the skiing is mostly drudgery that rarely even allows for some kicking and gliding.

Ben Saunders, a 27-year-old polar explorer, became the youngest to ski to the North Pole in 2004. In 2013 he was part of a two-person team that recreated the Robert F. Scott route by journeying 1,800 miles on foot to the South Pole and back. And surviving, unlike Scott's team.

On November 8, 2017 Saunders set out to attempt the first solo, unsupported, unassisted crossing of Antarctica. For 7 weeks he skied an average of 15.5 miles for 9 to 10 hours a day pulling a sledge with all of his supplies and gear. On December 29th he reached the pole after 660 miles, but decided not to continue on for an additional 30 miles that would have completed the crossing. His descriptions of the biggest challenges, particularly for a soloist, are a stark litany of what this kind of skiing in Antarctica is like.

"About 25 percent of the time on my trip, there was zero visibility, or close to it, because of snowfall, low clouds, fog or blowing snow. In a whiteout, all you can do is look down at your compass and try to keep travelling in vaguely the same direction… Sometimes I got this peculiar feeling almost like vertigo… At one point, it was like someone had spray-painted the inside of my goggles white…"

That last bit is the same thing people say about skiing the infamous Elk Mountain Traverse race from Crested Butte to Aspen through the middle of the night. When it's snowing and blowing and dark at 12,000 feet it's been described visually as like the interior of a ping-pong ball.

Saunders also talked about the monotony and boredom. "There were certain parts of the journey that were very memorable because there was lots going on – early on, I was travelling through mountains – but there were also days and days where nothing happened. I'd get up in the morning, go outside, take my tent down, travel for 10 hours south, and see nothing at all."

In terms of the skiing, it seemed he has, over the course of many polar expeditions, developed a fondness for the uniqueness of his circumstances in places where there are no hills, no jumps, no trees with powder shots or any of the other usual attractions of the sport. "I've no idea if there's an actual term for the phenomenon, but I had some of the best *whumphs* of my life on this trip," he said.

Anyone who's ever felt a substantial amount of snow settling under them knows what he's talking about. On a certain angle of slope it can be the paralyzing warning of an imminent slide. In the flat and featureless void of the Antarctic, there's none of that danger attached to it.

"I assume it's something to do with the weight of the snow settling," he explained. "But it's this sensation of the area of snow you're standing on suddenly dropping by an inch or two, accompanied by a sound like a muffled thunderclap. If you're lucky – as I have been – this sets of a chain reaction *whumph*, with a shockwave rolling out to the horizon in every direction. It's petrifying the first time you experience a *whumph* but once you realize they're harmless, it's extraordinarily satisfying – like being a snowfield chiropractor, clicking tons of snow back into the right place." It's an interesting example of the unusual pleasures polar skiing holds, in addition to all of the challenges.

Given how difficult it is to make it to either Pole today even with all the high tech gear, support, weather fore-casting and emergency rescue capabilities, it's hard to imagine what it was like when they first started making attempts. And in truth, the first completely verifiable successful trip to the North Pole on foot and by dog sled, didn't occur until 1969, on the 60th anniversary of Peary's disputed expedition, by one Wally Herbert. And it wasn't until 1995 that Richard Weber of Canada and Misha Malakhov of Russia became the first, and so far only, to reach the North Pole on foot (or skis) and return, with no outside help, no dogs, airplanes or resupplies. The fact that such a trip hasn't yet been repeated gives an indication of how truly extreme an endeavor it is.

Both the North and South Poles became such common goals for a variety of explorers that they've been reached by cars, planes, submarines, submersibles, snowmobiles and tractors, among other conveyances. In 2007 a 75-year-old black woman cancer survivor named Barbara Hillary inspirationally took a commercial trip to the North Pole, becoming the first black woman to have made the trip. Robert Peary's manservant Mathew Henson was the first black person, though it's by no means certain any of the crew actually made it to the Pole. If they did, then Henson was the first, arriving before Peary.

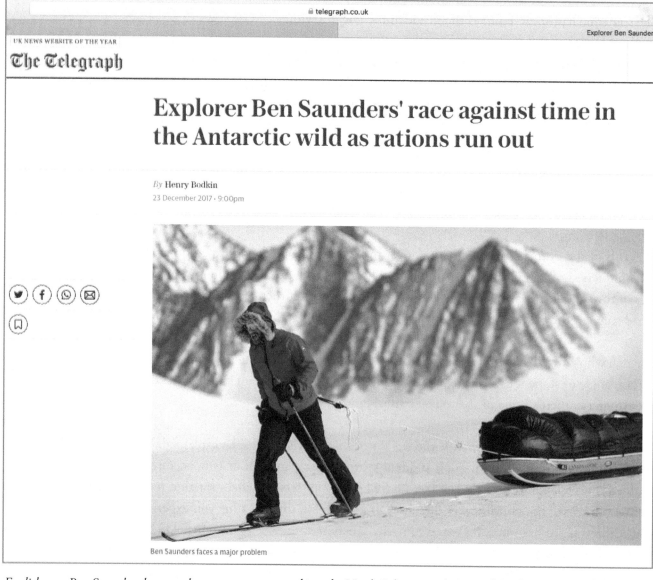

Explorer Ben Saunders

UK NEWS WEBSITE OF THE YEAR

The Telegraph

Explorer Ben Saunders' race against time in the Antarctic wild as rations run out

By Henry Bodkin
23 December 2017 · 9:00pm

Ben Saunders faces a major problem

Englishman Ben Saunders became the youngest person to ski to the North Pole in 2004. Screenshot of a story in telegraph.co.uk.

CHAPTER 39
MAJOR TRAVERSES

Following the Paths Taken by the Wild Animals

"The worst day ever was on Saint Gothard [Pass]: the weather was bad, but up to then I had never stopped so I set off nevertheless. I was hit full on by the storm… The wind blew me over twice and I simply couldn't see anything. I dived into a tunnel and since the weather wasn't getting any better I decided to turn back, but my tracks had already disappeared. I never thought about giving up, but had something irrepairable happened then I wouldn't have been too amazed. I always thought that I probably wouldn't finish the traverse, right up to the very end it was only a matter of luck."

In 2009, Italian Paolo Rabbia told this story to PanetMountain.com after attempting the first solo, full winter ski traverse of the Alps. Rabbia began in Forcella della Lavina at Mangart in the Julian Alps on December 29, 2008, headed to France, on skis as much as humanly possible and in the calendar months of winter. "I wanted to carry it out all on my own," he stated emphatically. He crossed ski slopes but didn't ride lifts, he walked along valley floors rather than ride buses, and he followed a route pioneered by Walter Bonatti and Lorenzo Longo in 1956 as closely as he could.

The winter of 2008 was one of heavy snowfall with high avalanche danger in much of the Alps. Due to conditions and other factors, such as large-scale development since Bonatti's trip, Rabbia wasn't always able to adhere to the route that had included multiple peaks. Rabbia's skis were a bit more modern, but as he pointed out, "not the lightest on the market" because, "when you descend on ice or crust with a 16kg pack, it's important that they don't play nasty tricks on you."

His pack only held the basics: clothes, thermal blanket, sleeping and bivvy bags, headlamp, satellite phone, a shovel, medicine, gas stove, food. "Thankfully I bivvied only three times. The Alps aren't the Himalayas," noted the man who became the first Italian to ascend an 8,000- meter peak in 2006, doing it without supplemental

Pioneering North American traverse, 1958, by (l-r) Bill Briggs, Barry Corbet, Sterling Neale, Roberts French. Photo by French courtesy American Alpine Club.

oxygen. "And despite the migration away from the peaks there are still some courageous people who still run their parent's lodgings."

After the first few days his trip was filled with high avalanche danger and, "I avoided saying anything so as not to worry my relatives at home." Because of closed slopes and backcountry due to the hazards, he didn't see many others when he was deepest in the mountains. But he was hosted along with other Italian skiing celebrities for part of a day at the World Championship ski races in Val d'Isere, where he felt honored but also like, "I gave the impression of being a real vagabond, with a long beard and truly famished."

He also met several legendary ski mountaineers along the way, including Clemente Berardo, "a mountain guide from Monviso," who was then over 70 and with whom he had dinner in Valle Maria. "At a certain point he turned to me and said, 'tell me, have you noticed how after a while you always end up following the paths taken by the wild animals?' And he was right."

Rabbia confessed that he started out relying on his GPS system, but completely ditched it halfway through. "Both in the forest and on open slopes, I realized that the best and most prudent route was always the one taken by the legitimate owners of nature: the animals."

Though other aspects of Rabbia's trip were distinctly modern in his ability to take advantage of lodging, good meals and various perks of the modern Alps, using animal trails for route finding harkened back to the forerunners of the big traverses in the Alps and around the world. In the end it helped the 43-year-old cover 1,800 kilometers (1,118 feet) and 45,720 vertical meters (150,000 feet) gained and lost over a span of 62 days until he arrived on February 28 at Garessio 2000 in the Ligurian Alps of northwestern Italy.

[DROP CAP] Given the location of the Alps, square in the middle of Europe, people have been finding ways through and around them for eons. Oetzi the Iceman is one of the most famous examples, hailing from somewhere between 3400 and 3100 BC, and found melting out of a glacier at the head of the Oeztal Valley on the border between Italy and Austria in 1991. His footwear consisted of boots made from bearskin, deer hide and bark netting, but no skis were found.

They also weren't employed by Hannibal in 218 BC when he tried (unsuccessfully) to surprise the Roman army by sneaking his own soldiers and all those famous elephants over a pass in the Alps. Nor did Napoleon use skis when had more success with basically the same ploy as Hannibal's in 1800.

The famous Haute Route in the Alps from the Matterhorn to Mont Blanc was first pioneered on foot by an English hiking club in 1861. It wasn't until 1903 when Dr. Payot, Alfred Simond, Jospeh Ravanel and Joseph Coutted used modified skis from Norway on parts of the journey. The first full ski tour of it took place in 1911. Since then ski traverses in the continent's most storied mountains have become legion.

French ski mountaineering pioneer and under-the-radar legend Leon Zwingelstein (aka Zwing) departed from Nizza in the Piedmont of Italy on the 12th of February in 1933 and spent 90 days covering 2,000 kilometers (1,242 miles), climbing 58,000 total meters (190,288 feet) of elevation and crossing more than 50 glaciers and 45 passes above 2,000 meters (6,561 feet), before reaching the Tyrol on April 6. His explanation of why may be as plain yet eloquent as it can get. "To create an objective, the crazier the better and to head off in search of it with nothing else in mind… devoting both body and soul to it with a sort of solemn rage, how wonderful." The "solemn rage" thing would make a great book title or band name.

In 1956, the great Walter Bonatti, along with Lorenzo Longo and occasional others, set the template for one of the most often repeated ski-traverse routes of the Alps. The Bonatti tour departed from the Yugoslavian border on March 14, 1956, and arrived in Colle di Nava in the Maritime Alps of France on May 18, making what is widely considered the first full and continuous ski traverse of the Alps.

According to one PlanetMountain account, a similar expedition "was carried out at the same time, with a couple of variations and gaps, also by L Dematteis and A. Guy, as well as by the Detassis brothers and A. Righini." In another account PlanetMountain says the other two trips were undertaken "a short while later." Whatever the case, it seems that all of the parties climbed together for some of the trip, but that only Bonatti and Longo made it uninterrupted by May 18.

As Rabbia said 52 years later, "I had the report of the Bonatti expedition and I used this wherever possible." That included following Bonatti's tracks through the Julian Alps at the start and in the Carnia, and off and on from there.

Bonatti and Longo's first ascent was in the South Tyrol up Cima Grande di Lavaredo. They next ascended the Valle Aurino, then the Val Passina, and the summits of Similaun and Ortles. From there they journeyed to Alpe

Galen Rowell's High and Wild book, 1979. The celebrated photographer/ ski mountaineer's 1980 Karakoram traverse was the first ever.

Devero, then Saas Fee via the Zwischenberg Pass. Their last big ascent was of Mont Blanc before reaching Colle di Nava, capping a trip of some 66 days along 1,795 kilometers (1,112 miles), with a colossal 73,193 meters (240,134 feet) of ascent, including multiple major summits.

Rabbia later commented in the press, "Three years ago, while repeating the 1956 great traverse of the Alps on skis, I felt so ashamed by what I read in newspaper articles, by those who had taken the liberty of describing it as a challenge against Walter Bonatti and, in doing so, comparing a nobody like myself to a living legend of alpinism, one evening close to Livigno I wrote him a letter of apologies." Bonatti responded and Rabbia described it being, "as if Pele had put pen to paper and written to a footballer in the favelas in Rio. I take my hat off to you Mr. Bonatti!"

It retrospect it seems clear that Bonatti's exceptional accomplishment ushered in an era of big ski traverses in the mountains of the world that hasn't ended yet. American ski mountaineering pioneer Bill Briggs, who is discussed in the Skiing High chapters, was a New England ski instructor who began exploring the Bugaboo Mountains (aka Bugs) in the Canadian Rockies in the last half of the 1950s. About the same time that Bonatti was making history in the Alps, Briggs devised a plan to ski, explore and climb a hundred-mile long traverse from the Bugs to Glacier Station near Rogers Pass.

As Lou Dawson wrote in his book Wild Snow, "At the time, most of the area was not mapped, and only one hut provided shelter along the way. What is more, no expeditions of this sort (using skis in an aggressive style on technical glaciers and passes) had been attempted in North America… His plan took the concept of a ski traverse into steeper and more technical terrain – a modern application of an old concept. As a consummate skier and mountaineer, Briggs had found what a fine tool the ski was. He wanted to share his insight with his mountaineering community. 'There was something to be said,' he remembers."

In 1958, Briggs assembled a crew from his New England operation of "superb mountaineers, expert skiers, single and ready for adventure," as Dawson notes. They consisted of Barry Corbet, Bob French and Sterling Neale. They set off into the literal unknown with new skis provided by Howard Head and astringently light pack loads.

Dawson relates, "With all their skill and planning – and luck with weather – the men's visionary ski traverse went off mostly without a hitch. For 10 days they climbed and skied through some of Canada's most rugged, unexplored mountains. They descended couloirs, crossed glaciers, forded rivers, and even chased a cougar."

In 2017 Andrew Findlay wrote on WildSnow.com, "Bugs-to-Rogers is one of North America's grand traverses, a bucket list item for any ski mountaineer. [The pioneers] completed the route in a monumental nine-day effort, ascending more than 32,000 vertical feet across 80 miles of mountain wilderness. It was remote and committing, and it required a gamut of mountain skills, from glacier travel to route finding, not to mention the ability to drop steep lines with a heavy pack." It's still a daunting task today for experienced backcountry skiers, as Findlay found out personally in that year when he and some friends attempted it and were turned back.

Given the state of the gear in 1958: fallback/rescue options (huh?); a complete absence of GPS, prior trip reports, sat or cell phones; and limited to non-existent snow condition monitoring, what Briggs and his crew accomplished was remarkable and game-changing. And Briggs and Corbet would soon collaborate on Briggs' first ski descent of the Grand Teton, thus authoring two of North America's most formative ski mountaineering achievements.

Heli-skiing pioneer Hans Gmoser, inspired by the Briggs traverse, put together a team the next year to take on what he called The Great Divide Traverse. It followed the Continental Divide by taking in passes and 9 high icefields between Lake Louise and Jasper along a nearly 300-kilometer(185-mile) trek that Dawson describes as staying, "classically true to the heart of Canada's greatest skiable alpine wilderness."

Brutal conditions prevented Gmoser's group from succeeding but planted seeds for those to follow. And in 1967 Canadian Don Gardner teamed up with fellow university students Chic Scott, Leil Liske and Charlie Locke and following 7 months of exhaustive planning and preparations, using lightweight Nordic cross-country gear, they knocked the route off in three weeks.

"Over the next 21 days an incredible adventure unfolded as we wended our way up beautiful and almost unknown valleys, over many an unknown col revealing ever new panoramas… it had been the finest experience of my life," concluded Chic Scott. As of 2018, noted Dawson, "The whole Great Divide Traverse has only been repeated once."

That took place on May 2, 2017, when four skiers finished their 320-kilometer trek in 21 days as well, 50 years after Chic Scott's group did it. And Alex Heathcott, Darren Farley, Lynnea Baker and Eliot Brooks were greeted by Scott at the end. "The one thing you can say about this trip is that it hasn't become much easier over the years," he observed. "It's not like a polar trip where you're going across a flat expanse of snow and ice. This is mountain terrain so you're going up and down and around. It's very complex."

Lynnea Baker told CBC.ca, "It's fun to go hang around with your friends for three weeks in the backcountry and challenge yourself and ski around, see cool terrain in places you would never go otherwise."

Alex Heathcott pointed out that it wasn't all fun. "You suffer from avalanche conditions, whiteouts, wind, rain, snow, anything nature can throw at you along the way."

But would they do it all again? "Oh, yes, absolutely," said Eliot Brooks.

Back across the pond, the first complete solo traverse of the Alps was attributed to Jean-Marc Bois in 1970, who began on January 30 at St.-Etienne-de-Tinee in the Maritime Alps of France, and ended April 25 in Bad Gastein, East Tyrol, Austria.

The next year, Austrians Robert Kitti, Klaus Hoi, Hansjorg Fabmacher and Hans Mariacher completed the entire traverse of the Alps from east to west on skis, starting near Vienna at Reichenau an der Rax and finishing in Contes, close to Nice in France. And instead of taking the most direct route they chose "an extremely challenging line" that included some of the highest mountains in the Alps such as the Grossglockner at 3,798 meters (12,400 feet), Piz Palau at 3,900, Dufourspitze at 4,634 (15,203 feet), and Mont Blanc at 4,808.

Across the Frozen Himalaya by Harish Kohli, 2000, recounts "impossible" winter traverse.

No one attempted the grueling route again until 2018 when the Red Bull Der Lange Weg expedition set out on March 17. An international team of Tamara Lunger, Nuria Picas, David Wallmann, Philipp Reiter, Bernhard Hug and Janelle and Mark Smiley, wanted to complete the 1,710-kilometer (1,062-mile) route, with a cumulative total of more than 85,000 meters (278,871 feet) of elevation gain, in less than the 41 days posted by the Austrians 47 years earlier.

As Mark Smiley, an IFMGA certified guide for Exum Mountain Guides, summarized for blog.arcteryx.com, "Our teammates were highly accomplished strangers, the stakes were high, and the terrain was literally foreign to us! All the ingredients for a true adventure." In common with nearly every account ever written of big-time ski expeditions, Mark and his wife Janelle, also an Exum guide and super accomplished ski-mo racer, were most amazed by the fact that they actually did it, in spite of frequent desires to quit.

Janelle wrote that on day 21 from Zermatt to Bourg-Saint-Pierre was her worst. "My sickness was catching up to me and I could start to feel the weakness moving through my body. As we were approaching hour 15 of moving, my legs completely gone, we came upon a 'no fall' ski descent on frozen chunder, I had to pull it together just to survive. It's amazing how deep you can dig when you feel like you have nothing left."

Some personality differences were to be expected amongst 7 extremely competitive and skilled individuals from multiple different countries who had only met for one day prior to the start of the trip. Significant tactical issues also arose from having differing approaches to pacing, as well as little real intel on many parts of the journey.

"A low point was the amount of risk we had to accept to make this traverse possible," wrote Mark Smiley. "It is not good avalanche mitigation practice to have external pressures to justify an action like, 'If we don't ski over this pass, we will have to go much further around,' or 'Plan B is to turn around and that will not allow us to reach our goal in 40 days.' Another challenge was having to onsight this huge amount of terrain. Occasionally we had a local that helped lead the way, but most of the time we were making decisions as they presented themselves using the information at hand to pick the best route possible… When our fatigue level was high, we accepted risk more often. That was just the reality."

When they arrived in Nice after 1,720 kilometers (1,069 miles) in just 36 days, many of those concerns were forgotten, or at least muted. It was a record-setting accomplishment by a group that included the first woman to ever complete a full ski traverse of the Alps (the other two who began the journey with the team had to quit). "There was a combination of peace, satisfaction, joy and disbelief that all blurred together in me. I was truly happy. We did it!" wrote Janelle.

In between the 1971 and 2018 Grand Alps Traverses, the rest of the world was opening up to the concept as well. In a 1981 story for the American Alpine Journal the multi-talented photographer, climber, naturalist and mystic Galen Rowell described the downside he saw to traditional mountain climbing expeditions in the Himalayas. It was their size. Due to the scale of the mountains, their inaccessibility, and the punishing conditions at high altitude in extreme cold, large numbers of support troops were generally required to get it done.

"If the root of the problem is all that gear needed to climb a mountain, why climb a mountain at all? With this non-objective firmly in mind, I organized the 1980 American Karakoram Traverse Expedition. Our goal was to traverse the highest range on earth, the Karakoram Himalaya, across northern Pakistan from the Indian border three-fourths of the way to Afghanistan."

Rowell's books such as High & Wild centered on his relationship with the environment and the ethos of traveling light. He didn't have much trouble finding like-minded companions from amongst the leading figures in the sport. The four-man crew consisted of Rowell, Ned Gillette, Kim Schmitz and Dan Asay, all of whom had climbed together and shared many of the same concerns about big expeditions.

It was a veritable Wild Bunch of some of climbing's most accomplished, bold and controversial figures. And they were following in the tracks of Orland Bartholomew's 1928/'29 revolutionary, solo three-month Muir Trail traverse in the Sierras. That epic feat redefined what was possible in the American mountains in winter and inspired generations to come. Including "extreme Bohemians" Doug Robinson and Peanut McCoy in 1970 who made the first repeat of the Muir Trail traverse.

In 1972, Ned Gillette, along with Jed Williamson, Wayne Merry and Jack Miller, made a 32-day traverse of Alaska's vast and remote Brooks Range. Then from April 2 through 28 in 1978, Gillette, Galen Rowell, Alan Bard and Doug Weins made the first ski circumnavigation of Denali. They accomplished it by going via Kahiltna Pass, Peter's Glacier, Muldrow Glacier, Traleika Glacier and Ruth Glacier. Two weeks later Gillette and Rowell climbed Denali in an unheard of single-day dash, a feat described by Martin Walsh – speaking for many – as "outlandish, dangerous and quite brilliant." For Gillette, even through the rest of his career, it was "the craziest thing I have ever done."

By 1980 Gillette and Rowell and Rowell's frequent partner Kim Schmitz, along with Yosemite legend Asay, were ready for a new foray. As Rowell wrote later for the American Alpine Journal (AAJ), "We would follow the greatest of all the world's high routes, an esthetic line over four of the largest glaciers outside the subpolar latitudes." They would do the vast majority of it without porters and only one food cache, while travelling "entirely above human habitation."

Each man hauled 120 pounds, with 50 on their back, another 60 on a kid's roll-up plastic sled and 10 more in a reverse fanny pack. The loads included lots of fuel for melting ice to get water since where they went, ice was all there was.

They started the 458-kilometer (285-mile) trek on March 27th from the village of Khapalu on nordic touring skis with enough climbing gear to do things like protect against crevasse falls, and traverse the south face of Sia Kangri at 6,858 meters (22,500 feet).

Though no one had been on these glaciers in winter and bothered to record the experience, there were many calamitous predictions of what the team would encounter, including "unconsolidated powder several feet deep at high altitudes." Instead, wrote Rowell, "What we found was a steady firm surface. It was too cold to form a crust, yet windblown enough to allow the leader to break trail almost as fast as the others could follow."

Being that cold wasn't always so helpful. They had to endure minus 31 Celsius (-25 degree Fahrenheit) temps at 4,876 meters (16,000 feet) on the Siachen glacier. And their progress was slow going uphill as they worked

Walter Bonatti, post-WWII father of ski mountaineering, after winter solo ascent of Monte Cervino, Zermatt, 1965. Photo: Wikidata.

toward the Baltoro Glacier, "spending only about five hours out of twelve actually skiing. Four hours were consumed setting up and breaking down camp, rest stops ate up another three."

And though in common with all such missions, much of the day was dull routine, there were plenty of challenges. A three-day traverse of the Sia Kangri chasm was likely the first of its kind; several runaway packs nearly disappeared into oblivion on icy mountainsides; large swings in temperature were seriously debilitating; and a long swath of brutal moraine presented, "jagged rocks toward the sun and a marginal snow layer in the shade. It was a skier's Hell."

Rowell wrote that, "Day after day we got up at 3:30 a.m., thrashed partly on skis, partly on foot with giant loads, ate the last of our food, and slowed from a peak speed of four miles an hour on the upper Baltoro to an agonizing four miles a day."

As Rowell was about to despair, Schmitz, who was serving as the team doctor and pharmacist, produced some form of cocaine he'd bought on the Khyber Pass. Through a tortured piece of logic he and Rowell, in true dope fiend fashion, decided they would keep the stimulant to themselves so that Gillette and Asay could serves as a control group for the "experiment."

This info can't go unremarked. I did not know Rowell, but I know his reputation, and this could be entirely true. But it's offered up in his own words for the AAJ so coyly as to seem like it could also be a joke. "Kim and I were tent-mates and we decided that our medical experiment needed a valid control group. Ned and Dan, unlike us, were not verbal complainers… We had been moving at relatively equal rates and we thought it fitting that the non-complainers should continue unaware. At noon that day we waited an hour and a half for them. In the evening we waited yet another hour."

Whatever the case, the traverse succeeded, and they arrived in Hunza on May 8. On the way they got to see sights from angles and in a season that no other westerners, or indeed possibly anyone, ever had. A pure marble moraine; massive outcrops of granite spires like organ pipes in the snows of the upper Biafo; profuse numbers of large mammals at higher altitudes; and a day with 16 miles of downhill powder skiing.

"What we found at the end of six weeks of the most intense physical activity of our lives was sensory and social deprivation," wrote Rowell. "Never on a mere peak-climbing expedition had any of us undergone such a shift… I no longer dream of that ideal expedition, isolated from the rest of humanity and any need to depend on it. I know the reality, the-trade offs and the strange mental filtration that has turned it into the favorite mountain adventure of my life."

Following the Karakoram High Route, Gillette proceeded almost directly to Mount Everest where he and Jan Reynolds executed the first circumambulation of the highest mountain on earth and came out of it with a compelling book called, Everest Grand Circle: A climbing and skiing adventure through Nepal and Tibet. "In an increasingly shrinking and competitive world," Gillette wrote for the AAJ, "style is the essential ingredient of adventuring: taking new approaches to old subjects."

The Grand Circle Route was done in two parts because the Tibetan-Nepal border was still closed at that time. Sponsored as the Camel Expedition for 1981/'82, it drew ample criticism for promoting cigarettes. But it came off after 120 days of skiing with several summits along the way, and help from a cast that included Steve McKinney, James Bridwell, Craig Colonica and Richard Barker on various legs.

This two-to-three-year period was historic for big new Asian traverses. In 1981/'82 Indian climber, explorer and adventurer Harish Kohli initiated the first on-foot traverse of the Himalaya, a 475-day project that covered 8,000 kilometers (nearly 5,000 miles).

Thirteen years later in 1995 Kohli accomplished the first ski traverse from the Karakoram Pass to Lipu Lekh Pass on the border between India, Nepal and Tibet. It was a 2,000-kilometer (1,242-mile) ski by an 8-man team in one of the coldest winters in two decades, across 20 passes, including three that were hitherto unknown, on a journey that many had declared impossible.

Indeed, that was the main reason Kohli did it. "The decision to undertake a winter ski traverse of the Himalaya was purely spontaneous because it was considered 'impossible'. There was danger of death from avalanches and deep crevasses, hypothermia and frostbite, but no one had ever attempted to put this assertion to the test. We dared."

The Karakoram Pass, where their trip began, rears up to 5,540 meters (18,176 feet) between India and China and is the highest point on the historic Silk Road connecting China to central Asia. It was where the king of Kashgar met his fate in 1531. From there (where fierce weather cost one team member seven fingers to frostbite) to Lipu Lekh the expedition dealt with avalanches, high winds and more debilitating cold. In a subsequent book, Across the Frozen Himalaya, Kohli even chronicled an ambush by a family of wolves and a life-or-death battle with a snow leopard. It's one of those accounts where events are routinely wild enough to sometimes suggest fiction.

Back in North America, another one of the big traverses that had been discussed for years and also roundly considered not even remotely likely, was attempted in 2001. A complete ski traverse in a single season from Vancouver, British Columbia to Skagway, Alaska, covering 2,015 kilometers (over 1,250 miles), was dismissed as "too logistically complicated, too long, too hard, too risky," wrote Geoff Powter for mountainculturegroup.com.

Nevertheless, several young friends with enough credentials and deep connections to the region to ignore the received wisdom began putting together an expedition. It's ethos was simple: "Put a pack on your back in the city and start walking, put your skis on as soon as you could, and then just keep heading north," wrote Powter. Not only did they intend to do the undoable, but they meant to do it by fair means.

Guy Edwards, a rising skiing and climbing star and the de facto ringleader of the expedition, invited his friend Vance Culbert to join them. Culbert had grown up in the Coast Range with a father who was one of the pioneers of serious climbing there. Another friend of Edwards, Dan Clark, had done trips with him in the Rockies and signed on for this one. And so did John Millar, a low-key, high-level local climber described as the group's "warrior monk" by Culbert.

Two equally qualified female believers in the concept, Lena and Ruby Rowat, learned about it too late to be able to join the boys at the start, but organized their own team and headed out after them just a few weeks later.

For the next six months, "So much happened on the trip, and yet, most days, very little. Every morning the two teams would just get up, eat, ski, eat, ski, eat, sleep," wrote Powter. Most days were very routine. But at other times, it was terrifying. For instance, Dan Clark was skiing by himself and trying to make up time when he took a bad fall, severely broke two vertebrae and had to be flown out. Doctors said later it was miraculous he hadn't been paralyzed.

For the women one of the worst days was in a storm and a days-long whiteout. With avalanches all around them and food running low, Lena became violently gut-sick and they nearly bailed. When the women contacted their father by SAT phone to discuss their predicament, he told them Edwards was offering Dan Clark's place on their team to Lena. All she had to do was get to Bella Coola with Ruby, then get from there to Terrace to meet the men for the second half of the trip. The ladies got to Bella Coola 54 days after leaving Vancouver and Lena hitched onward to Terrace.

Her addition may have given the men's team some renewed spark and the rest of the trip went "exactly as we had hoped," according to Culbert. Deep snow actually made parts of it much easier, and friends and partners flew in to join them for various legs. Six and a half months after leaving Vancouver they rolled down 1,128 vertical meters (3,700 feet) to Chilkoot Inlet, "and stepped back into the world on the Skagway docks," as Powter described it.

That physical act was hard to follow up psychologically, and everyone had trouble reacclimatizing. Dan Clark eventually healed but didn't climb again for years. Lena Rowat and John Millar had fallen in love and like everyone had more trips lined up, facilitated by their monumental accomplishment. In 2003 Rowat and her father, along with Millar and Edwards, attempted the Devil's Thumb Peak in Alaska that had stymied them on multiple efforts during the traverse. This time Edwards and Millar died on the peak.

A devastated Rowat continued to press on with her life. Having already added another 675 kilometers (420 miles) to the traverse in Alaska in 2002 beginning in Haines, she went back again and again to complete sections she'd missed by hitchhiking to Terrace. And in 2009 she finished the last 200 kilometers (124 miles) of the trip she had always thought was possible, becoming, as Powter wrote, "the only person who's completed the entire 2,700 kilometers [1,678 miles] of the extraordinary traverse, an accomplishment that stands as one of the most legendary known examples of human-powered travel."

CHAPTER 40
CROSS-COUNTRY SKI RACING

The World's Most Brutal Courses

Norway's very famous Birkebeiner is one of cross-country skiing's most influential and popular events and has inspired a namesake race in America. The original is staged in Lillehammer, one of Norway's Olympic locales, and has important historic underpinnings.

Participants in a political uprising in the 1170s in Norway were said by their opponents, who were in power, to be so poor they made their boots and shoes from birch bark. Instead of being shamed the opposition adopted the Birkebeiners (birch-legs) name. Torstein Kelva and Skjervald Skrukka were two of their loyalists who fought for Sverre Sigurdsson in the Norwegian civil wars. And in 1206 they spirited away the illegitimate two-year-old son of the country's King Hakon Sverresson from Lillehammer to Osterdalen to Trondeim over mountain passes and deep forests on skis in order to protect him. That child became King Haakon Haakonsson IV and brought a ceasefire to the civil wars.

It's an heroic tale worthy of having cross-country ski races as well as running and cycling ones held in its honor. All of them require participants to carry backpacks with a minimum of 3.5 kilos to represent the weight of the child. They're also a good excuse to require racers to pack food as well as clothing changes in order to respond to sudden shifts in the weather.

As with other big-time cross-country events, this one has become a festival with multiple races. But the centerpiece is 54 kilometers from Rena to the Olympic ski stadium in Lillehammer, running in the opposite direction from the original rescue mission, covering over 3,300 feet of elevation gain across two mountains. In 2011 the number of rapidly increasing participants was capped at 16,000.

One of Norway's best-known paintings, by Knud Bergslien (1869) depicts legend behind Birkebeiner race. The Ski Museum in Oslo via Wikimedia.

The first winning time in 1932 was 4:51:04 by Trygve Belsvag. Owing to harsh weather and widely varying conditions, times occasionally ballooned to almost an hour more. They also dropped to under four hours by 1938, but it was another 45 years in 1983 before Per Knut Aaland took it below three hours to 2:31:25. The current record was set by Petter Eliassen at 2:19:28 in 2015.

The women's race times went from 3:54:44 in 1976, the first year they were held, to the current record also set in 2015 of 2:41:46. Excellent and very fast track conditions that year were reflected in the new records for both the men and women that year.

It's sister race, founded in Wisconsin in 1973, quickly became the largest cross-country race in North America. Held annually in February it features a 50k (31 miles) skating event and the headlining 55K (34 miles) event in the classic style, both of them run between the towns of Cable and Hayward. The American Birkie was created by Tony Wise, who started the Telemark ski area in Cable in 1947. He added cross-country trails in 1972, giving a boost to efforts at the time to promote cross-country skiing in the US, and used the Birkie to publicize both.

The American event has also been a part of Worldloppet from the first, and racers come from virtually every state in the US and countries around the world. Registration was capped at 10,000 in 2013 and at least double that many spectators line the course. The event also features multiple races including the very popular 29k Kortelopet with many junior elite racers, and the more recreational 15k Prince Haakon.

Skiers start in alternating waves of skating and classical styles every five minutes for the main event, and spread out over one of the hilliest and most demanding courses of its length in the world. Firetower Hill near the beginning is a famous early test of strength; several tricky downhill sections are highlighted by Sledder Hill that's near a snowmobile trail where riders gather to watch and 'score' the competitors frequent falls. The so-called Bitch Hill gets similar spectators cheering them on up the steepest climb on the course, and crowds also line three blocks of Hayward's main street to urge racers on for hours throughout the day as they near the finish.

The 1973 inaugural event was won by a Swede, Eric Ersson in 2:48:16 for what was a 48k race. There was no women's event that year so Jacque Linkskoog raced with the men and was awarded the fastest women's time at 4:33:35. Dave Quinn of the US won the '74 race which was run at 50k, and the next year the first full 55k was run which Chris Haines from Alaska won in 3:00:34.

Since then the race has been run at 55k whenever possible, though differing conditions have forced occasional shortenings and reconfiguring and two cancellations, in 2007 and 2000. Due to ongoing track changes and adaptations to annual circumstances, it's difficult to really define course records. As of 2017, American Juergen Uhl from Vermont had the fastest time for the 54k classic style in 2010 at 2:28:39.4. And multiple winner Jennie Bender from the US set it for women at 2:50:53 in 2011

[DROP CAP] Structured and formalized events in all kinds of ski races sprang up fairly quickly once skiing started to spread as more of a sport than a necessity. In it's earliest forms it was simple: get from A to B the fastest. That soon evolved into doing the job within certain parameters such as set tracks and courses. And its purest form for the last couple of hundred years has been cross-country ski racing.

In virtually every length cross-country race run anywhere, the finish area becomes a kind of temporary graveyard where athletes collapse in heaps. There are few other athletic competitions in the world – bicycle racing, marathon running, long distance speed skating come to mind – where the end result is such a display of fully exhausted and spent competitors. It is an endurance sport that pushes people to their absolute limits in front of large crowds, and nowhere is that more true than at the Olympics.

Every Winter Olympics since the first one in 1924 in Chamonix, France, has featured cross-country ski racing as one of its premier sports. It all started with the 50- kilometer (31 miles) event that is still the longest cross-country race run in the games and the World Championships, as well as generally on the World Cup tour, with occasional exceptions.

Winning times in the 50k men's races and women's 30k (18.64 miles) vary from Olympics to Olympics due to the different tracks at each event, the amount of elevation gain overall, the weather and snow conditions, equipment and waxes and a variety of other influences, including the occasional doping scandals.

Norwegian Thorleif Haug won the first Olympic 50k in Chamonix in a time of 3 hours, 44 minutes and 32 seconds, a little less than two minutes ahead of second place. In the intervening years many adjustments have been made in the event, including limiting the overall elevation gains, the style of skiing employed (classical vs freestyle), and the form of the start (mass or individually).

When Alexander Legkov of Russia won the 50k at the 2018 Olympics (in 2022 it was shortened to 30k due to weather), it was a freestyle race with a mass start and his time was 1:46:55.2. He finished 7 tenths of a second faster than the silver medalist. In the 2014 games, where the event was last run in classical style, Finland's Iivo Niskanen won in 2:08:22.1.

Over the last nearly 100 years, racers have taken roughly two hours off the time that it takes to win an Olympic 50k event, cutting the records in half. They are now covering 31 miles in about the same time it takes the best marathon runners in the world to cover 24. An average Olympic 50k event is the rough equivalent of skiing from Vail to the top of Vail Pass and back down twice, then more than half way back up again. In two hours.

Since the first Scandinavian and Olympic races, cross-country events have flourished around the world in forms and distances that can vary significantly from the more standardized World Cup templates.

The Worldloppet Ski Federation of long-distance cross-country races was created in 1978 in Uppsala, Sweden, to promote the sport. As of 2015 it included 20 events across Europe, America, Asia and Australia ranging from 21 to 90 kilometers long. Actual distances vary from year to year based on each venue's conditions. Categories include full distance of at least 42 km (the length of a runner's marathon), plus shorter ones for less experienced skiers. Some races are freestyle and classic, while others allow only classic style.

Like Norway's Birkebeiner, Sweden's Vasaloppet is one of cross-country ski racing's most heralded events and a charter member of the Worldloppet. Started in 1922, today 16,000 participate in a 90k (56-mile) suffer-fest from the village of Berga to the town of Mora in the central part of the Dalarna Province. As in Norway this race also memorializes a royal escape, this time of a prince named Gustav Ericsson Vasa. In 1520 he fled from the troops of the tyrannical and unpopular Danish King Christian II, who had massacred most of the Swedish nobility including Gustav's parents. Vasa later rallied a rebellion against the king and won, dissolving the Kalmar Union that basically enslaved Sweden, and becoming the newly and permanently independent nation's first king.

One hundred and nineteen skiers took part in that first race, with Ernst Alm the winner in 7 hours, 32 minutes and 49 seconds. He is still the youngest ever at 22. Women had a difficult time gaining representation at the event "because it was considered bad for women's health to participate in such a competition." It seems more likely that it could have been really bad for their health if they ever beat some of the men. Nevertheless women raced in it as early as 1923 when Margit Nordin was the first. Later several women, disguised as men, also competed before they became fully welcomed into the Vasaloppet in 1997. Seventy-four years later.

As of 2022, Nils 'Mora-Nisse' Karlsson had won 9 titles with Janne Stefanson taking 7 and Sofia Lind tops among the women with four. The average winning time over the years is 5:11:38, while the record is 3:28:18 (a sizzling 2:19 average per kilometer, or almost 16.5 miles an hour average) by Tord Asle Gjerdalen of Norway in 2021.

Only 11 racers total have broken the four-hour mark. Out of the 10 fastest times, one was in the 1980s when

Facts and Figures for 93rd Vasaloppet

Share · Cross Country World Cup · 02 Mar 2017 · By Vasaloppet

Screenshot from FIS-Ski.com of the sea of racers (nearly 16,000) competing at the Vasaloppet in 2017.

Bengt Hassis of Sweden became the first; two were in the '90s, two in the 2000s, four in the '10s, and the one in the '20s. Jorgen Brink appears on the list twice. The race in 2021 when Gjerdalen set the men's record also saw the women's record established. Swedes have dominated their country's most famous race, with a only a handful of Finns and Norwegians occasionally interfering.

In 2023, 15,800 people participated, which is like half the entire town of Poughkeepsie, New York showing up for it. While all of the major Worldloppet races famously attract huge numbers of entrants, it has become such a problem that most have capped their numbers.

The Engadin Marathon in Switzerland, for example, is arguably the most famous large-scale cross-country race in the world. It sends out between 11,000 and 14,000 participants every year on the second Sunday in March to make a marathon-length blitz from near St. Moritz to Maloja. Started in 1969 it's an incredible spectacle at the upper end of the Engadine Valley – one of the country's most beautiful – and is a major winter sports event in the Alps. Participants only have to be 16 and older with no other qualifications required, but the field is capped according to pre-set limitations.

Categorized as a freestyle race, it also has tracks for classic style in most sections of the course. With a mass start that rolls out in colorful, jostling waves, it's famous for crashes and wholesale pileups that rarely cause injuries but can create major problems and gear carnage.

The winning men's time the first year was Swiss Karl Wagenfuhr's 2:19:38. Albert Giger won 5 times and took that time down to 1:38:25 by 1978. Bill Koch of the US won in 1981 with a 2:00:18. By 1990 multiple winner Konrad Hallenbarter, another Swiss, had it down to 1:24:54, before Frenchman Herve Balland won three times and set the existing record at 1:16:10 in 1994.

The first women's winner was Rita Czech from Switzerland with a 2:54:26. Another Swiss, Sylvia Honegger, set the existing record of 1:22:08, the same year as Herve Balland's mark. Those records may stand for a while since the race was altered in 1998, adding two kilometers to give it a full marathon distance with more challenging terrain.

One of the great features of the big cross-country events is that they include many racers who aren't pros or even top amateurs, but skiers just out to see what they can do. So while you have some of the best in the world giving it everything they've got, you also have others who are there as much for the gathering and the fresh air, lending a party atmosphere to what is also a significant sporting event.

The oldest major cross-country race in the world on the Wordloppet tour is the Holmenkollen, first run in Oslo, Norway in 1888 as part of the Husebyrennet. Thirty kilometer races were held at the big annual Holmenkollenrenne in 1900 and 1901, and the first 50k was run there in 1902 in the form of two 25k loops. It has been held every year since except when circumstances have forced cancellations or shortening, and is often called the most difficult 50k on the World Cup tour.

The slowest winning time in was 5:33:37 in 1906, by four-time winner Elling Rones. 1924 Olympic champion Thorleif Haug won 6 times from 1918 through 1924. Lauritz Bergendahl, who won 5 times, used to beat his closest competitors by more than 20 minutes. In more recent mass start versions, where times are closely bunched, there was actually a photo finish in 2015, with the winner Sjur Rothes setting a new record of 1:54:44.9.

The current track actually measures a full 53 kilometers. Norwegian star Peter Northug Junior has been quoted as saying, "It's not at all surprising that this is more than 50 km. This is a course that really sets skiers apart; it is very hard."

Since 2004, the maximum vertical gain allowed for World Cup courses has been 1,200 meters (3,937 feet) for the 30k and 2,000 (6,561 feet) for the 50k. The Holmenkollen 30k has the most on the WC tour with 1,193 meters, and their 50k is the most with 1,998, both numbers flirting with the max. The steep hills that have always characterized the race are such severe tests that the annual winner is widely considered the "toughest skier of the season" according to former Oslo sports Director John Aalberg.

A 50k skate and classic style race in Bavaria, Germany goes past a Benedictine monastery and the beautiful Linderhof Castle of mad King Ludwig in the Ammergau Alps. Begun in 1968 , the Koenig Ludwig Lauf, or 'Luggi' as its known on the tour, was attracting nearly 5,000 racers by the 2020s to what is considered one of the most elegant and forested tracks on the Worldloppet circuit.

The country's most interesting and original cross-country ski race, called the Miriquidi, is a 24-hour ordeal on a 6-kilometer (3.7 mile) loop trail running around the Scharspitze near Altenberg and the Czech border. It

Ernst Alm, winner of first Vasaloppet race in Mora, Sweden, 1922, began tradition of racers fully spent at the finish.

started in 2007 and is done in the classic style by single starters as well as teams of two and four, all of whom are required to carry headlamps for the night laps.

It's possibly the only race in the world that makes the 24 Hours of Aspen seem reasonable, because at least there it was all downhill. Of course in the Miriquidi you don't risk falling at 100 miles an hour. The course record as of 2020 was set by Ralf Grosse in 2017 who covered 348 kilometers (216.2 miles) on 58 laps with a grand total of 5,800 meters (19,028 feet) – or almost the height of Mount Kilimanjaro – of altitude gain.

The Gatineau Loppet in Quebec, Canada, features numerous races on a weekend in February in a park about three hours east of Montreal. At distances ranging from two to 53 kilometers, there are comps for cross-country skiers, snowshoers, and fat-tire bicyclists at one of the country's coldest but most popular cross-country venues. Their premier races are the Worldloppet sanctioned 53 and 29k events.

In an Olympic venue at Hokkaido, Japan, they hold an annual 50k race with substantial elevation gains and the kind of fluctuating width track that can produce actual hand-to-hand clashes. The Sapporo International Ski Marathon has been hosted for over 40 years in early February on two 25k laps of the Shirahatayama Open Stadium course.

Modeled after Norway's Holmenkollen Games, the marathon race started with 114 racers in 1981. The whole multi-race event quickly grew to over 2,000 participants by 1987, becoming the most popular ski event in Japan. Now only 500 men 49 and under are allowed to race in the 'free technique' main event of the marathon which was expanded from its original 30k to 50k in 1985, the same year it became a member of the Worldloppet.

Worldloppet races are also held in Argentina, Australia, the Czech Republic, Italy, France, Estonia, Finland, Russia, Poland, Iceland, China and New Zealand. A number of them now run longer than 50k. Italy's Marcialonga hosts a 70k classic style in Moena-Cavalese, and the Tartu Maraton in Estonia (where Worldloppet is head-quartered) holds 63k events in both classic and freestyle. The Finlandia Hiihto presents a 62k classic race, and the Dolomitenlauf in Lienz, Austria, features a 60k freestyle race at the Obertilliach.

That still leaves two of the most torturous races on the planet that fall outside the World Cup and Worldloppet tours. The Arctic Circle Race in Greenland includes two overnight stays in unheated bivouac tents, temperatures routinely below zero Fahrenheit, and the kind of stinging winds that drive the cold straight into the racers bones.

Billed as a combination extreme skiing and cultural event, competitors spend enough time in the start/finish town of Sismuit with its 5,500 inhabitants to give them a chance to make good contact with locals and indulge in the cultural aspect. Big climbs, fast descents and 160 kilometers (nearly 100 miles) of mountain-to-fjord skiing earn it the extreme label.

The big daddy of all cross-country races is undoubtedly in Jokkmokk, Lapland, Sweden. In the 1870s and '80s when Scandinavian explorers and resource hunters were drooling over the northern arctic regions and Greenland in particular, geologist Baron Nils Adolf Erik Nordenskjold, a Swede born in Finland, got in the mix. It was his Vega Expedition that opened the Northwest Passage in Greenland. And in 1883 he tried to cross the world's largest island in order to discover what lay in its interior. He was convinced it would be like Siberia with green fields and forests, but the expedition bogged down on its seemingly endless and inhospitable ice cap sheet.

When he was forced to turn back he dispatched two of the experienced Sami skiers to see if they could find the green valleys. Anders Pavasson and Pavva Lars Nilsson Tuorda were gone for 57 hours before returning to say they had skied 230 kilometers (143 miles) to the east before turning back and weathered a four-hour snowstorm in the process.

Hakan Stenlund, writing for swedishlapland.com, notes that, "According to Tuorda, Greenland was nothing but a great white mass – but an amazing place for a skier. He had never experienced better surface conditions. When the expedition made it home to Sweden again, they were met by heavy criticism." No one was convinced that the two Sami had gone 460 kilometers roundtrip on skis in 57 hours and, as Stenlund put it, "Nordeskjold's academic dignity was at stake."

In order to restore it he staged a race the next year from Jokkmokk to Kvikkjokk and back. On April 3, 1884, 18 racers including Pavva Tuorda (the so-called 'liar from the Greenland ice cap') set out. Eleven finished and Tuorda won, though only by 5 seconds over Per-Olaf Lanta. Most importantly, it was in an astonishing time of 21 hours and 22 minutes for 220k (136.7 miles) across untracked terrain with bad weather, cumbersome skis and few water/liquid breaks on the way. It also included a one hour and 45 minute break in Kvikkjokk "where they had a bit to eat and coffee and cognac for extra energy." Nordeskjold's dignity was restored and presumably a new respect was found for the Sammi skiers.

An Austrian named Wolfgang Mehl moved to Jokkmokk in 2009 and heard about the historic race and thought about updating it. When he approached Red Bull they were interested and in early April of 2016, 132 years after the original race, the modern Nordenskjoldsloppet was launched, with 335 skiers from 16 countries. For logistical reasons the course that first year was 'only' 190 kilometers (118 miles).

Like the first event, it had a very tight finish. Four top endurance racers were all still in it within view of the finish. Jorgen Brink, the lone Swede, buckled first, finishing fourth. John Kristian Dahl, Oyvind Moen Fjeld and Anders Aukland (all Norwegians) sprinted for the line with Dahl winning by a second in 8:35.17. The women's winner was Lina Korsgren in 9:23.55, just 10 seconds ahead of Britta Johansson-Norgren.

By the next year the course was at its permanent 220-kilometer length and nearly 400 competitors from 18 countries were greeted by numbing cold. In a reflection of what are frequent bursts of anger from racers at the finish about how bruising the race is, winner Andreas Nygaard of Norway said, "Its absurd to ski for that long, the craziest race I've ever done." His time was 11:48.07, a scant two seconds in front of countryman Fjeld who had taken third in the inaugural event.

The previous year's third place women's finisher Nina Lintzen won in 2017 by two hours over second place Emma Bergstrom, and her 13:01.01 was still a women's record at that distance as of 2023.

In 2018, defending champ Nygaard was coming off recent wins at the Vasaloppet and Birkebeiner. In going one and two again in Jokkmokk, he and teammate Fjeld were more than an hour and a half slower than in 2017 owing to brutal winds and sticky snow. Once again, only a second separated them at the finish, and there were only 6 seconds more to the third place finisher, Stanislav Rezac of the Czech Republic. For 2019 conditions improved and times came down to 2017 levels at 11:49.08, with Nygaard and Fjeld doing a three-peat, right down to the time differential of a second again.

Emma Lindstedt of Sweden took the 2018 women's race at 14:01.13, only giving up an hour to the ugly conditions, compared to the men's racers who were over 90 minutes off of the previous year's pace. She was also a blistering three hours ahead of the second place finisher Olivia Hansson. For 2019 Nina Lintzen was back as winner with Olivia Hansson finishing third.

A year off for Covid only upset the order a little on the ladies side when Lintzen and Hansson finished second and third in 2021 behind Frida Hallquist at 13:32.20. Hallquist won again the next year in 11:42.37, on a weather-shortened 200k course.

The men came back from the pandemic with a completely different lineup. Klas Nilsson of Sweden set a new men's mark by 5 minutes at 11:44.43, sharing it with Czech Jiri Pliska, who technically finished second. Norwegian Daniel Strand was third, not quite three minutes behind. He finished that way in 2022's shortened race as well, behind Johan Lovgren of Sweden in first and Frenchman Antoine Auger second.

Run in the classic style across everything from farmer's fields to crackling iced-over lakes, through deep woods and village streets, the punishing route has 19 feeding stations serving 300 liters of coffee, 800 liters of Red Bull, 1200 liters of blueberry soup, 2800 cheese sandwiches, 3800 buns and 5000 bananas, among other energy-boosting consumables. The ravenous carbo-loading athletes will burn up to 20,000 calories during the event, and some of them may need up to 30 hours to complete it. The Nordenskjoldsloppet AB is hosted by Jokkmokk SK, Sweden's oldest ski club, with Red Bull as the main sponsor and partner along with several local nonprofit associations.

The event took a break in 2023, vowing to return bigger and better than before in 2024. Whether that happens it has still been the most badass cross-country ski race on the planet so far and served as an example of what truly dedicated and slightly deranged competitors in the long distance events can do.

First ever women's 50K race, Holmenkollen 2023. Ragnhild Haga, Norway, 1st, Astrid Oeyre Slind, Norway, 2nd, Jesse Diggins, USA, 3rd. Photo by Nordic Focus via usskiandsnowboard.org

SECTION VIII
GOING DOWNHILL FAST

Winner of more WC races than anyone ever, Mikaela Shiffrin in 2017 in Killington, VT. Photo: Erich Spiess / Red Bull Content Pool.

CHAPTER 41
SPEED

A Crazy Liberation

Skiing fast is among mankind's most subversive pastimes. A crazy liberation occurs when unaided humans can skim along the surface of the planet at laughably high speeds. Maybe, then, anything is possible. This intoxication works well with the psyches of people who are also notable for abhorring restrictions. Fast skiing is one way of demonstrating that. It's a freedom cocktail distilled from equal parts control and abandon. As usual, the trick is in the mix.

There are two kinds of fast skiing: racing and recreational. The first is how the best in the world do it so that when you see it you just go, "Damn." The second is something lots of us can enjoy on a lesser level, depending on where and when we do it and how skilled we are. But it's complicated.

For racers, on the other hand, it's fairly simple. Get through a course to the finish line faster than anyone else. And they've been refining the process for a few hundred years at least, on a variety of different courses. The literal fastest ski racers in the world, on courses with gates (i.e not counting speed skiers), are the downhillers of the World Cup tour and they're covered in the next chapter. But there are also the fastest skiers in all of the other alpine racing disciplines, where the speed can be equally intoxicating and impressive, and it isn't just from going straight down a mountain.

When I talked to Olympic silver medalist and longtime ski racing announcer Christin Cooper about it she said that for her, "The sense of exhilaration comes from making beautiful turns a little bit faster than what is completely controlled. Just barely pulling it off makes every muscle and tendon come alive, and that's where the tingle of 'Yeah! This is great!' comes from."

AJ Kitt agreed. He was America's best downhiller in the early 1990s and won the season-opening World Cup downhill in Val d'Isere, France in 1992. "The key is going right to the edge of control without slipping over it." A big source of the adrenalin in recreational skiing comes from that kind of brinksmanship, and it's a driving force in the best ski racers.

When Jean-Claude Killy began standing out on a French ski team already loaded with talent in the mid-1960s and became one of the great ski racers of all time, part of the formula for his success was being not just comfortable with speed but craving it at every level. He wasn't happy with just having a good smooth slalom run, he wanted to be right on the edge in every gate and pressing to be faster all the way. And when it came to the downhill events, he went after them with a passion that was visceral, the kind of full-scale, edge of doom attack that presaged Franz Klammer and Bode Miller.

When Killy went on an historic tear from 1966 through 1968 and again as a pro in 1972, he was the fastest and best ski racer in the world and dominated the sport. He set the standard for the World Cup by having a perfect season in its inaugural year, winning all 5 downhills and giant slaloms, and most of the slaloms, along with crystal globes for the overall and all three disciplines, with the highest scores possible. He also won three gold medals at the Grenoble Olympics in his home country in 1968, only the second man to ever do that after Toni Sailer of Austria.

Mikaela Shiffrin and Marcel Hirscher with crystal globes as Overall women's and men's winners for World Cup season 2018/19. Photo courtesy Red Bull Content Pool.

Killy achieved all of this by looking for speed where others didn't. That included in the turns, where a combination of the French *avalement* technique and aggressive de-cambering and loading of the ski produced rebound and acceleration out of the turns where historically racers had just been hanging on. The results often appeared reckless but they were consistently fast.

Not all fast racers have approached it the same way. Some have preferred a smoother more fluid style to the all-or-nothing method, and been very successful at it. Sweden's Ingemar Stenmark comes quickly to mind for winning the second most World Cup races of all time with 86, all of them slaloms (40) and giant slaloms (46). Quiet and never seeming out of control, his strength and precision, along with focusing on the technical gate races, allowed him to win three overall World Cup globes, 7 Olympic and World Championship gold medals, and to be one of the most consistent racers in history over 16 seasons, from 1974 to 1989.

He also inspired several Americans, including the Mahre twins, who's power, technique and restraint led them to win 36 World Cup races combined. Phil managed to take three overall World Cup titles from Stenmark from 1981 through '83, by competing in occasional speed events, while still focusing primarily on the gate races.

On the women's side, Austrian Annemarie Moser-Pröll was a commanding presence from the time she first appeared on the World Cup stage at 15 in 1969. She followed firmly in the all-around tradition of her predecessors but favored the speed event, winning 36 downhills in 11 seasons. (She missed one in mid-career to care for her ailing father.) Added to 16 giant slaloms, 3 slalom and 7 combineds, her total of 62 is still third amongst women behind Schiffrin and Vonn. So far her 6 overall titles (5 of them consecutively) still leads them all, and her winning percentage is second only to Schiffrin's.

Moser-Pröll remains unusual to this day among women in being a downhill specialist who still won across the board, in all of the disciplines of her time. Vonn is the only other. MP is still the only woman to ever win 11 World Cup races in the same discipline (downhill) in a row. Very few women in the years since her accomplishments have even tried to race all the disciplines. Among them, Schiffrin, Vonn, Anna Parson, Tina Maze, Janica Kostelic, Pernilla Wiberg, Petra Kronberger and Nancy Greene are the only ones to have won in all of them.

Marc Girardelli, an Austrian racing out of Luxembourg, followed the same Mahre brothers' template to rack up 46 World Cup wins in 16 seasons from 1980 to '96, that included three downhills and 11 super-Gs. The latter was an event added to the WC tour in 1983 to try to balance out the opportunities for the overall title, which were skewing heavily in favor of the technical skiers. Girardelli won 5 overall titles under the new system, where it has to be noted he was also the first male ski racer to win across all 5 modern disciplines on the WC tour. And he and Kjetil Aamodt were also the first to win in all of the major disciplines of their era since Killy.

Vreni Schneider of Switzerland moved women's racing back in the direction of specialization by winning 55 times in a career from 1984 to '95 with all of them coming in slalom and GS, except for one combined. It brought home three overall titles, three Olympic gold medals, and the fourth most World Cup wins of any woman in history.

She was almost matched by Italy's Alberto Tomba during the same time period, as he reverted to the classic Stenmark tradition of just competing in slalom and GS for 13 seasons, and taking 50 World Cup wins in the process. His style was more like Girardelli's go-for-broke efforts than the Stenmark/Mahre approach. Restricting himself to the gate races only netted him one overall WC victory (in 1995), but made up for it by earning him three gold medals in two Olympics.

As the pendulum swung yet again, a new crew of Norwegians appeared on the scene to once more represent the all around racer. Lasse Kjus started his World Cup career in 1990, winning 18 times, including 10 downhills and zero slaloms, with two overall titles. He was possibly the first real speed specialist on the WC tour to win overall titles. His teammate Kjetil Andre Aamodt started the tour the same year as Kjus and had 21 wins in 16 seasons, including a downhill, 5 super-gs, 8 combineds, plus one overall title.

American Bode Miller countered the solid technical power of the Norwegians with a hell-bent assault as a gates specialist when he started the WC tour in 1998, notching 9 GS wins and 5 Slaloms during his 16-year career. But he added 8 downhills, 5 super-gs and 8 combineds to perfectly balance out his resume of 33 total wins and two overall titles, becoming the best all-around male racer of the modern era.

Sweden's Anja Parson (1998-2012) represented the distaff side of Miller's achievements, also racing in all disciplines and ending with 42 wins, 28 in the technical events, but also 10 in the speed races, along with two overall titles. Her haul of 17 Olympic and World Championship medals is the most in history for a woman, and second only to Kjetil Andre Aamodt all time.

When Ted Ligety of the US entered the fray on the WC Tour 5 years after Miller he carried specialization to a new height during 16 seasons, taking 24 of his 25 wins in the giant slalom. He was only competitive in one speed event ever, the Super G in the World Championships at Schladming in 2013, which he won.

In 2022, Ligety gave an Instagram interview that included an analysis of his famous GS turn where his extreme angulation causes his inside hip to touch the snow. As quoted on FedeWenzelski.com, Ligety emphasized that, "You always start a turn in this order: ankles, knees, and hips. Everything starts from the ground. You build angles from the ground up. I'm not trying to drive my hip to the ground. The hip gets to the ground because of the outside leg extension/push at the top of the turn. For me to build a high edge angle I need to drag my hip to the ground. That's because of my anatomy. Other guys in the world cup don't need to have the hip that close to the ground because they can drive the inside knee further in and get that same edge angle."

The most significant disciple of the specialists school of ski racing after Stenmark was Austrian Marcel Hirscher, who ended Ligety's reign as the king of giant slalom and went on to establish himself as one of the best male ski racers of all time. He did it by capturing a record-shattering 8 season-long World Cup overall crystal globes, along with two Olympic and 7 World Championship golds, and 67 World Cup wins. His consistency and power coupled with exceptional agility made him a latter day Stenmark as his 67 victories came almost entirely in slalom and GS, with only one super-g and three parallel slalom wins in a 12-year career.

It's important to add that qualifier of "male" because in 2023 American Mikeala Schiffrin broke Stenmark's record of most World Cup wins in a career, taking it to 88 after first surpassing teammate Lyndsey Vonn's women's record of 82. There aren't enough superlatives to describe what Schiffrin has accomplished in a relatively short period of time, but many of history's great ski racers including Stenmark have called her the best ever.

Adding to her resume is a great love of speed that first came to the fore in how she overpowers slalom and GS courses with a combination of cat-like reflexes and genius to go with her mastery of technique. And she has already developed a talent for the speed events that not all good gate racers do. And if they do its usually not until they've lost the quick feet required for slalom and giant slalom, but hers is coming while she's still at the top of her game in everything else.

RECREATIONAL FAST SKIING

Speed on skis is always relative to the circumstances. The fastest racer through a slalom course with all of its turns and combination gates, will always be going slower than one in a giant slalom, super-g or downhill, where speeds spike upward steadily from 30 miles an hour to 100 through the events.

For recreational skiers and boarders, circumstances are always changing and there are no ropes protecting our line on the mountain from casual intruders, or them from us. But speed doesn't always have to happen in a tuck in a straight line to be powerful and thrilling, as Mikeala Schiffrin or Marcel Hirscher can readily attest.

Marcel Hirscher, 8-time overall World Cup men's champion, at 2017 FIS World Championships. Photo by Jonas Ericcsoon.

As my friend and former US Ski Team and pro racer Mark Tache told me, "Anyone can drop into a tuck and go straight, but to fly down the mountain in big GS or Super G turns, where you're not skidding at all, just leaving perfect trenches in the snow, that's the best experience."

He singled out the Ruthies and Aztec side of Aspen Mountain where the men's downhill was held as also being one of his favorite routes for free skiing. "You have hard snow, you have a lot of undulating terrain, and its challenging from the word go. You can't fake it there."

Former Canadian Ski Team World Cup downhiller Chris Kent, who went on to make a habit of winning the 24 Hours of Aspen, voiced the same thoughts, saying, "Actually I like Spar Gulch, where the 24 Hours is run, for just cruising, too. You can crank some beautiful turns in there. And at speed you know when a turn's being done right and when it's being done wrong."

As much as he liked America's Downhill, AJ Kitt told me the same thing, "The most fun we have in Aspen is when they open the gondola early for us and we get to ski the mountain really fast."

Christin Cooper added to the equation of what makes speed fun. "I really like, when I'm going fast, to get a little air here and there. I look for a mogul, utilize the terrain, do a big turn, break it up with three little turns, then some air, so it really becomes kind of like a dance on the way down." That also happens to be a spot-on description of a modern Super-G course. "There's no feeling like it."

Then she added what is the crux of recreational haul-ass skiing. "That's probably the biggest frustration I've had since I quit racing: knowing what it feels like to carve an incredibly perfect dynamic turn and generate speed at 40 or 50 miles per hour – and to not be able to do it anywhere."

[DROP CAP] I've been around fast skiers for much of my life and came to really appreciate it during my racing days. And even when I left running gates behind, the speed was a hard habit to kick, so I haven't bothered. Back in the day, a small pack of us tooled around our home Aspen areas on 220s as often as not, in a time when there was still the space to do it and no reason not to. You could always find a run somewhere that was mostly empty and prime for stomping.

Aspen's cult of velocity as I first really encountered it in the 1970s encompassed a wide range of world-class athletes, from ski racers to pro tennis players to Indy racecar drivers, legendary surfers and professional extreme skiers. On any given day, Austrian skiing greats Anderl Molterer and Hias Leitner might lead a small funny-talker posse straight-lining Spar Gulch to see if they could get to Howard Awry's Skier's Chalet before their burgers were ready. If so, they'd be free. They'd called in the order from the Sundeck Restaurant on top of the mountain and all they had to do was get to Howard's before they were done.

The truth was, they skied Spar that way whether there were free burgers waiting or not, because that's just the way they rolled. Longtime Aspenite and former U.S. downhill star Andy Mill probably summed it up best when he told me, "I think speed is the essence of skiing. There are no limits, nothing is choreographed, and you're just out there experiencing where your spirit takes you."

Jean-Claude Killy with one of three gold medals he won at the 1968 Olympics in Grenoble, France. Photo by Ron Kroon.

That was the way we treated it then, and still do on some level. Skiing fast is transcendent, apart from time, an experiment in gravity and terrain, reaction and instinct, when you get a few seconds or minutes to just let it go.

By the 1980s Aspen Mountain's reputation as the Temple of Speed was certified with a season bookended by the 24 Hours of Aspen event is early December and the World Cup America's Downhill in late March.

Scott Nichols, the Aspen Skiing Company's director of ski racing for years, was also a competitor in the 24 Hours of Aspen, and a hang-glider pilot. He told me for a story I wrote in 1993 that what he valued the most in all of those pursuits was that they were expressions of his freedom. "I love the floating feeling, the lightness time. Speed heightens my awareness and I feel like I'm really living." Many others echo those sentiments in the following chapters.

For years the Aspen Skiing Company hosted a Town Downhill series at Buttermilk on the Tiehack side, where local hot shoes could have a place to train and race and basically go fast without anyone getting in their way. It was a treat and says something about how widespread the need for speed was, and may still be.

I also talked to Indianapolis 500 winner Danny Sullivan for that 1993 story. He lived in Aspen then and said he thought there was something in some people's makeup that allowed them to go fast and feel in control. "I've always liked speed, whether it was on a dirt bike or in a car or wherever, as long as I was in charge."

As noted in the next chapter, Formula 1 race car driver Divina Galica said that she too always loved speed, and that nowhere did she feel like she was going faster than when she was on skis. That probably has to do with the close proximity to the surface whipping by under you, just a scant couple of inches under your feet.

Given the difficulty finding anywhere safe to do it, skiing fast recreationally is usually best early in the morning with no one around and the corduroy is crispy quick. You can be riveted on the immediate future, fully involved in the elemental beauty and soft geometry of long straight lines and big carved turns.

The key is the degree to which you are able to control that speed, bringing us back to where we started. The rush and liberation of going fast only works if you survive it. And as Danny Sullivan noted, a feeling of control may sometimes be illusory. He got used to skiing fast with his friend Andy Mill, and usually related it to race car driving.

"My first time at Indy I went into turn three at over 200 miles per hour, and the fiberglass body on my car just failed and came off, and I had a little accident," he said with a small laugh. "And while it was happening, I felt so exposed. And I thought, I can't believe I really feel secure out here. But rightly or wrongly, I did."

And that may be at the core, not just of why we ski fast but why we ski at all. Because lurking just outside our façade of being composed and in charge is some wild thing waiting to consume us. And we believe implicitly that it won't, while being dangerously curious about what will happen if we're wrong.

Skiing likely originated as a way of simply facilitating travel over snow, then quickly mutated in multiple ways. But going fast has always remained a part of the gig, both as a means of getting somewhere quicker, and for fun.

One of the conclusions researchers have reached is that in addition to being a valuable survival skill for mankind, going fast (running, driving, sky diving, etc.) is enjoyable. Probably because its closely associated with surviving, and therefore scary and stimulating. We have not only required a certain amount of speed over the eons to avoid predators, and to hunt our own prey, we've liked it for the rush. We enjoy the stimulation of putting ourselves in situations where our control over them is stretched so thin that it means trusting entirely on our skills, instincts and luck.

High speeds add spice to almost any situation and bring out something fundamental in our DNA: react now, think later. The consequences involved can often be significant, whether you're driving at Indy, riding a bicycle down the Col du Galibier in the Tour de France, or racing the Hahnenkamm Downhill in Austria.

Many of the things skiers and snowboarders do have immediate results, mostly physical. When a golfer shanks a shot, it may cost them money and strokes for the lost ball, but they don't get the physical shit kicked out of them by the course. The falls and miscues and failures that all boarders and skiers are subject to often involve sudden contact between the body and ski slope. It's as if every other time a bowler threw a gutter ball it dragged them with it headfirst. Or if every third time a tennis player missed a backhand, it hit them in the face.

The severity of skiing's consequences go up with speed. That much is unquestionable and a part of what makes it exciting. There's also the indescribable feeling of being able to lay a ski up on edge, stand against it and take it through a big accelerating carved turn. It has that pure, wind-in-your-hair sports car appeal that comes from the simple joy of stepping on the gas.

I've been writing about fast skiing for years, including in defense of it in a Powder magazine point-counterpoint column in the early 80s. It seems like about once every decade or so a big hue and cry goes up over the dangers to all life on earth posed by fast skiers. And the unhappy truth is that a high percentage of skiing collision accidents involve one or both parties skiing at what can be considered "excessive speeds" and "out of control." Those are fraught phrases that no one really wants to have to go to court over. But it happens.

Another major contributor to collisions is our increasingly crowded slopes, which are obviously also a major issue for fast skiing. It shouldn't have to be said that high speed skiing and boarding aren't appropriate, polite or safe for anyone when there are lots of people on any given run, mountain, hill or footpath. I throw that last one in not just to be a smartass, but because there are many walking and uphill-ski-climbing trails on the edges of ski slopes in the Alps, and more all the time in North America. It's up to skiers to be aware of this and behave responsibly, including not going mach down marked *wanderwegs* and pedestrian trails.

Busy slopes have made it increasingly difficult to ski fast, or ski at all, safely. There have been discussions about roping runs off just for fast riders. Some areas have even followed up on it and it has been well received. I think it has a lot of merit, especially on runs that don't get much traffic anyway. Legal issues involving appearing to encourage dangerous riding could be a problem, though resorts have gotten around that with their Terrain Parks, so it can't be an insoluble obstacle.

Phone apps that provide feedback on our skiing, including speed, have incited a new wave of reckless riding by poseurs and wannabes who want to post something impressive, and are often totally unconcerned with anyone else on the run. That's a problem in general at resorts, where too many people ride like they're the only people on the mountain, never looking around for other traffic or double-checking last second decisions. There is very little of what ski patrollers call "situational awareness," and its lack increasingly complicates the whole experience.

For fast skiers it basically means throttling back except when you've got lots of room. Big high-speed arcs in appropriate settings are still easy enough to control and modulate that they can be done around limited numbers of other skiers. But tucking something for an Alpine Trace reading – which I'm still not immune to doing – demands an empty line at the least, and spotters if there are blind areas.

Realistically, does that always happen? No. But we all need to be fully aware of the issues, which are substantial. They start with, you might injure or kill someone else, and that person could be a child. There are a lot of other lesser possibilities, but with that even on the menu it demands serious consideration.

We also need to understand that the person going the fastest in any collision will inevitably get the bulk of the blame. Witnesses and bystanders will finger you instantly, and stone you to death if given the option. I exaggerate, but only slightly.

Though most ski resort managers would prefer to have as few regulations as possible for a variety of procedural, legal and PR reasons, they're also obligated to provide some security for their most vulnerable customers who are the young and the old. It makes no sense to force their hands on the matter.

The vast majority of good, fast riders know and understand all of this. Those who don't usually don't last long and you just hope there's no collateral damage when they go. For the rest of us, we will bend our own rules because that's our nature and part of the thrill, and because we paid for our tickets just like everyone else.

But I also don't want to cripple/kill someone else or myself just because I need a primal adrenalin boost on a regular basis. I'd also rather not have to take up bungee jumping or alligator wrestling to get my thrills, but at least those would only endanger me. In the end, we can complain that we should be able to enjoy ourselves on the slopes as much as everyone else. But the "fire in a crowded theater" principal applies. Especially since skiing has become a very crowded theater. We aren't allowed, nor should we be, to get our jollies by putting other people's welfare and lives at risk.

Yes, it can be argued that we do that in uncounted ways every day through completely unanticipated causes and effects that can't be legislated for. But basically that's a sophomoric dodge. We have to be accountable at some level.

On the other hand, if other skiers aren't paying any attention to what they're doing or where they are because they expect everyone else to watch out for them – or because they're just completely oblivious to the rest of us in their world – well, then there's ample room to debate responsibility for unhappy interactions. All in all, it's best if the question of who was at fault doesn't arise.

I sometimes think about a story Christian Pravda told me when I first me him in Kitzbuhel. He was in his 60s and had been injured recently. He still rode a very flat ski and went out almost every day and cruised a couple of fast runs. He told me he was skiing down a catwalk near the bottom of the Hahnenkamm mountain and came around a corner with some momentum only to find a group of skiers from Japan blocking the way.

"I had to hit the trees or hit the Chopanese," he told me.

"What did you do?"

"I hit the Chopanese."

Pravda broke a couple of ribs, the Japanese gentleman he sideswiped was fine.

As in life, there are no immutable rules in fast skiing, only choices.

CHAPTER 42
DOWNHILL RACING

On The Edge

The 1976 Winter Olympics was a star-crossed affair originally scheduled to take place in Colorado. But when the voters in the state held a referendum and rejected the ill conceived and planned event, Innsbruck, Austria – site of the 1964 Games – was chosen as the last-minute substitute. If the games had taken place as initially planned the most famous single downhill ski racing run in history would never have happened.

On February 5, 1976 as Austrian farm boy Franz Klammer slid into the starting gate wearing bib number 15, you could have heard a pin drop in any home in the country. Literally hundreds of millions around the world were tuned in and I was one. But in Austria you might have had your citizenship revoked if you weren't watching and holding your breath.

The defending Olympic champion in the event, Bernhard Russi of Switzerland, had already run in the number three position and was leading. It was an optimal start number given the conditions and he held on to first through the next 11 racers. "There was only Klammer left," Russi recalled years later for the In Search of Speed video series by Jalbert Productions. "There were 60,000 people in the stadium and the whole mountain started to shake."

Klammer and his fans had hoped for a better start number, but in terms of spectator drama it couldn't have been better if they'd scripted it. In one of the most highly anticipated competitions of the entire Games, ABC announcer Frank Gifford – no stranger to big time sports – would later say that he had "never in my life seen one man under so much pressure."

The 22-year-old Klammer entered the race as the World Cup downhill champ from the previous season,

Sports Illustrated's cover of Franz Klammer's gold medal winning run at Innsbruck Olympics, 1976. Photo by Helmut Gritscher / Sports Illustrated.

during which he had won an unprecedented 8 of the 9 events, only losing in Megeve where he stepped out of a binding. That year he also prevailed in the Olympic warm-up race on this Patscherkofel course (where Egon Zimmerman had won gold in 1964), beating Russi by close to half a second. And he was coming off of three straight downhill wins for the '76 season, including his second of back-to-backs on Kitzbuhel's Hahnenkamm, the world's most demanding course.

"When I went out of the starting gate, I knew I was going to win that race. Whether I win it or crash, there was nothing in between," he later recalled. And it seemed like it might be the latter all the way down the mountain.

At about the 24 second mark, in a big right hand turn he leaned in a little and his downhill ski came off the snow and he went wide to recover, but was still carrying speed, then faltered slightly on the next left turn. Play by play announcer and former US Ski Team coach Bob Beattie said, "trouble already Frank, he's right on the edge."

Gifford breathlessly responded, "right on the edge of disaster." At the first intermediate time 30 seconds into the race Klammer was two one-hundredths behind Russi. A few seconds later he roared around a big right with a bump in it and got too much air and came out of his tuck with his skis splitting and Gifford issued the first of several shuddering "oohs."

"He almost went down Frank!" exclaimed Beattie, by which time Klammer was wide right, out into the pine boughs marking the course edges and nearly into the fence, but still hauling ass.

At the second midway time he was two tenths behind, losing time to Russi and still "all over this mountain," as Beattie described it. The rough course bucked him around as he fought to hold his tuck and strayed outside the normal race lines and "nearly into the hay bales!" Beattie narrated. In real time it looked pretty out of control but it wasn't costing him a disastrous amount of time.

As Klammer later recounted, "Then halfway down the run I was looking at the crowd and kind of thinking, now I better do something to win the race. So I changed the line completely, and I felt the crowd really pushing me."

Russi agreed. "Really, the whole mountain was shaking when Franz came down and I personally think," he said with a smile on the video interview for the In Search of Speed episode, "that its from there, that power from spectators that they can pull him down. I think that gave him that extra kick, there was something in the air, he couldn't lose that race, no way. Finally he also skied a line in the final pitch which I am not sure he was ever recognizing. Nobody went there ever to see if it was possible or not. He just went straight down a line that normally everyone said was impossible. And he did it."

As Klammer remembered it, "And when I heard the crowd at the finish I knew I had won the greatest race of my life. With all of my other wins, without the Olympic title it would have been a good career, but not a great career." One of the first to congratulate him was Russi, which Klammer said was one of the best things about the day, and they've remained friends ever since.

You would be hard pressed to this day to find a ski racer who has known Klammer, let alone a living soul in Austria, who doesn't regard him highly as both a competitor and human. And a story that sounds almost too

Super-fast bottom third of the Streif course, Hahnenkamm downhill, Kitzbuhel. Photo by Michael Fleischacker.

much like a Hollywood fable was finally made into a feature film called Chasing a Line and released in 2021, with Daron Rahlves performing the stunt-skiing.

In America on that Olympic day, while I think most of us also gasped and shouted and cheered for Klammer, we also had a strong rooting interest in our Aspen hometown star of Andy Mill. America's top downhill hope, he skied the race on a right ankle that he'd kept stuck in the snow and an ice bucket up until minutes before his start, in order to reduce the swelling of a recent injury. He later said that he had very little feeling in the leg for his run, which complicated the left turns and made him look almost as wild as The Kaiser. But also like Klammer, he was fast and ended up 6th, one of the best American men's Olympic downhill finishes ever to that point.

That it was live on TV on the biggest possible stage showcasing what makes downhill ski racing so exciting, had a profound effect on the sport. Klammer's wild ride, accomplished in a canary-yellow downhill suit with red helmet and boots, made him a global media poster boy. Sports Illustrated, one of America's most widely read magazines, put him on the cover of its next issue with the tag line, "Winter Olympics Franz Klammer's Sensational Downhill."

Eight years earlier, at the Grenoble Olympics in France, America had gotten some of its first television coverage of the alpine skiing events. With international star Jean-Claude Killy a favorite to win three gold medals in his home country, ski racing was front and center at the Games.

The downhill got a big spotlight as the first of the alpine events. And Killy had a comfortable lead as the race went deep into the second seed. Starting number 29, American downhiller Jim "Moose" Barrows from Steamboat Springs, Colorado, was prophetically introduced by ABC announcer Jim McKay this way: "Moose has been hurt two or three times in the past year, but gee he heals quickly, doesn't he?"

Barrows was pressing hard about two-thirds of the way down and getting bounced around on the deteriorating course when he came through a left turn and over a jump off balance. He landed wide of the line, skipped off another small bump, then got compressed into a dip before a big roller in the next gate. He crashed through the poles of the gate and got absolutely launched, 20 feet high in places, spinning backwards and finally upside down nearly 200 feet in the air before landing on his head and shoulder. He stuck hard, with very little sliding to scrub speed, taking all of the impact on his body, dislocating a hip and earning him an airlift off the course.

It resulted in a two-page foldout spread in Sports Illustrated and probably more television play than Killy's winning run. In the process it also helped establish downhill ski racing as one of the most dramatic and compelling winter sports in the world. And Franz Klammer's run in '76 seriously underscored the point.

Downhill racing, like skiing itself, was progressing by leaps and bounds. Klammer's time on the Patscherkofel course was 30 seconds faster than Egon Zimmermann's just 12 years earlier. Technique, equipment and waxing had all undergone the kind of major transformations that took place regularly from the time the sport was first introduced.

When exactly that was is open to debate, of course. Just as we do with when and where skiing really started, we can speculate endlessly about when people first began racing each other downhill at it. In terms of organized and recorded ski racing, Scandinavians and indigenous arctic people such as the Sammi were probably racing on cross-country-style gear for centuries. And Norway is also recognized for hosting some of the earliest "alpine" ski events in Western Europe.

Sondre Norheim, as discussed in a previous chapter, was instrumental in launching skiing in Norway, and is also credited with staging and winning its first race. A short, multi-gate event run alongside of, and in combination with, a ski jump, it was held in 1868 in Oslo.

Around that time straight speed events with minimal to no gates were being held, and made record of, in the mining camps of the Sierra Nevadas in California. As cited in the following chapter, those were the first recorded speed skiing events in America, and more closely resembled modern day downhill racing than Norheim's gate race. The latter came to be called 'slaloms' by the early 1900s.

Alpine-style ski racing, with locked down heels and gates, seems to have developed later in the Alps. As per John Fry in Skiing Heritage (now Skiing History) magazine, the Kitzbuhel Winter Sports Club held a "Ski Race for the Club Master" on the Hahnenkamm Mountain above town in 1906, and they have documents to support the claim. As of this writing that would appear to make it the first such race in recorded history in the Alps.

The timed course was 3 kilometers (1.86 miles) long, with a vertical drop of 624 meters (2,047 feet), and won by Sebastian Monitzer in 8 minutes and one second. The vertical drop and route of the course was said by the Winter Sports Club to be "almost identical to the Super G of today." Other 'pure downhill' races, including a team race in 1910, were held in subsequent years.

The first Roberts of Kandahar (named after a famous British colonial General) downhill was held in Crans Montana, Switzerland in 1911. When Englishman Arnold Lunn formed the Kandahar Ski Club in Murren, Switzerland in 1924, it was to introduce the Swiss and their British guests to alpine ski racing. He did that by hosting an annual event consisting of a slalom and downhill that eventually evolved into the Arlberg Kandahar race series staged annually on the World Cup tour today as it rotates between multiple resorts.

The downhill portion of the event in Murren, first held in 1928, became known as The Inferno. Supposedly the world's oldest amateur downhill, it is without a doubt the longest at nearly 15 kilometers (9.258 miles) down a 2,170-meter (7,119 feet) vertical drop. Anyone can enter – after some rudimentary screening – and 1,850 are accepted, which means that racers are started every 12 seconds, one after the other, all day long.

If that doesn't give you pause, you aren't paying attention. Helmeted, cat-suited, long-board-riding thrill-seekers pouring down the same mountainside in the Alps that James Bond did in On Her Majesty's Secret Service, one after the other all day long on the same race course, sounds like a bonkers stunt for that film, rather than a serious annual event that's nearly a century old.

In that 1928 debut, an Englishman named Harold Mitchell won in an hour and 12 minutes. The next year's victor took 27 minutes off that mark. The current record is held by Swiss racer Kuno Michel, set in 2013, at 13:20.53, translating to an average of roughly 42.5 miles per hour the whole way, including several long flats and an uphill portion. The women's record is held by Nicole Bartschi at 14:45. Those marks are for the full length of the course, which conditions don't always permit to be run. And the start was moved down about 75 meters from the Piz Gloria summit in 1988 for safety reasons.

The Roberts of Kandahar downhill held in Crans Montana in 1911, was moved to Wengen, Switzerland, in 1912, across the Lauterbrunnen Valley from Murren, and called the Roberts of Kandahar Ski Challenge. In 1927 it was changed to the Lauberhorn Ski Cup and today is one of the oldest continuously held ski races in the world.

The annual Lauberhorn Downhill in early January is one of the crown jewels of the World Cup season, with the longest course and the fastest average speed on the tour. At 4.27 kilometers (2.65 miles) it's a full kilometer longer than the average WC course and can typically take up to 30 seconds longer than most of them, making it a serious test of endurance.

It's so long, in fact, that it has a dozen named sections, several of them derived from famous racers who've competed there. The *Russisprung* (Russi jump) near the start was named after Swiss downhill great Bernhard

Russi, one of the top course designers in the world who designed the Lauberhorn feature for a television show, then event officials decided to keep it for the race.

About a third of the way down, the *Hundschopf* (dog's head) is the race's signature air over a rock nose. Following it comes the *Minsch-Kante* (Minsch Ledge) jump, named for Josef Minsch who fell there in 1965 and was in the hospital for weeks afterward.

Similarly, the long fall-away right hand turn of Canadian Corner honors "Crazy Canucks" Ken Read and Dave Irwin who really attacked this part of the course in 1976 and both crashed.

The *Kernen-S* of consecutive right then left 90-degree turns with a small bridge connecting them, was renamed from the *Bruggli-S* after 2003 winner Bruno Kernen burned-in spectacularly there in 2006.

One of the most famous sections is the *Wasserstation* where a short tunnel passes under the railroad line. It's the only such element on any World Cup course in the world. And it was featured in the *Downhill Racer* movie when Robert Redford and a fellow competitor took the course side-by-side in training and the other guy didn't make it through.

Map of downhill and slalom for the Lauberhorn event in Wengen, Switzerland. Photo by Reto Nyffenegger.

The *Silberhornsprung* (Silverhorn Jump) debuted in 2003 with the ultra-photogenic wedge of the Silberhorn Mountain looming in the immediate background for the TV cameras. And the infamous "Austrian Hole" (*Osterreicherloch*), a series of high-speed ripples that were removed years ago, got its moniker in 1954 after nearly the entire Austrian team fell there, including Toni Sailer.

The *Ziel-S* is an S-turn just before a big roll jump and the finish line. Coming at the end of a punishingly long race, it has spelled disaster for many over the years. American Andy Mill, in the last event of his career, fell hard there through the finish and broke his neck. Had he not ended up in just the right position, he might have been paralyzed.

In 1991 a young Austrian named Gernot Reinstadler was far less lucky on a training run when he got off line above the roll, smashed into the netting on the side of the course and sustained fatal internal injuries, dying where he fell. In recent years the profile of the jump in the *Ziel-S* has been modified.

Italian Kristian Ghedina's winning time in 1997 of 2:24.23, is still a course record as of this writing, reflecting a blistering average speed of 106.33 kph (66.1 mph). Johann Clarey of France posted the highest speed ever reached in a World Cup race in 2013 on the super-fast *Haneggschuss* section when he hit 161.9 kilometers per hour (100.6 mph).

Austrians have won the race 31 times versus 29 for the Swiss. That has to be galling to the host country, especially since they were the only nationality racing there during the WWII years, when Karl Molitor won it 6 times from 1939 to 1947. Since then, Austrians Toni Sailer and Karl Schranz each had four total, and Franz Klammer three. Swiss downhill ace Beat Feuz won it three times starting in 2012.

The first North American to win the Lauberhorn was Canadian Ken Read in 1980, the only win so far by that country. Billy Johnson became the first from the US in his golden winter of 1984, when he skied clear out of the course at one point but carried so much speed that he still won. One of the top Austrian racers that day, taken completely by surprise, characterized Johnson in a quote to the press as "some nose-picker from the back of the pack." Kyle Rasmussen of the US won in '95, Daron Rahlves in 2006, and Bode Miller back-to-back in '07 and '08 to finish an unusual three-years-in-a-row sweep by Americans.

Kitzbuhel, Austria's Hahnenkamm downhill is another beast entirely. That's what help makes it and the Lauberhorn such ideal counterparts as the two best downhill races in the world for the last 75+ years. Where Wengen's event tests the racer's endurance and gliding ability, the Hahnenkamm's focus is squarely on balls and the ability to make high-speed turns right out of the starting gate.

The mountain where the downhill and slalom and sometimes a Super G are run is the Hahnenkamm, or cock's comb, rising right up out of Kitzbuhel. The course for the downhill is known as the *Streif* (Streak). As with the Lauberhorn, there is also a very prestigious combined trophy at the Hahnenkamm event that includes the downhill and slalom. But when people talk about "the Hahnenkamm" they're usually talking about the downhill, not the overall event or the mountain.

Andy Mill, who raced it several times, described the *Streif* for me a few years before I got to see it strictly as a tourist. "You stand in the starting gate looking across the valley at these beautiful peaks, and then you start looking down and down between your tips and finally between your bindings before you see the first three gates. And when you reach the first one, in about 8 seconds, you're going 60 miles an hour."

That 160-meter-long (525 feet) tilt is called the *Startschuss* and drops racers into a hard left over the course's steepest pitch and biggest air at the *Mousefalle* where they sail up to 40 meters (130 feet). Toni Sailer's father named it "the mousetrap" in the mid-1950s because racers fly off it into an abyss.

In 1991 American Bill Hudson crashed here and broke a shoulder blade and a vertebrae and suffered lung damage. Austrian Hans Grugger incurred traumatic head and chest injuries in the same place in 2011, then underwent a 5½ hour emergency operation in Innsbruck and a medical coma before recovering and retiring.

After a successful landing on the *Mousefalle* the racers crank a 180-degree right turn with over 3g's of centrifugal force leading onto the *Steilhang*. Canadian Steve Podborski, who grew up skiing on the firm slopes of eastern Canada, told me, "I couldn't stand up on the *Steilhang* the first time I skied into it from the side for course inspection. Literally. They soak it with fire hoses and its solid ice and really steep."

Pod went on to become the first North American to win the overall World Cup for Downhill in 1982. He also took back-to-back firsts at the Hahnenkamm in '81 and '82, in the middle of a four-year Canadian sweep of the event led by Ken Read in '80 and bookended by Todd Brooker in '83.

The *Steilhang's* extended right turn is on a nearly 36-degree slope that drops the racers at mach speed onto a road with high plastic mesh fencing all along the downhill side, where many racers have ended up over the decades. Bode Miller literally bounced off of it, skiing briefly along part of it with his left ski on his way to placing second in 2008.

Canadian Brian Stemmle got out of shape there in 1989 and slammed into the fence and one ski ripped through it. The resulting torque ruptured his pelvis and he nearly bled to death lying alongside the course. After a medically induced coma for five days, 25 blood transfusions and weeks in intensive care he was well enough to leave and begin pursuing his career again. That included several more Olympics and another fall at the Hahnenkamm before retiring in 1999.

After the *Steilhang* the *Streif* turns into a glider's haven along a road and some lower-angle straights until a small jump is followed by the first crazy fast sidehill section, aka the *Alte Schneise* (Old Corridor). And that leads into the *Seidlalmsprung*, a big jump with a blind landing that was built in 1994 at the halfway point of the course. Racers have to know exactly where they are to position themselves for a sweeping right-hand turn following the air.

The nearby Seidlalm gasthaus is where Serge Lange, Bob Beattie and Honore Bonnet founded the World Cup tour in 1966. It's also where legendary gold-medal-winning racer Ernst Hinterseer lived and worked when he was ski racing. His son Hansi grew up there and skied to school every day on the bottom of the world's greatest downhill course.

From the *Seidlalmsprung* to the finish is a final terrifying 30 seconds. The brutal, icy, side-hill *Querfahrt* (Traverse) portion sends racers chattering at 80 miles an hour across an icy washboard that's produced spectacular falls over the years. One of the worst was in 1987 in a full-tilt training run on Friday when Todd Brooker's downhill ski peeled off in the roughest part. Brooker tried to lay it down coming into the *Hausbergkante* jump but was knocked out and catapulted off of it into a tumbling, rag-doll series of tomahawks that horrified spectators and left him unconscious against the snow fencing.

Brooker later described what happened. "I rammed into the gate at the end of the side hill right on the jump. My head connected with the very bottom of the gate right where it attaches to the snow and it didn't move. That's when I got knocked out. At the time the gates weren't made out of plastic… [they were] made out of saplings, where somebody has to peel the branches off. They would water them and they were iced into the hill so they wouldn't move… I was absolutely amazed that I wasn't paralyzed, that I didn't break my neck or back… I had a concussion, a broken nose and I wrecked three ligaments in my left knee… I'm really lucky. I should have broken my neck."

Brooker had to be helicopter evacuated and he ended his ski-racing career after that season. That notorious part of the course is also where Italian Pietro Vitalini skied away from a serious cartwheeling fall through a snow fence in 1995. Austrian downhill gold medalist Patrick Ortlieb, like Brooker, was a prior winner on the *Streif* when he got sideways on the *Hausbergkante* in 1999 and fell hard, injuring his hip and knee and prematurely ending his career.

The evacs from this section and several others are especially dramatic because the choppers don't have room to land so they dangle the patient and a medic from a long line as they lift them out.

If a racer survives the *Hausbergkante,* the fastest part of the course comes next as it straightens out toward the *Zielschuss* (Finish Schuss) and one last, huge roller. I watched Lasse Kjus, who had won the 'sprint' downhill the day before, come to the *Zielsprung* with the lead for the full course event going around 150 kilometers per hour (93 mph). He got forced down into the compression for it and then missed his pre-jump by a fraction, came off a little back and opened up slightly. It cost him the victory by a few hundredths.

Other have fared far worse there, only seconds from the finish. On his 30th birthday in 2008, American Scott McCartney got too much air, crashed badly, whiplashed his head into the snow, lost his helmet and slid unconscious across the finish line where he lay convulsing. The brain injury required inducing a medical coma. But very happily, three days later he walked out of the hospital and resumed racing at Lake Louise in November of that same year.

Swiss star Daniel Albrecht had a similar accident in 2009 that also left him unconscious and with crushed lungs. He didn't come out of the induced coma for three and a half weeks and he missed the rest of the 2009 and all of the 2010 season before he returned to the World Cup tour for another two years.

Following a rash of bad falls and serious injuries throughout the 2000s, several parts of the course including the *Zielsprung* were modified to try to make them slightly safer. The race has also been cancelled or shortened on a number of occasions due to weather and/or snow conditions. And it is sometimes run twice to make up for other race cancellations. Swiss star Beat Feuz won two times in three days in 2021 when they ran a make-up for the Covid-cancelled Lauberhorn.

The first time the downhill was held on the *Streif* course was in 1937, followed by an 8-year hiatus due to WWII. Thaddaus Schwabl won that '37 premier with a 3:53.1, and when he also won the 1946 race he took 49 seconds off his time.

Fritz Huber, part of the legendary "Kitzbuhel Wonder Team" that was better than any other entire country on earth at that time, won in 1950. His fellow team members Christian Pravda, Toni Sailer and Anderl Molterer each won twice over the next 7 years, with Pravda the first to break the three-minute mark in 1951 setting a course record again in '54. That was broken by Molterer in '56, who set another record in '58.

Then American great Buddy Werner shocked the European racing world by winning in 1959 and lowering the course record by 7 seconds in the process. According to no less an authority than Toni Sailer, it heralded the arrival of a competitive presence from across the pond, although it would be two more decades before another American won a downhill on the *Strief*.

More record times have since been established on the course by a who's who of downhillers including Adrien Duvillard, Egon Zimmermann, Karl Schranz, Jean-Claude Killy, Roland Collombin, Franz Klammer and Harti Weirather. The current mark of 1:51.58 for the full course was set by Fritz Strobl in 1997, at an overall speed of 106.9 kph (66.4 mph). That's an *average* on a course with a long road in the middle of it.

Swiss superman Didier Cuche won the race a record 5 times, with two of them on shortened tracks. Franz Klammer won four on the full course, including three in a row from '75 through '77. His fourth came 7 years later in 1984, in what he has called his proudest race ever, after having fallen so far in the world standings that he didn't even make the Austrian Olympic team one year. Karl Schranz also won four on the full course, including three in a row from '69 through '72.

The racer who has won the most major downhills on the men's side of the event is hard to determine for the years prior to the introduction of the World Cup tour, though Karl Schranz, Toni Sailer, Jean Claude Killy, Bernhard Russi and several others captured many. Since the start of the WC in 1967, Franz Klammer still holds the record for his 25 wins, which is 6 more than Peter Mueller of Switzerland, who also won two super-g speed events. The latter weren't introduced until 1982 when Mueller won the first one, and it was 1986 before they were awarded their own separate trophy.

The great Austerian Hermann Maier, who won 54 World Cup races total, took 15 in the downhill and 24 in the super-g (the record so far), making him arguably the best of all time in the speed events. Franz Heinzer of Austria also won 15 downhills, and Dominik Paris of Italy has taken 17 along with 4 super-g's so far in his career which is ongoing as of 2023. Aksel Lund Svindal of Norway took 14 downhills and 17 super-g's which is currently the second most in history for that event. Another Norwegian, Kjetil Jansrud won 8 downhills and the third highest number of super-g's at 13.

Some of the first recognized women's downhill events were held at Kitzbuhel's Hahnenkamm starting in 1932,

Winningest World Cup downhiller in history, Lindsey Vonn (US), in Austria, 2017. Photo: Erich Spiess / ASP / Red Bull Content Pool.

They weren't included in the Federation Internationale de Ski (FIS) events until 1950. The first year at the Hahnenkamm the winner of the downhill and slalom and combined was Austrian Rini Andretta. Baroness Grazia Schimmelpenninck from the Netherlands dominated the women's comp in 1935 and '36.

Following the hiatus during WWII the Hahnenkamm winners were limited to local women for a while because Germans weren't technically allowed to compete for the title. Andrea Mead Lawrence from the US ended that Austrian dominance with a combined win in 1951, to become the first American to win at the Hahnenkamm.

Two years later a couple of women were hurt in training and voices were raised about how the course was too dangerous for the ladies. In 1954 the American team withdrew from the downhill saying it was too difficult. That changed with the presence of teenagers Penny Pitou from the US and Austrian Traudl Hecher. Their determination and talent kept the women's side of the Hahnenkamm alive for a few more years. In 1959 Norwegian Astrid Sandvik won the first of her back-to-back combination titles, then Traudl Hecher won in 1960 and '61. But political scheduling requirements of the FIS soon combined with the alarms over the Hahnenkamm being too dangerous for women, and the last race for them was Hecher's second win in 1961. It was 30 years before consideration was given to having women race again at the Hahnenkamm, but weather conditions along with persistent safety concerns scotched efforts in 1990 and '98.

Ultimately, there wasn't overwhelming support for women's downhills to be held there again even amongst the racers. Popular German star Rosi Mittermaier won 10 World Cup races, including an overall World Championship in 1976, and two golds at the '76 Olympics. When asked by Die Welt magazine how she felt about the Hahnenkamm, she replied that she could "do without this hell ride. I was never jealous of the men and their Kitzbuhel race, not at all."

Lindsey Vonn of America, unquestionably the greatest female downhiller of all time, disagreed and finally got her chance to do a ceremonial night-run on it in 2023, four years after she had retired from regular competition. "Only when you ski the Streif are you a real downhiller," she commented. "The Streif is the pinnacle of all downhills, the most difficult course in the world."

Given a chance at 38, four years after she retired, to do a demonstration night-run sponsored by Red Bull, she grabbed it. In spite of her numerous injuries throughout her career and the added drama of skiing 100 kilometers per hour (60 mph +) at night, albeit on a well-lit track, she said, "I'm an adrenaline junkie… I live for a challenge like this." After the run was successfully completed she added, "I've always had respect for the men that raced down the Streif, but I have even more respect now."

Vonn won the most World Cup downhills of any woman ever, with 43, along with 28 super-g's. Austrian Annemarie Moser Proell captured a very strong 36 downhills in the era before super-g's. Another Austrian, Renate Goetschl, took 24 downhills and 17 super-g's making her one of history's greatest women's speed events skiers. German Katja Seizinger won 16 of each event, while Micheala Figinia of Switzerland took 17 downhills along with 3 super-g's. And current Italian sensation Sofia Goggia has won 17 downhills and 5 super-g's so far.

Any international level downhill or super-g is dangerous for men and women alike. There are features that make the Hahnenkamm and Lauberhorn especially so, but racers have been badly hurt and killed on other courses around the world.

Two-time World Cup Super-G champion Ulrike Maier from Austria was the only mother racing on the tour in 1994 when she hooked a tip going 60 miles an hour on the downhill in Garmisch, Germany, one of the fastest women's courses in the world. She spun off the track and hit a frozen pile of man-made snow headfirst, fatally breaking her neck. Her daughter was 5 at the time and it sent shock waves throughout the athletic world. Initial fears were that she had hit her head on a timing post, but that was established in court not to have been the case and no fault was found with the FIS or race organizers. It didn't lessen the dimensions of the tragedy, nor the concern that women were at special risk in the speed events.

Nevertheless they have continued to compete in them safely and successfully to this day as they have at Speed Skiing where they have been continually drawing closer to the men's velocities.

Everyone involved in the speed events of ski racing knows they are dangerous and can be deadly, and they just choose not to dwell on it. Bernhard Russi has said in interviews, "In skiing and downhill in particular, there is a permanent risk. We all put on a helmet when we go skiing. That means we take a risk… At the end of the day, it's a choice to take the risk or not. We'll never be in a position of 'there's no more danger'."

Norwegian downhiller Kjetil Jansrud has noted that, "You have to compartmentalize things, and its tough. We talk about it, we know the sport has a lot of risks. I've tried not to think too much about it because that brings fears, a lot of nerves, I'll try to keep that away so that I don't make any mistakes myself."

Since records of such things have been kept, there have been deaths in the downhill. One of the earliest that was noted was of successful Italian Olympic skier Giacinto Sertorelli. He was racing in Garmisch-Partenkirchen in January of 1938 when he fell on what was described as "a seriously deteriorating track" and hit a tree, dying two days later.

In 1959, John Simmelink of Canada crashed near the end of that same Arlberg-Kandahar downhill on a foggy race day where he apparently pre-released and careened into a rocky gully where his leather helmet did little to protect him from serious head injuries that proved lethal. According to Hank McKee in Ski Racing, "The next season helmets (not leather) were required for Olympic racing."

An Australian teenager named Ross Milne was training for the Innsbruck Olympic downhill at Patscherkofel in 1964 when he veered off course, possibly to avoid other racers congregated on the track, and struck a tree and died.

Rising French star Michel Bozon was only 20 in 1970 when he flew off the Emille Allais World Cup downhill course in Megeve, France, at the bottom of the very steep *Mur de Borne* section. He fractured a leg and his skull and died two hours later. Another accident on the course resulted in the race being discontinued in 1975.

Austrian Sepp Walcher retired from a good World Cup downhill career in 1982 that saw him win World Championship gold in 1978, to go with 5 World Cup victories. Then in 1984 he fell in a benefit race in his hometown of Schladming and died.

The 1991 death of Gernot Reinstadler in training at Wengen added to the body count and highlighted a problem with the safety fencing that was meant to keep racers from hitting trees and lift towers and other immovable objects, but was causing problems as well.

Ultimately of course there is no way to entirely accident-proof courses. Frenchwoman Regine Cavagnoud hit German coach Markus Anwander at full speed during World Cup training on the Pitztaler Glacier in 2001. Both suffered serious skull injuries and were rushed to hospital in nearby Innsbruck where she died two days later. And in 2004 promising 17-year-old US development team skier Shelly Glover died of head injuries three days after a bad training crash on Mount Bachelor.

Though casualties among male racers have historically far exceeded those amongst the women, it hasn't dissuaded some observers from continuing to claim that the women are at greater and unnecessary risk. Yet modern female competitors in the speed events have demonstrated an indomitable attitude and strength that's been personified by the likes of Vonn. She survived numerous bad falls and injuries in downhills and super g's only to get up and go win Olympic gold and three bronzes, and a staggering *82 World Cup races*, a massive all-time record only recently surpassed by Mikaela Schiffrin.

And Vonn's speed events successor Sofia Goggia from Italy is famous for her go-for-broke attitude that's resulted in multiple disabling accidents along with 19 World Cup wins-and- counting, including 14 in Downhill along with a gold medal for the event in Korea in 2018.

In 2017 the deaths of two male racers training and competing in Canada brought the discussion of safety in ski competitions back into sharp focus. On November 13, French downhiller David Poisson had an accident at Nakiska where he was training for the season-opening World Cup downhill. It was reported that he tumbled hard after catching an edge and losing a ski at high speed, then crashed through the safety netting and into a tree.

After investigations were completed by various officials including ones with the French National Team, the latter stated there was nothing wrong with safety measures at Nakiska Ski area. The general manager of the French Team, Fabien Saguez, said, "These are training conditions we know very well. The French Team has been training here since 1992 with all the safety conditions in place that you would expect at a training course of this caliber."

Three weeks later, 17-year-old Max Burkhart of Germany was competing in a NorAm downhill at Lake Louise when he "lost control" and fell into the fencing and safety netting, suffering serious injuries to his lower body. Emergency first-aid was immediately provided at the scene and he was airlifted to a Calgary hospital, but died there the following day.

Aksel Lund Svindal had a brutal somersaulting fall at the Hahnenkamm in 2007 that was one of several crashes that day leading to the cancelling of the event after 30 racers had run. The World Championships and Olympic gold-medal-winning star admitted to being shaken following Poisson's death 10 years later. "It was a shock to your system. We know the risk and we've known it since we were teenagers. We sort of put that away, as we must to continue to do this thing we love. But then, you know, when it's something like that…" he said, trailing off and never finishing the sentence.

Current US record-holder Ross Anderson set the mark at 247.93 kph (154.06 mph) in 2006. Photo courtesy of Ross Anderson.

CHAPTER 43
THE FASTEST NON-MOTORIZED HUMANS ON THE PLANET

Learning From the Wind: The Ballistic Art of Speed Skiing

As Italian speed skier Ivan Origone folded himself into a tight tuck and started whistling through the top half of the Vars, France speed skiing track, he wasn't as together as he would have wished. About a third of the way down a left ski wandered slightly and then his right one twitched out of the track. Already going well over 161 kilometers per hour (100 mph), it wasn't the kind of queasy bobble he could afford.

Like most other speed skiers, Origone has fallen at high speeds and walked away from it, or at least survived. There was the time when he hooked a right ski just as he was crossing the finish line at 166 kilometers per hour (103 mph) and went down face first before sliding to a stop with only a dislocated shoulder and some road rash.

But this was March 20 of 2016 on a very fast day, with the event starting from the uppermost point on the ridge above a near-vertical headwall, down a course with an average gradient of 52.5% for the 490-vertical-meters (1,607 vertical feet) it covers. And Origone's skis were getting twitchy in the narrowest part of the track, within 20 or 30 feet of rock ridges on the skier's left side.

The next year, just below the same spot at speeds around 240 kilometers per hour (just under 150 mph), Frenchman Simon Billy, one of the top racers in the world, hooked an edge and tumbled and slid for 26 seconds. That's about how long it would take Usain Bolt to run the length of three football fields. Way, way longer than your average car wreck even if it goes off a cliff.

"When does it stop?" he asked himself. "I broke my knee, my ankle, my elbow, one finger. In the helicopter I said I want to stop it."

But he soon realized he still had the need for speed. His first race the next season was back at Vars, the toughest on the tour, without any warm-up races due to poor snow conditions throughout the Alps. He felt ready in his body but not in his mind and in the end he withdrew. "This track is a monster, and we are taking so much risk because we are ready to do it," he said in an interview with Jan Farrell. This time he wasn't ready, but he did return to the tour later that winter.

In 2016, Origone flirted with disaster at Vars, then pulled it together and with the customary sound of a jet taking off that accompanies a speed skier down the mountain, he crossed the finish timing line. "I didn't do a perfect run," he said later. "I had problems in the middle of the track and my skis opened. Then I thought I had to do a perfect run after that."

When he started to open up after the finish to slow down the force of the wind against his body made him realize he'd been fast. And then it flashed across the tote board as the announcer started shouting: 254.958 kilometers per hour (158.424 mph)! His brother Simone Origone had set the world record three times since 2006, and Ivan had just broken it by 2.5 mph.

Fellow Italian Valentina Greggio also set the women's speed record that day at 247.038 kph (153.502 mph) with a much different experience. "When I go down I think it's so simple, so it's not a good time," she said. Then she crossed the finish line and heard the announcer getting excited. Watching the replays the run is truly so stable and smooth that it's deceptive, just the way the great speed skiers say it often is when everything clicks above a certain velocity.

The way it did on March 22, 2023, when Simon Billy, 7 years after his bad fall, came back at Vars to set a new world record of 255.500 kilometers per hour (158.760 mph). "I felt it was my day," he told fellow speed skier and YouTube video host Jan Farrell afterward. "The Nature gave us the perfect day, the track was good, the snow was good... The run felt pretty easy, I had the perfect run. It was cool and relaxed at the top and I knew it was my day." Ivan Origone had held the record for an impressive 7 years, and on this day when he lost it, his brother Simone finished second.

[DROP CAP] Skiing fast isn't a difficult thing to understand. Especially compared to ski flying, skiing 8,000-meter peaks, skiing to the North Pole, traversing the Karakoram, getting dragged by a horse, kite-skiing cliffs in Switzerland, or cartop skiing. The latter of which is genetically related to speed skiing.

The DNA of fast skiing became easier to trace in the last 150 years. People we consider to be speed skiing pioneers were really just the first ones to clock how fast they were going and write it down. As with other records on skis and snowboards, it probably all got started with a bet, or a point of honor, or trying to impress someone. And the easiest way to prove you were faster was to get from point A to point B before anyone else you were racing.

Dick Dorworth is an American speed skiing pioneer and world record holder who has also researched and written about the sport. In a 2015 posting he noted that, "The first recorded speed skiing record was in 1867 in La Porte, California, by a woman with the provocative name of Lottie Joy, who traveled 48.9 mph/79.003kph.

Pictured in Vars in 2019, Frenchman Simon Billy set the speed-skiing world record there in 2023. Photo courtesy Simon Billy.

The length of her run and the method of timing are unknown."

Her feat was reported in The Mountain Messenger, and her run was assumed to be on the same track the men used for their regular speed trials, though that wasn't stated. According to Wikipedia, it wasn't until 1898 that Tommy Todd at La Porte put a watch and a distance measurement (1,230 feet) on a speed run he made that was reported as 140 kilometers an hour (87 mph). Which was clipping right along for the time, and is still fast today even for World Cup downhillers. The fact that it took 49 more years for anyone to go faster also casts some doubt on Todd's mark.

But maybe he had a secret. Dorworth noted that Todd was part of a Norwegian gold mining community that passed the long winters by staging skiing competitions. They used long wooden skis and, "Each racer's secret formula for wax was closely guarded, but persistent reports indicate that human sperm was a key ingredient of the best recipes. These concoctions were called 'dope'."

Yes, it could have been one of the first cases of doping in American sports… if not quite the same thing that still goes on today. And skiers in Europe, while undoubtedly using waxes of their own devising, may have neglected the pearl jam. In any event it was 1930 in St. Moritz, Switzerland before the first 'official' speed skiing record was set by Gustav Lantschner at 105.674 kilometers per hour (65.588 mph).

The next year Leo Gasperl attached hay hooks to the front of his skis that he held onto with his hands, and by

Italian Valentina Greggio set women's speed skiing world record in Vars, France in 2016. Photo © Louis Billy.

"having a rudimentary aerodynamic cone strapped to his butt," wrote Dorworth, he managed to attain a kind of missile shape and a considerably faster speed of 136.6 kilometers per hour (84.692 mph).

It took another 16 years until 1947 to break that record, when the great Italian downhill racer Zeno Colo went 159.292 kilometers per hour (98.761 mph) in his home country at Cervinia. After that there is some controversy over who first broke the 100 mph barrier.

In 1955 American ski racers Buddy Werner, Ron Funk and Marvin Melville participated in an event in Portillo, Chile staged by French star Emile Allais. Funk fell at almost 100 mph using bear trap bindings and long thongs and was badly hurt. American Ralph Miller was accorded a speed of 174.402 kilometers per hour (108.7 mph) by Allais who was using a hand held stopwatch. Because such manual timing is always subject to slight variations, it was unofficial. "He may have only gone 99 mph," noted Dorworth, "but it is just as likely he went 112 mph. People who have raced on the Portillo track and know where he started tend to believe Miller was the first to go over 100 mph."

Edoardo Agraiter then appears on the official list going 160.174 kilometers per hour (99.307 mph) in Sestriere, France in 1959. I've come across few further details on where exactly this apparently one-off speed event took place in the resort, or Agraiter's background including even his nationality.

It was Luigi DiMarco in 1960 who was the first to go over 100 mph with a certifiable clocking of 163.265 kilometers per hour (101.224 mph) in Cervinia. In July of '63 Alfred Planger attained a 168.224 kilometers per hour (104.298 mph) in Cervinia. And in September of that year Americans Dick Dorworth and C.B. Vaughn tied for a record of 171.428 (106.520 mph) in Portillo at a race put on by Ron Funk that used electric-eye timing, as in Cervinia. Then the next year DiMarco took the record back in Cervinia with a 174.757 (108.349 mph).

Nine decades after Lottie Joy set the first known speed skiing record, the first 'official' women's record was established in 1963 in Cervinia by Emanuel Spreafico going 127.138 kilometers per hour (78.82 mph). Kristl Staffner bumped that up by nearly 10 miles an hour the next year with a 143.230 (88.802 mph) mark also in Cervinia.

That four-year burst of records really signaled the beginning of speed skiing as an ongoing competition with regularly scheduled events. Because of that the equipment began to evolve and some of it – like body-wrapping ski poles with dollar-sized baskets, flat-tipped skis and non-porous speed suits – also made the transition into more traditional ski racing.

In 1965 Dorworth witnessed 19-year-old Italian junior champion Walter Mussner fall in Cervinia. Because of the helmet design and the style of tuck at the time, "The most aerodynamic position using them was to put the head down and essentially to ski almost blind," Dorworth wrote. "One element in Mussner's fatal accident was that he had put his head down and was unaware his line was taking him off the prepared track."

Dorworth's recounting of the appalling accident at the time in his journal was graphic. "At the top of the timing area he began to veer right. What happened when he fell is something I don't think I will ever forget as long as I live. With incredible force and speed he went end over end, feet and then head hitting the snow, and each turn wrenching his body unbelievably. Afterward 11 holes were counted in the snow… He lived a little more than five hours… He fractured his skull, broke two vertebrae in his neck, pulverized his entire pelvic region, broke one femur and tore loose the femoral artery, and he tore himself open from the anus to the navel. He had acute hemorrhages of the brain, stomach and leg."

It's a description to curdle the blood of anyone even thinking about watching the sport let alone trying it. And it came during a period when downhill ski racing was also getting a closer look from the public at large, which soon resulted in more attention to safety from the sponsors and stagers of such events.

For downhill courses there were certain obvious things that could be done to reduce the risks. They couldn't stop racers from falling but they could try to make it less ruinous when they did by erecting fences between the courses and the trees and padding lift towers and other permanent fixtures nearby.

For speed skiing it was a little different. Starting in the early 1990s events began grooming the courses with winch cats to smooth out the rolls and bumps and reduce the effect of multiple racers going in the same tracks. That made them safer, yet also faster, something multiple record holder Franz Weber attested to. Certain requirements were also established and enforced for the run out areas at the speed tracks, some of which were dangerously short for racers traveling as fast as they were.

In attempting to standardize the speed records from the 1930s onward, it had been generally accepted that recognized speed venues have tracks one kilometer long, with a timing area of 100 meters. Because that timing area usually occurs not far from the finish, racers have room to build up maximum speeds. They also need a lot of room after that to slowly stand up and turn the 240-centimeter planks they're on.

The length of the tracks were soon regulated at one kilometer for fear that longer ones would just encourage greater and more dangerous speeds until it would be little more than sky diving with skis on.

But there hasn't been much the FIS and other event sponsors can do for racers once they fall. Downhill racers on the World Cup tour were restricted from using super slick speed suits that could cause them to actually accelerate once they fell, thus increasing their risks of injury. For speed skiers it was in some ways better for them to slide to the run out area where they could stop slowly rather than abruptly.

As the old adage states, it isn't the speed that kills, it's the sudden stops. But equipment modifications have continued to be vital components of efforts to go faster, while simultaneously making accidents in the sport at least survivable. Helmets that had been the same standard issue as downhill ski racers used were adapted to the specific needs of speed skiers, providing them with better head and neck protection, while also streamlining their overall tucks to create less friction and wind resistance.

The latex speed suits have gradually incorporated more under armor in them as well as fire retardant qualities to reduce road rash and friction burns. They also have built in fairings that streamline the back of the racer's calves to reduce drag and turbulence.

Advances in ski technology, waxing and the ability to computer-model and wind-tunnel-test effective tucks have also helped produce incrementally faster speeds over the years. On site medical teams and helicopter evacuation capabilities have improved the availability of help for those who do get injured.

But in the end it is still a very dangerous game with little room for error. And the racers know it. "Everyone knows his life is on the line," said Tom Simons, who set the record in 1976, "and though many don't admit it, that's one of the reasons we race. There's a basic need in man that lures him into pushing his limits all the way."

Dick Dorworth agreed, noting, "Life is richer and more poignant when it is risked; it is so through a deep desire to go on living." He fell twice at high speed and broke a leg in one of them at about 100 mph. He has written that, "There is an infinitely fragile line of balance at 100 mph. You are more like a projectile than a skier, and once that line is broken it does not mend easily. You may breed a contempt for big speeds, forgetting respect through the grace of being atop your skis each run. No one on his back at 100 miles per hour will ever after have contempt for speed."

On the other hand, Yuichiro Miura (the Japanese athlete who skied – and fell – down Everest as recounted in an earlier chapter) fell 8 times going over 100 mph during a week he spent at the KL in 1964. Each time he got up and walked away, "bruised but unbowed" as Dorworth put it.

And when American legend Steve McKinney was dominating speed skiing in the 1970s and early '80s, setting 4 world records on three different tracks, he had several encounters with mortality and brushed them off. After crashing at 196 kilometers per hour (122 mph) in Portillo he commented, "I curled up like a noodle, bounced for several hundred yards, got up and did it again."

In 1974 he was waiting to run at Cervinia behind Swiss skier Jean-Marc Beguelin who tucked his head so low – in what was commonly referred to as the 'kiss your ass goodbye pose' – that he went blindly off course at 165.7 kilometers per hour (103 mph) and into avalanche debris where he was killed. McKinney set his first record the next day.

Through the 1970s and '80s speed skiing was a tough ticket to sell and the professional circuit that made Franz Weber a star collapsed by the end of the '80s. That left the FIS to pick up the pieces in preparation for having it as a demonstration event at the 1992 Olympic games in Albertville, France.

By all accounts it was a big success and French surgeon Michel Prufer, who had set the world record in Portillo and then again in Les Arcs in 1987, upped it again at the Olys with 229.299 kilometers per hour (142.165 mph). Torja Mulari of Norway broke the women's record with 219.245 kilometers per hour (135.931).

On the morning of the final day of the speed skiing, top 27-year-old Swiss skier Nicholas Bochatay was free skiing with other racers and catching air on a bump on an open public run, not the speed skiing track, when he unfortunately collided with a snowcat and died. Many believe that the accident, in spite of not happening in the event or training for it, tipped the scales in favor of not making speed skiing an Olympic sport due to its inherent danger.

In echoes of how other competitive skiing had come to be treated by governing bodies of the sports, the FIS soon moved to restrict the speeds that racers could reach during events on the World Cup tour. Just as with ski jumping, the idea was to make speed events safer and to have them won on merits other than breaking world records. As a result, two or three pro events annually aimed specifically at record breaking were organized without FIS sanctioning and held at Les Arcs, Vars, and Velocity Peak in Silverton, Colorado.

The World Cup tour for Speed Skiing has suffered from fewer viewers since it made the decision to stop chasing records. But events are still held at about half a dozen tracks around the world each year, from Andorra to Japan, depending on conditions and other factors. And as of this writing the pro record-setting attempts have been reduced to once a year at Vars in The Speed Masters Championships under the stewardship of the FSV (France Ski de Vitesse).

Some longtime venues have been abandoned as speeds have outgrown them or the tracks have become untenable. At Cervinia, where the course was on a glacier, it grew unusable due to crevasses opening up in the ice. Velocity Peak in Silverton, a privately owned site with no lifts, had financial difficulties. Portillo's popular Kilometro Lanzado, which was always speedy owing to its high altitude and lack of air resistance, was discontinued due to insufficient run-out room. And Les Arcs was closed in 2007 after the deaths of Marco Salvaggio and Caitlin Tovar.

The last two are part of the list of five fatalities attributed to speed skiing events over the years of the sport's existence. Given what the athletes are doing, that seems a remarkably small number, though that obviously isn't any consolation for the friends and families of those who have died. However, it's a simple fact that three of the 5 deaths attributed to the sport didn't occur during either racing or practice.

Nicolas Bochatay's death hitting a snowcat while free skiing, while tragic, shouldn't even be connected to speed skiing. What happened to him has happened to literally scores of recreational skiers around the world. It's one reason most ski resorts no longer use cats to groom while the slopes are open during the day, and do it at night instead.

With both Salvaggio and Tovar, they died as a result of problems they encountered before ever starting the race at Les Arcs. Race officials and competitors had apparently complained for years about the Les Arcs speed track being located immediately adjacent to a steep mogul run. The concern was that speed skiers veering off the track might be badly hurt because of it.

Marco Salvaggio, with his speed skis and suit on and *skiing down to the start area*, apparently clipped a rock and fell. And because of the speed suit, he slid the length of the mogul field and sustained fatal head injuries.

Following this horrible mishap, the FIS made it mandatory for racers to wear clothing over their speed suits from the lift access to the race track. According to an online post from a friend and teammate of Caitlin Tovar's, "this regulation is vigorously enforced." That friend witnessed the British racer's accident two years after Salvaggio's at the same track for the Pro World Championships.

On the second day of the event, as is usual, the women started after the top 10 men had run. Race organizers

Dick Dorworth, Portillo, Chile 1962. The next year Americans Dorworth and C.B. Vaughn tied for world record in Portillo. Photo courtesy of Dick Dorworth.

decided that Tovar and Japanese racer Tomoko "should start from a lower start and effectively act as forerunners for the ladies." Both had already lined up with the rest of the women, taken off their over-clothing and put on their long speed skis. When it was their turn they made their way very carefully over tricky frozen snow toward their lower start area, doing all of this inside the netted track area.

"As Caitlin approached the level of the start and attempted to traverse into position on the track, she lost her balance, her skis slid from under her and she began to slide," wrote her teammate on the Snowheads forum. After what had happened to Salvaggio, she wrote, "there was instant alarm."

At that moment there was no one who could help her since all the competitors were on their big skis and fully suited, and no one else was there who could have stopped her. She broke through the fencing on the edge of the course and out into the bumps where she bounced at high speed down the 45-degree slope for a full 3,000 feet and died. The race was cancelled.

"No one outside the incredibly close community of speed skiers can comprehend the horror, desperation and impotence that we felt during her fall," wrote her teammate. "It was truly a living nightmare in which we were powerless to alter the outcome. It was a cruel, cruel day."

It was ultimately made even worse by being held up as an example of how lethally dangerous the sport is. It would be like condemning speed skating because one of the racers slipped and fell on the ice before starting or even putting their helmet on, and cracked their head and died.

On the other hand it's true that the low fatality number only applies to "sanctioned" speed events. There is no doubt that there have been other deaths connected with speed skiing before records were really kept, and even since then on tracks that weren't holding official events. Still, as risky as the sport is, and given its 100-year existence, the fatality rate is very low. Certainly less than bobsledding, for example, or even traditional alpine ski racing, two stalwart Winter Olympic sports.

Part of what the World Cup Speed Skiing Tour is trying to accomplish is a legitimizing of the sport by proving it can be conducted safely and deserves to be in the Olympics. Racers fall while doing it and walk away far more often than not. French speed skier Bastien Montes survived the fastest crash in history at 243 kilometers per hour (151 mph) that left him with fourth-degree burns from shoulder to buttocks. But they didn't have to bury him and he returned to racing.

Speed skier Jan Farrell – who in 2016 had a well-publicized crash at 217 kilometers per hour (135 mph) and sustained heavy bruises and second-degree burns – returned to competition and has been a tireless promoter of the sport. He noted to journalist Simon Usborne in 2018 that, "In 1992, speed skiing was exotic and spectacular and one of the most viewed sports of the [Olympic] games. But we haven't made progress visually since then. It's every speed skier's dream to be Olympic again, but if we don't reinvent ourselves we won't attract spectators or new athletes."

In the meantime, "some opportunistic landscaping at Vars made it smoother – and faster," wrote Usborne for

Men's Health magazine. The records started being made again and getting noticed. And the World Cup speed tour continues, though financial rewards for the skiers are slim. From here on when more records are set they are likely to be by small increments. As evidence would be the fact that the world record hadn't been raised in 7 years prior to March of 2023, and the top speed by an American was set in 2006 and still stands as of this writing.

The latter was established by Coloradoan Ross Andrews at 247.93 kilometers per hour (154.06 mph) in Les Arcs, it's still the 9th fastest run ever. To this day the only Native American to compete on any World Cup skiing tour, he was also one of the very rare people of color there. Also the most successful, with 6 National Championships and a bronze at the FIS World Championships in Cervinia in 2005, among other achievements.

He told Dick Dorworth for a story in Skiing History magazine, that given "there's little presence of anyone of color [in the sport], and it's at the World Cup level," he thinks his story can be inspirational. "I hope kids who read this will realize that if they stick with their subject or their dreams or whatever they want to do in their lives, there will definitely be accomplishments."

Even while Andrews was helping broaden the sport's appeal on one front, as Jan Farrell noted, it was struggling overall. The absence of new records has certainly played a role, and there are multiple causes for that.

"Now, in the 2000s, innovation seems to have stalled," wrote John Cox as he discussed the issue in a scholarly data study in May of 2021. "Some recent methods of increasing speed include a starting ramp for the skiers made from turf. However, this had only slight affects on the skier's speed. Some modern skiers even take to smoothing out the bumps on their kneecaps for their runs to become more aerodynamic."

The most visible trend in recent history has been the dramatic narrowing of the margins between men and women racers, with the ladies steadily narrowing the now slender gap.

And overall, speed skiers continue to be the fastest non-motorized humans on the planet. That's a pretty big deal and the language of that characterization is important because it states, "on the planet." Skydiving, for instance, doesn't take place exactly "on the planet" but rather in its atmosphere. And it's often held out as an example to compare to earthbound skiing.

The current world speed record for skydiving as approved by the Federation Aeronautique Internationale (FAI) is held by Marco Hepp of Germany. It was set in Eloy, Arizona on October 22, 2022, at 529.77 kilometers per hour (329.18 mph), during the 4th FAI World Speed Skydiving Championships. Henrik Raimer of Sweden achieved the fastest speed ever recorded in competition in 2016 during the FAI World Championships in Chicago. It was 601.26 kilometers per hour (373.6 mph).

The wide spread between those numbers and so-called terminal velocity is achieved by aerodynamics. Without their assistance the maximum speed of a falling object is 120 mph until it gets a boost through design by the wind that's funneled around it as it falls. Aerodynamics is of course also the reason that speed skiers exceed terminal velocity. Obviously they have some ways to go before catching skydivers.

As far as skiing's other competitors on the planet go, just for comparison, Usain Bolt has been clocked running at 27.79 mph and his time for the 100 meters is 9.58 seconds. Ivan Origone covered that distance in 1.41 seconds. Speed skiers go from 0 to 60 mph in 3 seconds, hitting 120 mph in 6 seconds, speeds generally compared to Formula 1 racecars.

Wind-powered sports are also fast. While the windsurfing speed record, set in 2008, is only 103.67 kilometers per hour (61.3 mph), the land sailing record is much more impressive. It was shattered by Team New Zealand's America's Cup crew in 2022 on a 46-foot long carbon-fiber land yacht with wheels and a rigid wing sail, that reached 222.4 kilometers per hour (138.2 mph) on a dried-sand lake bed in Australia. There is reason to think they can go even faster and may someday prove a real challenge to skiing records. It will, however, likely always be considered an "assisted" speed due to the sail. While it can be argued that speed skiers also get an assist from the wind, it's wind they are generating. And in fact much natural wind at all can be ruinous to speed skiing.

In 2012 a skateboarder clocked 130 kilometers per hour (80.74 mph), and in 2010 an ice luger reached 154 kph (95.69 mph). But most of the non-motorized land speeds remotely comparable to skiing come from other snow-based efforts. Cycling is the top contender with 227.7 kph (141.5 mph) on a treacherous snowpack posted in 2000. A series of brutal accidents seriously clouded the future of speed snow-biking shortly after that, so it's hard to say if it will ever be fully competitive with skiing.

One-legged skier Michael Milton went 213.7 kph (132.8 mph in 2006). Frenchman Xavier Cousseau reached around 80 kph (128 mph) on a monoski in 2005. Snowboarder Darren Powell was just behind at 126.4 mph in 1999. English blind speed skier Kevin Alderton clocked an even 100 mph in 2006. And Yann Grandjean from Switzerland got a 'snowscoot' up to 87.8 mph in 2008.

We may speculate about other non-motorized speed sports that could someday break all the records skiing sets. But it seems unlikely that any other sports – not counting politics and show business – will ever see any players whose careers can go downhill faster.

PHOTO PERMISSIONS

FRONT COVER

1) Women's speed skiing world record holder Valentina Greggio. Photo © Louis Billy, used with his and her permission.

2) Kite skier Jon Devore during the filming of The Unrideables: near Anchorage, AK, USA on 27 April, 2014. Photo credit: Scott Serfas / Red Bull Content Pool.

CHAPTER 1

[Page 2] Egon Zimmermann's jump over a Porsche on the Flexenpass in Austria was taken by Hans Truol and was on the front of a postcard that Zimmermann handed out at his restaurant/hotel. The jump and postcard are cited in the book, as is Hans Truol. This image is from a postcard given to the author by Zimmermann.

[Page 7] Movie poster for film with Rick Sylvester's Baffin Island cliff jump w/parachute. The jump, the film and the image are discussed in this chapter. In the public domain for editorial purposes.

[Page 10] Jesper Tjäder's final run at Red Bull Playstreets in Bad Gastein, Austria, February 10, 2023. Photographer Credit: HYPERLINK "https://www.redbullcontentpool.com/search?facet:photographerCredit=Simon%20Rainer%20 %2F%20Red%20Bull%20Content%20Pool&layout=advanced" Simon Rainer / Red Bull Content Pool.

CHAPTER 2

[Page 12] Reidar Andersen. HYPERLINK "https://commons.wikimedia.org/wiki/File:Reidar_Andersen_ hopper_i_Holmenkollen_%281938%29.jpg" \t "_blank" File: Reidar Andersen hopper in Holmenkollen (1938). jpg - Wikimedia Commons. Creator: HYPERLINK "https://www.flickr.com/people/29160242@N08" Municipal Archives of Trondheim from Trondheim, Norway. Eier/Owner Institution: Trondheim byarkiv, The Municipal Archives of Trondheim Arkivreferanse / Archive reference: Ranheim Papirfabrikk: Saksarkiv - Scankraftmøte 1938 - Memoarer (1938 - 1940) This file is licensed under the HYPERLINK "https://en.wikipedia.org/wiki/en:Creative_ Commons" Creative Commons HYPERLINK "https://creativecommons.org/licenses/by/2.0/deed.en" Attribution 2.0 Generic license. You are free: to share – to copy, distribute and transmit the work, to remix – to adapt the work, Under the following conditions: attribution – You must give appropriate credit, provide a link to the license, and indicate if changes were made. You may do so in any reasonable manner, but not in any way that suggests the licensor endorses you or your use.

[Page 15] Holmenkolrendet with Ragnar Omtvedt, no date. Bildet er hentet fra Nasjonalbibliotekets bildesamling holmenkollbakken,Holmenkollen, Oslo, Unknown author - HYPERLINK "https://en.wikipedia.org/wiki/en:National_Library_of_Norway" National Library of Norway Public Domain, copyright expired, photographer unknown.

[Page 18] Upper image: H. Smith,Norwegian, 1907, location unknown, in the pubic domain due to age, no copyright and unknown photographer.

[Page 18] Lower image: Holmenkollbakken in 1904, after the stone take-off had been built. HYPERLINK "https://en.wikipedia.org/wiki/Anders_Beer_Wilse" Anders Beer Wilse (1865–1949) - HYPERLINK "http://www.nb.no/cgi-bin/galnor/gn_sok.sh?id=59560&skjema=2&fm=4" Galleri NOR Tilvekstnummer: NF.W 02189 Internnr: NBR9404:01975. Holmenkollbakken ski jump in Oslo, Norway. HYPERLINK "https://commons.wikimedia.org/wiki/File:Holmenkollbakken_1904.jpg?uselang=en" \l "Licensing" \t "" Public Domain. File:Holmenkollbakken 1904. jpg. Created: 1 January 1904. This image is in the HYPERLINK "https://en.wikipedia.org/wiki/public_domain" public domain in Norway because images not considered to be "works of art" become public domain 50 years after creation, provided that more than 15 years have passed since the photographer's death or the photographer is unknown. This is according to HYPERLINK "https://lovdata.no/lov/2018-06-15-40/%C2%A723" § 23 in the Norwegian HYPERLINK "https://no.wikipedia.org/wiki/%C3%85ndsverkloven" Åndsverkloven. Under the former photo law, protection ended 25 years after creation, provided that more than 15 years had passed since the photographer's death or the photographer is unknown. The image is in the public domain if the protection ended before 29 June 1995 under the older term. Images uploaded to Wikimedia Commons must also be in the public domain in the United States. A Norwegian work that is in the public domain in Norway is in the public domain in the U.S. only if it was in the public domain in Norway in 1996 and no copyright was registered in the U.S. (This is the effect of 17 USC 104A with its critical date of January 1, 1996.)

CHAPTER 3

[Page 20] Vinko Bogataj falling in ABC Wide World of Sports clip. Screenshot from YouTube video. The accident and the video clip of it are written about in the book. In the public domain for editorial use.

[Page 23] Bergisel Ski Jump, Austria, by Zaha Hadid Architects. HYPERLINK "https://commons.wikimedia.org/wiki/File:Bergisel_Ski_Jump_Tower.jpg" \t "_blank" File:Bergisel Ski Jump Tower.jpg - Wikimedia Commons, Top of the Bergisel Ski Jump tower, Tirol, Austria, Date of image: 7 October 2006; Uploader's own original photograph; Author: QEDquid; Permission: GFDL. I, the copyright holder of this work, hereby publish it under the following license: This file is licensed under the HYPERLINK "https://en.wikipedia.org/wiki/en:Creative_Commons" Creative Commons HYPERLINK "https://creativecommons.org/licenses/by-sa/3.0/deed.en" Attribution-Share Alike 3.0 Unported license. Permission is granted to copy, distribute and/or modify this document under the terms of the GNU Free Documentation License, Version 1.2 or any later version published by the Free Software Foundation; with no Invariant Sections, no Front-Cover Texts, and no Back-Cover Texts. A copy of the license is included in the section entitled HYPERLINK "https://commons.wikimedia.org/wiki/Commons:GNU_Free_Documentation_License,_version_1.2" GNU Free Documentation License. You are free: to share – to copy, distribute and transmit the work, to remix – to adapt the work. Under the following conditions: attribution – You must give appropriate credit, provide a link to the license, and indicate if changes were made. You may do so in any reasonable manner, but not in any way that suggests the licensor endorses you or your use. Share alike – If you remix, transform, or build upon the material, you must distribute your contributions under the same of compatible license as the original.

[Page 24] Bjørn Wirkola at the 1966 World Championships. Wikipedia. No restrictions. File: Bjorn Wirkola 1966. JPG. Created: 1 January 1966. The copyright is in the public domain because it has exoired; or it was injected into the public domain for other reasons, such as failure to adhere to required formalities or conditions; i.e. The institution owns the copyright but is not interested in exercising control; or the institution has legal rights sufficient to authorize others to use the work without restrictions. Verdensmesterskapet pa ski i Oslo 1966. Arkivreferense: Riksarkivet – RA/PA/0797/

U/Ua/3894_Lasse_010 Billedbladet NA/Klaeboe/ Riksarkivet (National Archives of Norway) – Bjorn Wirlola og Kjell Sjoberg

[Page 26] Copper Peak Ski Jump, HYPERLINK "https://creativecommons.org/licenses/by-sa/3.0" \t "_blank" CC BY-SA 3.0 File: Copper Peak Ski Flying Hill.JPG, Created: 5 August 2008, Copper Peak Ski Flying Hill, from the chairlift. HYPERLINK "https://en.wikipedia.org/wiki/User:Cbradshaw" Cbradshaw at HYPERLINK "https://en.wikipedia.org/wiki/" English Wikipedia, Own work (Original text: I created this work entirely by myself.) Wikimedia Commons. I, the copyright holder of this work, hereby publish it under the following licenses: This file is licensed under the HYPERLINK "https://en.wikipedia.org/wiki/en:Creative_Commons" Creative Commons HYPERLINK "https://creativecommons.org/licenses/by-sa/3.0/deed.en" Attribution-Share Alike 3.0 Unported license. You are free: to share – to copy, distribute and transmit the work, to remix – to adapt the work Under the following conditions: attribution – You must give appropriate credit, provide a link to the license, and indicate if changes were made. You may do so in any reasonable manner, but not in any way that suggests the licensor endorses you or your use. share alike – If you remix, transform, or build upon the material, you must distribute your contributions under the HYPERLINK "https://creativecommons.org/share-your-work/licensing-considerations/compatible-licenses" same or compatible license as the original. Permission is also granted to copy, distribute and/or modify this document under the terms of the HYPERLINK "https://en.wikipedia.org/wiki/en:GNU_Free_Documentation_License" GNU Free Documentation License, Version 1.2 or any later version published by the HYPERLINK "https://en.wikipedia.org/wiki/en:Free_Software_Foundation" Free Software Foundation; with no Invariant Sections, no Front-Cover Texts, and no Back-Cover Texts. A copy of the license is included in the section entitled HYPERLINK "https://commons.wikimedia.org/wiki/Commons:GNU_Free_Documentation_License,_version_1.2" GNU Free Documentation License.

CHAPTER 4

[Page 32] National Ski Jumping Centre, China, by TeamMinus (2020) Photo courtesy of Team Minus and Beijing 2022.

[Page 35] Stefan Kraft, in Klingenthal 2017. FIS Ski Jumping Summer Grand Prix Klingenthal 2017 on 2017-10-03 Stefan Kraft. File:2017-10-03 FIS SGP 2017 Klingenthal Stefan Kraft Flug.jpg. Created: 2017-10-03 16:12:52. FIS Ski Jumping Summer Grand Prix Klingenthal 2017 on 2017-10-03 Stefan Kraft. HYPERLINK "https://commons.wikimedia.org/wiki/User:Wikijunkie" Christian Bier -Own work. I, the copyright holder of this work, hereby publish it under the following license: This file is licensed under the HYPERLINK "https://en.wikipedia.org/wiki/en:Creative_Commons" Creative Commons HYPERLINK "https://creativecommons.org/licenses/by-sa/4.0/deed.en" Attribution-Share Alike 4.0 international license. You are free: to share – to copy, distribute and transmit the work to remix – to adapt the work Under the following conditions: attribution – You must give appropriate credit, provide a link to the license, and indicate if changes were made. You may do so in any reasonable manner, but not in any way that suggests the licensor endorses you or your use. share alike – If you remix, transform, or build upon the material, you must distribute your contributions under the HYPERLINK "https://creativecommons.org/share-your-work/licensing-considerations/compatible-licenses" same or compatible license as the original.

[Page 38] Ema Klinec of Slovenia, pictured in 2016 at Hinzenbach, holds the official women's world record at 226 m (741 ft). Photo by Ailura. 2016-02-07. Author" Ailura. Own work. CC BY-SA 3.0 at File: 20160207 Skispingen Hinzenbach 4431.jpg 13:01:02 Community content is available under CC-BY-SA unless otherwise noted. Wikis Using the CC BY-SA license. To grow the commons of free knowledge and free culture, all users editing or otherwise contributing to wikis that use the CC BY-SA license agree to grant broad permissions to the general public to re-distribute and re-use their contributions freely for any purpose, including commercial use, in accordance with the CC BY-SA license. Such use is allowed where attribution is given and the same freedom to re-use and re-distribute applies to any derivative works of the contributions. Supported by WMAT. Copyright: © Ailura. Wikipedia, prosta enciklopedija. The making of this work was supported by Wikimedia Austria.

[Page 41] Olympic gold medalist Ryōyū Kobayashi of Japan jumping during the Four Hills Tournament in Bischofshofen, Austria on January 06, 2023. Production Date: January 05, 2023. Project / Event: HYPERLINK "https://www.redbullcontentpool.com/search?facet:source=FIS%20Ski%20Jumping%20World%20Cup%20 2022%20-%202023%20Four%20Hills%20Tournament&layout=advanced" FIS Ski Jumping World Cup 2022 - 2023 Four Hills Tournament. Topic: HYPERLINK "https://www.redbullcontentpool.com/search?facet:topic=Ski%20Jumping&layout=advanced" Ski Jumping. Location: Bischofshofen. Person / Team:

[Page 41] New Holmenkollen jump being built, summer of 2010. https://commons.wikimedia.org

CHAPTER 5

[Page 44] Fred Harris, Class of 1911, Founder of the Dartmouth Outing Club, ca. 1958. Title Fred Harris, Class of 1911, Founder of the Dartmouth Outing Club, ca. 1958. Rights Copyright Undetermined. Available Online At https:// libarchive.dartmouth.edu/cdm/

Ref/collection/photofiles/id/70299 Bibliographic Citation Fred Harris, Class of 1911, Founder of the Dartmouth Outing Club, ca. 1958, Iconography, Icon1647-0686-0000012A, Rauner Special Collections Library. Image posted by exhibits.library.dartmouth.edu

[Page 46] ARMAND CHARLET Charlet on the cover of Vocation Alpine. Photographer Unknown - Original publication: On the cover of the book Immediate Source

HYPERLINK "https://www.amazon.co.uk/Vocation-alpine-Armand-Charlet/dp/2842304438" https://www.amazon. co.uk/Vocation-alpine-Armand-Charlet/dp/2842304438 Armand Charlet on the cover of Vocation Alpine Fair Use.

[Page 49] The cover of Jan Reynolds book The Glass Summit, One Woman's Epic Journey Breaking Through. Image courtesy of Jan Reynolds.

[Page 50] Irving Langmuir, reading. File:Langmuir-sitting.jpg Uploaded: 2015-03-09 19:30:31. Langmuir c. 1900. Unknown author - Unknown source. URL: HYPERLINK "http://www.geocities.com/bioelectrochemistry/langmuir. htm" http://www.geocities.com/bioelectrochemistry/langmuir.htm Date: c. 1900. This work is in the HYPERLINK "https://en.wikipedia.org/wiki/public_domain" public domain in its country of origin and other countries and areas where the HYPERLINK "https://en.wikipedia.org/wiki/List_of_countries%27_copyright_lengths" copyright term is the author's life plus 100 years or fewer.

CHAPTER 6

[Page 54] Davo Karnicar – image in blue and yellow credited to him. This image of him has run everywhere before and after his death, almost always with no credit. One version has a digital stamp in the lower right corner that reads La Legende Davo Karnicar. One outlet ran it with a credit saying it belonged to Davo Karnicar, which I think is the case. As run with a story written about in this book, and as an image that has run in connection with multiple stories on his death in media around the world, usually with no attribution for the image, would place it in the public domain. Photo credit: Davo Karnicar

[Page 57] Kit Deslauriers, photo of her starting her ski descent of Everest, courtesy of photographer Bryce Brown via his written permission.

[Page 58] Adrzej Bargiel, skiing down Yawash Sar II during his Ski Expedition in Karakoram, Pakistan on April 28, 2021. Photographer Credit: HYPERLINK "https://www.redbullcontentpool.com/search?facet:photographerCredit=Jakub%20Gzela%2C%20Bart%C5%82omiej%20Pawlikowski%20%2F%20Red%20Bull%20Content%20Pool&layout=advanced" Jakub Gzela, Bartłomiej Pawlikowski / Red Bull Content Pool.

[Page 60] Hans Kammerlander at slide show in the HYPERLINK "https://commons.wikimedia.org/wiki/Eifel" Eifel. Photographer: Thomas Mitterer. Source:

 HYPERLINK "http://bergfieber.de/berge/bergsteiger/pics/kammerlander" http://bergfieber.de/berge/bergsteiger/pics/kammerlander Created: 1 January 2001. HYPERLINK "https://creativecommons.org/licenses/by/3.0" \t "_blank" CC BY 3.0 File: Hans Kammerlander.jpg This work is HYPERLINK "https://freedomdefined.org/Definition" free and may be used by anyone for any purpose. If you wish to HYPERLINK "https://commons.wikimedia.org/wiki/Commons:Reusing_content_outside_Wikimedia" use this content, you do not need to request permission as long as you follow any licensing requirements mentioned on this page. The Wikimedia Foundation has received an e-mail confirming that the copyright holder has approved publication under the terms mentioned on this page. This correspondence has been reviewed by a HYPERLINK "https://commons.wikimedia.org/wiki/Template:PermissionTicket/Users" Volunteer Response Team (VRT) member and stored in our HYPERLINK "https://commons.wikimedia.org/wiki/Commons:Volunteer_Response_Team" permission archive. The correspondence is available to trusted volunteers as HYPERLINK "https://ticket.wikimedia.org/otrs/index.pl?Action=AgentTicketZoom&TicketNumber=2008121510016801" ticket #2008121510016801. This file is licensed under the HYPERLINK "https://en.wikipedia.org/wiki/en:Creative_Commons" Creative Commons HYPERLINK "https://creativecommons.org/licenses/by/3.0/deed.en" Attribution 3.0 Unported license. You are free: to share – to copy, distribute and transmit the work, to remix – to adapt the work under the following conditions: attribution – You must give appropriate credit, provide a link to the license, and indicate if changes were made. You may do so in any reasonable manner, but not in any way that suggests the licensor endorses you or your use.

CHAPTER 7

[Page 62] Skiing in the Vallee Blanche at Chamonix, one of the world's longest vertical-foot ski runs. Photo © Jay Cowan.

[Page 65] Mike Wiegle Heli-Skiing stock photo courtesy of Mike Wielge Heli-Skiing.

[Page 66] A special newspaper insert was published by the Aspen Times for every 24 Hours of Aspen event. Referenced in this chapter, in the public domain for editorial use. The author's image of the author-owned insert.

[Page 71] Kilian Jornet. HYPERLINK "https://commons.wikimedia.org/wiki/File:Ski_Mountaineering_World_Cup_Font_Blanca_20170121_072-95_%2832332824031%29.jpg" \t "_blank" File: ISMF Ski Mountaineering World Cup Font Blanca 20170121 072-95 (32332824031).jpg - Wikimedia Commons. Photographer: Jorge Millaruelo. This file is licensed under the Creative Commons Attribution-Share Alike 2.0 Generic License. You are free: to share – to copy, distribute and transmit the work, to remix – to adapt the work. Under the following conditions:attribution – You must give appropriate credit, provide a link to the license, and indicate if changes were made. You may do so in any reasonable manner, but not in any way that suggests the licensor endorses you or your use. Share alike – If you remix, transform, or build upon the material, you must distribute your contributions under the HYPERLINK "https://creativecommons.org/share-your-work/licensing-considerations/compatible-licenses" same or compatible license as the original.. This image originally posted to Flickr by Jorge Millaruelo at HYPERLINK "https://flickr.com/photos/127708545@N04/32332824031" https://flickr.com/photos/127708545@N04/32332824031 (HYPERLINK "https://web.archive.org/web/20200626173449/https://www.flickr.com/photos/127708545@N04/32332824031" archive). It was reviewed on 12 Juky 2018 by FlickreviewR2 and was confirmed to be licensed under the terms of cc0by-sa-2.0.

CHAPTER 8

[Page 76] Powder magazine memorial cover for Doug Coombs. Photo © Ace Kvale. Courtesy of Ace Kvale and Powder magazine / Dave Reddick.

CHAPTER 9

[Page 85] Lone Mountain at Big Sky MT, with the Big Couloir marked. Courtesy of Big Sky Resort.

[Page 86] Cosmiques Couloir at Chamonix, France. Written about in this chapter. Provided without credit online at Chamonix.net, Chamonix News, and planetchamonix.com. Courtesy of Chamonix Tourist Office and in the public domain.

[Page 91] Route lines of the Trifides Couloirs at La Grave, France. Courtesy of Skier's Lodge and Guide Service, La Grave.

[Page 92] Highland Bowl Trail Map, Aspen, CO. Courtesy of Aspen Skiing Company.

CHAPTER 10

[Page 98] Poster advertising the Academy Award-winning movie about Yuichiro Muira. Poster referenced in this chapter, in the public domain for editorial use.

[Page 101] Image of book co-written by Anselme Baud. Referenced in this chapter. In the public domain for editorial use.

[Page 104] Heini Holzer on Wikipedia. Image of gravesite memorial to Holzer, Sie können diese Datei unter folgenden Bedingungen weiterverwenden: Die Datei wurde unter der Lizenz „Creative Commons Namensnennung-Weitergabe unter gleichen Bedingungen Deutschland" in Version 3.0 (abgekürzt „CC-by-sa 3.0/de") veröffentlicht. Den rechtsverbindlichen Lizenzvertrag finden Sie unter HYPERLINK "https://creativecommons.org/licenses/by-sa/3.0/de/legalcode" https://creativecommons.org/licenses/by-sa/3.0/de/legalcode. Es folgt eine vereinfachte Zusammenfassung des Vertrags in allgemeinverständlicher Sprache ohne juristische Wirkung. Grabstätte Heini Holzers, Friedhof Schenna HYPERLINK "https://de.wikipedia.org/wiki/Benutzer:Nerenz" Nerenz (HYPERLINK "https://de.wikipedia.org/wiki/Benutzer_Diskussion:Nerenz" Diskussion) - selbst fotografiert. Grabstätte Heini Holzer, Friedhof Schenna HYPERLINK "https://creativecommons.org/licenses/by-sa/3.0/" \t "_blank" CC BY-SA 3.0 File:Grabstätte Heini Holzer.JPG. Erstellt: 29. September 2018

CHAPTER 11

[Page 106] Book about Pierre Tardivel co-written by him. Mentioned in my book, in the public domain for editorial use.

[Page 111] Jean-Marc Boivin. Photo © René Robert, all rights reserved. Written permission for use in this book.

[Page 112] Patrick Vallencant. Photo by Chris Noble © 2011, all rights reserved. Written permission for use in this book.

[Page 115] Lou Dawson. Image of his Wild Snow book cover w/Dawson's photo of Art Burrows on Mount Hayden. Written permission from Lou Dawson for its use in this book © Lou Dawson. All rights reserved.

CHAPTER 12

[Page 118] Image of Eric Pehota & Trevor Petersen skiing together. Photo © Scott Markewitz, all rights reserved. Written permission for use in this book.

[Page 121] Kristen Ulmer jumping off rocks. Photo © Adam Clark, all rights reserved. Written permission of Kristen Ulmer for use in this book.

[Page 122] Photo of Marco Siffredi riding the Nant Blanc on the Aiguille Verte. Photo © René Robert, all rights reserved. Written permission for use in this book.

[Page 126] Ptor Spricenieks image at La Grave, France. Photo © Cedric Bernardini, all rights reserved. Written permission for use in this book.

CHAPTER 13

[Page 131] Andrew McLean skiing Grizzly Gulch and Wolverine Cirque. Photo used with his permission for this book.

[Page 132] Cover of Powder magazine with image by Jeremy Nobis in Alaska. Photo © Wade McKoy, used with his permission for this book. Cover courtesy of Powder magazine/Dave Reddick.

[Page 135] Image of Shane McConkey labeled as, "Shane McConkey shows off during one of the training runs at Red Bull Snow Thrill of Alaska in Haines, USA on March 26th 2002." Photographer Credit: HYPERLINK "https://www.redbullcontentpool.com/search?facet:photographerCredit=Ulrich%20Grill%20%2F%20Red%20Bull%20Content%20Pool&layout=advanced" Ulrich Grill / Red Bull Content Pool.

[Page 139] Chris Davenport image courtesy of Chris Davenport with written permission for use in this book.

CHAPTER 14

[Page 142] Skier Adam U at Geto Kogen in Japan. Photo by © Kevin McHugh and used with his written permission for this book.

[Page 147] Japan's "Snow Canyon." HYPERLINK "https://commons.wikimedia.org/wiki/File:080504_Tateyama_otani-road_Tateyama_Japan02s3.jpg" \t "_blank" File: 080504 Tateyama otani-road Tateyama Japan02s3.jpg - Wikimedia Commons. Yukino-ōtani of HYPERLINK "https://en.wikipedia.org/wiki/Tateyama_Kurobe_Alpine_Route" Tateyama Kurobe Alpine Route in HYPERLINK "https://commons.wikimedia.org/w/index.php?title=Tateyama&action=edit&redlink=1" Tateyama, HYPERLINK "https://commons.wikimedia.org/wiki/Toyama_prefecture" Toyama prefecture, HYPERLINK "https://commons.wikimedia.org/wiki/Japan" Japan. Creator: HYPERLINK "https://ja.wikipedia.org/wiki/user:663highland" 663highland – Own work. HYPERLINK "https://ja.wikipedia.org/wiki/user:663highland" 663highland, the copyright holder of this work, hereby publishes it under the following licenses: This file is licensed under the HYPERLINK "https://en.wikipedia.org/wiki/en:Creative_Commons" Creative Commons HYPERLINK "https://creativecommons.org/licenses/by/2.5/deed.en" Attribution 2.5 generic license. Attribution: HYPERLINK "https://ja.wikipedia.org/wiki/user:663highland" 663highland. You are free: to share – to copy, distribute and transmit the work, to remix – to adapt the work, under the following conditions: attribution – You must give appropriate credit, provide a link to the license, and indicate if changes were made. You may do so in any reasonable manner, but not in any way that suggests the licensor endorses you or your use.

CHAPTER 15

[Page 150] Alta interlodge sign. Unknown photographer. Referenced in this chapter. In the public domain for editorial use and as non-original content.

[Page 153 & 154] Images from Mount Baker of snowstakes and chairlift from the record winter of 1998/'99. Courtesy of Mount Baker Ski Area.

[Page 156] Color weather map of the HYPERLINK "https://www.google.com/url?sa=i&url=https%3A%2F%2Fen.wikipedia.org%2Fwiki%2F1993_Storm_of_the_Century&psig=AOvVaw3fqAXOuem9peC5o6nm7Xg-C&ust=1690824585540000&source=images&cd=vfe&opi=89978449&ved=0CA8QjhxqFwoTCKi_k9D6toAD-FQAAAAAdAAAAABAI" \t "_blank" 1993 Storm of the Century. Wikipedia. Satellite image by HYPERLINK "https://en.wikipedia.org/wiki/NASA" NASA of the HYPERLINK "https://en.wikipedia.org/wiki/1993_North_American_Storm_Complex" 1993 North American Storm Complex on HYPERLINK "https://en.wikipedia.org/wiki/March_13" March 13, 1993 at 10:01 HYPERLINK "https://en.wikipedia.org/wiki/UTC" UTC. Author: NASA.

Source: NASA. HYPERLINK "https://commons.wikimedia.org/wiki/File:Storm_of_the_century_satellite.gif" \t "" Public Domain. File: Storm of the century satellite.gif. Uploaded: 2010-11-10 17:43:30. HYPERLINK "https://commons.wikimedia.org/wiki/File:Storm_of_the_century_satellite.gif?uselang=en" \l "Licensing" \t "" Public Domain. This file is in the HYPERLINK "https://en.wikipedia.org/wiki/public_domain" public domain in the United States because it was solely created by HYPERLINK "https://en.wikipedia.org/wiki/NASA" NASA. NASA copyright policy states "NASA material is not protected by copyright unless noted".

[Page 159] Alta's Katie Hitchcock in January of record season of 2022/'23. Photo by Chloe Jimenez, courtesy of Alta Ski Resort for use in this book.

CHAPTER 16

[Page 162] Author's van in Seefeld, Austria in the winter of 1999. Photo © Jay Cowan.

[Page 165] Cortina, Italy during the winter of 1999. Photo © Jay Cowan

[Page 168] The always ungroomed Schindlergrat in St. Anton, Austria. Photo © Jay Cowan.

[Page 171] Cross-country skiing by Linderhof Palace near Garmisch-Partenkirchen, Germany. Photo © Jay Cowan.

CHAPTER 17

[Page 172] The village of Andermatt, Switzerland. File: 00 0372. Andermatt im Urserrental – Schweiz.jpg. Wikimedia Commons. Photographer W. Bulach. This file is licensed under the Creative Commons Attribution-Share Alike 4.0 International license. I, the copyright holder, hereby publish it under the following license: You are free: to share – to copy, distribute and transmit the work, to remix – to adapt the work. Under the following conditions: attribution – You must give appropriate credit, provide a link to the license, and indicate if changes were made. You may do so in any reasonable manner, but not in any way that suggests the licensor endorses you or your use. Share alike – If you remix, transform, or build upon the material, you must distribute your contributions under the HYPERLINK "https://creativecommons.org/share-your-work/licensing-considerations/compatible-licenses" same or compatible license as the original.

[Page 175] Deep skiing image from the Vallee Blanche in Chamonix, France. Photo © Jay Cowan.

[Page 178] Skiing in La Grave/La Meije in the Hautes-Alpes Department of southeastern France. Photo © Jay Cowan.

[Page 183] Le Serac hotel in La Grave, France, receiving a snowstorm. Photo © Jay Cowan.

CHAPTER 18

[Page 188] Northern lights (aurora borealis) behind a night-lit ski area in Lapland, Finland. Photo © Hari Tarvainen, courtesy of VisitFinland.com

[Page 193] Mountain ski resort in Vostok, Primorsky Kray, Russia. Photographer: HYPERLINK "https://commons.wikimedia.org/w/index.php?title=User:Russian.dissident&action=edit&redlink=1" Russian.dissident - Own work. HYPERLINK "https://commons.wikimedia.org/wiki/File:Vostok_ski_resort.jpg?uselang=en" \l "Licensing" \t "" Public Domain. File:Vostok ski resort.jpg.. Uploaded: 2010-12-19 15:59:18. I, the copyright holder of this work, release this work into the HYPERLINK "https://en.wikipedia.org/wiki/en:public_domain" public domain. This applies worldwide. In some countries this may not be legally possible; if so: I grant anyone the right to use this work for any purpose, without any conditions, unless such conditions are required by law.

[Page 195] Mountain restaurant at Baqueira, Spain, with deep snow on roof and groomed slopes all around. Baqueira 1800. HYPERLINK "https://commons.wikimedia.org/wiki/User:Faras" Faras - Own work. HYPERLINK "https://creativecommons.org/licenses/by-sa/4.0" \t "_blank" CC BY-SA 4.0. File: Baqueira 1800.jpg. Created: 1 January 2005. I, the copyright holder of this work, hereby publish it under the following licenses: Permission is granted to copy, distribute and/or modify this document under the terms of the HYPERLINK "https://en.wikipedia.org/wiki/en:GNU_Free_Documentation_License" GNU Free Documentation License, Version 1.2 or any later version published by the HYPERLINK "https://en.wikipedia.org/wiki/en:Free_Software_Foundation" Free Software Foundation; with no Invariant Sections, no Front-Cover Texts, and no Back-Cover Texts. A copy of the license is included in the section entitled HYPERLINK "https://commons.wikimedia.org/wiki/Commons:GNU_Free_Documentation_License,_version_1.2" GNU Free Documentation License. This file is licensed under the HYPERLINK "https://en.wikipedia.org/wiki/en:Creative_Commons" Creative Commons Attribution-Share Alike HYPERLINK "https://creativecommons.org/licenses/by-sa/4.0/" 4.0 International, HYPERLINK "https://creativecommons.org/licenses/by-sa/3.0/deed.en" 3.0 Unported, HYPERLINK "https://creativecommons.org/licenses/by-sa/2.5/deed.en" 2.5 Generic, HYPERLINK "https://creativecommons.org/licenses/by-sa/2.0/deed.en" 2.0 Generic and HYPERLINK "https://creativecommons.org/licenses/by-sa/1.0/deed.en" 1.0 Generic license. You are free: to share – to copy, distribute and transmit the work, to remix – to adapt the work. Under the following conditions: attribution – You must give appropriate credit, provide a link to the license, and indicate if changes were made. You may do so in any reasonable manner, but not in any way that suggests the licensor endorses you or your use. Share alike – If you remix, transform, or build upon the material, you must distribute your contributions under the HYPERLINK "https://creativecommons.org/share-your-work/licensing-considerations/compatible-licenses" same or compatible license as the original.

[Page 195]) "In this mostly cloud-free true-color scene, much of Scandinavia can be seen to be covered by snow." From left to right across the top of this image are the countries of Norway, Sweden, Finland, and northwestern Russia. The Baltic Sea is located in the bottom center, with the Gulf of Bothnia to the north (in the center) and the Gulf of Finland to the northeast. This image was acquired on March 15, 2002, by the Moderate-resolution Imaging Spectroradiometer (MODIS), flying aboard NASA's HYPERLINK "http://terra.nasa.gov/" \t "outlink" Terra satellite. Image courtesy Jacques Descloitres, HYPERLINK "http://rapidfire.sci.gsfc.nasa.gov/" \t "outlink" MODIS Land Rapid Response Team at NASA GSFC. NASA images in the public domain for editorial use.

CHAPTER 19

[Page 196] House in Jahorina after avalanche. Wikipedia. HYPERLINK "https://creativecommons.org/licenses/by/3.0" \t "_blank" CC BY 3.0. File: Jahorina - panoramio (3).jpg. Created: 18 February 2012. Attribution: BrsJvnvc. This file is licensed under the Creative Commons Attribution 3.0 Unported license. You are free:to share – to copy, distribute and transmit the work, to remix – to adapt the work. Under the following conditions: attribution – You must give appropriate credit, provide a link to the license, and indicate if changes were made. You may do so in any reasonable manner, but not in any way that suggests the licensor endorses you or your use.

[Page 199] Cable cars at Jasná Ski Resort in the Tatra Mountains. Wikipedia Commons. Photographer: HYPERLINK "https://commons.wikimedia.org/wiki/User:Pudelek" Pudelek (Marcin Szala) - Own work. Kosodrevina – Chopok. HYPERLINK "https://creativecommons.org/licenses/by-sa/3.0" \t "_blank" CC BY-SA 3.0. File: Jasná Ski Resort - gondola lift Kosodrevina - Chopok (4) jpg. I, the copyright holder of this work, hereby publish it under the following license: This file is licensed under the HYPERLINK "https://en.wikipedia.org/wiki/en:Creative_Commons" Creative Commons HYPERLINK "https://creativecommons.org/licenses/by-sa/3.0/deed.en" Attribution-Share Alike 3.0 Unported license. You are free: to share – to copy, distribute and transmit the work, to remix – to adapt the work. Under the following conditions: attribution – You must give appropriate credit, provide a link to the license, and indicate if changes were made. You may do so in any reasonable manner, but not in any way that suggests the licensor endorses you or your use. Share alike – If you remix, transform, or build upon the material, you must distribute your contributions under the HYPERLINK "https://creativecommons.org/share-your-work/licensing-considerations/compatible-licenses" same or compatible license as the original.

[Page 200] Screenshot of CNN News report of a "snownado" in Greece. Cited in the book, in the public domain for editorial use.

[Page 204] Jahorina Ski Resort in Bosnia and Herzegovinia. Wikimedia Commons. Photographer: nikola_pu. File:Jahorina - ogorjelica - 2011 - panoramio - nikola pu (3).jpg. This file is licensed under the Creative Commons Attribution-Share Alike 3.0 unported license. Attribution: nikola_pu. You are free: to share – to copy, distribute and transmit the work to remix – to adapt the work Under the following conditions: attribution – You must give appropriate credit, provide a link to the license, and indicate if changes were made. You may do so in any reasonable manner, but not in any way that suggests the licensor endorses you or your use. share alike – If you remix, transform, or build upon the material, you must distribute your contributions under the same or compatible license as the original.

CHAPTER 20

CHAPTER 21

attribution – You must give appropriate credit, provide a link to the license, and indicate if changes were made. You may do so in any reasonable manner, but not in any way that suggests the licensor endorses you or your use.

[Page 225] Night Skiing at Alpensia, Korea. Wikimedia Commons. Photographer: HYPERLINK "https://commons.wikimedia.org/w/index.php?title=User:Albert_Lee1&action=edit&redlink=1" Albert Lee1 - Own work. HYPERLINK "https://creativecommons.org/licenses/by-sa/4.0" \t "_blank" CC BY-SA 4.0. File: Alpensia.jpg. Created: 2014-12-30. I, the copyright holder of this work, hereby publish it under the following license: This file is licensed under the HYPERLINK "https://en.wikipedia.org/wiki/en:Creative_Commons" Creative Commons HYPERLINK "https://creativecommons.org/licenses/by-sa/4.0/deed.en" Attribution-Share Alike 4.0 International license. You are free: to share – to copy, distribute and transmit the work, to remix – to adapt the work. Under the following conditions: attribution – You must give appropriate credit, provide a link to the license, and indicate if changes were made. You may do

so in any reasonable manner, but not in any way that suggests the licensor endorses you or your use. Share alike – If you remix, transform, or build upon the material, you must distribute your contributions under the HYPERLINK "https://creativecommons.org/share-your-work/licensing-considerations/compatible-licenses" same or compatible license as the original.

[Page 226] Powder skiing at Geto Kogen Resort, Japan. Photo © Kevin McHugh, courtesy of his written permission.

[Page 230] Record 2008 snowfall in Hefei, Anhui Province, China. Source: Benlisquare at English Wikipedia. Wikimedia Commons. HYPERLINK "https://creativecommons.org/licenses/by-sa/3.0" \t "_blank" CC BY-SA 3.0. File: 2008 China storms Anhui.JPG. Created: 27 January 2008. Benlisquare at English Wikipedia, the copyright holder of this work, hereby publishes it under the following licenses: This file is licensed under the HYPERLINK "https://en.wikipedia.org/wiki/en:Creative_Commons" Creative Commons HYPERLINK "https://creativecommons.org/licenses/by-sa/3.0/deed.en" Attribution-Share Alike 3.0 Unported license. Attribution: Benlisquare at English Wikipedia: You are free: to share – to copy, distribute and transmit the work, to remix – to adapt the work. Under the following conditions: attribution – You must give appropriate credit, provide a link to the license, and indicate if changes were made. You may do so in any reasonable manner, but not in any way that suggests the licensor endorses you or your use. Share alike – If you remix, transform, or build upon the material, you must distribute your contributions under the HYPERLINK "https://creativecommons.org/share-your-work/licensing-considerations/compatible-licenses" same or compatible license as the original. Additional license: Permission is granted to copy, distribute and/or modify this document under the terms of the HYPERLINK "https://en.wikipedia.org/wiki/en:GNU_Free_Documentation_License" GNU Free Documentation License, Version 1.2 or any later version published by the HYPERLINK "https://en.wikipedia.org/wiki/en:Free_Software_Foundation" Free Software Foundation; with no Invariant Sections, no Front-Cover Texts, and no Back-Cover Texts. A copy of the license is included in the section entitled HYPERLINK "https://commons.wikimedia.org/wiki/Commons:GNU_Free_Documentation_License,_version_1.2" GNU Free Documentation License.

CHAPTER 22

[Page 232] The Blizzard of Oz of 2017 is written about in the book. This online screenshot is from ABC.net.au's coverage of the story, and in the public domain for editorial purposes. The image accompanying the ABC story was lifted by them from Facebook.

[Page 235] The Lewis Glacier on Mount Kenya. Wikipedia. Public Domain. File: MtKenya gletscher.jpg. Created: 7 October 2006. This work has been released into the HYPERLINK "https://en.wikipedia.org/wiki/en:public_domain" public domain by its author, HYPERLINK "https://en.wikipedia.org/wiki/nl:User:Josski" Josski at HYPERLINK "https://en.wikipedia.org/wiki/nl:" Dutch Wikipedia. This applies worldwide. In some countries this may not be legally possible; if so: HYPERLINK "https://en.wikipedia.org/wiki/nl:User:Josski" Josski grants anyone the right to use this work for any purpose, without any conditions, unless such conditions are required by law.

[Page 236] Snowboarding in Las Lenas, Argentina's abundant powder. September 12, 2005. Boarder: Sigi Grabner. Photo by Gustavo Cherro / Red Bull Content Pool.

[Page 243] The upper half of New Zealand's Tasman Glacier. Wikipedia. HYPERLINK "https://creativecommons. org/licenses/by-sa/3.0" \t "_blank" <u>CC BY-SA 3.0</u> File: Upper Tasman Glacier.jpg. Created: 21 December 2009. I, the copyright holder of this work, hereby publish it under the following licenses: This file is licensed under the HYPERLINK "https://en.wikipedia.org/wiki/en:Creative_Commons" Creative Commons HYPERLINK "https:// creativecommons.org/licenses/by-sa/3.0/deed.en" Attribution-Share Alike 3.0 Unported license. You are free: to share – to copy, distribute and transmit the work, to remix – to adapt the work. Under the following conditions: attribution – You must give appropriate credit, provide a link to the license, and indicate if changes were made. You may do so in any reasonable manner, but not in any way that suggests the licensor endorses you or your use. Share alike – If you remix, transform, or build upon the material, you must distribute your contributions under the HYPERLINK "https://creativecommons.org/share-your-work/licensing-considerations/compatible-licenses" same or compatible license as the original. Additional license: Permission is granted to copy, distribute and/or modify this document under the terms of the HYPERLINK "https://en.wikipedia.org/wiki/en:GNU_Free_Documentation_License" GNU Free Documentation License, Version 1.2 or any later version published by the HYPERLINK "https://en.wikipedia.org/ wiki/en:Free_Software_Foundation" Free Software Foundation; with no Invariant Sections, no Front-Cover Texts, and no Back-Cover Texts. A copy of the license is included in the section entitled HYPERLINK "https://commons. wikimedia.org/wiki/Commons:GNU_Free_Documentation_License,_version_1.2" GNU Free Documentation License.

 HYPERLINK "https://www.abc.net.au/news/2017-08-07/blizzard-of-oz-creates-winter-wonderland-at-australian-snowfield/8780612" \t "_blank"

CHAPTER 23

[Page 248] 1984 Chevrolet Suburban compressed into half its normal width by an avalanche. Photo © Jay Cowan

[Page 251] Winter of Terror 1951. B&W image with men and women probing avalanche directly adjacent to buildings on all sides in Vals, Switzerland. Image posted on SLF.CH site, in the public domain for related press articles/editorial use. As quoted in this book in chapter 23, "Avalanche risk management recognized as UNESCO cultural heritage. Managing avalanche risk was inscribed in the Representative List of the Intangible Cultural Heritage of Humanity on 29 November 2018. The dossier supporting the application was produced by the WSL Institute for Snow and Avalanche Research SLF together with several partners." Copyrighted. WSL and SLF provide the artwork for imaging of editorial articles relating to this media release for free. Photographer unknown. Photo courtesy of SLF Archive.

[Page 252] Avalanche 2006, ligne SNCF from Saint-Gervais - Vallorcine. France. Author: Poudou - Own work (source familiale). HYPERLINK "https://creativecommons.org/licenses/by/3.0" \t "_blank" CC BY 3.0 File: Ligne Saint-Gervais - Vallorcine - avalanche 2006 - 08.jpg. Created: 6 March 2006. This file is licensed under the HYPERLINK "https://en.wikipedia.org/wiki/en:Creative_Commons" Creative Commons HYPERLINK "https://creativecommons. org/licenses/by/3.0/deed.en" Attribution 3.0 Unported license. You are free: to share – to copy, distribute and transmit the work, to remix – to adapt the work. Under the following conditions: attribution – You must give appropriate credit, provide a link to the license, and indicate if changes were made. You may do so in any reasonable manner, but not in any way that suggests the licensor endorses you or your use.

[Page 255] Large, 3,000-meter-long avalanche in Nepal. Photo © Jay Cowan.

CHAPTER 24

[Page 258] Clearing the road from Zernez to Brail in Switzerland after an avalanche during the Winter of Terror in 1951, near Punta Nova. Wikimedia Commons. Unknown author -This image is from the collection of the ETH-Bibliothek has been published on Wikimedia Commons as part of a cooperation with Wikimedia CH. CC BY-SA 4.0 File: Lawinenwinter 1951 Punt Nova.jpg. Created: January 1951date QS:P571,+1951-01-0T00:00:00Z/10. This file is licensed under the Creative Commons Attribution-Share Alike 4.0 International License. You are free: to share – to copy, distribute and transmit the work, to remix – to adapt the work. Under the following conditions: attribution – You must give appropriate credit, provide a link to the license, and indicate if changes were made. You may do so in any reasonable manner, but not in any way that suggests the licensor endorses you or your use. Share alike – If you remix, transform, or build upon the material, you must distribute your contributions under the HYPERLINK "https://creativecommons.org/share-your-work/licensing-considerations/compatible-licenses" same or compatible license as the original.

[Page 261] Graveyard at the parish church in Galtur, with crosses representing the lives lost in the 1999 slide. Photo © Jay Cowan.

[Page 262] Construction of massive avalanche-deflecting wall in Galtur, Austria, the summer following the tragic avalanche of 1999. Photo © Jay Cowan.

[Page 267] 1970 avalanche in Val d'Isere, France. Screenshot of an online story mentioned in book. From archives of ledauphine.com, in the public domain for editorial use.

CHAPTER 25

[Page 270] Memorial for victims of the Montroc and Le Tour Avalanche, Chamonix 09/02/1999. Wikipédia. Photographer: 5053PM, Pierre Martin (géotechnicien) - Own work. HYPERLINK "https://creativecommons. org/licenses/by-sa/3.0" \t "_blank" CC BY-SA 3.0. File: PM.Chamonix.JPG. Created: 2005-03-30 16:43:14. I, the copyright holder of this work, hereby publish it under the following license: This file is licensed under the HYPERLINK "https://en.wikipedia.org/wiki/en:Creative_Commons" Creative Commons HYPERLINK "https:// creativecommons.org/licenses/by-sa/3.0/deed.en" Attribution-Share Alike 3.0 Unported license. You are free: to share – to copy, distribute and transmit the work, to remix – to adapt the work. Under the following conditions: attribution – You must give appropriate credit, provide a link to the license, and indicate if changes were made. You may do so in any reasonable manner, but not in any way that suggests the licensor endorses you or your use. Share alike – If you remix, transform, or build upon the material, you must distribute your contributions under the HYPERLINK "https://creativecommons.org/share-your-work/licensing-considerations/compatible-licenses" same or compatible license as the original.

[Page 273] La Mort Blanche (The White Death). The front page of Swiss daily newspaper Le Matin, February 23, 1999, with a headline and story cited in the book. In the public domain for editorial use.

[Page 274] The 2017 Rigopiano, Italy avalanche destroyed the Hotel Rigopiano. Image of the position of the crushed hotel (yellow lines) before (right panel) and after (left panel), relative to the structurally stable edge of the spa area (red lines). Still image downloaded and reproduced by the authors of the research paper under Creative Commons license CC-BY 3.0, extracted from YouTube uploaded by TvSEI.

CHAPTER 26

[Page 279] Alpine Meadows, 1982. Image of the poster from the 2021 movie "Buried" about the tragedy. The movie is discussed in this chapter of the book. In the public domain for editorial use.

[Page 284] The Davos avalanches of 1968 included this one that buried the rail line and road under several meters of snow. Photo by E. Wengi, courtesy of the copyright holder SLF, which with the WSL provide the artwork for imaging of press articles relating to this media release for free. The press release is referenced repeatedly in the chapter.

[Page 285] View from ski slopes above St. Anton with the slide path through the trees from the Wolfsgrubben avalanche of 1988 visible on the upper right. Photo © Jay Cowan.

CHAPTER 27

[Page 289] Highland Bowl, Aspen, patrol-triggered slide in 1989. Photo © Matt Power, used with written permission.

CHAPTER 28

[Page 300] Avalanche blasting in French ski resort of Tignes at 3,600 meters. Author: Alexander Joss (original upload by HYPERLINK "https://en.wikipedia.org/wiki/User:Jossy89" Jossy89 at HYPERLINK "https://en.wikipedia.org/ wiki/" English Wikipedia). Transferred from HYPERLINK "https://en.wikipedia.org/" en.wikipedia to Commons by Liftarn using Commons Helper. Location: HYPERLINK "https://en.wikipedia.org/wiki/Alps" French Alps, lower slopes of [Tignes] (3600m). Public Domain. File: Avalanche Blasting.jpg. Created: February 2006. This work has been released into the public domain by its author: Jossy89 at English Wikipedia. This applies worldwide. In some countries this may not be legally possible; if so: Jossy89 grants anyone the right to use this work for any purpose, without any conditions, unless such conditions are required by law.

[Page 303] Man digging snowpit for avalanche evaluation. Photographer: HYPERLINK "https://commons. wikimedia.org/wiki/User:Clayoquot" Clayoquot - Own work. HYPERLINK "https://creativecommons.org/licenses/ by-sa/3.0" \t "_blank" CC BY-SA 3.0. File: Avalanche testing snow pit.JPG. Created: 22 December 2009. I, the copyright holder of this work, I hereby publish it under the following licenses: This file is licensed under the Creative Commons Attribution-Share Alike 3.0 Unported license. You are free: to share – to copy, distribute and transmit the work, to remix – to adapt the work. Under the following conditions: attribution – You must give appropriate credit, provide a link to the license, and indicate if changes were made. You may do so in any reasonable manner, but not in any way that suggests the licensor endorses you or your use. Share alike – If you remix, transform, or build upon the material, you must distribute your contributions under the HYPERLINK "https://creativecommons.org/share-your-work/licensing-considerations/compatible-licenses" same or compatible license as the original. Additional license: Permission is granted to copy, distribute and/or modify this document under the terms of the HYPERLINK "https:// en.wikipedia.org/wiki/en:GNU_Free_Documentation_License" GNU Free Documentation License, Version 1.2 or any later version published by the HYPERLINK "https://en.wikipedia.org/wiki/en:Free_Software_Foundation" Free Software Foundation; with no Invariant Sections, no Front-Cover Texts, and no Back-Cover Texts. A copy of the license is included in the section entitled HYPERLINK "https://commons.wikimedia.org/wiki/Commons:GNU_ Free_Documentation_License,_version_1.2" GNU Free Documentation License.

[Page 304] Rega Eurocopter EC145. Wikipedia. Photographer: Matthias Zepper – Own work. Swiss rescue helicopter in action. Model BK 117-C2 (HYPERLINK "https://en.wikipedia.org/wiki/Eurocopter_EC_145" EC-145) of HYPERLINK "https://en.wikipedia.org/wiki/Rega_(air_rescue)" Rega with registration "HB-ZRE". I, the copyright holder of this work, hereby publish it under these licenses: HYPERLINK "https://creativecommons.org/licenses/by-sa/3.0" \t "_blank" CC BY-SA 3.0. File: Zepper-BK 117-C2-(EC145)- SchweizerischeRettungsflugwacht.jpg. Created: 2 January 2009. Permission is granted to copy, distribute and/or modify this document under the terms of the GNU Free Documentation License, Version 1.2 or any later version published by the Free Software Foundation with no Invariant Sections, no Front-Cover Texts, and no Back-Cover Texts. A copy of the license is included in the section entitled GNU Free Documentation License.

[Page 307] Radar station for avalanche monitoring in Zermatt. Photographer: Avalaw. Own Work. Radarstation zur Lawinenüberwachung in Zermatt.CC-BY-SA 4.0. File: ZermattRadar.jpg. Created: 21 January 2016. This file is licensed under the Creative Commons Attribution-Share Alike 4.0 International license. You are free: to share – to copy, distribute and transmit the work, to remix – to adapt the work. Under the following conditions: attribution – You must give appropriate credit, provide a link to the license, and indicate if changes were made. You may do so in any reasonable manner, but not in any way that suggests the licensor endorses you or your use. Share alike – If you remix, transform, or build upon the material, you must distribute your contributions under the same or compatible license as the original.

CHAPTER 29

[Page 314] Cavalese cable car disaster, 9 march 1976.

Unknown photographer. Wikimedia Commons. HYPERLINK "http://www.ilpost.it/2016/03/09/disastro-funivia-cermis/" http://www.ilpost.it/2016/03/09/disastro-funivia-cermis/ HYPERLINK "https://commons.wikimedia.org/ wiki/File:Cermis_disaster_1976_d.jpg?uselang=en" \l "Licensing" \t "" Public Domain. File: Cermis disaster 1976 d.jpg

Created: 9 March 1976. The HYPERLINK "http://www.wipo.int/wipolex/en/treaties/text.jsp?file_id=283698" \l "P113_17989" country of origin of this photograph is Italy. It is in the HYPERLINK "https://en.wikipedia.org/

wiki/Public_domain" public domain there because its copyright term has expired. According to HYPERLINK "https://web.archive.org/web/20170409054450/http://portal.unesco.org/culture/en/files/30289/11419173013it_copyright_2003_en.pdf/it_copyright_2003_en.pdf" Law for the Protection of Copyright and Neighbouring Rights n.633, 22 April 1941 and later revisions, images of people or of aspects, elements and facts of natural or social life, obtained with photographic process or with an analogue one, including reproductions of figurative art and HYPERLINK "https://en.wikipedia.org/wiki/Film_frame" film frames of HYPERLINK "https://en.wikipedia.org/wiki/Film_stock" film stocks (Art. 87) are protected for a period of 20 years from creation (Art. 92). This provision shall not apply to photographs of writings, documents, business papers, material objects, technical drawings and similar products (Art. 87). Italian law makes an important distinction between "works of photographic art" and "simple photographs" (Art. 2, § 7). Photographs that are "intellectual work with creative characteristics" are protected for 70 years after the author's death (Art. 32 bis), whereas simple photographs are protected for a period of 20 years from creation. This may not apply in countries that don't apply the HYPERLINK "https://en.wikipedia.org/wiki/rule_of_the_shorter_term" rule of the shorter term to works from Italy. In particular, these are in the public domain in the United States only if: it wasn't in copyright in the United States due to being registered for copyright there and was created prior to 1976 and published prior to 1978 — then it was out-of-copyright in Italy on the HYPERLINK "https://en.wikipedia.org/wiki/Wikipedia:Non-U.S._copyrights" \l "Dates_of_restoration_and_terms_of_protection" URAA date of restoration (January 1, 1996) (HYPERLINK "https://en.wikipedia.org/wiki/Title_17_of_the_United_States_Code" 17 U.S.C. HYPERLINK "https://www.copyright.gov/title17/92chap1.html" \l "104a" § 104A) (in most cases; for all cases, see HYPERLINK "https://commons.wikimedia.org/wiki/Template:PD-Italy/US" Template:PD-Italy/US). If so, please add HYPERLINK "https://commons.wikimedia.org/wiki/Template:PD-1996" {{PD-1996}} in addition to this copyright tag. If the image was created after 1975 or was published after 1977, please add {{USSRA}}.

[Page 317] A tram in St. Anton, hundreds of feet off the ground, illustrating why when something goes wrong with them it can be disastrous. Photo © Jay Cowan.

[Page 318] Chairlift evacuation at Buttermilk near Aspen. Photo by Jeremy Wallace for the Aspen Times. The story is discussed in this chapter. In the public domain for editorial use.

[Page 321] T-Bar in Sweden. Wikipedia. Permission by Fri användning. Public Domain. File: T-bar lift.JPG. Created: 4 August 8 by Jag, cropped by HYPERLINK "https://commons.wikimedia.org/wiki/User:Ludmi%C5%82a_Pilecka" Ludmiła Pilecka. HYPERLINK "https://commons.wikimedia.org/wiki/File:%C3%85re_Tv%C3%A4r%C3%A5valvsliftarna.JPG" File: Åre Tväråvalvsliftarna.JPG. This work has been released into the HYPERLINK "https://en.wikipedia.org/wiki/en:public_domain" public domain by its author, HYPERLINK "https://commons.wikimedia.org/wiki/User:Skistar" Skistar. This applies worldwide. In some countries this may not be legally possible; if so: HYPERLINK "https://commons.wikimedia.org/wiki/User:Skistar" Skistar grants anyone the right to use this work for any purpose, without any conditions, unless such conditions are required by law.

CHAPTER 30

[Page 322] 1976 Vail, Colorado gondola 10,000-word story in Sports Illustrated, referenced in this chapter, in the public domain for editorial purposes.

[Page 325] Le Mont-Dore cablecar accident 1965. Eikidata. Gondel van kabelbaan near bergstationvan de Puy de Dome. Photographer: Arie M dem Toom. CC BY-SA 4.0. Puy de Dome 1.jpg. Created: 21 June 2017. I, the copy right holder of this work, hereby publish it with the following license: This file is licenses under the Creative Commons Attribution-Share-Alike 4.0 International license. You are free: to share – to copy, distribute and transmit the work, to remix – to adapt the work. Under the following conditions: attribution – You must give appropriate credit, provide a link to the license, and indicate if changes were made. You may do so in any reasonable manner, but not in any way that suggests the licensor endorses you or your use. Share alike – If you remix, transform or build upon the material, you must distribute your contributions under the same or compatible license as the original.

[Page 326] Front page of the New York Times with story on the Vail gondola accident in 1976. Story is written about in this chapter. In the public domain for editorial use.

[Page 329] Squaw Valley 1978 cablecar disaster. Photo of the destroyed tram car which is posted frequently without attribution or copyright. In the public domain for editorial use.

CHAPTER 31

[Page 336] Cavalese, Italy 1998 cablecar disaster. Screenshot of theaviationist.com story about the lift accident, as referenced and quoted in this chapter. US Air Force photo by Senior Airman Greg L. Davis. 1st Combat Camera Squadron. In the public domain for editorial use.

[Page 339] Screenshot of Kaprun funicular disaster aftermath on dallasmorningnews.com as referenced in this chapter. In the public domain for editorial use.

[Page 342] Gudauri lift rollback accident in the Republic of Georgia. Screenshot of online news and YouTube video shown widely around the world and referenced in this chapter. In the public domain for editorial use.

[Page 341] Kaprun, Austria funicular disaster 2000. Transferred from HYPERLINK "https://en.wikipedia.org/" en.wikipedia to Commons. The Kaprun train photographed by Adrian Pingstone a few weeks before the disaster. Released to the public domain. File: Kaprun train.jpg. Created: 25 February 2003. This work has been released into the HYPERLINK "https://en.wikipedia.org/wiki/en:public_domain" public domain by its author, HYPERLINK "https://en.wikipedia.org/wiki/User:Arpingstone" Arpingstone at HYPERLINK "https://en.wikipedia.org/wiki/" English Wikipedia. This applies worldwide. In some countries this may not be legally possible; if so: HYPERLINK "https://en.wikipedia.org/wiki/en:User:Arpingstone" Arpingstone grants anyone the right to use this work for any purpose, without any conditions, unless such conditions are required by law.

CHAPTER 32

[346] Skijoring with motorcycles, Augustusburg, Germany, 1963. CC BY-SA File: Bundesarchiv Bild 183-B0128-0006-003, Augustusburg, Skijöring, J. Riedel, H. Rösch.jpg. Created: 27 January 1963 date QS:P571,+1963-01-27T00:00:00Z/11. This file is licensed under the Creative Commons Attribution-Share Alike 3.0 Germany license. Attribution: Bundesarchiv, Bild 183-B0128-0006-003 / Gahlbeck, Friedrich / CC-BY-SA 3.0. You are free: to share – to copy, distribute and transmit the work, to remix – to adapt the work. Under the following conditions: attribution – You must give appropriate credit, provide a link to the license, and indicate if changes were made. You may do so in any reasonable manner, but not in any way that suggests the licensor endorses you or your use. Share alike – If you remix, transform, or build upon the material, you must distribute your contributions under the same of compatible license as the origin. This image was provided to Wikimedia Commons by the HYPERLINK "http://www.bundesarchiv.de/" German Federal Archive (Deutsches Bundesarchiv) as part of a HYPERLINK "https://commons.wikimedia.org/wiki/Commons:Bundesarchiv" cooperation project. The German Federal Archive guarantees an authentic representation only using the originals (negative and/or positive), resp. the digitalization of the originals as provided by the HYPERLINK "http://www.bild.bundesarchiv.de/" Digital Image Archive. Riedel, Joachim: Skisportler, Bruder von Eberhard Riedel, DDR (auf dem Motorrad). Heinz Rösch, Skisportler (an der Zugleine).

[Page 347] Heather Adeney skijoring with dogs at the IFSS World Championship race, Dawson City, Yukon, 2005. Public Domain. File: Skijor worlds.jpg. Uploaded: 2015-01-20 21:32:35 from en:wiki, uploaded there on 22 November 2006 by Heathera skidog. This work has been released into the public domain by its author, Heathera skidog at English Wikipedia. It applies worldwide. In some countries this may not be legally possible; if so: Heathera skidog grants anyone the right to use this work for any purpose without conditions, unless such conditions are required by law.

[Page 349] Competitive skijoring in St. Moritz, 1928, with the horses controlled by the skiers rather than a rider. Nationaal Archief / Spaarnestad Photo, SFA008000941 "Skijoring": een wintersport waarbij deelnemers op ski's door galopperende paarden (of honden of motoren) worden voortgetrokken. Saint-Moritz, 1928. Nationaal Archief Collectie Spaarnestad Voor meer informatie en voor meer foto's uit de collectie van Spaarnestad Photo, bezoek onze Beeldbank:http://www.spaarnestadphoto.nlPermission details: At the time of upload, the image license was automatically confirmed using the Flickr API. No Restrictions. File:Skijoring - Skijoring (4275596213).jpg. Created: 2010-01-15 09:56:36. This image was taken from Flickr's The Commons. The uploading organization may have various reasons for determining that no known copyright restrictions exist, such as: The copyright is in the public domain because it has expired; The copyright was injected into the public domain for other reasons, such as failure to adhere to required formalities or conditions; The institution owns the copyright but is not interested in exercising control; or The institution has legal rights sufficient to authorize others to use the work without restrictions. This image was originally posted to Flickr by National Archief at HYPERLINK "http://flickr.com/photos/29998366@N02/4275596213" http://flickr.com/photos/29998366@N02/4275596213. It was reviewed on 27 November 2016 by FlickreviewR and was confirmed to be licensed under the No Known copyright restrictions.

[Page 348] A Leadville Ski Joring team at the 2009 event in Leadville, Colorado. Photographer Kaila Angello. CC BY-SA 3.0. File: Leadville Ski Joring.jpg. Created: 8 March 2009. I, the copyright holder of this work, herby publish it under the following licenses: This file is licensed under the Creative Commons Attribution-Share Alike 3.0 Unported license. You are free: to share – to copy, distribute and transmit the work, to remix – to adapt the work. Under the following conditions: attribution – You must give appropriate credit, provide a link to the license, and indicate if changes were made. You may do so in any reasonable manner, but not in any way that suggests the licensor endorses you or your use. Share alike – If you remix, transform, or build upon the material, you must distribute your contributions under the same or compatible license as the original. Permission is granted to copy, distribute and/or modify this document under the terms of the GNU Free Documentation License, Version 1.2 or any later version published by the Free Software Foundation; with no Invariant Sections, no Front-Cover Texts, and no Back-Cover Texts. A copy of the license is included in the section entitled GNU Free Documentation License.

CHAPTER 33

[Page 352 Shaun White in the Aspen Super Pipe for Winter X. Photo © Matt Power, used with his written permission.

[Page 355] Aerial of much of the Winter X Games venue under the lights at night. Courtesy of Aspen/Snowmass, posted on their website promo for the 2023 event.

[Page 356] Skier in white from above and behind, way out of the pipe with his skis in an X. Photo © Jay Cowan.

[Page 359] Screenshot of Aspen Times story about Chloe Kim, referenced in this chapter. In the public domain for editorial use.

CHAPTER 34

[Page 362] Photo-shopped image of famous surfer Bruce Irons designed by Aspen Sojourner magazine. Irons photo by Brian Bielmann, mountainous background by David Hiser. Courtesy of Bruce Irons.

CHAPTER 35

[Page 366] Screenshot from International Paralympic Committee website's page for Alana Nichols who is shown competing in Alpine sit-ski. Nichols is featured in this chapter. Image in the public domain for editorial use.

[Page 371] The Bash for Cash. Poster image by Tony Gauba. Poster courtesy of Richard Allen's Vintage Ski World. Poster is referred to in this chapter. In the public domain for editorial use.

[Page 375] Mammoth Mountain, CA's annual pond skim, like many others, always showcases plenty of bikinis. Photo courtesy of Mammoth Mountain.

[Page 378] Image of Sean Cridland setting the cartop world speed record at Utah's Bonneville Salt Flats. Photo © Wake McKoy, courtesy of McKoy and Sean Cridland.

CHAPTER 36

[Page 380] Kite skiing on the Col du Lauteret Pass, France. Photo © Jay Cowan.

[Page 383] In a sequential image Andy Farrington jumps off a cliff and into a spiraling barrel roll during the filming of The Unrideables: Alaska Range in the Tordrillo Mountains near Anchorage, AK, USA, on 22 April, 2014.

Photographer: Scott Serfas / Red Bull Content Pool. Licensed for editorial use.

[Page 384] Three speed gliders fly through the middle of a glacier field during the filming of The Unrideables: Alaska Range in the Tordrillo Mountains near Anchorage, AK, USA, on 29 April, 2014. Photo credit: Scott Serfas / Red Bull Content Pool.

[Page 386] Jon Devore kite skis during filming of The Unrideables: Alaska Range in the Tordrillo Mountains near Anchorage, AK, USA on 29 April, 2014. Photo credit: Scott Serfas / Red Bull Content Pool.

CHAPTER 37

[Page 390] Image of two men and two women holding their skis. Titled: Skiing party near Golden Gate of Yellowstone Park, undated, uncopyrighted. National Park Service / Photographer unknown. Images credited to NPS without any copyright symbol are public domain.

YEL_1_034, 6/13/12, 4:33 PM, 16C, 7692x8975 (266+978), 100%, Repro 2.2 v2, 1/160 s, R57.0, G30.0, B43.4

[Page 393] Bison in the road near Tower Junction with cross-country skier stopped in the foreground. National Park Service / Jacob W. Frank. Images credited to NPS without any copyright symbol are public domain.

[Page 394] Modern skiers at eruption of Old Faithful Geyser in Yellowstone National Park. National Park Service/Neal Herbert. Images credited to NPS without any copyright symbol are public domain.

[Page 395] Three members of the US Army with captured poacher Ed Howell. Photographer: Frank Jay Haynes. Downloaded from National Park Service:

HYPERLINK "http://www.nps.gov/features/yell/slidefile/history/1872_1918/military/Images/11550.jpg" http://www.nps.gov/features/yell/slidefile/history/1872_1918/military/Images/11550.jpg, Pelican Valley, Yellowstone National Park, March 1894. Public Domain. File: Capture of Poacher Ed Howell 1894.jpg. Created: 1 March 1894. This work is in the public domain in its country of origin and other countries and areas where the HYPERLINK "https://en.wikipedia.org/wiki/List_of_countries%27_copyright_lengths" copyright term is the author's life plus 70 years or fewer. You must also include a HYPERLINK "https://commons.wikimedia.org/wiki/Commons:Copyright_tags/Country-specific_tags" \l "United_States_of_America" United States public domain tag to indicate why this work is in the public domain in the United States. Images credited to the NPS with no copyright symbol are in the public domain.

CHAPTER 38

[Page 398] Jade Hameister's book, referenced in this chapter. Its cover is in the public domain for editorial use.

[Page 401] Plumb-bobbing on 1911 Amundsen Antarctica Expedition. The Photographic Archive of Roald Amundsen's Icy Expedition made available by Lomography.com. Language accompanying images as posted on the site: "Images are from the public domain. 2018-07-29. From the 1910 – 1912 Antarctica Expedition."

[Page 402] Scott and his men at the South Pole. Lawrence Oates – National Library of Australia (PIC FH/1165 LOC Cold store PIC HURL 324/13). Public Domain. File: Robert F. Scott at Polheim.JPG. Created: 18 January 1912. This work is in the public domain in its country of origin and other countries and areas where the copyright term is the author's life plus 100 years or fewer. You must also include a United States public domain tag to indicate why this work is in the public domain in the United States. This file has been identified as being free of known restrictions under copyright law, including all related and neighboring rights in the U.S.

[Page 404] Story about Ben Saunders in The Telegraph online, as referenced in this chapter. In the public domain for editorial use.

CHAPTER 39

[Page 406] Photo of Bill Briggs, Barry Corbet, Sterling Neale, Roberts French. Photo by Roberts French, licensed for use in this book by the American Alpine Club.

[Page 408] Image of High and Wild book, published in 1979 by Galen Rowell, profiled in this chapter where this book is mentioned. In the public domain for editorial use.

[Page 411] Image of the book Across the Frozen Himalaya by Harish Kohli (2000) is referenced in this chapter. In the public domain for editorial use.

[Page 414] Walter Bonatti pictured after solo winter ascent of Monte Cervino, Zermatt, 1965. Source: Wikidata.

CHAPTER 40

[Page 418] Skiing Birchlegs Crossing the Mountain with the Royal Child, painted by HYPERLINK "https://en.wikipedia.org/wiki/Knud_Bergslien" Knud Bergslien. Painting located at HYPERLINK "https://en.wikipedia.org/wiki/Holmenkollen_Ski_Museum" The Ski Museum. Holmenkollen, Oslo, Norway. File: Birkebeinerne på Ski over Fjeldet med Kongsbarnet (cropped).jpg. Created: 1869. QS:P571,+1869-00-00T00:00:00Z/9. The official position taken by the Wikimedia Foundation is that "faithful reproductions of two-dimensional works of art are public domain". This is a faithful reproduction of a two-dimensional public domain work of art. The work of art itself is in the public domain for the following reason: The author died in 1908, so this work is in the public domain in its country of origin and other countries and areas where the copyright term is the author's life plus 100 years or fewer. The work is in the public domain in the United States because it was published (or registered with the US copyright office) before January 1, 1928. This file has been identified as being free of known restrictions under copyright law, including all related and neighboring rights.

[Page 421] Facts and Figures for the 93rd Vasaloppet. Screenshot of story on fis-ski.com that is referenced in this chapter. In the public domain for editorial use.

[Page 426] The podium at the first 50k women's race at Norway's Holmenkollen in 2023. As referenced in this chapter. In the public domain for editorial use. Photo by Nordic Focus, via the United States Ski Association (usskiandsnowboard.org).

[Page 423] Ernst Alm, the first winner of the Vasaloppet in Mora, Sweden, 1922. Unknown author. Public Domain. File: Vasaloppet 1922.jpg. Created: 19 March 1922. Photographer unknown. This Swedish photograph is in the public domain in Sweden because one of the following applies: The photograph does not reach the Swedish threshold of originality (common for snapshots and journalistic photos) and was created before 1 January 1973 (SFS 1960:729, § 49a). The photograph was published anonymously before 1 January 1953 and the author did not reveal their identity during the following 70 years (SFS 1960:729, § 44). For photos in the first category created before 1969, also HYPERLINK "https://commons.wikimedia.org/wiki/Template:PD-1996" {{PD-1996}} usually applies. For photos in the second category published before 1928, also HYPERLINK "https://commons.wikimedia.org/wiki/Template:PD-US-expired" {{PD-US-expired}} usually applies. If the photographer died before 1953, {{PD-old-70}} should be used instead of this tag. If the author died before 1926, also {{PD-1996}} usually applies. You must also include a United States public domain tag to indicate why this work is in the public domain in the United States. The photographer is unknown and no US copyright is known to exist. In any event the photographer undoubtedly died more than 70 years ago. And the image is being used editorially to depict an event written about in the book. The photograph was published anonymously before 1 January 1953 and the author did not reveal their identity during the following 70 years (SFS 1960:729, § 44).

CHAPTER 41

[Page 428] Mikaela Shiffrin is pictured here at the November 2017 World Cup event in Killington, VT. Photo Credit: Erich Spiess/Red Bull Content Pool.

[Page 430] Mikaela Shiffrin and Marcel Hirscher with the big crystal globes for their victories in the overall World Cup season 2018/19 during the allover winner Ceremony of the FIS Alpine Skiing World Cup finals in Soldeu, Andorra on March 17, 2019. Photo courtesy of Red Bull Content Pool.

CHAPTER 42

remix – to adapt the work. Under the following conditions: attribution – You must give appropriate credit, provide a link to the license, and indicate if changes were made. You may do so in any reasonable manner, but not in any way that suggests the licensor endorses you or your use. Share alike – If you remix, transform, or build upon the material, you must distribute your contributions under the same or compatible license as the original.

[Page 450] Lindsey Vonn at the FIS Alpine Skiing World Cup in Zauchensee, Austria on January 15, 2017. Format: JPEG 24bit RGB. Photo by Erich Spiess/ASP/Red Bull Content Pool.

CHAPTER 43

[Page 454] Speed skier Ross Anderson. Image courtesy of Ross Anderson.

[Page 457] Frenchman Simon Billy at Vars, Haute-Alpes, France in 2019. CC BY-SA 4.0. File:DAM1681.jpg. Author: Simon Billy, Source: Own work. March 22, 2019. I, the copyright holder of this work, hereby publish it under the following license: This file is licensed under the Creative Commons Attribution-Share Alike 4.0 International license. You are free: to share – to copy, distribute and transmit the work, to remix – to adapt the work. Under the following conditions: attribution – You must give appropriate credit, provide a link to the license, and indicate if changes were made. You may do so in any reasonable manner, but not in any way that suggests the licensor endorses you or your use. Share alike – If you remix, transform, or build upon the material, you must distribute your contributions under the same of compatible license as the original.

[Page 458] Valentina Greggio at Vars, Photo © Louis Billy, used for this book with his and her written permission.

[Page 463] American Dick Dorworth on the speed track in Portillo, Chile 1962. Photo courtesy of Dick Dorworth.

BACK COVER

[Top Image] Olympic gold-medal winning Nordic jumper Ryoyu Kobayashi at the Four Hills Tournament in Bischofshofen Austria, January 26, 2023. Photo credit: Limex Images / Red Bull Content Pool.

[Bottom Left] Kit Deslauriers on Everest. Photo © Bryce Brown, used with his and her permission.

[Bottom Right] Grotto in an iceberg frames some of the British Antarctica Expedition 1911 – 1913, 5 Jan 1911. National Library of New Zealand. CCO. File: Grotto in an iceberg.jpg. Created: QS:P571,+1911-01-05T00:00:00Z/11. This file is made available under the Creative Commons CCO 1.0 Universal Public Domain Dedication. http://flic.kr/p/7doxMR. This image was originally posted to Flickr by National Library NZ on The Commons at HYPERLINK "http://flickr.com/photos/32741315" http://flickr.com/photos/32741315

@NO6/4078337967. It was reviewed on 2017-08-03:38:31 by FlickreviewR, who found it to be licensed under the terms of the No known copyright restrictions, which is compatible with 'The Commons." It is, however, not the same license as given above, and it is unknown whether that license was ever valid.

Made in the USA
Monee, IL
01 February 2024

52309190R00273